# The Perfection of Wisdom in First Bloom

# The Perfection of Wisdom in First Bloom

## Relating Early *Aṣṭasāhasrikā Prajñāpāramitā* to *Āgama* Literature

Bhikkhu Anālayo

*Foreword by*

His Holiness the Dalai Lama

Wisdom

Wisdom Publications
132 Perry Street
New York, NY 10014 USA
wisdom.org



*Library of Congress Cataloging-in-Publication Data*
Names: Anālayo, 1962– author.
Title: The perfection of wisdom in first bloom: relating early Aṣṭasāhasrikā Prajñāpāramitā to Āgama literature / Bhikkhu Anālayo.
Description: New York, NY, USA: Wisdom, [2025] | Includes bibliographical references and index.
Identifiers: LCCN 2024042417 (print) | LCCN 2024042418 (ebook) | ISBN 9781614299998 (hardcover) | ISBN 9781614299967 (ebook)
Subjects: LCSH: Mahayana Buddhism—History. | Mahayana Buddhism—Sacred books. | Mahayana Buddhism—Doctrines.
Classification: LCC BQ7364 .A63 2025 (print) | LCC BQ7364 (ebook) | DDC 294.3/92—dc23/eng/20250211
LC record available at https://lccn.loc.gov/2024042417
LC ebook record available at https://lccn.loc.gov/2024042418

ISBN 978-1-61429-999-8 ebook ISBN 978-1-61429-996-7

29 28 27 26 25
5 4 3 2 1

Cover image: Prajñāpāramitā. Photo by Gunawan Kartapranata / CC BY-SA 4.0.
Cover design by Marc Whitaker. Interior design by Gopa & Ted 2. Set in DGP 11.25/14.9.

The index was not compiled by the author.

As an act of Dhammadāna, Bhikkhu Anālayo has waived royalty payments for this book.

Wisdom Publications' books are printed on acid-free paper and meet the guidelines for permanence and durability of the Production Guidelines for Book Longevity of the Council on Library Resources.

Printed in the United States of America.

Prajñāpāramitā might be interpreted also as the "translation" of significant parts of traditional Buddhist thought and practice into a new system of thought and language.

(Zacchetti 2015b, 176)

# Contents

# Foreword by His Holiness the Dalai Lama

In *The Perfection of Wisdom in First Bloom*, Bhikkhu Anālayo offers a profound exploration of the early stages of the Prajñāpāramitā tradition, tracing its origins to Lord Buddha's teachings found in the Āgama and Pāli Nikāya traditions.

The author reminds us that wisdom arises not in isolation but through compassion and understanding. The dialogue between Śāriputra and Subhūti reflects the universal journey we all share—transcending intellectual understanding to directly realize interdependence and emptiness. Bhikkhu Anālayo's scholarship and dedication draw readers to the timeless relevance of these teachings in today's world.

The book serves as a valuable guide for both practitioners and academics. It emphasizes not only the importance of study but also the embodiment of wisdom's transformative power in daily life. Bhikkhu Anālayo's engagement with early texts and his humility in presenting their insights embody the spirit of Lord Buddha's teachings.

*The Perfection of Wisdom in First Bloom* inspires those seeking to follow the path of wisdom and compassion. It reminds us that, as we cultivate inner transformation, we must also contribute to the harmony and well-being of all sentient beings.

January 28, 2025

# Acknowledgments and Dedication

I AM INDEBTED to Bhikkhu Bodhi, Chris Burke, Bhikkhunī Dhammadinnā, Paul Harrison, Yuka Nakamura, Jan Nattier, Michael Radich, and Peter Skilling for commenting on a draft version of this book and to the staff, board members, and supporters of the Barre Center for Buddhist Studies for providing me with the facilities needed to do my writing. My exploration in the following pages has considerably benefitted from research published by Karashima Seishi (1957–2019) and Stefano Zacchetti (1968–2020). Working on the present study has been a way for me to connect to the legacy left by these two outstanding scholars, with whom I had a warm personal relationship. I would therefore like to dedicate this book to their memory.

# Introduction

THE PRESENT BOOK explores a selection of central notions and protagonists in the "Perfection of Wisdom in Eight Thousand [Lines]," *Aṣṭasāhasrikā Prajñāpāramitā*,[1] more specifically in its two earliest versions currently available. One of these is a manuscript belonging to the so-called Split Collection, written on birchbark in the Gāndhārī language and Kharoṣṭhī script, with radiocarbon dating locating the production of this manuscript in the environs of the first to the earlier part of the second century of the present era.[2] The other version is a translation into Chinese undertaken by Lokakṣema and his collaborators in the later part of the second century,[3] presumably based on a Gāndhārī original.[4] Given the foundational role of members of the *Aṣṭasāhasrikā* textual family for *Prajñāpāramitā* literature in general,[5] these two versions provide a window on an early stage in a mode of thought and practice that was to be of lasting influence on later Buddhist traditions.

My exploration intends to complement existing perspectives on *Prajñāpāramitā* literature, often based on later traditions, by providing instead a relationship to ideas and developments that form part of the teachings of early Buddhism.[6] Because in what follows I attempt to provide a different perspective, my discussions of relevant dimensions of early Buddhism need to take up, at times in quite some detail, areas that are not necessarily of direct relevance to the passage at hand from the Perfection of Wisdom. In other words, I will regularly indulge in digressions, as these enable me to provide what I deem necessary for a full appreciation of the overall perspective on the Perfection of Wisdom that I attempt to develop.

For the purpose of exploring relevant early Buddhist ideas and developments, I rely on *Āgama* literature as my source material, that is, on texts stemming for the most part from the Pāli *Nikāya*s and their *Āgama* parallels,[7] extant mainly in Chinese but also at times in Gāndhārī, Sanskrit, and Tibetan. Throughout, my presentation does not intend to promote monocausal explanations, instead of which relevant aspects of early Buddhist thought are meant to be seen as just one type of influence operating within a broad web of interrelated causes and conditions responsible for the phenomenon or development under discussion. It is thus only due to the particular angle I have adopted for the present investigation that this type of influence receives the main share of attention.

Due to the same limitation, the result of my attempt to explore an early stage in the emergence of *Prajñāpāramitā* thought in this way can only be an additional perspective. In other words, my study is certainly not supposed to present any kind of final word on the meanings and implications of *Prajñāpāramitā* teachings. Instead, it is just a humble attempt, situated within the confines of my limited knowledge of Mahāyāna thought, to further our understanding of this fascinating dimension in the history of Buddhist philosophy and soteriology by adopting one specific perspective.

My presentation follows the thirty chapters of Lokakṣema's translation, a division that differs from the thirty-two chapters of the Sanskrit text; the divergence starts with the third chapter. To facilitate consultation of my exploration alongside what, for the Sanskrit version, is still the standard translation, I refer to the relevant section in Conze (1973/1975) at the outset of each of my chapters. The first chapter in Lokakṣema's translation (as well as in the other versions) is particularly long and rich, hence even just commenting on a selection of its presentations has resulted in a rather long discussion. Several subsequent chapters in Lokakṣema's translation, however, are comparatively short and call for less comment, wherefore in such cases I combine more than one such chapter in my treatment.[8] In the conclusion, I attempt to relate my exploration in the preceding pages to the much-discussed topic of the origins of Mahāyāna.

Each of my chapters begins by briefly identifying the main ideas that have been introduced in this part of the text and that I will be taking up for closer study.[9] These identifications are only meant as reference points, which due to their succinctness do not reflect the full richness of the material found in the respective parts of the text. Moreover, as I tend to disregard repetitions of themes already mentioned in earlier chapters, my brief introductions do not adequately reflect the structure of the whole text.[10] At times, I take up a certain topic only when commenting on a chapter in which this becomes particularly prominent and thus not invariably at its first occurrence in the whole text.

Following these brief introductions, the remainder of each of my chapters works through the selected topics, exploring the textual developments that appear to provide a perspective on the particular idea or notion under discussion. My hope is that in this way the present book could be consulted alongside reading through the *Aṣṭasāhasrikā Prajñāpāramitā*, or else readers may choose particular topics from the list of contents that seem to them to be of interest. The end of each of my chapters offers a summary of the main points that have been covered, in the form of at first recapping the chief topics in a single sentence and then providing more details, which could be relied on for deciding whether my actual treatment merits a full reading.

A colophon to the Gāndhārī manuscript refers to the copied text just as "the Perfection of Wisdom" (*prañaparamida*).[11] The title of Lokakṣema's translation also does not mention eight thousand or any other number (道行般若經), and Karashima (2011, 111) surmises that at an earlier stage its title may have just been "the Perfection of Wisdom" or else the same together with the qualification of being "Great."[12] This hopefully justifies my use of just the phrase "the Perfection of Wisdom" in the following pages to refer to the two texts that form the basis of my study as well as to the quality or realization that is their central concern,[13] in the understanding that the reference in the title of the Sanskrit version to eight thousand lines would be the result of a later development.[14] When referring to material from the *Nikāya*s and *Āgama*s, I in turn just use the expression "*Āgama* literature."[15] On the relatively rare occasions of referring to the traditional commentary, the *Abhisamayālaṃkārālokā Prajñāpāramitāvyākhyā* by Haribhadra,[16] I do so by using just the name of its author.[17]

Overall, I have endeavored to present the main part of my discussion in each chapter in a way that remains accessible to a general audience, relegating more specific points of scholarly interest to the endnotes.[18] Although it is not really possible to draw a hard and fast line between these two parts of my presentation, as a rule of thumb the text in the main body of the book is aimed at a readership of Buddhist practitioners, in order to introduce these to current research, including my own, in a way that can supplement a reading of the Perfection of Wisdom. Conversely, the notes are for the most part written with my academic colleagues in mind.

I also would like to alert readers from both of these audiences to the fact that my main area of research is early Buddhism, wherefore by venturing into the field of early Mahāyāna I am exploring an area in which I have less expertise.[19] In addition, I lack the language abilities required for consulting relevant research published in Japanese.[20] It follows that assessments I offer of early Mahāyāna thought, unless these rely on other scholars specializing in the field, are probably best taken with a grain of salt.[21]

Lokakṣema's translation of the Perfection of Wisdom comes with a preface written by the fourth-century Chinese scholar-monk Dào'ān (道安), in which he introduces the text to the Chinese audience by highlighting some of its significant features and teachings. In the course of this preface, Dào'ān provides an illustration of the depth of the Perfection of Wisdom that can perhaps also serve as a preface to the ensuing pages. The relevant part reads as follows:[22]

> One who ascends it, however high one may go, can still not mount it; one who wades into it, however deep one may go, can still not fathom it. One who considers it, though one is vitally concerned, cannot encompass it; one who inquires after it, though one may measure it, cannot take its full measure.

# On Chapter 1

The first chapter of Lokakṣema's translation of the Perfection of Wisdom, which aligns with the first chapter of the Sanskrit version translated by Conze (1973/1975, 83–95), begins with the Buddha inviting Subhūti to expound the Perfection of Wisdom to bodhisattvas in the audience. This invitation occasions a dialogue between Śāriputra and Subhūti, following which Subhūti approaches his task by way of exemplification, that is, by speaking from the viewpoint of the Perfection of Wisdom itself, in order to deconstruct the very notion of a "bodhisattva." The remainder of the first chapter then continues engaging in what could be referred to as "the rhetoric of emptiness," applied to the five aggregates, for example, as well as expounding the nature of a bodhisattva or *mahāsattva*, a "great being," and of the Mahāyāna.

In what follows I will explore three main topics: the evolution of the bodhisattva ideal (with a closer look at the same phenomenon in the Pāli traditions), the roles accorded to Śāriputra and Subhūti, and the rhetoric of emptiness.

## The Bodhisattva Path

After reporting the Buddha's whereabouts, the text continues in the dialogue mode, which characterizes most of the Perfection of Wisdom, except for its last chapters. The onset of this dialogue mode takes the form of the Buddha addressing Subhūti, which in the Gāndhārī manuscript version proceeds in the following manner:[23]

> There the Blessed One addressed the venerable Subhūti: "As to the Perfection of Wisdom of a [bodhisattva], a great being, reveal, [Subhūti], how a bodhisattva, a great being, may set out in the Perfection of Wisdom."

This opening statement conveniently reflects the centrality of the bodhisattva ideal for the whole of the Perfection of Wisdom. Behind the genesis of this bodhisattva ideal stands a complex interaction of various trajectories. In subsequent chapters I will have occasion to take up in more detail the notion of a particular way of conduct over a series of past lives that leads to the realization of Buddhahood (see below p. 93), the idea of receiving a prediction of becoming a Buddha in the future (see below p. 106), the intrinsic superiority of those on the bodhisattva path over other Buddhist practitioners (see below p. 194), the need to have a male body for progress to Buddhahood (see below p. 203), and a narrative involving a bodhisattva in quest of the Perfection of Wisdom (see below p. 250). Leaving aside these dimensions for the time being, in the present chapter I begin by summarizing the findings of other scholars regarding the level of development of the bodhisattva ideal evident in the Perfection of Wisdom. Then I look at stages in the development of the bodhisattva concept evident in *Āgama* literature. By way of further contextualization, I survey related developments manifesting in later Pāli literature.

Before delving into these three topics, however, I need to say a few words on *Āgama* discourses as my source material for discerning stages in the development of the bodhisattva ideal and for exploring various other topics in the course of my study. A complete set of such discourses from one reciter tradition is extant in Pāli; similar material transmitted by other reciter traditions is extant mainly in Chinese, Gāndhārī, Sanskrit, and Tibetan. Unlike the Pāli discourse collections, a complete set of these discourse collections has not been preserved by other transmission lineages.

As a rule of thumb, basic agreement between different extant parallel versions of a particular teaching can generally be considered to provide evidence for early Buddhism. The term "early Buddhism" here is meant to designate mainly the development of Buddhist thought during the pre-Aśokan period, characterized by reliance on solely oral means of textual production and transmission.[24] Needless to say, the employment of the term "early Buddhism" is not intended to convey the idea of some sort of monolithic entity, instead of which it refers to a period during which a range of different developments took place.

In principle, an agreement between discourse parallels is stronger evidence for such early Buddhist thought than a teaching found in a discourse only extant in a single reciter tradition. Although this can simply be the outcome of the vagaries of transmission, in particular the circumstance that we do not have complete discourse collections of other reciter traditions, the evidence provided by such a discourse is not as strong as it would be if the position or teaching in question were to be preserved also by parallel versions from other reciter traditions. Conversely, when parallel versions disagree in relation to a particular position or teaching, then examining such variation can help illuminate developments underway in one form or another in the respective reciter traditions, whether they stem from errors in oral transmission or new perspectives and ideas that have influenced this transmission.

In general, the process of committing these discourses to writing appears to have begun before the beginning of the Common Era. In the case of the Pāli discourses, it seems that their oral transmission had already reached a stage of closure, in terms of no longer incorporating major new developments, by about the time of King Aśoka, roughly speaking.[25] The main reason appears to be that by then attention increasingly shifted to other forms of textual articulation, mainly the evolving Abhidharma for doctrinal exegesis as well as various narratives, such as stories of the Buddha Śākyamuni's past lives, for other teaching purposes. These became the arenas for formulating innovative ideas during the ongoing process of negotiation between the teachings believed to originate from the Buddha and the various exigencies of the social, cultural, and geographical situations in which the reciters and teachers of Dharma found themselves.

For the parallels to the Pāli discourses extant in Chinese translation a similar scenario probably holds, with one notable exception in a collection of numerically ascending discourses, the *Ekottarikāgama*. This collection differs from the other extant discourse collections by showing clear evidence of having incorporated material at a relatively late stage, namely as part of a revision of the previously undertaken translation, both occurring in China.[26] In relation to the evolution of the bodhisattva ideal, this collection shows clear influence of already existing, mature Mahāyāna thought.[27] For this reason, it needs to be set apart from other discourses as source material for early Buddhism. As a way of signaling that I am excluding this collection from a particular assessment of early Buddhist thought, I will use the phrase "the Pāli discourses and their parallels (leaving aside the *Ekottarikāgama*)." This phrase intends to convey a more restricted scope, in the sense of not taking into account occurrences in the *Ekottarikāgama*, in particular those not supported by parallels in other discourse collections, which is indeed characteristic of most, though not all, of the instances that contain interpolated material found in this collection.

In general, I think it is fair to propose that the main teachings found in the Pāli discourses and their parallels (leaving aside the *Ekottarikāgama*) form a backdrop to the setting within which the Perfection of Wisdom would have evolved. Nevertheless, in the course of my exploration of the emergence of the bodhisattva ideal and related notions, I try to leave open the possibility of influences operating in both directions,[28] allowing for the very nature of the developments examined to reveal, whenever and to whatever extent that is possible, which cluster of ideas influenced the other.

### *The Stage of Evolution Evident in the Perfection of Wisdom*

For appreciating the stage of evolution of the bodhisattva ideal evident in the *Aṣṭasāhasrikā Prajñāpāramitā*, in what follows I survey selected assessments by other scholars. Zacchetti (2015b, 173) offers the following observation: "Supreme awakening [of a Buddha] is not proposed as a universal goal by Prajñāpāramitā texts, and in fact the *Aṣṭasāhasrikā* is very explicit in depicting the bodhisattva path as a difficult career for a few exceptional individuals."[29] In the same vein, Nattier (2003a, 175 and 132) points out that the *Aṣṭasāhasrikā Prajñāpāramitā* and other early Mahāyāna texts "stop short of urging all beings to become bodhisattvas. On the contrary, they recognize that not all beings have the capacity to become Buddhas, and that the *śrāvaka* and not the bodhisattva path is appropriate for some," adding that "this nonuniversalist position was actually quite widespread, especially in the early stages of the production of Mahāyāna literature." In fact, "the expectation that a bodhisattva's compassion should be manifest in the world here and now appears to have been largely unknown in medieval India."

Lethcoe (1977, 273) explains that a dominant theme, particularly among the early versions of the *Aṣṭasāhasrikā Prajñāpāramitā* textual family, is that "a Bodhisattva's primary efforts should be directed towards winning enlightenment and *then* fulfilling the vows to teach in a spirit of friendliness to all beings." Lethcoe (1977, 270–71) also notes that a bodhisattva's gaining of "irreversibility represented an opportunity to escape this world and to roam henceforth from one pure Buddhafield to another listening to Tathāgatas preaching the Dharma." The *Aṣṭasāhasrikā* "does not respond to the criticism that irreversible Bodhisattvas who only course from pure Buddhafield to Buddhafield have abandoned beings, but we may surmise that its response would be that this is the fastest way of winning enlightenment, i.e. gaining the state where one can best benefit others."

In fact, a significant feature particularly evident in the stage of development attested in the Gāndhārī manuscript version and Lokakṣema's translation appears to be the lack of a central role accorded to compassion. Karashima (2013c, 173) observes: "It is quite remarkable that expressions concerning compassion . . . are often wanting in the oldest versions, namely the first three Chinese translations, though later ones give a great deal of elaboration on this theme."

Commenting on Lokakṣema's translation of the Perfection of Wisdom, Fronsdal (1998/2014, 131) remarks that "contrary to later Indian (as well as modern) views of the bodhisattva as an altruistic practitioner, performing deeds for the benefit of others does not appear as a significant activity for the bodhisattva." In fact, "[e]ven the frequently promoted practice of giving others copies of the Perfection of Wisdom is advocated because of the great merit to be gained by the giver" (134–35). Moreover, "there is no indication of an ideal to postpone one's buddhahood in order to work for the benefit of all beings while one is still a bodhisattva. There is, however, a concern with becoming a buddha quickly, in as few lifetimes as possible" (136). In sum, the position taken in this way in the Perfection of Wisdom "suggests that at the time of its composition the original motivation for attaining buddhahood was not centrally concerned with altruistic regard for others" (132).[30] In relation to early Mahāyāna texts in general, Nattier (2003a, 147) offers the following assessment of such motivation:

> [P]art of the appeal of the bodhisattva path was the glory of striving for the highest achievement that the Buddhist repertoire had to offer. It is thus to the mentality of such people as Olympic athletes ("going for the gold") or Marine Corps recruits ("the few, the proud, the brave") that we probably should look if we want to understand what propelled these pioneering bodhisattvas to take on such a gargantuan task. It is equally clear that such a difficult career would never have appealed—and indeed, was never intended to appeal—to all members of the Buddhist community. The initial introduction of the bodhisattva path thus appears not as the *substitution* of the goal of Buddhahood for that of Arhatship but the *addition* of a new alternative for Buddhist practice, one that was viewed at least in the beginning as appropriate only for those "few good men" who would venture to take it on.

In sum, at the early stage in the evolution of the bodhisattva ideal evident in the Perfection of Wisdom, dedication to progress to Buddhahood emerges as an option for the few. A central concern of those rare beings who embark on this path appears to be the wish to reach their goal as quickly as possible, and acting for the benefit of others has its place primarily when Buddhahood has been successfully achieved.

### *Connotations of the Term "Bodhisattva"*

Har Dayal (1932/1970, 43) explains that "Gautama Buddha speaks of himself as a *bodhisatta*, when he refers to the time before the attainment of

Enlightenment. This seems to be the earliest signification of the word. It was applied to Gautama Buddha as he was in his last earthly life."[31]

When employed in this usage, the term "bodhisattva" mainly conveys the idea of Śākyamuni having gone forth in quest of awakening, without any explicit relationship to the compassionate wish to benefit others. At least in *Āgama* thought, his compassion does not feature as the motivational force leading to his awakening but much rather comes to the fore with his teaching activities once he had become a Buddha. The perspective that emerges in this way aligns with the stage of the bodhisattva ideal evident in the Perfection of Wisdom, where compassion has not yet reached the eminent position that it eventually was to acquire.

A Pāli discourse and its Chinese parallel explicitly depict the nature of Śākyamuni's motivation. This can best be illustrated with the following two excerpts taken from the Chinese version, the first of which concerns his aspiration to set out on the path to awakening and the second his report of having successfully reached awakening:[32]

> Formerly, when I had not yet awakened to supreme, complete awakening, I thought also like this: "I am actually subject to disease myself, and I naively seek for what is subject to disease; I am actually subject to aging, subject to death, subject to worry and sadness, subject to defilement myself, and I naively seek for what is subject to defilement. What if I now rather seek for the supreme peace of Nirvana, which is free from disease, seek for the supreme peace of Nirvana, which is free from aging, free from death, free from worry and sadness, and free from defilement?"

> Seeking for the supreme peace of Nirvana, which is free from disease, I in turn attained the supreme peace of Nirvana, which is free from disease. Seeking for the supreme peace of Nirvana, which is free from aging, free from death, free from worry and sadness, and free from defilement, I in turn attained the supreme peace of Nirvana, which is free from aging, free from death, free from worry and sadness, and free from defilement.

> Arousing knowledge, arousing vision, I was concentrated on the qualities pertinent to awakening. I knew as it really is that birth has been extinguished, the holy life has been established, what had to be done has been done, and there will be no experiencing of a further existence.

The Pāli version proceeds similarly, differing insofar as it does not refer to the qualities "pertinent to awakening" (*bodhipākṣika*). It additionally mentions the condition of being subject to birth alongside the predicaments of disease, aging, death, etc. Apart from such minor variations, however, the two parallels concord that Śākyamuni's motivation to set out in quest of awakening was to liberate himself.

The term "bodhisattva" in this usage would be applicable to Śākyamuni mainly for the narrative period between the first and the second of the two excerpts translated above, that is, from his going forth to his actual awakening. Yet, already in *Āgama* literature a broadening in the scope of meaning of the term can be discerned. Relevant to this broadening is the circumstance that, in order to refer to him before he went forth, the alternative possibility of using the name Gautama was clearly not considered appropriate. *Āgama* literature shows the employment of this name to be characteristic of non-Buddhists, in contrast to his disciples, who prefer to refer to him by an honorific epithet like "Blessed One" (*bhagavat*). In fact, a Pāli discourse and parallels in Sanskrit and Chinese report that the recently awakened Buddha explicitly told those who were to become his first disciples that they should not address him by his name, Gautama.[33] This procedure concords with an apparent general reluctance in the ancient setting to refer to a respected person by their name.[34]

Since at this stage in the evolution of Buddhist thought there was only a single bodhisattva—the Buddha Śākyamuni during the time of his quest for awakening—it would in a way be natural to extend the usage of the expression "*the* bodhisattva" to the time of his life preceding his going forth. An example in case can be seen in the Buddha's report that his mother passed away soon after his birth. In a Pāli discourse depicting various marvels related to the Buddha, this takes the following form: "Seven days after the bodhisattva has been born, Ānanda, the mother of the bodhisattva passes away and arises in the Tuṣita Heaven."[35] In this way, the Buddha here refers to himself as "*the* bodhisattva."

Notably, this discourse proceeds further, as it also covers Śākyamuni's previous life in Tuṣita. The Buddha reports, in obvious reference to himself, that "*the* bodhisattva" was born in Tuṣita, stayed there, and passed away from there endowed with mindfulness and clear comprehension.[36] The Chinese parallel does not mention the death of the mother at all; in relation to Śākyamuni's previous life in Tuṣita, it does not use the term "bodhisattva."[37] The significant contribution made by these Pāli passages appears to be that they extend the meaning of the term "bodhisattva" to comprise the period of Śākyamuni's life prior to his going forth, even to the extent of including his former life in the Tuṣita realm.

Another and similarly significant extension in meaning of the term "bodhisattva" can be seen in a discourse dedicated to providing details of the lineage of six previous Buddhas that according to the traditional account preceded Śākyamuni; the first of these is Vipaśyin and the last Kāśyapa. The Pāli discourses and their parallels (leaving aside the *Ekottarikāgama*) only know these six predecessors. With later tradition, the listing expands considerably and comes to comprise various other previous Buddhas, among them also Dīpaṃkara (see below p. 93).[38]

Although the set of six previous Buddhas must be comparatively early, the descriptions given in the relevant discourse are the result of some developments, based on incorporating textual material from the other discourse, just mentioned above, which depicts various marvels of the Buddha Śākyamuni. In a way such borrowing of portions of text is only natural, since the depiction of the lineage of Buddhas provides a template for central events that are believed to happen in the same basic manner in the lives of different Buddhas.[39] Hence, to rely on descriptions of the Buddha Śākyamuni in another discourse to provide more details to flesh out this template is an obvious choice. As a result, the parts of the Pāli discourse on former Buddhas that appears to incorporate textual material from the depiction of marvels naturally use the term "bodhisattva" that is already found in this depiction. However, in its new context, the term now refers to the former Buddha Vipaśyin. This usage contrasts with a subsequent part of the same discourse, which instead speaks of him as the "prince" Vipaśyin.[40] This change of terminology confirms the impression that an incorporation of textual material has taken place, and this has not been appropriately adjusted to its context. This could have been done by using the term "bodhisattva" continuously from then on or else by replacing occurrences of the term "bodhisattva" with the term "prince."[41]

As far as the term "bodhisattva" is concerned, its application to Vipaśyin significantly broadens its compass, as the term now refers no longer only to Śākyamuni but also to previous Buddhas during the time before their awakening. *The* bodhisattva has become *a* bodhisattva. Combined with the extension of the term to comprise not only the youth of a Buddha-to-be before going forth but even a past life, the generic concept of a bodhisattva emerges.

The above developments would in turn have set the stage for subsequent evolutions in meaning of the term "bodhisattva." This applies not only to the Perfection of Wisdom and other early Mahāyāna texts but also to later texts in the Pāli tradition, which I examine next. My discussion in what follows thereby moves beyond the general parameters of my exploration of the Perfection of Wisdom from the viewpoint of *Āgama* literature, to which I will return in the remainder of this chapter. At the present juncture, however, so as to enable an appreciation of the pan-Buddhist relevance of the bodhisattva ideal, I believe it is warranted to allow for a short diversion by taking a look at how this ideal evolved in later Pāli texts and influenced living Theravāda traditions.[42] Readers less interested in this exploration may prefer to shift directly to the next section (p. 22) on the roles of "Śāriputra and Subhūti" in the Perfection of Wisdom.

### *The Bodhisattva Ideal in Later Pāli Texts*

One instance pertaining to the category of references to the notion of a bodhisattva in later Pāli text occurs in the *Kathāvatthu*, found in the Pāli basket of Abhidharma. The work takes the position that a bodhisattva will not choose to be reborn in a lower realm.[43] This can be related to the observation by Lethcoe (1977, 271) that the *Aṣṭasāhasrikā Prajñāpāramitā* "holds that Bodhisattvas who are irreversible from the path cannot ever have an evil rebirth; presumably, they would never even choose to do so, since it would only retard their own speedy advancement to Tathāgata-hood," followed by noting that this attitude changes with the *Pañcaviṃśatisāhasrikā Prajñāpāramitā*. With this next stage of textual growth in *Prajñāpāramitā* literature, the perspective becomes rather that "irreversible Bodhisattvas do enter, by choice, the evil states to help beings there."[44]

In addition to the above instance from the basket of Abhidharma, relevant material can also be found in the fifth Pāli *Nikāya*, which differs from the other four *Nikāya*s collecting Pāli discourses by including a variety of textual material stemming from a broad range of time periods. One of the later members of this collection reports Śākyamuni's encounters with twenty-four past Buddhas during his former lives as a bodhisattva. This text, called *Buddhavaṃsa*, provides a list of eight conditions that need to be fulfilled in order to become a bodhisattva,[45] which reflects some degree of development in the theory of the path to Buddhahood.

Another such later text, the *Cariyāpiṭaka*, illustrates how Śākyamuni fulfilled the perfections in the course of his bodhisattva career.[46] In the Pāli tradition in general, the perfections to be cultivated by a bodhisattva amount to ten, rather than the six regularly mentioned in the Perfection of Wisdom, showing a distinct development of the common Buddhist notion of perfections required for progress to Buddhahood. This notion itself, unlike the qualities it comprises, is not found in the Pāli discourses and their parallels (leaving aside the *Ekottarikāgama*). These texts still reflect a stage when a need to single out qualities required for the path of a bodhisattva had not yet arisen, since progress to awakening was still concerned just with the four stages of stream-entry, once-return, nonreturn, and arhat-ship.

Another late Pāli text is the *Apadāna*, the first part of which, the *Buddhāpadāna*, refers to countless Buddhafields in the ten directions.[47] The same work quite explicitly speaks of a plurality of Buddhas existing in the present.[48] Another part of the *Apadāna* also refers to a plurality of Buddhas in the present.[49] It is remarkable to find such presentations in a text that, despite earlier disagreements over its status,[50] has gained acceptance in the Theravāda traditions of South and Southeast Asia for being "canonical."[51] Nevertheless, as long as these plural Buddhas live in different Buddhafields, this type of presentation would not conflict with the dictum in the Pāli discourses that there can be only one Buddha at a time, as this dictum explicitly applies only to the situation in a single world system.[52]

The recognition of a plurality of Buddhas coexisting in the present time is not confined to Pāli texts, as it also features as part of the living traditions, evident in a reference in a commonly recited Pāli verse to paying homage to "Buddhas of the present."[53] Given the dictum that there can be only one Buddha at a time in our world system, such usage would require the tacit acceptance of the existence of different Buddhafields, which in turn would confirm the widespread appeal of this notion. This suggests an at least implicit acceptance of different Buddhafields to be an integral part of the Pāli Buddhist traditions.

In the case of yet another late Pāli text, inclusion in the fifth *Nikāya* has remained a contested issue in the Theravāda traditions. This is the report of a debate between an Indo-Greek king and a Buddhist monk in the *Milindapañha*. This work presents a list of ten special qualities of bodhisattvas, which include their greatness (*mahantatā*) and their rarity (*dullabhatā*).[54] Such a reference to rarity appears to be similar to the position reflected in the Perfection of Wisdom that the path of a bodhisattva is a difficult career for a few exceptional individuals, which of course implies that bodhisattvas are rare beings.

Another type of text to be explored is Pāli commentarial literature. According to Endo (2005, 50), the commentarial tradition brought from India to Sri Lanka, which forms the basis for the Pāli commentaries, would have come to a close around the first century before the Common Era.[55] This would mean that those parts of the presently extant Pāli commentaries that reproduce this ancient commentarial tradition would be reflecting roughly the same time period that probably also saw the emergence of the Perfection of Wisdom.[56] Needless to say, precise dating is no longer possible. Nevertheless, it does seem reasonable to allow for the possibility that the Pāli commentaries may contain early material, preceding by several centuries their transposition into Pāli in the fifth century of the present era. This is especially the case when the relevant explanations seem to emerge quite naturally from the context set by the discourse on which they comment, without any evident need for external input.

Pāli commentaries that stand a higher chance of being comparatively early are those on the four main Pāli *Nikāyas*. One such Pāli commentary defines the term "bodhisattva"—which often in such contexts refers to Śākyamuni during his previous lives up to his realization of awakening—to stand for a being on the way to awakening who has received a prediction in the presence of former Buddhas and fulfilled the perfections.[57] A concern with receiving such a prediction is also evident in the Perfection of Wisdom, a topic to be explored in more detail in a subsequent chapter (see below p. 255). At times the Pāli commentaries use the term "great being" (*mahāsatta*) as an alternative to the term "bodhisattva."[58] The same usage can also be seen in the Perfection of Wisdom.[59]

The Pāli commentaries distinguish between three types of awakening, which are that of a disciple, of a Pratyekabuddha, and of a Buddha, the last being referred to as the attainment of omniscience.[60] These three types of awakening also feature in the Perfection of Wisdom, where the attainment of omniscience ranks as a topic of considerable interest (see in more detail below p. 237).

Another relevant commentarial passage describes the conduct of bodhisattvas who go forth under a former Buddha. Its presentation emerges quite naturally from the denouement of the narrative in the discourse on which it comments, which makes it possible that it reflects a relatively early tradition. According to the relevant passage, bodhisattvas will cultivate insight without making an effort to gain the paths and fruits (of stream-entry, once-return, nonreturn, and arhat-ship).[61] This presentation implies an intentional refraining from taking the cultivation of insight to its culmination in the breakthrough to Nirvana, ostensibly so as to be able to continue on the path to Buddhahood. The presentation in this commentary matches a recurrent theme in the Perfection of Wisdom of encouraging bodhisattvas to stay firm in their dedication to progress to Buddhahood rather than succumbing to the alternative option of becoming an arhat (or a Pratyekabuddha).

Whereas the passages surveyed above stem from commentaries on the four *Nikāyas* that give the impression of being moderately early, with the next passages my survey proceeds to a distinctly late type of commentary (on the in itself late work *Cariyāpiṭaka*). The relevant passage explains that out of compassion a bodhisattva accepts *dukkha* (Sanskrit: *duḥkha*), keeps arriving in the round of rebirths, faces *saṃsāra*, and has empathy for everyone.[62] This seems to reflect a stage in the development of the bodhisattva ideal that is clearly more evolved than what can be found in the early versions of the Perfection of Wisdom. Another passage in the same commentary speaks of a great being who embarks on the practice of the *mahābodhiyāna*—thereby using an expression that seems to involve a deliberate play on the term *mahāyāna*—who on having reached irreversibility truly deserves to be reckoned a bodhisattva.[63]

Although this choice of terminology must reflect influences from already existing Mahāyāna thought, the same need not hold for another presentation in the same commentary. The relevant part distinguishes three types of bodhisattvas according to their abilities. Some only need a succinct teaching, others necessitate more details, and still others require close guidance.[64] The distinction as such is already found in a Pāli discourse, although not applied to bodhisattvas.[65] Skilling (2002/2003, 99) notes that, even though the terminology employed here recurs in *Prajñāpāramitā* literature,[66] the application of the set of three terms to distinguish bodhisattvas of different capabilities is "a development unique to the Theravādins."[67] The same commentary also presents a distinction of each of the perfections into three levels as basic, intermediate, and supreme.[68] In conjunction with the typology of bodhisattvas, this work thereby presents classifications that "seem to be unique to the Theravāda" (Skilling 2013b, 115).

Another feature worthy of note is that Pāli texts do not employ the term *bodhicitta*, whose arousal is a defining characteristic of the fully evolved Mahāyāna conception of the path to becoming a Buddha.[69] Instead, some instances of Pāli formulations of the aspiration to gain the omniscience of Buddhahood for the sake of delivering sentient beings employ the Pāli counterparts to the Sanskrit terms *abhinirhāra* and *prārthanā*.[70] This would reflect a local development rather than a wholesale importation of the notion of aspiring for Buddhahood from some already existing, developed Mahāyāna tradition(s), as in that case it would have been more natural to use the established terminology.

The above exploration goes to show that a distinct contribution to articulations of the bodhisattva path can be found in the Pāli traditions. Moreover, this contribution is not confined to the realm of theoretical elaboration. Skilling (2002/2003, 101) points out that "[t]he typology of three bodhisattas pervaded religious thought in South-East Asia . . . Colophons and inscriptions show that the three types were . . . very much part of living Buddhism."

The degree to which the bodhisattva ideal has become part of the living tradition in the case of Sri Lanka can perhaps be exemplified with the help of figure 1, which shows a two-armed, single-faced Avalokiteśvara statue of 9.85 meters height carved out of stone probably in the second half of the eighth century and located in the area of Dambegoda, Sri Lanka.[71] According to Mori (1999, 68), in 1990 "the President of Sri Lanka, the late Mr. Ranasinghe Premadasa himself, paid a visit to the place and unveiled the Bodhisattva statue on the occasion of the completion of the restoration of the statue." Newspaper coverage at that time "clearly stated that it was a restored statue of Avalokiteśvara Bodhisattva." Mori (1999, 69) further reports that two weeks later, when visiting the statue himself, he "saw a group of visitors who had come there by a chartered bus to worship the large restored Avalokiteśvara statue." On another visit two and a half years later, he found that "[t]he number of pilgrims had increased from before: even Theravāda monks were found among them."

Figure 1.
Eighth-century
Avalokiteśvara statue.

Inscriptional evidence further supports the importance of the bodhisattva ideal for the living Theravāda traditions. One example is an inscription datable to the seventh century and found in Sri Lanka, which concludes with the donor's prayer that he may attain Buddhahood and thereby redeem mankind.[72] Another inscription datable to around the seventh to eighth century, which has been cut into the face of a rock in Sri Lanka, also ends with the donor's aspiration for Buddhahood.[73] A Sri Lankan inscription datable to the eighth or ninth century reports the donor's desire to become a supreme, perfect Buddha.[74] A stone inscription datable to the tenth century, found in a Sri Lankan monastery, expresses the desire of the donor to become a perfect Buddha who can quench the thirst of all people.[75]

Similar sentiments find expression in inscriptions in Thailand.[76] One such inscription reports the aspiration of the donor of a monastery not to be discouraged from progress to Buddhahood in order to rescue sentient beings.[77] A king of Sukhothai is on record in another inscription for aspiring to become a Buddha in order to lead all sentient beings out of the three worlds, just as a king of Ayutthaya wishes to lead all sentient beings to freedom from the fears of cyclic existence and the suffering of the woeful realms.[78] Skilling (2007b, 204) explains that "[t]he *bodhisattva* ideal had a strong following, not only among the nobility: high-ranking and ordinary monastics also recorded the aspiration . . . in colophons and inscriptions."[79]

Comparable aspirations can be found in inscriptions from Burma. An instance datable to the twelfth century reports the donor's aspiration to receive the prediction of his future Buddhahood from the next Buddha, Maitreya, indicating that his motivation is to redeem all beings from the miseries of *saṃsāra*.[80] Some such aspirations are also made by women. In one case, datable to the thirteenth century, the donor expresses her wish for future Buddhahood in terms of wanting to become omniscient.[81] Notably, in another inscription the same donor aspires to be free from the condition of being a woman,[82] reflecting the widespread belief that an advanced bodhisattva has to be a male. This is a topic I will explore in a subsequent chapter (see below p. 203). In a thirteenth-century inscription related to a lavish gift, a bodhisattva and princess clarifies that she loves

Buddhahood more than the property she has donated.[83] A queen wishes for omniscience and Buddhahood in order to be able to lead all beings to the great city of Nirvana.[84] One more inscription from the thirteenth century deserves to be mentioned, as it reports the aspiration to become a Buddha made by husband and wife together.[85]

By way of completing the picture that emerges in this way, the continuous relevance of the bodhisattva ideal can be seen from twentieth-century field work. Spiro (1970/1982, 62) reports that in Burma "there has been a long tradition of aspiration to Buddhahood" among a minority of the population. Bond (1988, 203) comments that recent developments in Sri Lanka show that the bodhisattva ideal appears to have "deep roots in popular tradition."[86] According to Tambiah (1976, 97), in Thailand it was "common practice for kings to take the title of *bodhisattva* and even sometimes to identify themselves with *maitreya*, the Buddha-to-come"; Skilling (2007b, 203–4) reports that "[t]he aspiration to Buddhahood of the kings of Sukhothai, Ayutthaya, Thonburi, and Ratanakosin was publicly proclaimed, in inscriptions, edicts, decrees, chronicles, and poems, and in their very names, titles, and epithets. That they were bodhisattvas was part of their image."[87] Sri Lankan and Burmese kings were similarly invested with the status of being bodhisattvas.[88]

In sum, it seems that the bodhisattva ideal, alongside some local variations, is probably best considered a pan-Buddhist phenomenon.[89] Despite accounts of the suppression of Mahāyāna by Sri Lankan kings,[90] the *bodhisattvayāna* has been of continuous relevance to Sri Lankan and Southeast Asian Buddhists. It clearly has impacted a range of Pāli texts as well as inscriptions and actual practice in the Theravāda traditions. Even *Prajñāpāramitā* literature made its appearance in Sri Lanka, as evident from seven gold leaves (size 63.5 to 5.8 centimeters) from an original that would have consisted of over thirty-five such leaves. The leaves, found in the surroundings of the Jetavanārāma of Anurādhapura, are inscribed in ninth-century Singhalese script with parts of the *Pañcaviṃśatisāhasrikā Prajñāpāramitā*.[91]

With this I have concluded my preliminary exploration of the bodhisattva path, covering the stage of its evolution evident in the Perfection of Wisdom, connotations of the term as such, and the development of the bodhisattva ideal in later Pāli tradition. A key point to be taken along from this discussion is that the conception of the bodhisattva path evident in the Perfection of Wisdom has much in common with the corresponding conception in later Pāli texts.

## Śāriputra and Subhūti

From a preliminary exploration of the bodhisattva ideal, a topic of continuous relevance to my exploration of the Perfection of Wisdom, in what follows I turn to two chief protagonists in the Perfection of Wisdom, in line with the suggestion by Silk (1994, 52) that "[o]ne way in which we may gain a better understanding of the tradition and currents of the literature of the early Mahāyāna is to investigate its protagonists."

The first part of the exchange between Śāriputra and Subhūti has been preserved in the Gāndhārī manuscript, taking the following form:[92]

> Then it occurred to the venerable Śāriputra: "How is it, will the venerable Subhūti here explain it by resorting to his own power or by the might of the Buddha?" Then the venerable Subhūti said to the venerable [Śāriputra]: "Venerable Śāriputra, whatever a disciple of the Blessed One says is entirely..."

Although the manuscript has not preserved the ensuing part (represented above by an elision mark), the context and what subsequently has been preserved make it clear that the missing portion must have conveyed the sense that what disciples teach originates from the might of the Buddha. This is the reading in the corresponding part of Lokakṣema's translation,[93] which additionally indicates that Subhūti had come to know of the thought in Śāriputra's mind,[94] something that is only implicit in the above passage.

Schmithausen (1977, 43) sees this exchange between Śāriputra and Subhūti as an early addition made for the purpose of authentication, prior to which the text would have proceeded directly from the Buddha's invitation to Subhūti's reply by deconstructing the notions of a bodhisattva (and of the Perfection of Wisdom). Authentication seems to be indeed an undercurrent in the present episode when the Buddha, instead of inviting his chief disciple Śāriputra to speak, chooses Subhūti,[95] and the latter is then shown to read the former's mind.[96] In this way, the roles accorded to Śāriputra and Subhūti respectively are sufficiently unusual to convey the impression that these choices must be communicating an important dimension of the overall message of the Perfection of Wisdom. Appreciating this requires a closer look at each of these two protagonists.

### *Śāriputra*

In *Āgama* literature, Śāriputra features as a particularly outstanding disciple of the Buddha, and a broad range of teachings given by him have made their way into the discourse collections. The dialogue style adopted in this first chapter of the Perfection of Wisdom, as well as in most of the ensuing chapters, is closely similar to the type of dialogue in which Śāriputra often engages with other disciples in various discourses.[97] This form of presentation avoids prolonged monologue and through its lively nature more easily captures the attention of the audience.

An example for such a dialogue in *Āgama* literature, which also shares with the Perfection of Wisdom the feature of proceeding from one topic to another, has Śāriputra and Mahākauṣṭhila as protagonists. Whereas in the Pāli and a partial Tibetan version the role of Śāriputra is to provide answers to questions by Mahākauṣṭhila, in a Chinese version Śāriputra is the one to ask questions.[98] This difference does not seem to carry significant implications, as the discourses recurrently showcase someone asking questions for the sake of others in the audience, rather than out of a need to receive personal clarifications. The Pāli commentary indeed allocates the present exchange to the category of questions posed just for the sake of discussion.[99]

The same perspective holds for another dialogue in which Śāriputra takes the role of questioner, which in this case he does in all versions. The task of responding to the questions falls to Pūrṇa Maitrāyaṇīputra, who also makes brief appearances in the Perfection of Wisdom. Other passages in *Āgama* literature laud Pūrṇa for his teaching abilities.[100] Nevertheless, the present exchange with Śāriputra appears to be the only discourse extant from different reciter traditions where Pūrṇa explicitly features as taking an active role as a speaker.[101] This makes it fair to allow for the possibility that his appearances as a speaker in the Perfection of Wisdom could have prompted members of the audience, as long as these were sufficiently familiar with *Āgama* literature, to recall this other discourse.

Exploring this possibility further, it is worthy of note that, in addition to having the same protagonists—Pūrṇa Maitrāyaṇīputra as one of its speakers and Śāriputra taking the role of asking questions—the discourse in question shares with the first chapter of the Perfection of Wisdom a concern with the highest type of wisdom as the final goal of the path of practice.

According to the introductory narration of the *Āgama* discourse, Śāriputra had earlier heard of Pūrṇa's outstanding qualities. When an occasion arises to meet the latter personally, he approaches the situation without revealing his identity, in order to elicit a manifestation of Pūrṇa's wisdom. The ruse works; in fact, all versions of the discourse agree that at the end of their exchange, once Pūrṇa realizes with whom he has been discussing, he explains that he would not have given such a detailed teaching had he known the identity of his questioner.[102]

The questions Śāriputra asks Pūrṇa are about the nature of the final goal: Can this be identified with different types of purification, such as purification of one's ethical conduct, of the mind, of one's view, etc.? Pūrṇa denies that any of altogether seven types of purification mentioned by his interlocutor could be identified as the final goal. In order to illustrate their merely instrumental purpose, Pūrṇa presents a simile of seven chariots used in relay by a king to proceed swiftly from one location to another. None of the seven chariots corresponds to where the king wants to arrive. Nevertheless, using these seven chariots one after the other he will arrive at the palace he wants to reach. In the same way, each of the seven purifications, even the seventh purification of knowledge and vision, is not the final goal but only a means to arrive at it.

By relying on the simile of the seven chariots, Pūrṇa aptly illustrates that the final goal of freedom from defilements, which another Pāli discourse and its Tibetan parallel equate to the peak of emptiness,[103] is beyond even the most refined levels of insight, even beyond purification of knowledge and vision. In view of the apt illustration provided by this teaching, I will mention the simile of the seven chariots repeatedly in my exploration of the Perfection of Wisdom.

Presumably aware of the challenges of adequately expressing the merely instrumental role of various levels of purification, within the narrative setting of the discourse Śāriputra can be envisaged to have chosen this profound topic deliberately in order to draw out Pūrṇa's wisdom. The context in fact makes it clear that Śāriputra is not in need of having the topic explained for his own sake.

The same can also be seen in a Pāli discourse without a known parallel in which he clarifies basically the same matter in a question-and-answer exchange with yet another monk.[104] Śāriputra points out that arrival at the final goal, here referred to in terms of making an end of *duḥkha*, does not come about by means of knowledge or conduct or even both. Yet, one who is without these will be completely unable to make an end of *duḥkha*. Both are necessary means but fall short of being the goal themselves. This presentation confirms the impression that *Āgama* literature reflects a keen awareness of the need to proceed beyond whatever means have been used to progress to the final goal. This is also a central theme in the first chapter of the Perfection of Wisdom, with a difference in setting being that here Śāriputra features as someone receiving instructions on the need to proceed further in order to arrive at a full realization of emptiness.

In *Āgama* literature in general, Śāriputra features as foremost in wisdom.[105] In fact, according to a Pāli verse Śāriputra has the role of keeping the wheel of Dharma rolling after it has been set in motion by the Buddha,[106] for which reason he is also known in other Pāli passages as the general of the Dharma.[107] A discourse extant in Pāli and Chinese provides a more specific relationship to the type of wisdom that is of particular interest from the viewpoint of the Perfection of Wisdom. The parallel versions report that the Buddha wants to know what meditation Śāriputra has been practicing, to which the latter replies that he has been meditating on emptiness.[108] The Buddha praises him for cultivating such meditation and then takes advantage of the occasion, provided by the example set by Śāriputra, to deliver a teaching on how to implement emptiness in a daily life situation, in particular when going to beg alms.

A Pāli verse, which according to the commentarial explanation was spoken in reference to Śāriputra, illustrates his role as a teacher of Dharma with the example of someone embarking on a boat who, knowing the means and being skilled, can ferry many others across.[109] The reference here to knowing the "means" and being "skilled" is intriguing. Pāsādika (2008, 439) reasons that this verse is "distinctly reminiscent of the Mahāyāna usage of *upāyakauśalya*," the notion of skill in means (to be examined in more detail below p. 214).

The usage of terminology closely related to the notion of skill in means, together with the image of ferrying others across, has a complement in another Pāli verse in the employment of the very term "perfection of wisdom" to designate what Śāriputra had "attained" (*paññāpāramitaṃ patto*).[110] The commentary adds that this of course intends the wisdom of disciples of the Buddha;[111] it does not include the wisdom of the Buddha himself, whom none of his disciples could surpass in this respect. Although strictly speaking this appears to be the only occurrence of exactly the term "perfection of wisdom" in Pāli discourse literature, a closely similar usage occurs in a Pāli discourse dedicated in its entirety to eulogizing Śāriputra. According to the relevant passage, Śāriputra "had attained perfection in noble wisdom" (*pāramippatto ariyāya paññāya*).[112] In the contextual setting of both instances, which as yet does not know the idea of a set of perfections to be cultivated in order to proceed to Buddhahood, the term "perfection" used in relation to wisdom simply refers to the peak of wisdom. In fact, the second instance applies the same idea of attaining perfection also to virtue, concentration, and liberation. The last is clearly not one of the perfections traditionally related to the path to Buddhahood.

In sum, in view of the above indications, Śāriputra would have been the most obvious choice for being invited by the Buddha to expound on the topic of the Perfection of Wisdom. In the different versions of the *Aṣṭasāhasrikā Prajñāpāramitā*, however, the role of Śāriputra is quite different. Appreciating this requires a brief look at the emergence of the Abhidharma.

Summarizing (and inevitably thereby simplifying) a complex development, aspects of which I have elsewhere studied in more detail,[113] the Abhidharma appears to have gradually arisen from within the growing body of commentaries on the discourses. Although summary lists and question-and-answer catechisms are important formal elements that have influenced the presentation of Abhidharma thought, these are not sufficiently specific to explain the dynamics at work in the emergence of Abhidharma thought as such, simply because they also occur in other contexts, even outside of Buddhist texts. The relevant dynamic can more fruitfully be understood to have served a central role in substituting for the loss of guidance and orientation caused by the Buddha's demise, who by this time had come to be considered omniscient (a topic I will explore in a later chapter; see below p. 237). In other words, a chief concern of Abhidharma thought appears to be to present doctrinal knowledge, in particular in relation to the path to liberation, in a manner as comprehensive and detailed as possible to ensure that disciples, wishing to progress to awakening, can avail themselves of a complete map of the path. For this purpose, the various teachings and forms of exposition in *Āgama* literature need to be streamlined and combined into a coherent system that is based on identifying their most essential features.

Besides comprehensive coverage, another important feature in this project is analysis, which has become a hallmark of Abhidharma thought. Already *Āgama* literature shows a penchant for analysis as a key tool for progressing to liberating insight. An example involving Śāriputra as the speaker provides a convenient illustration. His exposition, which this time takes the form of a monologue rather than a dialogue, proceeds from the four noble truths to the first truth. From that, he takes up the five aggregates mentioned in this first truth, then the first aggregate of form, and then the four elements as what make up the first aggregate. Then Śāriputra examines each of the four elements in detail, revealing their empty nature. His teaching eventually leads up to the famous statement that one who sees dependent arising (*pratītya samutpāda*) sees the Dharma.[114]

The approach taken in some Abhidharma traditions can be considered as following this basic procedure but with the assumption that it is not possible to take analysis beyond a certain point, such as in the present case the breakdown into the four elements as the final point at which Śāriputra arrived. These thereby can emerge as in some way ultimately real and endowed with an "intrinsic nature," *svabhāva*, sometimes alternatively rendered as "own-being."[115] Such a type of thinking in some Abhidharma traditions appears to have become a target of criticism in the Perfection of Wisdom,[116] a topic to which I will be returning repeatedly in the course of my exploration.

The emerging Abhidharma traditions, evidently due to the pervasively felt need for authentication, naturally took Śāriputra as their icon.[117] An example for this tendency relates to an *Āgama* discourse spoken by Śāriputra in order to ensure harmony among the disciples when the Buddha would no longer be among them. For this purpose, Śāriputra presents a long list of doctrinal items, arranged numerically, which are to be recited in unison as an expression of communal agreement and harmony.[118] A commentary on this discourse has become a canonical Abhidharma text of the Sarvāstivādins, with even this commentary at times being attributed to Śāriputra,[119] presumably influenced by the fact that in all versions he features as the speaker of the discourse.

The Pāli tradition, which attributes the delivery of the Abhidharma texts to the Buddha himself, nevertheless also accords a central role to Śāriputra in this respect. The actual teaching of the Abhidharma is situated in a heavenly realm, with the Buddha coming down daily to the human world to take a meal and afterward share the teachings of the day with Śāriputra.[120] In this way, Śāriputra acquires a central role in the transmission of the Pāli Abhidharma. Although this tale is only found in an Abhidharma commentary, it seems reasonable to assume that it builds on a common and relatively early tendency to associate Śāriputra with Abhidharma-type thought, in line with the style of teaching characteristic of several discourses attributed to him.

The reason the emerging Perfection of Wisdom did not make Śāriputra their key speaker, even though he would have been the most straightforward choice for this role, could perhaps be the circumstance that by then he had already become too closely associated with the emerging Abhidharma traditions. Given that the Perfection of Wisdom critically responds to some Abhidharma ideas, such association may well have already been in existence in some form when the Perfection of Wisdom began to emerge.

The Abhidharma-related associations Śāriputra appears to have acquired in this way would have made him instead the appropriate choice for exemplifying the need to proceed further. His role in this respect aligns with instances in *Āgama* literature of Śāriputra playing the part of a questioner requesting explanations, the main difference being that in the present context he is not just drawing out the other's wisdom. Instead, he is himself in need of instruction, by way of being encouraged to take analysis all the way to its culmination in the realization of the thoroughly empty nature of all phenomena without exception. Śāriputra needs to be taught what Pūrṇa so aptly clarified, namely the need to get off the seventh chariot so as to be able to enter the palace the king wanted to reach. Even the seventh purification of knowledge and vision is not yet an arrival at the final goal, for whose sake the seventh chariot needs to be left behind.

### *Subhūti*

In contrast to Śāriputra, in *Āgama* literature Subhūti features as a marginal figure about whom not much is known. His name comes up in only two instances of a discourse that receives support from a parallel version.[121] The first of these two, which is extant in Pāli and Chinese, with parts preserved also in Sanskrit and Tibetan, presents an analysis of the absence of conflict.[122] Since this topic relates closely to a chief characteristic of Subhūti, it may be opportune to take a closer look at the teachings in this discourse.

The main teaching begins by setting aside the two extremes of sensory indulgence and self-mortification, commending the adoption of a middle path aloof from these two, which is the noble eightfold path.[123] The problematization of sensual pleasures in this presentation concords with an alternative meaning of the key term taken up in this discourse, the "absence of conflict," *araṇa*, which can also convey the "absence of sensual passion."[124] A relationship between these two meanings can be established based on other discourses that identify the search for sensual gratification as a central driving force behind criminal activities, going to war, and other evils of human society.[125] From this perspective, then, overcoming sensual lust can be expected to make a significant contribution to dwelling in the absence of conflict.

The main part of the ensuing analysis of the absence of conflict takes up the need to avoid excessive praising as well as disparaging, instead of which one should just teach Dharma. The absence of conflict also benefits from discerning what types of speech are better avoided. This holds not only for untrue speech that is unbeneficial but also for true speech that is unbeneficial. It follows that one should endeavor to say only what is true and beneficial, with the additional stipulation that one should know the right time for engaging in such speech.

A practitioner seeking to abide without conflict should also avoid insisting dogmatically on particular linguistic expressions. The parallels exemplify this by listing different terms used for a particular item in various regions of ancient India. Instead of presuming that one's own familiar or preferred word choice is the only correct one, the advice is to go along with local customs and express what is to be said in the way familiar to the audience. In other words, rather than reifying a particular linguistic usage, the merely instrumental nature of language needs to be kept in mind, which facilitates adapting one's ways of speaking to the needs of the particular situation and contextual setting.

The above topics, selected from the presentation given in the discourse as a whole, would in principle stand a good chance of preventing conflict and contributing to equanimity. The Pāli commentary provides an additional indication in relation to the topic of just teaching Dharma. According to its report, Subhūti would teach without having any concerns in his mind regarding the good or bad qualities of those in his audience.[126] This indication ties in with qualities related to a realization of emptiness, which can be expected to make it easier to avoid clinging strongly to binary evaluations of good or bad. Another significant topic would be the need to avoid dogmatically clinging to particular words, in the understanding of the purely instrumental function of language. This would align well with the overall trajectory against reification of terms and concepts in the Perfection of Wisdom.[127]

The relationship of this whole exposition to Subhūti then comes up in the final section of the discourse. The Pāli version concludes with the Buddha highlighting that Subhūti cultivates the path of nonconflict.[128] The Chinese parallel, found in the *Madhyamāgama*, offers a more substantial reference to Subhūti:[129]

> In this way the son of a good family Subhūti, by dint of the path of nonconflict, subsequently came to understand the Dharma in accordance with the Dharma.

> Having known the Dharma as it really is,
> Subhūti spoke this verse:
> "This abiding is truly in emptiness,
> Being equanimous, this dwelling is pacified."

The two versions agree in associating Subhūti with the path of nonconflict. The Chinese version makes explicit what could be implicit in the Pāli version, in that this path was what made him gain an understanding of "the Dharma as it really is" (alternatively described as being an understanding of "the Dharma in accordance with the Dharma"). In the final two lines of the above verse, Subhūti extolls abiding in emptiness and identifies equanimity as being a dwelling in pacification. Such topics resonate well with central trajectories in the Perfection of Wisdom.

The second of the two instances in which Subhūti features in a discourse passage that receives support from a parallel version is a listing of eminent disciples, already mentioned above in relation to Śāriputra, which identifies those who are foremost in a particular quality. In the Pāli version, Subhūti features as foremost among monks in dwelling without conflict, followed by mentioning him once again as also foremost in being worthy of gifts.[130] The parallel in the *Ekottarikāgama* reckons Subhūti foremost among monks in regard to constantly delighting in meditating on emptiness and in analyzing the meaning of emptiness, followed by also listing him a second time, in this case as outstanding for being resolved on the peace of emptiness and for having sublime and virtuous conduct.[131]

The relationship established in the *Ekottarikāgama* to preeminence in matters of emptiness recurs in Lokakṣema's translation of the Perfection of Wisdom, which considers Subhūti to be foremost in the wisdom of emptiness.[132] One of the other Chinese versions belonging to the *Aṣṭasāhasrikā Prajñāpāramitā* textual family agrees in this respect,[133] whereas the Sanskrit, Tibetan, and remaining Chinese versions put a spotlight on Subhūti for being foremost in dwelling without conflict (one case instead speaks of dwelling in the forest, presumably the result of reading *araṇya* instead of *araṇa*).[134] In order to place these variations into a wider context, in what follows I briefly turn to relevant presentations in other *Prajñāpāramitā* texts.

Subhūti features as foremost in the absence of conflict in the *Vajracchedikā Prajñāpāramitā*, with the parallel versions agreeing with each other in this respect.[135] In the case of the *Pañcaviṃśatisāhasrikā* and *Śatasāhasrikā Prajñāpāramitā*, the Sanskrit version of the former does refer to the absence of conflict, whereas the latter speaks of dwelling in the forest (presumably the result of the same exchange of two similar terms just mentioned). Two Chinese versions of the Larger *Prajñāpāramitā* family also refer to the absence of conflict, whereas yet another rendering into Chinese by Dharmarakṣa, this being the earliest of the extant translations of Larger *Prajñāpāramitā* texts, brings in again the topic of emptiness.[136]

Now, the two references to the forest can easily be explained as the result of an interchange of terminology, although it is of interest to note that this is not merely a problem of translation into Chinese, as the same exchange can also occur in Sanskrit. In contrast, the references that reckon Subhūti as foremost in dwelling in emptiness do not seem to call for such an interpretation. Had this expression been found only in Lokakṣema's translation, for example, the assumption of some error would perhaps offer a plausible explanation; even in that case, however, a free translation would not seem to be a promising explanation.[137] Although the two meanings are related to each other, they seem too different to allow rendering one by translating the other, making it more probable that Lokakṣema's translation reflects a different Indic term in the original.

But once the same type of qualification recurs in a *Prajñāpāramitā* translation by Dharmarakṣa, as well as in two *Āgama*s rendered into Chinese by two different translators, of which at least the *Madhyamāgama* translator Gautama Saṅghadeva appears to be fairly reliable when it comes to fidelity to the Indic original,[138] it seems preferable to recognize the existence of two distinct, although related, lines of presentation. In fact, the combination of these two modes of presentation makes Subhūti a particularly attractive choice for the central role in teaching the Perfection of

Wisdom on behalf of the Buddha. Dwelling *without conflict*, based on a penetrative understanding of the limitations of language, aptly describes the outcome of insight into *emptiness*, and thereby would be of direct relevance to cultivating the Perfection of Wisdom. The appropriateness of this choice can be fleshed out further with a passage in Lokakṣema's translation of the Perfection of Wisdom in which the Buddha himself describes Subhūti's insight into emptiness in a way that closely relates to a penetrative understanding of the limitations inherent in language and concepts:[139]

> Whatever is being taught by Subhūti, he only teaches on matters of emptiness. Subhūti neither beholds that which is the Perfection of Wisdom, nor beholds one who cultivates the Perfection of Wisdom, nor beholds Buddhahood, nor beholds one who attains Buddhahood, nor beholds omniscience, nor beholds one who attains omniscience, nor beholds a Tathāgata, nor beholds one who attains Tathāgata-hood, nor beholds the nonarising [of dharmas] from anywhere, nor beholds one who realizes the nonarising [of dharmas] from anywhere.

In short, Subhūti does not reify anything at all, in full understanding of the limitations of any concept and the thoroughly empty nature of what is designated by any such concept, even when it comes to key notions of the very path to Buddhahood.

Another relevant consideration possibly influencing Subhūti's role in the Perfection of Wisdom could be that, since he is not on record in *Āgama* literature for having given specific teachings, there is no possibility of these somehow coming into conflict with the teachings he delivers now. This is the advantage of choosing someone less known, in that such a protagonist can more easily be accommodated to a new role without risking a conflict with some position or type of teaching he is already known for.

In addition—and this may be an important factor contributing to this choice—by placing an otherwise little-known arhat in the position of giving teachings to another arhat reckoned by tradition as being second only to the Buddha in matters of wisdom, the transformative power of the Perfection of Wisdom is thrown into full relief. In other words, the underlying message could be that even someone as relatively unknown as Subhūti can be transformed into a teacher of someone as famous as Śāriputra by dint of relying on the Perfection of Wisdom. This would tie in with a recurrent pattern throughout the Perfection of Wisdom of emphasizing its own transformative power.

In sum, the above survey suggests that Subhūti does indeed seem to be an excellent choice for assuming the role of teaching the Perfection of Wisdom. This is due to the qualities he embodies—absence of conflict and abiding in emptiness—together with the lack of records of conflicting teachings by him and his marginal role in *Āgama* literature, which makes his present central role attributable to the power of the Perfection of Wisdom.

There is, however, one more problem still to be examined. This is that Subhūti is invited to speak on a topic on which only the Buddha has actual expertise. The Buddha is the only one in the whole assembly who has successfully completed the bodhisattva career (at least when viewed from the traditional perspective of the belief in his prolonged career of a bodhisattva). In contrast, for Subhūti as an arhat to give teachings to bodhisattvas on how they should perfect their wisdom is not entirely straightforward. This problem comes up explicitly in Haribhadra's commentary, according to which Śāriputra thought that, since he was himself unable to expound this topic, in spite of being foremost in wisdom, Subhūti would hardly be able to do so on his own.[140] The Perfection of Wisdom itself solves this (only apparent) problem with the explicit indication, made right after Śāriputra's reflection, that Subhūti's exposition was facilitated by the power of the Buddha himself.[141]

A *Prajñāpāramitā* commentary extant in Chinese, the *Dà zhìdù lùn* (**Mahāprajñāpāramitopadeśa*), adds further information on the choice of Subhūti. According to its explanation, the exposition needed to be given by arhats, since bodhisattvas are still subject to the influxes and will for this reason not be trusted in the same way as an arhat.[142] The choice of Subhūti then is seen as motivated by his kind disposition toward others (reflected in his ranking foremost for being free from conflict), which aligns well with the basic disposition of bodhisattvas, and in his practice of the concentration on emptiness, which aligns well with the Perfection of Wisdom.[143]

The above considerations provide a perspective on the roles taken by the two disciples Śāriputra and Subhūti as protagonists in the Perfection of Wisdom. Although this cast must have had quite an effect on the ancient Indian audience, at least during the period when it was still a novelty, it needs to be kept in mind that the overall purpose is not to encourage a wholesale rejection of Abhidharma. Instead, the point appears to be only to lead Śāriputra, as the icon of Abhidharma thought, a step further by leaving behind any idea of an "intrinsic nature," *svabhāva*. At this stage in the development of Buddhist thought, the Perfection of Wisdom would have risked losing a considerable part of its prospective audience if it were to reject entirely all previous teachings formulated by the Abhidharma traditions. The first chapter in fact concludes with Subhūti's approval of a position taken by Śāriputra.[144] In later chapters, at times Śāriputra himself takes on the role of expounding the Perfection of Wisdom.[145] This confirms the impression that the issue at hand is not a wholesale dismissal but rather a conversion of Abhidharma practitioners to a new perspective that builds on—but leads beyond—Abhidharma analysis.

Another point to take away from the same setting is that, in being addressed to Śāriputra, Subhūti's teaching naturally takes a lot for granted. It presents a step to be undertaken *after* sustained analysis has already done its work in building a foundation in insight and in diminishing attachment. This provides a background for examining the rhetoric of emptiness, to be explored below. The point to be kept in mind is that these teachings are predominantly aimed at those already advanced in their progress on the Buddhist path. The purpose of the rhetoric of emptiness is not to explain why it is useful to employ a relay of seven chariots to travel swiftly from one location to another, let alone to give detailed instructions on how to drive a chariot. All of this is taken for granted, and the overall concern is mainly to establish the clear understanding that, when coming close to the final destination, even the seventh chariot needs to be left behind.

## The Rhetoric of Emptiness

Under the heading of "the rhetoric of emptiness" I will explore a central current in the teachings of the Perfection of Wisdom to deconstruct and undermine any tendency toward reification in order to clear the path for a full realization of the emptiness of all dharmas. Before examining actual instances of this rhetoric in the Perfection of Wisdom, however, I need to survey two relatively common modes of interpretation that I believe are in need of clarification, one relating to the "rhetoric" employed in the Perfection of Wisdom and the other to the conception of "emptiness" in the same text. The former interpretation takes the form of assuming that such rhetoric intentionally employs self-contradictory propositions, whereas the latter interpretation manifests in the belief that the conception of emptiness promoted in this way involves a radical departure from *Āgama* teachings.

### *A Hermeneutic of Self-Contradiction?*

In the context of exploring dimensions of Mahāyāna thought, Conze (1959/2008, 72) presents the following assessment: "In actual reality there are no Buddhas, no Bodhisattvas, no perfections . . . these conceptions have no reference to anything that is actually there, and concern a world of mere phantasy." This assessment then has its complement in a perception of the rhetoric of emptiness as self-contradictory, evident when Conze (1959/2008, 78) presents this type of reasoning: "If statements must be made, self-contradictory propositions are the ones most likely to bring out the truth of what there actually is." In another publication, Conze (1962, 200 and 202) comments on *Prajñāpāramitā* literature that "these texts are often more intent on mystifying the reader than on clarifying the problems they discuss"; in fact, "they observe the precaution of always cancelling out each statement by another one which contradicts it. Everywhere in these writings contradiction is piled upon contradiction." In the course of a study of what he refers to as "the ontology of the Prajñāpāramitā," Conze (1953, 126–27) then offers this appraisal:

> [T]he basic laws of logical thought are abolished. The principle of contradiction, in particular, is abrogated in emptiness.

> It is obvious that to say "X is empty of the own-being of X" amounts to identifying a *dharma* with its own negation. In a bold and direct manner, the *Prajñāpāramitā Sūtras* explicitly proclaim the identity of contradictory opposites, and they make no attempt to mitigate their paradoxes.

According to another relevant comment in Conze (1975/1984, 5), the teachings of the large *Prajñāpāramitā* can be summed up as conveying that "1. One should become a Bodhisattva . . . 2. There is no such thing as a Bodhisattva . . . ." Based on this assessment, he then reasons that the "solution of this dilemma lies in nothing else than the fearless acceptance of both contradictory facts."

The proposed reading of *Prajñāpāramitā* thought as calling for the acceptance of self-contradiction could to some extent be influenced by personal predilections, given the following assessment presented by Attwood (2022, 114–15):

> [In a book published before he began to write on *Prajnāpāramitā*]—*Der Satz vom Widerspruch: Zur Theorie des Dialektischen Materialismus* (1932)—Conze had already rejected Aristotle's principle of noncontradiction. His thesis was that logic is merely a social construct and, therefore, not universal. It is not that the principle of noncontradiction, along with all logic, is refuted in this way. Rather it is reconstrued as a matter of opinion. In his exegesis of *Prajnāpāramitā*, Conze takes this a little further, adopting the view that contradictory statements are all true.

Bastian (1979, 102) notes that the commentarial tradition following Haribhadra actually stands "in contrast to Prof. Conze's interpretation and translation" and does not consider *Prajñāpāramitā* texts "as presenting a dilemma solved by 'nothing else than the fearless acceptance of both contradictory facts.'" From their perspective, the injunction that one should not apprehend all dharmas intends that one "should not apprehend as 'truly existing' all dharmas." In other words, the statement by Subhūti that he does not apprehend a bodhisattva, instead of calling for a literal reading that there is no bodhisattva at all, much rather can be interpreted to intend not apprehending a bodhisattva as a truly existing entity. The target of this type of presentation would then be to foster a deconstruction of any tendency to reify by way of an intrinsic nature, *svabhāva*.

Based on a detailed study of passages in Sanskrit and Chinese *Prajñāpāramitā* texts related to selected formulations found in the *Prajñāpāramitāhṛdaya*,[146] Huifeng (2014, 91) reads an example of such a teaching as "referring not to the ontological status of phenomena, but to a subjective state—a meditative state if you will—which should rather be described as epistemological in nature."

In an introduction to his translation of a version of the *Vajracchedikā Prajñāpāramitā*, Harrison (2006, 137) explains: "When a word (X) is negated by the *a-* or *an-* prefix, one can translate it either as a *karmadhāraya* (not X, no X, non-X) or as a *bahuvrīhi* (X-less, lacking X, having no X)." Although in the case of *Prajñāpāramitā* literature in principle both readings are grammatically possible, "in my view the *bahuvrīhi* reading is more cogent philosophically" (138). On adopting this reading, the rhetoric of emptiness needs no longer be seen as "an expression of some kind of mystical paradoxicality" (140).

The suggestion that a different reading of the rhetoric of emptiness is more cogent philosophically can claim additional support from a consideration of the tetralemma as an integral dimension of Buddhist thought. *Āgama* literature presents the tetralemma mode of analysis as a feature commonly accepted in the ancient Indian setting. Its implementation comes up regularly in the context of a standard questionnaire to ascertain the view held by a particular teacher or practitioner. The Buddha is on record for consistently refusing to take up any of the positions envisaged in this questionnaire, apparently because these were based on wrong premises (see in more detail below p. 127).

Such a rejection, however, does not concern the tetralemma as such. In fact, several teachings in *Āgama* literature appear to be based on the basic mode of thought of the tetralemma.[147] The actual perspective proposed by the tetralemma calls for granting room to alternative possibilities alongside affirmation and negation.[148] This does not imply that at times a situation may not call for just one of these two options, and the Buddha is on record for making categorical statements on occasions when these were considered warranted. An example in case is the unequivocal statement in a Pāli discourse that misconduct by body, speech, and mind should not be done.[149] For other matters, however, it can be preferable to allow for the possibility that both affirmation and negation may be meaningful, or else neither of these two may fit the case.

An illustration of the potential of the tetralemma, whose four alternatives may at first sight be puzzling to someone from a cultural background influenced by Aristotelian logic, would be the contrast between the colors black and white. The sheet of paper on which the present words appear (or the background color of a digital file) is some shade of white, and the writing is in black ink. The contrast between these two colors facilitates written communication. But the whole world is of course not just like that. There can be shades of grey—which are both black and white—and there can be various colors like yellow, red, blue, etc.—which are neither black nor white. In this way, there clearly is room for allowing the tetralemma alternatives "both X and not-X" or else "neither X nor not-X."[150]

Such allowing of these alternatives does not result in a flat denial of the principle of noncontradiction. Instead, it only proposes that binary thinking in terms of two unreconcilable opposites is not always the most appropriate way of viewing a situation. The first and second options of the tetralemma are indeed "X" and "not-X," and these are clearly recognized as valid options. The point is only that these two do not exhaust all possible options, as there is also a third option, which allows for "both," and a fourth option, which sees "neither" of the two as fitting the case at hand.

The existence of the tetralemma mode as such implies that an exploration of ancient Indian thought needs to keep in mind that contrastive statements are not necessarily intended or perceived as contradictions. Instead, they may even be intentionally framed in this way to point in conjunction to a middle position. In relation to *Prajñāpāramitā* thought, Zacchetti (2015b, 173) explains that "Subhūti replies first by negating, through a typical negative epistemological approach, all the categories brought into the discourse . . . and then goes on declaring that if a bodhisattva who is instructed in this way does not become discouraged, depressed and terrified," then this is precisely what constitutes the Perfection of Wisdom.

In this way, the "dialectical structure of this passage . . . steers a middle course between absolute affirmation and absolute negation."

In sum, there do seem to be cogent reasons for going beyond the assumption of a hermeneutic of self-contradiction when reading the rhetoric of emptiness. This could even be viewed as following a precedent set by Conze (1975/1984, 19) himself. In the context of a discussion of the Larger *Prajñāpāramitā*, he proposes "that to say 'a thing is' is equivalent to 'it is eternally what it is,' 'it remains for ever what it is,' and that the formula 'it is destroyed' is equivalent to saying that 'it is not.' The whole doctrine of emptiness, as taught here, rests on this equivalence." Behind this assessment stands precisely the option of seeing contrastive statements as complementary pointers to a middle position, in this case the middle position between the extremes of eternal existence and total nonexistence. This precedent could be relied on to develop a different reading of what at first sight may indeed appear as contradictory positions. Such a different reading rather sees these positions as potentially complementing each other, in line with the third of the four options envisaged by the tetralemma mode of thought.

For the purpose of facilitating such a reading, here I present several excerpts from what I find to be a particularly helpful examination of the type of rhetoric employed in *Prajñāpāramitā* literature, offered by McMahan (2002, 36–37, 40, 33, 34, 40, and 41):

> [First of all,] it would be inadequate simply to interpret it, on the one hand, as convoluted and self-contradictory or, on the other, as an attempt to confuse the rational functioning of the mind in the service of mystical realization; for there exists a logic in this dialectic that is intelligible and at the same time attempts to show the authors' understanding of the relationship between words and their referents . . .
>
> The purpose of the dialectic is not to say *what* the unconditioned is, but to *show how* it is . . . [This takes the form of] a linguistic pattern that allows for the re-affirmation of language in a provisional sense that discourages essentializing its referents. This pattern is a seminal discursive structure found in the

Perfection of Wisdom texts . . . [it] is a unique pattern of paradoxical dialectic that arises from trying to solve the problems inherent in denying the ultimate validity of language while trying to preserve language in a practical sense . . .

[In the course of that,] the Perfection of Wisdom texts find themselves flirting with the boundaries of intelligible language. Their authors appear to have realized that the assertion of ineffability combined with the doctrine of emptiness threatens to shut down language altogether if pushed to its conclusions. Not only does language not adequately describe or refer to the actuality (*tattva*, *tathatā*) of things, this actuality is itself precluded from being anything inherently existent. In order to articulate this vision, the authors of the Perfection of Wisdom literature developed a dialectical discourse in which the rhetorical style itself is designed to disrupt the referential function of language, not to circumvent reason altogether, but to attempt to develop a linguistic 'game' that is transformative rather than strictly referential and that ultimately attempts to transcend words by means of words . . .

[This can have a] vertiginous effect on the reader of constantly having the rug pulled out from under one's feet. This, in effect, is part of the 'performative' aspect of the text, in that what it is supposed to do is more than just convey propositional meaning; it is designed to have a specific effect on the reader . . ..

The unique dialectical form put forth in the Perfection of Wisdom leaves the contradicting elements in tension, rather than resolving them in a final synthesis. Assertions give rise to negations, which in turn give rise to negations of the negations, not for the purpose of coming to a final conclusion—an endpoint in the dialectic at which the final truth can finally be stated—nor for the purpose of establishing an infinite regress. Instead, the movement of the dialectic itself shows the continual ungrounding of all affirmation and negation as the empty interplay of all binary opposition—indeed of all language. It is a demonstration of the endless shifting of perspectives that constitutes the emptiness of language and the lifeworld. This ungrounding dialectic, then, attempts to show what it cannot say by serving as a model that presents the ungrounded movement of things in general. It is, thereby, an attempt to use language to reveal the emptiness philosophers' understanding of the truth of things, not by means of unqualified propositional statements, but by a qualification and relativization of all such statements. Insofar as the dialectic resists any final closure or coming to rest in an unqualified statement of truth, it evokes the truth of what it cannot say by outlining the limits of propositional language, its paradoxes standing in sharp relief against the background of what is left unsaid and unsayable.

### *Emptiness of Persons or of All Phenomena?*

In what follows I turn to the other of the two terms that calls for clarification before embarking on a study of actual instances of the rhetoric of emptiness, namely the significance of the type of "emptiness" promoted in the Perfection of Wisdom. According to an opinion voiced by several scholars, this type of emptiness involves a substantial innovation in the history of Buddhist thought, as it extends the insight into not self from formerly having been applied to persons only to now qualifying all dharmas without exception.[151]

Such assessments fail to take into account that the application of emptiness to all dharmas or the whole world is already found in *Āgama* literature. Here are a few examples taken from Pāli discourses:[152]

The world is everywhere without an essence.
Having known about the world that "all this is unreal,"
A monastic leaves behind this shore and the other.

Being always mindful, Mogharāja,
You should contemplate the whole world as empty,
Having uprooted the view of a self.

> Ānanda, it is said that "the world is empty" because it is empty of a self and of what belongs to a self.

> All dharmas are without a self.

The world not only lacks any essence;[153] it is even unreal. Although the latter assessment needs to be read within its context in order to do it proper justice,[154] it can nevertheless be related to the emphasis in the Perfection of Wisdom on the illusory nature of the whole world of experience. The instruction to Mogharāja then links the contemplation of the world as empty to the view of a self, which needs to be left behind (this instruction, as well as the first reference to the world lacking an essence, are from Pāli verses for which no parallel is known).

In reply to a query by Ānanda regarding the statement that the world is empty, the Buddha clarifies that this refers to being empty of a self and what could belong to a self. The same qualification of being empty of a self and of what belongs to a self recurs elsewhere in ways ostensibly intended in a similarly comprehensive manner.[155] In the present case, a subsequent part of the same discourse, which I have not translated above, continues to apply the qualification of being empty of a self and of what belongs to a self to each of the senses, their objects, as well as the respective types of consciousness, contact, and feeling tones. The explicit inclusion of the objects in this presentation makes it clear that this conception of emptiness is not just about the person but indeed about the whole world.

These selected excerpts could be viewed as converging on the last statement in the list, according to which all dharmas are without a self. The verse in question indicates that this lack of a self in all dharmas is to be seen with wisdom. The same type of statement recurs in several other passages. One case is a Pāli discourse of which no parallel is known, where this statement features as a principle that holds quite independent of whether a Tathāgata (= a Buddha) has arisen or not; the relationship to a Tathāgata then is merely that he realizes and teaches to others that all dharmas are without a self.[156] The teaching that all dharmas are without a self also features in an instruction, extant in Pāli and Chinese, aimed at leading to a vision of the Dharma.[157] The same dictum recurs in another passage preserved in Pāli, Chinese, and Tibetan, which reports the Buddha explaining that to affirm the existence of a self would be contrary to what he has realized, namely that all dharmas are without a self.[158]

In this way, as pointed out by Deleanu (1993, 8), "we find very clear instances of early canonical sources speaking of the emptiness of phenomena." This much is in fact in line with an assessment made explicitly in the *Prajñāpāramitā* commentary *Dà zhìdù lùn* (**Mahāprajñāpāramitopadeśa*), which states that "in various places in the *Tripiṭaka* the emptiness of dharmas is taught."[159] The Perfection of Wisdom in turn reports an exchange in the course of which the Buddha queries if he has not constantly been teaching the emptiness of dharmas, which Subhūti confirms.[160] The way this exchange proceeds does not give the impression that such a teaching was considered an innovation.

Williams (1989/2009, 53) explains that, "[h]istorically, the teaching of absence of Self only in persons (in opposition to that of *dharmas*) is a feature of certain interpretations of the Abhidharma."[161] In other words, the main criticism voiced in the Perfection of Wisdom would not be aimed at an *Āgama* position but rather at a specific tenet of some Abhidharma traditions. Bronkhorst (2018, 124 and 126) presents the following relevant assessment:

> [T]he 'Perfection of Wisdom,' which is the subject matter of the *Aṣṭasāhasrikā Prajñāpāramitā* . . . only makes sense against the background of the overhaul of Buddhist scholasticism that had taken place in Greater Gandhāra during the last centuries preceding the Common Era. It was in Greater Gandhāra, during this period, that Buddhist scholasticism developed an ontology centred on the lists of dharmas that had been preserved. Lists of dharmas had been drawn up before the scholastic revolution in Greater Gandhāra, and went on being drawn up elsewhere with the goal of preserving the teaching of the Buddha. But the Buddhists of Greater Gandhāra were the first to use these lists of dharmas to construe an ontology, unheard of until then. They looked upon the dharmas as the only really existing things . . .

> The position taken in numerous Mahāyāna texts is that dharmas have no beginning (and no end). This makes perfect sense among thinkers who are steeped in Gandhāran scholasticism.

This assessment can be explored further with the help of a detailed study of the evolution of ideas related to the nature of dharmas in Sarvāstivāda Abhidharma thought by Cox (2004). Already an early canonical Abhidharma work, the *Saṅgītiparyāya*, appears to testify to a usage of the related term *bhāva* to attribute separate existence to the three periods of time, that is, the past, the present, and the future.[162] Cox (2004, 568) notes that in such usage the term "*bhāva* conveyed both an abstract sense as 'nature' and an ontological sense as 'mode of existence,'" reflecting an early period when "the more technical sense of *bhāva* was beginning to develop, but the clear distinction between *bhāva* and *svabhāva* typical of the later Sarvāstivāda materials had not yet solidified."

Cox (2004, 559, 562, 569, and 563) explains that the notion of *svabhāva* in turn appears to have developed mainly in "the context of categorization, where invariable criteria are demanded as the basis for unambiguous classification." In this role, "to be a *dharma* is to be determined by a distinctive intrinsic nature, which is never abandoned." Recognition of this *svabhāva* nature is in turn a crucial requirement for clear discrimination and the avoidance of confusion among dharmas. This then leads to the notion that "determination by intrinsic nature undergoes no variation or modification, and hence, *dharma*s, which are in effect types or categories of intrinsic nature, are established as stable and immutable." The point is that "determining individual dharmas through unique intrinsic nature also entails affirming their existence, as a natural function both of the etymological sense of the term *svabhāva* and of the role of *dharma*s as the fundamental constituents of experience." In sum, "*dharma*s as *svabhāva*s or as abstract categories are invariable and denote an atemporal, that is, inalterable existence."

Although concern with *svabhāva* in the sense of an intrinsic nature is mainly a preoccupation of Abhidharma compendia, the *Jñānaprasthāna* of the canonical Abhidharma collection of the Sarvāstivādins already reflects this notion.[163] The **Mahāvibhāṣā* compendium, an encyclopedic work of scholastic exegesis, in turn presents the fully developed notion by arguing that *svabhāva* exists, it is real, and it can be apprehended; moreover, it is never empty; thus, it is not the case that it has not existed, that it does not exist, or that it will not exist.[164] Such qualifications seem to be set in direct opposition to central positions taken in *Prajñāpāramitā* thought.

The gradual evolution of the notion of *svabhāva* in Abhidharma thought is also relevant for establishing a historical perspective on *Āgama* literature. Early Abhidharma clearly operates in close dialogue with the teachings in *Āgama* discourses. This is particularly evident in the earliest Abhidharma works, and it has its counterpart in proto-Abhidharma tendencies in some discourses that are usually not supported by their respective parallels and for this reason recognizable as reflecting later developments.[165] This pattern soon enough diminishes, and canonical works reflecting a more mature stage in Abhidharma thought can be seen to operate more and more independently, containing teachings that are in turn no longer reflected in *Āgama* literature.

An example in case is precisely the conception of *svabhāva*, which is not found among the teachings common to *Āgama* discourses of different reciter traditions.[166] Yet, an explicit dismissal of this notion can be found already in the Gāndhārī manuscript version of the Perfection of Wisdom, in the form of denying that any of the five aggregates is endowed with such an intrinsic nature.[167] Once the Perfection of Wisdom shows such clear evidence of responding to this notion and thus being in dialogue with an evolved stage in Abhidharma thought, the relevant passage would have to be allocated to a stage in Buddhist thought subsequent to that reflected in *Āgama* discourses that are supported by their parallels.

The perspective on the historical evolution that emerges in this way in turn supports my assessment earlier in this chapter (see above p. 8) that it seems reasonable to assume that the main teachings found in the Pāli discourses and their parallels (leaving aside the *Ekottarikāgama*) form the backdrop to the setting within which the Perfection of Wisdom would have evolved. Nevertheless, as announced earlier, I will continue to leave matters open and allow each individual instance surveyed in the course of my study to reveal in its own right what the most probable direction of influence would have been between a particular position taken in the Perfection of Wisdom and corresponding material from *Āgama* literature.

At this point, I have completed my survey of the two modes of interpretating the rhetoric of emptiness that I felt were in need of clarification. In what follows, I will examine the basic procedure of this rhetoric and then relate that to the nature of a sentient being and to insight into the five aggregates. The final topic in this chapter is the relationship between overcoming fear and gaining *samādhi*.

*The Basic Procedure of the Rhetoric of Emptiness*

The concerns underlying the rhetoric of emptiness employed in the Perfection of Wisdom can best be illustrated with a few excerpts from the Gāndhārī manuscript:[168]

> I do not find and do not apprehend what is named "a bodhisattva." Without finding and without apprehending [any, which] bodhisattva do I instruct in the Perfection of Wisdom?
>
> On being taught the Perfection of Wisdom, if a bodhisattva is not dejected and does not become afraid . . .
>
> This is a bodhisattva's *samādhi*, called "nonacquisition."

The first passage shows that, having been invited by the Buddha to teach the Perfection of Wisdom to bodhisattvas and having clarified that he will do so in reliance on the Buddha, Subhūti first of all deconstructs the key concept of this invitation: the bodhisattva.[169] The reference to being unable to apprehend something is a recurrent one in the Perfection of Wisdom; it can be understood to convey the sense of apprehending something as existing in itself,[170] that is, as something that has an "intrinsic nature," *svabhāva*. The second excerpt points to the importance of being able to accept this type of teaching without giving rise to fear. Once that has become possible, the mind can give rise to "collectedness" or "concentration," *samādhi*.[171]

In what follows, I will explore the type of deconstruction proposed in the first excerpt in detail, in particular in relation to the five aggregates.

Then I will turn to the topic of fear and the relationship of its absence to *samādhi*. Of course, more needs to be said on the topic of emptiness in the Perfection of Wisdom. Since the present first chapter has already by now become quite long and detailed, I will be taking up several related topics in later chapters, such as the injunction not to take a stance on anything (see below p. 79), the relationship of emptiness to impermanence (see below p. 119), the topic of taking up signs (see below p. 137), the nature of perception as a potential source of attachment (see below p. 141), the conception of omniscience (see below p. 237), and the doctrine of dependent arising (see below p. 246). In other words, what follows below is only a preliminary foray into the topic.

### *The Nature of a Sentient Being*

In the history of *Prajñāpāramitā* literature, the version that is now known as being in eight thousand lines appears to have been the starting point for a gradual process of expansion, leading to a version in twenty-five thousand lines, the *Pañcaviṃśatisāhasrikā Prajñāpāramitā*.[172] It can at times be helpful to turn to this version for additional indications, in the sense of potentially providing an explanation or perspective that is closer in time to the mode of thought reflected in the *Aṣṭasāhasrikā Prajñāpāramitā* than Haribhadra's commentary.

In the present case, a relevant passage can be found in the earliest Chinese translation by Dharmarakṣa of a version corresponding to what in Sanskrit is the *Pañcaviṃśatisāhasrikā Prajñāpāramitā*.[173] In the context of providing succinct explanations of each of the six perfections in what is the first chapter in this text—which to some extent serves to prepare the ground for a proper understanding of its subsequent chapters—Dharmarakṣa's translation offers the following explanation:[174] "The wisdom of understanding emptiness without assuming a self, this is the Perfection of Wisdom." This explanation offers a straightforward and succinct statement of emptiness as the perhaps most central concern underpinning the type of text under discussion.

In relation to Subhūti's statement that he does not find a bodhisattva, the *Pañcaviṃśatisāhasrikā Prajñāpāramitā* reports an additional clarification offered by the Buddha, explaining that this situation is similar to the case of a "sentient being," which can also not be obtained.[175] This indication enables relating the present discussion to the usage and problematization of the term "sentient being" in *Āgama* discourses.

Two different passages from *Āgama* literature can be relied on to present a contrast similar to the contrasting statements found regularly in the Perfection of Wisdom. One of these passages indicates that a sentient being cannot be obtained.[176] According to the other passage, a Tathāgata is foremost among sentient beings.[177] The context clarifies the difference. The first case is part of a reply given by a highly realized nun in order to deconstruct an attempt at reifying the notion of a sentient being. The idea behind this reification appears to have been that the term "sentient being" refers to an entity of sorts that has a creator and that must come from somewhere and disappear toward somewhere else. In the second case, however, the same term is used without reification.

The distinction to be made here can be related to two different definitions given in *Āgama* literature of what the term "sentient being" stands for. One of these is merely functional, pointing to the existence of the six sense spheres.[178] According to the other definition, however, the term "sentient being" stands for being attached to the five aggregates.[179] This presentation involves a wordplay, as Pāli *satta* could mean a "sentient being," Sanskrit *sattva*, or else refer to being "attached," Sanskrit *sakta*.[180]

A related sense appears to be relevant to a passage found in the version of the Perfection of Wisdom translated by Lokakṣema, located just before Subhūti's statement that he does not see or apprehend any bodhisattva. The relevant passage could be translated as follows: "The Buddha makes me teach the bodhisattvas. There being the name 'bodhisattva,' one then becomes attached to it. Is there the name 'bodhisattva' or is there no [such] name?"[181] The passage could be read to highlight the problem of latching on to the title of being a bodhisattva by way of attachment, leading to the query, presumably addressed to the bodhisattvas in the audience, if what designates their spiritual choice and identity is becoming a matter of attachment for them. The proposed reading would resonate with the following comment by Nattier (2003a, 135n62) on the *Aṣṭasāhasrikā* (and the *Vajracchedikā*) *Prajñāpāramitā*: "It is my strong suspicion that this 'rhetoric of negation' first emerged as a tactical attempt to undercut the potential for bodhisattvas' arrogance." Weaning bodhisattvas from any attachment or arrogance appears to be indeed a central concern of Subhūti's teachings in the Perfection of Wisdom.

Besides providing a pointer at such concerns, the quoted passage also confirms the relevance to the present context of the above definition in *Āgama* literature of a sentient being in terms of being attached. This definition is relevant to the case of a person who is reifying the notion of a sentient being; it is not applicable to a Tathāgata. As a fully awakened one, a Tathāgata is of course free from attachment. This is exactly why a Tathāgata is foremost among sentient beings. Being without attachment to the five aggregates, a Tathāgata no longer identifies with them. Due to not identifying with these, a Tathāgata can no longer be identified in terms of the five aggregates. This does not mean that a Tathāgata is without aggregates. It only means that a Tathāgata is beyond being identifiable by what a Tathāgata no longer identifies with.

Since this may appear perplexing, perhaps an illustration may be of use. Take the case of someone who has for many years held a leading position in some important institution and now has retired, perhaps even moved to a different country, making it impossible that she will ever take up that same position again. It no longer makes sense to refer to her by her previous title as the director or president of such-and-such institution. This is not a statement about the nonexistence of the institution but only about the definite severance of her relationship to that institution. In the same way, a Tathāgata has irrevocably retired from constructing a sense of identity, making it impossible that such constructing will ever happen again. It no longer makes sense to refer to a Tathāgata by way of constructing an identity. This is not a statement about the nonexistence of the aggregates but only about the definite severance of any relationship to the construction of identity based in one way or another on these aggregates.

Expressed in a contrastive type of language, a Tathāgata is a sentient being and is not a sentient being: The six sense spheres (or the five aggregates) are still there, hence to that extent one can still speak of a "sentient being" (definition 1). But any attachment to these is no longer there, hence to that extent it is no longer possible to speak of a "sentient being" (definition 2). As aptly clarified by another highly realized nun, a Tathāgata is freed from being reckoned in terms of any of the aggregates; at the same time—or perhaps precisely because of that—a Tathāgata is deep, immeasurable, and difficult to fathom, just like the great ocean.[182]

*Insight into the Five Aggregates*

In what follows, I continue exploring the rhetoric of emptiness in relation to the five aggregates. For doing that, an extract from the Gāndhārī manuscript can provide a convenient reference point:[183]

> Form itself, friend Śāriputra, is devoid of an intrinsic nature of form, and in the same way feeling tone, perception, volitional formations, consciousness, [friend] Śāriputra, is devoid of an intrinsic nature of consciousness.

The passage translated above presents in a nutshell a central teaching in the Perfection of Wisdom of rejecting an "intrinsic nature," *svabhāva*.[184] This applies to all phenomena without exception; in fact, the Gāndhārī manuscript version continues from the five aggregates to the very Perfection of Wisdom itself, which is also devoid of any *svabhāva*. Expressing the same basic point differently, the only *svabhāva* that can be found is the absence of *svabhāva*, hence the *svabhāva* of any phenomenon is emptiness. This is the pivotal point around which many of the discussions in the Perfection of Wisdom appear to revolve. At the same time, this is the teaching that Śāriputra—in his specific role as an icon of Abhidharma—needs help understanding, so that he can proceed beyond the level of understanding reached through Abhidharma analysis. It is presumably in this way, by avoiding any reification, that from the viewpoint of the Perfection of Wisdom it becomes possible to step out of the seventh chariot in order to be able to complete the journey.

An important practical tool to wean the mind from its ingrained tendency toward reification is to attend to the illusory nature of any aspect of experience. This can be illustrated with the following simile from Lokakṣema's translation (the relevant section is no longer preserved in the Gāndhārī manuscript):[185]

> It is just as if a master magician in a large, open space were magically to conjure up a great town, magically conjure up people to fill its interior, and then decapitate all the magically conjured up people.

In its context, this illustration serves to convey that bodhisattvas should have the proper attitude toward their aspiration to lead many sentient beings to liberation. Just as none of the magically conjured people has really been killed, in the same way should bodhisattvas view the sentient beings they are attempting to liberate. Now, if sentient beings were indeed as illusory as the magically conjured up people, it would be just as impossible to help them progress to awakening as it would be impossible to kill them. The context shows that the implication is not to give up helping others, in the realization that this is impossible, but much rather that bodhisattvas should do whatever possible to lead others to liberation while avoiding the error of taking themselves and their task too seriously by way of reification and attachment. The simile illustrates an attitude rather than being about ontology.

The analogy chosen in this way can be related to a simile employed in *Āgama* literature in the context of an exposition of the five aggregates. The simile in question serves to illustrate specifically the nature of consciousness, which turns out to be comparable to a magical illusion conjured up by a magician. Here, this image applies only to consciousness out of the five aggregates and thus is not an assertion of the illusory nature of the whole world. Several versions provide additional detail to this illustration by indicating that the magician conjures up different military troops.[186] Such imagery would accord with the idea of people being killed in the above illustration from the Perfection of Wisdom. In the course of elaborating the simile of the magician, Subhūti in fact brings in the topic of the five aggregates:[187]

> Form being like an illusion there is no being attached to it, no being bound by it, and no being freed from it. Feeling tone, perception, volitional formations, and consciousness being like

> an illusion there is no being attached to it, no being bound by it, and no being freed from it.

In this way, seeing each of the five aggregates as comparable to a magical illusion undermines any attachment to them and leads beyond the contrast between bondage and freedom. The passage continues by illustrating this with the example of space, which is similarly something one will not attach to, be bound by, or be freed from.[188] The position taken in this way can be compared to a teaching in *Āgama* literature on the implication of seeing consciousness to be comparable to a magical illusion:[189]

> Whatever consciousness there is, be it past, future, or present, be it internal or external, be it gross or subtle, be it sublime or repugnant, be it far or near, . . . there is nothing to it—nothing stable and nothing substantial—it has no solidity; it is like a disease, like a carbuncle, like a thorn, like a killer; and it is impermanent, *duḥkha*, empty, and not self. Why is that? It is because there is nothing solid or substantial in consciousness.

The underlying thrust of this teaching is to promote progress toward freedom from bondage, which becomes particularly evident with the commended evaluations of consciousness as being comparable to a disease, a carbuncle, a thorn, and even to a killer. The Perfection of Wisdom passage takes things a step further, as it were, by dismantling even such evaluations. At this presumably more advanced stage, the task is not just to overcome attachment in order to gain freedom from bondage, as even the very notions of being bound and its opposite in being freed are to be left behind as well.

A subsequent part of the present chapter in the Perfection of Wisdom turns to examining the nature of the self, showing that it is a notion devoid of any reality.[190] The topic of examining the nature of the self can in turn be related to a line in a verse extant in Pāli, with similarly worded parallels found in Chinese and Sanskrit. The verse provides an example for a type of formulation that at first sight can appear contradictory or incoherent, similar to the impression that at times can arise with statements in the Perfection of Wisdom. A very literal translation of this verse, to the extent of following the syntax of the original, would be as follows: "the self indeed for the self does not exist" (*attā hi attano n'atthi*).[191]

In this way, the existence of the self is explicitly denied but at the same time implicitly affirmed by referring to the self for which the denied item does not exist. From the viewpoint of grammar, the same term "self" features first as a nominative singular and then as a genitive/dative singular. Yet, the two occurrences carry substantially different meanings, which could be expressed by distinguishing between Self (first instance) and self (second instance). In other words, whereas the first instance concerns a reified sense of a self, the second instance is just a reflexive usage, serving as a pointer to subjective experience. The context involves a foolish person who worries about sons and wealth. The verse serves to point out that there is not even a "Self" to be owned by one-"self," much less sons and wealth.

The preceding line refers to the one who worries about sons and wealth explicitly as a "fool" (*bāla*), a term that could in principle also have been used in the line under discussion for the second instance of "self," thereby avoiding the juxtaposition of two occurrences of the same term carrying different meanings.[192] That this was not done gives me the impression that this juxtaposition may have been chosen intentionally, in that it has an important role to play by forcing the listeners to pause and reflect. This would be in line with a pedagogical strategy that *Āgama* literature shows the Buddha employing repeatedly, evident in instances reporting that he makes a brief statement and then leaves the puzzled monastics to themselves, who then ask some senior disciple to explain the matter for them.[193]

The basic pattern that emerges in this way has some similarity to the one adopted in the Perfection of Wisdom, where at first sight counterintuitive statements require pausing and reflecting in order to be fully understood. In the case of the above Pāli verse on the nonexistence of a self for the self, such an effect is well in line with what the whole verse apparently wants to achieve, namely a pausing and reflecting about the ingrained tendency of relating to things with a sense of ownership. Without such an apparently paradoxical formulation, the same statement would probably not achieve its effect to the same degree. A way of presentation that at first sight is puzzling seems necessary to stimulate the type of reaction that is to be achieved.

Although the main point of the line under discussion is of course not an instance of a perfection-of-wisdom type of teaching, it does seem to be related to emptiness in a wider sense. The verse can be read as an exemplification of a formulation, already mentioned above (p. 43), of a commendable way of contemplating emptiness: "This is empty of a self and what belongs to a self."[194] Once the first part is realized, the second follows naturally. Once it has become clear that there is not even a self to be owned, it follows naturally that sons and wealth are also not something that can truly be owned.

Particularly noteworthy is that the apparent paradox in the verse in question can fulfil its function even though *Āgama* literature does not yet know the distinction developed in later traditions between conventional and ultimate truths. In other words, such a type of statement must have been intelligible to the ancient Indian audience even without reliance on the notion of two truths. This is of course not meant to put into question that this notion can be fruitfully applied to emptiness rhetoric in the Perfection of Wisdom. Another scholar critical of the assumption that self-contradiction characterizes the thought of the Perfection of Wisdom, Williams (1989/2009, 52), relies precisely on the two-truths theory to make his point. He proposes that by shifting between these two levels of truth, "ultimate and conventional, it is possible to generate apparent paradoxes for pedagogic effect, but (*pace* Conze) it seems to me there are few if any genuine paradoxes, no real 'speaking in contradictions' in the Perfection of Wisdom literature."

The argument made in this way seems fair enough, and my additional observation is only that, at least from an ancient Indian perspective, even the distinction between conventional and ultimate truths is not indispensable for such apparently paradoxical statements to perform their pedagogic function. Since in the present study I attempt as much as possible to approach the Perfection of Wisdom from the viewpoint of *Āgama* literature, the distinction between two truths is not part of my proposed readings.[195] This does not mean that in some way this type of approach is being dismissed. Instead, the idea is just to provide another, additional perspective.

This additional perspective could perhaps be illustrated with the simile of the raft, whose relevance to reading *Prajñāpāramitā* literature is evident from its explicit use in the *Vajracchedikā*.[196] The raft is indispensable for crossing over. Once having crossed over, however, the raft is of no further use and needs to be left behind. The two perspectives that emerge in this way on the role of the raft do not require distinguishing between a conventional and an ultimate raft. Instead, the evaluation simply relies on the context: at first, when being on this shore or when crossing over, reliance on the raft is required; after having reached the other shore, letting go of the raft is required.

The same basic pattern can be applied to attempts to communicate key concerns of the Perfection of Wisdom. For such communication, using concepts is indispensable. Once the main point has been communicated, however, to keep holding on to the previously useful concepts risks turning into reification, comparable to carrying the raft along when continuing the journey on the other shore. In order to convey the two dimensions of a proper abiding in the Perfection of Wisdom, any concept that has been used needs to be deconstructed right after its usage has fulfilled its purpose. In terms of the raft simile: whoever takes up the raft needs to be ready to let go of it right after it has fulfilled its purpose. On this reading, the seemingly self-contradictory procedure can become quite meaningful. It inculcates and exemplifies what the practitioner has to do at every step along the long path to Buddhahood. This requires taking up the conceptual tools and letting go of them again right after they have fulfilled their purpose.

The basic notion of being a bodhisattva cultivating the Perfection of Wisdom is—at least from the perspective of the target audience of *Prajñāpāramitā* literature—indispensable for progress to Buddhahood. Yet, the very same basic notion can become a source of attachment and conceit. The notion as such needs to be brought in at first, as discarding the raft *before* crossing over would be even worse than carrying it along after having crossed over. But after a particular concept has been brought up initially, the very same concept needs to be deconstructed. This is precisely what Subhūti appears to be doing immediately after having been invited by the Buddha to teach the Perfection of Wisdom to bodhisattvas: He carries out his teaching task by exemplifying the procedure that bodhisattvas need to follow if they wish to progress speedily to Buddhahood. As explained by Orsborn (2012, 207):

> He seems willing to teach the *bodhisattva*s *Prajñāpāramitā*, but is unable to actually find any substantial thing which corresponds to either of them . . . Yet ironically, this very state of not finding a substantial living being (*-sattva*) as subject, or *Dharma* practice as object, is the teaching itself. Whoever is able to maintain this state of mind is in fact correctly practicing the *Prajñāpāramitā*, so long as they do not in turn reify this state itself.

The perspective that emerges in this way can be explored further with the help of another passage on the five aggregates, which takes the following form in the Gāndhārī manuscript:[197]

> When one becomes established in form, one cultivates the construction of form, [feeling tone, perception, volitional formations], if one becomes established in consciousness, one cultivates the construction of consciousness.

The passage seems to convey that becoming established in the five aggregates (presumably by way of reification and attachment) means that one is abiding in a "construction," *abhisaṃskāra*, rather than stepping out of construction.

The role of *abhisaṃskāra* in the construction of the five aggregates comes to the fore in an *Āgama* discourse extant in Pāli, Chinese, and Tibetan. The three parallels agree in placing a spotlight on the role of the fourth aggregate, the *saṃskāra*s, in this respect.[198] These "construct" the five aggregates—central dimensions of subjective experience—not just by way of the central role of *saṃskāra*s in the process of rebirth but also in every moment of present experience by providing a volitional input that will color the way unawakened perception appraises whatever happens.

According to another Pāli discourse and one of its two Chinese parallels, the term "world" can simply designate what arises in the six senses.[199] This does not appear to be meant in an idealist sense, instead of which it can best be read as a pointer to the construction of experience.[200] Ñāṇananda (1971/1986, 84) comments on the notion of the world as equivalent to experience through the six senses:

> Thus the world is what our senses present it [to] us to be. However, the world is not purely a projection of the mind in the sense of a thoroughgoing idealism; only, it is a phenomenon which the empirical consciousness cannot get behind, as it is itself committed to it. One might, of course, transcend the empirical consciousness and see the world objectively in the light of *paññā* [wisdom] only to find that it is void (*suñña*) of the very characteristics which made it a "world" for oneself.

The idea of the light of wisdom illuminating the empty nature of the "world" is quite in keeping with the concerns of the Perfection of Wisdom. A related perspective emerges in the following statement in a Pāli discourse: "Friend, wisdom is for the purpose of knowing directly, the purpose of knowing penetratively, and the purpose of abandoning."[201] In the setting of the Perfection of Wisdom, it seems that Subhūti is mainly concerned with the last of these three, with abandoning by way of stepping out of the seventh chariot in order to be able to enter the palace. This central instruction comes up in one way or another again and again.

### *Fear and Samādhi*

Repetition as such is a regular feature of Buddhist orality, where it serves to ensure that the main message is kept in memory and not easily forgotten. In the case of the Perfection of Wisdom, the rhetoric of emptiness clearly relies on this same feature of repeating its main message again and again, even though references to writing and books show that, at the time of composition, orality was no longer the sole mode of ensuring transmission of the text.[202]

The employment of repetition for delivering the message of the rhetoric of emptiness seems to be for a pedagogical reason, given that the tendency to reify rests on ignorance as an attitude rather than on ignorance as a lack of factual knowledge. This is indeed characteristic of the Buddhist conception of ignorance, which concerns a tendency to ignore, to avoid, to pretend otherwise.[203] In other words, the problem of ignorance is less about not being able to know as such and more about *not wanting* to know. Hence, it does not suffice to point out the truth of the matter once. Instead, the required remedy is to inculcate the tendency to deconstruct by dint of repeating the relevant instructions time and again, until such deconstruction has become almost like a reflex that occurs spontaneously.

From this viewpoint, the teachings given in the Perfection of Wisdom could even be considered to offer a kind of cognitive training aimed at a transformation of the audience's affectively held attitudes. The pattern employed for this cognitive training exemplifies what needs to be done again and again: take up any concept for whatever purpose it is needed and then right away let go of it again. The countermeasures taken in this way in turn target the affective dimension of experience, attempting to undercut attachment without going so far as to create excessive agitation. The last appears to be the problem that stands in the background of the warning that this type of instruction can arouse fear. In terms of the raft simile, being told to let go of the raft can naturally arouse fear of drowning. After all, preventing that has been the chief purpose of using a raft in the first place, and its usage thus far has precisely accomplished that. In the same way, the thorough deconstruction employed to encourage letting go of all dharmas can easily trigger fear of being deprived of what appears to be essential.[204]

In another part of the Perfection of Wisdom the Buddha explains specifically how best to instruct recent converts to the path to Buddhahood, namely by encouraging them to cultivate the six perfections aimed at supreme, complete awakening and to avoid becoming attached to the five aggregates.[205] This in a way presents the gist of what the rhetoric of emptiness is trying to convey but without actually employing it and thereby running the risk that someone unfamiliar with it becomes agitated and afraid.

Although the Perfection of Wisdom can in principle become a source of fear, especially for those who are not yet accustomed to the thorough deconstruction advocated with the rhetoric of emptiness, it can also help to face fear. The third chapter of Lokakṣema's translation commends learning, remembering, and reciting the Perfection of Wisdom as a means to remain fearless when encountering some hardship.[206] The Sanskrit version provides more details, as it lists different places where one may encounter such fear, including forest wilds and the root of a tree, in addition to which it also mentions the four bodily postures, as one could be walking, standing, seated, or reclining at that time.[207]

This description can conveniently be related to an *Āgama* discourse passage concerning the Buddha—*the* bodhisattva—during the time of his quest for awakening. The relevant Pāli discourse and its Chinese parallel report that the bodhisattva Śākyamuni was living in forest wilds in seclusion, where at times hearing unexpected noises would arouse fear in him. Whenever that happened, the bodhisattva would simply remain in the same bodily posture until the fear had subsided.[208] If he was walking, he would just keep on walking, and if he was standing, seated, or reclining, he would just remain in that same posture. The similarities that emerge in this way invite relating this description to the passage from the Sanskrit version of the *Aṣṭasāhasrikā Prajñāpāramitā*.

Now, when suddenly hearing some unexpected sound while being in the forest, it would be natural to change one's posture in order to try to identify the sound or to get a little bit away from whatever wild animal or other occurrence may be the source of that sound. Instead, the bodhisattva Śākyamuni would just stay quietly watching what was going on, and he was doing that, notably, not only on the outside but also on the inside, within his own mind. The main practice here appears to be a form of mindfulness,[209] in the sense that the bodhisattva would have been mindfully monitoring his own state of mind and at the same time his posture and thereby in a way embody a basic stance of mindfulness practice, namely receptive awareness without immediately reacting. On this reading, the cultivation of mindfulness in this passage would fulfil a function to some extent comparable to the role of recollecting—which is of course a mindfulness practice—the Perfection of Wisdom.

The function of the Perfection of Wisdom as a tool to counter fear in turn helps broaden the perspective on its various authentication strategies and self-promotions. In addition to the obvious agenda at work in such passages, instilling faith in the Perfection of Wisdom also has an important role in fortifying practitioners in their encounters with fear. The more they take the teachings on trust, the more their minds will easily settle and become composed, rather than succumbing to agitation. Eventually this process will lead to a supreme degree of inner certitude about the teachings on emptiness, in the form of the patient acceptance of the nonarising of dharmas (*anutpattikadharmakṣānti*), a topic to be explored in a subsequent chapter (see below p. 186).

Another passage from *Āgama* literature, concerned with cultivating calmness of the mind, describes how the bodhisattva Śākyamuni overcame, step by step, various mental obstructions to the deepening of mental "composure," *samādhi*, more usually translated as "concentration."[210] One such mental obstruction is indeed fear, whose recognition and overcoming enabled the bodhisattva Śākyamuni to progress in his cultivation of *samādhi*. His surmounting of fear (together with other obstacles) eventually led to his attainment of absorption (*dhyāna*). This presentation conforms to the basic pattern of facing fear and overcoming it, leading to the ability to gain *samādhi*.

The passage from the Perfection of Wisdom quoted earlier speaks of the *samādhi* of "nonacquisition," corresponding to the Sanskrit term *aparigraha*, which conveys a sense of renunciation and dispossession. Although a *samādhi* by this name does not feature among Pāli discourses, the notion of nonacquisition as characteristic of an advanced practitioner does occur in several Pāli verses.[211] Such references are, however, more about a level of development or condition of the mind than about an actual practice of meditation. Nevertheless, it may well be that the reference to *samādhi* in the Perfection of Wisdom has in mind such a mental condition. Be that as it may, an actual meditation practice to implement the principle of nonacquisition would be "signless concentration," *animitta samādhi*. In fact, the Gāndhārī manuscript version refers to the sign, *nimitta*, in its exposition of the *samādhi* of nonacquisition,[212] followed at a subsequent point of its exposition by indicating that one who proceeds in form (etc.) proceeds in signs.[213]

Exploring the problem posed by signs and meditative approaches of working with that, however, will have to wait until a subsequent part of my study (see below p. 137). The time has come to let this rather long chapter come to its end. Here and elsewhere, I conclude each chapter with a summary. This first condenses the whole content of the respective discussion in a single sentence, followed by a more detailed summary that surveys the main topics covered in the course of the chapter.

## Summary

In this chapter I have surveyed evidence for the bodhisattva ideal being a pan-Buddhist phenomenon, examined the roles of Śāriputra and Subhūti as exemplifying a concern with countering the position that dharmas have an intrinsic nature, and argued that the rhetoric of emptiness can be read as involving an internally coherent mental training in nonreification.

The Gāndhārī manuscript version and Lokakṣema's translation of the Perfection of Wisdom appear to testify to an interim stage in the development of the bodhisattva ideal. A characteristic of this stage is a lack of prominence of compassion as the chief motivation for embarking on the path to Buddhahood. At this point in the development of Buddhist thought, Buddhahood has not yet become the sole appropriate object for spiritual practice and rather features as a goal for the chosen few who aspire to become Buddhas as soon as possible.

A survey of relevant Pāli sources shows a gradual evolution of the bodhisattva ideal in the Theravāda textual traditions, with repercussions on actual Buddhist practice evident in South and Southeast Asia. The picture that emerges in this way makes it clear that the bodhisattva ideal is best considered a pan-Buddhist phenomenon, rather than being restricted to some Buddhist traditions only. In other words, the existence of the bodhisattva ideal as such, together with corresponding practices, cannot be used as an identifier of some Buddhist traditions in contrast to others, simply because it is a shared feature of the main, extant Buddhist traditions.

A gradual evolution is similarly evident in the different roles taken by Śāriputra. His position as foremost in wisdom among the Buddha's disciples must have made him a natural choice to serve as an icon for the emerging Abhidharma traditions. This in turn would have impacted the role given to him in *Prajñāpāramitā* literature as someone who needs to be taught how to proceed further, in line with the overall concern in this type of text to encourage proceeding beyond the results of Abhidharma analysis to a penetrative vision of the complete emptiness of all phenomena.

The role of the Perfection of Wisdom in this respect finds exemplification in the choice of Subhūti as its spokesman, who in *Āgama* literature stands for the absence of conflict and, in some reciter traditions, for abiding in emptiness. His selection can convey to the audience that even a disciple of only marginal importance in *Āgama* literature could, by dint of reliance on the Perfection of Wisdom, become a teacher of someone as outstanding in matters of wisdom as Śāriputra.

The quest for the supreme in wisdom is the central underlying current of the rhetoric of emptiness. This rhetoric is probably best approached while keeping in mind the ancient Indian tetralemma model of thought, rather than being read from a position of interpreting contrasting positions as involving a form of self-contradiction. Moreover, the concern with emptiness in this rhetoric does not appear to be an entirely novel development, as the absence of a self in all phenomena was clearly recognized in *Āgama* thought.

The basic concerns underlying the rhetoric of emptiness in the Perfection of Wisdom are reflected in instances of deconstructing key terminology, including the very notion of a "bodhisattva." Should this not result in agitating a mature practitioner, then such deconstruction has the potential of leading instead to a form of *samādhi*. The deconstruction itself appears to be aimed at countering any self-notion, including even just the idea of positing an intrinsic nature, and in this respect would be similar to the deconstruction of the notion of a "sentient being" in *Āgama* literature. Just as a sentient being, so too the five aggregates are devoid of any essence or intrinsic nature. A helpful way to contemplate this empty nature can be the metaphor of an illusion. Used already in *Āgama* literature to characterize the nature of consciousness, the Perfection of Wisdom applies the same image in a broader manner to help counter reification and attachment.

Another similarity can be found in the employment of at first sight paradoxical statements, whose usage is not confined to the Perfection of Wisdom but can also be identified in Pāli texts, such as in a verse indicating that a self does not exist for the self. An element of continuity between *Āgama* literature and the Perfection of Wisdom can also be seen in the employment of the parable of the raft to illustrate the need to let go of the very means for progress on the path, once the time has come to proceed further.

The repeated employment of deconstruction in the Perfection of Wisdom could be a kind of cognitive training, whereby bodhisattvas learn to let go of any conceptual tool on the spot, immediately after it has fulfilled its communicative purpose. The procedure of repeating the same message over and again would also foster gradually overcoming reactions of fear, which may be triggered by the deconstruction of notions and beliefs held to be indispensable for progress on the path to Buddhahood or even just for one's sense of identity as a Buddhist practitioner.

# On Chapter 2

THE SECOND CHAPTER of Lokakṣema's translation of the Perfection of Wisdom, which for the most part still aligns with the second chapter of the Sanskrit version translated by Conze (1973/1975, 96–102), sets in with various celestials joining the audience, including Śakra and Brahmā. The ensuing discussion marks the contrast between the traditional four levels of awakening and the path of a bodhisattva, which requires not taking a stance on anything.

In what follows I will explore two main topics: the roles of Śakra and Brahmā, respectively, and the recommendation on not taking a stance on anything.

## Śakra and Brahmā

The report that various celestials (*deva*) had come to join the assembly listening to the exposition of the Perfection of Wisdom takes the following form in Lokakṣema's translation:[214]

> At that time, Śakra, the ruler of the *devas* [of the Thirty-Three], came together with a following of forty thousand *devaputras*, joined the assembly, and sat down. The Four Heavenly Kings came with a following of twenty thousand *devaputras* from the Heavens, joined the assembly, and sat down. *Devas* of Brahmā's company came with a following of ten thousand *devaputras*, joined the assembly, and sat down. *Devas* from the Pure Abodes came with a following of five thousand *devaputras*, joined the assembly, and sat down.

The above report of celestials coming to join the assembly in the same manner as human beings reflects a basic pattern in Buddhist thought in general, which since the time of its inception has considered the supernatural to be entirely natural. In line with this principle, various celestials feature as an integral part of the Buddhist world, and their interactions with humans appear just as real as those among humans themselves. Reciprocation of their visits in turn apparently requires having developed one's mental powers sufficiently through meditation to enable levitating to the respective celestial realm.[215] Not all nonhuman beings are necessarily benevolent, however, hence the need to establish protection against those who might do harm (as well as against other calamities). Some discourses serve the function of providing such protection,[216] thereby presenting a counterpart to the role of the Perfection of Wisdom in this respect.

Another dimension of the passage translated above relates to authentication, a topic that already emerged in the first chapter in relation to the roles accorded to Subhūti and Śāriputra. The dynamics at work in this respect have been presented by Silk (2003a, 173–74) as follows:

> One challenge faced by the authors of the first Mahāyāna scriptures is . . . [that] they had among other things to convince their audience that their innovations were fundamentally no innovations at all, and thus that in fact their presentation of new scriptures, full of new ideas, in no way really represented any actual expansion of the established and accepted canon. The new, then, must appear as the genuinely real old.
>
> It is well known that one of the strategies that the authors of Mahāyāna scriptures employed in this effort to persuade their audience of the continuity and coherence of their compositions with the prevailing corpus of scripture was to place the newly composed discourses in a familiar setting. At least in the case of the earlier Mahāyāna scriptures now accessible to us . . . the setting is always one familiar from the earlier literature, and much of the audience and many of the interlocutors [are] the same . . . The placement of a new discourse in familiar surroundings signals the audience that it should attribute to this material

> the same authority and authenticity it attributes to the previously familiar discourses set in the same environment. The new discourse, preached by the same Buddha at the same spots and to, at least in part, the same audience, is therefore just as true and valid as the teachings already familiar to the audience.
>
> In fact, however, something more is also going on here. The inhabitants of the earlier Buddhist literary tradition are, as it were, co-opted by the rhetoricians of the Mahāyāna scriptures, not only to lend authority to their scriptures, but also to illustrate the superiority of those scriptures over the old, superseded revelation . . . Not only are Mahāyāna scriptures the authentic, genuine preaching of the Buddha, but in reality they are more true, more authentic and more genuine than the already accepted scriptures known to and acknowledged by all.

Although the eminent representatives of the heavenly realms of ancient Indian cosmology mentioned in the above passage from the Perfection of Wisdom make their appearance individually in various discourses, a congregation of the type described above is exceptional. In view of such clear articulation of celestial interest, the audience of the Perfection of Wisdom cannot fail to realize that the teachings presented here must be rather special and indeed of a superior type.

Alongside such a function, the same depiction also seems to signal, in line with the suggestions offered in the above quote, a continuity with the traditional way of presentation in a discourse, building on the indications given in this respect in the first chapter. These indications take the form of adopting the standard opening of a discourse, which reports the whereabouts of the Buddha and gives some information about those who were held to have been present on that occasion. Moreover, the first chapter presents its teachings in a dialogic manner that involves, besides the Buddha himself, some of his arhat disciples. By also bringing in celestials well known in *Āgama* literature, the opening of the second chapter builds on this and can perhaps be understood to offer the additional indication to the members of the audience that they can expect their heart will also in some way be touched and roused.

The elevating presence of celestials and literary tools involving, for example, inspiring narratives or striking similes belong to the standard repertoire of *Āgama* literature. With the early stages in the evolution of Abhidharma, however, such literary tools had to recede to the background at least to some extent. As mentioned in the first chapter, a chief concern of Abhidharma thought is to present doctrinal knowledge in as comprehensive and detailed a manner as possible. This requires streamlining the variety of teachings and forms of exposition in the discourses and combining them into a coherent system that is based on identifying their most essential features. In the context of such an undertaking, there is naturally less room for various tales, interactions with celestials, metaphors, and other such literary means. As a result, at least canonical Abhidharma works have in comparison less to offer to the heart than *Āgama* literature.[217]

The Perfection of Wisdom, and other early Mahāyāna *sūtras*, can perhaps be viewed as making up for this by ensuring that their doctrinal expositions come embedded in a literary context that is richly endowed with stories, imagery, and of course also the presence of celestials. Conze (1960/2008, 138) explains that "the *Prajñāpāramitā* deliberately supplements its abstractions with the personifications of mythology," in the realization that "a religion is bound to become emaciated if defined in terms acceptable only to highbrows and intellectuals." Harrison (1995, 66) offers the following reflection:

> [T]he magical apparitions and miraculous displays in Mahāyāna *sūtras* are not just some kind of narrative padding or scaffolding for the elaboration of doctrine; they are the very essence of the Mahāyāna's struggle to make a place for itself and to survive in a competitive environment.

One of the advantages of the dexterous move of availing themselves of the entire literary repertoire of *sūtra* literature, which combines analysis with lively metaphors and inspiring storytelling, would have been to put the proponents of the Perfection of Wisdom at a considerable advantage over some of their competitors in the ancient Indian arena of public appreciation. When viewed from this perspective, the appearance of Śakra and Brahmā, just as the tale of the bodhisattva Sadāprarudita in the final chapters (see below p. 250), can be viewed as integral to the transformative project of the Perfection of Wisdom. These narrative elements in a way provide the environment for the teaching on emptiness to flourish.[218]

Based on this overall assessment, in what follows I explore the role of Śakra as a Buddhist disciple, set in contrast to his former martial activities when being the Indra of ancient Indian mythology. Then I examine the function of Brahmā in protecting the Buddha's dispensation, in particular his intervention to convince the recently awakened Buddha to teach at all.

### *Śakra as a Buddhist Disciple*

A key element informing the depiction of Śakra in *Āgama* discourses is a rather substantial transformation of the ancient Indian warrior god Indra into a Buddhist disciple and stream-entrant.[219] Bingenheimer (2011, 183) highlights the contrast between these two by noting that "[c]ertainly the gentle and friendly Sakka bears little resemblance to the *soma*-quaffing, demon-beheading Indra of the Vedas." *Āgama* literature repeatedly negotiates this contrast in one way or another, often combined with a good dose of humor.

A telling episode takes off from a battle with the *asuras*, the "demons" or "titans" who in ancient Indian mythology are constantly at war with the celestials of Śakra's realm, the Heaven of the Thirty-Three. On this particular occasion, the *asuras* are victorious and Śakra is trying his best to escape from his enemies, who are in hot pursuit. His chariot heads for a forest, whose bird nests will be harmed if he continues his flight. On recognizing the harm that will be incurred in this way, Śakra tells his charioteer to turn back, as he prefers to let himself be caught rather than be responsible for harming innocent sentient beings.[220] This (at least for Indra) rather unexpected turn of events could not have failed to make an impact on the ancient Indian audience. The whole narrative then comes with a happy ending. On seeing Śakra suddenly turn around and drive toward them, the *asuras* get frightened and in turn take flight themselves. In this way, the virtues of nonviolence and compassion are successfully promoted as leading to victory in an otherwise lost battle.

The above episode still takes an actual battle as its setting. Although this is a requirement in order for the ensuing tale to deliver its chief message, actually engaging in warfare is in a way still too much on the side of Indra's former pursuits and does not fit particularly well the role of Śakra as a Buddhist disciple wholeheartedly committed to keeping the five precepts. This consideration appears to provide the backdrop to yet another tale that involves the same enmity between the *asura*s and the celestials of the Thirty-Three. On the verge of yet another battle, Śakra and the leader of the *asura*s decide they will instead engage in a contest of poetry, in the sense that whoever proclaims the better verses shall be reckoned the victor. Needless to say, Śakra wins the contest with a poem in praise of patience instead of retaliation.[221] Besides the predictable final outcome, the very idea that these two warriors would decide to forgo battle and instead have a poetry contest can safely be expected to have had quite an entertaining effect on its ancient Indian audience.

Although the above episodes show the degree to which Śakra had to leave behind his former warrior activities, his interest in sensual indulgence appears to have been a trait less easily overcome. This can be seen in a Pāli discourse that begins with Śakra approaching the Buddha with an inquiry about gaining liberation through the destruction of craving. Such an inquiry is in line with a standard procedure for a mature practitioner, usually a monastic, who wishes to withdraw into seclusion for intensive practice aimed at arhat-ship. Before doing so, such a mature practitioner will approach the Buddha for a succinct instruction that will inform and inspire the period of wholehearted dedication to progress toward the final goal.

In the present case, after having rejoiced in the Buddha's instruction and returned to the Heaven of the Thirty-Three, Śakra does the very opposite of this pattern, as he is found enjoying himself in the company of heavenly nymphs. This is of course not quite in keeping with the clarifications on the destruction of craving that he has just received. The relevant Pāli discourse and its Chinese parallels agree that it takes a visit and supernatural feat performed by Mahāmaudgalyāyana to rouse Śakra from his negligence.[222] The main story line, just as several of its narrative details, is pervaded by humor, thereby providing an entertaining framing for what at the same time is a rather profound teaching on the destruction of craving. These and other such tales in *Āgama* literature stand in a lively dialogue with the repercussions of Śakra's conversion and the contrast to his previous activities as Indra.

In the Perfection of Wisdom, a reference to Śakra's role in having to combat the *asuras* occurs in the next chapter. According to the relevant episode, other celestials have been urging Śakra to take up the Perfection of Wisdom. The Buddha joins in and informs Śakra that recalling or reciting the Perfection of Wisdom will suffice to cause the *asuras* to abandon any attempt to invade the Heaven of the Thirty-Three and give battle.[223] Compared to the episodes surveyed above, this offers an even better solution. Turning around in flight may have worked once, but who knows if the same will work again? Even the idea of a poetic contest with the leader of the *asuras* requires first of all that both sides agree, and it could at least in principle also end in the other's victory. Being in the possession of the Perfection of Wisdom, however, Śakra will be able to thwart any attack by the *asuras* on the spot and that without any risk. Such a way of dealing with an attack by the *asuras* also requires little effort, as it not only dispenses with having to take up arms but even avoids having to compose poetry. All that is required is to recall the Perfection of Wisdom, and that is anyway worth the effort needed to keep it in mind.

Although Śakra is not able to try out this new approach right away, simply because there appear to be no *asuras* around ready to launch an attack, soon enough he gets two opportunities to witness firsthand the efficacy of the Buddha's recommendation. The first of these opportunities involves a group of non-Buddhists who are about to intrude into the assembly. Śakra recites the Perfection of Wisdom, and they withdraw and leave.[224] The same approach works similarly to repel Māra, who also has come with the intention to disturb the assembly listening to the exposition of the Perfection of Wisdom.[225]

These two episodes exemplify the suggestion made at the outset of the present chapter that the Perfection of Wisdom avails itself of various literary modalities also used for teaching purposes in *Āgama* literature, including narratives. After the introduction of celestials that join the assembly at the outset of the present chapter, which can serve to call up a deepening of inspiration and perhaps even awe among the audience, the present turn of events may suddenly bring home the fact that not just anyone wanting to join the assembly will necessarily be welcome, as some may come to disturb. Perhaps this possibility should be read as reflecting actual experiences among those cultivating the Perfection of Wisdom, although it is in principle difficult to ascertain how far references to others criticizing or obstructing the teaching and spreading of the Perfection of Wisdom may have just served the purpose of strengthening a sense of group identity among adherents.[226] Be that as it may, the very Perfection of Wisdom can not only be viewed as an occasion for such unwanted intrusions but also serve as the means for dealing with them. In fact, as evident from the case of Śakra's perennial trouble with the *asuras*, it does so better than what *Āgama* literature has to offer for such purposes. In this way, those listening to or reading this episode are drawn in by the dramatic turn of events and thereby become ever more receptive to the main message: Behold the power of the Perfection of Wisdom!

### *Brahmā Sahāṃpati*

Brahmā Sahāṃpati is a celestial from the Pure Abodes, which were mentioned in the passage from the Perfection of Wisdom translated above in the form of reporting that five thousand celestials from these elevated celestial realms joined the assembly. He comes up by name in the next chapter, in the course of which he expresses his willingness to protect all those who engage with the Perfection of Wisdom.[227] From the viewpoint of narrative logic, he is best understood as implicitly mentioned in the present chapter's reference to the celestials from the Pure Abodes.

These Pure Abodes are somewhat of an *Āgama* counterpart to the Pure Land, with the difference of course that the Pure Abodes are not presided over by a Buddha. The basic requirement for residential rights in the Pure Abodes is the attainment of nonreturn. As a result of only admitting nonreturners, defilements like sensual desire and anger are simply unknown among the citizens in this world. As is the case with any Brahmā realm, the respective celestial inhabitants are genderless beings possessed of a fine-material body that does not require food or beverages and will not be affected by disease or other vicissitudes. Since in the case of the Pure Abodes everyone is a Buddhist disciple, and quite an advanced one at that, living in the Pure Abodes does seem to have much in common with the attractions of rebirth in the Pure Land.

The proposed relationship becomes particularly evident if compared with what appears to be an early stage in the development of Pure Land thought, namely the description of the Buddhafield of Akṣobhya.[228] Nattier (2000, 83 and 99) reports:

> The text describes at length how much easier it is to attain Arhatship in Akṣobhya's world than in our own. Innumerable listeners attain Arhatship each time Akṣobhya preaches the Dharma, and those who require four such lectures to progress step by step from stream-enterer to Arhatship are considered the "slow learners" of the group. No one, apparently, will require rebirth elsewhere before attaining final liberation; thus birth in Akṣobhya's land is tantamount to the last birth of the non-returner...
>
> [T]he fact that Abhirati provides an optimal setting for the rapid attainment of Arhatship makes it analogous to the "Pure Abodes" (*suddhāvāsa*)... the upper heavens of the Form Realm in which the non-returner (*anāgamin*) is reborn, attaining Arhatship there and never returning to our world.

The suggestion finds further support in the circumstance, noted by Nattier (2000, 91), that the relevant text explicitly indicates rebirth in this world to be impossible for those whose mind is still under the influence of lust.[229] The above parallelisms make it reasonable to propose that there is a marked affinity between descriptions of the Pure Abodes and of Akṣobhya's Buddhafield, even though the former lacks a Buddha and the latter is not a heaven but a whole world system.[230]

A Pāli discourse can be seen to take a significant step in the direction of bringing the Pure Abodes even closer to the Pure Land, as it presents an intriguing way of gaining rebirth in the former. Without any explicit reference to the need to progress through the lower levels of awakening, the discourse describes how a monastic endowed with faith, virtue, learning, renunciation, and wisdom hears of the rather attractive living conditions in the Pure Abodes. This motivates the monastic to form the aspiration to be reborn there. Fixing the mind on this aim and cultivating it in this manner will conduce to the desired rebirth.[231] Would it be going too far to consider this Pāli discourse to be indeed drawing close to Pure Land type of practices?

Be that as it may, Brahmā Sahāṃpati is not a recent convert, unlike Śakra. A Pāli discourse with no known parallel reports that Sahāṃpati had become a monk under Kāśyapa, the last Buddha to appear before the advent of Śākyamuni Buddha. Having successfully overcome sensuality, he was reborn in a Brahmā world; a Pāli commentary confirms what seems to be implicit in this indication, namely that at that time Sahāṃpati had progressed up to nonreturn.[232]

Elsewhere among Pāli discourses Brahmā Sahāṃpati features regularly in the role of a protector of the Buddha's dispensation, expressing his approbation or even offering advice to the Buddha. An example for approbation concerns the Buddha's decision to honor nobody else but the Dharma he has discovered. Becoming aware of this thought, Brahmā Sahāṃpati appears in order to express his approval.[233] The same happens when the Buddha reflects on the potential of the four establishments of mindfulness (*smṛtyupasthāna*) as the direct path to awakening, which similarly motivates Brahmā Sahāṃpati to voice his agreement.[234]

Alternatively, Brahmā Sahāṃpati may extoll the ideal monastic life.[235] In fact, he also takes a keen interest in communal harmony, intervening to reconcile the Buddha with a group of unruly monks.[236] A gibe at ancient Indian ritual customs can be seen in another episode in a Pāli discourse, featuring a brahmin woman who makes daily oblations to Brahmā. This ritual observance takes an unexpected turn when Brahmā Sahāṃpati suddenly appears in midair and tells her she would do better to take the food offered in oblation and give it to her son, who had become a Buddhist monk.[237]

The perhaps most famous episode featuring Brahmā Sahāṃpati takes place right after the Buddha's awakening. The Buddha is disinclined to teach what he has discovered to others. Brahmā Sahāṃpati realizes this and appears in front of the Buddha, requesting that he teach. Following this request, the Buddha reconsiders and decides to share his discovery with others.

Brahmā Sahāṃpati's rather crucial intervention at this juncture of events, without which Śākyamuni would presumably have taken up the career of a Pratyekabuddha, forms part of an account of the Buddha's quest for awakening in a Pāli discourse.[238] The same episode recurs in other Pāli discourses; in a discourse in the *Ekottarikāgama*; in several texts on monastic discipline, *Vinaya*; in an account of the founding of the Buddhist community, the *Catuṣpariṣatsūtra*; and in biographies of the Buddha, such as the *Lalitavistara* and other comparable works extant in Chinese.[239] A reference to the Buddha's hesitation to teach also features in the Sanskrit version of the *Aṣṭasāhasrikā Prajñāpāramitā*, although such an indication does not occur in the corresponding part of Lokakṣema's translation.[240] In addition to textual reports, this rather crucial intervention has also been taken up repeatedly in ancient Indian art, and the location associated with this episode was known to the Chinese pilgrims Fǎxiǎn (法顯) and Xuánzàng (玄奘).[241]

In an account of Brahmā Sahāṃpati's request that the Buddha teach, found in the *Jātaka* collection, Brahmā comes in the company of Śakra; the same also holds for a version of this request in a *Vinaya* text of the Mahāsāṃghika-Lokottaravādins, the *Mahāvastu*, and in a biography of the Buddha extant in Chinese.[242] This appears to reflect a gradual rise in importance of Śakra vis-à-vis Brahmā, which can also be seen in the circumstance that in the Perfection of Wisdom Sahāṃpati plays only a minor role, whereas Śakra occurs regularly and is more prominent in comparison.

The participation of Śakra in the important event of requesting the Buddha to teach occurs similarly in depictions in sculptures and reliquaries.[243] In such cases, however, it is not always certain if a particular image intends the actual request that the Buddha teach or else perhaps just depicts worship in general.[244] Nevertheless, such depictions definitely reflect a tendency to give Śakra as prominent a role as Brahmā. An example for such a depiction of Śakra together with Brahmā, which could be the request to teach but may alternatively be just a scene of worship, can be seen in figure 2.[245] This Gandhāran sculpture shows only an empty seat, presumably an aniconic representation of the presence of the Buddha, flanked on both sides by the gods Brahmā and Śakra, who have their hands folded in the traditional gesture of respect.

Figure 2. Brahmā and Śakra/Indra worshipping the Buddha, the latter represented by an empty seat.

The Pāli discourse giving an account of the Buddha's quest for awakening, which reports the hesitation to teach and Brahmā Sahāṃpati's intervention, has a parallel in Chinese, found in the *Madhyamāgama*. This discourse does not report any disinclination by the Buddha to teach and for this reason also does not mention any action taken by Brahmā (or anyone else) to convince the Buddha to share his discovery with others. The narrative flow of the *Madhyamāgama* discourse at this juncture is smooth, with no evidence that a loss of text has occurred.[246] Moreover, this *Madhyamāgama* discourse is not alone in reporting neither any hesitation nor an intervention by Brahmā, as the same occurs in relation to the awakening of the former Buddha Vipaśyin in two discourse versions, extant in Chinese and Sanskrit.[247] The situation that emerges in this way leaves open the possibility that the intervention of Brahmā could be a later development,[248] whose appeal would then have led to it being included in a range of textual accounts and artistic presentations. For my present exploration, ascertaining whether the episode of Brahmā's intervention was added in some texts or lost in others is of less consequence. What matters more is the very fact that this episode came into being, and about this there cannot be any doubt.

In the *Milindapañha*, the Indo-Greek King Milinda takes up the present episode in one of his dilemmas: how to reconcile the report that during incalculable eons the bodhisattva who was to become the Buddha Śākyamuni had prepared himself for the task of liberating sentient beings, yet, once he had awakened, he was disinclined to teach?[249] In reply, the Buddhist monk Nāgasena presents two arguments. One of these is that the hesitation should be understood to be just of the type of a doctor who hesitates, deliberating what medicine would be appropriate, or of an anointed king who hesitates, considering how best to protect his dependents. In the same way, when the Buddha surveyed the world with his omniscient knowledge and realized the contrast between the degree to which beings were under the influence of defilements on the one hand and the subtlety and profundity of what he had discovered on the other, he hesitated in the wish to make sure that beings indeed would be able to understand.[250]

The second argument is that it is an integral part of the standard pattern followed by all Buddhas that they are to be invited by Brahmā to teach. This serves to instill respect for their teachings in a setting in which Brahmā is held in high regard, on the principle that, once Brahmā bows down to a Buddha, the rest of the world will follow suit.[251] The Pāli commentary on the discourse that reports the episode under discussion adds that the Buddha of course knew that his hesitation would motivate Brahmā to intervene.[252]

Neither argument fits the actual Pāli discourse particularly well. The narrative setting of this discourse is an exposition given by the Buddha to an assembly of his monastic disciples on the topic of his quest for awakening. It makes little sense for the Buddha to inform his own disciples in quite explicit and unambiguous terms that he had been disinclined to teach,[253] if this had in truth and fact only been a pretense of sorts to get Brahmā to invite him to teach. There is hardly a way of reading the Pāli discourse other than as depicting an actual hesitation, without any hint at ulterior motives.

According to the temporal sequence of events in this discourse, the hesitation was followed by Brahmā's intervention, and only after that intervention did the Buddha survey the world. This goes to show that the idea of a survey of the world leading to a hesitation similar to a doctor or king does not work either, since it confuses the temporal sequence of events. In the discourse, the hesitation happens *before* the survey of the world, not after it. In fact, the actual survey leads the Buddha to the realization that some will understand what he has to teach, rather than instilling any hesitation. It functions as a confirmation of the appropriateness of Brahmā's request, rather than instigating any uncertainty regarding how to perform the task of teaching.

The *Buddhacarita* extant in Chinese translation attempts to resolve the same problem by having the recently awakened Buddha recall his former pledge before any intervention.[254] Brahmā then becomes aware of the Buddha's thought and nevertheless invites him. In line with the apparent tendency to improve on this intervention by bringing in Śakra, the Tibetan version of the *Buddhacarita* refers to the two supreme ones,[255] evidently in reference to Brahmā and Śakra. Whether Brahmā intervenes alone or in the company of Śakra, the described procedure does not solve the dilemma particularly well, since to the extent to which the Buddha had already recalled his mission, to that same extent there would no longer be any need for others to intervene. In this way, the dramatic intervention by Brahmā becomes merely an encouragement along the lines of what the Buddha had already decided to do.[256]

These various attempts at ironing out the problem caused by the idea that the Buddha hesitated to teach reflect the degree to which this episode is difficult to accommodate within a worldview that takes the bodhisattva path for granted. Whenever the narrative of Brahmā's invitation came into being and gained widespread acceptance, this must have happened in a setting that had not yet adopted the paradigmatic idea that Śākyamuni had prepared himself over many past lives with the intentional purpose of liberating sentient beings. Had this idea already been in place, it can safely be expected that it would have created as much cognitive dissonance as it did in later times, and this would have undermined the very spread of a narrative that shows the Buddha to be reluctant to teach others. From this perspective, the various instances of this episode in texts and art can be taken as pointers to the need for appreciating each stage in the gradual evolution of the bodhisattva ideal on its own terms. I will come back to this need in the next chapter.

## No Stance on Anything

From the widespread appeal of the narrative of Brahmā's intervention to convince the recently awakened Buddha to teach, whose very spread reflects an early stage in the gradual evolution of the bodhisattva ideal, in what follows I turn to an essential dimension of the path to Buddhahood (as well as of the path to awakening in general). According to the Perfection of Wisdom, following the path of a bodhisattva requires not taking a stance on anything. This much applies not only to the five aggregates but also to different levels or types of awakening:[257]

> One should not take a stance on form. One should not take a stance on feeling tone, perception, volitional formations, and consciousness. One should not take a stance on stream-entry, one should not take a stance on once-return, one should not take a stance on nonreturn, one should not take a stance on

> arhat-ship, one should not take a stance on Pratyekabuddhahood, and one should not take a stance on Buddhahood.

For appreciating the import of this instruction, it can be helpful to keep in mind that, alongside the main concern of the Perfection of Wisdom in guiding the practitioner dedicated to achieving Buddhahood, its teaching explicitly features as relevant also to those practicing for arhat-ship.[258] In other words, at least a rudimentary grasp of this type of teaching is required even for what the Perfection of Wisdom considers lower types of awakening, even though its full penetration remains the sole domain of those on the path to Buddhahood. It nevertheless follows that not taking a stance on the four levels of awakening, from stream-entry to arhat-ship, concerns the proper attitude of nonreification that would be required even by those who aspire for such goals. For bodhisattvas the most directly relevant part, in addition to the need to avoid any reification of the five aggregates, is in turn the final indication regarding Buddhahood.

The above listing appears to be by way of exemplification, in the sense that one should better not reify anything. In fact, the Sanskrit version expands on the above list by relating the same injunction also to the six senses, their objects, and the corresponding type of consciousness, to the six elements (earth, water, fire, wind, space, and consciousness), and to the qualities and practices "pertinent to awakening" (*bodhipākṣika*), which comprise the four establishments of mindfulness, the four right endeavors, the four bases of success, the five faculties and powers, the seven awakening factors, and the noble eightfold path.[259]

The need to avoid any reification is the central theme of an *Āgama* discourse extant in Pāli and Chinese, the former of which constitutes the first member in the collection of middle-length discourses, *Majjhimanikāya*, a position perhaps reflecting its importance. The challenging nature of this exposition becomes evident in the final part of both discourses. According to the conclusion of the Pāli version, the listening monastics were not delighted by the Buddha's instruction; according to its Chinese parallel, they did not accept this teaching.[260] Among Pāli discourses this appears to be the only instance of an instruction given to disciples that departs from the standard conclusion reporting the delighted reaction of the listeners.[261] Even though the Pāli commentary attributes the absence of delight to the inability of the listening disciples to understand the teaching,[262] an alternative explanation would be that their unusual reaction should be attributed to the fact that they did understand the thorough undermining of any tendency toward reification proposed in this discourse and precisely for this reason were unable to delight in it.[263]

This episode can be related to a passage in the **Kāśyapaparivarta*, another early Mahāyāna text, a version of which has been translated by Lokakṣema. Although the relevant passage does not occur at the end of the text as extant now, it similarly reports a group of monks to be rather displeased at having heard a profound teaching just given by the Buddha, to the extent that they actually get up and leave.[264] The possibility of such a drastic reaction also features in the Perfection of Wisdom as a hypothetical case, where Śāriputra describes how on hearing its teachings bodhisattvas may become afraid, reject it, and leave.[265]

In the above-mentioned Pāli discourse, the basic pattern of the actual exposition proceeds from the tendency of the worldling to conceive and reify to the need of the disciple in higher training to avoid any conceiving, followed by highlighting that arhats and Buddhas have gone beyond any such problematic ways of apperceiving. The resultant presentation works through three different modes of perceiving: the case of the worldling is characterized by conceiving and reifying, the disciple in higher training by refraining from these, whereas arhats and Buddhas are definitely beyond these. When taking up each of these three cases, the exposition covers a range of different objects that can be perceived in these different ways. In the Pāli version, these objects comprise the four elements, various celestials, the four immaterial spheres, experiences through the senses (what is seen, heard, sensed, and cognized), the notions of unity, of diversity, and of everything, and finally Nirvana itself. The resultant list seems to be intended to offer a fairly exhaustive account of different possible experiences.

The part perhaps most relevant as a juxtaposition to the instructions given in the Perfection of Wisdom would be the case of disciples in higher training, as these share with advanced bodhisattvas the condition of being fully dedicated to their respective paths without yet having reached the final consummation of their aspirations. The task faced by a disciple in higher training can perhaps best be exemplified with the final instruction regarding the perception of Nirvana itself:[266]

> Do not conceive "Nirvana," do not conceive "in Nirvana," do not conceive "from Nirvana," do not conceive "my Nirvana," and do not delight in Nirvana. Why is that? I say: "[Because] one should fully understand it."

Not even the final goal, Nirvana, is worth conceiving, worth being appropriated. Needless to say, this instruction needs to be read alongside repeated references in other discourses that encourage wholehearted dedication to progressing toward Nirvana, which clearly forms the overarching goal of early Buddhist soteriology. Nevertheless, as the present passage clarifies, one should not delight in it, which must be intending the type of delight that results from the previously depicted modalities of reification by conceiving and appropriating. These are problematized because they hamper full understanding—that is, they hamper perfecting one's wisdom. Although this passage does not go so far as to refer to Nirvana as being like an illusion, as is the case for the Perfection of Wisdom,[267] the underlying concerns in both texts seem to be similar. The above passage sounds a clear warning against becoming so carried away by the concept of Nirvana as to reify it, which is problematic precisely because it can prevent progress to the actual realization of Nirvana.

A presentation that is to some extent comparable to the above Pāli discourse can be found in the penultimate chapter of the Perfection of Wisdom, where it is precisely the exercise of the Perfection of Wisdom that results in penetrating, in the sense of comprehending, the various items listed.[268] This listing covers, among others, the elements, the aggregates, the gateways to deliverance, various classes of celestial beings, the four levels of awakening, the qualities pertinent to awakening, etc.[269] This passage supports the impression that the above Pāli discourse expresses concerns that are similarly relevant to the Perfection of Wisdom.

Another discourse extant in Pāli and Chinese applies a somewhat comparable deconstruction to virtuous conduct (*śīla*) and thus to the very foundation of the path as envisaged in *Āgama* thought. According to the narrative context, the Buddha has been asked his opinion regarding the claim that someone who refrains from ethically bad bodily and verbal actions, etc., can be considered highly accomplished. In reply, the Buddha points out that an infant would also fulfil such conditions, due to its inability to engage in ethically bad ways of acting or speaking, etc. Clearly, more is required for deserving to be reckoned a highly accomplished practitioner.

In exploring this topic further, the Buddha points out the importance of knowing that defiled states of mind form the roots of ethically bad forms of conduct and the absence of such defilements constitutes the root for ethically good forms of conduct. In addition, one should also know where ethically bad and good forms of conduct cease completely. The exposition of the latter takes the following form in the Pāli version:[270]

> One is virtuous but not made of virtue, and one understands as it really is that liberation of the mind and liberation by wisdom where those wholesome forms of conduct cease completely.

It is noteworthy that a cessation of wholesome conduct (*kuśala śīla*) here features in a positive light in a Pāli discourse. Of course, the passage needs to be read in conjunction with the previously mentioned cessation of unwholesome conduct. In other words, it certainly does not amount to commending acting in unwholesome ways. The reference to understanding as it really is liberation of the mind and liberation by wisdom confirms this (although this reference is not found in the Chinese parallel).

At the same time, however, the actual realization of liberation goes beyond any form of conduct. In preparation for such utter transcendence, the first part of the above indication can be of considerable help, enjoining that one should be virtuous but not made of virtue, not use it as a basis for creating a reified sense of identity, and not relate to it with attachment. Once again, the main issue appears to be the need to avoid any reification by not taking a stance on anything.

Another perspective on the same need not to take a stance on anything, including on the undertaking of ethical conduct, can be gathered from a poem that records a reply given by the Buddha in the course of an exchange with a non-Buddhist visitor. The exchange leads from an inquiry regarding what type of practice and teaching the Buddha advocates to the question of what he understands to be the attainment of peace. The Pāli report of his reply takes the following form:[271]

> It is not through a view, not through learning, not through knowledge, and also not through virtue and observances that I declare [the reaching of] purification, nor is it through the absence of view, through the absence of learning, through the absence of knowledge, through the absence of virtue, and through the absence of observances—it is also not in that way.

This mode of presentation is to some extent similar to the rhetoric adopted regularly in the Perfection of Wisdom, and Gómez (1976, 146) includes the present passage in a survey of what he refers to as instances of "proto-Mādhyamika" found among Pāli discourses. Compared to the discourse taken up above on not identifying with one's virtue, the present passage further broadens the perspective beyond the topic of virtue and corresponding modes of observance to include taking up a view, acquiring learning, and even knowledge presumably derived from some form of practice that is not further specified. As the next verse indicates, the task is to avoid any clinging to these and to be willing to let go of them in order to dwell independently and at peace. Of course, as the second part of the above poem clarifies, the idea is not that taking up a view, acquiring learning, etc., can just be dispensed with. The point would rather be that these have a merely instrumental function, and clinging to them becomes an obstacle to the very purpose they are meant to achieve.

The Buddha's interlocutor is not satisfied with the above explanation, as it seems to him to be a confused type of teaching. This is unsurprising for someone who, according to the narrative setting, is unacquainted with Buddhist teachings and apparently holds the belief that taking up a view, provided it is the "correct" one, can in itself be purificatory.[272] The Buddha replies by setting aside notions of being equal, superior, or inferior, which he identifies as sources for the arising of disputation; then he queries why one should even assert truth in contrast to falsehood?[273] This teaching seems to leave no place at all to take a stance on.

It is noteworthy that such indications are part of a teaching given to someone who according to the narrative setting has his first encounter with Buddhist doctrine and practice. This goes to show that this type of teaching, although particularly relevant to the last leg of the spiritual journey when one needs to get off the seventh chariot and leave the raft behind on the other shore, can also have a clarifying effect for someone who has yet to embark on the chariot or raft.

This theme ties in with a repeated concern voiced in the Perfection of Wisdom, in that someone who has only recently embarked on the path to Buddhahood could easily become afraid on hearing its teachings, whereby the very means to be employed for progress on this path are being deconstructed. On the other hand, however, if the purely instrumental purpose of these means can be clarified from the outset, forestalling any clinging or attachment to them, this would make for speedy and smooth progress. This suggestion could be supported by the background information provided in the Pāli commentary to the above discourse, according to which by the end of the exchange the interlocutor and his wife were sufficiently inspired to go forth under the Buddha and both in turn became arhats.[274]

Another relevant example concerns the issue of views. A Pāli poem describes the accomplished sage as one who "has shaken off all views right here," and another poem refers to the "wise one who is released from resorting to views."[275] A literal reading could lead to the impression that this type of teaching conflicts with the emphasis on the four noble truths as right view in many other discourses. Yet, such an impression may be missing the point. The passage translated above clearly combines the indication that reaching inner purification is not "through a view" with the indication that it is also not "through the absence of view." Both dimensions need to be kept in mind. In other words, it would be more fruitful to rely on the tetralemma perspective and allow for positions that may at first sight appear contradictory to be rather complementing each other.

The diagnostic scheme of the four noble truths can be immensely helpful in identifying craving and clinging, and that potential holds in particular when such craving and clinging are directed toward one's own views. Once this potential is fully appreciated, the apparent contradiction dissolves. This is yet another dimension that has much in common with the teachings of the Perfection of Wisdom, which are also most fruitfully read as conveying something more profound than an exercise in self-contradiction (see above p. 36).

In the case of *Āgama* literature, however, such indications are only found in a few passages. To a considerable extent this must be due to the circumstance that in *Āgama* literature such instructions often feature as being given somewhat impromptu in a particular situation. In the case of the narrative setting of the passage translated above, the Buddha's interlocutor was apparently ready for such deep teachings, even though these did not land with him right away. But such cases are not the norm for depictions of audiences and their concerns in *Āgama* literature. For this reason, it takes familiarity with *Āgama* literature and their thought to detect instances of this type of instructions. This situation changes with the Perfection of Wisdom, where this rather important dimension of the Buddhist teachings becomes a continuous and prominent theme that, unlike the case of *Āgama* literature, can hardly be missed.[276] It is thus with the Perfection of Wisdom that the importance of not taking a stance on anything receives the sustained and in-depth highlight it indeed deserves.

## Summary

This chapter has highlighted similarities, alongside differences in the details, between *Āgama* literature and the Perfection of Wisdom regarding the roles of Śakra and Brahmā Sahāṃpati as well as in respect to the all-important injunction not to take a stance on anything.

Celestials like Śakra and Brahmā Sahāṃpati are a common feature of Buddhist texts, which make their actions appear just as real as those of human beings. In the present case, the participation of celestials can be seen to convey that the Perfection of Wisdom avails itself of the whole range of literary means to communicate its message, including inspiring encounters with nonhumans as well as entertaining tales and illustrative similes.

The literary function of Śakra stands in close relationship to narrative entertainment, related to the conversion of the ancient Indian warrior god Indra to become the peaceful Buddhist disciple (and stream-entrant) Śakra. Negotiating this transition calls for a substantial reinterpretation of his warrior activities, evident when discourses show him risking defeat for the sake of avoiding harm to innocent birds or else substituting fighting battles with a poetry contest. Yet, the Perfection of Wisdom is able to offer an even better means, as the Buddha informs Śakra that reciting or recollecting the Perfection of Wisdom will stop his archenemies, the *asura*s, from any attempt to invade the Heaven of the Thirty-Three.

Unlike Śakra, Brahmā Sahāṃpati is not a recent convert, as he apparently became a nonreturner when being a monk under Kāśyapa, the previous Buddha. He presently resides in the Pure Abodes, which could be considered an *Āgama* counterpart to the Pure Land (albeit without a Buddha in residence). Brahmā Sahāṃpati features in *Āgama* literature as a protector of the Buddha's dispensation, intervening whenever this seems to be called for. His most famous intervention occurs right after the Buddha's awakening. Realizing that the Buddha is disinclined to teach others, Brahmā Sahāṃpati appears and successfully convinces the Buddha to teach.

This episode, found in a Pāli discourse but not in its Chinese parallel, has been of lasting appeal in texts and art. The very existence of a narrative that shows the Buddha reluctant to teach, together with its evident appeal and spread, testifies to a setting in which the bodhisattva ideal had not yet fully evolved. Had the idea already been in place that becoming a Buddha requires intentional cultivation over a series of lives under the overarching motivation of liberating sentient beings, this narrative would hardly have stood a chance of achieving the success that it did. The present case thereby serves as a reminder of the need to avoid defaulting to the perspectives of later tradition, so as to be able to appreciate instances of textual evidence that reflect the gradual evolution of the bodhisattva ideal.

Not taking a firm stance on anything at all is a central concern in the Perfection of Wisdom. This applies to any aspect of subjective experience, expressed in terms of the five aggregates, just as it does to different levels or types of awakening, including Buddhahood. Related indications can be found in *Āgama* literature, such as the injunction that those on the path to the four levels of awakening should not conceive of or even delight in Nirvana. The same texts also promote the idea of a cessation of wholesome conduct as something positive. This does not imply an encouragement to indulge in ethically reprehensible actions. Instead, the point appears to be rather that one should be virtuous but without identifying with that, without making it into a building block of one's sense of identity.

Another relevant passage proposes that inner peace and purification will not be achieved by holding a particular view, having acquired learning, being in the possession of knowledge, or cultivating virtue and undertaking related observances. Yet, in the absence of these, the same goal of inner peace and purification is definitely beyond reach. Although such indications can at first sight appear confusing, their potential benefit does not seem to be confined to only those who have reached the very final leg of the path. Even those just about to embark on the path can benefit from the clarification that the means to be used for progress have merely an instrumental value and should not be clung to in any way.

Indications in this respect, which have been considered to be "proto-Mādhyamika" in type, are found only occasionally and in different textual collections of *Āgama* literature. It is only with the Perfection of Wisdom that the overarching need to avoid taking a stance on anything comes fully out into the open, becoming a continuous theme that can hardly be missed.

# On Chapters 3 and 4

THE THIRD AND FOURTH chapters of Lokakṣema's translation of the Perfection of Wisdom no longer align with the Sanskrit version translated by Conze (1973/1975, 103–34), as their contents correspond to the third to sixth chapters in the latter.[277] The structural layout of Lokakṣema's translation also differs in having at the outset of its third chapter a reference to the Buddha Śākyamuni in one of his past lives meeting the former Buddha Dīpaṃkara, whereas the Sanskrit version has this episode at the end of its second chapter.[278] Other themes taken up in the present portion of the text are the potency of the Perfection of Wisdom as a protection against various calamities, its central role among the perfections to be acquired for progress to Buddhahood, and its exceptional merit-generating potential. In the course of showcasing the superior merit to be gained through engaging with the Perfection of Wisdom in various ways, the text turns to the topic of an imitation or counterfeit teaching on the sixth perfection, which takes the form of equating the impermanent nature of the five aggregates with their destruction.

Two topics to be explored below are former Buddhas from the viewpoint of the evolving bodhisattva ideal as well as the relationship of impermanence to wisdom.

## FORMER BUDDHAS

### *An Abundance of Merit*

Under the heading of former Buddhas, I will be exploring a range of related topics, beginning with the notion of merit, whose acquisition is a key requirement for progress to Buddhahood over a series of lives.[279] The third chapter in the Perfection of Wisdom provides a convenient occasion for an exploration of the notion of merit, as much of its discussion revolves around precisely this theme.

In *Āgama* texts, the topic of merit to some extent escapes the otherwise pervasive rhetoric on the need to avoid attachment. A Pāli discourse with parallels extant in Sanskrit and Chinese reports the Buddha emphatically addressing a monastic audience with the declaration that merits should not be feared, as these are a designation for happiness.[280] A set of Pāli verses present merit as the only treasure that one need not leave behind when proceeding from one life to another.[281] As a sort of spiritual currency, merit can lead to gaining all that one may possibly wish for. The verses present a fairly exhaustive survey of various possible wishes, which range from mundane possessions to spiritual attainments, culminating in awakening as an arhat, a Pratyekabuddha, or a Buddha.[282]

The last option is naturally of particular interest from the viewpoint of the Perfection of Wisdom. For progress on the path to Buddhahood, in the way this emerges in the Perfection of Wisdom, the acquisition of merit has indeed a central role to perform. In keeping with a trend evident in *Āgama* literature, the Perfection of Wisdom does not single out merit for sustained problematization in the way the otherwise-sweeping rhetoric of emptiness deconstructs terms like the "bodhisattva" or even the very "Perfection of Wisdom" itself (see also below p. 137). In other words, whereas those who seek merit, together with what in the present context features as a chief source for its acquisition, are so thoroughly empty that it becomes challenging even just to apprehend them, the reality of merit as such remains squarely evident, to the extent that the present chapter of the Perfection of Wisdom can confidently assert various hierarchies in matters of merit acquisition. Conze (1960/2008, 132) comments that "in so extravagantly praising the merit to be derived from Perfect Wisdom, the authors were, by appealing to the acquisitive instincts of mankind, in danger of sinning against the very spirit of the *Prajñāpāramitā*. To hoard 'merit' is surely better than to hoard money, titles and honours, but it is still hoarding."

The way the Buddha depicts different modalities of generating merit, with engagement in the Perfection of Wisdom invariably topping all other potential sources of merit, can be exemplified with an excerpt from the Gāndhārī manuscript:[283]

> [The Buddha said:] "If [a son of a good family or daughter of a good family] were to establish in the fruit of stream-entry all sentient beings in Jambudvīpa, what do you think, [Kauśika,] would that son of a good family [or daughter of a good family] generate much merit?"
>
> He replied: "Venerable sir, it would be much, Blessed One."
>
> [The Buddha said:] "Kauśika, that son of a good family [or daughter of a good family] would generate more merit by writing a book of the Perfection of Wisdom for someone else."

Establishing all inhabitants of the Indian subcontinent, Jambudvīpa, in the attainment of stream-entry is a feat that the Buddha Śākyamuni had certainly been unable to accomplish. From the viewpoint of the ancient Indian audience, this feat would imply a complete transformation of the entire country, with all competition with non-Buddhists completely vanishing as everyone is now a Buddhist. It would also imply the total disappearance of any unethical activities, as stream-entrants are characterized not only by their unshakeable faith in Buddha, Dharma, and Saṅgha but also by firm adherence to ethical conduct.[284] The merit accrued by the person responsible for this feat would indeed be stellar, yet this does not match the merit resulting from the simple act of writing down the Perfection of Wisdom in book form and giving it to someone else.

The Buddha does not stop with this already rather extraordinary scenario, as he keeps leading Śakra (whom he addresses as Kauśika) through ever more impressive depictions of merit generation.[285] Instead of stream-entry, what about establishing everyone in still higher spiritual realizations?[286] Instead of the inhabitants of Jambudvīpa, what about larger populations, up to as many world systems as there are grains of sand in the river Ganges?[287] All of these spectacular scenarios fall short of matching the merit that anyone in the audience can in principle gain by promoting the Perfection of Wisdom.

As an aside, it may be worth noting that the Chinese pilgrim Fǎxiǎn (法顯) reports that in early fifth-century India the *Prajñāpāramitā* was worshipped by practitioners of the Mahāyāna.[288] This report gives the impression that the promotion strategies evident in *Prajñāpāramitā* literature were indeed successful.

With this spotlight on the generation of merit in place, the time has now come to turn to the first main topic in the present chapter, the emergence of the bodhisattva ideal from the viewpoint of the notion of former Buddhas. In what follows, I begin with Dīpaṃkara's prediction and relate this to the motif of the physical repercussions of successful merit acquisition in the form of thirty-two special marks with which the body of a Buddha is endowed. Given the central importance of merit for progress toward Buddhahood, it is perhaps unsurprising that a Buddha should indeed be, quite literally, an embodiment of merit in this way.

A Pāli discourse presenting these marks takes the important step of detailing the particular deeds, done by Śākyamuni in the course of his past lives, as a result of which in his final life he was endowed with these thirty-two marks. The relationship established in this way between the marks and Śākyamuni's former lives appears to have provided a crucial input for the very idea of undertaking a particular conduct over a series of successive lives in order to achieve Buddhahood. The perspective toward Śākyamuni's past lives that emerges in this way has its complement in various narratives becoming *jātaka*s by dint of one of the protagonists being identified as a former life of the Buddha. A particularly significant instance of this pervasive tendency involves a tale found in *Āgama* literature, which depicts a past life of Śākyamuni at the time of Kāśyapa, the last Buddha prior to Śākyamuni's Buddhahood. In conjunction, these trajectories appear to have made a substantial contribution to the complex of causes and conditions impacting the evolution of the bodhisattva ideal.

In what follows, my presentation is to a considerable degree based on summarizing previous research of mine.[289] To the best of my knowledge, this has for the most part not encountered substantial criticism, wherefore I can present matters in line with what seems most directly relevant to providing a perspective on the Perfection of Wisdom. In the case of the topic of a past life of Śākyamuni at the time of Buddha Kāśyapa, however, my discussion of the idea that at that time he decided to embark on the path to Buddhahood has met with some criticism. My exploration of this topic will therefore be more detailed, in order to take into account such criticism, combined with more detailed replies in my annotations. Throughout, my central concern is an attempt to discern textual developments that seem to exemplify ideas that in one way or another would have contributed to the emergence of the bodhisattva ideal that stands in the background to the Perfection of Wisdom.

*Buddhahood and Its Embodiment*

The chief indication given in the prediction by Dīpaṃkara, in the way in which this is found in the Perfection of Wisdom, takes the following form:[290]

> In the future, in countless incalculable eons, you will become a Buddha, called by the name of Śākyamuni, becoming the most exalted one in heaven and on earth, well established in the world with a teaching that is superbly bright.

Although the Buddha Dīpaṃkara is unknown to the Pāli discourses and their parallels (leaving aside the *Ekottarikāgama*), Pāli versions of his predicting the future Buddhahood of Śākyamuni can be found in the *Buddhavaṃsa* and in the *Jātaka* collection.[291] The popularity of this tale can also be seen in art, an example in case being the Gandhāran relief in figure 3 below. A noteworthy feature of figure 3 is that the Buddha Dīpaṃkara has long hair, gathered in a topknot. This is a recurrent feature of Buddha statues, including those that portray the Buddha Śākyamuni.[292] In contrast to such depictions, *Āgama* literature clearly presents the Buddha Śākyamuni as shaven headed.[293] As a result of being depicted in art with some form of topknot, the idea appears to have arisen that the Buddha had some sort of protuberance on his head. This has become and still is a pervasive feature of Buddha statues.

This short look at depictions of the Buddha's head exemplifies a general pattern of cross-fertilization between textual accounts of his appearance, in particular descriptions of his thirty-two bodily marks

Figure 3. The youth who was to become the Buddha Śākyamuni expresses his devotion to the former Buddha Dīpaṃkara. In line with a standard procedure in ancient Indian art, the iconography combines several successive events in a single scene. To the bottom right Śākyamuni, in his past life, can be seen acquiring flowers, to the bottom left he scatters these flowers over Dīpaṃkara, and at the center of the bottom he has spread his hair on the ground for the Buddha Dīpaṃkara to step on.

(*lakṣaṇa*), and their portrayal in art. With the term "cross-fertilization" I intend to convey an ongoing process of mutual influence and interaction, where textual accounts would have inspired art, and the resultant presentation in art would in turn have impacted textual accounts. In the present case, a description of the roundness of the Buddha's head appears to have been reinterpreted, in the light of artistic presentations of a topknot, to intend that he had some kind of protuberance on the top of his head.[294]

As a result of presumably being influenced by artistic portrayal, textual descriptions of the thirty-two marks, in the way these now appear in the texts, are at times difficult to make sense of; in fact, some of these marks could even give the impression of referring to some physical deformity. Yet, several discourses indicate that the Buddha was not known for having had some unusual bodily feature that would have made it easy to recognize him.[295] In other words, at an early stage these thirty-two marks do not appear to have been about some abnormal features but rather were descriptive of subtle nuances. This impression receives support from references in *Āgama* literature to brahmins trained in the lore of these thirty-two marks.[296] In other words, these marks were conceived as something evident only to those who had learned the corresponding lore, rather than being so plainly evident that anybody who saw the Buddha could not have failed to notice them.

Another significant feature is that the thirty-two marks feature predominantly as a topic of concern among brahmin contemporaries of the Buddha, who relied on ascertaining their presence on Śākyamuni's body to decide if he was indeed a fully awakened one, or even to ascertain at his birth if he was destined to become a Buddha.[297]

Comparative study brings to light a gradual process of incorporating these thirty-two marks into the Buddhist fold. A first step taken in this direction consists in relating these marks to previous Buddhas. Closer inspection shows that the relevant Pāli discourse and its Chinese parallels, concerned with providing an account of six former Buddhas, introduce various aspects of their lives and qualities with the indication that for Buddhas these are an invariable feature, *dharmatā*. Yet, they no longer use this qualification in relation to the thirty-two marks.[298] Although another parallel extant in Sanskrit does use this qualification also for the thirty-two marks, in the remainder of the discourse this usage creates an inner incoherence and can for this reason safely be considered to reflect a standardizing without sufficient attention paid to the context.[299]

What emerges from this finding is that there is agreement regarding the possibility of predicting that someone endowed with the thirty-two marks at birth will become either a wheel-turning king or else, if he decides to go forth, a Buddha. However, at the stage in the development of Buddhology testified by these discourses, there is as yet no explicit indication that endowment with the thirty-two marks is an indispensable condition for becoming a Buddha (or a wheel-turning king). Nevertheless, this requirement appears to have soon enough been articulated more explicitly. A discourse in the *Ekottarikāgama* in turn refers to the future Buddha Maitreya's endowment with the thirty-two major and eighty minor marks.[300]

With later tradition, the role of the thirty-two marks as a means of conversion tends to expand and move beyond the circle of brahmins knowledgeable in the corresponding lore. As part of this process, the marks inevitably come to be conceived as more readily visible, to the extent that at times they even are endowed with luminescence.[301] Besides conversion, just seeing the Buddha's marks also acquires a function as a means of healing.[302]

It is against the background of a gradual incorporation of these thirty-two marks, together with an increasing fascination with them, that a Pāli discourse taking these marks as its main theme can best be appreciated. Before turning to this discourse and its apparent contribution to the evolution of the bodhisattva ideal, however, it may be opportune to acknowledge the challenge of staying clear of the tendency to rely on well-known and familiar notions when approaching descriptions originating from a time when these notions had not yet evolved. This requires a conscious effort to step out of some paradigmatic assumptions, so as to be able to do justice to early stages in the history of Buddhist thought on their own terms. In the present case this holds for the assumption that one becomes a Buddha through many lifetimes of practice intentionally dedicated to that aim. However much this may be paradigmatic in various Buddhist traditions and texts, this assumption needs to be set aside for the time being in order to be able to appreciate the gradual development that appears to have led to it. The conception of the nature of Śākyamuni Buddha in *Āgama* literature needs to be recognized as distinct from what in the course of time has become standard.

In support of the proposed distinction, a relevant example would be the reference to "writing a book" of the Perfection of Wisdom, mentioned in the quote given above in relation to the acquisition of merits (see p. 91). This reference reflects a shift from an entirely oral period of textual transmission to what could perhaps be called an aural/oral intertextuality, in the sense that writing has gradually acquired a role in supporting oral transmission and performance.[303] Whereas the Pāli discourses do not reflect the employment of writing for their own transmission, the Pāli commentaries refer to book(s)/manuscript(s),[304] which by their time had evidently come into use for recording Buddhist texts. This exemplifies that it is meaningful to consider such discourses to reflect an overall earlier period in Buddhist thought and practice than the Perfection of Wisdom or the Pāli commentaries, wherefore there is a basis for proposing a distinctly early Buddhist conception of the nature of Śākyamuni Buddha.

Nevertheless, in the remainder of my exploration of the Perfection of Wisdom I will not take this temporal perspective for granted and instead, as announced in my first chapter (see above p. 8), allow the nature of the developments examined to reveal, whenever possible, the direction of influence. The same holds for my present topic of the nature of the Buddha Śākyamuni in relation to the bodhisattva ideal, in that the basic distinction between the discourses found in *Āgama* literature and other texts is only meant to support the invitation to step out of paradigmatic assumptions so as to be able to appreciate the perspective that this particular textual genre can offer for developing a text-historical assessment.

The detailed description of the six former Buddhas, mentioned above, does not establish any direct, personal relationship between them and Śākyamuni.[305] The function of these six is merely to exemplify characteristics of a Buddha, thereby turning descriptions that appear to have originated in relation to Śākyamuni into a general template.[306] Despite the fairly mature stage of Buddhology evident in the discourse on the six former Buddhas, the parallel versions evince no sustained concern with the past lives of any of these Buddhas. Instead, their attention is mainly on what took place in the last life of each of these six, beginning with the moment they passed away from their former heavenly existence and entered their mother's womb. This concords with a tendency in *Āgama* literature to present Śākyamuni's Buddhahood mainly as the result of his striving for awakening in his present life, rather than as the outcome of an intentional cultivation undertaken during a series of past lives.

Yet, this is not the whole story, as can be seen with the Pāli discourse to be taken up next, the Discourse on the Marks (*Lakkhaṇasutta*). In fact, already the very notion of being endowed from birth with thirty-two special physical marks points to something more than just wholehearted dedication to the path to awakening after having gone forth in order to become a Buddha. Versions of the Discourse on the Marks are extant in Pāli, Chinese, and Tibetan. The three versions agree in taking as their main theme the thirty-two marks, indicating that one endowed with these will either become a wheel-turning king or a Buddha.

The Pāli and Tibetan versions show a peculiarity in relation to the description of the wheel-turning king, as their description of his realm offers some additional indications that have some similarity to depictions of Buddhafields in other texts. In the case of the Pāli discourse, in three out of four editions—the Burmese, Ceylonese, and PTS editions—the additional indications do not occur in the first part of the discourse, even though this otherwise gives exactly the same descriptions of the conditions in the world governed by a wheel-turning king. Nevertheless, the additional indications only manifest in a later part of the discourse that presents a detailed exposition of the thirty-two marks (this is the part most relevant to my present concerns).[307] Given the tendency of oral transmission to stereotype, this internal inconsistency is fairly clear evidence that a textual expansion has taken place by way of incorporating a description of a commentarial type. Whereas the Chinese version does not have any such addition, the Tibetan version also mentions two such qualities resembling descriptions of Buddhafields.[308]

This finding is, however, only a prelude to a more significant, major difference among the three versions. The Pāli discourse stands alone in following the listing of thirty-two marks with a detailed account of deeds done and qualities developed by Śākyamuni in his past lives that led to the respective physical mark(s) in his present life.[309] The quite detailed presentation of this topic proceeds by alternating prose and verse, the latter showing distinct signs of lateness in its meters.[310] From the viewpoint of textual evolution, this part of the discourse can with high probability be identified as a commentarial exposition that in the course of oral transmission has come to be integrated into the discourse itself.

Such incorporation of material of a commentarial nature is a fairly common procedure, with a number of examples identifiable in *Āgama* literature.[311] In a posthumously published monograph researching the *Prajñāpāramitā* commentary *Dà zhìdù lùn* (**Mahāprajñāpāramitopadeśa*), Zacchetti (2021, 1 and 11) offers the following general assessment:

> It is becoming increasingly clear that exegesis played a vastly more active role than we have generally appreciated in *shaping*—not just explaining and reflecting—all types of Buddhist scriptures . . . when these texts were recited, put to use for various purposes (ritual, etc.), or copied and transmitted across time and space, they were also *interpreted*. And at times, interpretations of words and passages (which we can call glosses) ended up being absorbed by the texts themselves, in the process modifying the texts to varying degrees.

The present "interpretation" of the thirty-two marks, to all appearances absorbed into the discourse and thereby modifying it, is of considerable significance, as it testifies to the very idea of relating Buddhahood to particular forms of conduct undertaken in former lives.[312] As mentioned above, appreciating the importance of this presentation requires setting aside, for the time being, well-known, paradigmatic assumptions about the path to Buddhahood prevalent in all Buddhist traditions. In order to evaluate this exposition within its textual setting, the question needs to be asked what the rationale behind this presentation could be.

Fortunately, the answer to this question is readily available, as the Pāli discourse offers quite an explicit indication in this respect. This takes the form of introducing the detailed exposition with the statement that, even though non-Buddhists know the thirty-two marks, they do not know what type of karma leads to gaining each mark:[313]

> Of a great man, monastics, outside seers also bear in mind these thirty-two marks of a great man, yet they do not know: "by the doing of this deed does one gain this mark."

In this way, alongside recognizing that knowledge of the thirty-two marks is common among those outside of the Buddhist fold, this introductory statement announces a distinctly Buddhist perspective on these marks. It thereby takes a step further along the trajectory mentioned above, whereby a formerly brahmanical concern gradually becomes accultured to Buddhist thought. This trajectory involves the possession of the thirty-two marks becoming an indispensable requirement for the achievement of Buddhahood, an expansion of their role in conversion beyond brahmins trained in their lore (as a result of which the marks themselves inevitably become more visible), and the function of seeing them as a means of healing. The present instance adds a doctrinal perspective to this thrust, which takes the form of using the thirty-two marks to exemplify the law of karma and its fruit. Its significance, as evident from the above introductory statement, is to provide a doctrinal home for the marks. Wimalaratana (1994, 29) reasons that "[t]he importance of the *Lakkhaṇa sutta* lies in the fact that it combines the concept of the Great Man with some of the fundamental tenets of Buddhism such as the doctrine of *kamma*, rebirth, the law of causation."

In this way, the Pāli discourse under discussion takes the entirely natural step of bringing the brahmanical concern with the thirty-two marks fully into the orbit of early Buddhist doctrine, which it achieves by endowing these marks with a karmic perspective. Such a move is fully in line with a pervasive interest in karma and its fruit, evident in *Āgama* literature. Note that at this stage the presentation does not function as an injunction to emulate the past deeds of the Buddha. Instead, the overall concern is simply to provide a specific Buddhist perspective on the thirty-two marks.

After this type of presentation has come into existence, however, it can of course easily be read as a psycho-somatic script for the path of a bodhisattva. Particularly once the idea has become established that achieving Buddhahood requires the acquisition of the thirty-two marks, the presentation offered in the Discourse on the Marks inevitably acquires a significance well beyond its explicitly stated concerns; it becomes prescriptive. The influence of this type of correlation of past deeds with the acquisition of the thirty-two marks can be seen reflected in the circumstance that a comparable presentation can be found in the *Bodhisattvabhūmi*—a part of the foundational treatise on Yogācāra, the *Yogācārabhūmi*, dedicated in particular to the path to Buddhahood—which explicitly introduces its exposition as stemming from a version of the Discourse on the Marks (*Lakṣaṇasūtra*).[314] This implies that the presentation in the Pāli version of the Discourse on the Marks, although not being supported by its extant parallels, is not unique, as a comparable discourse from another reciter tradition must have been in existence.[315]

Another text offering such an exposition is the *Pañcaviṃśatisāhasrikā Prajñāpāramitā*. Conze (1964, 225–26) introduces his edition of the relevant portion as follows:

> The Sūtra first enumerates the 32 *lakṣanas*, then explains them, and thirdly outlines both their cause and their consequence. As for the third part, it is of special interest as this section of the *Prajñāpāramitā* . . . deals with this aspect of the doctrine in some detail. It shows many similarities with the *Lakkhaṇa-suttanta* of *Dīgha-nikāya*.

### *The Jātakas*

An important trajectory in the evolution of the bodhisattva ideal, which can safely be assumed to have stood in close interrelation with the perspective afforded by the Discourse on the Marks, emerges with *jātaka* tales.[316] Nattier (2003a, 186 and 144) offers the following reflection:

> [I]f Mahāyāna sūtras are the precipitate, and not the initial cause, of bodhisattva practice, we must look to earlier traditions . . . as possible sources of inspiration. And the obvious source, in my view—and one frequently alluded to or even cited directly in Mahāyāna sūtras—is the collection of stories of Śākyamuni Buddha's former lives . . . It is thus to the transitional literature of the *jātaka* tales . . . that we should probably

> turn if we wish to gain a glimpse of the Mahāyāna in its formative stage...
>
> Given that the *jātaka* tales were considered to relate actual incidents in previous lives of Śākyamuni Buddha, and that bodhisattvas were attempting to retrace Śākyamuni's steps in order to attain Buddhahood themselves, the use of these tales as a source of guidelines for practice must surely have been widespread.

Given this apparent importance, it can be instructive to explore the evolution of such tales from a text-historical perspective.[317] *Jātaka* stories as such appear to have had considerable popular appeal since ancient times.[318] An early stage in the evolution of *jātaka*s finds reflection in several instances of this type of narrative found in *Āgama* literature. These are characterized by being in prose and involving former lives of Śākyamuni as a human protagonist, in contrast to the Pāli *Jātaka* collection, which is in verse—prose narrations are provided by the commentary—and which regularly features animals identified as former lives of the Buddha.[319]

An example of the early type of *jātaka* found in *Āgama* literature has as its narrative setting the Buddha's successful attempt to prevent a massive slaughter in a sacrifice, which he achieves by describing a different type of sacrifice undertaken in the past that did not involve any killing. Hearing this tale from the past, the brahmin about to perform the sacrifice on behalf of the king wonders what enables the Buddha to know about this event from ancient times. The relevant Chinese discourse presents his reflection as follows:[320]

> The recluse Gautama speaks about this matter without saying that he has heard it from another. I silently thought: "Will it not be that the recluse Gautama was that warrior king? Or perhaps he was that brahmin chaplain?"

Parallels extant in Pāli and Sanskrit report a similar reflection.[321] This conveniently encapsulates a basic reasoning that must have had a considerable impact on the interpretation of such tales. Since the Buddha will never speak an untruth, if he tells some story from the past, this must be based on his recollection of his own past lives. It follows that he must have been one of the chief protagonists in this tale. The same type of reasoning finds explicit expression in the *Bodhisattvabhūmi*, which indicates that the source of *jātaka* tales is the Buddha's recollection of past lives.[322] In the present case, as evident from the brahmin's reflection, the Buddha should be identified with one of the two main protagonists of that sacrifice, that is, either with the king, who ordered the sacrifice to be undertaken, or else with the brahmin chaplain, who took the leading role in the performance of the sacrifice.

Although the parallels agree regarding this basic reasoning, they disagree on which of these two chief protagonists should be reckoned a past life of the Buddha. According to the Pāli version, he was the brahmin chaplain, whereas according to the Chinese version he was rather the king.[323] These two contradictory indications seem to exhaust the possibilities for identifying one of the two eminent protagonists in this ancient sacrifice as a former life of the Buddha. Yet, the Sanskrit version offers still another perspective, as it reports the Buddha making the following statement:[324]

> Bhāradvāja, I indeed remember both [having been] the head-anointed warrior king, who was the sacrificer of this type of sacrifice, as well as the brahmin chaplain, who was the sacrifice-performer of this type of sacrifice.

This is, of course, impossible. Whoever was responsible for this formulation in the Sanskrit version must have been aware of both identifications and, in an attempt at harmonizing, combined them into the doctrinal incongruity of having the Buddha in a former life be two different persons at the same time in the same place.

In this way, the present *jātaka* not only explicitly formulates the type of reasoning that appears to have led to interpreting sundry tales as *jātaka*s but also confirms that such an identification is indeed a later step taken in relation to an already existing tale, rather than being part of it from the outset. The pedagogical function of the episode does anyway not require an identification of the brahmin chaplain or the king as a former life of the

Buddha, and the variations between the parallels in this respect, in particular the remarkable position taken in the Sanskrit version, clearly testify to the lateness of such identification. The impression that parables and fables became *jātaka*s at some stage during their oral transmission finds further confirmation on examining several other early *jātaka*s occurring in *Āgama* literature.[325]

Just to give one more example, a parable can be taken up that illustrates the potential of mindfulness practice. The illustration in question, extant in a Pāli discourse and its Chinese parallel, describes how a quail outwits a falcon.[326] In the (commentarial) prose part of the Pāli *Jātaka* collection, the same tale has become a *jātaka*, with the quail identified as a former life of the Buddha. The identification as such is obvious, as the falcon is hardly an attractive alternative for being considered a past life of the Buddha. At the same time, however, the discourse versions show that the tale of the quail does not require any such identification, which in a way even risks distracting from the lesson that the story encapsulates. Although in terms of the timing of the respective texts the direction of influence is already fairly obvious, the *jātaka* prose actually refers to the Pāli discourse as its source, providing not only its title but also a quote from the discourse and a reference to the discourse collection in which it is now indeed found, thereby showing that from an emic perspective its derivative nature was clearly recognized.[327] This concords well with the overall impression that what in the Pāli discourse features as a parable has indeed been turned into a past life of the Buddha.

The parable of the quail exemplifies Buddhist values, in particular illustrating how the cultivation of mindfulness can offer a dimension of protection.[328] The same is not necessarily the case, however, for a range of other fables that in the course of time became part of the Buddhist narrative repertoire, authenticated by being turned into *jātaka*s.[329] A case in point would be what is perhaps the most popular such tale,[330] a former life of the Buddha as the prince Viśvantara (Pāli: Vessantara). The prince is so wholeheartedly devoted to giving that he donates to brahmins whatever they may ask of him. Eventually he even gives away his own children to a cruel brahmin who starts beating them in front of their father. When they manage to escape, the prince returns them to the brahmin. The behavior depicted in this way conflicts with Buddhist ethical values. As their father, he should protect his children rather than cause them to suffer from abuse.

Closer inspection suggests that the tale may have originated from a brahmanical trope that serves to promote the self-serving notion that whatever a brahmin may ask for should be given without reservation.[331] Once this tale is transplanted into a Buddhist environment through identifying the prince as a former life of the Buddha, however, the net result is a depiction of irresponsible behavior that members of the Buddhist audience should better not emulate. Yet, with the arising and spread of the bodhisattva ideal, this is precisely the function acquired by *jātaka*s, namely illustrating the type of conduct that at least those on the path to Buddhahood should, to the best of their abilities, try to emulate.

The *Mahāvastu*, a *Vinaya* text of the Mahāsāṃghika-Lokottaravādins, explicitly indicates that the delivery of *jātaka* tales reveals the path of practice of a bodhisattva.[332] Given that many such tales stem from the general ancient Indian narrative repertoire, they often have only a loose connection to Buddhist doctrine, or even no such connection. As a result, it is certainly not always straightforward to take such *jātaka* stories as prescriptive for the acquisition of the perfections required for progress to Buddhahood. In particular the perfection of giving seems to have acquired dimensions in the course of time that appear to be out of proportion. In a subsequent part of my study, I will explore in more detail the promotion of giving away even parts or the whole of one's own body (see below p. 264).

The prose narrations of Pāli *jātaka*s conclude by reporting that the Buddha personally identified a particular protagonist in the respective tale as one of his former lives, a pattern that also holds for the case of Viśvantara/Vessantara.[333] In this way, the identification of the prince's irresponsible behavior as exemplifying the perfection of giving for the sake of progress to Buddhahood becomes authenticated by the Buddha himself. This type of procedure is not an unusual phenomenon in the Pāli textual traditions, and some distinctly late Pāli texts even employ the formula "thus have I heard" in order to pretend that they were spoken by the Buddha.[334] It follows that authentication strategies for promoting new texts are best reckoned a pan-Buddhist phenomenon, rather than being specific to

Mahāyāna literature. In fact, relating tales naturally stimulates literary creativity, something that holds not only for *jātaka*s but also for the stories that in *Vinaya* literature serve to provide the narrative context for rules and regulations.[335] From this perspective, the creativity evident in the production of early Mahāyāna *sūtra*s can be seen to continue an already well-worn track.

### *Meeting the Previous Buddha*

Another *jātaka* found in *Āgama* literature appears to have had a special role in the evolution of the bodhisattva ideal. The relevant episode involves an encounter between the Buddha Kāśyapa and a brahmin youth. The hero of the discourse in question is a potter, however, who in several episodes features as an exemplary lay supporter of the Buddha Kāśyapa. In one such episode, he goes to considerable lengths to convince, or perhaps even force, the brahmin youth to come along to visit the Buddha Kāśyapa. Although this brahmin youth is at first rather reluctant, to the extent of referring to the Buddha in disparaging terms,[336] his eventual encounter with the Buddha leaves him sufficiently impressed that he decides to go forth and become a monk. After that, nothing further is heard about him, and in the remainder of the discourse the spotlight continues to be on the potter.[337]

Given that the Buddha Śākyamuni relates this tale to his disciples, the same reasoning applies as in the above case of the story of a past sacrifice: from the perspective of the reciters of the discourse and their audience, knowledge about what happened in the past at the time of the Buddha Kāśyapa must be due to Śākyamuni's recollection of past lives. The potter in this tale would in principle have been an obvious choice for identifying a protagonist as a former life of Śākyamuni, in view of his exemplary conduct and the fact that he is clearly the central character. His only shortcoming is that he does not go forth as well, but that turns out not to be a shortcoming at all, as it reflects his obligation to look after his blind parents. Otherwise, despite remaining a lay person, he observes a type of conduct that is closely modelled on monastic ideals. Yet, identifying him as a past life of Śākyamuni is not feasible, as several versions indicate that he had already reached stream-entry.[338] This prevents considering him to have been an aspirant to Buddhahood, in line with a general principle of Buddhist thought, which happens to be stated explicitly in the Perfection of Wisdom:[339]

> By gaining the awakening of stream-entry, one can no longer gain the awakening of a bodhisattva. What is the reason? The reason is that one has closed off the path of births and deaths.

A little later, the Perfection of Wisdom explains stream-entry to imply that within seven lives one will exit (*saṃsāra*).[340] This complements the reference to having closed off the path of births and deaths in the above passage, showing that—fully in line with the conception of stream-entry in *Āgama* literature—one who has gained stream-entry will not be subject to the cycle of births and deaths for more than seven lives at most, as within that period full awakening will be reached. This is hardly sufficient time for bringing the path to Buddhahood to its successful completion, which requires remaining sufficiently long in *saṃsāra* to be able to acquire the vast amount of merit and cultivate the perfections required for becoming a Buddha.

As the potter could not be turned into a bodhisattva and therefore was not an option for identification with Śākyamuni, the choice has inevitably become the young brahmin. All versions of the discourse in question agree in reckoning the young brahmin to have been a past life of the Buddha Śākyamuni.[341] Due to such agreement among the extant versions, the present case is not as straightforward as the example of the sacrifice episode becoming a *jātaka*, discussed above, where substantial disagreements occur between parallel versions in matters of identification. Nevertheless, the agreement in the present case is not surprising, given that, similar to the case of the fable of the quail, there is hardly another alternative for identifying someone as a past life of the Buddha. That is, whereas with a king and a brahmin chaplain as the main protagonists in a sacrifice there is indeed a choice to be made, in the present case there is no such choice, wherefore no variations in identification could manifest. For this reason, it does not follow from such agreement in matters of identification that this discourse must have been a *jātaka* from the outset. In fact, the Pāli version of the present tale is not included in the Pāli *Jātaka* collection,[342] which would have been a natural move if the tale had indeed been perceived throughout as involving a past life of the Buddha.

The impression that this identification could be a later element finds further support when evaluating the discourse in its entirety, as its main concerns are clearly the exemplary nature of the potter. The brahmin youth is only secondary in comparison. Yet, had this brahmin youth been considered a past life of the Buddha already from the outset, the presentation would naturally have focused on him rather than on the potter.

Not only is the identification of this brahmin youth as a past life of Śākyamuni unnecessary for the tale to perform its pedagogical function, but it even creates problems. One such problem manifests in the form of an inconsistency in the *Madhyamāgama* version. In line with a recurrent pericope used in this discourse collection to qualify various past lives of Śākyamuni, in the present instance the *Madhyamāgama* also reports the Buddha concluding his account of the past by not only identifying one protagonist—in the present case the young brahmin—as one of his former lives but also declaring that the type of teaching he followed at that time did not lead to the supreme, unlike his own present teaching.[343] This type of declaration reflects a standard pattern in discourses in *Āgama* literature that involve past lives of Śākyamuni, which shows that at the time of becoming a *jātaka* the respective tales were not yet seen as an intentional step taken in the direction of future Buddhahood. To the contrary, they were seen as exemplifying a type of practice or teaching that does *not* lead to awakening.

In the present context in the *Madhyamāgama*, however, the application of this pericope results in a misfit, as the teaching followed by the young brahmin was imparted by the Buddha Kāśyapa and for this reason was just as capable of leading to the ultimate as the teachings of the Buddha Śākyamuni. The incoherence that emerges in this way could be explained by proposing that the addition to the discourse of the identification of the young brahmin as a former life of Śākyamuni took the form of importing the whole textual portion usually employed for such purposes, without noticing that this creates an inner incoherence.

In addition to such incoherence, problems also emerge on consulting the narrative context set by other relevant discourses. One of these relates to the discourse covering the lineage of six previous Buddhas. As mentioned above, this text does not establish any direct relationship between any of these six and Śākyamuni. Yet, if he had been a monk under the last of these six Buddhas, it is surprising that the coverage of Kāśyapa in this discourse does not even hint at the idea that Śākyamuni had been one of his monastic disciples. The parallel versions of this discourse explicitly indicate that the Buddha Śākyamuni gained detailed information about various circumstances related to each of these six past Buddhas during a visit to the Pure Abodes, where he encountered their former disciples who told him about their previous lives as followers of each of these Buddhas.[344] The relevant presentation includes such reports—given in abbreviation due to following the standard description adopted for other Buddhas—by the former disciples of the Buddha Kāśyapa.[345] The absence of any variation in this respect to make room for the unique—and for the audience certainly highly interesting—detail that in his case the disciples of the Buddha Kāśyapa are actually meeting one of their former companions makes it fair to assume that this depiction would have come into being at a time when the idea that Śākyamuni had himself also been a disciple of the Buddha Kāśyapa had not yet arisen.

The same perspective would also appear to be relevant to reports of the Buddha Śākyamuni's gaining of awakening. According to the standard account, the actual event of his awakening was preceded by him recollecting his past lives.[346] Since at the time of such recollection he was still in search of awakening, recalling his recent past life as a monk under the Buddha Kāśyapa should have naturally stood out as an opportunity to know directly about the type of teachings that lead to awakening. Had he recalled his former life at that time, however, it would no longer have been fitting to claim that he had reached awakening without a teacher,[347] which is the defining condition of a Buddha, namely being one who discovers the path to awakening on his own and then teaches it to others.

These various pointers at the probably late nature of the idea that the young brahmin who ordained under the Buddha Kāśyapa was a former life of the Buddha Śākyamuni provide the backdrop for appreciating why there is no report at all about the conduct and attainments of this young brahmin once he had gone forth. Given that, before this tale became a *jātaka*, its concern would just have been to depict the exemplary conduct of the potter, this is only natural.

With this type of perspective on the *jātaka* nature of the tale of the potter at the time of the Buddha Kāśyapa in place, the time has come to turn to a discourse from the *Madhyamāgama* that depicts various marvels related to the Buddha. The marvel to be taken up here is not found in the Pāli parallel and can safely be regarded as a later addition, in line with other marvels found in only one of the two parallel versions. This marvel takes the following form, with Ānanda being the speaker:[348]

> Practicing the holy life at the time of the Buddha Kāśyapa, the Blessed One made his initial aspiration/vow for Buddhahood. That practicing the holy life at the time of the Buddha Kāśyapa the Blessed One made his initial aspiration/vow for Buddhahood—this I remember as a marvelous quality of the Blessed One.

From the viewpoint of the fully evolved bodhisattva ideal, the encounter between Śākyamuni as a young brahmin and the Buddha Kāśyapa features as the last instance in a series of such meetings with previous Buddhas. Śākyamuni's decision to embark on the path to Buddhahood in turn had already taken place during his encounter with another Buddha, which in the case of the Perfection of Wisdom and the Pāli tradition is the Buddha Dīpaṃkara.

However, appreciating the significance this encounter had at an earlier stage in text-historical development, when the bodhisattva ideal must still have been in the process of gradually evolving, requires navigating the same challenge mentioned earlier, namely the need to beware of defaulting to well-known and familiar notions when approaching descriptions that reflect a time when these notions had not yet emerged. This is essential for being able to do justice to distinct stages in the history of Buddhist thought and understand each of these on their own terms. In the present case, the qualification of the aspiration or vow as an "initial" one clearly calls for a different perspective. Setting aside the paradigmatic assumption that the course of a bodhisattva involves repeated encounters with former Buddhas, is it possible to imagine a time when the very idea of such an encounter was a novelty?

It appears to be precisely the novelty of the idea that Śākyamuni had already in a past life dedicated himself to awakening—rather than only in his present life at the time of deciding to go forth—that must have motivated considering it a marvel. Such a consideration only makes sense in a setting that does not yet know of the idea that Buddhahood is to be achieved over a series of lives of dedicated practice. In a setting before the arising of this notion, for Śākyamuni to decide to aim for becoming a Buddha himself *already* at the time of the Buddha Kāśyapa can indeed appear as a marvel. Once he was believed to have taken such a decision already much earlier, a repetition of the same in the presence of the Buddha Kāśyapa would hardly have been considered marvelous. In other words, it is not only the qualification of being "initial" but also the fact of being considered a marvel that quite clearly points to the need to read this passage without defaulting to the well-known perspective of the aspiration for Buddhahood informing a long series of successive lives of a bodhisattva.

Within its text-historical setting, the main message of the present passage would be that the encounter with Kāśyapa, which all versions of the relevant discourse depict as so deeply inspiring that it transformed a reluctant and disrespectful young brahmin into a Buddhist monk, had an additional effect. It instilled such deep regard for the Buddha Kāśyapa in the young brahmin that he even aspired to become a Buddha himself in the future. The purpose of this presentation would be to provide an even stronger highlight on the young brahmin's willingness to let himself be transformed completely, together with showcasing the transformative power of meeting a Buddha.

Both highlights in combination offer an excellent perspective on the somewhat unsatisfactory presentation caused by turning the tale of the potter into a *jātaka*. The idea of the young brahmin aspiring for Buddhahood solves the problem that nothing is heard of him in terms of reaching some distinction after he has gone forth. Moreover, once the present episode features as the first instance of his decision to aim for Buddhahood, his earlier disrespectful behavior becomes a narrative asset, as it further enhances the transformation that took place: from a disdainful attitude of not even wanting to see a Buddha to wishing to become a Buddha himself. The episode of the disrespectful behavior can fulfill this role of a narrative asset only because at this stage in development it does not yet stand in contrast to the idea that Śākyamuni had already been a bodhisattva for many previous lives. As testified by the qualification of the aspiration or vow as the first of its kind and as a marvel, from the viewpoint of the passage quoted above it is only at the time of this encounter with Kāśyapa that the young brahmin decided to opt for Buddhahood.

The situation changes substantially once the fully evolved notion has become established that it took a vast number of lives of intentionally cultivating the perfections for Śākyamuni to become a Buddha. From that perspective, rather than being a narrative asset, the conduct of the young brahmin becomes problematic. How could it be that at the time of the distant Buddha Dīpaṃkara he behaved with such deep respect, but at the much closer time of the last Buddha to appear before his own Buddhahood, being himself a highly advanced bodhisattva who had received his prediction long ago, he would not only be unwilling to meet Kāśyapa but even refer to a Buddha in derogatory terms?

According to a discourse version and two other versions of the tale, the potter told the Buddha Kāśyapa that the young brahmin had no faith or respect for the Buddha, or else that he had no faith in the Buddha, the Dharma, and the Community.[349] A lack of faith or respect for the Buddha is also implicit in the other versions, despite not being explicitly stated. A *Vinaya* version and an *Avadāna* account even identify this disrespectful behavior as the karma responsible for Śākyamuni having to undertake ascetic practices in his present life before realizing awakening.[350] The inappropriateness of his contemptuous attitude was clearly not lost on tradition, in that the conduct and attitude of the young brahmin stand in stark contrast to the mature conception of the prolonged career of a bodhisattva, guided by the intention of eventually becoming a Buddha and involving the acquisition of the needed store of merits by serving and worshipping other Buddhas as much as possible.

From a text-historical perspective, the disrespectful behavior of the young brahmin worked well in the context of a text dedicated to extolling the potter, since it enhances his ability to convince the young brahmin to come and meet the Buddha Kāśyapa. The same narrative aspect becomes even more powerful when the ensuing meeting with Kāśyapa becomes the occasion for Śākyamuni to take the—in its textual setting unprecedented—decision of aiming for Buddhahood. Instead of only serving to eulogize a lay disciple, it now achieves the same for two Buddhas, as the amazing transformation that emerges in this way results from the impact of meeting Kāśyapa and testifies to Śākyamuni's openness to undergo a conversion as thorough as one could possibly imagine. With the evolved bodhisattva ideal fully established, however, this same episode becomes problematic. In this way, different readings of this tale can be appreciated from the viewpoint of their respective text-historical setting.

From the perspective of how *Āgama* texts tend to evolve during oral transmission and performance, it would be an entirely natural procedure to improve on an already existing effect by adding another episode that makes the same point in an even stronger manner. This is precisely what the marvel of Śākyamuni's initial aspiration or vow achieves. Moreover, the apparent motivation behind such a powerful addition to a listing of marvels is fully in line not only with the specific concerns of the discourse in which it occurs but also with a pronounced tendency in much of *Āgama* literature toward eulogizing Buddhas and their powers.

It thus seems fair to envisage that the effect of the present episode could be comparable to that of the Discourse on the Marks, which takes off from a concern with karma but to all appearances results in opening the door to the notion of intentionally progressing toward Buddhahood over a series of past lives. In a similar way, it is conceivable that the present marvel may reflect a setting that led to the very arising of the notion of formulating in the presence of a Buddha the aspiration or vow (*praṇidhāna*) to become a Buddha oneself.[351] Rather than a concern with karma, in the present case the apparent motivation leading to the development under discussion would simply have been the tendency of the reciters to exalt Śākyamuni (together with Kāśyapa).

A Pāli work on opinions debated among Buddhist schools, the *Kathāvatthu*, reports a statement made by Śākyamuni regarding his former life as a disciple of the Buddha Kāśyapa. Notably, this statement is not found in the relevant discourse. In this statement, the Buddha tells Ānanda that he lived the monk's life under the Buddha Kāśyapa for the sake of his future awakening.[352] A comparable position emerges in the *Saṅghabhedavastu* of the Mūlasarvāstivāda *Vinaya*, which reports Mahāmaudgalyāyana indicating that Śākyamuni lived the life of a monk under the Buddha Kāśyapa with the aspiration to reach awakening in the future.[353]

A *Vinaya* text of the Mahāsāṃghika-Lokottaravādins, the *Mahāvastu*, in turn reports how the young brahmin at that time formulated the aspiration or vow to become a Buddha.[354] According to the *Mahāvastu*, this happened when the Buddha Kāśyapa had just instructed his monk disciples that they should sit in meditation without getting up until their defilements are destroyed. This narrative detail seems to confirm the impression that the aspiration for Buddhahood serves to explain why the young brahmin is not on record for reaching any level of awakening, given that, as mentioned above, even just the realization of stream-entry would be an obstruction to the path to Buddhahood. The *Mahāvastu*'s resolution of the problem becomes fully apparent when, on becoming aware of the young brahmin's aspiration for Buddhahood, the Buddha Kāśyapa predicts that he will indeed become a Buddha in the future and set rolling the wheel of the Dharma in the Deer Park at Vārāṇasī.[355] His future Buddhahood explains why the young brahmin does not join the other monks in their wholehearted dedication to becoming arhats.[356]

In this way, the *Kathāvatthu*, the *Saṅghabhedavastu*, and the *Mahāvastu* testify to the continuity of the basic idea of interpreting the young brahmin's discipleship under Kāśyapa without reaching any noteworthy distinction as reflecting the circumstance that he was motivated by the wish to progress to Buddhahood. By the time of these texts, the aspiration for Buddhahood formulated in the presence of the Buddha Kāśyapa features as the last instance in a series of such encounters with previous Buddhas.

Based on the textual evidence surveyed above, it seems possible to envisage a gradual evolution from the *Madhyamāgama* marvel of a first aspiration for Buddhahood to the same becoming the last one in a series of such aspirations, which then combines with a corresponding prediction in the *Mahāvastu*. However, my suggestion in Anālayo (2010a, 84–92) regarding the possibility that the notion of the aspiration or vow to become a Buddha in the future may at first have been related just to the Buddha Kāśyapa, before shifting further into the past, has been received with some criticism.[357] First of all, it may be opportune to note that the textual evidence in question stems from the *Madhyamāgama*, which reflects a level of evolution of Buddhist thought comparable to that of the Pāli discourses and shows no evidence of having incorporated material as late as what can be found in the *Ekottarikāgama*.[358] This holds even though the *Ekottarikāgama* was translated earlier into Chinese than the *Madhyamāgama*. The present case thereby exemplifies that the date of translation can substantially postdate the time when a particular text reaches a date of closure in terms of no longer admitting major changes.

Another point to be kept in mind is that the translator of the *Madhyamāgama*, Gautama Saṅghadeva, was an Indian who had learned Chinese. To the extent to which the quality of his work can still be assessed now, his translations appear to be marked by a degree of accuracy and faithfulness to the Indic original superior to translators of other *Āgama*s into Chinese.[359] In other words, there are reasons to take the *Madhyamāgama* marvel seriously when it speaks of an "initial" vow to become a Buddha.

There is of course no reason to take for granted that this *Madhyamāgama* passage must definitely be earlier than the report of Śākyamuni's aspiration to Buddhahood in the *Mahāvastu*.[360] At the same time, however, this is not an improbable scenario, given that *Vinaya* texts overall have remained open to later influences for a longer period than the Pāli discourses and their *Āgama* parallels (leaving aside the *Ekottarikāgama*). Proposing such a probability does not in principle exclude an influence in the opposite direction, which would simply require identifying evidence that suggests such an influence.

The proposed probability can be explored further by evaluating the respective textual setting. In the case of the *Madhyamāgama* passage, this is the only instance—not only in this collection but also among Pāli discourses and their *Āgama* parallels (leaving aside the *Ekottarikāgama*)—testifying to the idea that in a past life Śākyamuni decided to become a Buddha in the future. From the perspective of the gradual beginnings of the bodhisattva ideal evident in this textual corpus, the idea as such seems a natural step to take, that is, to associate such a decision with an encounter with the immediately preceding Buddha. Such association is based on the only specimen among the relatively few instances of *jātaka*s found in *Āgama* literature that involve a past Buddha.

In addition, the tale of the young brahmin stands out for providing cogent reasons for the arising of the very idea that in a past life Śākyamuni aspired to become a Buddha in the future.[361] The idea of the decision to become a Buddha helps to smooth out a puzzling aspect that results from turning the tale of the potter into a *jātaka*. Rather than appearing almost like a failure, the encounter between the young brahmin and the Buddha Kāśyapa can even become a marvel,[362] because it resulted in the former's initial decision to pursue Buddhahood. The taking of such a decision is novel in its textual environment; *jātaka*s found in *Āgama* literature do not exhibit any concern with an intentional cultivation of the perfections for the sake of becoming a Buddha, instead of which they simply feature as stories of the past recalled by the Buddha. This perspective also holds for the Discourse on the Marks, which in its present form is just about a karmic background to the acquisition of the physical marks of Buddhahood; it does not require the idea that the actions it describes were undertaken intentionally by Śākyamuni in his past lives in order to acquire the marks and become a Buddha.

With the continued evolution of *jātaka* literature, however, the number of identifications of past lives of Śākyamuni rapidly increased. Once such past lives were seen as governed by an intentional decision to cultivate the perfections required for Buddhahood, a decision to become a Buddha at the time of Kāśyapa is of course much too close in time to Śākyamuni's awakening to be able to accommodate all these past lives.[363] Hence, an obvious response to the continuously increasing number of *jātaka*s, perceived as intentional steps on the path to Buddhahood, would be to shift the same decision to an earlier Buddha in the far distant past, such as Dīpaṃkara. The idea of formulating the aspiration or vow under Kāśyapa can be left in place as it is, just that it comes to be seen as a reaffirmation of something already formulated earlier and thereby no longer carries any particular significance; it certainly no longer appears marvelous in itself.[364]

In contrast to the scenario that emerges in this way, the *Mahāvastu* testifies overall to a considerably more mature stage in the development of the bodhisattva ideal. It abounds in *jātaka*s that also involve past lives as an animal, thereby reflecting a development that would have encouraged associating Śākyamuni's decision to embark on the path to Buddhahood with a distant past rather than with the most recent Buddha. The same work knows of a plurality of former Buddhas well beyond the six recognized in the Pāli discourses and their parallels (leaving aside the *Ekottarikāgama*) and testifies to a tendency to associate Śākyamuni's decision to embark on the path of a bodhisattva with ever more remote times.[365] In its narrative setting, the notion that the young brahmin formulates the aspiration or vow to become a Buddha at the time of his encounter with Kāśyapa is fully in line with other such elements found elsewhere in this work.[366] In fact, unlike the case of the *Madhyamāgama*, the aspiration or vow comes together with the reception of a prediction of future Buddhahood. This reflects a further stage in the trajectory of aligning this episode with central elements of the bodhisattva ideal. In this way, the *Mahāvastu*'s version of the young brahmin's aspiration or vow to become a Buddha, although reflecting some interesting narrative details that help appreciate the textual dynamics at work in this tale, overall is in accordance with other, similar elements in this *Vinaya* text, rather than giving the impression of having taken a novel, innovative step.

In sum, when comparing the two versions of Śākyamuni's aspiration or vow, it seems reasonable to conclude that the *Madhyamāgama* passage presents something unprecedented in its textual setting, which precisely for this reason has been considered a marvel. In contrast, the *Mahāvastu* passage testifies to an overall more advanced stage in the development of the bodhisattva ideal. It follows that the first of these two versions stands a better chance at providing indications regarding the very genesis of the notion that someone decides to become a Buddha in a future life. In terms of the history of ideas, it is the *Madhyamāgama* passage that stands out for possibly providing a hint, however faint and hypothetical it may be, to a transitional stage in the emergence of the conception of what eventually became a central element of the path of a bodhisattva, namely the aspiration or vow to embark on the quest for Buddhahood.

Needless to say, the evolution of the bodhisattva ideal must have been a highly complex process influenced by a broad range of different conditions. Moreover, even successfully identifying some such conditions only captures a fraction of the actual evolution, simply because complex systems of thought and practice are more than just the sum of their parts. At the same time, however, given its pan-Buddhist manifestations, it can safely be assumed that certain dimensions of Buddhist doctrine and practice would have influenced this evolution. This in turn makes it meaningful to explore relevant indications among the records of Buddhist doctrine and practice, which for the period in question are predominantly of the textual type. In clear recognition that these can only provide one window on aspects of this evolution, capture only one dimension out of many, a hypothetical sketch could still be drawn based on the material surveyed above:

A gradual process of transforming parables and fables into past lives of the Buddha can safely be considered to have offered a substantial contribution to the emergence of the bodhisattva ideal. The selected examples surveyed here confirm that such a transformation has taken place. One of these involves disagreements between parallel versions regarding which of the two main protagonists in a tale about a past sacrifice should be considered to have been the Buddha. The case taken up above is particularly entertaining in this respect: in addition to two parallels proposing opposite identifications, a third version combines these two alternatives and presents the Buddha as having been two persons at the same time. Another example of a parable's transformation into a *jātaka* comes with conclusive evidence for the direction of influence, as the latter explicitly refers to the former by name and location in a discourse collection.

An important shift in perspective emerges with the Discourse on the Marks, whereby emphasis proceeds from Śākyamuni's progress toward awakening during the period after his going forth to a concern with his past lives. One out of the three extant versions presents detailed information on types of conduct and qualities leading to each of the thirty-two bodily marks required for Buddhahood. A reference to a version of this discourse in the *Bodhisattvabhūmi* has a similar effect as the *Jātaka* reference to the Pāli discourse presenting the parable of the quail, in that it unmistakably establishes the direction of influence. The discourse itself quite explicitly testifies to its presentation taking off from a concern with karma, situated within the context of a gradual integration of the thirty-two marks into the Buddhist fold. The net result, however, is a form of presentation that can be reckoned as marking a major, distinct step in the emergence of the bodhisattva ideal.

Another significant piece of evidence is the tale of the brahmin youth who became a monk under the Buddha Kāśyapa. A particularly significant contribution made by this tale could be the very idea of aspiring for Buddhahood, here associated with the occasion of an encounter with the most recent previous Buddha and of course forming just one, significant condition in a causal network leading to the full emergence of this idea. In terms of the direction of influence, the reference to an "initial" instance of such an aspiration at the time of the Buddha Kāśyapa and its qualification as a marvel make it fair to conclude that this passage would not be influenced by an already existing, evolved bodhisattva ideal. In that case, with the idea of repeated meetings with former Buddhas in place, the idea of being an "initial" aspiration or vow could hardly have arisen, and it would also not have made much sense to include this passage in a listing of marvels. In other words, in this case, too, it seems as if the presentation results from developments within the same textual corpus.

As pointed out by Ruegg (2004, 52n91), "a given doctrine of a Śrāvakayānist Nikāya, as now available to us, is not *automatically and necessarily* earlier historically than a comparable idea of the *earlier* Mahāyāna." This is indeed the case. At the same time, however, the above exploration has spotlighted several indications that do establish the comparative earliness of the relevant passages, which makes it reasonable to take into account the information they may offer for developing a historical perspective on the evolution of the bodhisattva ideal.

## The Wisdom of Impermanence

In the midst of expounding the merits to be gained by engaging in various ways with the Perfection of Wisdom, the text turns to the topic of an imitation or counterfeit teaching, in the sense of a pretension to be advocating the Perfection of Wisdom when in reality this is not the case. This somewhat abrupt appearance can be explored further by taking a closer look at the mode of exposition adopted for the topic of merits. The exposition employs a form of presentation that has counterparts in *Āgama* literature, examples of which take the form of presenting a comparison that starts off with something already rather great, only to surpass that with something even greater.[367] The same pattern features in the Perfection of Wisdom in relation to the merit to be derived from engaging in it in various ways. The depiction of the superiority of such merits proceeds gradually and in a way that produces a crescendo effect, thereby presumably creating a sense of suspense in the audience. This type of crescendo effect, too, has counterparts in *Āgama* literature (the same holds for strategies of textual promotion).[368]

In view of the employment of such a gradual mode of depiction in the Perfection of Wisdom for capturing the audience's attention in a carefully crafted manner, it is unexpected for the passage under discussion to interrupt this crescendo effect. This gives the impression that it could have been added—with little regard for the dynamic created by the crescendo effect—to the already existing exposition of merits, to which it also does not seem to be particularly well related thematically.

The relevant part of this apparent addition begins in the Gāndhārī manuscript version by relating the imitation teaching on the Perfection of Wisdom to disclosing the impermanent nature of the five aggregates, followed by indicating what particular understanding of impermanence is intended here.[369] This takes the following form:[370]

> Kauśika, the impermanence of form should again not be seen by way of the destruction of form, [and so for] feeling tone, perception, volitional formations, consciousness. Kauśika, the impermanence of consciousness should again not be seen by way of the destruction of consciousness. [If] one sees it in this way, one is cultivating an imitation of the Perfection of Wisdom.

According to an explanation given in the commentary by Haribhadra,[371] "the impermanence of form is the momentary arising, discontinuity, and destruction of form." This gives the impression as if this imitation teaching would be an affirmation of the doctrine of momentariness. In other words, the teaching rejected here appears to be the notion that impermanence is tantamount to complete destruction (in every moment). The circumstance that this notion is presented as an imitation or counterfeit of the Perfection of Wisdom in turn suggests that its proponents would also be practitioners of the path to Buddhahood, given that they promote the teaching in question as a way of cultivating wisdom as one of the perfections.[372]

The doctrine of momentariness envisages that everything has only a momentary duration, in that any arising will be followed right away by a complete disappearance and cessation. Such a radicalization of impermanence appears to have gained traction in the environs of the first century of the present era,[373] making it just possible that the present passage could constitute an early reply to the beginning stages of this doctrine. Such a reply may have been added to the exposition of merits as a kind of afterthought and without being properly adjusted to its context, in order to take into account what at that time would have been a recent development. Whereas the Gāndhārī manuscript version just introduces the idea of an imitation or counterfeit teaching as such, Lokakṣema's translation presents it in a slightly negative light by referring to those who give such teachings as "bad friends" (*pāpamitra*).[374] Other versions go further by indicating that these teachers have not developed their body, morality, and mind as well as—of course, one might say—not developed their wisdom, being of a stupid type whose wisdom has disappeared.[375] Perhaps such growing censure in some versions can be read as expressing an increasingly felt need to distance the Perfection of Wisdom from this doctrine as a potential competitor in respect to ways of cultivating the wisdom needed to progress toward Buddhahood.

From the viewpoint of *Āgama* literature, a relevant indication would be an affirmation of continuity between arising and passing away. The relevant Pāli discourse and its Chinese parallel single out three characteristics of what is conditioned. These are that one can discern an arising, a ceasing, and a process of alteration (more literally "otherwiseness") that continues as long as what has arisen persists and has not yet ceased.[376] The

Chinese version stands alone in providing a practical illustration with the example of a human body. Its arising takes place with birth and its cessation with death. As long as it persists, between these two events of birth and death, there is a process of alteration manifesting in aging, etc. This provides quite a straightforward perspective. Although it can in principle happen that someone passes away right after being born, this is an exceptional case and most human bodies go through a more or less extended period of gradual alteration between the times of their birth and of their death.

The teaching found similarly in the Pāli and Chinese versions suggests that in early Buddhist thought the notion of time mainly functions as a conceptualization of the experience of change. This can be of the more sudden type when something arises or ceases, or else of the gradual type when something undergoes alteration while persisting. The three periods of time, to which I will return below, can then simply be understood as referents to what has already changed, what is right now changing, and what will change.

From the viewpoint of the characteristics of what is conditioned, the theory of momentariness focuses just on two of these three, namely on arising and ceasing, and then applies these also to the interim period of gradual alteration. In relation to the above example of the aging of a human body, this takes the form of conceiving such aging as involving a series of replacements of the body, where in each moment the old body disappears and is replaced by a new body that is just an infinitesimal bit older; the series of different bodies making up one individual are in turn held together by conditionality. The following comments by von Rospatt (1995, 176 and 217) provide helpful indications regarding this type of perspective:

> For envisaging the human body over the entire span of its existence, one may naturally come to the conclusion that at different stages in life one deals with completely distinct bodies . . . [hence] the observation that at every moment the body undergoes destruction and a new body arises may have come across as not all that contra-factual. This is all the more so

> because the principle that change implies substitution is more plausible in the case of the body where many changes entail evidently the origination of a new and the destruction of old entities . . . [leading to] the conclusion that the body is changing all the time, and that hence the experience of the constant substitution of the old body by a new one corresponds to reality.

The teachings of the Perfection of Wisdom can at first sight appear to do the opposite of the above tendency to reduce everything to an arising followed by an immediate ceasing, as the recurrent reference to nonarising and nonceasing, together with the recognition of an advanced level of progress toward Buddhahood involving the patient acceptance of the nonarising of dharmas (*anutpattikadharmakṣānti*), can give the impression that arising and ceasing as dimensions of impermanence are in some way being rejected.[377] The significance of this type of presentation can be explored with the help of the following passage from the Perfection of Wisdom:[378]

> As to those dharmas, on account of not having arisen anywhere, there is also no ceasing for dharmas; dharmas, too, do not arise from anywhere, and dharmas also do not cease toward anywhere. Among dharmas, one comprehends, there is not that which arises, and there is also nowhere toward which dharmas then cease.

Particularly helpful is the indication that dharmas do not arise *from somewhere* or cease *toward somewhere*. This suggests that the assertion of "nonarising" would actually be an assertion of "nonarising [from somewhere]" and "nonceasing," which already follows from nonarising, would intend "nonceasing [toward somewhere]." The criticism appears to be not of impermanence as such but much rather of the idea that entities come from somewhere when they appear and go somewhere when they disappear.[379] Another statement in the Perfection of Wisdom emphatically asserts that the dictum, according to which dharmas do not arise from anywhere, is in accordance with the teachings of the Tathāgata.[380]

The perspective that emerges in this way can be related to an *Āgama* discourse passage extant in Chinese, Sanskrit (fragmentary), and Tibetan. The relevant part takes off from the illusory nature of conditioned phenomena, a topic already explored above (see p. 51), and then proceeds to their arising and passing away. The pertinent part in the Tibetan version proceeds in the following way:[381] "Monastics, conditioned phenomena are like a magical illusion, like a mirage . . . they arise from being nonexistent; having arisen, they nevertheless disintegrate. For this reason, monastics, conditioned phenomena are empty." The Chinese parallel adds that the illusory nature of conditioned phenomena implies that they "do not really come and really go."[382]

A similar statement, but applied instead to the six senses, occurs in a discourse from another collection extant in Chinese: "At the time of the arising of the eye, when it arises one does not know from where it comes; at the time of the ceasing of the eye, when it ceases one does not know where it goes."[383] The same type of indication also features in the *Visuddhimagga*, which indicates that the sense spheres "do not come from anywhere before they arise, and they do not go anywhere after they cease."[384]

What these different passages appear to point to in one way or another is the dependently arisen nature of conditioned phenomena or of the sense spheres. These do not exist in some abstract form somewhere else, instead of which they are through and through the product of conditions in the here and now. This precisely reflects their empty nature. From this viewpoint, then, the assertion of nonarising in the Perfection of Wisdom would be an affirmation of dependent arising rather than a denial of impermanence.

A central concern of this affirmation appears to be in turn the undermining of any positing of entities as causal agents. Another perspective on the same basic problem can be garnered from a Pāli discourse and its parallels. In reply to an exposition related to the topic of dependent arising, a monk in the audience evinces the type of thinking that takes some type of an entity as a causal agent for granted, leading him to inquire who feels, who craves, who clings, etc.[385] The Buddha invariably rejects such questions as improper, clarifying that he does not teach that there is one who feels, craves, or clings. The proper question is rather to inquire after what serves as a condition for the arising of feeling tone, craving, clinging, etc. In other words, instead of thinking in terms of an entity, the approach should be based on looking at conditions.

The same basic problem recurs with a report of the Buddha's rejection of all of the four possibilities that according to the tetralemma mode of thinking exist for explaining the creation of pleasure and pain: created by oneself, by others, by both, or else just arisen by chance.[386] When the Buddha reportedly denies all four possibilities, his exasperated visitor wonders if this should be understood to imply that pleasure and pain do not exist at all. This goes to show the degree to which the refusal of adopting any of the four alternatives, considered to cover all possibilities exhaustively, was experienced as perplexing. The proper reply to the matter turns out to be once again conditionality: it is due to the appropriate conditions that pleasure and pain manifest. Here, as well, the problem appears to be that the inquiry is based on thinking in terms of entities as causal agents and for this reason cannot be answered in a way that would confirm the mistaken premise. The proper procedure is then to let go of entity-thinking and instead shift toward mere conditionality.

In this way, it seems that the affirmation of nonarising in the Perfection of Wisdom, despite employing a mode of expression that at first sight may well seem to be in direct contradiction to *Āgama* thought, instead appears to be making the basically same point as the above passages, in that there is no entity who feels, craves, or clings, who creates pleasure and pain, instead of which all of these phenomena result from their respective conditions.

The proclamation of nonarising is not yet the end of challenging positions taken in relation to impermanence, as elsewhere the Perfection of Wisdom appears to reject the notion that the three periods of time can be discerned. One such instance directly precedes the statement quoted above regarding dharmas arising from somewhere. The instruction commends the understanding that in regard to past, future, and present dharmas there is nothing to obtain, give up, know, or apprehend.[387]

A statement on the three periods of time found elsewhere in *Prajñāpāramitā* literature can help clarify the main point apparently made in the Perfection of Wisdom. The relevant part takes the following form:[388]

> Again, just as empty space, so what is earlier, later, and present can all not be apprehended . . . the past time is empty of past time, the future time is empty of future time, the present time is empty of present time. The three times are the same; the three times are the same in emptiness.

The formulation employed in this passage, in particular the reference to the three times being the same in emptiness, seems to imply that the rejection of the three time periods in the Perfection of Wisdom would be aimed at a substantialist notion of these three periods. This would tie in with another passage in the Perfection of Wisdom, according to which past, future, and present instances of the aggregates are equally without an intrinsic nature.[389] In that sense, dharmas in the three time periods are indeed beyond being apprehended. In other words, the point would not be to deny the ability to know the difference between something being past, present, or future,[390] instead of which the issue at stake would much rather be to criticize the notion of an absolute existence of the three time periods. Once again, the Perfection of Wisdom appears to stand in dialogue with a central tenet of Sarvāstivāda Abhidharma thought, in particular the notion that phenomena really exist in the past, the present, and the future.[391] Cox (1995, 136–37) explains the reasoning behind such a position in the following manner:[392]

> A given instance of perceptual consciousness is said to arise only in dependence upon two conditions: the sense organ and its corresponding object-field. This implies that perceptual consciousness arises only in conjunction with an appropriate and existent object; perceptual consciousness of a nonexistent object or without an object is, therefore, impossible. Since mental perceptual consciousness of past and future factors does indeed occur, in order to preclude the absurdity of perceptual consciousness without an object-field, these past and future factors too must be acknowledged to exist.

In this way, the perceived need for an actually existing object appears to stand in the background of this significant development in Sarvāstivāda thought. In a later chapter, I will come back to the topic of the object's role in experience (see below p. 234).

Although an attempt to refute such positions may explain the choice of wording in the Perfection of Wisdom, the net result is a lack of easy comprehensibility. The claim that dharmas of the past, present, and future cannot be known or apprehended can be misunderstood, and the same holds for the proclamation of the nonarising of dharmas. A comparable problem, however, occurs also in *Āgama* literature in reply to the question of whether the world is either eternal or else not eternal.[393] To the surprise of his interlocutors, the Buddha is on record for rejecting both alternatives whenever these were brought up for his judgment. This may seem puzzling at first sight, as a straightforward reply indicating that the world is of course not eternal would be in keeping with the teachings on impermanence in other discourses.

The two alternative positions under discussion form part of a standard questionnaire to ascertain the view held by a particular teacher or practitioner (see also above p. 38). The expectation in the ancient Indian setting was apparently that one of the alternatives should fit the case. In order to ensure that this is possible, some positions are presented in the tetralemma mode, leaving room for denying both alternatives or affirming that both fit the case. Yet, even in relation to such questions presented in the tetralemma mode, the Buddha is on record for rejecting all four alternatives. In the present case, which only involves two alternatives, the expectation is that one will either proclaim that the world is eternal or else will take the position that the world is not eternal. Why deny both?

The baffling nature of the Buddha's refusal to take up any of the positions in the standard questionnaire can be seen reflected not only in the reactions to this stance reported in *Āgama* literature but also in the rather substantial body of discussions of this topic in Buddhist studies.[394] The solution appears to be that each of these questions involves a premise the Buddha was not willing to accept. In the present case, the problem is the term "world," in the sense of what this term is taken to connote. From the viewpoint of the early Buddhist analysis of the construction of experience, the term "world" simply stands for what arises through the six senses. Yet, the concept of the "world" underlying the inquiry is a different one; it presumably involves a form of reification of the world as something existing on its own, about which then an eternal or noneternal nature can be predicated. Had the Buddha taken up the (in itself correct) position of denying eternal existence, he would have implicitly endorsed a conception of the "world" not compatible with insight into the construction of experience. Hence, the only choice left is to refuse both alternatives.

In this way, it seems as if the report of the Buddha's refusal to declare that the world is either eternal or else not eternal can be viewed as similar in nature to the position taken in the Perfection of Wisdom regarding the nonarising of all dharmas or the three periods of time.[395] In both cases, the formulation considered on its own can easily lead to misunderstandings. In order to avoid that, contextualization is required, in particular by ascertaining what each of these formulations stands in dialogue with, what they are responding to. The main concern appears to be reified notions—be it the world in the case of *Āgama* literature or dharmas in the case of the Perfection of Wisdom—wherefore the reply to such notions must be very circumspect to avoid in some way endorsing such reification. The Buddha of *Āgama* literature achieves this by simply refusing to take up any of the proposed positions. Since in the Perfection of Wisdom he does not feature involved in an actual debate or discussion with others who promote that dharmas are endowed with an intrinsic nature in past, present, and future times, the procedure is rather to refuse to employ any of the notions that usually come with this position. Such refusal then takes the form of deconstructing any such notion on the spot in the form of propounding nonarising, nonceasing, and so on.

Although affirmations of impermanence do not occur frequently in the Perfection of Wisdom, in contrast to their extensive manifestations in *Āgama* literature, Lokakṣema's translation does warn against succumbing to the four perversions of perception (*saṃjñāviparyāsa*), one of which is precisely mistaking what is impermanent for being permanent.[396] Such a warning would be superfluous if the proclamations of nonarising in the Perfection of Wisdom were intended to promote a dismissal of impermanence. This indication can be complemented with the following short exchange between the Buddha and Subhūti:[397]

> The Buddha said: "How is it, does the mind that earlier ceased arise again later?" Subhūti said: "No."
>
> The Buddha said: "Can the mind that has at first arisen [then] cease?" Subhūti said: "It can cease."
>
> The Buddha said: "What is subject to ceasing, could it be prevented from ceasing?" Subhūti said: "No."

This exchange conveys the impression that the dismissal of an entity arising—here presumably reflected in the proposal that the (same) mind arises again after having ceased—comes together with an affirmation of impermanence, in the sense that the mind arises and ceases, and that the latter cannot be prevented.

Actual contemplation of impermanence in turn comes up in the *Pañcaviṃśatisāhasrikā Prajñāpāramitā* as a practice commendable for bodhisattvas, as long as this is done with nonapprehension.[398] In other words, the recommendation is not to write off contemplation of impermanence as such but much rather to encourage undertaking it in a way that avoids any reification.

In sum, it seems that with the Perfection of Wisdom's proclamation of nonarising the same holds as in the case of its promotion of the emptiness of all dharmas, discussed earlier (see above p. 42), in that both positions need not involve a radical departure from the type of thought reflected in *Āgama* sources. Nevertheless, the mode of presentation chosen in the Perfection of Wisdom is clearly distinct and not without consequences. Before turning to these, however, at this point I would like to present an illustration in an attempt to bring together the different perspectives on impermanence surveyed above, that is, of *Āgama* literature, of Abhidharma traditions subscribing to momentariness, and of the Perfection of Wisdom.

For this purpose, the *Āgama* perspective could be compared to constantly changing clouds on a windy day raining down to form rivulets and rivers that are also constantly changing. The moving clouds in the sky, the rain pouring down, and the flowing water of the rivulets and rivers are all changing at their own speed, hence at times an arising and ceasing is more evident, such as in the case of rain drops, or else an alteration while persisting is more prominent, such as with moving clouds or flowing water in rivulets and rivers.

Momentariness could in turn be compared to the surface of a pond or lake impacted by the same rain, resulting in a quick succession of bubbles arising and immediately passing away due to the impact of the raindrops. The same basic effect would also manifest if due to a sudden drop of temperature hail were to form in midair and this hail were then to impact the surface of the pond or lake (as long as this has not yet frozen over). What this image intends to convey is that it is in principle possible to combine the doctrine of momentariness with the notion of phenomena as entities, comparable to solid bits of frozen water. This is less easily done with change conceived as a continuous flow like a river or moving clouds. But momentarily coming into existence and then disappearing can in principle involve entities.

This would be relevant for Abhidharma traditions that combine momentariness with an affirmation of the intrinsic nature of phenomena as existing in the past, the present, and the future. The possibility of such a combination goes to show that even a radical version of impermanence, in the form of momentariness, can coexist with the assertion of *svabhāva*. A helpful illustration relevant to this case has been offered by Kajiyama (1995, 138), in that the operation of *svabhāva* manifests in a way that is comparable to how "the frames of film on the reels of a projector, passing from upper to lower reel, project momentary ever-changing pictures on the screen, while existing permanently in the film on the reels."

In the context of the rain simile, the criticism of the *svabhāva* notion in the Perfection of Wisdom could in turn be illustrated by the opposite of a drop in temperature resulting in hail, namely an increase in temperature resulting in an evaporation of any water in the air that could form into rain drops. As a result, there will be no more rain—which successfully forestalls any further impact on the surface of the pond or lake—and the sky will become cloudless. In this way, only empty space remains, which is indeed a recurrent metaphor employed in the Perfection of Wisdom to articulate its vision of emptiness. Although the manifestation of just space successfully undermines any attempt to solidify, to create entities, with only space left the fact of change is also no longer fully evident; it has quite literally evaporated. What this intends to convey is that the attempt to counter a radicalization of impermanence in the form of momentariness can go overboard and result in a situation where even just plain impermanence is no longer fully apparent. In some strands of Mahāyāna thought there does indeed seem to be a tendency to place less emphasis on impermanence, a trend described by McMahan (2002, 78–80 and 188–89) in the following manner:

> While it would be misleading to say that the Mahāyāna abandoned the doctrine of impermanence, some texts implicitly de-emphasize it . . . While the very doctrine of emptiness derives from impermanence—things lack self-identity in part because they are in constant flux and interaction—emptiness takes on its own semantic life in the Mahāyāna, sometimes forgetting its basis in impermanence. Indeed, this foundational notion in Buddhism often recedes somewhat in Mahāyāna texts and becomes subservient to the now more privileged concept of emptiness, which assumes connotations beyond just lack of identity because of impermanence. Images and metaphors likening emptiness and dharmas to static space are among the vehicles whereby emptiness takes on such new semantic overtones . . .
>
> Rather than a plurality or hierarchy of dharmas, all dharmas in this Mahāyāna image are the same, sharing a fundamentally empty nature, and in this way leveled so that none is intrinsically higher or lower than others. Instead of the series of plural moments of existence arising and falling in time, we see the elements of existence as a continuity, without any essential differences, inactive, and unified in a homogeneous and infinite space. This de-temporalizing of time by representing it as subordinate to space is significant . . .

> [In this way], the Mahāyāna found ways to conceive of the transcendence of time within time itself. Part of this is the spatialization of time—assimilating temporality to the always present dimension of space, which presents a symbolic abrogation of temporality by representing the world not as a series of things coming and going, but as a space within which the events of the world are contained, events which are all present together as if unified in one ever-present field of vision. The representation of dharmas as static or contained in a spatial field is also conducive to the injunction not to cling to worldly phenomena. Descriptions of dharmas as equal, with none being more inherently attractive or repulsive than others, are meant to induce a sense of neutrality and equanimity toward all phenomena...
>
> [T]he valorization of space . . . occurs with the orthodox doctrine of impermanence as a background... the two are not necessarily in contradiction; the spatialization of temporality is, rather, a response to impermanence... Time is symbolically overcome by representing it as contained within the visual field.

## Summary

This chapter has covered two temporal perspectives related to the path to Buddhahood, namely the evolution and impact of the notion of former Buddhas and a shift in the degree of importance granted to the recognition that things change in the course of time, that they are impermanent.

The possession of sufficient merits is a central requirement for progress toward Buddhahood and for this reason is naturally an important concern of the Perfection of Wisdom. Articulations of this concern can take the form of somewhat hyperbolic depictions of various scenarios of merit accrual that are invariably bested by engaging with the Perfection of Wisdom.

The successful acquisition of merits has a bodily dimension, which manifests in being endowed with thirty-two special physical marks. *Āgama* literature presents the ability to recognize these marks as a brahmanical lore, serving to facilitate the conversion of brahmins by convincing them of the extraordinary nature of the Buddha. The Discourse on the Marks brings these thirty-two physical endowments more firmly within the orbit of Buddhist doctrine by providing a karmic perspective on their acquisition. This takes the form of delineating the conduct and qualities developed by Śākyamuni in past lives that led to his present endowment with the respective mark(s). Apparently originating from a commentary that in the course of oral transmission became part of the discourse, the resultant presentation seems to have had a considerable impact on the evolution of the bodhisattva ideal, opening up the vista toward progress toward Buddhahood over a series of lives dedicated to cultivating the required qualities.

Another, related perspective emerges with the *jātaka*s, which often result from identifying a protagonist in various parables and fables as a former life of the Buddha Śākyamuni, wherefore he can now relate what happened through his recollection of past lives. The integration of sundry tales from the ancient Indian narrative repertoire into the Buddhist fold in this way has resulted in incorporating a range of values and positions that do not necessarily sit easily with Buddhist doctrine and orientation. Yet, once these tales have turned into *jātaka*s, they can come to serve as a script for the conduct of a bodhisattva in quest of Buddhahood (after this notion itself has gained traction).

A *jātaka* that appears to have been of particular significance for the evolution of the bodhisattva ideal occurs in *Āgama* literature and involves the identification of a young brahmin, living at the time of the previous Buddha, as a past life of Śākyamuni. This young brahmin is at first unwilling to meet the Buddha Kāśyapa and even uses dismissive terms to refer to him. On being forced to come along and meet the Buddha Kāśyapa, he is sufficiently impressed to become a monk. However, the tale as such is mainly about the exemplary conduct of another person, a potter and lay disciple of Kāśyapa, and nothing further is heard about the young brahmin after he has gone forth.

The somewhat incongruent identification of the young brahmin as a former life of Śākyamuni appears to have created a fertile field of exploration for later traditions. An apparent solution to the problem takes the form of proposing that at that time Śākyamuni formed the aspiration or vow to become a Buddha in the future. A *Madhyamāgama* discourse reporting various marvels related to the Buddha Śākyamuni explicitly qualifies this vow or aspiration as the first instance of this type, as his "initial" decision to opt for the pursuit of becoming a Buddha in the future. This passage could be reflecting an early stage in the evolution of the motif of the aspiration or vow to become a Buddha, which naturally would have been related to the prior Buddha. Given that it is considered a marvel, it seems that this notion would have arisen in a setting that did not yet know the idea that Śākyamuni had already at a much earlier time decided to opt for Buddhahood.

A shift of this decision toward a considerably earlier point in time would have been an inevitable result of the increase in past life stories of Śākyamuni, especially once these were considered to reflect an overarching intention to cultivate the perfections for the sake of progress toward Buddhahood. With numbers of such stories in circulation, the period of time between the Buddha Kāśyapa and the time of the Buddha Śākyamuni would not have sufficed to accommodate all these past life tales, which must have led to a shift of the initial decision to embark on the path to Buddhahood to a far distant time, such as being associated with the Buddha Dīpaṃkara. In this way, the time span since Śākyamuni's resolve to embark on the path to full awakening appears to have gradually increased from a decision taken in the same life before his going forth, to the time of the Buddha Kāśyapa, and then well beyond that.

Whereas in this way a gradual increase in time can be observed, the opposite effect can be seen in the doctrine of momentariness, according to which whatever arises will cease and disappear on the spot. A reference to an imitation teaching in the Perfection of Wisdom appears to intend this doctrine of momentariness, in the sense of a particular understanding of impermanence by way of equating it with destruction (in every moment). A relevant perspective in *Āgama* literature posits a period of alteration while persisting that occurs between the arising and the ceasing of conditioned phenomena.

Whereas the doctrine of momentariness no longer acknowledges a more or less prolonged period of gradual change between arising and ceasing, the apparent response to such notions in the Perfection of Wisdom can at first sight seem to abrogate arising and ceasing with its proclamation of the nonarising and nonceasing of all dharmas. Closer inspection shows that such statements are best read as intending the nonarising from somewhere and nonceasing toward somewhere of dharmas—that is, they would serve to clarify that there are no entities that come from elsewhere, instead of which any dharma is merely the product of conditions interacting in the present.

In this way, the proclamation in the Perfection of Wisdom of the nonarising of all dharmas, or of the nonapprehension of the three periods of time, can be understood to employ somewhat challenging statements that need to be read with the context in mind, in particular taking into account the position they apparently intend to refute. A similar pattern holds for *Āgama* literature, in the form of the report that, in refusing to take up any of the positions delineated in a standard questionnaire, the Buddha not only rejected the proposal that the world is eternal but also the opposite proposition that the world is not eternal. This case, too, needs to be contextualized. The implication is not some reservation about impermanence, instead of which the reason would be that the conception of the "world" held by those promoting this questionnaire involved reification. Affirming any position based on such reification risks endorsing that premise.

In this way, closer inspection helps to make sense of positions taken in the Perfection of Wisdom. Nevertheless, the net result of such rhetoric does appear to be a diminishing of the importance granted to impermanence. Although the contemplation of impermanence can offer an important support for insight into emptiness, the all-out emphasis on the latter does seem to have resulted in a vision of empty space that no longer exhibits evident manifestations of change.

# On Chapters 5 and 6

THE FIFTH AND SIXTH chapters of Lokakṣema's translation of the Perfection of Wisdom correspond to the seventh and eighth chapters of the Sanskrit version translated by Conze (1973/1975, 135–48). A central theme in this portion of text is the need to avoid taking up a sign (*nimitta*) when dedicating one's merits to complete awakening. Another important topic is the role of the Perfection of Wisdom as one's teacher. Access to such teachings is due to past encounters with Buddhas; rejecting it leads to hell.

One of two topics to be explored below is the role of signs and meditative ways of cultivating their absence; the other topic is the notion of rebirth in hell.

## SIGNS AND THEIR ABSENCE

The problem with taking up signs (*nimitta*) is a recurrent theme in the Perfection of Wisdom, even in relation to merit. Merit, as noted in a previous chapter, is not a target for sustained problematization through the otherwise-sweeping rhetoric of emptiness. Nevertheless, the present chapter sounds a warning in regard to taking up the sign(s) of merit, presumably to avoid the basic problem of reification. The Perfection of Wisdom offers a simile to illustrate the problem with taking up signs, which affords a convenient occasion to explore this topic in more detail. The simile proceeds as follows:[399]

> One who therein takes up signs is like, for example, [food] mixed with poison. Why is that? Suppose attractive food

> has been prepared by putting poison into it. Its appearance is extremely excellent and fragrant; everyone would delight in it. Not knowing that there is poison in the food, foolish people eat it, being delighted and sated. When their appetite has disappeared, their bodies become very sick for a long time.

The idea of partaking of something delicious that is poisoned aptly conveys the problem of doing something that in the moment is experienced as pleasant but later turns out to have detrimental consequences. This is precisely the sense conveyed by a version of the simile of partaking of poison in a Pāli discourse and its Chinese parallels, with the minor difference that the illustration involves a beverage instead of food.[400]

Another occurrence of this simile in a different Pāli discourse concerns the topic of attachment to what is experienced through the senses, which naturally stands in close relationship to taking up signs. The simile describes how someone who knows the beverage is poisoned would not want to drink it.[401] This serves to illustrate the attitude of someone free from attachment toward possible acquisitions by way of the senses.

Yet another occurrence of this simile in a Pāli discourse and its parallels serves to illustrate the problem of mistaking any aspect of experience as permanent and a self (etc.).[402] This usage relates to the topic of signs, since such a mistaken perspective involves taking hold of the wrong sign, such as the sign of permanence, the sign of a self, etc. The problem identified in this way can easily be correlated with a central concern of the Perfection of Wisdom, whose employment of the rhetoric of emptiness appears to be predominantly motivated by the attempt to undermine the tendency to take up the sign of some sort of enduring essence in relation to any dharma.

This is precisely where wisdom would be called for in order to counter the propensity of delusion to act as a "maker of signs," a potential it shares with sensual lust and anger.[403] Needless to say, not all signs activate the three root defilements. As such, a sign is simply an aspect of the process of cognition and recognition, enabling the mind to process the data of the senses. Nevertheless, in the unawakened mind this seemingly innocent process tends to distort and rework any aspect of experience in line with the influence of the three root defilements.

The potential impact of the type of delusion that the Perfection of Wisdom attempts to counter could be exemplified with the case of taking up the sign of "a river."[404] At first sight, taking up such a sign seems fair enough, as it simply serves to cognize a flowing watercourse that proceeds toward a lower elevation until it reaches another body of water, usually the ocean. It seems natural to state, on witnessing this phenomenon, that "the river flows." Yet, there is no river that flows apart from the water. In fact, there is just water and no entity or thing that owns the water, so that even speaking of "its water" or the water "of the river" has no basis in something that actually exists. There is also no agent behind the flowing; it is not the case that there is something called "river" that gets the water to flow according to its design. The flow of the water is just a result of conditionality, in this case the natural tendency of water to flow from a higher to a lower elevation. If the water dries up, there will no longer be a river but just the dried-up riverbed. The designation of a particular track on the surface of the earth as "riverbed," too, depends on the water. If the course of the water is altered, perhaps by shortcutting an elongated bend, then that becomes the new "riverbed." In sum, on closer analysis it turns out that there is no "river" entity as such. It is, after all, just a sign taken up by the mind. The same holds in turn for the sign of "water," "riverbed," or any other sign. Under closer scrutiny each of these evaporates, so to say, as none of them stands for some sort of an entity. Signs are, after all, just signs.

In view of the potentially far-reaching repercussions of taking up signs, early Buddhist mental training gives considerable room to various ways of learning how to work with signs.[405] At a basic level this takes the form of sense restraint, which serves to prevent the arising of defilements when taking up signs by way of any of the senses. Building on this is the cultivation of the ability to stay with a bare cognizing of the data from the senses, without immediately giving rein to various proliferations. Eventually such mental training can lead to the experience of signlessness, a form of *samādhi* that is devoid of anything that is being cognized or that the mind might focus on. This type of experience can be described in complementary ways as either requiring not paying attention (*amanasikāra*) to any sign (*nimitta*) or else paying attention (*manasikāra*) to signlessness (*animitta*). In short, it involves the complete absence of any mental processing of content while the mind is still present and fully alert. Even when such practice is referred to as a form of not paying attention (*amanasikāra*), this does not mean that the mind is dull or that the practitioner is somehow semi-conscious or even unconscious. In fact, as the alternative formulation shows, the mental factor of attention is still there and operative. But instead of paying attention to this or that, it pays attention to the absence of any this or that.

Although such a condition of the mind has much in common with the breakthrough to the realization of Nirvana, *Āgama* literature indicates that this much is not in itself necessarily liberating. A telling case in this respect involves the report of a monastic who successfully attains signless *samādhi* but on subsequent occasions excessively socializes and eventually becomes overwhelmed by sensual lust to the extent of disrobing.[406] In other words, this episode conveys that an abiding in signlessness can just involve a condition of mental tranquility. Although such a form of practice could well have repercussions in the short term, it does not necessarily ensure a lasting transformation of the mind. Such a transformation would require combining signless meditative experiences with insight in some way, be it by way of preparation before abiding in signlessness or else by way of subsequent reflection. Expressed in terms of the relay of seven chariots or the raft, the thorough letting go that can result from cultivating signlessness comes into its proper place when the seven chariots have been used to reach the doors of the palace, when the raft has been used to arrive at the other shore. If by using the seven chariots or the raft the foundation for liberating insight has been put into place, then letting go can ensure that the momentum that has built up thus far leads to the final breakthrough.

In order to prepare for that, it would of course be helpful to train in letting go of signs in any situation, which is precisely why signless concentration is recommended as a general form of practice. Such a recommendation would not be meant to encourage getting off the chariots or leaving behind the raft before having used these for their intended purpose. Instead of being intended to deconstruct the very means for progress, such practice would only be meant to support deconstructing any clinging and attachment to those means for progress, thereby ensuring that, when the time has come, it will be easier to let go of them.

Besides, neither the means for progress nor even signs as such are a problem; in fact, a Buddha still uses signs. He is still able to take up the sign of a "river," for example, and the signs required to form the idea of a "raft" or any other means to be used to cross over that river.[407] The difference is that a Buddha sees through signs; for this reason, he is no longer affected by their potential to poison the food of experience.

A complementary perspective on the problem posed by taking up signs comes to the fore in the Perfection of Wisdom in an exposition by Subhūti:[408]

> One perceives form as empty; this is called becoming attached. One perceives feeling tone, perception, volitional formations, and consciousness as empty; this is called becoming attached. In the case of phenomena of the past, one perceives them as phenomena of the past; this is called becoming attached. In the case of phenomena of the future, one perceives them as phenomena of the future; this is called becoming attached. In the case of phenomena of the present, one perceives them as phenomena of the present; this is called becoming attached.

This teaching by Subhūti serves as a more detailed explanation of a succinct statement made earlier by the Buddha, in which he reveals that the condition that leads to becoming attached is perception.[409] The exposition by Subhūti conveys that even the crucial insight into the empty nature of the five aggregates can lead to becoming attached, rather than being liberative. The same holds for the basic distinction between the three periods of time. Subhūti's employment of the rhetoric of emptiness is as relentless as ever.

The above presentation can conveniently be interpreted from the viewpoint of the relay of chariots. The intention would not be to dismiss insight into emptiness or the basic distinction between the three periods of time. Both can serve as means for progress, just as the seven chariots. However, when the relay of seven chariots has led to the palace, even the seventh chariot will have to be abandoned. In the same way, the in itself correct perception of emptiness or of distinguishing the three periods of time can come with some degree of holding on. Allowing this vestigial degree of attachment to continue would be similar to being unwilling to get off the seventh chariot.

The role of perception is problematic to the extent that it tends to mix subjective evaluations and prejudices with the actual data of the senses. The net result is that what subjectively seems to be "out there" can in fact be merely a projection of what is "in here." That is, much of the outer world is constructed by perception, and this usually takes place unnoticed. Countering the impact of perceptual distortion as an ingrained aspect of unawakened experience is precisely why the training of perception receives such sustained attention in Buddhist thought. One type of such training concerns precisely emptiness, which can serve to wean the mind from projecting the notion of an entity or a self. Another training concerns impermanence, which is meant to undermine the tendency to latch on to some aspect of experience as everlasting. The scheme of the five aggregates can be of considerable help in deconstructing the notion of a self, just as attention to the three time periods can reveal the truth of impermanence. Yet, in the above passage even these valuable tools come in for deconstruction. They are, after all, just chariots to be used for the journey up to the doors of the palace. Entry into the palace, corresponding to stepping completely out of construction, requires leaving behind even the perception of emptiness.

The proposed reading of the above passage can also be employed for another challenging passage. In the context of exploring the liberating potential of the Perfection of Wisdom under the heading of "purity," Subhūti presents the tantalizing statement that "the self is pure,"[410] which the Buddha affirms. In his commentary, Haribhadra makes it clear that this statement does not intend to endorse the existence of such a self. He explains that it refers to the self that others imagine to be existing, and the qualification of being pure is meant to convey that even this imagined self is something that in an ultimate sense has not arisen.[411]

This clarification could in turn be related to a usage in a Pāli discourse of the term usually translated as "pure," which occurs in the context of an attempt to counter a reified notion of a sentient being. In this context, the term *śuddha* (Pāli: *suddha*) qualifies "formations," where the rendering "pure" is perhaps not the best choice, as this could be misunderstood to provide a contrast to being impure.[412] Instead, a sense of "sheer" or "mere" would fit the case better, in that what others may mistake to be a sentient being as a substantial entity turns out in reality to be a heap of mere formations or sheer formations. In this case, the qualification *śuddha* does not convey purity as such, instead of which it rather serves to communicate a sense of bareness by clarifying that there is nothing else in addition to those mere or sheer formations. Such usage could be compared to the employment of the English term "pure" in phrases like "pure nonsense" or a "pure accident," where similarly the idea is not to convey that the nonsense or the accident are in some way of an exalted, purified nature.

In relation to the statement by Subhūti, the point of employing the qualification "pure" does indeed appear to be to counter reification, by way of affirming nonarising. This suggestion receives support from a comment made in general, not related to the present passage, in the *Dà zhìdù lùn* (**Mahāprajñāpāramitopadeśa*), which takes the following form:[413]

> It is just as dust and water do not adhere to empty space, because of its pure nature; the Perfection of Wisdom is also like that: it is always pure, because it does not arise and does not cease. Just as empty space cannot be defiled, the Perfection of Wisdom is also like that . . . it cannot be defiled.

Such explanations offer welcome help when attempting to make sense of references to purity in the Perfection of Wisdom. These could then perhaps be read keeping in mind the alternative nuance of "sheer" or "mere," conveying a sense of bareness that may serve to promote nonreification, rather than taking the employment of *śuddha* and its equivalents to intend a state of purity as such. Nevertheless, even with these explanations in place it is still noteworthy that the Perfection of Wisdom would employ a term that could easily be misunderstood, and that all the more in relation to a topic as highly sensitive in Buddhist circles as the notion of a self. All this comes in close proximity to the depiction of the hellish rebirth to be expected of those who reject the teachings given in the Perfection of Wisdom. Presumably, the need to counter attachment at all costs stands in the background to the employment of a phrasing that is certainly challenging, if not at times shocking, when viewed from the perspective of an ancient Indian audience familiar with standard Buddhist doctrine.

Nevertheless, already *Āgama* texts do at times employ phrasing that is open to misunderstanding. An example would be a description in a Pāli discourse of a fully awakened person as one who "dwells with the *ātman* become divine" (*brahmabhūta*).[414] Here, the sense of *ātman* is reflexive; it just refers to "oneself." Yet, this phrase can and indeed has been misunderstood to imply the affirmation of a self.[415] This goes to show that the Perfection of Wisdom is not alone in presenting statements that risk being misconstrued.

## Rebirth in Hell

My next topic is rebirth in hell, which I will cover by first taking up relevant indications from the Perfection and Wisdom, after which I survey references to hell in *Āgama* literature. The prospect of rebirth in hell for opposing the Perfection of Wisdom can in a way be considered to form a counterpart to the exuberant descriptions of the merit to be gained by engaging in its promotion. The Buddha explains the former as follows:[416]

> Because of this offence of opposing the Dharma, at death they will enter the Great Hell. For many hundreds of thousands of years, for many hundreds of millions of crores of years they will suffer much in hell, fully experiencing painful feelings that are indescribable. Their lifespan ending herein, they will be reborn in the Great Hell of another world. Their lifespan ending again, they will in turn again be reborn by arriving in the Great Hell of another world.

The Great Hell features in Buddhist cosmology as a place of intense suffering that is beyond description. The time to be spent in this gruesome condition is also beyond imagination, especially when viewed from the perspective of the average life span of human beings. As if all this horror were not enough, in the above description finally passing away from this condition only leads to being reborn again in the same horrible situation. Avoiding such a predicament of course requires finding out what type of behavior will have such repercussions, which the Perfection of Wisdom indeed supplies. Those destined to end up in the Great Hell have acted in the following manner:[417]

> At the time when the profound Perfection of Wisdom is being recited, verbally expressed, or taught, they have doubts about this teaching in their minds and are also unwilling to train in it. They think and say this: "It has not been taught by the Tathāgata." They obstruct others, telling them: "Do not train in this!"

In other words, a central issue here is the perennial challenge of attributing new texts to the Buddha. Just as in matters of making merit the question is not just to engage with the Perfection of Wisdom oneself but also to pass it on to others, in the same way here the problem is not just oneself doubting that the Perfection of Wisdom was taught by the Buddha—here referred to as the Tathāgata—but also instilling such doubt in others.

The Buddha warns Śāriputra that he should not even sit together with such people, talk with them, or partake of a meal together with such slanderers of the Dharma, who are in the dark themselves and place others in the dark.[418] The activities described in this advice are common for ancient Indian monastics who live in the same monastery, so that an implementation of this instruction would require staying only in monasteries whose inhabitants are not opposed to the Perfection of Wisdom. Since to find such monasteries would probably not have been easy at least during an early period of the spread of the Perfection of Wisdom, the circumstance that the Buddha nevertheless gives such a recommendation reveals the degree to which doubts about the authenticity of the text are experienced as challenging.[419] In other words, it should be absolutely clear that the Buddha himself taught the Perfection of Wisdom as an integral part of his commendation to his disciples that they should emulate his example by embarking on the path to Buddhahood.

In what follows, I turn from the basic perspective on rebirth in hell in the Perfection of Wisdom to *Āgama* literature, where the dire prospect of rebirth in hell features as a recurrent theme. Some of the relevant instances even provide detailed descriptions of the various sufferings to be expected on being reborn in hell. I will explore several selected cases of relevant descriptions, in particular from the viewpoint of possible signs of developments in conceptions of hell that can be identified through comparative study.

A Pāli discourse and its Chinese parallel agree in contrasting heaven to hell, describing both just in terms of the six spheres of contact. Whereas in heaven these six are entirely pleasant, in hell they are entirely unpleasant.[420] According to the Pāli commentary, the reference to six spheres of contact experienced as entirely unpleasant should be understood to intend a specific hell by the name of Avīci.[421] The commentarial suggestion can to some extent be related to another Pāli discourse and two of its parallels that consider the term "six spheres of contact" to be one of several alternative names for referring to the Great Hell and thus indeed a specific hell.[422] Nevertheless, another two parallels do not have a counterpart to this indication.

The proposed identification is in fact not entirely straightforward, as the notion of "six spheres of contact" conveys the impression of intending unpleasant experiences through each of the six senses. In contrast, the Great Hell or Avīci seem to be predominantly about the experience of suffering through the fifth sense of the body (together with the sixth sense in the form of the resultant mental suffering). Witanachchi (1992, 430) reasons that the reference to six spheres of contact suggests an "early attempt to interpret metaphorically" some of the notions of heaven and hell prevalent in the ancient Indian setting, in that "[t]his could very well be a reference to the six types of sense experience, painful or pleasurable, one could experience in any place, especially in the human world." He notes that the commentary seems to allow for such an interpretation, as it explains that the terms "heaven" and "hell" can be used to designate experiences in the human realm, which in general consist of a mixture of pleasure and pain.[423] Such a notion of heaven and hell would leave open the possibility that perhaps a shift in meaning may have taken place in the form of the emergence of more literal notions of heaven and hell.

The impact of literalism can be seen in the case of a Pāli discourse with two Chinese parallels, which agree in reporting that witnessing a wildfire served as an occasion for the Buddha to expound to his monastic disciples the dire consequences of misconduct. The main pattern of this teaching involves presenting two alternative scenarios, one of which at first sight seems definitely preferable, yet the alternative scenario turns out to be the better one. In the first such case, the Buddha clarifies to his monk disciples that it would be preferable if they were to hug the blazing fire rather than hug a beautiful woman.[424] The point made in this way is that the second alternative risks leading to breaches of monastic celibacy, and these in turn will result in much greater suffering than just hugging a wildfire.

Although these stark images are clearly inspired by the vision of the wildfire, whose presence must have substantially supported the stern teaching, the motif of fire is just a metaphor. Its employment serves to drive home the predicament of misconduct leading to hell; it is not an actual description of hell. In fact, the fire imagery concerns the alternative that will prevent ending up in hell.

In one of the Chinese versions, however, the Buddha refers to seeing personally how immoral people end up in hell, where their bodies dry up and boiling blood comes out of their facial apertures, eventually leading to their deaths.[425] Here, the motif of fire has become part of a concrete description of torture in hell, where the culprit is roasted in fire such that the above-described effects occur. In this case, a concretization of an image related to hell is found in the discourse itself, rather than occurring only in the commentary.

Another feature of interest is an alternative illustration, found in all three of the parallel versions, which contrasts swallowing a burning metal ball to an immoral recipient accepting food offered by faithful donors. In line with the pattern evident in relation to the wildfire, the burning metal ball would of course be the preferable option. Whereas in one of the two Chinese versions the image concerns swallowing such a burning metal ball, in the Pāli and the other Chinese version the same effect is administered by someone else.[426] This thereby involves the need for an intervention by others who inflict some form of torture. In the present case, however, this is still metaphorical. It is only a comparison, although that comparison has by now become more alive and to some extent also more real through the action taken by those who impose swallowing the hot metal ball as a form of punishment. The metaphorical sense of the same image of swallowing a hot metal ball recurs in several other contexts. One example is a verse, extant in a range of versions, which makes the same basic point that an immoral recipient would be better off swallowing a burning iron ball rather than partaking of food offered in donation.[427]

A teaching that also employs fire-related imagery to sound a stern warning occurs in a discourse extant in Pāli, Chinese, and in part in Sanskrit fragments. The Pāli and Chinese versions work through the physical senses, each time indicating that it would be preferable to have the sense organ itself burnt with a hot metal implement or otherwise damaged rather than grasping at what is experienced through the respective sense organ, since this could lead to a lower rebirth, even in hell. The stark comparisons drawn in this way resonate with the image of hugging a wildfire or swallowing a burning metal ball, mentioned above. A difference between the two main parallel versions in this case is that the Chinese version's description of the prospect of falling into a bad realm indicates that this takes place "like a sinking iron ball."[428] This reference to an iron ball does not stand in any evident relationship to the images related to the senses themselves, and its absence from the parallels makes it fairly probable that this would be a case of a later addition. Due to not being required by the context, the reference to the iron ball may have earned its placing simply by dint of being associated with a bad rebirth, particularly with hell.

A case of an apparent later addition also manifests in a Gāndhārī manuscript version of a discourse extant additionally in Pāli and Chinese. Whereas the other two versions just refer to a hell in which all experiences through the six senses are disagreeable, the Gāndhārī version illustrates this case with the example of heated iron balls.[429] Although this presumably later addition to the version extant in Gāndhārī makes the reference to hell found in all versions come alive, this still functions by way of comparison in its narrative context. The three versions agree that a failure to understand the four noble truths is even worse than that hell.

A comparable case involves a discourse extant in Pāli that has several parallels in Chinese. The relevant exposition in all versions concerns the disadvantages (*ādīnava*, literally "danger") inherent in sensual pleasures, bodily form, and feeling tones. The parallels agree that in the latter two cases the disadvantage is the fact of impermanence. All versions also agree that a disadvantage of the first topic of sensual pleasures is that their pursuit can motivate criminal activities, being arrested for which can result in rather cruel punishments. Only one Chinese version takes up the topic of impermanence as a disadvantage of sensual pleasures, which forms the culmination of its exposition of this topic.[430] This presentation is in line with the pattern adopted for the other two topics in all versions and also aligns well with a general emphasis on the impermanent nature of sensual gratification in *Āgama* literature in general.

The other versions, however, instead of concluding their exposition with the theme of impermanence, rather turn to the prospect of a lower rebirth, such as in hell, due to those reborn in this way having undertaken evil deeds for the sake of sensual gratification.[431] This thereby shifts to the topic of disadvantages to be experienced in the afterlife in an exposition that otherwise concerns what is evident in the present life. It seems at least possible to envisage that the description of tortures suffered in this world on being arrested for criminal activities may have called up the topic of hell by association, which then came to serve as the finale of the exposition instead of the theme of impermanence.

A series of discourses extant in Pāli and Chinese report Mahāmaudgalyāyana's personal vision, by dint of his supernormal abilities, of various beings reborn as a sort of ghost who has to suffer the bitter fruition of the bad deeds done in the previous life as a human. For example, Mahāmaudgalyāyana reports seeing a sentient being pecked at by various birds of prey and reduced to a skeleton.[432] This and other such descriptions do not involve another human who actually inflicts the respective torture. In a comment on this set of discourses, Schmithausen (2000c, 268) explains that when some instances describe "a deformed human being flying through the air . . . chased and attacked by carnivorous birds," and the human beings in such depictions are then identified "to have been 'professional' killers of animals in their previous human existence . . . their being chased and attacked by aggressive birds" could be "a residue of the old idea of the animal victims retaliating upon the killer." This would be in line with comparable descriptions in non-Buddhist texts reflecting notions current in the ancient Indian setting, which in one way or another involve the conception of the victim taking revenge in the afterlife.

The Chinese version of the same set of discourses has another three instances of Mahāmaudgalyāyana's visions that involve the burning iron ball. This particular motif is not found in the Pāli set of parallel discourses and could be a later addition. In keeping with the pattern already mentioned, the relevant passages in the Chinese discourses proceed without any indication that some external agent is involved.[433] This changes with a description of Mahāmaudgalyāyana's personal visions in the *Mahāvastu*, a *Vinaya* text of the Mahāsāṃghika-Lokottaravādins, the relevant part of which involves the guardians of hell who force open the mouths of their hungry victims and throw burning iron balls into them, telling the culprits to eat these.[434] This example points to the apparent attraction of the motif of the hot iron ball and to a tendency toward narrative embellishment by way of the guardians of hell entering the scene and administering the relevant torture.

The repeated occurrence of the motif of the hot iron ball in Buddhist discourse can be appreciated with the help of extracts from a detailed and informative study by Marino (2019, 31, 37, 32, and 42–43):

> Early Buddhist texts were first being composed and compiled during South Asia's Iron Age, and thus contain many references to iron and other metal technologies . . . the blacksmith's furnace found its way into the imagination and everyday language of people in the Buddhist heartland along the Gangetic plains in the mid-to-late first millennium BCE . . .

> [T]he iron ball drew upon the imagery of a vibrant industry with a tangible, everyday presence . . . the smelting process is foreboding. It is loud, volatile, mysterious, and to a certain degree violent. Combined with the massive risks involved with superheated metal, it is no wonder that references to hot iron take on a decidedly infernal connotation . . .
>
> [In particular,] the red-hot iron ball becomes a horrific mimesis of the *piṇḍapāta*, which is the lump of almsfood offered to the monastic community by lay devotees. Moreover, its appearance in gruesome tortures in hell testifies to its role as a symbolic karmic result for a lack of discipline, especially designated for those who compromise the alms exchange . . .
>
> Eating the iron ball as a result of food-related misdeeds is also found in Brahmanical texts . . . [i]nstead of warning against overindulging in alms, or taking alms without proper discipline, a particularly Buddhist monastic concern, the *Manusmṛti* warns against eating offerings designated for ancestors despite one's ignorance of the Vedas, a Brahmanical concern. The trope is the same for both: abuse of the food offering will result in consuming red-hot iron food in the next world . . .
>
> The iron ball as a torture device also sheds light on the relationship between Buddhist conceptions of hell and notions of juridical punishments in ancient India, real or imagined . . . in some cases punishments in Buddhist hells are echoed in the *Arthaśāstra*, suggesting that both Buddhist and normative political literatures drew upon similar tropes, and possibly that certain Buddhist hell tortures were also the fate of criminals at that time.

In a way, some depictions of hell in Buddhist discourse can be viewed as "a smith's furnace gone awry" (Marino 2019, 41). This provides a meaningful background to the description of some hellish tortures given in a Pāli discourse on the topic of the divine messengers and in its parallels. Commenting on this description, which involves the guardians of hell forcing the culprit to swallow a burning iron ball,[435] Marino (2019, 40) notes that "[t]here is no specific alms-related crime mentioned here . . . the symbolic meaning of this hell torture comes in part from its intertextual relationship to other occurrences of the image in Buddhist texts."

From the viewpoint of my present exploration, a particularly significant aspect of such hell tortures described in this discourse is the role played by the guardians of hell in administering these punishments. This involves forcing the culprits to swallow burning iron balls and various other tortures described in the discourse. Notably, the Pāli description of various tortures reports the Buddha explicitly asserting that his account of such torments is not based on hearsay but rather on having seen it all himself.[436] Since such a remark is not found in the parallels, it is possible that it has been added in the course of the transmission of the Pāli version, which in turn would suggest a felt need to endorse and empower this mode of presentation. The Pāli commentary in fact explicitly refutes the opinion that the guardians of hell do not really exist.[437]

Similar depictions of hellish torture occur in another discourse extant in Pāli, which has a parallel in Chinese, in addition to which parts of the presentation are also preserved in another discourse in Chinese and in a discourse quotation in Tibetan. The overall topic in the two main versions is the contrast between a foolish and a wise person. The former does evil and therefore must face dire retribution, including rebirth in hell, whereas the latter does good and therefore can look forward to pleasant rewards, including rebirth in heaven. A depiction of this contrast in the main Chinese version employs the motif of the six spheres of contact, already mentioned above, to designate both hell and heaven. The occurrence of this image invites exploring the relevant context provided in this version.

In the case of the heavenly outcome to be experienced by the wise for thinking, speaking, and acting in wholesome ways, rebirth in the good destiny called "six spheres of contact" involves of course entirely pleasant experiences.[438] Although it is not possible to describe this adequately, it can be illustrated with the example of the happiness experienced by a wheel-turning king. If the supreme delight experienced by a wheel-turning king is like a small pebble the size of a pea, then the happiness of a heavenly rebirth compares to mount Himālaya.

Conversely, rebirth in the hell similarly called "six spheres of contact" is of course entirely unpleasant.[439] The suffering experienced there can in turn be illustrated with the help of another simile, which describes a thief caught and punished by being stabbed repeatedly with spears. Once again, if the thief's suffering compares to a pebble, then the suffering of the hellish rebirth compares to mount Himālaya.

Although the coverage of heaven and hell correspond to each other in these ways, in the case of hell the Chinese discourse adds a detailed description of various tortures. This detailed description stands to some extent in contrast to the Buddha's explicit declaration: "Monastic, hell cannot be completely described, that is, the suffering in hell."[440] The whole purpose of the simile of the thief is precisely to stand in place of an actual description, in line with the pattern adopted for heaven. Yet, after the completion of the simile of the arrested thief, the Chinese discourse continues with a *description* of actual tortures in hell. It seems fair to allow for the possibility that this internal lack of coherence could result from an addition of the description of tortures in hell at some stage in textual development, even though such a description receives support from a comparative perspective, as it is also found in the full Pāli parallel and the partial Chinese parallel.[441] Without the hell tortures, which in this case throughout involve the guardians of hell inflicting cruel punishments,[442] the exposition on hell in this Chinese discourse would proceed in analogy to its coverage of heaven. Given that the parallel versions agree in depicting a series of earthly punishments inflicted by the local government on those who break the laws,[443] it would not take much for the precedent set in this way to stimulate a depiction of what are in several respects similar punishments inflicted by the guardians of hell in the afterlife.

The role of the guardians of hell in such depictions of various tortures can be illustrated with the help of figure 4 below, which shows two depictions from Borobodur, Java, both of which involve fire-related punishments.[444] In the first case, a guardian of hell throws evildoers into fire, whereas in the second case two guardians of hell make sure evildoers remain in a cauldron, where they are being boiled.

Figure 4. In the scene at left, a guardian of hell has taken hold of an evildoer by the throat and a leg to throw him head over heels into the fire, while at the same time giving a push with his left leg to another evildoer who is toppling into the same fire. A third evildoer is already suffering greatly due to the extreme heat, with his hands held together as if praying to be somehow relieved from his plight. The scene at right depicts the related punishment of being boiled alive, with five evildoers suffering in a cauldron heated over a fire. One of the five in the righthand scene, to the left, also holds his hands together as if praying to be relieved. The one next to him on the right has his mouth wide open as if shouting in agony while being pushed down into the cauldron by a guardian of hell who wields a club, ready to beat down anyone trying to escape. The other guardian of hell just watches, presumably ready to intervene should anyone try to escape.

Now, the overall concern behind references to hell in *Āgama* literature is karma, in particular by way of providing a spotlight on the repercussions of unwholesome ways of acting. The main point is to drive home the fact that, even though a delinquent may escape earthly punishment by the local government, punishment in the next world will inevitably occur. There is thus a bitter price to be paid for indulging in unwholesome behavior.

In the context of such a concern, it would be only natural if during oral performance the dire repercussions of unethical conduct come to be depicted in ever more graphic ways, as this will help ensure that the main lesson sinks in. Hence, stark images depicting revenge taken by those who have been harmed or imagery related to the smith's furnace come in handy. Yet, the net result of such attempts at enhancing the main message appears to have been the introduction of an element that conflicts with the Buddhist karma theory, precisely in relation to the central topic of the repercussions of intentionally undertaken unwholesome deeds. This takes the form of guardians of hell who intentionally inflict punishment in the form of excruciating suffering. How does this square with the very law of karma the whole depiction of rebirth in hell is meant to illustrate? Are these guardians of hell sentient beings?

A discourse extant in Chinese indicates that the guardians of hell are without kindness (*maitrī*) and are not human beings.[445] Yet, since they converse with their victims, they must be sentient in some way. If so, is it due to their previous karma that they now have such a role? Are their present cruel acts exempt from the law of karma or will they suffer karmic retribution for inflicting horrible punishments on others? In terms of the two scenes in figure 4, should there not be some karmic results for throwing others into fire or pushing them down into a boiling cauldron, ready to take more drastic measures with a club in hand if anyone should try to escape?

This problem has not escaped traditional exegesis, and a Pāli work reporting opinions debated among Buddhist schools, the *Kathāvatthu*, defends the position that the guardians of hell are real against those who think otherwise.[446] The *Abhidharmakośabhāṣya*, an influential treatise on Sarvāstivāda Abhidharma in the form of an auto-commentary by Vasubandhu, reports the argument that the guardians of hell are not real.[447] Besides the question of retribution for their deeds, another problem is how these guardians are able to move around amidst fire (at times walking over ground made of blazing iron) but are not burnt.[448] Such discussions confirm that the notion of guardians of hell who administer torture does not fit smoothly into the general framework of Buddhist ethics.

The difficulties that emerge in this way in turn align with the impression that the notion of hell guardians may be an outcome of literalism and narrative embellishment without sufficient consideration granted to the resulting problems. This would be in line with a fairly pervasive tendency in *Āgama* texts of such influences to precipitate consequences that are not in line with, or are even contrary to, the intended purposes (see also below p. 271).

The problem of a lack of doctrinal coherence offers needed support to the findings that emerge from a comparative study of relevant textual evidence surveyed above, the results of which are not as clear-cut as in the case of central dimensions of the evolution of the bodhisattva ideal, studied in the previous chapter. The development in conceptions of hell realms appears to have set in too early to leave distinct tracks of the type found, for example, in the case of the evidently late depiction of Śākyamuni's deeds in past lives leading to his present endowment with the thirty-two marks.

In the present case, the starting point for the apparent impact of literalism and narrative embellishment could perhaps have been the idea of contrasting heaven to hell in terms of the six spheres of contact. Just as these will be highly pleasant in the case of heaven, they will be thoroughly painful in the case of hell. Such a reference occurs together with a description of regret in the Chinese discourse contrasting fools to the wise, discussed above. This description of regret, found similarly in the Pāli parallel and in the partial Chinese parallel, concerns the earthly repercussions of unwholesome conduct, which manifest at a time when the evildoer is sick and in pain:[449]

> It is just as when in the late afternoon the sun goes down [behind] a tall mountain and its shadow hangs over the ground. In the same way, what evil bodily conduct, evil verbal and mental conduct the [culprit] has [done], that hangs over him at that time. He has this thought: "This is my evil bodily conduct, evil verbal and mental conduct hanging over me. In former times I have not done what is meritorious; I have done much evil."

The illustration conveys that being sick and in pain, perhaps on the verge of death, puts engaging in unwholesome actions into perspective. Whether these were motivated by a desire for power, for example, or for sensual gratification, all of these rationales break down in the face of death. Power will now have to be relinquished anyway, and sensual gratification is now out of reach. Once these motivational forces fall away and the fear of death manifests, the stark realization arises: "I have done much evil."

This depiction fulfills its function without any need for positing actual hell guardians that administer various tortures.

Needless to say, the above exploration is not to pretend that the notion of hell at some early point had no cosmological dimension at all; the point is only that this dimension need not have been formulated in as concrete and detailed a manner as it eventually was. Psychology and cosmology are closely interrelated in *Āgama* thought, and states of mind correspond to states of existence; hence, it would be quite natural for notions of hell to combine from the outset a psychological with a cosmological dimension.

Nevertheless, the textual evidence surveyed above, together with the doctrinal problems resulting from the motif of hell guardians, make it fair to assume that there has been a development in depictions of hell. It does not take much for the regret experienced by an evildoer to become personified in Yama, who reminds the culprits that they did witness the divine messengers, which should have served as a deterrent from evil conduct.[450] Along similar lines, it would also not take much for the idea of hell as a referent to six spheres of entirely unpleasant contact to be given a specific name such as "the Great Hell." This could still be reflecting a stage of conceiving of just a single hell, which van Put (2007, 205) considers the starting point for a subsequent multiplication of hells. In line with the same pattern of hell descriptions becoming more detailed and concrete, the imagination of the tortures to be experienced could gradually have become more detailed and concrete, eventually leading to the introduction of those who administer such tortures: the guardians of hell.

I need to emphasize that the above sketch is only hypothetical, as the textual evidence is suggestive but not conclusive. Nevertheless, at least as far as the notion of hell guardians administering tortures is concerned, it seems reasonable to consider their appearance to result from narrative embellishment without sufficient attention paid to the resulting doctrinal problems.

The development surveyed above in *Āgama* literature can to some extent also be related to *Prajñāpāramitā* literature, along the lines of its apparent, gradual expansion from eight thousand to twenty-five thousand and eventually to a hundred thousand lines. Lokakṣema's translation of the Perfection of Wisdom does not describe suffering in hell in a way that requires hell guardians who take the role of inflicting punishments, and it also does not envisage bodhisattvas being reborn in hell (at least as long as they do not dismiss the Perfection of Wisdom as something not taught by the Buddha). A shift in perspective emerges with later *Prajñāpāramitā* texts, which describe bodhisattvas willing to face even rebirth in hell for the purpose of saving sentient beings. Whereas in the *Pañcaviṃśatisāhasrikā Prajñāpāramitā* such a description just speaks of being in hell for as many eons as there are grains of sand in the Ganges, the corresponding indication in the *Śatasāhasrikā Prajñāpāramitā* concretizes the suffering experienced in hell by describing the undergoing of various tortures.[451] Although this description does not refer explicitly to the guardians of hell, the gradual increase in narrative detail evident in this way illustrates the type of development that can eventually result in the need for someone to inflict the described punishments on those who have ended up in hell.

Another perspective on the torments experienced in hell emerges in the *Prajñāpāramitā* commentary *Dà zhìdù lùn* (**Mahāprajñāpāramitopadeśa*), which reports that a bodhisattva, on seeing such suffering, will be even more determined to make a wholehearted effort to cultivate the six perfections in order to be able to deliver sentient beings from the type of ignorance that leads them to suffer in such rebirth destinies.[452] In addition to seeing such suffering—be it in meditation or in a dream—perhaps the same may also hold for hearing about it. From this perspective, then, vivid descriptions of hell tortures could serve not only to deter evildoers but also to inspire bodhisattvas.

## Summary

This chapter has covered the role of signs and their absence, which serves as a convenient backdrop to exploring an apparent tendency toward a literal interpretation of signs influencing the evolution of descriptions of suffering in hell and precipitating the eventual appearance of hell guardians who administer various tortures.

The potentially detrimental repercussions of grasping at signs, a concern shared by the Perfection of Wisdom and *Āgama* literature, can be illustrated with the example of partaking of poisoned food. Although the sign as such is needed for cognition and recognition—and in this function will still be present for a Buddha—the case of the unawakened mind taking up a sign usually comes inexorably intertwined with the impact of defilements. Even the simple apperception of a "river" that flows can easily lead to barely noticeable tendencies to reify this river, even though on close inspection no river can be found, as the sign "river" just refers to flowing water. In the arena of meditation, working with signs can progress from sense restraint to bare cognizing of sense data and then to the experience of signlessness. Such an experience can be described either as requiring nonattention to signs or else as involving attention paid to the absence of signs. Both descriptions refer to the same mental condition of being free from distraction and endowed with clarity but devoid of any processing of experience, that is, devoid of any cognizing that relies on a conceptual label. In this way, exploring signs and their absence highlights the need to avoid the poisoned food of indiscriminately taking up signs when abiding in the Perfection of Wisdom.

Rejecting the Perfection of Wisdom as not taught by the Buddha risks the dire retribution of rebirth in hell. Descriptions of hell in *Āgama* literature may have evolved from a relatively simple reference to the six spheres of contact being entirely unpleasant. Comparative study brings to light several instances in *Āgama* literature where imagery related to fire or burning iron balls seems to have been intended metaphorically but in the course of transmission has become a literal description of something that actually takes place.

Such apparent narrative embellishments appear to be responsible for the emergence of the notion of hell guardians, whose task is to inflict various punishments on culprits reborn in hell. Although this notion would have developed as part of an overarching concern to inculcate Buddhist ethics, its ramifications do not sit particularly well with the basic principle of karma and its retribution. The problem is that since these hell guardians function as if they were sentient beings and intentionally inflict cruel tortures on others, what about the karmic results of their deeds? The manifestation of this problem supports the in itself not conclusive textual evidence garnered through comparative study, yielding the impression that descriptions of hellish tortures in *Āgama* literature appear to be the result of some degree of development, influenced by a pervasive tendency toward literalism and narrative embellishment that in one way or another has impacted much of Buddhist literature.

# On Chapters 7 to 9

THE SEVENTH TO NINTH chapters of Lokakṣema's translation of the Perfection of Wisdom correspond to the ninth to eleventh chapters of the Sanskrit version translated by Conze (1973/1975, 149–71). The Buddha's teaching of the Perfection of Wisdom meets with acclaim from a host of celestials for amounting to turning the wheel of Dharma again, an acclaim the Buddha on the spot deconstructs through the rhetoric of emptiness. Having the good fortune of encountering the Perfection of Wisdom can be taken to reflect being already fairly advanced on the path to becoming a Buddha, in the sense that such bodhisattvas will soon receive a prediction of their future Buddhahood or else have already received it in a previous life. Still, obstacles created by Māra are to be expected, as he is ever set on obstructing those who dedicate themselves to progressing toward awakening and thereby to going beyond his realm of power. After the Buddha's final Nirvana, the Perfection of Wisdom will spread to various parts of India.

Two topics to be explored below are the turning of the wheel of Dharma and the role of Māra.

## Turning the Wheel of Dharma

The celestial acclaim of the Buddha's teaching of the Perfection of Wisdom as constituting a turning again of the wheel of Dharma meets with a short response by the Buddha, which he then expands in a more detailed manner. Below I translate both sections together, beginning with the actual acclaim:[453]

> All the celestials from the trichiliomegachiliocosm, who were flying above and observing it all, in turn raised their voices and together exclaimed: "On the grounds of Jambudvīpa we see again the turning of the wheel of Dharma."
>
> The Buddha said to Subhūti: "The wheel of Dharma is not being turned twice, and one should also not have the idea that there is a single turning of the wheel of Dharma. What does not turn, that is the Perfection of Wisdom."

> The Buddha said to Subhūti: "In emptiness there is nothing being turned [forward] and likewise no being turned backward, there is likewise no sign, likewise no aspiration, likewise no birth and death, likewise nothing from which to arise, and there exists likewise no turning [forward] and likewise no turning backward. One who speaks thus is teaching the Dharma."

The idea of investing a particular teaching with increased authority by borrowing from the phraseology employed in what tradition reckons to have been the first sermon given by the recently awakened Buddha can also be found in *Āgama* literature. The relevant reference occurs in a context clearly meant to forestall possible objections, which takes the form of detailing in what ways those who dare to contradict or refuse this teaching will incur censure. The statement in the respective Pāli discourse takes the following form: "The Dharma teaching [titled] 'The Great Forty' has been set rolling and cannot be rolled back by any recluse, brahmin, celestial, Māra, or Brahmā in the world."[454] The formulation of this passage clearly takes inspiration from the phrasing employed in the Pāli version of the Buddha's first sermon, even though it does not explicitly refer to a turning of the wheel of Dharma.[455] Counterparts to the above statement in Chinese and Tibetan, however, explicitly employ the wheel imagery, as they refer to what has been set rolling as the "wheel of Brahmā."[456] This further strengthens the relationship to the "wheel of Dharma" set in motion by the Buddha with his first teaching.

The count of forty in the title of the above discourse concerns the ten factors of the path of an arhat, which are right view, intention, speech, action, livelihood, effort, mindfulness, concentration, liberation, and knowledge (the last two occur in the opposite sequence in the Pāli version). These ten factors, together with the ten wholesome states resulting from them, stand in contrast to the ten wrong path factors, together with the resultant ten unwholesome states. The overall count of four sets of ten then makes up the "great forty." In other words, the teaching authenticated in this way concerns what in *Āgama* thought ranks as the highest accomplishment of wisdom possible for a disciple, namely the realization of full awakening by an arhat.

In this way, the present discourse employs imagery and phrasing from the Buddha's first sermon to authenticate and defend a teaching on the peak of wisdom that is anticipated to meet with contradiction and rejection. This proceeds in a way comparable to the claim in the passage translated above from the Perfection of Wisdom, in that its presentation of the supreme accomplishment in wisdom, similarly anticipated to encounter contradiction and rejection, can be considered to amount to turning the wheel of Dharma again.

The explicit reference in the extract translated above to seeing "again" a turning of the wheel implies that the text recognizes the priority of the first turning. It follows that an exploration of the narrative setting and content of the first turning of the wheel can help ascertain the significance of the notion that the wheel of Dharma is being turned again. The event of the first turning itself can be exemplified with figure 5 below, which shows the Buddha turning the wheel of Dharma.

According to the preceding narrative, after the recently awakened Buddha has decided to share his discovery (see the discussion above p. 74), he first thinks of sharing it with two teachers under whose guidance he had cultivated the immaterial spheres of nothingness and of neither-perception-nor-nonperception. Yet, this idea has to be discarded, as both had by then passed away. The relevant Pāli discourse and its Chinese parallel agree in reporting the Buddha's reflection that he had expected these two would have quickly understood what he had discovered.[457] This anticipation conveys the impression that, even though from an *Āgama* perspective the attainments of nothingness and of neither-perception-nor-nonperception are not considered as liberative in themselves, their

Figure 5. The Buddha has his hands in the teaching gesture and is flanked by a celestial on each side. The wheel beneath his seat serves to identify the teaching to be his first sermon, whereby he set in motion the wheel of Dharma. To the sides of the wheel are two antelopes, representing the location where the first sermon was given, and the five who were to become his first disciples, listening with their hands in the gesture of respect.

mastery can provide a convenient springboard for further progress to the realization of Nirvana, therefore warranting the assumption that these two teachers would have quickly understood.

Next, the Buddha decides to teach the five who were indeed to become his first disciples, though notably the texts no longer report any expectation that they will quickly understand. In the narrative setting, these five had attended on him when he engaged in asceticism and had left him in disgust when he gave it up. On his way to meet them, the Buddha has an encounter with a wanderer who at first seems quite impressed by the

Buddha's bearing and appearance. But when the Buddha proclaims his spiritual victory, this wanderer remains unconvinced and leaves.[458] This episode conveys quite clearly that a mere proclamation by the Buddha of his realization will not necessarily suffice to convince a prospective disciple.

In sum, according to the narrative frame, the Buddha has to find a way of communicating his discovery to his five former companions, who hold the view that liberation requires asceticism. Already the previous encounter with the wanderer has made it clear that mere claims will not be sufficient. In addition, there is also not as much common ground as there would have been with proponents of the immaterial spheres of nothingness and of neither-perception-nor-nonperception. Hence, a way needs to be found to communicate the extremely subtle nature of Nirvana in a situation not particularly favorable to this task.

The first part of what according to tradition became the first sermon spoken by the Buddha establishes the notion of a middle path aloof from not only sensuality but also asceticism, these two being extremes that are better avoided. This clarification would reflect the need to address the assumptions held by the audience, since the five were under the impression that Śākyamuni had reverted to sensual indulgence by giving up asceticism. That there could be another option, apart from these two opposite approaches, appears to have been novel to them.

With this much established, the actual teaching would in some way have to find common ground with the mindset of the five former companions, in order to lead them from that common ground to an understanding of what the Buddha had discovered. It seems to be in this narrative context that the employment of the scheme of four truths is probably best understood. The presentation as such appears to stem from an ancient Indian medical diagnostic scheme, probably known at least at a popular level.[459] This would presumably have been something familiar to the five, providing a starting point for articulating the common aim of finding a way to be free of the "disease" of *duḥkha*. The pragmatic approach of relying on medical diagnosis takes the form of identifying craving as the pathogen and the noble eightfold path as the cure, leading to the state of health of Nirvana. This mode of presentation met with success, as the different versions of the Buddha's first sermon agree in reporting that one of the five members of the audience realized stream-entry.[460] This realization appears to be the key requirement for a successful setting in motion of the wheel of Dharma—that is, the outcome of the teaching needs to be that someone in the audience realizes Nirvana.[461]

The realization of Nirvana is in turn also the key aspect of the teaching on the four noble truths.[462] This holds even for a more complex presentation that according to tradition was part of the Buddha's delivery of his first sermon, in the form of breaking down the four truths into twelve aspects. These result from proceeding though each truth according to a threefold pattern: every single truth needs to be understood, the particular activity it calls for needs to be undertaken, and that undertaking has to be brought to its successful conclusion. In the setting of ancient India, apparently teeming with various philosophies and views that at times were believed to be capable of bringing about purification by dint of being merely accepted,[463] an important point of this presentation is the clarification that something needs to be done. It is not enough to accept the four truths. Moreover, each truth calls for a specific activity, namely understanding (first truth), abandoning (second truth), realizing (third truth), and cultivating (fourth truth).

The actual breakthrough to Nirvana then corresponds to the activity of realizing, relevant to the third truth, along with which at the same time *duḥkha* will be fully understood (first truth), craving will be abandoned (second truth), and the path will have been successfully cultivated (fourth truth). In the case of the first breakthrough to Nirvana with stream-entry, these four dimensions have not yet been brought to their full completion, which will only be achieved with full awakening.

Although the chief concern of this teaching still seems to be to point to the single realization of Nirvana—be this communicated by way of four truths or by further analysis in the form of a twelvefold presentation—the complexity of this presentation could easily be read as conveying the idea of a series of distinct insights.[464] This is precisely the perspective adopted in Sarvāstivāda exegesis, which presents the realization of the four truths as involving a series of sixteen discrete moments, each offering its own distinct contribution to a realization of the four truths.[465]

The Perfection of Wisdom refers explicitly to the three modes and twelve aspects of turning the wheel of Dharma,[466] showing an awareness of this form of presentation. The *Pañcaviṃśatisāhasrikā Prajñāpāramitā* in turn provides further details in relation to the activities related to each truth. Notably, the activity related to the first truth takes the form of understanding not just *duḥkha* but its nonarising.[467] This thereby brings in the distinct perspective of the rhetoric of emptiness.[468] At the same time, this mode of presentation also confirms the suggestion made above (see p. 123) that references to nonarising are preferably not read literally. In the present case, a literal reading would conflict with the description of the ensuing second truth in the same text, which of course concerns the "arising" of *duḥkha*. In view of this indication, made in the *Pañcaviṃśatisāhasrikā Prajñāpāramitā* in keeping with the standard accounts of the first sermon, the previous reference to the nonarising of *duḥkha* is best understood as a strategy for countering any reification of *duḥkha*, rather than as implying that *duḥkha* does not arise at all.

The insight into the nonarising of *duḥkha* can then be taken to exemplify the specific *Prajñāpāramitā* perspective on the four truths, in line with the pervasive concern to encourage letting go of the seventh chariot so as to be able to enter the palace as the ultimate destiny of the relay of chariots. Attachment to the last of the seven chariots, however valuable it was for arriving close to the final goal, will prevent full arrival at that final goal.

From this perspective, then, several of the teachings in the Perfection of Wisdom could indeed be viewed as attempts to set the wheel of Dharma in full motion again, in the sense of clearing the path to the realization of awakening. Although the main concern has by now become awakening to Buddhahood, the same teaching is clearly seen as relevant to the traditional four levels of awakening,[469] including the first of these in the form of stream-entry, which formed the successful outcome of the Buddha's first turning of the wheel of Dharma.

The notion of turning the wheel of Dharma again can then be considered as finding its expression in teachings given in the Perfection of Wisdom that encourage a comprehensive application of emptiness without exempting any dharmas. Such an application comes together with a relentless emphasis on not taking a stance on anything. As a backdrop to this emphasis, there is a clear awareness of the problems involved in taking up signs as well as of the deluding nature of perception and the construction of experience. Other related topics, to be explored in subsequent chapters of my study, are an articulation of skill in means as a form of monitoring one's own progress and an approach to gaining omniscience that emphasizes seeing through anything rather than being concerned with seeing everything in all its details. Taken together, these rich perspectives promoted in the Perfection of Wisdom would indeed offer a substantial contribution to turning the wheel of Dharma.

## Māra

Māra has already made an appearance in earlier chapters, although it is only with the ninth chapter of Lokakṣema's translation that his misdeeds receive a detailed coverage. In this context, the Perfection of Wisdom reveals Māra to be at work behind a range of possible obstructions to the reception of its teachings. One example involves the recurrent theme of succumbing to the attraction of the paths to becoming an arhat or a Pratyekabuddha. The relevant passage illustrates the situation in this manner:[470]

> [The Buddha said:] "In this way, Subhūti, in the future there will be bodhisattvas who give up the profound Perfection of Wisdom, instead seeking for twigs and branches by means of pursuing the study of other teachings, and then falling to the level of the awakening of arhats and Pratyekabuddhas. It is as if a man apprehending an elephant examines [just] its feet. What do you think, Subhūti, is that man clever?"
>
> Subhūti said: "He is not clever."
>
> The Buddha said: "This bodhisattva who, being a virtuous person, becomes one among the two types of people [who aspire to become arhats or Pratyekabuddhas], gives up the profound Perfection of Wisdom and departs, studying instead other teachings to attain the awakening of arhats and

> Pratyekabuddhas—what do you think, Subhūti, is this bodhisattva clever?"
>
> Subhūti said: "He is not clever."
>
> The Buddha said: "In this way, one should realize that this is Māra's deed."

A reference to taking hold of just twigs occurs in *Āgama* literature in the context of a simile illustrating how someone goes forth but then settles for mundane gains or lower attainments rather than continuing the path all the way through to the final goal of full liberation. This compares to a person in need of heartwood who goes into the forest and cuts down a tree but then only takes its twigs rather than the heartwood.[471] Obviously, these will not serve the purpose of whatever that person was planning to make out of heartwood.

The idea of examining the foot of an elephant can be fleshed out with the help of other members of the *Aṣṭasāhasrikā Prajñāpāramitā* textual family, which indicate in various and complementary ways that the person in question was not able to see the elephant properly or that it was in the dark.[472] This gives the impression that the present case may be a partially preserved reference to the simile of the blind men and the elephant. This simile describes getting several blind men to touch different parts of an elephant.[473] When asked about the nature of an elephant, each gives a substantially different description, since one has touched the foot, another the tail, another the trunk, etc. Each of their perceptions were valid and based on direct personal experience, but due to their blindness they mistook their limited experience for the whole picture, believing that touching just a part of the elephant sufficed to arrive at a comprehensive assessment. If the above reference to examining the feet of an elephant should indeed be a remnant of this simile, its employment in the present context would be particularly apt. On this interpretation, the omniscient knowledge to be gained with the attainment of Buddhahood would correspond to a comprehensive vision of the whole elephant, whereas the awakening of an arhat or Pratyekabuddha is similar to taking hold of a part of an elephant, mistaking it to be the whole animal.

It appears to be precisely such a comprehensive vision by realizing Buddhahood that Māra, in the role he takes in the Perfection of Wisdom, wants to prevent at all costs. In his similarly obstructive tendencies in *Āgama* literature, it is rather the escape from *saṃsāra*—by dint of attaining arhat-ship as well as the three lower levels of awakening that eventually lead to the same transcendence of the cycle of births and deaths—that Māra quite definitely wants to obstruct. The shift of emphasis evident in the Perfection of Wisdom would reflect the repercussions to be expected from the teaching activities of a Buddha. This perspective emerges explicitly in another chapter, which reports that on two occasions Māra, on witnessing the sincere dedication of a bodhisattva, decides to intervene out of apprehension that this bodhisattva will liberate many others.[474] In this way, the path to becoming an arhat (or a Pratyekabuddha) becomes a lesser evil, when evaluated from the perspective of Māra, if in this way at least the progress of a bodhisattva on the path to Buddhahood can be thwarted.

Māra's obstructive role in much but not all of Buddhist literature—exceptions to which I will briefly mention at the end of this chapter—differs from Śakra and Brahmā. Whereas these two reflect a reinterpretation of already well-known protagonists of the Indian world of thought, Māra appears to have been something of a novelty in the same setting. Presumably as a result of this, he does not have a clear-cut place in ancient Indian cosmology, in the way this is reflected in *Āgama* literature. Śakra as the Buddhist version of Indra rules over the Heaven of the Thirty-Three, and the dominion of Brahmā(s) are of course the Brahmā worlds. Apparently for want of a cosmological realm of his own, Māra was eventually allocated to the outskirts of the sensual celestial realms.[475] He is indeed considered a celestial (*deva/devaputra*) rather than a hell being, and his concerns are mainly to keep others within the dominion of the sensual realms and thereby under the sway of his powers.

In addition to his actual appearance as a celestial being, *Āgama* literature also uses him in a symbolic manner to represent death and defilements, as well as to signify clinging to the aggregates. A proper appreciation of Māra requires keeping these alternative dimensions in view, in line with the basic interrelatedness in ancient Indian thought of the inner and the outer worlds, of psychology and cosmology.[476] It would not be appropriate to opt for only one of these two perspectives, such as his symbolic function, as the only relevant one. For example, when Māra challenges the Buddha or his fully awakened disciples, then this does not imply that such episodes reflect their inner uncertainties.[477] Instead, in these cases his role can reasonably be understood to represent challenges posed by outsiders, to which those being challenged then respond in a manner exemplifying how such a situation can best be faced.

One of many examples of the type of mischief for which Māra can be responsible in *Āgama* literature involves his attempts to distract a group of monastics intent on listening to a teaching given by the Buddha. To achieve this effect, Māra transforms himself into a bull and starts walking near the place where the monastics had left their bowls, thereby causing them to become apprehensive that the bull will break their bowls.[478] The Buddha, however, is quick to clarify that this is just a ruse of Māra. This solves the issue in a way that reflects a standard pattern. Comparable to something experienced in a bad dream that disappears on waking up, once Māra has been recognized, this spells his defeat, and he has to leave. Becoming distracted by looking left and right or else having a state of mind that is not focused also feature in the Perfection of Wisdom as being due to the influence of Māra.[479] Another of his ruses is to advocate the enjoyment of the five strands of celestial pleasures, found similarly in the Perfection of Wisdom and in *Āgama* literature.[480]

Other examples of Māra's devious deeds stand in closer relationship to the topic of insight into emptiness. *Āgama* literature reports him taking the role of advocating a reified notion of a sentient being, presumably both reflecting his own lack of insight into emptiness and his hope that he might confound those he has accosted. This hope, however, is quickly shattered, as he has twice made the mistake of trying to challenge highly realized nuns with such ideas. Both easily dispatch him. One of the two nuns does so by revealing that his query about a creator of bodily form reveals his lack of insight into conditionality, as bodily form is neither created by oneself nor by another.[481] The other nun clarifies that his questions regarding whence a sentient being has arisen and where it will go are utterly misconceived. They reveal his confused assumption of the actual existence of a sentient being, when all that is there are just empty aggregates. The position taken in this way seems to be quite in line with the teachings of the Perfection of Wisdom. This second nun then delivers the famous simile of the chariot to elucidate the situation.[482] A chariot is but an assembly of different parts. Just as a chariot is not an entity but something composite, in the same way there is no entity to be found in what is referred to as a sentient being. This simile, so dexterously devised by this nun, has become a lasting source of inspiration for later Buddhist traditions.[483]

A similar discomfiture awaits Māra when he advocates the belief, apparently not uncommon in the ancient Indian setting, that a woman is by nature incapable of reaching spiritual realization. Once again, he has made the mistake of trying to challenge a nun who has already reached realization. With the inner certitude of having attained precisely what Māra wants to call into question, this nun easily dismisses his silly ideas, clarifying that entering a meditative attainment has no relationship to having a female (or a male) body.[484] Hence, Māra would be better off talking to those who are still caught up in the concepts of being a "man" or a "woman." This reply also shares some similarities with the deconstruction strategies employed in the Perfection of Wisdom. It is noteworthy that this instance is the only passage in *Āgama* literature where the ability of women to reach spiritual perfection is openly questioned. In this single instance, such an idea features as a silly prank by Māra. More needs to be said on the topic of the position of women and their abilities to gain realization, however, a topic to which I will turn in more detail in a subsequent chapter (see below p. 203).

Regarding Māra's various misdeeds, the above survey exemplifies that his role in the Perfection of Wisdom stays close to its *Āgama* counterparts, except of course for his now central concern to obstruct bodhisattvas. In a later chapter of the Perfection of Wisdom, he even magically conjures up hells filled with large numbers of bodhisattvas in order to confuse and obstruct those who have dedicated themselves to the path to Buddhahood.[485] There seems to be no limit to the various ruses he may devise in order to prevent bodhisattvas from realizing the goal of their aspirations.

Although my exploration of various aspects of the Perfection of Wisdom proceeds predominantly from the viewpoint of relevant *Āgama* discourses, it may be of interest to cast a brief glance at further developments of the conception of Māra in other Mahāyāna *sūtras*. According to the *Saddharmapuṇḍarīka* (popularly referred to as the "Lotus sūtra"), Māra and his followers will be converted to the Buddhist fold under the future Buddha Raśmiprabhāsa.[486] A perhaps even more intriguing perspective emerges in another *sūtra* in the course of a teaching delivered by the eminent householder Vimalakīrti to the monk Mahākāśyapa. As an aside, I would like to note briefly that the role taken by Vimalakīrti in this way has a counterpart in the householder Citta, who in several discourses in *Āgama* literature delivers profound teachings to monks.[487] The development in the conception of Māra evident with Vimalakīrti's teaching takes the form of revealing that Māras should be recognized for being bodhisattvas, whose task is to mature sentient beings through their deployment of skill in means.[488]

## Summary

This chapter has covered the motif of turning the wheel of Dharma, which represents the success of the Buddha's teachings in enabling someone else to realize Nirvana, and the chief adversary to such teachings in the form of Māra.

The acclaim of the Buddha's teaching of the Perfection of Wisdom as amounting to turning again the wheel of Dharma implies a recognition of the first turning, which according to tradition occurred when the Buddha's first sermon resulted in one of his first five disciples becoming a stream-enterer. The teaching on the four noble truths in this sermon emerges in the narrative context as an ingenious way of communicating the realization of Nirvana, by way of relying on an ancient Indian scheme of medical diagnosis. Just as the diagnosis has as its focal point the regaining of health, so are the four noble truths centered on the realization of Nirvana.

The employment of the scheme of four truths appears to reflect the narrative context and the challenge of expressing in words what by its very nature is beyond language and concepts. Nevertheless, the complex presentation in the first sermon—applying three perspectives to each truth, resulting in a twelvefold scheme—can easily be read as implying a series of distinct insights.

The Perfection of Wisdom appears to attempt to clear the path toward the actual realization of awakening as the key aspect of turning the wheel of Dharma, although of course from the perspective of preferably leading to the awakening of Buddhahood. Several of the teachings in the Perfection of Wisdom seem to align with such a concern, especially the rhetoric of emptiness and the relentless emphasis on the need to avoid any reification by not taking a stance on anything.

In contrast to such teachings aimed at keeping the wheel of Dharma rolling, Māra throughout tries his very best to prevent precisely the progress of Buddhist disciples to liberation. He thereby continues his mischievous activities known from *Āgama* texts, with the difference that Māra's concerns in the Perfection of Wisdom are geared particularly toward obstructing bodhisattvas from reaching Buddhahood. Faced with the prospect of bodhisattvas delivering liberating teachings, once they have become Buddhas, Māra is compelled to intervene and do his best to prevent them from successfully reaching their aim. From his perspective, even an escape from his realm of power through the attainment of arhat-ship becomes a lesser evil, if in this way at least progress toward Buddhahood can be stalled. Conversely, this means that when a bodhisattva succumbs to the attraction of attaining arhat-ship, then this can be attributed to the work of Māra.

# On Chapters 10 to 15

THE TENTH TO FIFTEENTH chapters of Lokakṣema's translation of the Perfection of Wisdom correspond to the twelfth to seventeenth chapters of the Sanskrit version translated by Conze (1973/1975, 172–208). The Perfection of Wisdom emerges as the root of the Buddha's comprehensive knowledge. Among other aspects, this comprises full knowledge of the nature of the mental states that people experience. The Buddha's revelation of the nature of the Perfection of Wisdom as unfathomable by thought or calculations leads to various attainments among the audience; the same happens on a second occasion after an exposition on suchness. This second occasion also leads to a group of beginner bodhisattvas becoming arhats. Such an outcome will not happen in the case of irreversible bodhisattvas, who will also remain unperturbed by any of the tricks of Māra.

Two topics to be explored below are contemplation of mental states and progress toward awakening, the latter in relationship to the two reports of different levels of attainments reached when the Perfection of Wisdom was taught.

## The Nature of the Mind

The Buddha, here referred to as the Tathāgata, has a comprehensive knowledge of the mental states of others. The first part of the description of such knowledge shows similarities to the standard instructions in *Āgama* literature for the third establishment of mindfulness (*smṛtyupasthāna*), contemplation of mental states. The relevant passage in the Perfection of Wisdom proceeds as follows:[489]

> If someone has a lustful mental state, [the Tathāgata] knows it for being a lustful mental state; if someone has an angry mental state, he knows it for being an angry mental state; if someone has a deluded mental state, he knows it for being a deluded mental state. He knows that the lustful mental state is originally a mental state without lust; he knows that the angry mental state is originally a mental state without anger; he knows that the deluded mental state is originally a mental state without delusion. Subhūti, this is because I, [the Tathāgata], have attained omniscience with the Perfection of Wisdom.
>
> Why is that? Tathāgatas have mental states without lust. Due to having mental states without lust, they fully know that those mental states are originally also mental states without lust, the reason being that Tathāgatas have mental states without lust.
>
> Why is that? Tathāgatas have mental states without anger. Due to having mental states without anger, they fully know that those mental states are originally also mental states without anger, the reason being that Tathāgatas have mental states without anger.
>
> Why is that? Tathāgatas have mental states without delusion. Due to having mental states without delusion, they fully know that those mental states are originally also mental states without delusion, the reason being that Tathāgatas have mental states without delusion.
>
> In this way, Subhūti, Tathāgatas, arhats, Fully Awakened Ones, keep revealing it to the world by dint of the Perfection of Wisdom.

In the course of surveying other mental states,[490] the Buddha then notes that mental states themselves cannot be apprehended, explaining that this is so "because mental states are originally pure and devoid of signs."[491] The reference to being originally pure in this statement in Lokakṣema's translation does not recur in the parallel versions, as those that have a similar presentation only refer to the absence of signs.[492] Nevertheless, in the course of the same discussion the Sanskrit version does affirm that mental states are by nature luminous,[493] a term that often features as an alternative to being pure. In what follows I will first examine contemplation of mental states and then turn to the notion of an original purity or luminosity of the mind.

### *Contemplation of Mental States*

The description of contemplation of mental states in one of the two extant Chinese versions of the Discourse on the Four Establishments of Mindfulness (Pāli: *Satipaṭṭhānasutta*) offers the following instruction for the three mental states of sensual desire, anger, and delusion, which came up in the extract translated above from the Perfection of Wisdom:[494]

> What is the establishment of mindfulness by contemplating mental states as mental states? Having a mental state with sensual desire, monastics know, as it really is, that they have a mental state with sensual desire; having a mental state without sensual desire, they know, as it really is, that they have a mental state without sensual desire. Having a mental state with anger, without anger; having a mental state with delusion, without delusion . . .
>
> In this way monastics contemplate internal mental states as mental states, and they contemplate external mental states as mental states. They establish mindfulness in mental states and have knowledge, vision, understanding, and penetration. This is reckoned how monastics contemplate mental states as mental states. If a monk or a nun contemplates mental states as mental states in this way even for a short time, then this is reckoned the establishment of mindfulness by contemplating mental states as mental states.

The treatment of mental states being with or without anger and with or without delusion is abbreviated and should be completed in line with the full text given for the case of mental states with or without sensual desire. In each of these instances, practitioners need to recognize the condition of the mental state "as it really is." The passage qualifies the practitioner as being a monastic, which is best understood to be exemplifying the lifestyle that in the ancient setting was considered most conducive to such practice. *Āgama* literature explicitly refers to lay practitioners of the four establishments of mindfulness (*smṛtyupasthāna*), thereby making it clear that the qualification in the above instruction of the practitioner as a monastic is not meant to restrict the instructions to those who have received ordination.[495]

The distinction made in the second paragraph of the above passage between internal and external modalities of the four establishments of mindfulness is a recurrent one in *Āgama* literature. The main implication appears to be that practitioners should cultivate mindfulness not only of themselves but also of others.[496] This is the sense relevant for contemplation of mental states according to an early work of the Pāli Abhidharma collection.[497] The presentation in this text is particularly significant, as it testifies to a stage in the evolution of descriptions of the four establishments of mindfulness earlier than the corresponding Pāli discourses, which seem to have continued to evolve subsequent to the stage of finalization of the relevant part in this early Abhidharma work.

Such evolution appears to be responsible for introducing some degree of ambiguity or uncertainty regarding the significance of the distinction between internal and external mindfulness practice. One relevant addition to descriptions of the first establishment of mindfulness in *Āgama* literature involves an extract of the first few steps from a scheme of sixteen steps of mindfulness of breathing.[498] This incorporation of just an extract from the full scheme forms part of a gradual reduction of rather sophisticated and remarkably efficient instructions on the cultivation of mindfulness of breathing to eventually becoming just a focus on the touch sensation caused by the inhalations and exhalations (see also below p. 234). Of particular relevance for my present concerns is the circumstance that the addition of the first few steps from this scheme to the first establishment of mindfulness involves a practice for which the distinction between internal and external no longer makes practical sense. Unlike being mindful of one's own breathing, to do the same in relation to the breaths of another hardly provides a similarly straightforward, practicable option.

Another relevant addition, this time to the fourth establishment of mindfulness, concerns the six senses and their objects.[499] This brings in a different sense of externality and thereby further complicates the basic idea of cultivating mindfulness either in relation to oneself or else in relation to another. As a result of such developments, exegetical traditions came up with a range of different interpretations of this basic distinction between mindfulness cultivated internally and externally.

In the case of contemplation of the mind, envisaging such practice undertaken by the Buddha is of course unproblematic, as he has telepathic powers. This must stand in the background to the above indication in the Perfection of Wisdom that the Tathāgata knows if someone else has a particular mental state. However, the same is also within range, albeit to a lesser degree, of the average practitioner who does not possess telepathic powers. Another person's facial expression, gestures, tone of voice, and physical movements can provide the needed information. In fact, the ability to detect another's emotional state of mind is learned at an early stage in human development.[500] Although of course not as precise as the telepathic abilities of a Buddha, this much can nevertheless be relied on to develop an external cultivation of mindfulness, which in the extract from the Perfection of Wisdom covers the presence of lust, anger, and delusion.

Whereas this extract concerns more specifically the Tathāgata, that is, the Buddha, an instruction on the cultivation of the four establishments of mindfulness to be undertaken by bodhisattvas in general can be found in the *Pañcaviṃśatisāhasrikā Prajñāpāramitā*. The relevant exposition unfortunately presents the second to fourth establishments only in abbreviation, but at least the first establishment of contemplating the body receives a detailed exposition. What characterizes the relevant instructions, when compared to their *Āgama* counterpart, is the recurrent emphasis on the importance of being equipped with nonapprehension (*anupalambhayoga*).[501] That is, the otherwise similar indications regarding how to cultivate any of the exercises pertaining to the first establishment of mindfulness, and thus by implication also those of the other three establishments, become a cultivation of the Perfection of Wisdom if the practitioner keeps to nonapprehension, avoiding any reification in relation to what is being contemplated. This appears to be part of a general pattern,[502] described by Deleanu (2000, 69) as follows:

> [T]raditional Śrāvakayāna meditative practices . . . are reinterpreted in the light of the Prajñāpāramitā relativism, with special emphasis on the idea of practising without a support . . . the main innovative effort of this trend was not directed towards the creation of new meditative techniques. Its chief contribution rather appears to lie in a new hermeneutic approach towards the spiritual cultivation. The most important point here is not what a *bodhisattva* practises, and usually he works with traditional methods and categories, but how he practises, to be more precise, how he practices without practising.

A passage relevant to the present exploration occurs in the **Pratyutpanna-samādhisūtra*, another early Mahāyāna text that was apparently translated by the same team and in tandem with the Perfection of Wisdom, as both were reportedly completed at the same time.[503] The **Pratyutpanna-samādhisūtra* also shares with the Perfection of Wisdom that some parts of its exposition are extant in a Gāndhārī manuscript belonging to the Split Collection,[504] and in both cases the originals used for translation were recited or read out by the same Indian monk.[505]

The version of the **Pratyutpannasamādhisūtra* attributed to Lokakṣema offers brief instructions on each of the four establishments of mindfulness. For the case of contemplation of the mind, the relevant instruction distinguishes between contemplation of one's own mind and that of others—the formulation used in the Chinese passage clearly corroborates the above proposed understanding of external mindfulness practice—and then indicates that with both modalities the practitioner should have a clear awareness that any such state of mind originally lacks [an intrinsic nature of] the mind.[506] The phrasing used here is literally "originally not" or a bit less literally "from the beginning nonexistent" (本無). In the course of a survey of Lokakṣema's employment of this phrase in the Perfection of Wisdom, Karashima (2010, 29) notes that it can also form the counterpart to references in the Sanskrit version to "suchness" (*tathatā*) and "not otherwiseness" (*avitathatā*), whereby it takes a more affirmative nuance. The main point in the present context would presumably reflect the overarching concern to debunk the positing of an intrinsic nature, *svabhāva*.

On this understanding, perhaps the instructions in the *Pañcaviṃśatisāhasrikā Prajñāpāramitā* and the **Pratyutpannasamādhisūtra* can be read as complementing each other, together pointing to the basic challenge of avoiding any reification. This calls for being "equipped with nonapprehension," in the realization that whatever is being contemplated lacks an intrinsic nature. This would then be the decisive perspective a bodhisattva should keep in mind when cultivating contemplation of the mind or any of the other establishments of mindfulness. The basic practice appears to remain the same, with the additional requirement that for such contemplation to become part of a cultivation of the Perfection of Wisdom, the practitioner needs to avoid any reification.

### *The Mind's Original Purity*

The passage from the Perfection of Wisdom translated at the outset of the present chapter proceeds from the distinction between defiled and undefiled mental states to the affirmation that these mental states are originally without defilement. A subsequent part then refers to the notion that the mind is originally pure (alternatively also qualified as luminous in some other texts).

The notion of a luminosity of the mind can already be found in *Āgama* literature, although such instances are not supported by parallels. Elsewhere I have studied the relevant passages and developments in detail,[507] which allows me to present here just in brief what is actually a rather complex matter. The basic trajectory at work appears to be a fascination with imagery related to light and fire in some reciter lineages of the discourses belonging to *Āgama* literature, particularly in the Dharmaguptaka and Theravāda traditions. Such fascination builds on common ground among different reciter lineages in recognizing inner experiences of luminosity as the outcome of concentrative practices. These experiences have their cosmological counterpart in the luminosity of celestial beings dwelling in those heavenly realms that correspond to the meditative states gained through cultivating higher levels of concentration.

The further development of this common ground in the Dharmaguptaka and Theravāda reciter traditions can be exemplified with a portrayal of the Buddha as actually emanating fire. Whereas one such case in a Pāli discourse just indicates that the Buddha had attained the fire element, another case, found in a different Pāli discourse, specifies that, having attained the fire element, he emanated a flame as high as seven palm trees. In both cases, the presentation in the respective Pāli discourse does not receive support from the parallel versions.[508] Another relevant instance occurs in the *Dīrghāgama* extant in Chinese—a collection that appears to have been transmitted by Dharmaguptaka reciters—in the form of a report that the Buddha entered meditation on fire while seated in a cave, as a result of which the whole mountain appeared to be on fire.[509] In this case, too, the parallels do not relate such an effect to the Buddha's meditation practice. Yet another case concerns the Buddha's footprint, which according to a Gāndhārī manuscript version of the discourse in question was endowed with luminescence, a presentation that is without support from the parallels.[510] A similar application of luminescence to a footprint can be found in another *Dīrghāgama* discourse in relation to the former Buddha Vipaśyin.[511]

A Pāli discourse with no known parallel indicates that the Buddha's body becomes more luminous as a result of his meditation practice.[512] Other instances in Pāli discourses involve qualifying a particular level of equanimity or else a cultivated state of mind as luminous, a presentation not supported by the parallels.[513]

The above examples set the background for appreciating a reference to the luminous mind in a Pāli discourse that appears to have been particularly influential in later times.[514] Although this discourse has no known parallel, a quotation in an Abhidharma work probably belonging to the Dharmaguptaka tradition offers a similar presentation, differing in using the qualification "pure" instead of "luminous."[515] The attraction exerted by this type of presentation appears to be largely due to an embedding of the notion of the luminous or pure mind in a context that speaks of adventitious defilements being either present or absent. This combination appears to have served as a fertile ground for the emergence and spread of the idea that the mind is by nature luminous or pure.

From the viewpoint of *Āgama* thought as reflected in other discourses, however, to speak of any defilement as "adventitious" (*āgantuka*) is problematic, since defilements do not exist somewhere independently and then come to invade the mind. This relates to a point repeatedly made in the Perfection of Wisdom, in that defilements or other states of mind do not arise from somewhere and on ceasing do not proceed toward somewhere.

Moreover, the idea that the mind is originally pure does not sit easily with the explicit indication in *Āgama* literature that there is no beginning point discernible for sentient beings faring on under the influence of craving for existence.[516] In other words, this type of text does not envisage purifying the mind as involving a return to an original condition but rather sees it as a departure from an original condition, since the mind has been defiled all along. In this respect the *Āgama* perspective differs from the later part of the passage in the Perfection of Wisdom on the Tathāgata's knowledge of mental states.

What underpins the *Āgama* instructions for mindful contemplation of mental states from the viewpoint of their defiled or undefiled condition is conditionality. The distinction between being defiled and undefiled calls for a clear recognition of the operation of conditionality in the present, without requiring an original state of purity to explain why the mind can in principle be free from defilements. Such freedom simply occurs when the conditions for defiling the mind are not operating, without any need for a precedent from the distant past.

The position taken in this way could be illustrated with the example of fruit ripening on a tree. There is no need to postulate the ripe fruit as having existed in some way in the corresponding blossom that earlier grew on the tree. Nor is there a need to postulate the next tree as already existing in the seed now found inside of the fruit. All that is needed for explaining the growth of the fruit from the blossom, and the seed of that fruit subsequently leading to the growth of another tree with its blossoms and fruits, is conditionality.

Nevertheless, and this may well be a rationale underpinning some depictions of the mind as originally pure or luminous, the undefiled condition can easily be experienced as more natural. In fact, the passage from the Perfection of Wisdom explicitly indicates—in relation to the third defilement of delusion, for example—that "Tathāgatas have mental states without delusion. Due to having mental states without delusion, they fully know that those mental states are originally also mental states without delusion." From a practical viewpoint, this provides a powerful incentive for bodhisattvas to emulate the Buddha's example by striving to emerge from being overwhelmed by delusion (or other defilements). The Buddha's example not only inspires but also confirms that it is indeed possible to be free from delusion.

From the perspective of a practitioner of the Perfection of Wisdom, perhaps the divergent *Āgama* position of conceiving of a purification of the mind without positing an originally pure and luminous condition can still be read in a meaningful way. In keeping with the basic trajectory of the Perfection of Wisdom, this indication could be read as an encouragement that any experience of mental purity or luminosity should not be allowed to give rise to attachment or reification, given that what really matters in the end is progress toward supreme liberation of the mind through awakening to Buddhahood.

## Progress toward Awakening

Progress toward liberation is in turn the topic that will occupy me for the remainder of this chapter. The first of two instances reporting the occurrence of liberating attainments among the audience listening to the Buddha expound the Perfection of Wisdom proceeds as follows:[517]

> When the Buddha spoke this teaching, five hundred monks in the community and twenty nuns all attained arhat-ship. Sixty male lay disciples and thirty female lay disciples all attained the awakening of stream-entry. Twenty bodhisattvas all reached the patient acceptance of the nonarising of dharmas; they will all receive their prediction in this auspicious eon.

The description given in this way clearly shows that references elsewhere in the Perfection of Wisdom to its transformative potential being relevant also for those on the path to arhat-ship should be taken seriously. The two reports of attainment found in the text, the second of which I will take up below, include both stream-entry and arhat-ship. In this way, becoming an arhat or else progress toward Buddhahood are seen from the perspective of the Perfection of Wisdom as alternative outcomes of its teachings, with the latter of course featuring as the superior option. The relevance in general of such an element of continuity has already been highlighted by Ruegg (2004, 8), who notes that in Buddhist texts in general "*arhant*—alongside *bhagavant* and *samyaksambuddha*—is a regular and altogether standard epithet of a *buddha*."[518] This goes to show that "it cannot correctly be held that, in all circumstances, the ideal of Arhatship is antithetically opposed to (and even contradictory with) that of bodhisattvahood or buddhahood." Another relevant observation offered by Nattier (2000, 94n68) takes the following form:

> Much confusion has been created by the widespread practice of interpreting all negative comments found in Mahāyāna sources about "falling to the level of the *śrāvaka*s and *pratyekabuddhas*" (to use the wording found in the *Aṣṭasāhasrikā*) as if they were criticisms directed toward a competing Buddhist school. On the contrary . . . they are better understood as the exhortations of a professor to a Ph.D. student not to take a terminal M.A. degree and be done with it, but to strive to complete the much more demanding doctoral degree, at which point the student (having become a professor) can then teach others, leading them to the attainment of the (admittedly lower) B.A. and M.A. degrees.

The apt comparison with university degrees illustrates the main point behind the emphasis on the superiority of the path to Buddhahood, which as yet has not totally eclipsed the alternative paths to arhat-ship and Pratyekabuddhahood.

In addition to providing a clarification regarding the potential of the Perfection of Wisdom for progress toward stream-entry or arhat-ship, the above attainment report states that bodhisattvas gained the patient acceptance of the nonarising of dharmas (*anutpattikadharmakṣānti*).[519] The present passage already implies that such patience marks a mature stage in progress toward Buddhahood, as all the bodhisattvas who have gained this type of decisive realization are bound to receive their prediction within this same eon.

In what follows, I will examine the notion of patience as a mature stage of insight in some *Āgama* discourses and then turn to another attainment report, according to which a teaching on suchness led to some bodhisattvas rather becoming arhats. Then I take up the motif of the Pratyekabuddha as a supposedly viable alternative to becoming either an arhat or a Buddha. In the final part of this chapter, I explore the notion that a bodhisattva is by nature superior to other practitioners, even when these have reached various stages of awakening.

### *Patience*

The notion of a form of patience as a token of maturing practice has a counterpart in *Āgama* literature. A Pāli discourse with no known parallel indicates that seeing Nirvana as *duḥkha* will prevent a practitioner from having the type of patience required for being able to attain any of the four levels of awakening. The opposite case of seeing Nirvana as happiness proceeds as follows:[520]

> It is possible that one who considers Nirvana to be happiness will be endowed with patience in conformity (*anuloma*). It is possible that one who is endowed with patience in conformity will enter upon the fixed course of rightness. It is possible that one who enters upon the fixed course of rightness will realize the fruit of stream-entry, the fruit of once-return, the fruit of nonreturn, or arhat-ship.

Viewing Nirvana (which is of course free from any arising) as productive of happiness results in a type of patience qualified as being in conformity. This type of patience in turn forms the necessary condition for progress toward the realization of Nirvana with the attainment of stream-entry or higher levels of awakening.[521]

The implications of patience that is in conformity can be explored with the help of a Pāli exegetical work, the *Paṭisambhidāmagga*, which explains that the patience described in this discourse calls for conformity with insight. In relation to the five aggregates, such conformity can occur when seeing the aggregates to be, for example, void, vain, empty, not self, and without an essence.[522] Each of these perspectives, on being applied to the aggregates—representative of central dimensions of subjective experience—can lead to the type of patience or acceptance that facilitates the breakthrough to Nirvana.

The Pāli terms corresponding to the qualifications of being void, vain, and without an essence recur in a Pāli discourse that takes the nature of these five aggregates as its main topic.[523] That each of these five is void, vain, and without an essence finds expression in a series of similes, found similarly in parallel versions extant in Chinese and Tibetan. The first aggregate of bodily form compares to a lump of foam carried away by a river, feeling tones are like bubbles on the surface of water during rain, perception is similar to a mirage, volitional formations are comparable to a plantain tree (which has no heartwood), and consciousness is like an illusion created by a magician.

These similes bring out the implications of the insight perspectives that can lead to being endowed with patience that is in conformity. In other words, such patience could result from accepting the following perspectives: The body is indeed just as brittle and unstable as a lump of foam, carried away by the river of impermanence. What is subjectively felt as a crucially important distinction between what is pleasant and what is unpleasant, with its repercussions leading to likes and dislikes, turns out to be just as fleeting as water bubbles arising and quickly vanishing again. The way the world is perceived, although subjectively taken to be an accurate reflection of reality, tends to be rather like a mirage. The ability to take decisions and exert control, however solid and essential this may seem from the viewpoint of the one who feels in charge, lacks any true core, just as a plantain tree has no heartwood. Identification with consciousness is so deeply ingrained, yet it is just a magic trick. Accepting these perspectives could well be expected to correlate to an attitude of patience that in turn will set the stage for progress toward liberation.

It is noteworthy that the type of patience that is in conformity can stand in a close relationship to insight into emptiness, which appears to be a central theme underlying the above similes. Insight into emptiness is also central for the type of patience required of a bodhisattva, namely the patient acceptance of the nonarising of dharmas (*anutpattikadharmakṣānti*). In relation to the same term used in another translation by Lokakṣema, Harrison (1998a, 106) explains that this type of patience stands for "a decisive realisation by the bodhisattva of the emptiness of all dharmas, i.e., the absence of inherent existence in them."

The requirement of a form of patience resulting from maturing insight into emptiness—be it in the form of seeing the five aggregates as void, vain, and without an essence or else in the form of accepting that phenomena are not entities for which an arising from somewhere can be predicated—points to some degree of similarity between the path to stream-entry and the notion of having become an irreversible bodhisattva.[524] This apparent similarity finds confirmation in a statement in the Perfection of Wisdom that compares the certainty of being an irreversible bodhisattva to the certainty of someone who has gained stream-entry.[525] Just as an irreversible bodhisattva is called such because of being definitely destined to become a Buddha, in a similar way one who has gained stream-entry is definitely destined to become an arhat; both are unable to fall away anymore and are certain to reach the respective attainment. The same even holds for someone on the path to stream-entry, as several Pāli discourses explicitly highlight that such a practitioner is unable to pass away without having realized stream-entry.[526]

In terms of future lives, those who have reached stream-entry are in turn certain to be free from the prospect of rebirth in hell or in any other lower realm.[527] This has a counterpart in the position taken in the Perfection of Wisdom that advanced bodhisattvas will also no longer be reborn in hell or in any other lower realm.[528] In sum, the above shows some intriguing similarities between mature practice of the path to Buddhahood and mature practice of the path to the traditional levels of awakening. This in turn raises the question whether a possible direction of influence can be discerned. Since the path to stream-entry is known in *Āgama* literature and in the Perfection of Wisdom, whereas the path to Buddhahood features only in the latter, it would be reasonable to assume that, if there has been an influence of one of these two path conceptions on the other, then the depiction of the path to stream-entry could have provided a template for the developing conceptions of the path to Buddhahood.

### *A Teaching on Suchness*

The second report of attainments in the Perfection of Wisdom offers the following information about the outcome of the teaching that had just been given:[529]

> At the time when suchness was being taught, two hundred monks in the community all attained arhat-ship, five hundred nuns all attained the awakening of stream-entry, five hundred celestials all attained the patient acceptance of the nonarising of dharmas, becoming established therein. Sixty beginner bodhisattvas all attained the awakening of arhat-ship.
>
> The Buddha said: "During their past lives, these sixty bodhisattvas each worshipped five hundred Buddhas, their giving was in quest of material [benefits], their upholding of morality, their patience, and their energy was in quest of material [benefits], their meditation bereft of an understanding of emptiness, being apart from emptiness. They did not gain the Perfection of Wisdom and skill in means.

The term "suchness" (*tathatā*) already features in *Āgama* literature, where it can serve as a designation for the principle of dependent arising (*pratītya samutpāda*).[530] Ñāṇananda (2015, 87) explains that here "*tathatā* asserts the validity of the law of dependent arising, as a norm in accordance with nature." Another discourse indicates that seeing dependent arising equals seeing the Dharma.[531] This would implicitly place this particular notion of suchness right at the center of a penetrative understanding of the teachings of the Buddha as recorded in *Āgama* texts.

A similarly central position emerges in the statement in the Perfection of Wisdom that "a bodhisattva who attains true suchness is named a Tathāgata,"[532] a statement of such importance that it is followed by six earthquakes. One of several functions of the occurrence of earthquakes in Buddhist literature, which fortunately do not result in any damage, is to express approbation.[533] This function must be the one relevant to the present case.

*Āgama* literature conveys the impression that the term *tathāgata* was in general use in the ancient Indian setting to designate someone who had reached the acme of spiritual perfection. They also show the Buddha to have preferred using this term when referring to himself. Although in principle the term *tathāgata* can just designate an arhat, this meaning would not be relevant to the above statement in the Perfection of Wisdom, which must rather be intending a Buddha. This relates true suchness to the final goal of a bodhisattva's path.

The description in the Perfection of Wisdom of the repercussions of the exposition on suchness comes with an imbalance already evident in the report of the earlier occasion resulting in attainments: in both cases women do not match men. In the first case, arhat-ship is realized by five hundred monks but only by twenty nuns, and stream-entry by sixty male lay disciples but only by thirty female lay disciples. In the present case, although the five hundred nuns exceed the number of monks, who are only two hundred, these two hundred attain arhat-ship whereas the five hundred nuns only attain stream-entry. I will return to the topic of this type of imbalance, which seems to place the abilities of women at a lower level than that of men, in my next chapter (see below p. 203).

Particularly noteworthy in the passage translated above is the reference to beginner bodhisattvas, literally bodhisattvas who are "newly training," who instead become arhats. In a part of the text that I have not translated above, the Buddha explains that these sixty are comparable to a large bird without wings: when it tries to fly, it will just fall down.[534] According to an interpretation of this simile offered by Vetter (2003, 66), the largeness of the bird represents the acquired merits, the lack of wings exemplifies the lack of training in *prajñāpāramitā* and skill in means (*upāyakauśalya*, a topic I will explore in a subsequent chapter; see below p. 210), the attempted flight corresponds to hearing a teaching like the present one on suchness, and falling down of course takes the form of attaining arhat-ship.

The illustration starkly exemplifies the predicament of having lost the path to Buddhahood. The circumstance that these sixty bodhisattvas attained arhat-ship rather than just becoming stream-enterers, for example, should presumably be attributed to the merits they had accumulated by worshipping five hundred Buddhas in their past lives. Elsewhere the Perfection of Wisdom does envisage bodhisattvas just becoming stream-enterers, which features among various misdeeds of Māra.[535] In the present case, despite such a formidable accumulation of merits, they were still beginners and had not gained the Perfection of Wisdom. In this way, even though some degree of the Perfection of Wisdom is required even for those on the path to arhat-ship—and in the present case an exposition on its key teaching on suchness precisely leads to such attainment—at the same time its full comprehension remains the sole domain of those firmly on the path to Buddhahood.

### *Pratyekabuddhas*

The above description of attainments concords with another passage in the Perfection of Wisdom, which similarly points out that, due to lacking the sixth perfection and skill in means, bodhisattvas will fall to the level of arhats and Pratyekabuddhas; this will not happen if they are endowed with these two qualities.[536]

Although such dangers are a recurrent theme in the Perfection of Wisdom, the second report of attainments, translated above, exemplifies that such a fall to a lower level can result in becoming an arhat (or one on the path to arhat-ship, such as a stream-entrant, etc.), whereas the option of becoming a Pratyekabuddha is not relevant at a time when a Buddha has arisen or even when his teachings are still available. The Perfection of Wisdom thereby shares a feature with Pāli discourses and their parallels (leaving aside the *Ekottarikāgama*), in that the Pratyekabuddha features more as a theoretical possibility than an actual option. In *Āgama* literature, this concerns mainly hierarchical listings of meritorious recipients of offerings, where the Pratyekabuddha ranks below the Buddha but above an arhat (I will return to this ranking in the next section of this chapter).[537]

In the absence of a living Buddha, a Pratyekabuddha then becomes the topmost recipient of gifts.

References to Pratyekabuddhas tend to become more frequent in the Pāli *Jātaka* collection as well as in the *Ekottarikāgama* extant in Chinese translation. The latter in fact abounds in tales and references to Pratyekabuddhas, many of which lack parallels in other discourse collections.[538] Such references even comprise instances of actual predictions that someone in the distant future will become a Pratyekabuddha.[539] This makes the option of the path to Pratyekabuddhahood come more alive.

A relevant instance that does have parallels concerns an invitation by the Buddha that, in view of his advanced age, Mahākāśyapa may give up his ascetic conduct and adopt a less stringent lifestyle. The *Ekottarikāgama* has in fact two versions of this episode. One of these brings in the notion of Pratyekabuddhahood, which is not found in the other *Ekottarikāgama* version or in parallels extant in Pāli and other Chinese *Āgama* collections.[540] The discourse as such shows the impact of later developments, evident in a reference to the three *yāna*s.[541] According to this *Ekottarikāgama* discourse, Mahākāśyapa's reply took the following form:[542] "I will not follow the Tathāgata's injunction now. The reason is that if the Tathāgata had not accomplished supreme, complete awakening, I would have accomplished Pratyekabuddhahood."

This statement implies that Mahākāśyapa's abilities and accumulation of merits had reached such a level of maturity that, even if Śākyamuni had not become a Buddha, Mahākāśyapa would still have become a fully awakened one. Rather than becoming an arhat disciple of the Buddha Śākyamuni, he would have become a Pratyekabuddha. This thereby combines in the figure of Mahākāśyapa what a bodhisattva should avoid at all costs, namely becoming either an arhat or else a Pratyekabuddha.

The various references in the *Ekottarikāgama* convey the impression that, at least for some time, the motif of the Pratyekabuddha did carry some practical relevance. In an attempt to explore the possible reasons for this presumably only brief period of actual significance, it may be relevant that the motif of the Pratyekabuddha embodies the possibility of gaining awakening at a time when a Buddha is not in existence and his teachings have disappeared.[543] Such a motif could have acquired increasing significance after the Buddha Śākyamuni's demise, when his followers were struggling to ensure the survival of his teachings in the face of various hardships and the ongoing competition with other religious traditions in the ancient Indian setting. In this context, the Pratyekabuddha motif may have provided a sense of reassurance. Even if the teachings of the Buddha Śākyamuni and the monastic lineage he had started were to disappear completely, it would still be possible to reach awakening, and those who wished to gain merits by making offerings and performing acts of worship would still stand a chance of encountering worthy human recipients in such Pratyekabuddhas.

This appears to be precisely what the Mahākāśyapa episode communicates, namely that he would nonetheless have reached full awakening and become a highly meritorious recipient of offerings and worship. From this perspective, Śākyamuni's attainment of Buddhahood is no longer as decisive a matter as one may have otherwise thought, as it only makes a difference regarding what type of full awakening Mahākāśyapa reached: due to encountering the Buddha, he became an arhat instead of a Pratyekabuddha.

With the emergence of the bodhisattva ideal, however, the aspiration to become a Pratyekabuddha would soon have lost whatever attraction it may have held earlier, if this is indeed the implication of the above passages. Although the limitations of the textual evidence, in particular in the case of the *Ekottarikāgama*, make it impossible to draw a firm conclusion, it seems at least possible that the motif of the Pratyekabuddha enjoyed a short period of popularity, situated in between the Buddha's final Nirvana and the gaining of traction of the bodhisattva path. Such a short period of popularity would explain why texts like the Perfection of Wisdom continue to refer to the option of becoming a Pratyekabuddha as if this were indeed a valid alternative to the aspiration for Buddhahood, one that is to be taken as seriously as the alternative possibility of becoming an arhat.

### *The Superiority of Bodhisattvas*

The standard model in *Āgama* literature of progress through the four levels of awakening involves altogether eight stages. This presentation does not exclude the possibility that a particularly gifted practitioner, endowed with the required accumulation of merits, may proceed directly to becoming an arhat. Unlike such exceptional cases of *sudden* attainments, however, in the more ordinary case attaining the final goal involves a *gradual* progress that can be expressed with the help of the following eight levels:

1. path to stream-entry
2. stream-entry
3. path to once-return
4. once-return
5. path to nonreturn
6. nonreturn
7. path to arhat-ship
8. arhat-ship

Due to the progressively higher degree of spiritual maturation reached with each stage, these eight levels feature in listings of increasingly meritorious recipients of gifts. Out of these eight, the arhat naturally figures as foremost in this respect. Such listings also tend to incorporate references to those who are even superior in merit, which are a Pratyekabuddha and, even better than that, a Buddha. The final two no longer stand in a practical relationship to the previous eight, as becoming a Pratyekabuddha or a Buddha takes place apart from the gradual progress to arhat-ship. In fact, even the first level of being on the path to stream-entry would set the practitioner's course toward arhat-ship and for this reason not toward becoming a Pratyekabuddha or a Buddha.

An interesting variation on this type of list of gift recipients can be found in a discourse in the *Ekottarikāgama*, of which no parallel is known. The relevant part proceeds as follows:[544]

> Offering food to someone who is proceeding toward stream-entry, one obtains merit that cannot be calculated. How much more [on giving to] someone who has accomplished stream-

> entry; still more [on giving to] to someone who is proceeding toward once-return [or who even] has attained the awakening of once-return; still more [on giving to] to someone who is proceeding toward nonreturn [or who even] has attained the awakening of nonreturn; still more [on giving to] to someone who is proceeding toward arhat-ship [or who even] has attained the awakening of an arhat, still more [on giving to] to someone who is proceeding toward Pratyekabuddhahood [or who even] has attained Pratyekabuddhahood, still more [on giving to] to someone who is proceeding toward becoming a Tathāgata, arhat, a Fully Awakened One, and still more [on giving to] someone who has accomplished Buddhahood and [at the same time giving also] to his monastic community.

The first part of this presentation proceeds in accordance with a standard hierarchical listing of the gradual progression toward becoming an arhat, with each stage building on those mentioned previously. Beyond these eight then come Pratyekabuddhas and Buddhas as superior recipients of donations. The peculiar feature of the above passage is that it presents these two together with a reference to their respective paths. The addition of these two paths—to Pratyekabuddhahood and to Buddhahood—in the above passage could simply be the result of influence from the previous part of the text. Given that being on the path has been mentioned four times already, it does not take much to repeat the same for the final two items in the list. In the context of oral transmission, such an addition can easily occur.

However, the net result is a misfit. Even though it is in principle of course meaningful to apply the notion of being on the path to those who will become Pratyekabuddhas or Buddhas, the problem is fitting this notion into the hierarchical listing of recipients of gifts. There is in principle no reason why someone on the path to becoming a Pratyekabuddha or a Buddha should be more advanced in practice and therefore a more meritorious recipient of gifts than an arhat. Yet, this is what the above presentation communicates. In fact, since those on the path to becoming a Pratyekabuddha or a Buddha have not yet eradicated their defilements, according to the rationale that underpins the hierarchical listing they should be placed well below the arhat, even perhaps below the stream-enterer, rather than above these. As mentioned above, the notion of a mature bodhisattva shares some similarities with the depiction of one who is on the path to stream-entry. The net result of the above mode of presentation is rather to convey that a bodhisattva, due to being on the path to Buddhahood, ranks superior even to arhats and Pratyekabuddhas.

Although this is just an isolated example, it can be related to a tendency in some texts and even inscriptions to use the term "Buddha" when strictly speaking the term "bodhisattva" would be more accurate, particularly in the case of Śākyamuni. For example, a Pāli verse speaks of Śākyamuni's mother as "the mother of the Buddha,"[545] even though according to tradition she passed away soon after his birth and thus well before he actually became a Buddha. As Rhi (1994, 209n12) explains, "Māyā can be called the 'mother of the Buddha' regardless of time, because this describes the general status of Māyā." An Aśokan inscription in turn commemorates the location of Śākyamuni's birth in terms of "here the Buddha was born, the Śākyan sage."[546] Such instances are in line with a general tendency for commemorative plaques related to the birth of a person by referencing their later accomplishments.

Some degree of actual conflation of the status of a bodhisattva with that of a Buddha can be seen in the Perfection of Wisdom. An example occurs after an extended exposition of how bodhisattvas should practice. The passage in question states:[547] "Bodhisattvas of a type like this should not be called 'bodhisattva,' but should be called 'Buddha.' Why is that? It is because they will now soon become a Buddha." In such instances, a perhaps somewhat playful use of terminology does result to some extent in blurring the distinction between one who is still on the path to Buddhahood and one who has indeed achieved it, thereby making the bodhisattva share to some degree the superiority of a Buddha.

The notion of the superiority of bodhisattvas can also be seen in a Pāli discourse listing various marvels related to the Buddha. One such marvel, which is not found in the Chinese parallel and may well be a later element,[548] reports that right after being born the bodhisattva Śākyamuni made the following proclamation (see also figure 6 below):[549] "I am supreme in the world, I am the highest in the world, I am the first in the world; this is my last birth, there will be no further existence."

Figure 6. Queen Māyā is giving birth in the standing posture. To her right the bodhisattva stands on a lotus, his whole body surrounded by an almond-shaped halo, with his right hand raised as if he is making a proclamation. Above the bodhisattva two celestial beings pour out water to bathe him.

From the viewpoint of *Āgama* doctrine in general, this proclamation is not unproblematic, since at that time Śākyamuni had not yet purified his mind of defilements. After all, he was merely an unawakened bodhisattva. It follows that he could not have claimed to be supreme, highest, and first in the world, nor could he have been completely certain that this was his last birth, a statement appropriate only after full awakening has been reached. Silk (2003b, 864) highlights the resultant contrast, where "the infant Gautama . . . is virtually fully awakened ('enlightened') from the moment of his birth," whereas subsequent events show that he was still ignorant, so that "[t]he infant, upon his birth, knows everything; the young man he becomes knows nothing."

Other passages show Śākyamuni before his awakening to have been under the influence of ignorance and thus certainly in a condition that would not allow him to claim to be the first and foremost in the world. From this perspective, it is only after becoming a Buddha that a claim to superiority would be appropriate. In other words, with the above presentation superiority is no longer based on what the claimant *has achieved* but what the claimant *will achieve* in the future. This appears to be precisely the reasoning underlying the notion of the superiority of bodhisattvas.

In the case of the infant Śākyamuni, this type of claim was quite successful in captivating ancient audiences, as can be deduced from its recurrence in several biographies of the Buddha extant in Sanskrit and Chinese.[550] These document that this proclamation of superiority did not remain confined to the Pāli traditions. They also show that what from a doctrinally normative perspective may seem problematic can be deeply inspiring from the viewpoint of a living tradition. Although at the outset this proclamation would have been simply part of the general trend toward exaltating the Buddha—which is quite evident throughout the whole discourse in question—its repercussions in later times could easily have been to contribute to authenticating the notion of the superiority of bodhisattvas. This combines with an implicit indication that Śākyamuni had undertaken the real work to progress to Buddhahood in his previous lives rather than in the present one, wherefore already at his birth he could be absolutely certain of reaching Buddhahood in that same life.

The superiority of bodhisattvas comes up explicitly in the Perfection of Wisdom in an indication made in the context of describing various qualities of an irreversible bodhisattva in the following form: "Their mental states are very pure, a purity that is beyond that of those on the path to arhat-ship and Pratyekabuddhahood."[551] Consulting the parallel versions to this statement suggests that the underlying point may perhaps be that the purity of the mental orientation of irreversible bodhisattvas will lead them beyond the stage of an arhat or a Pratyekabuddha, in the sense that they are beyond the possibility of succumbing to the attraction of attaining these lower levels of awakening. On this reading, the point at stake would not be that the mental states of an irreversible bodhisattva are necessarily more highly purified in terms of eradication of defilements than the mental states of those who are on the path to becoming an arhat or a Pratyekabuddha. In the case of one who is on the path to becoming an arhat, such a practitioner would in fact be a nonreturner and thus would have eradicated all sensual desire and aversion. Such a level of eradication of defilements does not form a necessary condition for becoming an irreversible bodhisattva.

Whatever the final word on the implication of this passage in the Perfection of Wisdom may be, it remains beyond doubt that in the course of time the spiritual status of an irreversible bodhisattva came to be located precisely at the same place where someone who is on the path to Buddhahood is found in the listing of recipients of offerings in the *Ekottarikāgama* passage translated above, namely above everyone else except a Buddha, thereby becoming superior not only to stream-enterers but even to arhats and Pratyekabuddhas.

## Summary

This chapter has surveyed the related topics of cultivating insight into the nature of the mind and the repercussions of insight leading to different levels of attainment, be these along the lines of the traditional four levels of awakening or in terms of a bodhisattva's progress toward Buddhahood.

According to the Perfection of Wisdom, a dimension of the Buddha's comprehensive knowledge takes the form of insight into the mental states of others. The formulation employed here shows some similarities compared to instructions in *Āgama* literature on the third of the four establishments of mindfulness (*smṛtyupasthāna*). An external modality of such practice can take the form of knowing the state of mind of others. Such practice is not confined to the exercise of telepathy, as it can rely on an observational skill already possessed by infants, namely deducing the state of mind of another by noting their facial expression, tone of voice, gestures, and posture. Bodhisattvas are to cultivate the four establishments of mindfulness with the proviso that such practice should be combined with nonapprehension, that is, without giving any room to reification.

The notion that the mind is originally luminous or pure appears to result from a development influenced by a fascination with fire-related imagery in some reciter traditions. From the perspective of *Āgama* literature, just as there is no need for a fruit to be already found in the tree blossom that will eventually lead to the fruit, in the same way there is no need to postulate an original condition of purity for being able to achieve purification of the mind. Since no beginning point can be found for the influence of craving subjecting sentient beings to the endless cycle of birth and death, the removal of craving appears to be much rather an innovation, a departure from the condition of having been in the grip of defilements all along.

Besides the need to overcome defilements, the path to Buddhahood shares with the path to stream-entry the need to cultivate a form of patience that entails being able to put up with potentially destabilizing forms of insight. Irreversible bodhisattvas are certain to become Buddhas in a way comparable to the certainty that stream-entrants will eventually become arhats. At the stage in the development of the bodhisattva ideal reflected in the Perfection of Wisdom, mature bodhisattva practitioners also share with stream-entrants the assurance that they will not take birth in a lower realm.

Lack of maturity as a bodhisattva can result in the attainment of arhatship on hearing a delivery of the profound teachings of the Perfection of Wisdom, thereby falling away from the path to Buddhahood. In addition to the alternative options of becoming an arhat or a Buddha, the texts regularly refer to a third option, which is to become a Pratyekabuddha. The inclusion of this somewhat theoretical option might perhaps reflect a short period of popularity of the notion of Pratyekabuddhahood, situated after the Buddha's final Nirvana and before the bodhisattva path gained traction.

A recurrent element in depictions of the bodhisattva path is a sense of its practitioners' intrinsic superiority. A precedent to this notion can be found in a proclamation by the infant Śākyamuni right after his birth, in which he claims to be supreme in the world.

# On Chapters 16 to 20

THE SIXTEENTH to twentieth chapters of Lokakṣema's translation of the Perfection of Wisdom correspond to the eighteenth to twenty-third chapters of the Sanskrit version translated by Conze (1973/1975, 209–44). On hearing an exposition of the different sources of fear to be confronted by those on the path to Buddhahood, a female bodhisattva declares herself to be endowed with the required fearlessness. The Buddha smiles and predicts her future Buddhahood. Subhūti queries how a bodhisattva meditates on emptiness, in reply to which the Buddha explains how such practice is undertaken without it resulting in a full realization of emptiness. Such undertaking of practice without full realization requires skill in means. A dimension of Māra's mischief is to mislead bodhisattvas into believing they already received a prediction of their future Buddhahood in the past. The Perfection of Wisdom, as the leading quality among the six perfections, is like a good friend (*kalyāṇamitra*) to a bodhisattva.

Two topics to be explored below are the impact of being a woman on the quest to become a Buddha and the role of skill in means in preventing a bodhisattva from falling to the level of an arhat or a Pratyekabuddha.

## WOMEN AND BUDDHAHOOD

The position of women in the Buddhist traditions, from ancient to contemporary times, is marred by pervasive and systemic discrimination. The Perfection of Wisdom is unfortunately no exception to this. In what follows, I first survey pertinent instances from the Perfection of Wisdom and then turn to relevant passages in *Āgama* literature.

### *Women in the Perfection of Wisdom*

An episode in the Perfection of Wisdom involves the female disciple Gaṅgadevā, who receives a prediction of her future Buddhahood. This prediction takes the following form:[552]

> The Buddha said: "In the future this female disciple Gaṅgadevā, in a future age during an eon called Constellation, will be a Buddha here by the name of Golden Flower Buddha. This female disciple will hereafter discard her female body and rather receive a male bodily form. In the future, (s)he will be reborn in the Buddhafield of Akṣobhya. Departing from Akṣobhya's Buddhafield, (s)he will again reach a Buddhafield, and from one Buddhafield be reborn in [another] Buddhafield . . . from one Buddhafield reaching again [another] Buddhafield, this female disciple will always be beholding a Buddha."

The assurance of her future Buddhahood comes with the indication that her next rebirth will be in the Buddhafield of Akṣobhya,[553] following which she will be reborn in one Buddhafield after another. In addition, Gaṅgadevā will change to having a male body.[554] Elsewhere, the Perfection of Wisdom explicitly indicates that an irreversible bodhisattva will no longer be reborn in a lower realm and will not have a female body.[555] Besides treating female rebirth on a par with rebirth in lower realms, this statement implies that a woman cannot be an irreversible bodhisattva.

Similar indications can be found in texts not pertaining to *Prajñāpāramitā* literature. The **Mahāvibhāṣā* lists five conditions for truly deserving to be called a bodhisattva, the third of which is having a male body.[556] The *Bodhisattvabhūmi* explains that a woman will never realize the awakening of a Buddha, because advanced bodhisattvas already leave the female state behind and will not be reborn as a woman again.[557] The *Mahāvastu* confirms that those who progress through the ten stages (*bhūmi*) to Buddhahood are males.[558] The Pāli *Jātaka* collection even relates receiving the prediction of future Buddhahood to being a male.[559]

Although the Perfection of Wisdom at least envisages the possibility that a woman may receive such a prediction, the overall situation remains the same: Gaṅgadevā will have to become a male in order to be able to progress further on the path to Buddhahood. Harrison (1987, 78–79) offers the following comments on the situation in general:

> Compared with the situation in the Pāli Canon, in which women are at least as capable as men of attaining the highest goal, arhatship, the position of women in the Mahāyāna has hardly changed for the better, since women cannot attain buddhahood, and even the title of *bodhisattva* is withheld from them. Of course all this reflects the attitudes of the men (probably monks) who produced these texts, but this does not make the conclusion any less inescapable: although both men and women can ride in the Great Vehicle, only men are allowed to drive it.

The stricture of not allowing women to acquire a driver's license for the Mahāyāna, to stay with the apt illustration provided in the quote above, comes together with other hints that women are somehow of lesser value, spiritually speaking. In fact, according to Nattier (2003a, 99–100), "the emergence of the goal of Buddhahood (as opposed to Arhatship) brought with it a perceptible drop in women's status in those circles that embraced it";[560] "while the 'Mahāyāna' is often portrayed in 20th-century publications as more welcoming of women than earlier Buddhism had been, the reality appears to have been the opposite."

An episode relevant to such assessments occurs in the twenty-ninth chapter of Lokakṣema's translation as part of an extended narrative to which I turn in more detail in my last chapter (see below p. 264). The parts relevant to my present concerns can be summarized as follows: A male bodhisattva and a woman with a following of five hundred women perform an act of self-sacrifice by offering up their own blood in order to help prepare the place where a teacher will soon be expounding the Perfection of Wisdom. The male is referred to by name, whereas all the five hundred women, including their leader, remain nameless. Śakra witnesses the feat and applauds the male bodhisattva for his heroism, without a word about the five hundred women who have performed the same deed.[561] Since

Śakra has to restore all of them to health, the male just as much as the five hundred females and the woman who is their leader, it is clear that they all have undertaken the same action. Nevertheless, only the male gets praise for it.

After hearing the teacher expound the Perfection of Wisdom, the five hundred women are so deeply inspired that they wish to offer themselves up as servants to the male bodhisattva, together with all their wealth.[562] The male bodhisattva then in turn offers them, together with himself, to the teacher. In order to enable the male bodhisattva to accrue merits, the teacher accepts the five hundred women and their wealth, after which he returns them to the male bodhisattva. The celestials rejoice at the meritorious deed done by the male bodhisattva, without even a passing reference to the women. In the course of this transaction, the nameless women have let themselves become a sort of property that the two named males can pass on to each other.

Eventually the male bodhisattva receives a prediction of his future Buddhahood, revealing the name he will have at that time. The five hundred women also receive a prediction, but this does not mention their future names and indicates only in general terms that at an unspecified later time they will also become Buddhas. They and their female leader remain as nameless as they have been throughout.[563] On hearing this prediction, however, they all magically transform into males.[564] The perceived need for such a transformation succinctly embodies the underlying attitude that pervades the whole narrative, which is unfortunately quite in line with the passages quoted earlier regarding Gaṅgadevā having to turn into a male so as to be able to make further progress toward Buddhahood.

The same pattern can also be seen in another report of women aspiring to Buddhahood, found in a different early Mahāyāna text whose translation's attribution to Lokakṣema remains uncertain. The relevant passage involves a large group of women (84,000) who aspire to become Buddhas but at the same time are aware that this is difficult to accomplish for a woman.[565] The Buddha responds with a teaching offering a list of conditions with the potential of leading women to a quick rebirth as males in progress toward Buddhahood; eventually the Buddha predicts that they will indeed be reborn as males.[566]

The attitude expressed in this way is not confined to Buddhahood. As evident in the attainment reports discussed in my previous chapter, when it comes to reaching arhat-ship or even just stream-entry, men are shown to outperform women. This is evident in the numbers employed in the following indication: "Five hundred monks in the community and twenty nuns all attained arhat-ship. Sixty male lay disciples and thirty female lay disciples all attained the awakening of stream-entry."[567] When it comes to arhat-ship, the ratio is twenty-five times as many males as females, and in the case of stream-entry it is still twice as many males compared to females.

This unequal presentation can be contrasted to a report of the attainments reached in general by Buddhist disciples, found in a Pāli discourse and its two Chinese parallels. The three versions agree in giving the same count of realized disciples for males and females respectively, and that in relation to becoming either arhats, nonreturners, or stream-enterers.[568] In each case, there is no hint that females have somehow been outperformed by males.

The other report of attainments in the Perfection of Wisdom actually presents a higher number of nuns compared to monks, but then the nuns only reach stream-entry whereas the monks all become arhats:[569] "Two hundred monks in the community all attained arhat-ship, five hundred nuns all attained the awakening of stream-entry." If there were so many nuns present during the delivery of this teaching, why did none of them manage to reach what each of the two hundred monks was able to accomplish? Whereas in the previous case there could still be uncertainty if the idea in the background may have been that there were simply many more males in the audience, the present case shows that enough women must have been present so that there could in principle have been a substantial number of female arhats. It follows that the central idea promoted in this way is indeed to attribute lesser spiritual abilities to women.

The Perfection of Wisdom is not alone in presenting such indications. Another instance can be found in the version of the **Pratyutpanna-samādhisūtra* attributed to Lokakṣema. The relevant passage reports that eight hundred monks and five hundred nuns became arhats.[570] Once again, women are simply no match for men.

### *Women in Āgama Literature*

The impact of the attitude held by the monks responsible for textual composition and transmission makes itself similarly felt in *Āgama* texts, a prime example being the account of how the order of nuns came into existence. What in principle should have been a story of success has instead become an occasion for voicing various deprecations of women. Comparative study of the extant versions of this account allows identifying such tendencies and thereby reconstructing an earlier narrative of this important episode that is less influenced by male biases.[571] Nevertheless, the basic attitude evident in the account of the establishment of the order of nuns has continued over the centuries and still impacts the current situation on the ground.[572]

In relation to the specific case of restricting access to the higher echelons of the path to Buddhahood, a relevant development can be discerned through comparative study of a part of an *Āgama* discourse that offers a survey of various impossibilities. According to the Pāli version "it is impossible, it cannot come to be that a woman should be an arhat who is a Samyaksambuddha."[573] Although most parallels agree, a version of the discourse extant in the *Madhyamāgama* does not mention the impossibility of a female becoming a Buddha at all.[574]

A comparative study of the different parallel versions brings to light a recurrent tendency toward textual expansion.[575] This impression finds corroboration in the *Prajñāpāramitā* commentary *Dà zhìdù lùn* (**Mahāprajñāpāramitopadeśa*), which in relation to the section on impossibilities in this discourse explicitly indicates that the listing given by the Buddha was further expanded by the treatise masters.[576] This shows that the topic was prone to stimulate expansions by adding more instances of what was considered to be impossible, making it fair to assume that the same type of motivation could already have had an impact during the formation of the discourse itself.

The common core exposition in the case of the impossibilities appears to have been to stipulate that the following is out of the question: the simultaneous arising of two Buddhas or two wheel-turning kings (explicitly specified in the Pāli version to refer to a single world system), bad conduct having good results or good conduct having bad results, and a stream-enterer committing the five heinous crimes (to kill one's mother, one's father, or an arhat, to create a schism, and intentionally to cause physical harm to the Buddha).[577]

In relation to what is impossible for women, the versions that do take up this topic at all agree on mentioning the impossibilities of becoming Śakra, Brahmā, and a Buddha, with some versions additionally referring to becoming a wheel-turning king, a Pratyekabuddha, and a Māra.[578] All of these indications occur right after the topic of the impossibility that two Buddhas or two wheel-turning kings could coexist, making it probable that these two indications, found also in the *Madhyamāgama* discourse, formed the starting point for a process of textual expansion in the other versions.

Now, a wheel-turning king rules over the whole world (as conceived in ancient Indian cosmology), making it obvious that there cannot be two of this type. From the viewpoint of ancient Indian social hierarchy, it would also have been unthinkable that such a position could be occupied by a female. The same holds for celestial rulership, such as occupying the position of Śakra or Brahmā. At least at the outset, the reasoning leading to these additional impossibilities would have been mainly that a woman cannot fulfil any of these roles at present, since in the setting of the ancient Indian patriarchal society such leadership positions have to be occupied by males. In short, these stipulations appear to originate from conceptions of rulership and not, at least in the early stages, from notions related to spiritual inferiority. As already pointed out by Kajiyama (1982b, 64), since at the time of the composition of this discourse "no one, neither man nor woman, aspired to Buddhahood," it follows that "[t]he dictum that a woman cannot become a Buddha thus did not have a target to which it could have been directed."

The situation changes with the gradual emergence of the bodhisattva ideal. Of particular importance in this respect appears to have been the tendency, discussed in a previous chapter (see above p. 101), of turning various narratives and fables into *jātaka*s by identifying a protagonist in these stories as a past life of the Buddha Śākyamuni. In view of the vast array of different protagonists singled out in this way, covering not only humans in all different possible social situations but also a range of animals, maleness must have naturally emerged as a characteristic capable of providing at least some degree of continuity, thereby helping to string together widely different roles and behaviors attributed to Śākyamuni in his past lives. The in itself natural tendency to choose male protagonists, however, would in turn have impacted the conception of the bodhisattva path. Appleton (2010, 96) explains that since "the Bodhisatta always happens to be male in his *jātaka* stories . . . After the association of the stories with the *bodhisatta* path, his consistently male character influenced the idea that a *bodhisatta* must be male."

Notably, elsewhere *Āgama* literature offers a detailed exposition of the impact of karma on various aspects of one's living conditions—in terms of lifespan, health, beauty, etc.—but does not mention the difference between being born as a male or as a female.[579] This gives the impression that, at the time of the textual composition of this discourse, the difference between being male or female was considered only incidental to the question of rebirth. In other words, being born as a woman is here not singled out as in principle a result of bad karma.

Nevertheless, textual proliferation oriented along notions of rulership together with maleness as a narrative requirement for stringing together past-life tales of the Buddha Śākyamuni appear to have contributed to the emergence of the doctrinal position that higher stages of progress toward Buddhahood require a male instead of a female body.[580] The present case thereby exemplifies what appears to be a recurrent pattern in the gradual evolution of various dimensions of the bodhisattva ideal, in that textual trajectories and developments inspired by concerns that have little or nothing to do with the path to Buddhahood can in the course of time come to determine essential dimensions of this path.

## Skill in Means

In the remainder of the present chapter, I will explore the notion of skill in means from the viewpoint of two different modalities, the first of which takes the form of monitoring one's own practice, whereas the second concerns the Buddha's role as a teacher.

### *Skill in Monitoring One's Own Practice*

The first of these two modalities of skill in means can be exemplified with the help of a passage from the seventeenth chapter of the Perfection of Wisdom, which starts with the following exchange:[581]

> Subhūti said to the Buddha: "How do bodhisattvas cultivating the Perfection of Wisdom enter into emptiness? How do they develop concentration on emptiness?"
>
> The Buddha said: "Bodhisattvas cultivating the Perfection of Wisdom contemplate form, feeling tone, perception, volitional formations, and consciousness as empty. They should undertake this contemplation, with unified mind undertake this contemplation, without seeing their true nature. In this way, not seeing their true nature, they do not gain a realization of their true nature."[582]
>
> Subhūti said: "The Buddha said: 'They do not gain a realization in emptiness.' How are bodhisattvas established in concentration without gaining a realization in emptiness?"
>
> The Buddha said: "Bodhisattvas are completely mindful of emptiness without attaining realization; they undertake this contemplation without obtaining realization. They undertake this contemplation; they contemplate and penetrate this sphere. Only at the time of wishing to proceed, they do not obtain realization. They do not penetrate the concentration of the mind free from attachment. At that time, they do not lose the essence of the nature of being bodhisattvas; they do not attain realization midway. What is the reason? The reason is their original aspiration to take care of all sentient beings; the reason is their supreme compassion."

The gist of this passage appears to be that the task of bodhisattvas is to contemplate the empty nature of the five aggregates but at the same time avoid that this results in the breakthrough to Nirvana. Subhūti's second query then leads to more details on how this can be achieved. It requires cultivating meditative understanding as far as possible but without taking the final step whereby such insight will result in actual realization. How to achieve such an outcome can be elucidated further with the help of another explanation by the Buddha:[583]

> So as to protect all sentient beings fully, these bodhisattvas develop emptiness concentration proceeding to the gateway to Nirvana, keeping this distinction in their mind. What is that distinction? It is developing emptiness concentration, signless concentration, and wishless concentration [without obtaining realization]. That is the distinction. Due to their skill in means, these bodhisattvas do not obtain realization midway. What is the reason? The reason is that they are protected by their skill in means. Because they keep all sentient beings in their mind. Because of their upholding of this recollection, they acquire skill in means and do not obtain realization midway.

The three concentrations mentioned in the above excerpt are traditionally considered to facilitate the realization of Nirvana.[584] One way to understand the implications of this set of three is to view the first as pointing to the foundational insight into the empty nature of reality. In a way this can be considered as the other side of the coin of dependent arising, in that emptiness here stands for the absence of any entity or essence in phenomena, which are seen to be in their entirety the product of conditions. Since such a vision of emptiness also undermines the assumption of a substantial separation between subject and object, the next in the set of three concentrations naturally presents a more epistemologically related perspective in terms of signlessness, with which the potential unfolds of gaining insight into the construction of experience. Insight into the construction of experience in turn has its complement in a thoroughgoing transformation of the mind by way of establishing insight-related equanimity in the form of wishlessness. The third concentration thereby embodies the soteriological orientation that underpins the whole set of three, their convergence on liberation from *duḥkha*.

The challenge for bodhisattvas is to cultivate these three rather profound concentrations but alongside that keep in mind their aspiration to become a Buddha for the welfare of all sentient beings. Mindfully recollecting this and keeping it in mind then prevents their meditation on emptiness, signlessness, and wishlessness from proceeding beyond the threshold to Nirvana to its actual realization. This is their skill in means (*upāyakauśalya*), and such skill in means was precisely lacking in the case of those sixty bodhisattvas who became arhats, discussed above (see p. 189).

A complementary perspective on this type of skill in means can be based on an extract from the previous, sixteenth chapter of the Perfection of Wisdom, which addresses basically the same issue from the viewpoint of signs (*nimitta*):[585]

> One who is in quest of the cessation of signs, one who is set up for the cessation of signs—if they should indeed cease—in turn attains arhat-ship. This is the skill in means of bodhisattvas: they do not [let] signs cease to attain realization; they proceed toward the signless in accordance with this instruction.

In this way, skill in means ensures that the cultivation of signlessness does not issue in the cessation of signs and therewith the realization of Nirvana.[586] This passage presents the same basic injunction as the previous extracts, this time phrased in terms of signlessness. Throughout, the task of skill in means is to ensure that premature realization can be avoided in order to enable continuous progress toward Buddhahood.

The distinct perspective on the role of skill in means that emerges from the above passages can be explored further by consulting relevant *Āgama* discourses.[587] The notion of skill in means occurs in two Pāli discourses in the context of a set of three skills.[588] For one of these two Pāli discourses no parallel is known; the other has Śāriputra as its speaker, who presents a list of doctrinal items to be recited in unison as an expression of communal harmony. The parallel versions expand this list in different ways, and the three skills in question are only found in the Pāli version. Whereas this Pāli discourse just lists the three skills, the other Pāli discourse presents them as part of a set of six qualities that will help a practitioner grow in what is wholesome. The set of three common to both Pāli discourses comprises the following:

- skill in progression
- skill in retrogression
- skill in means

The implication of this threefold presentation can be drawn out further based on explanations provided in an early Abhidharma text, the *Vibhaṅga*.[589] According to its presentation, skill in progression (*āya*) requires understanding with wisdom how to direct attention so that what is unwholesome or unskillful diminishes and what is wholesome or skillful increases. Skill in retrogression (*apāya*) then corresponds to understanding with wisdom what type of attention has the opposite result. These two are supported by skill in means (*upāya*), representative of the wisdom that enables choosing the appropriate means.

This type of skill in means appears to be relevant particularly to monitoring one's own practice from the viewpoint of growth in what is wholesome. Such a concern with monitoring one's own practice would be quite in line with the type of skill in means described in the above passages from the Perfection of Wisdom.[590] Expressed in the terminology found in the two Pāli discourses, in the setting of the Perfection of Wisdom skill in *progression* to Buddhahood would have its counterpart in skill in *retrogression* by avoiding the level of an arhat or Pratyekabuddha, and skill in *means* would be the ability to foster the former and prevent the latter. As the passages translated above indicate, such skill in means enables cultivating emptiness without proceeding to the realization of emptiness or cultivating signless without proceeding to the cessation of signs.

### *The Buddha's Skill in Means*

In addition to providing a counterpart to this particular modality of skill in means found in the Perfection of Wisdom, Pāli texts feature another type of occurrence of the term that relates to the more widely known modality of skill in means used by the Buddha when teaching others, rather than serving to monitor one's own practice. The former modality is typically employed by the Buddha to adapt his ways of teaching to the particular needs and propensities of his audience. Such a usage becomes evident in a Pāli verse in which the Buddha's half-brother, the monk Nanda, reports that he became an arhat and successfully overcame his sensual lust and fondness for adornment due to the Buddha's skill in means.[591]

The relevant teachings given by the Buddha are reported elsewhere in *Āgama* literature. Relevant to the topic of adornment is an occasion when Nanda revealed his fondness in this respect by walking around all dressed up. According to a Pāli discourse and two of its three Chinese parallels, this led to the Buddha recommending that Nanda should undertake the ascetic practices of living in seclusion in forest wilds, subsisting on begging food (rather than accept invitations for meals), and wearing rag robes (rather than accept ready-made robes as gifts).[592] His other problem of being prone to sensual lust comes up in another Pāli discourse and its parallels extant in Chinese, Sanskrit, and Tibetan, which present a set of mindfulness-related practices to help Nanda live the life of celibacy despite his lustful disposition. These are guarding the sense doors, moderation with food, wakefulness by purifying the mind of unwholesome states during the first and last watches of the night, and contemplating impermanence.[593] Nanda apparently took the practice of guarding the sense doors particularly to heart, as the listing of outstanding disciples reckons him foremost in this respect.[594]

The practices presented in this way are standard in *Āgama* literature for countering fondness of adornment and the challenges of sensual lust. Although none of these instances explicitly uses the term "skill in means," the same could in principle be applied to the respective teachings, in the sense that the practical instructions given here exemplify the Buddha's skill in means.[595]

A different perspective emerges in a narrative found in a Pāli collection of inspired utterances, *Udāna*. This collection results from a gradual process of textual formation with a tendency to supplement inspired utterances with prose narrations.[596] At times, such narrations show clear signs of lateness, even to the extent of reflecting a misunderstanding of the inspired utterance in question. An example in case is a metaphorical reference to not having any need for a well, found in an inspired utterance on the topic of the destruction of craving.[597] The prose narrative adopts a literal reading of this reference, describing an actual well that had been filled with chaff to prevent the Buddha and his disciples from drinking the water.[598] The resultant tale misses the point made by the verse.

This instance exemplifies that prose narrations found in this collection of inspired utterances can be considerably later than the discourses surveyed above regarding instructions given to Nanda to curb his fondness of adornment and sensual lust. The same also holds for two Chinese parallels to this particular Pāli tale, as these also occur in textual collections with material that can be distinctly later than *Āgama* literature in general.

According to the relevant narrative, Nanda is overcome with sensual lust to the extent that he wants to disrobe.[599] The Buddha takes him by the arm and teleports him to the Heaven of the Thirty-Three, showing him beautiful heavenly nymphs that, as Nanda has to admit, are much more attractive than the human woman he is hankering for. The Buddha promises that Nanda will gain such heavenly nymphs in his next rebirth if he stays in robes. The ruse works, Nanda does not disrobe, and eventually he even becomes an arhat. Since as an arhat he will no longer be reborn and has also gone completely beyond sensual lust, the prospect of gaining heavenly nymphs is no longer relevant.

Further developments of this basic trope in some texts even portray the Buddha as having tricked Nanda into becoming a celibate in the first place.[600] At the end of a meal, the Buddha hands his bowl to Nanda and does not take it back, thereby forcing Nanda to follow him to the monastery. When they have arrived at the monastery, the Buddha tells him to ordain; out of respect for the Buddha, Nanda is unable to refuse. A version of this developed tale appears to have inspired the Gandhāran relief shown in figure 7 below.

Even without this embellishment, the tale of Nanda shows several noteworthy features. One of these concerns the Buddha teleporting him to the Heaven of the Thirty-Three. A closer study of relevant passages in *Āgama* literature gives the impression that at an early stage celestial travel was perceived as something performed with the mind-made body, while the physical body remains behind, still seated in meditation.[601] The tale of Nanda, however, clearly involves actual physical teleportation, with the Buddha using his powers to lift Nanda up to the Heaven of the Thirty-

Figure 7. The relief to the right shows Nanda's beautiful fiancée checking her appearance in a mirror. She is surrounded by three female attendants, one of whom is combing her hair. Nanda leaves with the Buddha's bowl in his hands, looking back longingly at his fiancée. In the scene at the left, he returns the bowl to the Buddha, who in turn will give him ordination.

Three. The promise of heavenly nymphs is also not without problems, as it does not fit the early Buddhist theory of karma and its fruition particularly well. According to this theory, the actual fruition of karma is rather complex, and the circumstances of one's next rebirth do not depend solely on the ethical quality of one's present conduct.[602] It follows that it would not be possible to be absolutely certain that merely staying in robes will indeed lead Nanda to be reborn in the Heaven of the Thirty-Three in the company of beautiful heavenly nymphs. In fact, as the remainder of the story shows, this indeed did not happen.

A perhaps even more significant departure from the general approach in *Āgama* thought, which is more directly relevant to the topic of the Buddha's skill in means, emerges when comparing the present episode to the instructions to Nanda surveyed earlier. These recommended undertaking ascetic practices, guarding the sense doors, moderation with food, wakefulness by purifying the mind from unwholesome states during the first and last watches of the night, and contemplating impermanence. In the present case, however, the approach is rather to stimulate sensual lust (for heavenly nymphs) to prevent Nanda from disrobing due to his already existing sensual lust (for a human female). Such an approach differs substantially from the teachings given in the other instructions to Nanda, as here lust is encouraged as a means to motivate celibacy. Although the idea is to stimulate his lust so that he continues a life of celibacy, the approach to keep him in robes is rather unorthodox.[603] Pāli commentaries identify the procedure adopted by the Buddha to quench Nanda's sensual lust with the promise of gaining superior objects of sensual lust as an instance of skill in means.[604]

The perspectives that emerge from the above exploration of skill in means tie in with tendencies evident in surveying the evolution of the bodhisattva ideal in Pāli texts (see above p. 14), in that the supposedly clear-cut boundaries between Mahāyāna and not-Mahāyāna tend to become considerably more porous when inspected more closely. In the present case, an apparently early notion of skill in means as a way of monitoring one's own mental states and progress, found in some Pāli discourses, closely resembles a type of skill in means advocated in the Perfection of Wisdom to ensure that a bodhisattva keeps progressing to Buddhahood rather than falling to the level of arhats or Pratyekabuddhas. At the same time, the notion of skill in means as an approach employed by the Buddha when teaching others also finds reflection in Pāli sources, with one particular tale, related to the Buddha's half-brother Nanda, presenting a way of dealing with the challenges of sensual lust that differs substantially from the standard methods described in *Āgama* literature for such purposes.

## Summary

This chapter has offered a critical assessment of the tendency to deny or underrate women's potential to progress toward Buddhahood and provided a spotlight on the potential of skill in means as a quality of monitoring one's own progress toward the same goal.

The Perfection of Wisdom is unfortunately not an exception to a pervasive tendency in Buddhist traditions to discriminate against women. When the female disciple Gaṅgadevā receives a prediction of her future Buddhahood, this comes with the stipulation that from now on she will only have male bodies. Again, a substantial group of female bodhisattvas remain unnamed and their heroic deeds unnoticed, but on receiving a prediction of their future Buddhahood they all transform into males. The lack of balance evident in this way is not confined to the path to Buddhahood. When it comes to arhat-ship or stream-entry attainment, the Perfection of Wisdom adopts a similarly disproportionate mode of presentation that conveys the impression that women have lesser spiritual abilities.

Already in *Āgama* literature the dictum occurs that only a male can be a Buddha, which comparative study reveals to be a later addition. The textual expansion apparently leading to this dictum seems to have taken off from the indication that it is impossible for two wheel-turning kings or two Buddhas to coexist in the same world system, leading to the addition of other stipulations to the effect that a woman cannot occupy rulership positions in the ancient Indian patriarchal setting. Combined with the tendency to identify male protagonists in various *jātaka*s as former lives of the Buddha Śākyamuni, the notion would have become established that it takes a male body to complete progress toward Buddhahood. Since the time of its apparently somewhat-accidental origins, this belief has continued to impact the situation of women in pursuit of Buddhahood.

The Perfection of Wisdom presents a specific modality of skill in means in the form of bodhisattvas monitoring their own practice to prevent realization midway, which would forestall their continued progress toward Buddhahood. This modality has a counterpart in descriptions of skill in means in two Pāli discourses, which are similarly concerned with monitoring oneself rather than being about teaching and guiding others. Nevertheless, this other-directed form of skill in means is also known to Pāli sources, with one comparatively late Pāli discourse even reporting that the Buddha weaned his half-brother Nanda from sensual lust in a way that involves a distinct departure from the standard approach for such purposes described in *Āgama* literature.

# On Chapters 21 to 25

THE TWENTY-FIRST to twenty-fifth chapters of Lokakṣema's translation of the Perfection of Wisdom correspond to the section from the twenty-fourth to the first part of the twenty-eighth chapter of the Sanskrit version translated by Conze (1973/1975, 245–70). Ānanda takes on a prominent role in this portion of the text, dialoguing with the Buddha on topics related to the Perfection of Wisdom, including challenges posed by Māra. In reply to a question by Subhūti, the Buddha expounds how to train for gaining omniscience. He also mentions the names of bodhisattvas practicing under the Buddha Akṣobhya. A substantial group of monks get up and pay respect to the Buddha, who smiles and predicts their future attainment of Buddhahood, when all of them will have the same name, Avakīrṇakusuma. The Buddha for the first time entrusts the Perfection of Wisdom to Ānanda (he will do so again at the end of the thirtieth chapter). Through the Buddha's power, the members of the audience are able to see the Buddha Akṣobhya teaching his disciples.

The two main topics to be explored below are the role of Ānanda and the attribution of omniscience to the Buddha Śākyamuni.

## Ānanda

In the course of the twenty-fifth chapter, the Buddha entrusts the Perfection of Wisdom to Ānanda for the first time in the following manner:[605]

> The Buddha said to Ānanda: "I take this Perfection of Wisdom and entrust it to you . . . The other teachings that have been constantly taught by me and received by you, suppose you

> were to let them all be lost, all be forgotten. Even if this were to happen, that would only be a minor transgression. Suppose the Perfection of Wisdom you have received from the Buddha were to be lost, suppose it were to be forgotten, that would be a very great transgression, not a minor one.

The passage reflects Ānanda's role as the guardian of the Buddha's teachings. Having been the Buddha's attendant for many years, he was naturally present on many occasions when the Buddha delivered a discourse. The different *Vinaya*s report that, soon after the Buddha had passed away, the monks gathered to perform a communal recitation, *saṅgīti*—sometimes less appropriately rendered as the first "council"—of the various teachings believed to have been given by the Buddha and his eminent disciples. In the setting of this *saṅgīti*, Ānanda was a natural choice for reciting the teachings.[606] It is in his role as the custodian of the teachings that he is now being entrusted with the Perfection of Wisdom. In this way, the Perfection of Wisdom comes to be placed not only in a position similar to the teachings believed to have been recited at the first *saṅgīti* but, according to the explicit indication given by the Buddha in the above passage, it even supersedes them all in importance. If Ānanda should forget all the other teachings he has received from the Buddha, this would not be as bad as forgetting the Perfection of Wisdom. This warning thereby complements a repeated advocacy of the importance of the Perfection of Wisdom, engaging with which serves as an incredible source of merit, just as rejecting it leads to rebirth in hell. In the same way, let all the other teachings be forgotten, as long as the Perfection of Wisdom remains.

In what follows, I explore the role of Ānanda as a disciple with a keen interest in teachings related to emptiness; I also take up his prosocial attitude, which to some extent contrasts with an apparent development of the arhat ideal in a direction that may perhaps explain the arising of criticism for seeming to lack compassion. A qualification of Ānanda's *maitrī* as nondual then affords me an occasion for exploring the significance of nonduality in *Āgama* literature and in the Perfection of Wisdom.

### *Ānanda's Interest in Emptiness Teachings*

Besides his role in the transmission of the teachings, Ānanda features on several occasions in *Āgama* literature as a disciple with a particular interest in topics related to emptiness, which thereby makes him an appropriate choice for being one of the protagonists in the Perfection of Wisdom. According to his own report, given in a Pāli discourse and its Chinese parallel, his stream-entry took place based on hearing a penetrative instruction on patterns of identification in regard to the five aggregates.[607] In other discourses he features repeatedly as inquiring, presumably during the time before he had a personal experience of Nirvana through attaining stream-entry, into a mental condition that is conscious but at the same time does not take up any object at all. In an example from a Pāli discourse with no known parallel, he formulates this type of inquiry in terms of paying attention, *manasikāra*. When the Buddha confirms that there is indeed such a mental condition, Ānanda wants to know how this could be. The relevant exchange proceeds as follows:[608]

> [Ānanda asked:] "Venerable sir, but in what way could there be an attainment of concentration for a monastic of such a type that one would not pay attention to the eye, not pay attention to form, not pay attention to the ear, not pay attention to sound, not pay attention to the nose, not pay attention to smell, not pay attention to the tongue, not pay attention to taste, not pay attention to the body, and not pay attention to touch?
>
> One would not pay attention to earth, not pay attention to water, not pay attention to fire, not pay attention to wind, not pay attention to the sphere of infinite space, not pay attention to the sphere of infinite consciousness, not pay attention to the sphere of nothingness, and not pay attention to the sphere of neither-perception-nor-nonperception.
>
> One would not pay attention to this world, not pay attention to another world, and also not pay attention to what here is seen, heard, sensed, cognized, attained, sought for, and pursued by the mind. Yet, one would still pay attention."

> [The Buddha replied:] "Here, Ānanda, a monastic pays attention like this: 'This is peaceful, this is sublime, namely: the calming of all constructions, the letting go of all supports, the extinguishing of craving, dispassion, cessation, Nirvana.'"

Ānanda's long description works its way through all the various dimensions of experience that one could possibly pay attention to. He begins with the five senses and their objects, then takes up the four elements and the four immaterial spheres. As if this were not enough already, he next mentions this world and another one, and then summarizes all possible avenues of paying attention from the viewpoint of modalities of mental activity. These are not only related to the senses by way of seeing, hearing, etc. but also include the notion of attaining something, of seeking to attain something, and of anything that the mind may pursue. With all such potential avenues for paying attention set aside, could one still be paying attention?

The Buddha confirms that this is indeed the case, namely by paying attention to Nirvana. Although his reply employs concepts, the idea behind this reply is quite probably not to encourage a conceptual reflection along the lines of the maxim. The reason is simply that reflecting would still fall within the range of what Ānanda's query has already set aside. Instead, the Buddha's reply can more meaningfully be understood to point to the very experience of Nirvana, the cessation of the whole world of experience.

In addition to showing a sustained interest in a form of paying attention that could be called nonattention, *amanasikāra*, Ānanda also features as the central dialogue partner in two detailed teachings by the Buddha on the topic of emptiness. In the background to one of these two teachings stands a tendency by Ānanda to display an excessively prosocial inclination. To some degree a strengthening of such a prosocial tendency would have been a natural outcome of his role as the Buddha's attendant, due to which *Āgama* literature often shows him having the task of conveying messages on behalf of the Buddha or else intervening on behalf of his co-disciples with the Buddha. In an apparent attempt to restrain his tendency to become excessively busy with such affairs, evident in the present case in his congregating with other monastics to make robes, the Buddha begins by censuring a proclivity for delighting in company and then expounds on internal and external emptiness.[609] The ensuing teaching shows how emptiness can be applied not only in meditation but also to a variety of daily life situations.

The other detailed teaching on emptiness begins with an inquiry by Ānanda about the Buddha's own abiding in emptiness.[610] In order to show how such an abiding can be emulated, the Buddha describes a gradual progression through a series of perceptual experiences that involve a step-by-step deconstruction of how the world is normally perceived.[611] The progression culminates in signlessness as a springboard for the realization of Nirvana, the supreme emptiness in *Āgama* thought.

The progression up to signlessness would be relevant to the concerns expressed in the Perfection of Wisdom of finding a way to deepen insight into emptiness without prematurely proceeding to the realization of Nirvana. The gradual deconstruction of perceptual notions proposed in this way, especially if not taken beyond the stage of signlessness, would be well in keeping with the overall thrust evident in the Perfection of Wisdom.

### *Ānanda's Kindness*

In a different part of the Buddha's first entrustment of the Perfection of Wisdom, another dimension of Ānanda's role as attendant comes to the fore. Here is the relevant passage:[612]

> If you have a mental attitude of kindness toward the Buddha, you should keep in mind the Perfection of Wisdom, you should worship it, pay respect to it, and make offerings to it. Setting up such activities, you are fully worshipping the Buddha, by way of repaying his kindness, and you have worshipped past, future, and present Buddhas. Your esteem of the Buddha, your worship, and your recollection of the Buddha do not equal your worship of the Perfection of Wisdom. Be careful not to forget a single sentence!

The reference to Ānanda's kindness toward his teacher can be related to an indication found in the parallel versions of a discourse that provides an account of the Buddha's final Nirvana. According to the narrative context, Ānanda has left the Buddha's presence and is crying at the thought that his teacher is about to pass away. The Buddha summons him back and comforts Ānanda by highlighting the outstanding ways he has performed his duties as the Buddha's attendant. According to most of the parallel versions, the Buddha highlights that Ānanda had served him with loving kindness, *maitrī*.[613]

In *Āgama* literature, Ānanda features in general as a particularly kind person. Nyanaponika and Hecker (1997, 154) report that, "[b]ecause of his natural kindliness and compassionate concern, Ānanda was especially solicitous for the welfare of all four classes of disciples, not only monks and laymen, but also nuns and laywomen." A case in point is the report of his intervention on behalf of Mahāprajāpatī Gautamī's petition that the Buddha found an order of nuns, mentioned in the previous chapter (see above p. 208).

Another dimension of the depiction of his kind and compassionate disposition is his failure to progress to arhat-ship while the Buddha was still alive. This is implicit in the episode on the eve of the Buddha's final Nirvana, as Ānanda's sorrow reflects his condition of not yet having reached the final goal, whereby one goes beyond all sorrow and grief. The depiction of Ānanda breaking out into tears on this occasion is a recurrent motif in texts and art. An example of the latter is figure 8 below, a Gandhāran relief showing the Buddha's final Nirvana and Ānanda overwhelmed by grief.

In terms of how the texts portray his personality, Ānanda could be viewed as somewhat of a proto-bodhisattva in terms of mental qualities (leaving aside the notion of aspiring to Buddhahood itself). He is full of compassion and always ready to help or intervene on behalf of others, at the expense of his own progress toward awakening. Moreover, he does not discriminate and, contrary to the norms of ancient Indian androcentrism, gives his full support to the cause of women. Besides, he plays a central role in textual transmission, a topic of considerable interest among the promoters of the Perfection of Wisdom and other early Mahāyāna texts, which tend to exhibit a clear focus on ensuring their own transmission. Only when his task of supporting the Buddha to the best of his abilities has ended, because his teacher has passed away, does Ānanda find the

Figure 8. The Buddha is lying on his side, with his face covered by his robes, conveying the fact that from now on his disciples will no longer be able to see him or be seen by him. Directly below the covered face is his attendant Ānanda, overwhelmed by grief, with the standing Aniruddha holding him by his arm as if trying to help him overcome his sorrow.

time to dedicate himself wholeheartedly to progress to arhat-ship. His inability to accomplish this earlier comes up implicitly in the introductory section of the Sanskrit version of the *Aṣṭasāhasrikā Prajñāpāramitā* and most of its Chinese parallels, which make a point of mentioning that Ānanda was the only one among the monks present on this occasion who had not yet become an arhat.[614]

The same failure of Ānanda, if it can be called such, also comes up in reports in different *Vinaya*s of the first *saṅgīti*, already mentioned above, a communal recitation believed to have been held shortly after the Buddha's demise.[615] As the Buddha's attendant who had been present on many occasions when teachings were given, being moreover, according to tradition, endowed with an exceptional memory, Ānanda should in principle have been the most important person in such an undertaking. However, the *Vinaya* accounts instead accord a central role to Mahākāśyapa, to the extent that some versions even report that he at first refuses to let Ānanda participate in this communal recitation at all. In one *Vinaya*, Mahākāśyapa argues that to let Ānanda, who was not an arhat, enter the assembly would be comparable to letting a jackal enter a pride of lions.[616] In another *Vinaya*, Mahākāśyapa only agrees to allow Ānanda to join the assembly on the condition that he serve as attendant by supplying the other monks with water, which Ānanda humbly accepts.[617]

Having joined the assembly, in all *Vinaya* accounts Ānanda becomes the target of a series of accusations, which include his intervention on behalf of women to get the Buddha to found an order of nuns.[618] As pointed out by several scholars, the roles accorded to Mahākāśyapa and Ānanda in this way seem to reflect an underlying tension in the monastic community that broke out into open conflict after the teacher had passed away.[619] On this reading, the narrative of the first communal recitation held shortly after the Buddha's demise serves to articulate a contrast between two different currents or attitudes, with the faction upholding a more stringent attitude toward regulations and a more austere ideal of spiritual perfection emerging victorious.

The impression of a shift in attitude toward a less prosocial ideal of spiritual perfection finds corroboration in an otherwise unrelated discourse extant in Pāli and Chinese. The chief protagonist is an arhat monk who reveals his own qualities in the course of a discussion with a non-Buddhist practitioner; one such quality is that he has been a Buddhist monk for eighty years.[620] This implicitly locates the delivery of this discourse several decades after the Buddha's demise. Even if this monk had been among the first to take ordination, his eighty years of monkhood substantially exceed the about forty-five-year span of the Buddha's teaching career.[621]

The two versions agree that this monk had become an arhat soon after his ordination.[622] It follows that descriptions of his conduct depict the behavior of an arhat. This is worthy of note, since several of his other qualities point to a marked lack of prosocial concern.[623] According to the Chinese version, he never greeted a nun; the Pāli parallel clarifies that he never taught any woman, be she lay or monastic. In fact, according to the Chinese version, he also never taught laity; according to the Pāli version, he never gave others the going forth or the higher ordination—that is, he also did not act as a teacher within the monastic community. It is difficult to understand why an arhat, who has removed sensual desire for good, needs to shun women to such an extent. The same holds for giving teachings to others. With the task of purifying his own mind already completed, why not dedicate at least some time to helping others to achieve the same?

Note also that this is not just presented as an isolated instance of an extremely introverted person. In both discourses, these descriptions feature as praiseworthy qualities, alongside his observance of several ascetic practices. That is, this is a model arhat, rather than an exception. In fact, both versions follow the description of each of his qualities with a repetition of the same in the form of an acclamation by the reciters in praise of his wonderful and marvelous qualities. For *Āgama* literature this is a rather unusual procedure and highlights the degree to which the reciters wanted to emphasize the type of arhat that emerges in this way. In conjunction with the narrative of the first communal recitation, *saṅgīti*, the textual evidence points to a recasting of the arhat ideal.

Although the reciters evidently found inspiration in this type of arhat ideal, the *Aśokāvadāna* reports that King Aśoka was not at all impressed. Being taken on a tour of *stūpa*s of eminent disciples, the king makes lavish donations each time he hears their respective qualities. In the case of the monk under discussion, however, on being told that he never taught others, not even as little as a two-line stanza, Aśoka reacts by donating just a small coin, explaining that he fails to be inspired by someone who does not benefit others.[624] Aśoka may not be alone in finding this type of arhat uninspiring.

The apparent shift of the arhat ideal that emerges in this way can in turn be related to the somewhat negative way in which arhats are depicted in some Mahāyāna texts. Similar to the case of emptiness teachings being applied to all dharmas, which stand in dialogue with trends in some Abhidharma traditions rather than with early Buddhism (see above p. 42), in the present case it also seems as if the criticism of selfish arhats may stand in dialogue with the above-described development. In fact, elsewhere *Āgama* literature shows arhats being motivated by compassion, willing to teach and guide others.[625] Such instances would hardly provide a natural occasion for any criticism of being selfish, whereas the same type of censure could easily have arisen in relation to the promotion of a different arhat ideal of the type evident in the texts surveyed above. Since this ideal indeed appears to stand in contrast to the prosocial motivation of benefitting others, a move toward such a more austere ideal, at the expense of compassion, may well have motivated a critical response in the opposite direction of emphasizing compassion, feeding into the promotion of the superiority of the bodhisattva ideal.

### *Nonduality*

The second entrustment to Ānanda, which occurs at the end of the thirtieth chapter, shares with the first entrustment a reference to his kindness:[626]

> Ānanda, what you should have done, it has all been done: You have been with kindness by the body, with kindness by speech as well, and also with kindness by the mind; you have filial respect for the Buddha; it could not be said that you have been without filial respect . . . I tell you, Ānanda, should you forget a single word from among this Perfection of Wisdom, should you abandon it, should you neglect it and not write it down, by all of this you would be without kindness and filial respect for the Buddha; you would no longer be seeing me. Ānanda, by this you would no longer be worshipping the Buddha. Ānanda, by this you would no longer be following the Buddha's teaching.

Similar to the first entrustment, the main message is that Ānanda should redirect his attitude of kindness toward transmitting the Perfection of Wisdom without allowing any loss to occur. A minor difference is that the present passage draws out the way in which Ānanda's kindness toward the Buddha manifested, namely by way of bodily activities, by speech, and as a mental attitude. This indication concords closely with a formulation adopted in most *Āgama* accounts of the Buddha's final Nirvana. According to the relevant versions, the Buddha specified that Ānanda's loving kindness toward his teacher indeed comprised bodily, verbal, and mental activities.[627] Unlike the part from the Perfection of Wisdom translated above, however, several versions offer additional information on the quality of loving kindness cultivated by way of the three doors of action, as they qualify Ānanada's loving kindness as "immeasurable" (*apramāṇa*) and also as "nondual" (*advaya*), which in the present context could less literally be rendered as "undivided."

The qualification of being immeasurable is a recurrent one in *Āgama* literature, employed regularly for loving kindness, *maitrī*, and the other three *brahmavihāras* of compassion, sympathetic joy, and equanimity. In fact, each "divine abode," *brahmavihāra*, can alternatively be designated as a state that is "immeasurable," *apramāṇa*. Being immeasurable or boundless, in the sense of all-encompassing without any exception, naturally relates to the idea of being undivided or even nondual, even though this qualification is not standard, unlike the reference to being immeasurable. Among Pāli discourses the term *advaya* occurs in fact only rarely. Apart from the present instance, it mainly features in descriptions of meditative experiences of "totality," *kṛtsna* (Pāli: *kasiṇa*). These feature in a standard list of ten, which comprises the four elements, four colors, space, and consciousness.[628]

The relatively rare occurrence of the notion of nonduality in *Āgama* literature has a counterpart in the Perfection of Wisdom, which also does not evince a sustained interest in this topic. The notion does occur in a statement by the Buddha to the effect that "there are no dual dharmas. For this reason, they are originally pure and therefore they are said to be one."[629] With the Sanskrit version of the *Aṣṭasāhasrikā Prajñāpāramitā* and later Chinese translations, however, an interest in nonduality becomes more prominent. Since nonduality is clearly a topic of considerable importance in developed *Prajñāpāramitā* literature, it seems worthwhile to take the present instance related to Ānanda as an opportunity to explore the information that *Āgama* literature has to offer on the notion of nonduality.

A term related to the idea of nondual meditative experiences, employed on several occasions, is "unity" (*ekatva*), which stands in contrast to "diversity" (*nānātva*). The two together can simply represent different modalities of perception.[630] When used in the context of meditative practice, the term "unity" designates a superior level of mental composure compared to the absence of such unity.[631] In this role, unity can also qualify different perceptive experiences to be cultivated in a gradual meditation on emptiness,[632] mentioned above as involving a step-by-step deconstruction of how the world is normally experienced and being a form of practice inspired by the Buddha's own abiding in emptiness (see p. 225).

Another type of terminology serves to designate a mental condition as being "unified" (*ekāgra* or *ekoti*). This qualifies the meditative experience of the four absorptions and immaterial spheres;[633] at times it can also refer to a less deeply concentrated condition, such as the state of mind resulting from successfully implementing sense restraint.[634] *Āgama* literature clearly recognizes and values such unitary mental experiences, but this appears to be mainly for instrumental purposes. What counts is not just abiding in an absence of duality as such but freedom from attachment. This can be exemplified with the concluding part of a discourse extant in Pāli, Chinese, and Tibetan. After a survey of various avenues for reaching profound, unitary meditative experiences, the parallel versions agree in pointing out that any attachment to these will prevent progress toward liberation.[635]

Just as *Āgama* literature does not accord liberating value to the mere absence of duality, it also does not problematize its presence. An example in case is a Pāli discourse without known parallels, which in its entirety is dedicated to commending contemplations by way of dyads.[636] Most of the contemplations presented in this discourse build on the basic contrast between the first two noble truths, *duḥkha* and its arising, and the third and fourth noble truths, the cessation of *duḥkha* and the path leading to that. Such forms of contemplation would indeed amount to relying on a dualistic distinction. At the same time, however, this is just one possible perspective among several. Since there are four of these noble truths, it would equally well be possible to contemplate them from a fourfold perspective. Seeing them as together pointing to a single realization of Nirvana, yet another approach could focus on that single aspect, where the direct realization of the cessation of *duḥkha* implies the other three.

A positive evaluation of a specific type of duality features in an account of the type of approach cultivated by the Buddha-to-be during his progress toward realizing Nirvana. This approach takes the form of contrasting thoughts of a wholesome type to those of an unwholesome type, on the grounds that the latter lead to affliction of oneself and others, unlike the former. The relevant Pāli discourse and its Chinese parallel report the Buddha explaining that he intentionally divided his thoughts into these two opposite types.[637] Although this explanation does not explicitly use the term "dualistic," it clearly involves such a distinction. In its contextual setting, this dualistic distinction facilitates the bodhisattva Śākyamuni's progress toward awakening. This neatly exemplifies that, alongside emphasis on the construction of experience and the need to avoid taking a stance on anything, the basic ethical distinction and cognitive discernment between what is wholesome and what is unwholesome remains central in *Āgama* thought.

A type of presentation also relevant to the topic of duality is when *Āgama* literature contrasts the senses to their objects, which happens regularly. However, another mode of presentation instead lists the senses, their objects, and the corresponding type of consciousness. This results in a triad required for the occurrence of contact as the event of experience.[638] A similar triadic pattern can be seen in a mode of presentation that helps to explain the continuity of existence during life and from one life to another.[639] This continuity involves a reciprocal conditioning between consciousness on the one side and name-and-form on the other. Here, "form" stands for the material dimension of experience and "name" for those mental factors that are involved in giving a name to things, in recognizing them.[640] These mental factors, together with the material side of what they cognize, rely on consciousness to be known, just as consciousness relies on these for the content of what is known. The mode of presentation that emerges in this way is clearly not about positing a mind-matter duality.

Now, the starting point for my present exploration of nonduality was a difference between descriptions of Ānanda's attitude toward the Buddha, where the Perfection of Wisdom just mentions his *maitrī* by way of body, speech, and mind, whereas corresponding descriptions in some discourses add the qualification that his *maitrī* was "nondual," or perhaps "undivided." A relationship of *maitrī* to nonduality can also be identified in a passage in the *Pañcaviṃśatisāhasrikā Prajñāpāramitā*, which offers a description of the cultivation of *maitrī* in general (without any relation to Ānanda). This description comes with the explicit qualification that such cultivation of *maitrī* is nondual.[641]

Several Mahāyāna texts in turn describe a cultivation of *maitrī* (or even of all four *brahmavihāras*) that is without an object.[642] Examples are the *Śikṣāsamuccaya*, a compendium of the training for bodhisattvas, and the *Mahāyānasūtrālaṃkāra*, an important treatise on the bodhisattva path. These two works agree in presenting an objectless form of *maitrī* as the domain of bodhisattvas who have reached the patient acceptance of the nonarising of dharmas (*anutpattikadharmakṣānti*).[643] In other words, objectless *maitrī* features as a comparatively advanced type of practice.

The notion of cultivating *maitrī* without an object can be compared to the standard way in which *Āgama* literature describes its cultivation (as well as that of the other *brahmavihāras*). The relevant instructions are simply to dwell pervading all directions with a mental attitude of *maitrī*, without any reference to specific recipients of such pervasion and thus without a clearly delineated object.[644] Given that no recipients are mentioned, not even a generalized notion, such as "all sentient beings," the type of practice depicted in this way seems to have some similarity to the above-mentioned descriptions of the practice of advanced bodhisattvas.

A different perspective emerges with exegetical treatises like the *Visuddhimagga* and the *Abhidharmakośabhāṣya*. Both works present various individuals as objects toward which *maitrī* should successively be directed.[645] This has become the standard approach to the cultivation of *maitrī* in later times, with the result that the intrinsic quality of being immeasurable is no longer fully evident during the early stages of actual practice, which for the most part involve a focus on specific objects.

A comparable evolution can be discerned in relation to mindfulness of breathing, where later developments have also become the standard approach to meditation practice in the course of time. These developments have their starting point in *Āgama* literature in a sophisticated scheme of sixteen steps of practice that require cultivating mindfulness in such a way that the experience of the inhalations and exhalations combines with an awareness of various aspects of subjective experience.[646] Such a practice explicitly features as a way of actualizing the four establishments of mindfulness rather than being aimed merely at focused concentration. A gradual reduction of this scheme of sixteen steps can be discerned in various texts,[647] with the final result that mindfulness of breathing becomes just focusing on the sensation caused by the breath, to be replaced in the course of progressive practice by a mental image, usually experienced as a form of inner light. In this way, what appears to have started as a cultivation of a broadly receptive mindfulness of the process of breathing *together* with other dimensions of subjective experience has evolved into an exclusive focus on a single object.

Textual accounts of the attainment of absorption (*dhyāna*) also to some degree testify to this type of pattern. In *Āgama* literature, the standard descriptions of absorption are concerned with what happens in the mind, delineating which particular mental factors and qualities are characteristic of a specific level of absorption.[648] Objects are not mentioned in these standard descriptions.[649] With the *Visuddhimagga*, however, these come to the forefront, evident in the circumstance that the scaffolding of Buddhaghosa's exploration of the topic of absorption attainment relies on distinguishing different objects. After a general discussion of the nature of concentration as such, he begins providing practical instructions based on the example of earth as the object of concentration.[650] Having developed this in much detail, Buddhaghosa then continues with other possible objects for attaining absorption, detailing in what ways these differ from his first example of earth. This approach is dominated by the importance granted to the objects of the cultivation of concentration.

The example of taking earth as the object for cultivating absorption involves one of the totalities, already mentioned above. With these totalities, a change in meaning of the relevant Pāli term (*kasiṇa*) can be observed, as in its usage in the *Visuddhimagga* this term now refers to the device on which the meditator should focus in order to arouse an inner image that is then to be used to enter absorption.[651] The device can be a disk, which in the case of earth should be covered with earth. In this way, the very term *kṛtsna* (Pāli: *kasiṇa*), connoting a perceptual "totality," has come to be narrowed down to designating a disk as the object of a perceptual focus. This change of meaning and understanding makes it difficult to accommodate consciousness as one of the totalities listed in the discourses. The *Visuddhimagga* in fact drops consciousness from its presentation—perhaps in recognition of the difficulties of turning consciousness into an object, let alone cultivating a perception of consciousness based on some kind of a disk or round aperture—replacing it with light (*āloka*) as an alternative object. This should be cultivated by looking at a circle of light resulting from a lamp or else the sun or the moon shining through a hole.[652]

A change of meaning in terminology holds even for the very term used in later Pāli texts to designate an "object," *ārammaṇa* (Sanskrit: *ālambana/ārambaṇa*). In Pāli discourses this term conveys the sense of a "foundation" or a "basis," in the sense of what one depends on, what serves as a means for some purpose or other.[653] The shift in meaning of this term in later Pāli texts to designate an "object" aligns with an overall increasing concern with precisely such objects. At the same time, however, it needs to be acknowledged that this emphasis is not absolute, as the Pāli commentaries recognize that meditation can be not only on objects but also on qualities or characteristics (*lakṣaṇa*).[654] The latter category could in principle accommodate, for example, a contemplation of emptiness that does not apprehend any specific, circumscribed object.

Several of the examples mentioned above reflect Theravāda developments. Nevertheless, a concern with objects is also plainly evident in Sarvāstivāda thought. As mentioned above (p. 126), here the perceived need to posit an actually existing object applies even to mental experiences concerned with what is already past or what will be in the future. This appears to stand in the background of the very reification of dharmas as truly existing.

In view of the above developments reflecting a preoccupation with objects in exegetical literature, together with its repercussions on actual practice, it is perhaps unsurprising if in later *Prajñāpāramitā* literature and other Mahāyāna texts an increasing emphasis on nonduality can be discerned.[655] Perhaps this may originate from an attempt at counterbalancing the above-described developments. If this should indeed be the case, however, attempts at correction can take on a life of their own, proceeding beyond the needed return to a state of balance and resulting in an imbalance in the opposite direction. This could take the form of investing nonduality with a value in its own right, as a result of which the qualification of being dualistic then can come to express an evaluation of something as just flat wrong. At least from the viewpoint of *Āgama* literature, at times it can be quite meaningful to adopt a dualistic perspective, such as for discerning the difference between ethically wholesome and unwholesome actions (or, say, between healthy and poisonous food).[656] Moreover, the significance of any nondual experience remains subordinate to the need to stay free from attachment and reification. This is clearly the overarching concern in *Āgama* literature just as in the Perfection of Wisdom, becoming even more prominent in the latter, and that evidently for good reasons.

## Omniscience

The twenty-second chapter in Lokakṣema's translation begins with a discussion of the training of a bodhisattva in omniscience. This affords me a convenient occasion for exploring the topic of omniscience as an important equivalent to Buddhahood in the Perfection of Wisdom, wherefore this notion as such already featured in previous chapters. By way of introduction, I present a few selected excerpts from these previous chapters relevant to appreciating the implications and role of omniscience:[657]

> From omniscience one attains Buddhahood.
>
> Omniscience is accomplished through the Perfection of Wisdom.
>
> Overall, it is through training in the Perfection of Wisdom that one gains accomplishment in omniscience.
>
> One who takes refuge in the Perfection of Wisdom has taken refuge in omniscience.
>
> The wisdom of omniscience is illuminated by this Perfection of Wisdom. For one who is established in the Perfection of Wisdom, there is nothing that wisdom does not understand.

> The Buddha said: "The mind that proceeds toward omniscience: this is contemplation of the Perfection of Wisdom."
>
> Subhūti said: "How is the mind said to be proceeding toward omniscience?"
>
> The Buddha said: "The mind that proceeds toward emptiness: this is contemplation of omniscience."

The above quotes begin by clarifying the basic position that omniscience is integral to becoming a Buddha. This can in turn be accomplished through the Perfection of Wisdom, as it is training in the latter that will lead to omniscience. The same close interrelation can also be expressed in terms of taking refuge. In fact, the wisdom of omniscience results from the illumination provided by the Perfection of Wisdom. The exchange between Subhūti and the Buddha then highlights that emptiness is the key here.

The twenty-second chapter brings these perspectives to the forefront by setting out with Subhūti's inquiry into how a bodhisattva trains in omniscience. The ensuing discussion reveals once again that training in the Perfection of Wisdom corresponds to training in omniscience.[658]

> Training like this is training in omniscience. Training like this is training in the Perfection of Wisdom. Training like this is training in the level of a Tathāgata, is training in the powers [of a Tathāgata], is training in the fearlessness [of a Tathāgata], and is training in all the qualities of a Buddha.

The relationship of the Perfection of Wisdom to omniscience is probably best viewed as an integral part of its overall leading role in relation to all aspects of the path to Buddhahood. Nevertheless, the resultant presentation is of considerable significance, in that omniscience results from the illumination provided by the Perfection of Wisdom and from a cultivation of emptiness. In other words, the type of omniscience that would fit the above indications seems to be more about seeing through anything than about knowing everything. This distinction can be kept in mind when turning to the early Buddhist perspective on omniscience, which can be approached by first surveying indications in *Āgama* literature regarding what the possession of omniscience was believed to entail.

The relevant descriptions occur in the context of a depiction of teachers whom one should better not follow. One such teacher claims to be omniscient but then undergoes various misfortunes. According to the Pāli account, such a teacher may go begging and receive no food, or else be bitten by a dog, or may encounter a fierce elephant, horse, or bull.[659] According to a Sanskrit fragment parallel, such a teacher may also fall into a sewer or cesspool.[660] An otherwise unrelated discourse extant in Chinese translation offers a similar description, which also mentions encounters with fierce animals or else falling into a cesspool.[661] Needless to say, such misadventures are what anyone in ancient India (or elsewhere) would rather avoid. When any of these nevertheless happens, a teacher claiming to be omniscient will be forced to take the position that this just had to happen. In other words, the teacher knew that this was in store but did not go to a different place to beg or take a road that avoids encounters with animals or bypasses the cesspool due to the knowledge that this was bound to happen anyway. Such weak excuses are hardly convincing, and the presentation in these discourses makes it clear that one should not place confidence in teachers who in this way do not live up to their own claims.

It follows from the above that in the ancient Indian setting omniscience comprised the ability to foretell the future. One who is truly omniscient should know where alms can be gotten and go there rather than where none will be given. Such a one should similarly know of the danger posed by fierce animals on certain roads and avoid these by taking a different road or else know where a cesspool is found and therefore be able to avoid falling into it.

The first of the above misfortunes is particularly interesting, as *Āgama* literature reports that on one occasion the Buddha went to beg without receiving anything.[662] The account of this episode, extant in a Pāli and two Chinese versions, would be reflecting a time when the Buddha was as yet not considered omniscient, given that the narrative conflicts directly with what is to be expected from an omniscient teacher. This is not the only such case, as already pointed out by Gombrich (2007, 206–7), who explains that "the idea that the Buddha was omniscient is strikingly at odds with the picture of him presented in every Vinaya tradition." These "show that the Buddha did not anticipate what rules would be needed, he even occasionally made a false start and found it necessary to reverse a decision." In terms of the notion of omniscience as it emerges from the passages surveyed above, it would follow that the relevant narratives on the promulgation of rules in the different *Vinaya* traditions must have come into existence in a setting that had not yet conceived of the Buddha as an omniscient law giver. The situation that emerges in this way finds confirmation in an explicit statement attributed to the Buddha and reported in a Pāli discourse with no known parallel, to the following effect:[663]

> Those who speak like this: "The recluse Gotama is omniscient and all-seeing; he claims to have complete knowledge and vision: 'Walking or standing, sleeping or awake, knowledge and vision are continuously present to me without interruption'"—they are not speaking what has been said by me; they are misrepresenting me with what is untrue and false.

The formulation employed in this passage to describe omniscience recurs in other Pāli discourses in reports of a claim to omniscience by Mahāvīra, the leader of the Jains.[664] As already pointed out by several scholars, in view of the ongoing competition between Buddhists and Jains in the ancient Indian setting, it would be unsurprising for the Buddha's disciples to promote their teacher to the same rank by attributing omniscience to him as well.[665] This soon enough appears to have become a common tenet of the different Buddhist traditions, to the extent that at times some later texts even apply the qualification "omniscient" to the bodhisattva Śākyamuni.[666] This phrasing can best be understood to intend the bodhisattva who is *in quest of* omniscience.

In an attempt to bolster the attribution of omniscience to the Buddha, the Pāli commentators read another passage extant in a Pāli discourse as implying a claim to omniscience made by the Buddha himself. The relevant passage proceeds as follows:[667]

> Monastics, in the world with its celestials, Māra, and Brahmā, among its population of recluses and Brahmins, celestials and humans, what is seen, heard, sensed, cognized, attained, sought for, and pursued by the mind—all that the Tathāgata has awakened to. For this reason, he is called "Tathāgata."

A parallel extant in Chinese translation indicates that "whatever there is that is completely correct, the Tathāgata has understood, seen, realized, and attained all that."[668] The import here appears to be a seeing through, in the sense of understanding, rather than a form of omniscience that enables a comprehensive access to all details. The same appears to be the required meaning in the case of another passage extant in Pāli, according to which without knowing and understanding everything, it is not possible to eradicate *duḥkha*; the Chinese parallel formulates the same requirement in terms of the need to understand all as it really is.[669] Since the eradication of *duḥkha* is a feat accomplished by every arhat, unlike gaining omniscient knowledge, here the reference to knowing all must be meant in a penetrative sense rather than in the comprehensive sense envisaged by the ancient Indian notion of omniscience.

The foregoing suggests a development from a penetrative knowledge as a form of insight to a comprehensive knowledge of everything as a quality eventually attributed to the Buddha by later generations in order to draw equal with the Jains. Such a shift toward giving increasing importance to detailed and all-inclusive forms of knowledge would in turn be characteristic of Abhidharma thought. Alongside the impact of formal elements like summary lists and the question-and-answer format, which are frequently used in early Abhidharma but at the same time not confined to it, it appears to be this drive toward covering everything in all its details that would have been of central influence in the early stages of the evolution of Abhidharma thought.[670]

*Prajñāpāramitā* literature promotes a different attitude in this respect. This comes to the fore in the extracts translated above, according to which the very Perfection of Wisdom leads to omniscience. Particularly telling are the indications that "for one who is established in the Perfection of Wisdom, there is nothing that wisdom does not understand," and "the mind that proceeds toward emptiness: this is contemplation of omniscience." All of this points to penetrative insight rather than to a gathering of exhaustive information on all details.[671]

## Summary

This chapter has presented a survey of Ānanda's qualities that have commonalities with those of a bodhisattva and an examination of omniscience as a dimension of Buddhahood.

In his role as the guardian of the Buddha's teaching, Ānanda is naturally the one to be entrusted with the preservation of the Perfection of Wisdom, to which he should dedicate himself fully in order to ensure that not a single sentence will be lost. Such a task would be in line with his role as a disciple who is not only endowed with exceptional textual memory but also with a personal interest in teachings related to emptiness. The care with which he should devote himself to the task of transmitting the Perfection of Wisdom should mirror his attitude of kindness toward the Buddha.

Accounts of a communal recitation, *saṅgīti*, reportedly held soon after the Buddha's demise, appear to reflect an underlying tension in the monastic community, resulting in a move away from the type of behavior and attitude embodied by Ānanda and in favor of a more ascetic ideal. The same can also be seen in a discourse depicting another monk, who features as praiseworthy for a type of conduct that could even be considered selfish had he not been an arhat. These passages, which are later than the bulk of the discourses in *Āgama* literature, point to a change in the conception of what makes an ideal arhat. This conception becomes more closely aligned with ancient Indian values of asceticism at the expense of prosocial attitudes. Such an apparent shift may stand in the background of criticism of arhats in texts promoting the bodhisattva ideal, which perhaps may stand in dialogue with this later conception of an arhat.

Ānanda's loving kindness toward the Buddha comes with the specific qualification in *Āgama* literature of being "nondual," *advaya*, or less literally "undivided." This is one of the relatively rare occurrences of this term in the Pāli discourses and their parallels, which mirrors a similar lack of concern with nonduality in the Perfection of Wisdom. With later *Prajñāpāramitā* literature, however, the topic of nonduality receives increasing emphasis. This may be standing in dialogue with a tendency in exegetical texts of the Sarvāstivāda and Theravāda traditions to focus on objects. Manifesting in a range of ways, a result of this tendency appears to be an increasing emphasis on the subject-object duality.

From the viewpoint of *Āgama* literature, nondual and dual modes of perception are not intrinsically right or wrong, as their appropriateness or inappropriateness simply depends on the context of their usage. What counts overall, and in this respect *Āgama* literature aligns closely with the Perfection of Wisdom, is avoiding reification and attachment in order to progress toward liberation.

Although the original conception of the Buddha's successful progress toward liberation does not seem to have included the achievement of omniscience, in view of claims to omniscience made by other teachers in the ancient Indian setting it is hardly a surprise that soon enough similar claims were made on his behalf. Such an attribution of omniscience to the Buddha can be seen to involve a shift from seeing through anything to seeing everything, from a penetrative knowing to knowing every single detail. From the perspective of this shift, the Perfection of Wisdom seems to emphasize seeing through anything when it presents the path to omniscience as requiring, above all, insight into emptiness.

## On Chapters 26 to 30

THE TWENTY-SIXTH to thirtieth chapters of Lokakṣema's translation of the Perfection of Wisdom correspond to the textual portion beginning with the second part of the twenty-eighth up to the end of the thirty-second chapter of the Sanskrit version translated by Conze (1973/1975, 270–300). In both versions these are the final chapters, which begin with the Buddha expounding how a bodhisattva should survey dependent arising in order to avoid falling to the level of arhats or Pratyekabuddhas. Then the literary style of presentation changes from the dialogue format mainly employed thus far to a predominantly narrative mode of presentation. The narrative in question has the bodhisattva Sadāprarudita as its main protagonist, who exemplifies wholehearted dedication to the quest for the Perfection of Wisdom.

In his wish to make an offering to his prospective teacher of the Perfection of Wisdom, Sadāprarudita starts dismembering himself when he has found a prospective buyer for parts of his body. The prospective buyer reveals himself to be Śakra in disguise. Sadāprarudita's body is restored to his former condition and a woman, who has witnessed his dedication, joins him in his quest for the Perfection of Wisdom, together with a following of five hundred women. Eventually they hear a public teaching of the Perfection of Wisdom by the eminent lay teacher and bodhisattva Dharmodgata. In preparation for Dharmodgata's next teaching, Sadāprarudita and the five hundred women sprinkle their own blood to settle any dust, as Māra has hidden all water that could be used for that purpose. Śakra transforms the blood into scented water. Dharmodgata expounds the Perfection of Wisdom and Sadāprarudita as well as the five hundred women receive a prediction of their future Buddhahood. After the narrative has come to its end, the Buddha once more entrusts the Perfection of Wisdom to Ānanda. The text closes by locating the teaching event in the thirtieth year after the Buddha's awakening, followed by the standard conclusion reporting the delighted reaction of the members of the audience.

Two topics to be explored below are the doctrine of dependent arising and the tale of the bodhisattva Sadāprarudita, in particular in relation to the notion of making an offering by relinquishing parts or even all of one's body.

## Dependent Arising

The clarification regarding how a bodhisattva should contemplate dependent arising in a manner that avoids falling to the level of an arhat or a Pratyekabuddha proceeds as follows:[672]

> Suppose a bodhisattva, when cultivating the Perfection of Wisdom, pays attention to the twelve-fold dependent arising not becoming extinct. One who pays such attention goes beyond and leaves behind the path to arhat-ship or Pratyekabuddhahood and is correctly established in the path to Buddhahood.

The passage continues by indicating that failure to pay attention in the proper way can result in realization midway and thus becoming an arhat or a Pratyekabuddha. The present indication thereby restates a problem already taken up earlier with respect to meditation on emptiness and related topics (see above p. 211). In that context, the task was to avoid penetrating the concentration of the mind free from attachment, or taking emptiness concentration, signless concentration, and wishless concentration up to the level of actual realization. With all these forms of cultivation, there is a need to avoid going so far as to gain full realization by relying on skill in means, which also features in the same role in relation to the passage translated above, namely as the key quality preventing a full realization of dependent arising. Throughout, the task of a bodhisattva is to mature insight as much as possible but at the same time avoid realization midway, that is, avoid the breakthrough to Nirvana as long as the gradual process of inner maturation is not yet sufficient for this breakthrough to issue in Buddhahood.

The recommendation given in this way can be explored by turning to teachings on dependent arising in *Āgama* literature. Since I have surveyed these elsewhere in more detail, in what follows I can present the matter succinctly. First of all, it may be worth noting that the early Buddhist teaching on dependent arising is not about promoting some form of general interdependence or interconnectedness, where everything is seen as being in some way or other causally related to everything else.[673] Of course, all phenomena in the world are conditioned. But the point of the teaching of dependent arising is more precisely to discern, within this general state of affairs of phenomena being conditioned, those conditions that are directly relevant to the issue at hand. Such specific conditions are indispensable for the arising of whatever phenomenon is being investigated, and their absence inevitably leads to its ceasing. In short, the concern is with those conditions that really matter, rather than surveying all conditions regardless of whether these have a clear, tangible impact.

The overall pragmatic orientation of *Āgama* thought toward gaining liberation then finds its expression in focusing the inquiry into dependent arising in particular on the arising (and ceasing) of *duḥkha*. That is, the conditions that contribute to the arising of *duḥkha* need to be identified in order to be able to reach freedom from *duḥkha* through their cessation. The key element at stake is specific conditionality, which often but not invariably finds expression in a series of twelve links leading from ignorance to *duḥkha*. This twelve-link presentation appears to stand in dialogue with a Vedic creation myth.[674] From this perspective, a significant shift in perspective articulated with the teaching on dependent arising would be that the series of links, instead of issuing in the celebrated event of creation, lead up to the manifestation of *duḥkha*. Moreover, in addition to the arising mode, the same teaching also comprises the complementary ceasing mode, where the overcoming of ignorance leads via the cessation of the intervening links to freedom from *duḥkha*.

The key for realizing such freedom with the attainment of Nirvana would thus be less about any of the twelve links and more about a thorough letting go that makes it possible to experience the cessation of all conditions. This can be illustrated with the report of how Śāriputra and Mahāmaudgalyāyana attained stream-entry.[675] In both cases, the relevant texts indicate that this took place based on hearing a brief statement on conditionality that does not mention any of the twelve links. This confirms that these links can serve as an exemplification of a principle, and it is insight into this principle that would have the potential of issuing in realization.

The impression that the twelve links are not the key for realization finds further support in the report that the Buddha cultivated insight into the links of dependent arising already before his actual awakening.[676] The description in the relevant discourses appears to intend a form of mental reflection. From the viewpoint of the concern in the Perfection of Wisdom with avoiding a realization midway, this much would appear to be unproblematic for any bodhisattva. The same would also hold for some degree of realization of dependent arising, in the form of recollecting one's own past lives and witnessing the passing away and rebirth of others with the divine eye. These are profound meditative visions, based on a deeply concentrated mind, but they are nonetheless not considered to be liberating in themselves.[677]

In the case of the Buddha's own awakening, *Āgama* literature provides an account of the night of his awakening that only describes the three higher knowledges attained in the first, second, and third watch of the night, without drawing out how these relate to each other.[678] The actual description of his recollection of past lives just mentions that he was able to remember his past names and families, the food he ate, and the pleasure and pain he experienced. Of course, with each past life, these would have been substantially different. A *Vinaya* text of the Mūlasarvāstivādins reports that the wish to understand the causes underlying the process of his rebirths then motivated him to cultivate the divine eye.[679] The discourses describing his attainment of the second higher knowledge, developed in the second watch of the night of his awakening, emphasize wholesome and unwholesome conduct leading to rebirth in pleasant or unpleasant forms of existence. This would then imply a firsthand realization of the principle of karma and its fruit as what connects one life to the next, revealing the causes and conditions considered responsible for the individual circumstances of each rebirth and its particular experiences (such as the pleasure and pain felt in any such former life).[680]

If this way of reading should be correct, then the third knowledge gained in the night of the Buddha's awakening would have confirmed the growth of insight into dependent arising acquired with the first two higher knowledge through a realization of the unconditioned. In *Āgama* thought, this realization corresponds to the supreme accomplishment in emptiness, which reveals that there is nothing at all stable or substantial, no entity or thing as such, as all that is there is the empty interplay of causes and conditions. With this realization, the whole range of conditionality will be fully understood by dint of stepping outside of it, which at the same time reveals the illusory nature of any notion of a self, a notion that turns out to be merely a construct superimposed on the operation of causes and conditions.

This type of direct realization would be what a bodhisattva, according to the injunction given in the Perfection of Wisdom, should definitely avoid. It is perfectly fine to pay attention to the twelvefold dependent arising, but this should take place without proceeding to the point where its operation becomes extinguished. The point could then be that a direct realization of the cessation of dependent arising, of the unconditioned, should be sidestepped until the bodhisattva has matured sufficiently to be able to become a Buddha. It would be by avoiding premature realization in this way that the bodhisattva "goes beyond and leaves behind the path to arhat-ship or Pratyekabuddhahood" and remains "correctly established in the path to Buddhahood." In terms of the relay of seven chariots, bodhisattvas can and should leave the seventh chariot behind. However, instead of charging forward to reach the final goal of the long journey, they await the right time for entering the palace.

## The Sadāprarudita Tale

The Perfection of Wisdom reports the Buddha giving the rationale for introducing the tale of Sadāprarudita in the following way:[681] "One who wishes to become a Buddha quickly should be like the bodhisattva Sadāprarudita in seeking for the Perfection of Wisdom." This touches on a theme of considerable importance throughout the Perfection of Wisdom, namely speedy progress to Buddhahood, a prospect that must have been of considerable appeal among its audiences. To achieve this requires wholehearted dedication of the type exemplified by Sadāprarudita.

In what follows, I explore the tale of Sadāprarudita from the viewpoint of its contribution to the teachings in the Perfection of Wisdom and thus to speedy progress toward Buddhahood. In this context, I also examine its indication that embarking on the bodhisattva path can take place in reliance on visionary experiences of Buddhas, and I survey literary dimensions of how the tale depicts Sadāprarudita's gradual maturation. Another topic to be examined is the rhetoric of self-sacrifice in this tale. This leads me to a survey of other instances of this rhetoric, in particular in relation to the motif of self-immolation. In this way, whereas it was possible to deal with my first topic of dependent arising in a fairly brief manner in this chapter, my second topic of the Sadāprarudita tale requires quite a detailed examination.

In the context of a study of the composition of the *Aṣṭasāhasrikā Prajñāpāramitā*, Conze (1952/2008, 170) offers the following comments on the Sadāprarudita narrative, which he assigns to the latest stage of textual growth of the whole text: "The almost turgid devotionalism of these chapters is very unlike the lucid rationality which marks the sober and highly intellectual discussions between the Lord and his disciples in the first chapter of the *Aṣṭa*°." In another publication, Conze (1959/2008, 64) reasons:

> [The tale of Sadāprarudita] is indeed a pure fairy-tale, showing complete disregard for common sense and this mundane world. Everything about it is otherworldly, the excessive regard for the Dharma and its representatives . . . and also the almost

> naïve belief in the power of Truth. To the spiritually minded it nevertheless illustrates the inescapable fact that the readiness to sacrifice all is an indispensable condition for the acquisition of wisdom.

Without intending to deny that the Perfection of Wisdom in its present form would be the product of a gradual textual expansion and therefore combine earlier and later layers, my approach to this tale is mainly oriented toward attempting to understand its message. After all, the tale is already fully in place in Lokakṣema's translation. Moreover, I think it is important to avoid that in-themselves meaningful distinctions between earlier and later textual strata shade into value judgments. This can easily lead to a tendency to ignore what is deemed later and thereby miss out on important dimensions of the text under discussion. I believe we can be quite sure that members of the audiences of the Perfection of Wisdom would have listened to or read the Sadāprarudita tale with just as much interest as previous chapters of the same text. This makes it meaningful to try to understand the message delivered by this tale.

### *Profound Teachings*

An evaluation of the Sadāprarudita tale can benefit from paying attention not only to its more devotionally oriented narrative elements but also to practical advice given to the bodhisattva Sadaprarudita. A passage illustrating this dimension takes the form of an instruction on how Sadāprarudita should conduct himself when walking in the direction of the east in his quest for the Perfection of Wisdom:[682]

> When you are walking, disengage attentionally from the left, disengage attentionally from the right, disengage attentionally from the front, disengage attentionally from behind, disengage attentionally from above, disengage attentionally from below, disengage attentionally from walking.
>
> When you are walking, disengage attentionally from what is frightful, disengage attentionally from what is delightful, disengage attentionally from eating, disengage attentionally

from drinking, disengage attentionally from sitting, disengage attentionally from walking on the path, disengage attentionally from stopping halfway, disengage attentionally from lust, disengage attentionally from anger, disengage attentionally from delusion, disengage attentionally from cultivation, disengage attentionally from something to be attained, disengage attentionally from the internal, disengage attentionally from the external.

Disengage attentionally from form, disengage attentionally from feeling tones, perception, formations, and consciousness, disengage attentionally from the eyes, disengage attentionally from the ears, disengage attentionally from the nose, disengage attentionally from the mouth, disengage attentionally from the body, disengage attentionally from the mind, disengage attentionally from earth, water, fire, and wind, disengage attentionally from space, disengage attentionally from people, disengage attentionally from yourself, disengage attentionally from life.

Disengage attentionally from the presence of emptiness, disengage attentionally from the absence of emptiness, disengage attentionally from cultivating the path of a bodhisattva, disengage attentionally from the presence of teachings, disengage attentionally from the absence of teachings, disengage attentionally from rebirth in heaven, disengage attentionally from rebirth in the world, disengage attentionally from a bodhisattva being good, disengage attentionally from a bodhisattva being bad.

All those penchants for engaging attentionally, abandon them completely and be everywhere without attachment to anything!

This passage offers a remarkably thorough instruction on nonattention (*amanasikāra*), in the sense of disengaging attentionally from any sign (*nimitta*), thereby thoroughly undermining the basis on which attachments usually thrive. The instruction given in this way could fruitfully be compared with Ānanda's inquiry about a way of paying attention that does not involve any of the possible objects or mental activities that one usually pays attention to, discussed earlier (see above p. 223). The two passages share the instruction that one should not pay attention to the senses, the four elements, or the idea of having attained something. The present teaching to Sadāprarudita places more emphasis on the need to avoid evaluations and defiled mental states, and it brings in various bodily activities related to the walking posture in which this practice should be cultivated.

Another remarkable passage takes the form of the first teaching given by Dharmodgata. Sadāprarudita had earlier experienced meditative visions of Buddhas and now wants to know where they came from and where they went to.[683] Here is an excerpt from the first part of Dharmodgata's reply:[684]

> Emptiness does not originally come from anywhere, and on passing away it also does not arrive anywhere; Buddhas are also like that. Signlessness does not originally come from anywhere, and on passing away it also does not arrive anywhere; Buddhas are also like that . . . Nirvana does not originally come from anywhere, and on passing away it also does not arrive anywhere; Buddhas are also like that.

This type of teaching is well in line with previous chapters of the Perfection of Wisdom.

With this basic assessment in place, at this point I depart briefly from my exploration of the tale of Sadāprarudita and explore the question about where Buddhas, being experienced in vision, come from with the help of another text whose translation by Lokakṣema and his team was apparently completed at the same time as his translation of the Perfection of Wisdom. This is the **Pratyutpannasamādhisūtra*, which tackles what appears to be basically the same question regarding the provenance of a Buddha encountered in visionary experiences in the following manner:[685]

> One has this thought: "Where did the Buddha come from? Where did I go to?" One thinks to oneself: "The Buddha came from nowhere, and I also went nowhere." One thinks to oneself: "The three realms—the sensual realm, the fine-material realm, and the immaterial realm—these three realms are just made by the mind. Whatever I think, I then see. The mind constructs the Buddha. The mind itself sees him. The mind is the Buddha. The mind is the Tathāgata."

In a way, this takes the teachings on the illusory and constructed nature of reality found in the Perfection of Wisdom to their logical conclusion.[686] With this proposition I am not intending to promote an idealist interpretation but rather to propose reading the above, including the tantalizing statement that the three realms are made by the mind, as a pointer to the source of the construction of experience, which is of course none other than the mind. Such a reading is clearly the appropriate one for a verse that stands at the outset of what is probably the most popular collection of Pāli poetry, the *Dharmapada* (Pāli: *Dhammapada*). The first part of the verse in question proceeds as follows:[687]

> Phenomena are preceded by the mind,
> They are led by the mind,
> And they are made by the mind.

This verse and the extract quoted above from the *Pratyutpanna-samādhisūtra* can be brought into a closer relationship to each other with the help of a passage found in the version of the *Aṣṭasāhasrikā Prajñāpāramitā* translated by Zhī Qiān (支謙). The relevant quote also relates the three realms to the mind, followed by indicating that the same holds for the six sense spheres and the five aggregates. To express the basic equation, the relevant passage uses two Chinese characters that could be rendering an Indic original corresponding to *manomaya*, "mind-made",[688] as the first of the two Chinese characters renders "the mind" and the other could be a misunderstanding of "made". Should this indeed be the case, then it would concord with the last line in the Pāli verse quoted above that phenomena (like the three realms, the six sense spheres, and the five aggregates) are "made by the mind."

After this short excursion for the purpose of rounding off a topic of recurrent interest in the Perfection of Wisdom, the time has come to return to the tale of Sadāprarudita and more specifically to Dharmodgata's second sermon, delivered after he had withdrawn for a long period to abide in meditation. The profundity of his teaching can be illustrated with the following excerpt:[689]

> The Nirvana of an arhat is empty; it does not arise from anywhere. In the same way the Perfection of Wisdom is also empty; it does not arise from anywhere. The Nirvana of a Tathāgata is originally the same, without any difference. In the same way the Perfection of Wisdom is also originally the same, without any difference.

The situation finds illustration in a fire that similarly does not come from anywhere and upon ceasing does not go anywhere. This illustration can conveniently be related to the simile of a fire employed in a Pāli discourse and its Chinese and Tibetan parallels to convey the nature of a Tathāgata, in the context of an attempt to counter any reification. As long as the fire exists, it can be located due to the material that is burning. But once the fire has gone out, it can no longer be located.[690]

The position taken in this way in *Āgama* literature seems to express concerns quite similar to those relevant to the above passage in the Perfection of Wisdom, which also relies on the image of fire and then indicates that "Buddhas are also like that." In both cases, the central motivation appears to be an attempt to undermine any tendency to turn a Buddha or a Tathāgata into an entity of sorts that originates somewhere and on disappearing arrives somewhere else.

### *A Vision of Buddhas*

The tale of the bodhisattva Sadāprarudita and the five hundred women who follow him in his quest for the Perfection of Wisdom also provides a perspective on whether at this comparatively early stage in the development of the Mahāyāna traditions an encounter with a living Buddha was considered indispensable for the path of a bodhisattva.[691] The tale itself is explicitly situated at a time when the previous Buddha had already passed away long before, and one could no longer even hear his discourses or meet members of his monastic community.[692] This would imply that the narrative exemplifies the conduct of a bodhisattva at a time when no living Buddha (or even his dispensation) is in existence. Given the early date of Lokakṣema's translation, indications that can be gathered from this version of the narrative can safely be expected to throw significant light on the type of beliefs held at an early stage in the development of the Mahāyāna traditions.

Two episodes in combination are relevant to this topic. The first of these episodes reports the bodhisattva Sadāprarudita explaining to a woman who had witnessed his heroic conduct that he wishes to learn the Perfection of Wisdom from the teacher Dharmodgata in order to become a Buddha. Impressed by his sincere dedication, she decides to join him, together with her following of five hundred servant women. The episode does not give any indication that she or her followers should be viewed as already being aspirants for Buddhahood. In the narrative setting, the main reason for her decision to follow Sadāprarudita appears to be his willingness to sacrifice himself for the sake of receiving teachings. Given the belief that a male body is integral to being an irreversible bodhisattva, discussed above (see p. 204), it can safely be taken for granted that in the present narrative setting the role of these women is not that of advanced bodhisattvas, precisely because they are still women.

The other relevant episode occurs at the end of Dharmodgata's second teaching, when all the bodhisattvas in the assembly experience a vision of the Buddhas of the ten directions.[693] Sadāprarudita and the whole group of five hundred women receive a prediction of their future Buddhahood, whereupon the women magically transform into males.[694] The prediction of the five hundred women does not stipulate when they will become Buddhas or what their names will be. Although it falls short of the characteristic traits of a standard prediction—traits evident in the prediction given at the same narrative juncture to the bodhisattva Sadāprarudita—it is still a prediction.[695] Since no living Buddha is present at that time and in that location, the predictions of Sadāprarudita and the women are given by the Buddhas of the ten directions whom those who receive the prediction encounter in a mental vision.

Such a type of procedure would in principle be available at any time, rather than requiring a living Buddha to be in existence in the same geographical area. The indication given in this way in Lokakṣema's translation of the Perfection of Wisdom does not seem to be unique in this respect, as a similar procedure appears in the translation of the **Pratyutpannasamādhisūtra* attributed to Lokakṣema. The relevant passage concerns the meeting between the Buddha Dīpaṃkara and the bodhisattva who was to become Śākyamuni Buddha. In an intriguing variation on the standard depiction of this meeting, the one who was to become the future Buddha Śākyamuni has a vision of the Buddhas of the ten directions, and these are then responsible for proclaiming that he will become the Buddha Śākyamuni.[696] This gives the impression that, even when a living Buddha is present, his presence may still not have been considered indispensable for receiving what for all practical purposes appears to be a prediction of future Buddhahood.[697] Such a prediction can also be conferred by the Buddhas of the ten directions whom the bodhisattva encounters in a meditative vision.

The narrative of Sadāprarudita differs from the **Pratyutpannasamādhisūtra*, as it is situated at a time when no Buddha is present and even his monastic community is no longer in existence. Due to their different settings, the two episodes from the **Pratyutpannasamādhisūtra* and the Sadāprarudita tale complement each other by covering the two alternatives of a Buddha being present or not present. For the latter case, the above denouement would exemplify the procedure that can be adopted in such a situation, namely relying on visionary experiences of Buddhas. It is in reliance on this expedient—which is a central theme in the **Pratyutpannasamādhisūtra*—that the tale of Sadāprarudita is able to portray a progression toward a level of being predicted as a future Buddha without any explicit hint that a personal encounter with a living Buddha was considered necessary.

Once a Buddha living in the same location is not absolutely necessary for receiving a prediction, it would be unsurprising for the same to hold in relation to taking the decision to embark on the path to Buddhahood. The Perfection of Wisdom definitely testifies to the former, the receiving of a prediction. Moreover, its depiction of the five hundred women reads most naturally as also pointing to the latter, in the sense that the chief source of their inspiration was witnessing other bodhisattvas—the heroic conduct of Sadāprarudita and the profound teachings of Dharmodgata—rather than encountering a living Buddha.

In sum, the above episode makes it reasonable to conclude that, at the stage in the development of Mahāyāna thought reflected in Lokakṣema's translations, a direct meeting with a Buddha living at the same place and time was not considered indispensable for becoming a bodhisattva whose future Buddhahood has been predicted.[698]

### *Sadāprarudita's Spiritual Maturation*

In addition to providing such indications regarding the need or dispensability of a direct meeting with a Buddha, the version of the Sadāprarudita tale found in Lokakṣema's translation has, as noted by Lancaster (1968, 203), "literary as well as religious merits. There is a structure and plot with movement from one event to another in a logical and understandable sequence."

The name of the hero of the tale is Sadāprarudita, "Ever Tearful." This name already hints at an emotionally stirring dimension in his role, which in turn can be taken to reflect an attempt to communicate the Perfection of Wisdom in a way that touches the heart. This dimension can be appreciated by surveying instances in the narrative when he starts crying.

This first happens after Sadāprarudita has heard a divine voice in a dream telling him to search for the Dharma. On waking up he does not know where to search, wherefore he breaks out into tears. The celestials of the Thirty-Three, on witnessing him crying day after day, give him the name Sadāprarudita.[699] The indication provided in this way helps to clarify the import of his name, which does not imply that he is continuously in tears. From the viewpoint of the entire narrative, it appears that the celestials have chosen this name to express his propensity to break out into tears easily. In view of this, the name Sadāprarudita would convey that this bodhisattva has a penchant for being easily moved or affected emotionally. In the setting of an actual delivery of the tale, his breaking out into tears can be expected to impact the audience, who may well sympathize with his plight in living in a location and at a time where it is so difficult to encounter the Dharma.

Once Sadāprarudita is asleep and dreaming again, the celestials of the Thirty-Three reveal to him the name of a former Buddha. Sadāprarudita wakes up full of joy and is so deeply inspired that he goes to dwell in a secluded place deep in the mountains.[700] On realizing that he is unable to see a Buddha or hear the Dharma, however, he weeps again.[701]

A celestial voice tells him to stop crying, informing him of the Perfection of Wisdom. Since he is not asleep at this time, Sadāprarudita can ask questions, so he requests detailed instructions on how he should proceed to find the Perfection of Wisdom. It is at this point that he receives the instructions translated above regarding how he should conduct himself when walking in his quest for the Perfection of Wisdom. Sadāprarudita once again is overjoyed and proceeds in pursuit of his quest, only to realize that he does not know how far he should travel to find the Perfection of Wisdom, whereupon he starts crying again.[702]

This time the vision of a magically created Buddha appears before him and gives him a teaching that already contains basic indications similar to those found elsewhere in the Perfection of Wisdom, in addition to also offering more detailed information on where he will meet his teacher, Dharmodgata. On hearing these teachings and instructions, Sadāprarudita is once again overjoyed and gains a *samādhi* that enables him to see all the Buddhas of the ten directions,[703] who praise and encourage him. When he emerges from his *samādhi*, he wonders where all these Buddhas have come from and where they went, which causes him to break out into tears once more.[704] On this fourth occasion, however, no intervention by others is needed to rouse him from his sorrow, as he remembers the instruction he has already received and continues his journey toward his teacher Dharmodgata, whom he will then ask about the appearance and disappearance of the Buddhas.

Based on a detailed comparative study of the tale of Sadāprarudita as found in Lokakṣema's translation of the Perfection of Wisdom,

Lancaster (1968, 205–6) highlights how the above instances of Sadāprarudita breaking out in tears reflect a gradual building up of the narrative:

> At first he hears only a voice of an unidentified *deva*; this is followed by a second revelation from a *deva* of the *trayastriṃśa*. The third time there is a voice in the sky, and finally . . . a magically created Buddha is manifested. From these four events, the developing awareness of the Bodhisattva can be traced . . .
>
> When Sadāprarudita received the initial revelation, he was asleep and dreaming . . . The second experience is also in an unconscious state of sleep . . . The dream state is in turn superseded by a state of consciousness in which he first hears a voice in the sky and then sees a Buddha body . . . In this second series, Sadāprarudita is actively involved with the messenger and is able to carry on a dialogue with the Buddha figure . . .
>
> It is after this more concrete vision of the Buddha body and the teaching which is given that Sadāprarudita matures to the degree that he no longer needs initiative other than his own . . . he is able in the fourth instance to handle doubts without an external visitation . . . he needs no revelation to quiet his sorrow . . . At this point he has become a self-directed individual and with the strength of his inner achievements he is able to set out on the journey.

In this way, the narrative of these successive occasions of Sadāprarudita breaking out into tears, in keeping with his name, at the same time reflect a gradual process of inner maturation. This proceeds until he becomes self-reliant, able to deal with his own sorrow.

The gradual progression evident in this way also has a visual dimension. In what follows I will explore this aspect as well, so that it can be tied into the overall trajectory of Sadāprarudita's spiritual maturation. A visual dimension comes to the fore with the waking experience of a magically created Buddha, eventually leading to a vision of all Buddhas of the ten directions in a *samādhi* experience. Moreover, when Sadāprarudita receives instructions on how he should proceed to meet his teacher

Dharmodgata, the magically created Buddha combines these instructions with a detailed description of the beauty of the location where Dharmodgata lives, which has seven walls made of the seven precious substances (which usually stand for gold, silver, and various jewels) and trees made of the same seven precious substances, with the same material being used to adorn curtains as well as boats found in seven concentric moats surrounding the walls.[705] Before continuing to explore the visual dimension of Sadāprarudita's gradual maturation, this particular type of description merits closer inspection.

In relation to a passage in the *Larger Sukhāvatīvyūha* that elaborates on what is basically the same mode of lavish and detailed description in considerably more detail, Harrison (2003, 122) proposes the following:

> [There can be] a new way of reading the text, as a template for visualization . . . What we are left with on the printed page resembles the wiring diagram for a television set, of interest only to electricians, baffling and tediously complex to anyone else. But when we "do" the text rather than read it, when we perform its operations ourselves . . . we get quite different results . . . texts like this are not to be read, in our usual modern fashion, but performed . . . in this light it might be better if we saw them as more like the scripts for plays, or scores for pieces of music.

Textual depictions of this type are not confined to Mahāyāna texts, as a comparable description of seven walls made of the seven precious substances, together with trees made up of the same, etc., also features in a Pāli discourse with a range of parallels.[706] The narrative is situated at a time close to the Buddha's final Nirvana. Ānanda worries that this is about to take place at a location of little importance. The Buddha corrects him and reports that in former times this location was a flourishing city, the description of which then proceeds similarly to the way the magically created Buddha in the Perfection of Wisdom depicts the location where Dharmodgata lives. Both texts share the employment of a particular textual modality that can serve to stimulate visual imagination.

*Āgama* literature in general is rife with metaphors and similes,[707] several of which have a visual component. In addition, at times teachings take off from something visible in the actual surroundings.[708] For example, the Buddha sees a log being carried away by a river and uses that to illustrate progress toward liberation.[709] Another such instance involves witnessing a wildfire, which provides the occasion for a sermon on the dire consequences of ethical misconduct. The instruction given in this way was apparently so powerful that a group of sixty monastics became arhats and another group of sixty decided to disrobe.[710] It seems fair to propose that the vivid images taken from the environs made a substantial contribution to the impact of the orally delivered teaching, even though the actual text does not contain any explicit reference to visualization.

Such an explicit reference can be found, however, as part of the standard instruction in *Āgama* literature on the first establishment of mindfulness, contemplation of the body. One of the exercises described similarly in the Pāli version of the relevant discourse and its two Chinese parallels directs mindfulness to the vision of a decaying corpse. The injunction is to draw the inference that the practitioner's own body is of the same nature and will similarly fall apart. The instructions in the Pāli version give the impression of intending an act of visualization, whereas the phrasing in the Chinese parallels reads more as if an actual vision of a corpse is intended.[711] The same instructions recur in the *Pañcaviṃśatisāhasrikā Prajñāpāramitā*, in which case the instructions suggest an actual vision of a corpse.[712]

From a practical perspective, it seems reasonable to assume that practitioners of this mindfulness exercise will not invariably need to find a corpse every time they cultivate this contemplation. This finds confirmation in a discourse extant in Sanskrit and Chinese. The two versions agree in explicitly indicating how a practitioner, having seen a corpse, returns to the monastic dwelling, washes the feet, and then sits down to meditate on a mat or seat.[713] In other words, for quite probably the majority of meditators cultivating this type of mindfulness practice would require a form of visualization, more specifically a mindful recollection of an earlier visual experience.[714] Since the four establishments of mindfulness constitute the direct path to awakening in *Āgama* thought,[715] the present type of practice can be considered as carving out a place for a vision-related meditation practice that is located right at the heart of the early Buddhist path to liberation.[716]

In the case of the Sadāprarudita tale, the emphasis on the visual dimension introduced with the help of the detailed description of Dharmodgata's location is part of a progression of visionary experiences. It is preceded by his vision of the magically created Buddha, and it leads to Sadāprarudita having a vision of the Buddhas of the ten directions; at a later narrative junction, the whole assembly has such a vision. All of this suggests a gradual buildup of visionary elements perhaps similar to the gradual evolution of the motif of Sadāprarudita's crying. In a way, these two trajectories complement each other, with the progressive instances of the crying motif showing his gradual inner maturation and the succession of visionary elements leading to the outcome of this inner maturation in the form of his spiritual accomplishment. In combination, these two trajectories culminate in the peak of his development when he receives a prediction of his future Buddhahood, with which he has been completely transformed from a state of despondency and uncertainty to the supreme certainty of being sure to achieve his goal of becoming a Buddha.

Such a prediction as a culmination in his spiritual quest and maturation is well in line with a recurrent concern in other parts of the Perfection of Wisdom with receiving a prediction and acquiring the status of being an irreversible bodhisattva. All of this goes to show that the tale of Sadāprarudita in several ways complements the previous chapters in the Perfection of Wisdom, making its teachings come alive, and thereby offers a significant contribution to its overall message.[717]

The employment of a narrative to substantiate a doctrinal point or teaching is also a regular feature of *Āgama* literature. An example occurs in relation to the claim by brahmins that, by dint of their birth, they are superior to members of other social classes in the ancient Indian setting, to the extent that only brahmins can supposedly achieve purification. The Buddha counters such claims with one argument after another, but then he switches to the narrative mode to relate a tale that confirms his position in a way quite different from his previous arguments.[718] This goes to show that the delivery of a narrative can have its place even in the context of a public debate. The same would hold in turn for the tale of Sadāprarudita when viewed from the overall setting of the Perfection of Wisdom, in that this narrative has its place and offers its own distinct contribution.

Orsborn (2012, 366) notes that, while clearly acknowledging the difference in literary style between the present tale and the preceding textual material, we should nevertheless "be careful not to let such polarizing categorization blind us to similarities within the deep structures of the text or parts of the text in question." Giddings (2014, 236) explains that, within the overall setting, the function of the Sadāprarudita tale "is to provide a vivid scenario in which the various topics discussed by the principal interlocutors [of the Perfection of Wisdom] become dramatized." In this way, "the tale of Sadāprarudita then, rather than serving as a simple illustration, serves to provide a complete scenario, an account of someone on the bodhisattva path to whom all the best and worst eventualities occur." In short, the tale can be seen as a means "towards accessing the meaning of the text as a whole."

### *Sadāprarudita's Self-Sacrifice*

Having attempted to establish that the tale of Sadāprarudita has much to offer that is in line with teachings in previous chapters of the Perfection of Wisdom, in what follows I need to complement that by turning to what appears to be mainly responsible for the references by Conze (1952/2008, 170) to an "almost turgid devotionalism" and a "complete disregard for commonsense" (1959/2008, 64). I take it that these remarks would refer to the descriptions of Sadāprarudita's self-sacrifice.

According to the instruction Sadāprarudita receives from the magically created Buddha, he should offer what he possesses to Dharmodgata.[719] Since he is poor, the direction set in this way naturally leads to the perceived need to accumulate some wealth in order to make an offering to his prospective teacher. In this way, the instruction by the magically created Buddha forms the point of departure for a narrative development that leads to Sadāprarudita's unsuccessful attempts to sell his body so as to make an offering to Dharmodgata from the proceedings. Māra prevents everyone from hearing or seeing Sadāprarudita, wherefore no buyer can be found.[720] Finally, however, Śakra disguised as a brahmin approaches

Sadāprarudita and expresses interest not in Sadāprarudita's whole body but only some of its parts:[721]

> The brahmin said to the bodhisattva Sadāprarudita: "I wish to make a great sacrifice now, son of a good family, [for which] I wish to get human blood, I wish to get human flesh, I wish to get human bone marrow, and I wish to get a human heart. If you are able to give that to me, I will benefit you by giving you wealth."
>
> The bodhisattva Sadāprarudita was highly elated and replied: "I wish to give that to you." The bodhisattva Sadāprarudita took a knife and personally stabbed both his arms. Much blood came out, which he took and gave away. Again, he cut flesh from the inner part of both his thighs, took it, and gave it away. Again, he personally smashed up his bones, took the marrow, and gave it away. Again, right away at that time he personally wanted to cut open his own chest.

Before Sadāprarudita is able to cut out his heart to complete his offerings, a woman who has watched the whole episode intervenes and, after finding out about his motivation, promises him the wealth needed to make an offering to his prospective teacher, adding that she would like to join him in his quest for the Perfection of Wisdom. Śakra then reveals his true identity and Sadāprarudita's body is restored to his former healthy condition.[722]

Sadāprarudita's willingness to give up even parts of his own body comes up again later when he has set out to clean up the place where Dharmodgata will give teachings. He looks in vain for water needed to sprinkle the dusty ground, as Māra has once again intervened, this time by hiding all water. Sadāprarudita and the group of five hundred women who have joined him in his quest thereupon take knives and stab themselves, intending to sprinkle the ground with their own blood.[723] Once again Śakra enters the scene, praises Sadāprarudita's conduct, transforms the grounds, and restores the health of Sadāprarudita and the group of women.

These two episodes of the gift-of-the-body trope pertain to what

Ohnuma (2007, 22 and 4) considers as "constituting a discrete subgenre of Indian Buddhist narrative literature," whose main articulations tend to manifest in the following manner:

> Over and over again, throughout his long career . . . the bodhisattva quite literally gave of himself, repeatedly jumping off cliffs or into fires, drowning himself in the ocean, slashing his throat, cutting the flesh from his thighs . . . gouging out his eyes . . . He offered his body as food, as drink, as medicine to cure all ills, as a raft to hang onto in pursuit of the other shore, as ransom for the life of another—or for no good reason at all, but merely because someone had asked. And always with the same motivation—to benefit other beings out of selflessness and compassion, to fulfill the "perfection of generosity" (*dāna-pāramitā*), and ultimately to win the highest state of Buddhahood.

From the viewpoint of the narrative context in the Perfection of Wisdom, it is worth noting that in both cases the actual episodes are framed by the contrast between Māra and Śakra. In both cases, the offering up of one's own body parts is occasioned by a misdeed of Māra. Although Śakra at first seemingly collaborates in this misdeed by instigating Sadāprarudita to sacrifice himself, in both instances he makes sure that in the end no lasting harm results. In the ancient Indian setting, this type of narrative framing would have made it clear to the audience how the tale should be appraised. This holds from the time of the explicit indication that Śakra has transformed himself into a brahmin out of the wish to test the extent of Sadāprarudita's dedication.[724] This type of action is typical for Śakra's role in such stories, which in turn makes it obvious that the narrative moves toward some kind of a miraculous solution.[725] Sadāprarudita's actions therefore need to be read from the viewpoint of the expectation that whatever he does just serves to illustrate his wholehearted dedication and will not have any actual consequences for himself, as a miracle of some type is already in the air. Once that setting is in place, the same pattern then applies to the second instance of Sadāprarudita and the group of women offering up their own blood.

Besides, a literal reading would fail to make sense. If Sadāprarudita dismembers himself and is even ready to cut out his heart, which would result in his death, he would be unable to make any offering to Dharmodgata or even just receive the wealth promised by the brahmin. Again, a ground sprinkled with blood is hardly an appropriate way to prepare the scene for a Dharma talk. In other words, both tales seem to be designed in such a way that they discourage a too-literal reading and at the same time foster the expectation of a happy resolution. This sets the context for the somewhat exuberant fantasies of complete self-relinquishment to illustrate the overarching desire to be taught the Perfection of Wisdom.

Needless to say, those hearing or reading this tale are right then and there in the precious situation of being taught the Perfection of Wisdom, and without any need to offer up parts or the whole of their bodies. This thereby follows the same pattern as the section on merit, discussed above (see p. 89), where an accrual of dazzling amounts of merit results from engaging with the Perfection of Wisdom, which is of course what the recipients of this information are actually doing right at that time. In other words, one of the effects of hearing the Sadāprarudita tale could well be that members of the audience congratulate themselves on their good fortune of having encountered the Perfection of Wisdom.

Lancaster (1968, 208) considers the tale of Sadāprarudita's self-sacrifice to be a parallel to the *jātaka* tale of King Śibi.[726] The basic story line in this case involves King Śibi granting protection to a pigeon being chased by a hawk (or a hunter)—the latter is Śakra in disguise—who objects to being deprived of food. King Śibi offers his own flesh in recompense, but however much he cuts off from his body to put on a scale to outweigh the pigeon, it is never enough. When he is ready to relinquish his whole body, Śakra reveals his identity and restores the king to health.

The tale of King Śibi can be seen to stand in dialogue with notions related to Vedic sacrifice,[727] making it no surprise that versions of basically the same tale can also be found in brahmanical literature.[728] In other words, this tale appears to be in line with a general pattern of *jātaka*s discussed above (see p. 106), where the story line does not necessarily reflect Buddhist values and orientations. It is mainly the identification of one of the protagonists as a former life of the Buddha, with the king in the present case being an obvious choice, that furnishes a Buddhist veneer to a tale adopted from the general ancient Indian narrative lore.

Nevertheless, once this identification is in place, the tale can of course come to function as an exemplification of the conduct it takes to become a Buddha. The **Pratyutpannasamādhisūtra* explicitly encourages cutting off the flesh of one's own body and giving it to one's teacher.[729] The context is set by the Buddha reporting how in a past life he had heard in a dream about a particular type of meditation, and on waking up he went in search of someone who could teach him. Even though he found a teacher and served him for a long period of time, due to interventions by Māra he did not learn the meditation. This description has several elements in common with the Sadāprarudita tale.

Again, a description of the perfection of giving in the *Pañcaviṃśatisāhasrikā Prajñāpāramitā* mentions donating one's head, limbs, flesh, blood, and marrow to those who want them.[730] A commentary on this *Prajñāpāramitā* text, the *Dà zhìdù lùn* (**Mahāprajñāpāramitopadeśa*), presents the tale of King Śibi as an exemplification—the only one given in this context—of how to fulfill the perfection of giving.[731] Elsewhere the same work adds a distinction, in that King Śibi's gift needs to be evaluated from the viewpoint of the presence or absence of wisdom.[732] The point here is not to question whether it is wise for a king to mutilate himself and even be ready to kill himself for the sake of saving a mere pigeon. The act itself is clearly considered praiseworthy, particularly if it is done without any regret. The question of wisdom concerns rather whether the act is undertaken while having the notion of a giver, a gift, and a recipient, as only the absence of these three would fulfil the requirements of the Perfection of Wisdom.[733]

Another tale in the *Dà zhìdù lùn* provides further illustration of the notion of giving away part of one's own body. The relevant narrative purports to explain why Śāriputra, after having followed the practice of a bodhisattva for sixty eons, renounced the goal of becoming a Buddha.[734] On being asked by a beggar to offer up his eye, Śāriputra objects that his eye would not do any service to the beggar, offering instead his body or possessions as alternatives. When the beggar insists on being given the eye, enforcing his demand with a reference to Śāriputra's cultivation of the practice of giving, the latter eventually pushes it out of its socket and gives it away. The beggar throws the eye on the ground, steps on it, and spits on it. On witnessing this behavior, Śāriputra decides to change course and rather opt for becoming an arhat and thereby be liberated sooner from the cycle of births and deaths. The point of this tale is once again not to problematize the act of giving away one's eye to someone who does not have any use for it. Instead, the purpose is to illustrate the problem of failing to remain equanimous when the gift of one's own eye is treated in such a disrespectful manner.[735]

### *Self-Immolation*

The tale of Sadāprarudita's self-sacrifice has continued to attract the attention of later Buddhist traditions. In the *Prasannapadā*, a commentary on Nāgārjuna's *Mūlamadhyamakakārikā*, Candrakīrti presents a summary of the tale and reports how Sadāprarudita drew his own blood to prepare the place for Dharmodgata's teaching.[736] The same event features also in Śāntideva's *Śikṣāsamuccaya*, together with the other episode of Sadāprarudita selling his body to a potential buyer.[737] These references reflect the degree to which his conduct was experienced as inspiring.

In order to explore the emic perception of self-sacrifice as inspiring, I now turn to another two such tales, following up on the identification proposed by Rawlinson (1977, 6) of similarities between Sadāprarudita's self-sacrifice and instances of self-sacrifice reported in the *Samādhirājasūtra* and the *Saddharmapuṇḍarīka*, in that "[a]ll three versions are concerned with the sacrifice of the body out of a desire for the Dharma." In what follows, I once more depart from the general parameters of my exploration of the Perfection of Wisdom from the viewpoint of *Āgama* literature, as I did in my first chapter in relation to the evolution of the bodhisattva ideal in later Pāli texts and related traditions. The present case serves as a complement to the perspective that emerged from that earlier exploration, both instances sharing an attempt to broaden perspective by taking a brief glance at related developments in later traditions (without, of course, thereby intending to propose a linear development of this type of notion).

The relevant episode in the *Samādhirājasūtra*, an influential Mahāyāna text, is situated at a time when the previous Buddha has passed away. A king has made various offerings, including offerings of lights, to *stūpas* containing relics of that Buddha. A recently ordained monk and bodhisattva by the name of Kṣemadatta decides to make an offering that surpasses the king's offering.[738] He wraps his right arm with cloth drenched in oil and sets it on fire.[739] The light of his offering outshines all the other lights, and with a declaration of truth Kṣemadatta restores his arm to its former condition.[740]

The *Saddharmapuṇḍarīka* episode is situated at a time in the past when a Buddha was in existence. Wishing to make an offering, the bodhisattva Sarvasattvapriyadarśana swallows incense and drinks oil over a long period of time, and through the power of his mental determination eventually sets himself on fire.[741] His body burns for a long time, illuminating all directions, after which he passes away. In his next rebirth, he burns his arms as an offering to *stūpas* of a recently deceased Buddha,[742] and with a declaration of truth restores the arms to their former condition.[743]

These two tales seem to exhibit some significant differences compared to the story of Sadāprarudita. The report of his actions still reflects a concern with presenting a compelling motivation, namely selling his body to be able to make offerings to his teacher and preparing the place where the latter will give teachings. In both cases the responsibility for the dramatic turn of events rests with Māra.

In the case of Kṣemadatta, however, the aim of the self-sacrifice is just to make an offering of light, and the motivation is merely to best the king in that respect. With Sarvasattvapriyadarśana the same aim of just making an offering features on both occasions. In other words, in these two tales the gift of the body has acquired sufficient traction to be in itself sufficient for motivating action, no longer needing a narrative frame that forces the protagonist to undertake the act of self-sacrifice.

There is also no evident sign at the outset of these narratives for the audience to know that a happy resolution can be expected. This nevertheless happens in the two cases of burning arms, based on the trope of a declaration of truth. But in the case of the whole-body offering by Sarvasattvapriyadarśana even that no longer happens. After many years of preparation by eating incense and drinking oil, he successfully immolates himself and passes away.

These two tales share with the story of Sadāprarudita that they all belong to the same genre of gift-of-the-body narratives. Since the motif of setting oneself on fire as a form of offering is more easily adapted to different circumstances than the idea of giving away one's body parts for a sacrifice or using one's blood to clean up a place for preaching, they stand a greater chance of inspiring other, similar narratives or even actions. That is, they stand a better chance of occasioning literalism. Such a tendency has been a significant factor in the evolution of Buddhist thought and practice in general. As pointed out by Gombrich (1996, 21), "unintentional literalism has been a major force for change in the early doctrinal history of Buddhism."

The same pattern has continued in later times. Benn (2009, 107–8) reports that the impact of literalist interpretations of the example set by Sarvasattvapriyadarśana burning himself, as described in the chapter on the Medicine King in the *Saddharmapuṇḍarīka*, can be seen in the following examples:[744]

> Beginning around the end of the fourth century of the Common Era, and continuing sporadically into modern times, some Chinese Buddhists have drawn inspiration from the *Lotus Sūtra* for a style of religious practice involving burning a finger or the whole body . . .
>
> The *Lotus Sūtra* provided not only a template for auto-cremation, by showing readers how and why it might be performed, but also the liturgy: self-immolators chanted the chapter on the Medicine King as they enacted it, thus making the scripture into a kind of performative speech . . .
>
> The offering of fingers and burning of incense on the skin (another symbolic act of self-immolation) still occur in China, Taiwan, and Korea. The tradition of making small burn marks on the crown of the head as part of the ordination ceremony for Chinese monks and nuns ultimately derives from the example of [the] Medicine King.

Besides burning marks on the crown of the head as part of the ordination ceremony,[745] the practice of setting the whole body on fire also continues. The perhaps best-known case occurred on the eleventh of June 1963, when the Vietnamese monk Thich Quang Duc set himself on fire in protest against the persecution of Buddhism by the South Vietnamese government; see figure 9.

Figure 9. Monument commemorating the Vietnamese monk Thich Quang Duc, located at the road intersection in Saigon (now Ho Chi Minh City) where he set himself on fire.

His self-immolation is not an isolated case, however, and its fame is to a considerable extent due to the worldwide impact of the news report of his sitting immobile while the flames were consuming his body. Similar actions have been and still are being undertaken, even though they have not been able to capture public attention in the same way. A series of well over a hundred instances in recent years of self-immolation by Tibetan Buddhists occurred to protest discriminatory policies by the Chinese government.[746] Another instance in 2022 in Washington, DC, involved an apparent Buddhist convert setting himself on fire to draw attention to the problem of climate change.[747]

Undertaking self-sacrifice through immolation is not confined to Mahāyāna traditions. Sheravanichkul (2008, 769) reports that in "the early nineteenth century, at Arunratchawararam Temple in Bangkok, two faithful Buddhists, *Nai Ruang* and *Nai Nok*, burnt themselves as an offering to the Buddha and aspired to attain Buddhahood." Although their "self-immolation was praised by many people," the king objected to such action.

In the context of a discussion of wisdom as one of the perfections recognized in the Pāli tradition, the eminent Burmese scholar-monk Mingun Sayadaw (1991, 62) refers to the practice of the "offering of one's own limbs at the Pagoda or of . . . burning oneself after wrapping up the whole body with cloth and pouring oil on it." He cautions those who may feel critical of such actions, reasoning that if someone "very courageously makes an offering of his own body, even to the extent of abandoning his life, he is actually worthy of praise as a donor of the gift of one's own person, *ajjhattika-dāna*."

A scriptural model can be found in a comparatively late Pāli text, which reports how a bodhisattva wraps himself in cloth soaked with oil and burns himself in front of the Buddha Kāśyapa (Pāli: Kassapa) with the aspiration to gain omniscience.[748] Kāśyapa predicts the future Buddhahood of this bodhisattva, whose body continues to burn throughout the whole night until he passes away. The text continues by indicating that the merit of this offering will ensure that as a Buddha he will have various endowments. Due to making a gift of the body, he will have an extraordinarily large body. Due to sacrificing his life, he will have an exceptionally long lifespan. On account of having burnt his body throughout the whole night, as a Buddha he will emanate rays that will overpower even the light of the sun and the moon.[749]

The idea of matching particular aspects of making a gift of the body with specific future outcomes can also be found in a Pāli commentary (on the *Cariyāpiṭaka*). According to its presentation, the motivation for making a gift of one's feet is to achieve feet marked with wheels (a feature characteristic of Buddhas), a gift of one's hands will enable giving sentient beings "the hand" of Dharma to help them get across the flood of defilements, and offering up one's ears, nose, etc. will ensure acquiring the five spiritual faculties (*indriya*). In the case of the eyes, relinquishing these will enable one to become all-seeing, and giving away flesh and blood, etc., is done in the wish that one's body may become a means of life for the whole world. Finally, the gift of one's head will lead to becoming supreme in the world.[750]

An actual instance of self-cremation can in turn already be found in a Pāli discourse and its two Chinese parallels. To be precise, this episode features in two consecutive Pāli discourses. The first reports the actual event, whereas in the second the Buddha relates this event to a group of monastics. This is a rather unusual procedure for Pāli discourses and is not found elsewhere in this form, that is, as two consecutive discourses in the same collection. Perhaps this reflects the importance of the story from the viewpoint of the reciters, which motivated them to present it twice, by way of relating it to two difference verses. The textual collection in question is the *Udāna*, which I mentioned earlier contains at times quite late material, as a result of a gradual process of textual formation during which several already existing inspired utterances appear to have occasioned the creation of prose narrations (see above p. 215).

The Pāli prose narration depicts an arhat monk who, in the presence of the Buddha, rises up in the air, enters a concentrative attainment related to the fire element, and miraculously burns himself up, leaving no ashes or soot; a similar depiction can be found in the Chinese parallels.[751] These also agree with one of the two Pāli versions in associating this episode with a twin verse that compares the impossibility of pointing out the destiny of an arhat after death to the inability to know the destiny of a blazing spark or pellet that has gone out. The idea behind this image seems to be that a smith beats a heated piece of iron, due to which a blazing spark or pellet flies off into the air and then becomes extinguished. Here is a translation of the relevant verse from one of the Chinese versions:[752]

Just as a burning iron pellet
That is blazing up in flames,
When its heat eventually comes to be extinguished,
No one knows to where it has returned.

So, too, well liberated ones
Cross over the mire of defilements,
Having cut off all torrents forever,
No one knows where they have gone.
Having attained imperturbability,
They enter Nirvana without remainder.

Note that in this poetic image, just as in its parallels, the reference to fire serves as an illustration; it is metaphorical. It does not mean that arhats somehow burn up physically. In fact, the verse is not about what causes arhats to pass away or what happens to their body but rather about their postmortem destiny.[753] In relation to that, the twin verse illustrates the inability to point them out in any way, just as the extinct spark or pellet can no longer be located.

The episode of this monk auto-combusting appears to be another instance in this Pāli collection of a poetic image in a verse triggering a literalist interpretation that then finds expression in the corresponding prose. The present narrative, which seems to be the only instance of such an auto-combustion found in an *Āgama* discourse that receives support from parallel versions, can with considerable probability be considered the outcome of literalism.

A connection between this particular monk and pyrotechnic abilities can also be seen in an entertaining story found in different *Vinaya*s, possibly inspired by the association with mastery of the fire element that results from the tale of his spectacular passing away. Having the task of allotting quarters to incoming monks, this monk would magically set one or more fingers of his hand, or even the whole hand, on fire to illumine the path for those who arrive after dark.[754] This feat did not result in any actual harm to his fingers or hand.

It seems fair to propose that these two narratives, his auto-cremation and his setting parts or the whole of his hand on fire to provide light, may have provided a blueprint for the episodes involving Kṣemadatta and Sarvasattvapriyadarśana.[755] Their burnings also take place in front of a Buddha (or his relics) and succeed in illuminating the surroundings. Burning the hand or arm does not result in permanent harm (here due to the power of a declaration of truth to restore these to their former condition), whereas burning the whole body entails actual death.

At this juncture, I am coming close to the end not only of the present topic but also of my exploration of the Perfection of Wisdom from the viewpoint of *Āgama* literature. At the outset of this book, when embarking on my first topic, I explained that my exploration of the evolution of the bodhisattva ideal and related notions will be informed by the attempt to leave open the possibility of influences operating in both directions, rather than assuming from the outset that *Āgama* literature invariably forms the backdrop to the setting within which the relevant notions in the Perfection of Wisdom would have evolved (see above p. 8). Adopting this procedure was meant to allow for the nature of the developments examined to reveal on their own, whenever and to whatever extent possible, which cluster of ideas influenced the other. Coming now to the end of the exploration of my last topic and looking back at the relevant themes surveyed in the preceding pages, it seems to me that in the case of most of these the direction of influence does indeed appear to be from *Āgama* literature to the Perfection of Wisdom,[756] in line with what the general history of the development of Buddhist thought and texts would suggest. In what follows I will illustrate this briefly just in relation to the evolution of the bodhisattva ideal, as a backdrop to the tale of Sadāprarudita and narratives involving the gift of the body.

An attempt to situate the thirty-two marks—as something inherited from brahmanical lore—more clearly within a Buddhist context naturally proceeds by presenting a karmic perspective on these. The relevant Pāli discourse in fact explicitly introduces this type of description as a distinctly Buddhist perspective beyond the knowledge of outsiders. The emerging perspective that it takes certain deeds in past lives to acquire these marks is a natural outcome of the narrative setting, and it would not be reasonable to propose that this must be a motif inherited from already existing Mahāyāna thought. The resultant presentation, in the way it is exemplified in this discourse, can be assumed to have offered a rather substantial contribution in a historical context that, to the best of our knowledge, had not yet conceived of the very idea that Buddhahood requires a series of lifetimes of intentional preparation.

The closely related case of the *jātaka*s takes off from the common ancient Indian passion for storytelling. The first specimen of this type, found in *Āgama* literature, does not show any evident relationship to Mahāyāna thought. The understandable reasoning that the Buddha must have personally witnessed the stories he taught seems to have set in at a comparatively early stage, leading to identifying a protagonist in any story he reportedly told as necessarily involving a past-life experience of the Buddha. Even at this stage, there is no evidence of any influence of already existing Mahāyāna thought. In the case of a particular *jātaka* in *Āgama* literature, with the narrative setting situated at the time of the former Buddha Kāśyapa, the identification of one of its protagonists as a former existence of the Buddha Śākyamuni creates a fertile field of friction, leading to further elaborations that appear to have been influential in the development of the bodhisattva ideal.

The same also applies to the motif of bodhisattvas setting parts or the whole of their bodies on fire in the *Samādhirājasūtra* and the *Saddharmapuṇḍarīka*. It would not be reasonable to propose that such narrations of self-immolation led to the metaphorical reference to a blazing pellet in a verse found in *Āgama* literature. Instead, it is the verse that must have given rise to a literalist interpretation in the form of a prose depiction of an auto-combustion, and this in turn would have inspired further narratives of self-immolation.

The limitations of textual sources are such that it is hardly ever possible to draw definite conclusions, and in addition to these there is a whole range of other conditions impacting developments in the Buddhist traditions. Nevertheless, based on the textual evidence to which we still have access, it seems as if the repeated impact of literalism has been such that a poetic spark set human fires burning all the way through the history of Buddhism up to present times.

## Summary

This chapter has covered dimensions of the conduct of a bodhisattva, which requires insight into dependent arising without realizing its cessation and wholehearted dedication of the type exemplified—in a somewhat extravagant form that in the text under discussion here was to all appearances not yet meant to be taken literally—by the tale of Sadāprarudita's quest to receive teachings on the Perfection of Wisdom.

The proper approach for a bodhisattva contemplating dependent arising is to give full attention to this teaching but avoid a realization of its cessation, in order to remain on the path to Buddhahood. The concern of *Āgama* teachings on dependent arising is not to proclaim a general type of interdependence or interconnectedness but to encourage the identification of central conditions leading to *duḥkha*, so as to be able to overcome them. As a doctrinal teaching, dependent arising concerns specific conditionality, often illustrated with the help of a list of twelve links that lead in a causal sequence from ignorance to the manifestation of *duḥkha*, a mode of presentation that appears to stand in dialogue with a Vedic creation myth.

Full insight into dependent arising through experiencing its cessation comes with the realization of Nirvana, which could result in stream-entry or else even in becoming an arhat. The same holds in principle for becoming a Buddha, although in this case sufficient preparations need to be in place, wherefore a bodhisattva needs to beware of prematurely attaining Nirvana before having completed the necessary groundwork required for becoming a Buddha.

The path to Buddhahood is indeed a demanding one, and its challenges can be illustrated with the tale of Sadāprarudita's quest for the Perfection of Wisdom. This tale can be seen to offer its own distinct contributions to the teachings in the Perfection of Wisdom as a whole. Examples for such contributions take the form of detailed instructions on the cultivation of nonattention during any activities as well as teachings on the empty nature of Buddhas and Nirvana. The same narrative also clarifies that being in the presence of a living Buddha was at this early stage in the development of *Prajñāpāramitā* literature not considered indispensable for becoming a bodhisattva. Even receiving a prediction of one's future Buddhahood could take place in reliance on the visionary experience of the Buddhas of the ten directions.

The narrative of his quest portrays Sadāprarudita's spiritual maturation through a progression of instances causing him to burst into tears. These gradually build up until he has gained mastery over himself. The depictions of him crying combine with another literary dimension of the tale related to visual experiences, which become ever more distinct until eventually he reaches a peak of his spiritual quest when he receives the prediction of his future Buddhahood.

Another significant aspect of the tale is the description of Sadāprarudita's self-sacrifice, which pertains to a series of tales on gifts of the body found in the Buddhist narrative traditions. A common characteristic of such tales is the eulogizing of acts of self-mutilation or even destruction of the body under the overarching aim of fulfilling the perfection of giving. A particular modality of such narratives involves the motif of self-immolation. From an apparent starting point in a literal interpretation of a poetic reference to a burning spark or pellet, repeated instances of literalism appear to have turned this particular motif into a script to be acted out, with actual self-immolations stretching from the distant past to present times. These exemplify the impact of literalism in the development of Buddhist thought and practice. The tale of Sadāprarudita, however, does not go quite that far. Besides its narrative cast being less easily amenable to imitation, its contextual setting in the Perfection of Wisdom, with its rhetoric of emptiness and continuous concern with undermining any reification, could be expected to counter excessive literalism of this type.

# Conclusion

THE PRECEDING PAGES would hopefully have shown that a closer study of central positions taken in the Perfection of Wisdom can benefit from taking into account relevant *Āgama* teachings. The perspectives that emerge in this way are in line with the indication offered by Conze (1948/2008, 166–67) that "Prajñāpāramitā texts are . . . full of hidden hints, allusions, and indirect references to the pre-existing body of scriptures and traditions circulating in the memory of the Buddhist community at the time. They are more often than not an echo of older sayings."[757] In the context of a discussion of Mahāyāna Buddhism in general, Conze (1959/2008, 75) similarly explains that "Buddhism throughout its history has the unity of an *organism*, in that each development takes place in continuity from the previous one." In relation to the specific case of the *Aṣṭasāhasrikā Prajñāpāramitā*, Rawlinson (1977, 15–16) in turn proposes that "[t]he mythological, historical and geographical background of the *Aṣṭa* is that of traditional Buddhism . . . [d]octrinally, also, the *Aṣṭa* is much more of a *restatement* of traditional Buddhist views than is sometimes supposed."

According to Ruegg (2004, 56–57), "the Mahāyāna appears not so much as a radical break in the course of Buddhist thought—one that is markedly discontinuous with the rest of the 'Buddha-Word' (*buddhavacana*) or the Buddha's teaching (*dharma, śāsana*)—but rather as continuing elucidation and persistent elaboration." That is, "[a] good number of the fundamental ideas of the Mahāyāna in fact turn out to have antecedents, precursors or prefigurations in the old canonical scriptures (Āgamas/Nikāyas) and their commentaries." Skilling (2013b, 98–99) reasons that "[t]he study of the Śrāvaka Piṭakas was essential to the Mahāyāna masters, and the great Mahāyāna sūtras cannot be understood without a thorough grounding in the Śrāvaka Piṭakas."

It follows that my survey in the preceding pages, rather than presenting a novel discovery, has merely supported such assessments with detail. Moreover, my study remains, as already stated in the introduction, just one out of many different perspectives, without the least claim of having resulted in the one and only definitive assessment. My presentation definitely comes without any pretension to be providing a complete account of influences relevant to the arising of central notions of early Mahāyāna, which are far too complex and intricate to allow for any monocausal explanation.

Nevertheless, it seems to me that exploring related perspectives from *Āgama* literature enriches reading the Perfection of Wisdom. The evidence for continuities between the early Perfection of Wisdom and the discourses found in *Āgama* literature in turn provides a convenient backdrop for situating the text I have studied in relation to the much-discussed topic of "the origins of Mahāyāna," which I will do in the remainder of this concluding part of my study. Since each of the preceding chapters already comes with a summary of the respective main points, the task of providing a synopsis has already been taken care of, wherefore the present conclusion can instead take the form of a chapter in its own right by way of placing things into a wider perspective.

I begin by attempting to relate the Perfection of Wisdom and its salient characteristics to the notion of Mahāyāna. Then I turn more specifically to the quest for origins, which I explore also in relation to the related terms "Buddhism" and "Theravāda."

## The Perfection of Wisdom and Mahāyāna

Before embarking on my exploration, I need to repeat something already said in my introduction, in that my main focus of research is early Buddhism, wherefore with the present book I have been venturing into an area in which I have less expertise. Whatever assessments I may present in this conclusion are only relevant to the specific text I have taken up, and these are moreover based on a reading of this text limited for the most part to relevant perspectives provided by *Āgama* texts. Even just a full appreciation of the Perfection of Wisdom would require taking into account a range of other influences operative in the religio-historical setting in which this text emerged and evolved, such as competition with brahmins, royal patronage, and so on.[758] It follows that what I present here can only be, and is only meant to be, of limited significance.

A first step in pursuing my present exploration would be to ascertain if the application of the term "Mahāyāna" is justified in the case of the text under discussion.[759] Confirmatory evidence from within the text comes from its first chapter, which appears to be a particularly important (and generally considered early) part of the version of the Perfection of Wisdom translated by Lokakṣema. A relevant passage takes the form of a proclamation by Subhūti to the following effect: "Among people in heaven and on earth, the Mahāyāna very much excels: there is nothing that can compare with it."[760] The same first chapter refers to bodhisattvas who set out in this Mahāyāna.[761] This much suffices to show that the basic sense of identity appears to be in place, even if the term may not yet have acquired its fully-fledged institutional sense.[762] Particularly noteworthy in this respect is that the sole reference in the Sanskrit version of the *Aṣṭasāhasrikā Prajñāpāramitā* to the Hīnayāna, pursued by those who abandon the Mahāyāna, has no counterpart in Lokakṣema's translation of the Perfection of Wisdom.[763] Presumably, the perceived need for such derogatory terminology had not yet arisen at this early stage.[764] In sum, external and internal indications make it safe to allocate Lokakṣema's translation of the Perfection of Wisdom to the category of texts that—by the time its evolution had reached the stage in which we are now able to access it—proceed from the viewpoint of a Mahāyāna sense of identity.

This concords with the perspective taken in later tradition, evident from the fact that a catalogue of Chinese translations compiled toward the end of the sixth century lists Lokakṣema's translation under the header of Mahāyāna *sūtras*.[765] Together with the indications found in the text itself, this much should satisfy the condition mentioned by Silk (2002, 370) "that those scriptures identified by tradition, for instance in the Tibetan and Chinese canonical collections, as Mahāyāna sūtras should be so considered," adding that it needs to be kept in mind, however, that "the classification of scriptures in China and Tibet (and doubtless in India too) was a polemical activity, motivated by a multitude of forces. These sources are not 'objective'" (370n37).

With this much ascertained, according to a recommendation by Silk (2002, 369) "we must stop referring, at the very least provisionally, to 'the Mahāyāna' in the singular." Instead, we should approach a particular scripture from the viewpoint of it potentially representing "a different community, a different Mahāyāna." In the present case, following this compelling recommendation is a must, because the textual evidence surveyed here is only representative of an early stage in the development of one particular text/textual family. This calls at the very least for rephrasing the topic to be explored as the "*Prajñāpāramitā*-Mahāyāna." This would still not be entirely adequate, however, given that according to Lethcoe (1977) a development can be distinguished leading from the bodhisattva ideal of the *Aṣṭasāhasrikā* to that of the *Pañcaviṃśatisāhasrikā Prajñāpāramitā*,[766] the latter reflecting the next stage of textual growth in *Prajñāpāramitā* literature. Even limiting the topic just to the "*Aṣṭasāhasrikā-Prajñāpāramitā*-Mahāyāna" is still not sufficiently concise, as an increasing emphasis on the crucial quality of compassion can be discerned between earlier and later versions of the *Aṣṭasāhasrikā Prajñāpāramitā*.[767] Such an increase amounts to a significant difference from the viewpoint of the present inquiry. It would follow that a further refinement of the topic is required, and my discussion should rather be about the "Early-*Aṣṭasāhasrikā-Prajñāpāramitā*-Mahāyāna." Since this long phrase becomes a bit unwieldy, in what follows I will abbreviate it to "Early-*Aṣṭa*-Mahāyāna."

As a next step in my exploration, I will now attempt to relate Early-*Aṣṭa*-Mahāyāna to a few selected suggestions made in the history of Buddhist studies regarding the origins of Mahāyāna in general. What follows is just meant as a short checklist, without trying to be comprehensive or reflect the details and nuances of the relevant positions and their respective criticisms, simply by way of briefly noting their relevance or lack of relevance to the specific case of Early-*Aṣṭa*-Mahāyāna.

Early-*Aṣṭa*-Mahāyāna does not show evidence of being anti-clerical in orientation.[768] Leaving aside celestial beings, the main protagonists of the text are monastics, and the basic ideal of monastic renunciation is not the target of any sustained criticism. The overall interest of the discussions seems to be to promote anti-reification as the path to Buddhahood rather than anti-clericalism. Human lay practitioners take an active role mainly in the final part of the Perfection of Wisdom concerned with the tale of Sadāprarudita, situated in the distant past.[769] In this case, the prominence of laity would simply be a reflection of the location of the narrative at a time when the dispensation of the previous Buddha had completely disappeared and members of his monastic community were no longer in existence. Moreover, promoting the Perfection of Wisdom as superior to *stūpa* worship is a recurrent theme.[770] In other words, the Early-*Aṣṭa*-Mahāyāna does not give the impression of reflecting a supposedly early period of the rise of Mahāyāna as a lay movement centered around *stūpa* worship.[771] It also does not provide evidence in support of the assumption that a cult of celestial bodhisattvas was a central concern.[772]

Regarding a possible relationship to the lifestyle of dwelling in forest wilds (*araṇya*), a passage in Lokakṣema's translation commends the memorization and recitation of the Perfection of Wisdom to prevent fear arising when dwelling in a remote place.[773] Such a potential would be quite relevant for those who dwell in forest wilds. At the same time, however, the passage does not amount to commending such a lifestyle in itself. Instead, the point appears to be just that the advantages of the Perfection of Wisdom hold an attraction also for those who live in forest wilds.

In fact, in another passage in the Perfection of Wisdom the Buddha quite emphatically states that he does not instruct bodhisattvas to dwell in the seclusion of solitary and remote places.[774] This proclamation forms a reply to Māra commending such a lifestyle. Nattier (2003a, 94n31) comments that this passage takes an "antiforest stance, referring to wilderness dwelling as 'the detachment recommended by Māra.'"[775] It thus seems that, alongside showing that the Perfection of Wisdom is also relevant to dwellers in forest wilds, those who have adopted such a way of life should nevertheless be wary of granting excessive importance to such external forms of conduct, as what really counts are their internal qualities, in particular their understanding of, and dedication to, the Perfection of Wisdom.[776] The last is really the key concern throughout the Perfection of

Wisdom, rather than any promotion of a particular lifestyle, be it lay cults or monastics dwelling in forest wilds.

With this much ascertained, the next step would be to try to identify significant, unprecedented contribution(s) evident in the Early-*Aṣṭa*-Mahāyāna when viewed in its ancient Indian setting. As discussed in detail earlier in my exploration (see above pp. 36 and 79), the vision of emptiness promoted in the Perfection of Wisdom does not seem to involve a substantial innovation, even though the language used to convey this teaching is distinctive and novel.[777]

An important topic in the Perfection of Wisdom is the promotion of the bodhisattva path. However, it is not as easy as perhaps expected to detect a substantial difference between the bodhisattva path of the Early-*Aṣṭa*-Mahāyāna and the bodhisattva path in Pāli sources. Since, at least according to popular perceptions, the Theravāda traditions should furnish a clear-cut example of "non-Mahāyāna" against which to delineate "Mahāyāna," the situation that results from attempting to identify a substantial contribution made by the Early-*Aṣṭa*-Mahāyāna in terms of the bodhisattva ideal is not straightforward.[778]

For such purposes, minor differences would not suffice. A candidate for marking a distinct perspective would be the universalization of the bodhisattva ideal, in the sense of the path to Buddhahood becoming the sole viable option for spiritual practice.[779] This indeed results in a substantial difference in comparison with the bodhisattva path in Pāli sources.[780] On adopting the universalization of the bodhisattva ideal as the decisive marker for the designation "Mahāyāna," however, it would follow that the Perfection of Wisdom should no longer be considered Mahāyāna, since it does not promote the bodhisattva path as the only viable option.[781] Such a conclusion would not accord with the indications found in the text itself as well as the perspective on this text in later tradition. In other words, such a conception of Mahāyāna appears to be too narrow to fit the present case.

It follows that a broad conception of the term as a nonexclusivist path to Buddhahood appears to be required for accommodating the Perfection of Wisdom. In other words, the case of the Perfection of Wisdom confirms that the popular supposition, according to which Mahāyāna should stand by definition in contrast to Hīnayāna or Theravāda, does not work particularly well. The term "Hīnayāna" itself is a polemical construct that does not reflect an actually existing tradition or monastic institution in the history of Buddhism,[782] wherefore its usage tends to obscure rather than clarify the actual situation. Leaving behind the polemical legacy may require more than just replacing Hīnayāna with Theravāda, however, because the very framing of Mahāyāna as the other in a polemic contrast is not necessarily compelling, and relevant observations have already been offered in this respect by several scholars.

Silk (1994, 3) notes that "the crux of the matter is this: we must avoid any suggestion of an organizational or institutional discontinuity between Mahāyāna and non-Mahāyāna Buddhism." Gombrich (1998, 55) comments on Theravāda and Mahāyāna that in the past "[d]ifferences between the two were exaggerated and the internal heterogeneity within each was brushed under the carpet." Rectifying this requires "abandoning these stereotypes and realizing that both within the Mahāyāna and within the other forms of Buddhism there has been an enormous range of diversity." As pointed out by Ruegg (2004, 56), "for the history of the Mahāyāna we shall no doubt need to adopt in many a case a 'both . . . and' view," which requires "renouncing the specious clarity and simplicity of some stark 'either . . . or' dichotomy." In other words, "[w]e shall surely have to eschew any generalizing reductionism that transforms the whole of the Mahāyāna into some one-sided dogma or praxis." Skilling (forthcoming, 4–5) offers the following overall assessment:

> [T]he foundations of the late nineteenth and early twentieth century understanding of Buddhism lay in a two-track or binary paradigm of Hīnayāna versus Mahāyāna. This paradigm was a kind of caricature of saṃgha history: it ignored the importance of Vinaya—the eighteen Vinaya schools or monastic orders—and the complexity of centuries of philosophical and ideological evolution. Early studies failed to recognize the central ideas and shared core (*coeur*, heart) of Buddhism, or to see Buddhism as an organic and integral aggregate of practices and ideas. Modern scholarship reified the dialectics of

> intellectual development and the natural antagonism of ideas into opposing and exclusive camps. Difficult indeed it was for the Europeans who had been brought up in a world of single and exclusive "faiths" to fathom the dynamics of Buddhist inclusivism.

Tsai (1997, 20–21) speaks of an "imaginative projection of a dichotomy between Mahāyāna and Hīnayāna [that] completely overwhelms disciplined prudence," adding that "[i]t may be that the great proliferation of this dichotomy, which occupies a place in virtually every introductory book on Buddhism, has prevented many scholars from reexamining the appropriateness of its construction."[783] Schopen (2005, 109) identifies what I would refer to as an element of circularity in this respect, as "any description or characterization of an early Mahāyāna necessarily depends on a comparison or contrast—whether explicit or not—with what it is supposed to have diverged from." As a result, however, "how one describes what it is supposed to have emerged from will, in fact, determine how that Mahāyāna is then itself described." Drewes (2011, 361) observes that "[s]ince the beginning of the study of Indian Mahāyāna, scholars have persistently tended to imagine early Mahāyāna as a group or groups that split off from the main body of ancient Buddhists. Attempts to determine which Buddhists split off and why they did so have proceeded primarily on *a priori* grounds."

The basic assumption of an opposition or rebellion as the central defining element of Mahāyāna has of course its roots in emic perspectives articulated in later Buddhist traditions.[784] The inherited paradigm of an irreconcilable confrontation then unsurprisingly leads to focusing on one monastic tradition (the Mahāsāṃghikas) separated from others by what tradition reckons to have been the first schism as the decisive point of origin. When that no longer works, the same paradigm can inspire a shift to the lay-monastic divide, with lay disciples protesting a supposed monastic monopoly on spiritual practice. When that also no longer works, the same paradigm can continue in the form of opting for the divide between dwellers in forest wilds and in villages, with the former defying laxity and decadence among the latter. Judging from the detailed discussion of this hypothesis offered by Drewes (2018), it seems as if that also no longer works so well.

Now, in the case of the Gāndhārī manuscript version and Lokakṣema's translation of the Perfection of Wisdom, the actual textual evidence indeed gives the impression of articulating a perspective that was perceived as distinct and important by those involved in formulating and promoting it. At the same time, however, this perspective not only fails to fit one of the above three scenarios but also comes without a clear-cut framing in terms of an opposition to an "other," however defined, as the central characteristic of Early-*Aṣṭa*-Mahāyāna.

The recurrent emphasis on the superiority of the path to Buddhahood, as aptly clarified by Nattier (2000, 94n68; quoted above p. 185), can be read as comparable to promoting the superiority of a PhD degree compared to a BA or MA degree in the context of university education. In fact, the two attainment reports discussed above (see p. 184) showcase the potential of the Perfection of Wisdom in leading among other things to the realization of stream-entry and arhat-ship. Of course, progress to Buddhahood is vastly superior to these, but highlighting this superiority does not result in a wholesale rejection of alternative realizations. As noted by Nattier (2003a, 85), "we are dealing here with a type of 'in-house' discourse, which is not necessarily intended to be universal in its implications." It just involves urging "someone who is already on the bodhisattva path not to abandon his vocation," which needs to be differentiated from "urging all Buddhists to become bodhisattvas."

Even in relation to Abhidharma teachings, the position taken in the Perfection of Wisdom is considerably more nuanced than a flat antagonism. Rather than promoting a wholesale rejection of Abhidharma thought, Early-*Aṣṭa*-Mahāyāna can more profitably be understood to build on and improve such thought, the latter in particular by deconstructing the notion of an intrinsic nature, *svabhāva*. In fact, those portrayed in the text as resistant to this deconstruction are (novice) bodhisattvas themselves, who may become afraid and lose their faith on being exposed to such teachings. Just like the question of the superiority of Buddhahood over arhat-ship, adverse reactions to the rhetoric of emptiness seem to be less about a conflict with other Buddhist traditions or institutions and more about an internal problem. The same appears to hold for the apparent proposition of momentariness as an imitation of the Perfection of Wisdom (see above p. 119). Its proponents seem to be fellow practitioners of the path to Buddhahood, given that the proposal as such is articulated within the context of promoting the cultivation of the sixth perfection.

The overall attitude to Abhidharma teachings can perhaps be illustrated with the simile of the relay of chariots, to which I have been returning repeatedly in the preceding pages: Early-*Aṣṭa*-Mahāyāna does not attempt to demolish and discard the seven chariots, whose usefulness is never put into question and thus not the issue at hand. Instead, the concerns are more specifically that some may become afraid of leaving behind the seventh chariot and for that reason be unable to enter the palace.

The main challenge indeed posed by others, as reflected in the textual evidence for Early-*Aṣṭa*-Mahāyāna, appears to be the judgment that the teachings of the Perfection of Wisdom were not spoken by the Buddha and for this reason should not be followed. Given that the composition of new texts is a pan-Buddhist phenomenon, such a contestation is part of a type of problematization that also happened in relation to new non-Mahāyāna texts, such as those of the Abhidharma.[785] At the same time, however, from the viewpoint of adherents of the Early-*Aṣṭa*-Mahāyāna such a dismissal is of course perceived sufficiently problematic to require being addressed. Be it in reaction to actual occurrences of such rejection or based on apprehensions that this may happen, the text devotes quite some attention to this matter and offers tools to deal with it, such as identifying a rejection of the Perfection of Wisdom's status as taught by the Buddha himself, when commending that his disciples adopt the bodhisattva path, to be the result of Māra's influence and threatening those who advocate such a stance with rebirth in hell (see above p. 144).

Conversely, advocates of such a rejection would hardly have needed any further arguments, as the simple assessment that the text in question is not from the Buddha would have settled the case for them. This may explain the observation by Bareau (1955, 299), made in the context of a discussion of the origins of Mahāyāna, that recurrent references in Mahāyāna texts to being criticized do not really have a counterpart in a comparable body of actual criticism articulated in non-Mahāyāna texts.[786] In a similar vein, Deleanu (2000, 89) notes that "the scarcity of direct references and attacks against Mahāyāna in Śrāvakayāna sources is surprising." From the viewpoint of the textual evidence provided by the Gāndhārī manuscript version and Lokakṣema's translation for Early-*Aṣṭa*-Mahāyāna, this is perhaps precisely what we should expect.

In sum, except for participation in pan-Buddhist apologetics in order to authenticate novel texts, the paradigmatic assumption of being embattled in some fundamental conflict does not seem to fit the case of the Early-*Aṣṭa*-Mahāyāna particularly well.[787] In the hope that I am not entirely off target with the perspective present here—based on relating assessments offered by a range of scholars to what emerges from my study of the Perfection of Wisdom—then a solution to the problem may be to recognize the polemic conception as an unwarranted projection, at least as far as the Early-*Aṣṭa*-Mahāyāna is concerned. If it should be possible to step out of the entrenched contrast and shift to an alternative perspective, perhaps we can simply consider texts and practices related to the path of a bodhisattva as a pan-Buddhist phenomenon that emerges in the post-Aśokan period. This would work well for the Perfection of Wisdom, and it would enable viewing relevant texts and practices found in the Pāli traditions as additional articulations of the bodhisattva path.

The proposed pan-Buddhist relevance of the bodhisattva path could then perhaps be viewed as comparable to the notion of Abhidharma as a referent to particular texts and practices, in this case articulating an Abhidharma type of thought. A key drive in the evolution of such Abhidharma thought appears to have been the attempt to emulate the Buddha's omniscient wisdom by providing an analytical map of reality that is as detailed as possible.[788] A key driving force in the evolution of Early-*Aṣṭa*-Mahāyāna and related strands of Mahāyāna thought appears to have been the Buddha's omniscient wisdom as well. Here, a chief concern would be to re-enact it by realizing such perfect wisdom oneself. For the sake of such realization, the texts of Early-*Aṣṭa*-Mahāyāna provide instructions to bodhisattvas on the cultivation of perfect wisdom in a way that is as penetrative as possible. This takes off from and incorporates much of early Buddhism and early Abhidharma while at the same time articulating a sustained criticism of aspects of Abhidharma thought that are perceived as focusing too much on details of the map at the expense of becoming less penetrative in matters of realization. Just as the rise of Abhidharma is simply a stage in development in Buddhist thought that took place after the period of early Buddhism, the rise of Early-*Aṣṭa*-Mahāyāna could perhaps also simply be viewed as another such development that also took place after the period of early Buddhism.

Such Early-*Aṣṭa*-Mahāyāna could then be regarded as having in common with early Abhidharma a trajectory of taking off from previous developments in Buddhist thought and practice, to which each of these two is indebted, with which they at times stand in critical dialogue, and to which they contribute by providing important new perspectives. In the case of Early-*Aṣṭa*-Mahāyāna such an interactive, dialogic relationship holds not only in relation to early Buddhism but also in relation to early Abhidharma. The overall perspective that emerges in this way can perhaps best be sketched with the help of a few excerpts from Dhammajoti (2023, 54–55, 4, 26, and 34):

> Since the Buddha's own time, the disciples, including the foremost Arahants, had been overwhelmed by the superiority of the Buddha's Wisdom ... continuous pondering over ... his incomparable perfect Wisdom and the path leading thereto ... may be considered one of the major threads inspiring the origin of the Mahāyāna ...
>
> [T]he Sarvāstivāda tradition articulated the doctrine of non-defiled nescience ... The Buddha alone is perfect in wisdom, because he alone has absolutely abandoned the non-defiled nescience ...
>
> [T]he early Mahāyāna scriptures subsequently derived much inspiration from this Abhidharma doctrine, in which they found an adequate and satisfactory doctrinal basis for the formulation of their Bodhisattva ideal culminating in the attainment of Perfect Buddhahood—perfect wisdom in contrast to the inferior wisdom/knowledge of the two *yānas* ...
>
> In brief, the doctrine that came to be formulated in the Prajñāpāramitā is that the Buddha's perfect Wisdom ... is to be

achieved through the practice of *prajñāpāramitā* in the equipoise state of not grasping at any *dharma* at all, and this is the new Bodhisattva praxis.

## The Quest for Origins

At this point, another trajectory of investigation to be pursued would be to explore how the notion of "origins" has fared with other, related concepts. Obvious examples would be the terms "Buddhism" and "Theravāda." Since I have examined both cases elsewhere in detail,[789] in what follows I can present the matter succinctly. In the case of the term "Buddhism," a corresponding Indic term would be *śāsana* (Pāli: *sāsana*),[790] which in its usage in *Āgama* literature usually refers to the Buddha's "teaching." However, already in a Pāli verse the same term occurs as the object of going forth.[791] Going forth by taking ordination requires some kind of institution, hence with this occurrence the meaning of *śāsana* can be seen to acquire a more institutionalized sense. In later Pāli literature this becomes a prominent meaning, which would correspond to the English usage of the term "Buddhism." A global sense of religious identity then manifests, for example, when in the early fifth century a group of Sri Lankan nuns had the remarkable courage to travel all the way to China to transmit a women's ordination lineage to a location that had previously received only transmissions of men's ordination lineages.[792]

A comparable evolution in meaning can be seen for the term *theravāda*, whose earliest occurrence features in Pāli discourses describing the Buddha's pre-awakening apprenticeship with two ancient Indian teachers.[793] In this context, to my mind the most straightforward understanding of the term *theravāda* would be to take it to refer to a body of explanations of theoretical aspects related to the meditative attainments promoted by these two ancient Indian teachers.[794] This usage is specific to Pāli discourses, as the term does not occur in relevant parallels.[795] With commentarial Pāli literature, the same term comes to convey what appear to be two interrelated senses: an orally transmitted body of explanations of the texts believed to have been recited at the first communal recitation (*saṅgīti*) held shortly after the Buddha's demise, and the monastic tradition of reciters responsible for passing on these texts together with relevant explanations.[796] An eighteenth-century inscription then testifies to a usage of the term "Theravāda" in relation to a pictorial representation of an otherwise unknown *jātaka* tale,[797] an occurrence that appears to be in line with the general usage of the term nowadays.

In both cases, the attempt to pinpoint an exact time and place of origin fails, as all that can be identified are gradual developments. The earliest occurrences of *śāsana* carry a meaning that differs from the term "Buddhism," just as the earliest occurrence of *theravāda* differs from the usage of "Theravāda" as an umbrella term for the Buddhist traditions of South and Southeast Asia. For this reason, these earliest occurrences are not good candidates for identifying an origin of "Buddhism" or "Theravāda." At what point exactly in their gradual developments these terms acquired the senses they carry nowadays then depends on how this sense is defined. In other words, whatever definition of "Buddhism" or "Theravāda" is preferred will in turn determine what particular stage of the gradual development can be identified as the respective origin.

In order to pursue this line of reasoning with the term *mahāyāna*, in what follows I first need to survey occurrences of what appear to be instances of the term in *Āgama* literature.[798] One of these occurrences—all of which manifest in Chinese translations and are for this reason more easily open to external influences from already existing Mahāyāna thought—features in the accounts of the last journeys and teachings of the Buddha before his final Nirvana. The relevant passage concerns his miraculous crossing of a river, after which he delivers a poem that plays on the metaphorical sense of the notion of a vehicle used to cross over. In this context, two versions preserved in Chinese translation, one as part of an *Āgama* collection and the other as an individually translated discourse, agree on mentioning the term *mahāyāna* (大乘) to designate the Buddha's means for taking celestials and humans across.[799] Although the term is not found in the Pāli and Sanskrit parallels,[800] its occurrence in the present context does not seem to be carrying later connotations, as it could just refer to the idea of a large means of transportation. Since the task is to take celestials and humans across, it would make sense to qualify the vehicle used for that purpose as "great."

Of further interest is a phrasing employed in a version of this episode in a *Vinaya* text. The relevant part uses the same Chinese characters that make up the standard translation of the term *mahāyāna* (大乘), but in the opposite sequence, to express the idea of "embarking" (乘) on a "great" (大) boat.[801] This confirms the impression that a reference to a large means of transportation need not be influenced by acquaintance with full-fledged Mahāyāna thought and can simply reflect the context.

Another occurrence in a Chinese *Āgama* collection forms part of a series of *yāna*-related terms that serve to eulogize the noble eightfold path.[802] According to the narrative setting, Ānanda has witnessed people in town expressing their amazement at a beautiful chariot. He reports this to the Buddha, who in reply presents the noble eightfold path as truly deserving praise for being an exceptional vehicle. Although the Pāli version does not have a counterpart to the term *mahāyāna* (大乘), its occurrence in the present context in the parallel Chinese *Āgama* discourse is fairly natural.[803] The term here simply conveys the meaning that the noble eightfold path functions as a great vehicle, just as it is also a divine vehicle, an expression common to the Pāli and the Chinese versions.[804]

In sum, in these two instances the occurrence of the term *mahāyāna*, although probably a later addition, appears natural and simply serves to convey the notion of a vehicle that is great. In the first case such greatness expresses the sense of being large, and in the second case it involves a sense of superiority. Although in these passages the sense of a "vehicle" is clearly the prominent one, it is quite possible that ancient Indian audiences would have perceived *yāna* terminology as bridging both the senses of a "vehicle" and a "path."[805] Keeping the inherent complexity of meaning in mind may perhaps be the best way of approaching its usage, rather than trying to pin down which occurrence definitely reflects the meaning of a "vehicle" and which instead points to a "path."[806]

In contrast to the above two cases, the remaining three occurrences to be discussed seem to reflect influences from already existing Mahāyāna thought. One of these instances features in the context of a description of the Buddha's qualities and behaviors, which also covers the repercussions of his sitting in meditation. The Pāli version and a parallel in a Chinese *Āgama* collection relate his meditation practice to the welfare of the world.[807] A discourse individually translated into Chinese presents a long list of items supposedly related to the Buddha's meditation practice, culminating in a reference to the four types of equality of the Mahāyāna whereby he had crossed over and delivered sentient beings.[808] This instance can safely be reckoned to reflect the impact of already existing, full-fledged Mahāyāna thought.

Another instance in a different individually translated discourse has as its context a comparison of the Buddha's teachings to the ocean, which has a single, salty taste. In the same way, according to most versions of the relevant passage the Dharma has the single taste of liberation. Some versions expand on this idea and mention several tastes. This is also the case for the individual translation in question, which additionally has the taste of the Mahāyāna, followed by referring to the aspiration to deliver people.[809] Such a taste is not found in parallel versions that also broach the topic of taste(s).[810] It seems fair to conclude that this taste, involving the term *mahāyāna*, reflects a textual expansion inspired by already evolved Mahāyāna thought.

Yet another instance occurs in the *Ekottarikāgama* in the course of an exchange, first in prose and then in verse, on the topic of assessing when someone will make an end of *duḥkha*. The first three lines of the verse in question are still related to this topic, whereas the fourth speaks of "the quest for practicing in the Mahāyāna."[811] Even though the lack of parallels prevents a comparative study, the context conveys the impression that this reference is a misfit. It thus seems to be in line with several other instances in this *Āgama* collection extant in Chinese translation of incorporating Mahāyāna-related material.[812]

The above survey suggests a pattern shared by the terms *theravāda* and *mahāyāna* as reflected in *Āgama* literature. In the former case, the type of occurrences that can be identified among Pāli discourses, which are not supported by their parallels, carry a sense that is clearly unrelated to the notion of "Theravāda Buddhism." Nevertheless, from presumably designating a body of explanations of theoretical aspects of pre-Buddhist meditation practice as the probable starting point, the term can be seen to evolve to refer to a body of explanations of Buddhist teachings together with those responsible for its oral transmission, until it eventually acquires its sense of designating Theravāda Buddhist traditions. In the case of the term *mahāyāna*, terminology and meanings related to the notion of a *yāna* may similarly have provided a background for the emergence of the term,[813] in the form evident in the first two instances surveyed above. Similar to instances of the term *theravāda* among Pāli discourses, these two instances of the term *mahāyāna* are not supported by their parallels. These suggest a starting point where the term *mahāyāna* would have simply referred to the Buddha's salvific activities as comparable to a large vehicle and his central teaching of the noble eightfold path of practice as a vehicle far superior to any ordinary chariot. It would not be surprising if these two senses should eventually coalesce into the idea of a *superior* path of practice that emulates the *large* compass of the Buddha's salvific activities.[814]

A next step to be taken at this point would be to try to ascertain what the Early-*Aṣṭa*-Mahāyāna has to say about the term *mahāyāna*. In line with my procedure adopted throughout, the exploration at present will have to be confined to occurrences of the term in Lokakṣema's translation (the term does not occur in the Gāndhārī manuscript).[815] As already mentioned above (see p. 283), in one relevant passage Subhūti expresses the basic sense of superiority by proclaiming that "among people in heaven and on earth, the Mahāyāna very much excels; there is nothing that can compare with it."[816] This can easily be related to the above-mentioned notion of a superior path of practice as a meaning of the term *mahāyāna* in *Āgama* literature.

Another relevant indication in the Perfection of Wisdom, this time given by the Buddha, clarifies that "the Mahāyāna has no limits, and one cannot arrive at its boundaries."[817] Just a few lines later, Subhūti offers an explanation that can be relied on to draw out the meaning of the absence of any limit or boundary, in that "the Mahāyāna covers uncountable, innumerable people; for this reason it is called 'Mahāyāna.'"[818] These two passages in conjunction clarify that the sense of greatness is grounded in the vast scope of the Mahāyāna, which takes the form of embarking on the path to Buddhahood with the aspiration of benefitting "uncountable, innumerable people." The sense that emerges in this way squares with the notion of Mahāyāna as a large vehicle found in the *Āgama* reference mentioned above.

In a subsequent part of the Perfection of Wisdom, Subhūti explains that "bodhisattvas, great beings, being armed with the great amour (*mahāsaṃnāhasaṃnaddha*) have set out (*saṃprasthita*) in the Mahāyāna."[819] The notion of being "armed with the great amour" can be appreciated with the help of a gloss provided elsewhere in the Perfection of Wisdom by the same Subhūti, according to which this expression stands for a bodhisattva, a great being, who delivers incalculable people, bringing them all to Nirvana, without becoming afraid on hearing that not a single person attains Nirvana.[820] Combining these two explanations by Subhūti provides a more specific orientation for the usage of the term *mahāyāna*, by establishing a close relationship to the key insight that the Perfection of Wisdom endeavors to inculcate. This brings to the fore another dimension of greatness, particularly relevant to the cultivation of the perfections, namely that bodhisattvas do their very best without any attachment to, or even any notion of, achieving something or even being on a path. Their great armor thereby combines such wholehearted dedication with the most thorough deconstruction of any trace of reification.

Yet another relevant passage in Lokakṣema's translation, spoken by the Buddha, describes how on "hearing the Perfection [of Wisdom] a son of a good family or a daughter of a good family thereby gains supreme joy in the virtues of the Mahāyāna and draws still closer to supreme, complete awakening."[821] This description provides an additional spotlight on the gaining of supreme joy, which is of course the opposite to becoming afraid on hearing teachings involving the rhetoric of emptiness. Providing such a counterbalance, by way of emphasizing the positive quality of inspirational joy, offers a pointer to another, equally important dimension of the type of Mahāyāna under discussion. Devotion, joyful inspiration, concern with merits—all of these are significant facets of the other side of the coin of emptiness in the way this emerges in Early-*Aṣṭa*-Mahāyāna. Both sides of this coin are indispensable for progress toward Buddhahood, and for this reason both are integral dimensions of the conception of Mahāyāna in the Perfection of Wisdom.

The above exploration to ascertain what the Early-*Aṣṭa*-Mahāyāna has to say about the term *mahāyāna* can additionally be related to occurrences of the term *bodhisattvayāna* in the same text.[822] The relevant instances in the Perfection of Wisdom share the feature of involving the qualification *bodhisattvayānika* to designate persons who aspire for Buddhahood.[823] This seems quite straightforward, and another occurrence indicates that the Buddha rejoices in such *bodhisattvayānika* sons or daughters of a good family.[824] The wisdom of emptiness also has its place, of course, as such *bodhisattvayānika* persons will know in regard to past, future, and present dharmas that there is nothing to obtain, give up, know, or apprehend.[825] However, not all adherents of the *bodhisattvayāna* will have this type of insight. In the future, some *bodhisattvayānika* persons get to hear the profound Perfection of Wisdom but do not approve of it and leave it behind to search for omniscience among the teachings of the other two *yāna*s; according to another, similar passage the same reaction of disapproval can lead to adopting *śrāvaka* teachings in order to gain omniscience and become a Buddha.[826] Needless to say, the Perfection of Wisdom makes it clear that these are rather foolish persons.

Overall, the above instances can be seen to complement the usage of the noun *mahāyāna* surveyed above, giving the impression that the two terms express the same basic meaning.[827] The overall sense appears to be that a *bodhisattvayānika* person is simply a follower of the Mahāyāna,[828] albeit not always successfully, as evident with the instances of future disapproval.

In sum, references to the term "Mahāyāna" in the Perfection of Wisdom unsurprisingly relate the term closely to embarking on the path to becoming a Buddha, and those who do so embark on the *bodhisattvayāna*. The Mahāyāna is "great" due to several interrelated reasons. A prominent reason is the vastness of its scope, due to the aspiration to liberate uncountable sentient beings. This makes it superior to alternative paths aimed at the awakening of an arhat or a Pratyekabuddha, and such superiority in turn constitutes a closely related dimension of its greatness. Yet another facet of greatness emerges with the need to combine wholehearted dedication to liberating others with a thorough insight into emptiness as revealed in the Perfection of Wisdom, which calls for deconstructing any reification or attachment that may manifest.

The breadth of topics covered in the thirty chapters of the Perfection of Wisdom translated by Lokakṣema illustrates that this vision of emptiness comes embedded in a network of other, related qualities and practices, the Sadāprarudita tale being a good example in case (see above p. 250). This is yet another dimension of greatness, in that the devotional and inspirational dimensions of actual practice are given full attention as well.

The Early-*Aṣṭa*-Mahāyāna that emerges in this way, in all its luxuriant complexity and beauty, appears to be influenced, among others, by a range of strands and trends gradually emerging in the history of Buddhist thought and practice, which never were and never resulted in some kind of unitary entity. In a way, already the Early-*Aṣṭa*-Mahāyāna is so rich in diversity, of which my lengthy study has only scratched the surface, that it is not possible to subsume it under a single trajectory. In terms of the quest for origins, the answer may simply be that there is no specific point of origin.

Nevertheless, as I believe the preceding pages would have shown, within the textual records of early Buddhism a range of notions can be identified that stand in close relationship to teachings of the Early-*Aṣṭa*-Mahāyāna. Appreciating these developments does not require identifying a single agenda, in the expectation that something unique, even exceptional, must have happened.[829] Instead, the main, significant developments that can be identified in this way appear to evolve naturally and in a plurality of manifestations from the seeds sown in the early Buddhist period. This would be in line with what also holds for "Buddhism" and "Theravāda." In other words, rather than trying to single out a specific act of creation, gradual change and adaptation seems to do better justice to the evidence we have.

In addition to the need to do justice to such evidence, however, there is also a need to take into account the perspective of living tradition. In a survey of developments in Japanese scholarship, Sasaki (1997, 79) notes that, once it had become clear "that the Mahāyāna sūtras were not the Buddha's word," the question arose: "[I]f the Buddha did not establish Mahāyāna Buddhism, who then compiled the Mahāyāna sūtras?" The significance of this inquiry for members of the tradition can be appreciated further in the light of the following comment offered by Shimoda (2009, 6 and 8):

> Those who seek to explore Mahāyāna Buddhism while abandoning questions about its origins understand it as a process that took place over a period of time involving a multiplicity of interlinked factors. In contrast, those who focus on its origins see the Mahāyāna as a substantive entity possessing some sort of self-identity. In Japan, with its awareness of its own well-established religious orders that are based on a Mahāyāna Buddhism that is perceived as existing as part of an unbroken line reaching back to ancient India, the Mahāyāna is a substantive reality . . .
>
> While consciously distinguishing between these two methodological approaches, it is best to draw on both of them. If the former can be characterized as a descriptive stance that examines Mahāyāna Buddhism analytically from the outside, the latter represents a hermeneutical stance rooted in tradition. While the commentators' arguments defending the Mahāyāna against the view that it did not represent the teachings of the Buddha cannot offer a full picture of the historical reality, unless one gives ear to voices within the tradition, one will be unable to solve the riddle of why complex and multifarious phenomena came to be conceived of as a single movement.

In an attempt to take into account traditional perspective(s) as well, I think it is possible to identify a specific episode that stands out as the central source of inspiration for the rise of Buddhism, the rise of not only Early-*Aṣṭa*-Mahāyāna but even Mahāyāna in general, and the rise of Theravāda. This would be what according to the traditional account happened under the *bodhi* tree in the final part of the night of the Buddha's awakening. The textual memories of this event are the seeds that in the course of time led to what we now refer to as Buddhism, Mahāyāna, and Theravāda.

The realization that, from a historical perspective, the Mahāyāna *sūtras* were not spoken by the historical Buddha applies also to what I would venture to identify as a decisive text for the evolution of the pan-Buddhist bodhisattva ideal, the Pāli version of the discourse on the karmic background to the Buddha's thirty-two marks (see above p. 98), as the relevant part is clearly a later addition. Moreover, even in the case of Pāli discourses that are supported by their parallels, it is impossible to determine the words of the Buddha with certainty.[830] A difference is that quite a few teachings in *Āgama* literature could in principle have been spoken in this way by the Buddha, even though there is no way to be certain about this, whereas with the karmic background to the thirty-two marks or the Perfection of Wisdom such a possibility does not hold in a comparable manner. Nevertheless, without intending to deny this difference, early Buddhism and Early-*Aṣṭa*-Mahāyāna share the inability to establish themselves as definite records of *the* teachings given by *the* historical Buddha.

What is within reach are much rather teachings of the Buddha as a literary figure in the various texts that have been preserved and can therefore still be accessed. His role as a literary figure has undergone a development comparable to the different roles assumed by Śāriputra (see above p. 23). There is indeed a difference between the Buddha depicted in *Āgama* literature and in Early-*Aṣṭa*-Mahāyāna, and I believe the present study confirms that it is meaningful to consider the former depiction to be on the whole earlier than the latter. At the same time, however, there is also a remarkable degree of continuity that can easily be missed. In fact, at times a passage in Early-*Aṣṭa*-Mahāyāna can even do better justice to the basic message of the Buddha's awakening, a case in point being the thorough emphasis in the Perfection of Wisdom on not taking a stance on anything (see above p. 79).

A pointer to an element of continuity related to the same topic of not taking a stance on anything affords me a convenient way of concluding my exploration of the Perfection of Wisdom. This pointer takes the form of an injunction attributed to the Buddha in a Pāli discourse, an injunction that could equally well have been spoken by the Buddha of *Prajñāpāramitā* literature:[831]

All dharmas are not worth adhering to.

# Abbreviations

| | |
|---|---|
| Abhidh-k | *Abhidharmakośabhāṣya* |
| AN | *Aṅguttaranikāya* |
| Ap | *Apadāna* |
| Ap-a | *Apadānaṭṭhakathā* |
| As | *Atthasālinī* |
| $B^e$ | Burmese edition |
| Bv | *Buddhavaṃsa* |
| Bv-a | *Buddhavaṃsaṭṭhakathā* |
| CBETA | Chinese Buddhist Electronic Text Association |
| $C^e$ | Ceylonese edition |
| Cp | *Cariyāpiṭaka* |
| Cp-a | *Cariyāpiṭakaṭṭhakathā* |
| D | Derge edition |
| DĀ | *Dīrghāgama* (T 1) |
| Dhp | *Dhammapada* |
| Dhp-a | *Dhammapadaṭṭhakathā* |
| DN | *Dīghanikāya* |
| $E^e$ | Pali Text Society edition |
| EĀ | *Ekottarikāgama* (T 125) |
| $EĀ^2$ | partial *Ekottarikāgama* (T 150A) |
| It | *Itivuttaka* |
| Jā | *Jātaka* |
| Khp | *Khuddakapāṭha* |
| Kv | *Kathāvatthu* |
| MĀ | *Madhyamāgama* (T 26) |
| Mil | *Milindapañha* |

| | |
|---|---|
| MN | *Majjhimanikāya* |
| Mp | *Manorathapūraṇī* |
| Nidd I | *Mahāniddesa* |
| P | Peking edition |
| Paṭis | *Paṭisambhidāmagga* |
| Pj | *Paramatthajotikā* |
| Pp | *Puggalapaññatti* |
| Ps | *Papañcasūdanī* |
| PTS | Pali Text Society |
| SĀ | *Saṃyuktāgama* (T 99) |
| SĀ$^{2}$ | partial *Saṃyuktāgama* (T 100) |
| SĀ$^{3}$ | partial *Saṃyuktāgama* (T 101) |
| S$^{e}$ | Siamese edition |
| SHT | Sanskrithandschriften aus den Turfanfunden |
| SN | *Saṃyuttanikāya* |
| Sn | *Suttanipāta* |
| Spk | *Sāratthappakāsinī* |
| Sv | *Sumaṅgalavilāsinī* |
| T | Taishō edition (CBETA) |
| Th | *Theragāthā* |
| Th-a | *Theragāthāṭṭhakathā* |
| Thī | *Therīgāthā* |
| Thī-a | *Therīgāthāṭṭhakathā* |
| Ud | *Udāna* |
| Ud-a | *Udānaṭṭhakathā* |
| Up | *Abhidharmakośopāyikāṭīkā* |
| Vibh | *Vibhaṅga* |
| Vin | *Vinaya* |
| Vism | *Visuddhimagga* |

# Notes

1. Here and elsewhere, I have adopted the standard rendering of *prajñā* as "wisdom," thereby not following the reasoning proposed by Wayman 1955, 253 and 256–57 that "a consideration of etymology (*nirukti*) and usage (*rūḍhi*) indicates that *jñāna* and *vidyā* are satisfactorily translated by their respective cognates, *knowledge* and *wisdom*," and that "[t]he usual translation of *prajñā* has been with *wisdom*, but as this word appears more appropriate for *vidyā*, the expression *insight* . . . can be considered a just equivalent for *prajñā*." In order to examine these suggestions further, in what follows I briefly survey a few selected instances of relevant usage in *Āgama* literature.

The term *tevijjā* can stand for Brahmanical knowledge of the three *Vedas* (e.g., MN 100 at MN II 211,12: *brāhmaṇā tevijjā*, with a parallel in Sanskrit fragment 347v5, Zhang 2004, 12: *traividyā nāma brāhmaṇāḥ*). From a Buddhist perspective, knowledge of the three *Vedas* is not necessarily a matter of wisdom. Even in its reinterpreted Buddhist usage, this notion comprises recollection of past lives and the divine eye. The former of these can lead to the arising of eternalist views according to DN 1 at DN I 13,11 and its parallels DĀ 21 at T 1.1.90a9, T 1.21.266a14, Weller 1934, 16,13, and Up 3050 at D 4094 *ju* 143a7 or P 5595 *tu* 164b6, whereas the latter can lead to mistaken conclusions about the workings of karma according to MN 136 at MN III 210,9 and its parallels MĀ 171 at T 1.26.707b7 and Up 5004 at D 4094 *ju* 264b4 or P 5595 *thu* 7b1. Such views or conclusions are the very opposite of Buddhist wisdom. Another relevant case occurs in DN 11 at DN I 213,14 in the form of a reference to *gandhārī nāma vijjā*, which designates a charm that enables the performance of magical feats. The same phrase can be found in a parallel in Sanskrit fragment 387r2, Zhou 2008, 2: *gāndhārī nāma vidyā*; another parallel, DĀ 24 at T 1.1.101c19, has 瞿羅呪; see also Abhidh-k VII 47, Pradhan 1967, 424,17. Knowing such a charm would also not necessarily be a case of wisdom, at least from an early Buddhist perspective. Another relevant case without support from parallels, as the whole relevant section appears to result from a textual expansion (see Anālayo 2014b, 47–50), is DN 1 at DN I 9,2, which thus can be taken to reflect a slightly later usage than the instances already mentioned above. The relevant passage introduces various types of prognostication that feature as wrong forms of livelihood with the term *tiracchānavijjā*; several individual instances of such prognostication are compounds whose second member is *-vijjā*. Wrong forms of livelihood are indubitably not a matter of Buddhist wisdom.

Needless to say, this is not to propose that any charm or spell is necessarily outside of the scope of wisdom; in fact, as noted by Karashima 2010, 651, Lokakṣema's translation employs 祝, "an incantation, a charm," to render what in its Sanskrit counterpart is a reference to *vidyā*, and this usage can clearly carry positive connotations. The point is only that the translation "wisdom," although possible for occurrences of *vidyā*/*vijjā* in other contexts, would not fit the instances surveyed above. In fact, according to an assessment of the usage of the Pāli term *vijjā* provided by Rhys Davids and Stede 1921/1993, 617, at times this term can function as "a general, popular term for lore in the old sense, science, study, esp. study as a practice of some art (something like the secret science of the medicine man)." The case of *prajñā*/*paññā* differs in this respect, as it has a much closer relationship to matters of liberation and does not comprise types of lore in general; it would be difficult to identify instances of its usage similar to those surveyed above for *vidyā*/*vijjā*. As far as I can see, actual usage in *Āgama* literature would make "wisdom" a more suitable candidate for translating *prajñā*, whereas the more general "knowledge" would fit the broader compass of *vidyā*/*vijjā*. Besides matters of wisdom, *vidyā*/*vijjā* can also include types of knowledge that in the Buddhist perspective are not necessarily wise.

The term "insight" in turn appears to be a good fit for *vipaśyanā*, given that the prefix *vi-* can express an intensification and *paś* in turn a form of seeing. Wayman 1955, 257 instead suggests "higher vision" for *vipaśyanā*, but that is not without drawbacks, as the term "vision" is already somewhat of a standard rendering for *darśana* (together with "view" for *dṛṣṭi*). This case reflects a basic problem in introducing a change of translation terminology, at least as long as this involves terms already in use like "wisdom" or "insight," in that a change in relation to one Indic term can have a ripple effect and require adjustments to be undertaken also with other terms. It seems to me that the inconvenience of a series of changes would only be justified if the translation under discussion is indeed misleading (which is the case, for example, for the standard rendering of *duḥkha* as "suffering"; see, e.g., Anālayo 2013b). This, however, is not the case for translating *prajñā* as "wisdom," which instead emerges from the above survey as a fairly good fit, as far as *Āgama* usage is concerned, and this usage is sufficiently close to the period of early Mahāyāna thought to be relevant for my exploration of the Perfection of "Wisdom."

2. The manuscript has preserved substantial parts of the first and fifth chapter (the latter corresponds to the last part of the third chapter in Lokakṣema's translation); see Falk and Karashima 2012 and 2013 respectively (with a correction to the latter in Harrison 2022, 657n20), which can be consulted for more fine-grained comparisons between this text and T 224; see especially Falk and Karashima 2013, 97–100 on each text representing a distinct line of transmission. Regarding the dating of this manuscript, Falk 2011, 20 reports that the C14 dating gave "two-sigma ranges from AD 25–43 (probability 14.3%) and AD 47–147 (probability 81.1%)," adding that "[o]n palaeographic ground[s] a date in the first century AD would not surprise." Falk 2011, 20 also notes that the "Gāndhārī text looks archaic and is less verbose than what Lokakṣema translated," when viewed within the context of an overall development evident in the different extant versions "from a simple to a more developed text." According to Falk and Karashima 2012, 20 and 22, "Lokakṣema . . . translated a version already slightly enlarged in comparison to our [Gāndhārī] manuscript, so that our manuscript can be regarded as representing the forerunner to the one Lokakṣema knew." This manuscript, in turn, "was copied from another one which was written in Kharoṣṭhī as well." On the significance of this manuscript in the context of Mahāyāna literature from Gandhāra see also Allon and Salomon 2010, 10.

3. T 8.224.425a3, for which I rely on the critical edition by Karashima 2011, with the support of the glossary by Karashima 2010, both of which have been indispensable for my study (in keeping with my general approach of using the same English style of punctuation for quotes in other languages, I have adjusted the Chinese punctuation, such as replacing the exclamation mark after a proper name used in direct address with a comma; on the rare occasion of adopting a punctuation that otherwise differs from Karashima 2011, I have indicated this with the help of square brackets; I have not been able to come up with a way of marking the highly exceptional instances where I deleted his punctuation). Here and elsewhere, my use of the expression "Lokakṣema's translation" is meant as a shorthand to refer to the whole translation team involved in the production of T 224.

The completion of this translation can be dated more precisely based on the indications provided in T 55.2145.47c5. Harrison 1993, 142 summarizes the available information as follows: "It informs us the translation was made (completed?) on October 26, 179 C.E.; that Lokakṣema worked on it together with the Indian *śramaṇa* Chu Fo-shuo . . . who had brought the text from India and who on that occasion recited the original . . . and that Lokakṣema's oral rendering in Chinese was taken down in writing by several Chinese assistants." Harrison 2019, 703 points out that the Indian *śramaṇa* may well have played a considerably more central role in the actual translation; see T 55.2145.96a1.

In the context of my present research, my interest is mainly in the earliest extant versions, the Gāndhārī manuscript and Lokakṣema's translation. My concerns in what follows are decidedly not to carry out a comparative study of the different surviving versions, instead of which I attempt to read these two early versions on their own respective terms (rather than, for example, approaching T 224 through the lenses of the later Sanskrit version, in keeping with the comment by Zacchetti 2015a, 178 that "evaluating early Chinese translations in the light of later Sanskrit parallels can be a dangerous affair"). Nevertheless, on a few occasions, by way of providing an outlook on how a particular passage developed in later times, I refer to some of the other versions or consult the Sanskrit text in an attempt at evaluating the possible Indic original underlying a particular rendering adopted by Lokakṣema. Parallels extant in Chinese translation, listed in chronological order, are:

1. T 8.225.478b19, attributed to Zhī Qiān (支謙), who was active in the third century, although Nattier 2008/2010 has shown that the first chapter must be by another, unknown translator.
2. T 8.226.508b17, attributed to Zhú Fóniàn (竺佛念), who was active in the fourth century; the attribution appears to be uncertain. This version lacks a counterpart to what in T 224 are the last ten chapters.
3. T 8.227.536c15, translated by Kumārajīva in the early fifth century.
4. T 7.220.865c2 to 920b16, an earlier version translated by Xuánzàng (玄奘) in the seventh century.
5. T 7.220.763b2 to 865a26, a later version translated by Xuánzàng (玄奘) in the seventh century. The tale of Sadāprarudita, found in the final chapters of the other versions of the *Aṣṭasāhasrikā Prajñāpāramitā* textual family (except, of course, for T 226), has its counterpart in Xuánzàng's encyclopedic translation of *Prajñāpāramitā* texts (T 220) instead in T 6.220.1059a16 to 1073a8, which is thus

in the final part of his rendering of a version of the text whose extant Sanskrit version goes under the title of being the *Śatasāhasrikā Prajñāpāramitā*.

6. T 8.228.587a3, translated by *Dānapāla in the late tenth century.

For a comparison of the translation style of Lokakṣema in T 224 with that of Zhī Qiān in T 225 see Zürcher 1991, 280–81 and Nattier 2008/2010, 309–17, and for the problematic translatorship attribution of T 226 the information collected by Michael Radich at https://dazangthings.nz/cbc/text/181/. In addition to these Chinese translations and the Sanskrit text (on which see below note 16), another version has been preserved in Tibetan translation, D 12 *ka* 1b1 or P 734 *mi* 1b1. According to Schmithausen 1977, 73n5, the Tibetan version closely resembles the Sanskrit text and for this reason is not of much use for a text-historical comparison: "Die tibetische Version der *Aṣṭa* ist für die Textgeschichte unergiebig, da sie bis ins Detail der überlieferten Sanskrit-Version entspricht."

4. On the Indic original see Karashima 2013c. Regarding the translator Lokakṣema in general, Harrison 2019, 704 offers the following comments: "Lokakṣema's archaic translations are important because, until very recently, they were our oldest surviving evidence for Mahāyāna Buddhism in India (Harrison 1993). While this position has now been usurped by the materials discovered in Gandhari, nevertheless, given the fragmentary nature of most of these Gandhari texts now coming to light, Lokakṣema's translations are likely to remain an indispensable resource for historical investigations."
5. Zacchetti 2015b, 177 explains that "the theory that the original Prajñāpāramitā text is to be found in the group (or subfamily) of texts related to the *Aṣṭasāhasrikā* was advocated with a very detailed analysis by Kajiyoshi (1980 [1st ed. 1943], 515–567), and his conclusions, at least in this respect, have been generally accepted. In particular, Kajiyoshi (1980, 568–633) identified part of the first chapter of the *Aṣṭasāhasrikā* (corresponding to T. 224 [VIII] 425c6–427a4 in the earliest Chinese translation; Kajiyoshi, 1980, 576–581) as the original, very short Prajñāpāramitā scripture." My ignorance of Japanese prevents me from consulting Kajiyoshi's analysis myself; for a survey of the same in English see Hanayama 1966, 47–51.
6. On the notion of early Buddhism see Anālayo 2023e, 1–12 and 2024d, 14–19. A few selected examples illustrative of the potential of an approach that grants importance to *Āgama* literature when exploring *Prajñāpāramitā* texts would be the rich annotations in Lamotte 1944/1981, 1949/1981, 1970, 1976, and 1980, Gómez 1976 (which is more specifically on the related topic of Mādhyamika thought), Huifeng 2016, and Walser 2018, 162–81. Huifeng 2016, 217–18 argues that "it is at least as important to look into material that *precedes* the *Prajñāpāramitā* in order to understand it, as it is to look to *later* commentaries . . . When these early Mahāyāna texts were first compiled in and around the turn of the millennium, it would have been the earlier material that was in the minds of the anonymous authors of the time, not the systems developed in later centuries."
7. In the case of quoting passages in Chinese, I tend to mention variants only when I have adopted them, given that the existence of other variants is readily evident in the annotations in the Taishō edition. This is not the case in the same way for the Pāli discourses, wherefore I attempt to report variants, based on comparing the PTS with three Asian editions, when quoting a particular passage even when I have not adopted them (I will not report variations in the degree of abbreviation but simply give the fullest version). I have not been able to do the same for other Pāli texts, due to lacking

access to print versions of these texts in different editions. For quotations in Tibetan, I have relied just on the Derge and Peking editions.

8. Conze 1978, 49 comments on the Sanskrit version that "often the chapters are linked together. In many cases the argument simply goes on, as between 3–4–5, 7–8–9, 11–12, 15–16, 25–26 and 30–31. Similarly, 18, 19, and 20 . . . once formed one continuous argument, which was then interrupted by the insertion of the episode of the Ganges Goddess."
9. These selections are of course rather subjective and do not intend in any way to convey that what has been chosen is necessarily the most important aspect of the portion of text under discussion. The material is so rich that I could probably have continued to produce a series of books commenting on it. What this study presents is thus only a fraction of what might possibly have been covered, and the boundaries of this fraction have been determined by my personal interests and my anticipation that, within the confines of the limitations of my knowledge and prior research, I may perhaps be able to provide a meaningful perspective on the chosen topic. In addition, another factor at times impacting my choices is that some topics are not as clearly articulated in Lokakṣema's translation as they are in the later versions.
10. For a study of the structure of the text from the viewpoint of the theory of chiasmus see Orsborn 2012 (whose publications during his time as a monk appear under his monastic name, Huifeng Shi), with a critical comment on the problem that successfully identified structural integrity does not necessarily have to reflect the original composition in Walser 2018, 133.
11. See Falk 2011, 23, who comments that this "shows that the title Prajñāpāramitā is not accompanied by a number." Falk and Karashima 2012, 24 note that differences in writing style show that the colophon was not written by the copyist but rather "by the person who had commissioned the manuscript to be written"; on this colophon see also Strauch 2014, 811–12 and Baums 2022, 28–32.
12. For a survey of different titles that have been used for T 224 see Lancaster 1975, 33.
13. In principle, it should have been possible to distinguish between the Perfection of Wisdom as a text and the perfection of wisdom as a quality or realization to be cultivated. However, in actual usage these two meanings tend to blend and shade into each other, making it challenging, if not impossible, to disentangle each and every occurrence in order to allocate it to one of these two meanings; see also below n. 206. As noted by Zhao 2020, 253n1, "Prajñāpāramitā literature does not make a distinction between the Prajñāpāramitā text and the *prajnāpāramitā* (perfection of wisdom) in the sense of the teaching of the Buddha, or the corresponding practice." Harrison 2022, 652 refers to this type of phenomenon in general as a form of "[f]uzzy self-reference, in which the text refers indeterminately to itself and to whatever it is—the *samādhi*, the *dhāraṇī*, the quality, etc.—that it teaches." Perhaps the recurrent emphasis throughout the text on the supremacy of the sixth perfection over the other perfections and on its crucial, decisive role for progress to Buddhahood will make the use of capitalization appear acceptable even in cases where the issue at stake appears to be indeed mainly the quality or realization rather than the text.
14. Zacchetti 2015b, 180 comments that "the definition of early texts such as the Gandhari manuscript or Lokakṣema's *Dao xing jing* as *Aṣṭasāhasrikā* is almost certainly not accurate from a historical point of view," since this term results from a "comparatively late categorization." In a similar vein, Harrison 2022, 656n13 reasons that "[i]t is anach-

ronistic to refer to this text as the AsPP [= *Aṣṭasāhasrikā Prajñāpāramitā*], since it is highly unlikely for it in this form to have been 8,000 ślokas (i.e. 256,000 syllables) long. The Gāndhārī version, like the Indic text translated by Lokakṣema, must have been a much shorter work." The mention of the *Aṣṭasāhasrikā Prajñāpāramitā* in the title of my present study is therefore not intended to designate T 224 specifically but rather to alert potential readers to the family of texts known under this name, in the sense that what I present in the following pages can in principle accompany a reading of the Sanskrit version or its English translation by Conze 1973/1975, which is precisely why I start each chapter with a reference to the relevant pages in the latter.

15. The term *āgama* (in the singular) features in Pāli discourses and *Vinaya* to refer to the body of discourses in circulation; see Anālayo 2016a, 9–12. This precedent hopefully suffices to allow for my approach of extending the usage of the same term (in the plural) from collections of discourses transmitted by other reciter traditions to include also those transmitted by Theravādins, even though the latter tend to use *nikāya* to refer to such collections; in fact, as noted by Gethin 2020, 6n2, the Pāli commentaries also employ *āgama* to refer to the four discourse collections; see also Skilling 2024, 383.
16. Wogihara 1932/1935, which conveniently presents the commentary together with the text commented on, wherefore I rely on his edition for the root text as well, rather than on Mitra 1887/1888 or Vaidya 1960; in fact, Sander 2000a, 5 considers Wogihara's edition to be "the most reliable one" of the three; positive evaluations of his edition can also be found in Lamotte 1944/1981, ixn3 and Sparham 2006, ix. For a portion of text missing in all three editions see Conze 1952/2008, 183–84 or Karashima 2013a. On what before the discovery and identification of the Gāndhārī manuscript ranked as the oldest Indic-language witness to *Aṣṭasāhasrikā Prajñāpāramitā* texts see Sander 2000a and 2002.
17. About this author, Harter 2022, 497 reports that "Haribhadra (c. eighth century CE) is renowned as one of the foremost specialists in the literature of Perfect Wisdom (*prajñā-pāramitā*) in late Indian Buddhism."
18. Although these notes do contain some critical engagement with positions taken by other scholars, listed below, I have abstained from voicing criticism on each occasion when this would in principle have been possible, as my main purpose here is not to provide a critical review of current scholarship. Due to my inability to consult relevant publications in Japanese, carrying out such a review would in fact not be feasible for me. When I quote a statement from a particular publication, this does not entail that I am necessarily in agreement with other positions taken in that publication or even with all the conclusions the respective author may have drawn based on the part quoted by me. Positions taken by other scholars that in some of my notes have nevertheless received a more detailed critical review—leaving aside just brief clarifications—involve the following publications, listed here for ease of reference: Drewes 2021 on becoming a bodhisattva in the presence of a Buddha n. 691 and 698 (see also n. 357); Fronsdal 1998/2014 on aspects of T 224 in n. 30, 283, 552, and 762; Karashima 2015a on the origins of the term *mahāyāna* in n. 814; Orsborn 2012 and Osto 2015 on the role of Subhūti in the *Aṣṭasāhasrikā* in n. 141; Ray 1994 on the promotion of life in forest wilds in the *Ratnaguṇasaṃcayagāthā* in n. 775; Schopen 2000/2005 on the appeal of *prajñāpāramitā* in ancient India in n. 288; Skilling 2023 on the role traditionally accorded to Ānanda in textual transmission in n. 606; Tournier 2017 on the evolution of the bodhisattva ideal in n. 358, 360, 361, and 524 (see also n. 347); Vetter 1994a,

2001, and 2003 on aspects of T 224 and the promotion of *prajñāpāramitā* in n. 288, 671, 759, 770; and Wayman 1955 on translating *prajñā* in n. 1.

19. Here and elsewhere, references to "early Mahāyāna" intend the term "early" only in relation to what is attested and can still be accessed nowadays, in clear awareness of the fact, pointed out by Harrison 1993, 139–40, that the earliest extant texts already reflect a considerable degree of sophistication and complexity, pointing to the existence of a prior period of evolution.
20. The English summary of relevant Japanese scholarship kindly provided by Hanayama 1966 leaves me at a stage of research reached some sixty years ago, which is better than nothing but still way too far behind.
21. The limitations of my research of early Mahāyāna, articulated in more detail in Anālayo 2025b, 130 apply to the present case as well.
22. I have basically just adopted the translation offered by Hurvitz and Link 1975, 422, with the difference of replacing "he" in their translation with "one" in order to make the passage become more gender inclusive. The original is found at T 8.224.425a24: 陟者彌高而不能階, 涉者彌深而不能測, 謀者慮不能規, 尋者度不能盡 (adopting the 元 and 明 variant 涉 instead of 陟 and the 明 variant 深 instead of 高).
23. Falk and Karashima 2012, 28: *[tatra ho bhagava aiśpa suhuti amaṃtreti]: [paḍi]* + + + + + + + + + *mahasetvasa prañaparimidu aradhya yasa bosisatve mahasa[tv]e* + + + + *[mi]dae ṇiyayae*. Colons and question marks, etc., are not found in the manuscript and have been added by me. According to the conventions employed by the editors, square brackets indicate partially preserved letter(s), a double period a letter too poorly preserved to enable reconstruction, and round brackets letter(s) not preserved that can nevertheless be reconstructed from the context; plus signs convey how much of the same line has not been preserved due to loss of bark. In my translations, I restrict the use of square brackets to signal only when a word has not been preserved at all. I would also like to acknowledge that here and elsewhere I benefitted considerably from consulting the translation of the Gāndhārī manuscript by Salomon 2018, 347, even though in the end I have decided to present my own rendering, mainly motivated by the wish to maintain some degree of consistency in translation terminology with other passages I translate from different sources in the remainder of this book.
24. The evolving Abhidharma and early Mahāyāna in the post-Aśokan period appears to reflect instead an environment of textual transmission that, due to a gradually increasing reliance on writing, is substantially impacted by the opening up of new avenues for the preservation of thoughts and ideas; see in more detail Anālayo 2023e, 2–4.
25. See in more detail Anālayo 2012d and 2022d, 189–90.
26. See Anālayo 2014/2015, 2015d, and Kuan 2019.
27. See Anālayo 2013c. Qing 2001, 33 notes a case that reflects the influence of *Prajñāpāramitā* thought, as EĀ 32.6 at T 2.125.678c28 has the following formulation: 無我者即是空; 空者非有, 非不有. Whereas the indication in the first part of the quote that not self corresponds to emptiness is fully in line with *Āgama* thought, the ensuing statement that "emptiness neither exists nor does not exist" is typical for the type of formulation found in *Prajñāpāramitā* literature. It seems safe to propose that this instance may result from an addition by the translator Zhú Fóniàn (竺佛念); see also Schmithausen 1987, 318–21.
28. In adopting this procedure, I am trying to address concerns expressed by Harrison 2018, 17 as follows: "As far as the relationship between Mahāyāna and the Mainstream

canons is concerned, one conclusion we ought not to jump to is that everything that is Mainstream or Śrāvakayāna must predate everything that is Mahāyāna. Put this way it looks like a statement of the obvious, but it may in fact take some effort to envisage a far more complex situation where Mainstream and Mahayana texts developed simultaneously, influencing each other . . . The unfortunate upshot of such a situation, however, is that any attempt to plot proto-Mahāyāna elements in the Nikāyas and Āgamas of the Mainstream canons, no matter how carefully carried out, is open to questions about the direction of influence. It is not easy to see how to resolve this problem, which is especially acute when the argument comes to rest on only one or two texts."

In an earlier consideration of this problem in Anālayo 2020b, 2720–21, I proposed drawing a distinction between the case of the *Ekottarikāgama*, which shows several instances of being influenced by at times fairly mature Mahāyāna thought, and material from other discourse collections that rather suggests an influence in the opposite direction. One such case is the *Lakkhaṇasutta*; for a discussion of which see p. 98. The same distinction can fruitfully inform an evaluation of the various topics I will be covering in the present study. In other words, it would be good to keep in mind the question of how far a certain position taken in *Āgama* literature seems to arise naturally from its narrative or doctrinal context, comparable to the case of the *Lakkhaṇasutta*, or whether there is evidence suggesting external influences, such as is clearly the case for several discourses in the *Ekottarikāgama*. A few selected examples of the latter, taken from the more detailed survey in Anālayo 2013c, are recurrent references to the three *yānas* or else the recommendation to cultivate the attitude of a bodhisattva, e.g., EĀ 48.5 at T 2.125.792c9+17; a teaching to Śāriputra on four matters that followers of the *hīnayāna* are unable to understand, EĀ 26.9 at T 2.125.640a5 (on this case being clearly a later interpolation see also Deeg 2006, 112); a reference to an *ekajātipratibaddha* bodhisattva, EĀ 20.10 at T 2.125.601a4 (on this case as reflecting Mahāyāna influence see also Huyên-Vi and Pāsādika 2002, 49n4); or Mahāmaudgalyāyana visiting another Buddha in a different Buddhafield, EĀ 37.2 at T 2.125.709c28 (on this case being a clear instance of later interpolation see Kuan 2019). These examples confirm the importance of the concerns expressed by Harrison 2018, 17.

At the same time, however, they also provide a telling contrast to cases like the *Lakkhaṇasutta*, where a crucial notion indispensable for the emergence of the very idea of a path to Buddhahood undertaken over multiple lives naturally arises from within the narrative and doctrinal context of the discourse itself. Even though this is only a single discourse, its testimony is rather significant and stands in contrast to the rest of the Pāli discourse collections, which do not reflect the idea of observing a particular mode of conduct over a series of past lives in order to become a Buddha. To my mind, this is relevant evidence even though it "comes to rest on only one or two texts." Evidence reflecting an interim stage in development is of such a nature that it often occurs only in one or two texts. It seems to me that, even though such instances do need to be handled with caution, for an understanding of the history of the evolution of Buddhist thought it would be preferable to take into account this type of evidence. See also below p. 93 and p. 276.

29. For examples see, e.g., Karashima 2011, 69,4 and 409,13 (= T 8.224.432b5 and 465a19).
30. Fronsdal 1998/2014, 132 introduces the above statement by speaking of "the lack of any emphasis on a bodhisattva's compassionate concern for others throughout the *Daoxing jing*" (= T 224). This does seem to be a bit of an overstatement, as references

to a bodhisattva's compassionate concern for others can be found; for examples see below n. 581.

31. See also Anālayo 2010a, 15–19.

32. MĀ 204 at T 1.26.776a26: 我本未覺無上正盡覺時, 亦如是念: 我自實病法, 無辜求病法, 我自實老法, 死法, 愁憂慼法, 穢污法, 無辜求穢污法. 我今寧可求無病無上安隱涅槃, 求無老, 無死, 無愁憂慼, 無穢污無上安隱涅槃耶, and at T 1.26.777a13: 我求無病無上安隱涅槃, 便得無病無上安隱涅槃, 求無老, 無死, 無愁憂慼, 無穢污無上安隱涅槃, 便得無老, 無死, 無愁憂慼, 無穢污無上安隱涅槃. 生知, 生見, 定道品法. 生已盡, 梵行已立, 所作已辦, 不更受有, 知如真, parallel to MN 26 at MN I 163,9 and 167,9; see also Anālayo 2011a.

33. MN 26 at MN I 171,33, Waldschmidt 1957, 136,8, and MĀ 204 at T 1.26.777c12 (another parallel, EĀ 24.5, is overall rather brief and does not have a clear-cut counterpart to this injunction). The Sanskrit fragment belongs to the *Catuṣpariṣatsūtra*, which is strictly speaking not a parallel to MN 26; it is nevertheless relevant to the present case, as it covers the same episode.

34. An example would be Vin I 92,37, which reports that, out of respect, Ānanda would not refer to Mahākāśyapa by his name; see von Hinüber 1991, 124.

35. MN 123 at MN III 122,2: *sattāhajāte* ($S^e$: *sattāhaṃ jāte*), *ānanda, bodhisatte bodhisattamātā kālaṃ karoti, tusitaṃ kāyaṃ* ($S^e$: *tusitakāyaṃ*) *upapajjatī ti* ($E^e$: *uppajjatī ti*). In a counterpart to this indication in Ud 5.2 at Ud 48,6, Ānanda is the speaker and he uses the more respectful "Blessed One": *sattāhajāte bhagavati bhagavato mātā kālam akasi, tusitaṃ kāyaṃ* ($E^e$: *tusitakāyaṃ*) *upapajjatī ti* ($C^e$: *upapajjī ti*). When the Buddha confirms this state of affairs, he then speaks of plural bodhisattvas and their mothers, Ud 5.2 at Ud 48,8: *sattāhajātesu bodhisattesu bodhisattamātāro kālaṃ karonti, tusitaṃ kāyaṃ* ($E^e$: *tusitakāyaṃ*) *upapajjantī ti*, thereby turning a single instance into a general pattern. Ud 5.2 does not appear to have a parallel in T 212; on the relation between these two collections of inspired utterances see also Anālayo 2009b, and on the reference to the mother's death in MN 123 Anālayo 2010a, 32–33.

36. MN 123 at MN III 119,19: *sato sampajāno* ($E^e$ adds *uppajjamāno*), *ānanda, bodhisatto tusitaṃ kāyaṃ upapajjī ti . . . sato sampajāno, ānanda, bodhisatto tusite kāye aṭṭhāsī ti . . . sato sampajāno, ānanda, bodhisatto tusitā kāyā cavitvā mātu kucchiṃ okkamī ti.* Unlike the case of Ud 5.2, when Ānanda repeats these statements in MN 123, he continues using the term "bodhisattva."

37. MĀ 32 at T 1.26.470a14: 世尊在兜瑟哆天, 於彼命終, 知入母胎. This corresponds to the third case in the previous note, as MĀ 32 does not report his mental condition on being reborn or remaining in Tuṣita, only mentioning this in relation to the time of passing away from Tuṣita and entering his mother's womb. The term used here to refer to him, 世尊, corresponds to *bhagavat* used in Ud 5.2 by Ānanda; see above n. 35.

38. For an excellent study of references to former Buddhas in textual and epigraphic records see Tournier 2019.

39. Rhys Davids and Rhys Davids 1910: 1 refer to the "six forerunners of the historical Buddha, each constructed . . . in imitation of the then accepted beliefs as to the life of Gotama."

40. DN 14 at DN II 12,3 to 15,14 uses the term *bodhisatta* when describing various marvels also found in MN 123. For the period from birth to going forth, however, which is not covered in MN 123, DN 14 at DN II 16,1 to 30,5 instead uses the term "prince," *kumāra*, but at DN 14 at DN II 30,10 reverts to *bodhisatta*. Particularly noteworthy is

the contrast between the employment of the term *bodhisatta* in descriptions of marvels occurring after his birth, DN 14 at DN II 14,3 to 15,14, whereas from DN 14 at DN II 16,1 onward the report given to his father of his birth and the examination of the infant by brahmins skilled in the lore of prognostication uses the term *kumāra*, even though the events pertain to the same period of his life. Similarly noteworthy is that the usage of *kumāra* continues in relation to various aspects related to his going forth, up to DN 14 at DN II 30,5, but then from DN II 30,10 onward the term *bodhisatta* is used to refer to that very same condition of having gone forth. It seems highly unlikely that these changes of terminology reflect an intentional choice.

41. See in more detail Anālayo 2010a, 47–49.
42. My exploration below could fruitfully be complemented by consulting the study of the bodhisattva ideal in Sarvāstivāda texts offered by Fujita 2009; see also Dhammajoti 2011.
43. Kv 23.3 at Kv 623,1.
44. For comparative observations on versions of the *Pañcaviṃśatisāhasrikā Prajñāpāramitā* see also, e.g., Lethcoe 1976 and Watanabe 1994.
45. Bv 2.58 at Bv 12,28; one of these qualities is to be a male, a topic I explore in more detail on p. 204. According to von Hinüber 1983a, 8, Pāli was a foreign language to the person(s) responsible for composing the *Buddhavaṃsa*.
46. Cp 1–37. In an apparent wordplay on the claim implicit in the title of this work to be an actual basket, a *piṭaka*, Ratnayaka 1985, 89 reasons that "it may be proper to say that the *Cariyāpiṭaka* is a *Bodhisattva-Piṭaka* in the Theravāda *Tripiṭaka*."
47. Ap 1.64 at Ap 5,19: *disā dasavidhā loke . . . buddhakhettā asaṅkhiyā*; see also Ap 1.3 at Ap 1,10: *yāvatā buddhakhettesu*. Barua 1946, 184 comments that the "main interest of the Buddhāpadāna . . . centres round the romantic conception of the *Buddhakhetta*, an ideal land of art and beauty. It is an ideal educational institution, situated in the midst of the most beautiful and sombre natural surroundings." Another relevant reference can be found in Ap 485.10–11 at Ap II 429,7+9, which mentions a plurality of fields and then the present Buddhafield, *yathāpi bhaddake khette . . . tath' ev' idaṃ buddhakhettaṃ*. A comparable reference to the present, single Buddhafield, in the context of qualifying an offering as supreme, occurs in Mil 176,27: *yaṃ imasmiṃ buddhakkhette asadisaparamadānaṃ*, on which Zhutayev 2010, 155n4 comments that this passage is "obviously using the word in the sense of a cosmological unit." Another relevant reference occurs in Th 1087: *yāvatā buddhakhettamhi*. On precedents to the notion of a Buddhafield in *Āgama* literature see in more detail Anālayo 2025a, 97–104.
48. Ap 1.20 at Ap 2,22: *ye ca etarahi atthi buddhā loke anuttarā* and Ap 1.76 at Ap 6,13: *samāgatā bahū buddhā*.
49. Ap 6.148 at Ap 48,5: *abbhātītā ca 'me buddhā vattamānā anāgatā*; Ap-a 293,31 explains: *ye ca buddhā vattamānā idāni jātā ca ye buddhā*. As noted by Henry 2020, 131, "the *Buddhāpadāna* . . . contains cosmological notions analogous with contemporary Indian Mahāyāna works exemplified by the *Sukhāvatīvyūha Sutra* (for example, the idea of 'Buddha fields' or *buddha-khetta* in Pali)."
50. Sv I 15,22 reports that the reciters of *Dīghanikāya* disagreed with the reciters of the *Majjhimanikāya*, who included the *Apadāna*, together with the *Buddhavaṃsa* and the *Cariyāpiṭaka*, in their conception of the fifth *Nikāya*; see also, e.g., Lamotte 1957, 344–45, Norman 1983, 9, Abeynayake 1984, 33–46, von Hinüber 1996/1997, 42–43, Endo 2003, 7, and Baba 2005.

51. Bechert 1976, 47 notes a reference in this work to a count of the perfections that is otherwise only known from Theravāda sources, making a wholesale import from some Mahāyāna source less likely. He also points out that the language and style of the *Buddhāpadāna* stands in continuity with other and comparably late Pāli literature; see also the assessment in general by Bechert 1964, 535 that traces of the bodhisattva ideal in non-Mahāyāna texts appear to reflect natural developments rather than external influences. Norman 1983, 91 comments that a "simpler and doubtless earlier idea of the *Buddhakhettas* is found elsewhere in the Apadāna, and also in the Theragāthā and the Milindapañha . . . The form of classification which Buddhaghosa adopts for the *Buddhakhettas* shows that the concept was widespread by his time . . . Whether any Mahāyānic influence should be seen in the idea is doubtful. It has been rightly pointed out that many ideas in Buddhism follow from the dynamics of *Āgama* thought, which lead to the existence of one and the same idea in two forms in two different traditions. Linguistic evidence suggests an unusual origin for this Apadāna . . . but there is no reason to see here anything more than an idea which was carried further in this text than in any other Theravādin text." Nevertheless, for a case of external influence on the *Apadāna* see Hofinger 1954, 22 and Salomon 2008, 28. Moreover, as already noted by Zhang 2020, 30, Kv 21.6 at Kv 608,22 reports a refutation of the idea that Buddhas persist in all directions.
52. MN 115 at MN III 65,14 and AN 1.15 at AN I 27,38; both cases come with the specification that the arising of two Buddhas is impossible in "a single world system," *ekissā lokadhātuyā*; see in more detail Anālayo 2025a, 94. As noted by Vetter 2001, 67n32, "[w]hat seems implicit here . . . is the acceptance of the existence of several *lokadhātu*s."
53. Skilling 2013b, 116 refers to "the commonly recited verse: *ye ca buddhā atītā ca, ye ca buddhā anāgatā, paccuppannā ca ye buddhā, ahaṃ vandāmi sabbadā*," commenting that "[h]ere the devotee pays homage not only to the Buddhas of the past and the Buddhas of the future, but also to the Buddhas, plural, of the present."
54. Mil 276,10. The whole part in which this indication occurs is without a counterpart in the (earlier) Chinese version; for a comparative study of the two versions see Minh Chau 1964.
55. Endo 2005, 50 explains that "there is no literary evidence whatsoever to prove that the class of basic Sīhaḷa sources of the present Pāli Commentaries called '*Aṭṭhakathā*' was expanded and added new elements after the time of King Vaṭṭagāmaṇī-Abhaya. This positively suggests that the expansion of the 'Sinhala Version of the Original Commentaries' had come to a completion by the time of this king, when the Buddhist texts were committed to writing."
56. The idea as such has already been suggested by Warder 1970/1991, 367, who proposed that the Pāli "commentaries and the Eight Thousand seem to be contemporary in origin."
57. Spk II 21,9: *buddhānaṃ santike byākaraṇassa laddhattā avassaṃ anantarāyena pāramiyo pūretvā bujjhissatī ti bujjhanakasatto ti pi bodhisatto.*
58. The term occurs in the context of a discussion of the entry of bodhisattvas into the womb of their mothers, Sv II 430,21: *mahāsattānaṃ paṭisandhi na aññesaṃ paṭisandhi sadisā*. See also Th-a I 9,8, which uses the term *mahābodhisatta* as distinct from the *paccekabodhisatta* and the *sāvakabodhisatta*.
59. Lokakṣema's translation, Karashima 2011, 15,3 (= T 8.224.426c18), refers to bodhisattvas, *mahāsattvas*: 菩薩, 摩訶薩, an instance reflecting a recurrent usage in the text

suggesting that the two terms can function as synonyms. According to an explanation offered by Haribhadra (in the *Abhisamayālaṃkārālokā Prajñāpāramitāvyākhyā*), Wogihara 1932/1935, 22,13, the combination of the two terms clarifies that the persons intended are not *śrāvaka*s, to which the term "bodhisattva" on its own could be taken to refer, nor are they altruistically disposed non-Buddhists, to which the term *mahāsattva* on its own could be taken to refer; see also the discussion in Kajiyama 1982a, 265–66.

60. Sv I 161,1: *sāvakabodhim pi paccekabodhim pi sabbaññutam pi pāpuṇanti*. The basic distinction made in this way recurs in the context of practical advice on how to cultivate one's meditation practice in Vism 116,19, which quotes from an unknown source a recommendation on six types of inclination of the mind that are equally relevant to progress toward these three types of awakening, *chahi ākārehi sampannajjhāsayena bhavitabbaṃ. evaṃ sampannajjhāsayo hi tissannaṃ bodhīnaṃ aññataraṃ pāpuṇāti*. This conveys the impression that this basic distinction was considered of practical relevance to meditators, rather than being merely a theoretical construct.
61. Ps III 282,16: *bodhisattā hi buddhānaṃ sammukhe pabbajanti . . . vipassanaṃ vaḍḍhetvā yāva anulomaṃ ñāṇaṃ āhacca tiṭṭhanti, maggaphalatthaṃ vāyāmaṃ na karonti*. The passage comments on the past life of Śākyamuni as a brahmin youth who goes forth under the Buddha Kāśyapa; discussed in more detail above p. 106. See also Unebe 2012 on the idea of explicitly opting for future Buddhahood, set in contrast to becoming an arhat or a Pratyekabuddha, as documented in the *Paññāsajātaka*.
62. Cp-a 289,30: *karuṇāya dukkhaṃ sampaṭicchati . . . karuṇāya vaṭṭaṃ pāpuṇāti. tathā karuṇāya saṃsārābhimukho hoti . . . karuṇāya sabbe pi anukampati* (the introduction to this discussion at Cp-a 289,19 mentions *mahākaruṇā*). In the overall context, these indications come in conjunction with references to *paññā* as a complementary factor, which in relation to *dukkha* has the function of arousing *nibbidā* and thereby complements facing *saṃsāra* with facing Nirvana, *nibbānābhimukho hoti*, and ensures that there is no delight in *saṃsāra*.
63. Cp-a 284,15: *mahāpuriso mahābodhiyānapaṭipattiṃ otiṇṇo nāma hoti niyatabhāvasamadhigamanato tato anivattanasabhāvattā bodhisatto ti samaññaṃ paṭilabhati*. Bodhi 1978/1992, 253 conveys the apparent wordplay by translating the term *mahābodhiyāna* as the "great vehicle to awakening."
64. Cp-a 329,18: *tividhā hi bodhisattā abhinīhārakkhaṇe bhavanti: eko ugghaṭitaññū, eko vipañcitaññū, eko neyyo ti*.
65. In AN 4.133 at AN II 135,9 these three are part of a list of altogether four types, the fourth being, according to the explanation given in the *Puggalapaññatti*, Pp 41,35, unable to reach realization in that same life. Since this option is not relevant to the path of a bodhisattva, which extends over many lives, it is natural that only the other three have been taken up.
66. Two of the three terms occur in the *Aṣṭasāhasrikā Prajñāpāramitā* in relation to teaching the Dharma, Wogihara 1932/1935, 515,6.
67. Skilling 2002/2003, 98 points out the usage of just one of the three terms in relation to bodhisattvas in the *Saddharmapuṇḍarīka*, Kern and Nanjio 1912, 473,7: *udghaṭitajñā hi kulapitraite bodhisattvā mahāsattvāḥ*.
68. Cp-a 320,25: *dasa pāramiyo, dasa upapāramiyo, dasa paramatthapāramiyo ti samatiṃsa pāramiyo*. By in this way arriving at a total count of thirty, the Theravādins were, in the words of Skilling 1996a, 179, "surpassing the figures given by other Śrāvaka schools,

and also the mainstream Mahāyāna. On the subject of Buddhology the Theravādins were far from conservative: they seem to have been the most innovative of the known Śrāvaka schools."

69. For example, the *Bodhisattvabhūmi*, Wogihara 1930/1936, 12,1, describes the initial arousal of the mind by resolving for supreme, complete awakening and the establishing of all sentient beings in Nirvana, and indicates that with the arousal of *bodhicitta* one has entered the Mahāyāna of supreme awakening and comes to be reckoned a bodhisattva: *iha bodhisattvasya prathamaś cittotpādaḥ sarvabodhisattvasamyakpraṇidhānānām ādyaṃ . . . sa khalu bodhisattvo bodhāya cittaṃ praṇidadhad evaṃ cittam abhisaṃskaroti vācaṃ ca bhāṣate: aho batāham anuttarāṃ samyaksaṃbodhim abhisaṃbudhyeyaṃ sarvasattvānāṃ cārthakaraḥ syām atyantaniṣṭhe nirvāṇe pratiṣṭhāpayeyaṃ . . . tasya ca bodhicittasya sahotpādād evāvatīrṇo bhavati bodhisattvo 'nuttarabodhimahāyāne, bodhisattvo bodhisattva iti ca saṃkhyāṃ gacchati.*

70. Bv 2.54–58 at Bv 12,20 reports the reflection of the one who was to become the Buddha Śākyamuni at the time of his meeting with Dīpaṃkara, when he rejected the possibility of becoming an arhat and rather decided to aim for omniscience and for taking across many people, followed by stating *iminā me adhikārena katena*. After quoting these verses, Jā 15,13 (for the Tibetan version see Gaffney 2003, 331,3) reports Dīpaṃkara reflecting that this ascetic—that is, Śākyamuni in his past life—has made a resolution (*abhinīhāra*) for Buddhahood, wondering if this resolution (*patthanā*) will be successful: *ayaṃ tāpaso buddhattāya abhinīhāraṃ katvā nipanno, ijjhissati nu kho imassa patthanā udāhu no?* The passage reflects the usage of two distinct terms to express the same basic meaning, namely *abhinīhāra* and *patthanā*; on these two terms as apparent equivalents to *bodhicitta* see also Wangchuk 2007, 81 and on *abhinīhāra* in particular Cooray 1961, Nanayakkara 1972, 184, and Tournier 2017, 153n96. In Pāli discourses, the verb *abhinīharati* conveys the sense of inclining the mind toward awakening in DN 2 at DN I 83,35 (used together with *abhininnāmeti*); the term *patthanā* expresses a strong wish in SN 12.63 at SN II 99,33 (used together with *cetanā* and *paṇidhi*), here in particular the longing to get away from being dragged toward a burning charcoal pit. These instances suggest that the basic notion of aspiring for Buddhahood may have been expressed with the help of terminology chosen from such precedents.

At the same time, however, a terminological overlap can be found in the term *praṇidhāna/paṇidhāna*. A Pāli usage of this term to convey the sense of the aspiration for Buddhahood can be seen, e.g., in Bv-a 59,13: *buddhabhāvāya kadā paṇidhānaṃ katan ti?* This forms a comment on a verse in Bv 1.75 at Bv 6,25 that rather employs the noun *abhinīhāra* and the verb *pattheti* (= the noun *patthanā*). In the *Critical Pāli Dictionary*, Trenckner, Andersen, and Smith 1924, 361 list *paṇidhāna* and *patthanā* as synonyms to *abhinīhāra*.

71. On this statue in more detail see Mori 1999, 57–71; on Avalokiteśvara in Sri Lankan Buddhist traditions see Holt 1991.

72. Dohanian 1977, 24.

73. Dohanian 1977, 20.

74. Dohanian 1977, 25.

75. Dohanian 1977, 25.

76. Assavavirulhakarn 2010, 242n89 refers to *Charuek nai Prathet Thai*, 1986, Bangkok: National Library of Thailand, vol. 5 pp. 83, 84, and 187 for instances in Thailand. My ignorance of Thai prevents me from following this up. Fortunately, after reading a draft

version of the present book, Peter Skilling kindly directed me to two of his publications that cover relevant material from Thailand.

77. Skilling and Pakdeekham 2013, 199: "[M]ay I not be discouraged from [my goal to realize] awakening as a bodhisatva . . . and concentrate only on rescuing beings from the suffering of *samsara* so that they can gain the happiness of Nibbāna."
78. Skilling 2007b, 188.
79. See also Ooi 2022, 128: "The tradition of aspiring to become a Buddha has been present in Thailand since the formation of the Siamese state around the fourteenth century, as evidenced by epigraphic inscriptions . . . such aspiration continued to be a popular option for donors and scribes from the seventeenth to nineteenth centuries . . . the desire to become an omniscient Buddha was expressed by all layers of society, not just by the nobility or by high-ranking monks."
80. Tun 1956/1978, 71: "May I receive from Maitreya the prophecy (of my future Buddhahood) . . . so that I may be able to redeem all beings from the miseries of *saṃsāra*." In a general comment unrelated to this inscription, Holt 1991, 55 notes that "the wish to be reborn in Metteyya's time and in *cakkavatti* Sankha's kingdom of Ketumatī is comparable to the Mahāyāna desire to be reborn in Amitābha's Sukhāvatī and has been long an intrinsic part of lay Buddhist aspirations in Sri Lanka."
81. Tun 1956/1978, 73.
82. Tun 1956/1978, 74; her wish is "that I also may be freed from this womanhood and in all my wanderings (i.e., future existences) . . . I may be a man who is endowed with piety."
83. Tun 1956/1978, 73: "I dedicate so much property not that I do not love it but that I love Buddhahood more."
84. Tun 1956/1978, 74; on the "city" of Nirvana see Anālayo 2023d, 177n187.
85. Tun 1956/1978, 74: "May I and my wife without fail get the boon of Buddhahood."
86. On the appeal of the path of a bodhisattva among Sri Lankan monks in particular see also Hemasiri and Sangjingyu 2022.
87. Skilling 2007b, 204 adds that "[n]ot only kings, but also other members of the royal family, were *bodhisattvas* by birth."
88. Holt 1991, 54 reasons that "the tradition of associating bodhisattvahood with kingship is clearly referred to within early Pāli biographical accounts of the life of Gotama, wherein Siddhartha is portrayed as having been born as a prince into the royal Śākyan clan" and "was prophesied to become either a buddha or a *cakkavatti*"; see also the discussion by von Hinüber 2009, 50–51 of the description of the Buddha's cremation.
89. As already noted by Boucher 2008, 77, "the bodhisattva path seems to have functioned as a pan-Buddhist option."
90. For a comparative study of the relevant accounts see Mori 1999, 11–33; on the *vetullavāda* see also Skilling 2013b, 88–94.
91. See von Hinüber 1983b.
92. Falk and Karashima 2012, 30: *asa ho aiśpasa śariputrasa edad ahoṣi: kim ayaṃ ausa subhu[ti] + + + + yeṇa valadhaṃdaṇeṇa ṇidiśiśasi asa [h]i b(u)dhaṇ(u)bhaveṇa? asa ho aiśpa suhuti [aiśpa] + + + + + + [doya]: kiṃci ausa śaripu(t)ra bhagavado ṣa[vaga maṃt]r(e)[ti] [sa]r[va t] + + + + + + ++ + + +.*
93. Karashima 2011, 3,1 (= T 8.224.425c14): 皆持佛威神; see also below note 141.
94. Karashima 2011, 2,7 (= T 8.224.425c12): 須菩提知舍利弗心所念. However, this does

not rank in T 224 as a feat exclusively attributed to Subhūti and the Buddha, as on one occasion Śakra reads Ānanda's mind; see Karashima 2011, 399,2 (= T 8.224.463c23).

95. According to MacQueen 1982, 50, "when the Buddha invites Subhūti to speak . . . The invitation constitutes a certification before the event and indicates that the discourse is a form of extended *buddhavacana*." Nattier 2003a, 12 comments that "the degree of concern expressed in a number of places in the *Aṣṭa* with establishing the legitimacy of dharma-discourses *not* preached by the Buddha suggests that something more than the use of an alternative speaker as a narrative device is at stake. In the opening lines of the sūtra, before Subhūti has uttered a single word, Śāriputra begins to experience doubts about the legitimacy—that is, the authoritativeness—of what he is about to say."

96. Nattier 2003a, 210n25 notes that later versions of the *Aṣṭasāhasrikā Prajñāpāramitā* indicate that it was through the power of the Buddha that Subhūti was able to read Śāriputra's mind, which she considers to be an example of a tendency where "the Buddha's level of influence increases and the importance of the follower's initiative is reduced."

97. My comments on Śāriputra in what follows, as well as other references in my study to any of the different protagonists of *Āgama* literature and the Perfection of Wisdom, do not intend to convey certainty that these are actual historical persons who did precisely what the texts report. The use of expressions like "the Buddha explains," etc., is just meant to reflect what the texts report.

98. MN 43 at MN I 292,7, MĀ 211 at T 1.26.790b13, and Up 9008 at D 4094 *nyu* 81a4 or P 5595 *thu* 127a4; for a discussion of this difference see Anālayo 2007c, 29–32.

99. Ps II 337,20.

100. According to the listing of outstanding disciples, Pūrṇa Maitrāyaṇīputra was exceptional for his teachings; see AN 1.14.1 at AN I 23,25: (*etad aggaṃ, bhikkhave, mama sāvakānaṃ bhikkhūnaṃ*) *dhammakathikānaṃ* and EĀ 4.5 at T 2.125.557c18: (我聲聞中第一比丘) 能廣說法, 分別義理. Pūrṇa's teaching ability comes up again in SN 14.15 at SN II 156,7 and its parallels SĀ 447 at T 2.99.115b13 and EĀ 49.3 at T 2.125.795c17.

101. He features implicitly as a speaker in the context of an indication given by the Buddha's attendant Ānanda, SN 22.83 at SN III 105,10 and SĀ 261 at T 2.99.66a6, according to which the latter attained stream-entry based on receiving a penetrative instruction from Pūrṇa Maitrāyaṇīputra; on this instruction see also Anālayo 2023d, 147–48.

102. MN 24 at MN I 150,28, MĀ 9 at T 1.26.431b29, EĀ 39.10 at T 2.125.735b2, and SHT II 163.bR5–6, Waldschmidt, Clawiter, and Sander-Holzmann 1968, 16; see also the discussion in Anālayo 2005, 133–35.

103. MN 121 at MN III 109,1 and Skilling 1994, 178,2. Although the parallel MĀ 204 does not have an explicit statement to this effect, the same is implicit in the overall presentation shared by the three versions.

104. AN 4.175 at AN II 163,25.

105. The listing of outstanding disciples in AN 1.14.1 at AN I 23,17 refers to his great wisdom, *mahāpaññā*, and its parallel EĀ 4.2 at T 2.125.557b5 highlights his inexhaustible wisdom and ability to resolve all doubts, 智慧無窮, 決了諸疑.

106. Sn 557.

107. Ud 2.8 at Ud 17,29 and Th 1083.

108. MN 151 at MN III 294,4 and its parallel SĀ 236 at T 2.99.57b10; the same is also found in the partial parallel EĀ 45.6 at T 2.125.773b24.

109. Sn 321: *so tāraye tattha bahū pi aññe, tatrūpāyaññū* ($B^e$, $E^e$, and $S^e$: *tatrūpayaññū*) *kusalo mutīmā* ($S^e$: *matimā*); for the commentarial identification see Pj II 325,24.
110. Th 1015.
111. Th-a III 105,14: *paññāpāramitaṃ patto ti sāvakañāṇassa pāramiṃ pārakoṭiṃ patto.*
112. MN 111 at MN III 29,6 ($E^e$: *ariyā*). Ps IV 91,17 explains that this refers to him having attained complete accomplishment: *pāramippatto ti nipphatti patto.*
113. Anālayo 2014c.
114. MN 28 at MN I 190,37 and MĀ 30 at T 1.26.467a9.
115. Garfield 1995, 89n4 has chosen to render *svabhāva* as "essence," noting at the same time the potential problem of calling up resonances related to the usage of this term in Western philosophical traditions. Yet, compared to such calling up of unintended resonances, which is to some extent unavoidable in translation, "[r]etaining the original term is worse, as it conveys nothing to the reader not already conversant with Tibetan, Sanskrit, and Buddhist philosophy. And using one of the ugly neologisms frequently introduced conveys the misleading impression that the original introduces such an ugly neologism." Nattier 2003a, 294n565 agrees, reasoning that "the term 'essence' better conveys to Western readers the underlying Sanskrit than do such literalistic alternatives as 'own-being', 'self-nature,' and so on."

    In appreciation of the above reasoning, it seems to me that a perhaps still better alternative would be "intrinsic nature," following the example set by Cox 1995, 12. One of the meanings conveyed by *bhāva* is "nature" (as a state or condition), and "intrinsic" seems successful in capturing the sense taken in the present context by *sva*, which in general stands for what is (one's or another's) "own." Combining "intrinsic" and "nature" results in a rendering that avoids a literalist translation difficult to understand but at the same time reflects the original more closely than does "essence." In what seems fairly standard procedure, "essence" often serves to render *sāra*. The qualification of being without an essence, *asāra*, occurs, e.g., in SN 22.95 at SN III 141,2 in relation to the five aggregates and in Sn 937 in relation to the whole world. These instances reflect a period in the evolution of Buddhist thought before the arising of Abhidharma notions regarding *svabhāva*. Employing the same English term to render the notion of *asāra* and the denial of *svabhāva*, besides not reflecting the fact that different Indic terms are involved, would also risk incurring a loss of clarity in respect to this doctrinal development. For this reason, to my mind "intrinsic nature" appears as the most convenient choice for rendering *svabhāva*.
116. In the context of a survey of *Prajñāpāramitā* literature, Harvey 1990, 96 speaks of the concern "that *Abhidharma* analytical thinking could lead to a subtle form of intellectual grasping: the idea that one had 'grasped' the true nature of reality in a neat set of concepts." Gethin 1998, 236 explains that "[f]rom the perspective of perfect wisdom . . . the conceptual constructs of Buddhist theory are *ultimately* no less artificial and arbitrary entities than the conceptual constructs of the ordinary unawakened mind, which sees really existing persons and selves. The mind can grasp at the theory of dharmas and turn it into another conceptual strait-jacket."
117. See, e.g., Migot 1954, 519–23 and Li 2019, 416.
118. DN 33 at DN III 210,18, Stache-Rosen 1968, 44,19, DĀ 9 at T 1.1.49c6, and T 1.12.227b5.
119. This is the *Saṅgītiparyāya*, 阿毘達磨集異門足論, an early member of the Sarvāstivāda Abhidharma collection, whose Chinese version reports an explicit attribution of the commentary itself to Śāriputra, T 26.1536.367a5: 尊者舍利子說; see also Anālayo

2014c,153n76. An association with Śāriputra appears to hold as well for another Abhidharma text, in this case presumably belonging to the Dharmaguptaka tradition (see Anālayo 2014c, 88n119), titled **Śāriputrābhidharma*, 舍利弗阿毘曇論, T 28.1548.525a3.

120. As 16,19; see in more detail Anālayo 2012f.

121. Instances among Pāli discourses without a parallel are AN 11.15 at AN V 337,12, where Subhūti receives a teaching from the Buddha on what makes a monastic worth being called "faithful," which turns out to be a whole range of practices and accomplishments from moral restraint to the three higher knowledges; Ud 6.7 at Ud 71,10, where the Buddha speaks an inspired utterance on seeing Subhūti seated in thought-free concentration (according to the commentary, Ud-a 348,19, he was seated in the fruition attainment of arhat-ship, based on the fourth absorption); and Th 1, where he refers to his own well-concentrated and liberated mind in verse; different verses by him are recorded in Mil 386,26 and 391,7.

    In the Chinese *Āgamas*, at first sight a reference in SĀ$^2$ 324 at T 2.100.482b4 appears to mention his name, yet closer inspection suggests this to be a textual error to be corrected by adopting a 宋, 元, and 明 variant reading. Several references to his name can be found in the *Ekottarikāgama*. One example is EĀ 13.7 at T 2.125.575b1, which could be a composition rather than a translation by Zhú Fóniàn (竺佛念), with the first part being modelled on the introductory narration in DN 21, leading on at T 2.125.575c12+18 to Subhūti on Mount Vulture Peak giving the following teaching to Śakra: 善哉, 拘翼, 法法自生, 法法自滅, 法法相動, 法法自息 and 一切所有皆歸於空. This reads more like what one would expect to find in *Prajñāpāramitā* literature. Again, EĀ 36.5 at T 2.125.707c18 reports Subhūti having the following reflection: 一切諸法皆悉空寂, 無造, 無作, which makes it probable that this episode belongs to the same category. The same discourse at T 2.125.706a12 reports the making of a Buddha image on behalf of King Udayana; for a discussion of this evidently late tale see, e.g., Rowland 1948, 183–84, Lamotte 1958, 704, Soper 1959, 259–60, Carter 1990, 6, Bareau 1997, 28n25, and Kuan 2013, 150–63 (with a critical reply to the last in Anālayo 2013c, 9–10). EĀ 36.5 also refers to the Buddha arousing in others the *bodhicitta*; T 2.125.703b18: 未發菩薩心, 令發菩薩意. These instances give the impression that references to Subhūti in this discourse are probably the result of later influences.

122. For a comparative study see Anālayo 2011b, 793–96.

123. Based on noting similarities between the eightfold path and the ten courses of action in Pāli discourses and then somewhat surprisingly considering these to imply that the latter is the source of the former, Skorupski 2022, 399 arrives at the rather unconvincing conclusion that the eightfold path is a later development. From a methodological viewpoint, assessments of the relative earliness or lateness of early Buddhist teachings need to be based on a comparative study of discourses preserved by different reciter traditions. In the case of what tradition believes to have been the first sermon by the Buddha, the extant parallels agree in presenting a reference to the eightfold path as an integral part of this first teaching; see Anālayo 2012b and 2013a. This agreement does not turn the report into a historical truth, but it does provide textual evidence that needs to be taken into account.

124. Rhys Davids and Stede 1921/1993, 563.

125. See, for example, MN 13 at MN I 86,27 and its parallels MĀ 99 at T 1.26.585a29, T 1.53.847b2, EĀ 21.9 at T 2.125.605a28, and T 17.737.539c26 (the references are to fight-

ing battles in a war; for a comparative survey of the various detrimental repercussions of the pursuit of sensual gratification taken up in each version see table 2.7 in Anālayo 2011b, 119).

126. Ps V 31,15: *subhūtittherassa pana dhammadesanāya ayaṃ puggalo appaṭipannako anārādhako ti vā ayaṃ sīlavā guṇavā lajjī pesalo ācārasampanno ti vā n' atthi, dhammadesanāya pan' assa ayaṃ micchāpaṭipadā ayaṃ sammāpaṭipadā tv' eva paññāyati.*

127. An example for this trajectory would be the succinct indication by Subhūti that bodhisattvas, great beings, in relation to all namable dharmas no longer grasp at a name; see Karashima 2011, 15,3 (= T 8.224.426c18): 菩薩, 摩訶薩一切字法不受字. This conveniently exemplifies a central concern underlying the rhetoric of emptiness.

128. MN 139 at MN III 237,15: *subhūti ca pana, bhikkhave, kulaputto araṇapaṭipadaṃ paṭipanno ti.*

129. MĀ 169 at T 1.26.703c8: 如是須菩提族姓子, 以無諍道, 於後知法如法. 知法如真實, 須菩提說偈: 此行真實空, 捨, 此住止息. The prose part and the first two lines of the ensuing verse are spoken by the reciter(s) of the discourse, who are also responsible for providing the standard introduction and conclusion to a discourse as well as any background information required to follow the progress of a dialogue or teaching, by way of identifying the speakers, etc. A relationship between Subhūti and the path of nonconflict as well as a realization of the Dharma in accordance with the Dharma features also in the **Mahāvibhāṣā*, T 27.1545.900a15, introduced as a *sūtra* quotation: 善現苾芻修無諍行證法隨法.

130. AN 1.14.2 at AN I 24,8 lists him as foremost among *araṇavihārīnaṃ*, followed by doing the same for *dakkhiṇeyyānaṃ*. The commentary on MN 139, Ps V 32,23, explains in relation to this second, alternative commendation that, when begging alms, Subhūti would briefly enter absorption on *maitrī* while waiting for the food to be brought, thereby purifying the gift; see also Maithrimurthi 2004, 205–8. Subhūti as foremost in worthiness to receive gifts recurs in the **Karmavibhaṅgopadeśa*, Lévi 1932, 161,17. His rank as outstanding in dwelling without conflict in turn recurs in the *Avadānaśataka*, Speyer 1909/1970, 131,5.

131. EĀ 4.8 at T 2.125.558b15+16: [我聲聞中第一比丘] 恒樂空定, 分別空義, and 志在空寂, 微妙德業. A relationship to understanding emptiness comes up also in EĀ 30.3 at T 2.125.663a4: 解空須菩提 (preceded by 由本布施報, 今獲此功德), and his rank in being foremost in this respect can be seen in the context of a survey of various distinguished disciples found in EĀ 49.3 at T 2.125.795c22: 汝等頗見須菩提比丘不乎? 諸比丘對曰: 唯然, 見之. 佛告之曰: 此諸上人皆是解空第一. In relation to the last case of EĀ 49.3, however, the parallels SN 14.15 at SN II 155,10 and SĀ 447 at T 2.99.115a28 do not include Subhūti in their survey of disciples. Walleser 1917, 12 notes a reference to Subhūti in the context of a listing of ten outstanding disciples in the 翻譯名義集, T 54.2131.1063a18, where he features foremost in the understanding of emptiness, 須菩提解空, with detailed explanations at T 54.2131.1063c1.

132. Karashima 2011, 6,1 (= T 8.224.426a4): 空身慧而說最第一. The basically same role of Subhūti appears to be evident also in the 阿閦佛國經, on whose attribution to Lokakṣema see below n. 229. The main topic of this *sūtra* is Akṣobhya and his Buddhafield, which the Buddha describes to Śāriputra and Ānanda. In addition to these two, Subhūti makes a brief appearance at T 11.313.760b11. After a revelation of the remarkable living conditions in Akṣobhya's Buddhafield has taken place, Ānanda turns to Subhūti in an attempt to find out what the latter has to contribute to the matter.

Subhūti invites Ānanda to look up at the sky. Ānanda replies that he only sees the empty sky (rather than having any vision of Akṣobhya or his Buddhafield). Subhūti replies that Akṣobhya, his disciples, and his Buddhafield should be regarded just as the empty sky. This entertaining episode may be a textual expansion, as the ensuing question Śāriputra asks the Buddha does not do justice to Subhūti's profound indication. However, the same question relates directly to what the Buddha has said just before Ānanda turns to Subhūti. As already noted by Kwan 1985, 139, Ānanda and Subhūti "come into the scene too suddenly" and their exchange "not only disturbs the smooth flow of the text but it also engages in a discussion of the teaching not quite in keeping with the rest of the scripture." The choice of Subhūti for introducing this touch of *prajñāpāramitā* emptiness into the otherwise fairly realistic description of Akṣobhya's Buddhafield shows the degree to which he has come to be associated with the role of being foremost in expounding the wisdom of emptiness.

133. T 8.226.508c24: 空身慧所說最第一. In principle, it is possible that the reference in the listing of outstanding disciples in EĀ 4.8, quoted above in n. 131, could have been influenced by this version of the Perfection of Wisdom; see also above n. 27.

134. Wogihara 1932/1935, 40,19: *'raṇāvihāriṇām agratāyāṃ* (although, as already noted by Walleser 1917, 4, Mitra 1887/1888, 6,9 instead reads *'raṇyāvihāriṇām*), D 12 *ka* 3b1 or P 734 *mi* 3b5: *nyon mongs pa med pa la gnas pa'i mchog tu*, T 7.220.763c26 + 867b27: 住無諍定最爲第一, T 8.227.538b9: 於無諍三昧人中最爲第一, and T 8.228.590a7: 於無諍三昧行中最勝第一 (as already noted by Walser 2018, 236, these Chinese versions add the indication that the absence of conflict takes the form of being a *samādhi*). However, T 8.225.479a4 reads: 山澤行實爲第一. In a discussion of translation terminology employed in T 225, Nattier 2008/2010, 321 notes the use of 山澤 for *araṇya* as a terminological choice that had already been introduced by the early translators Ān Xuán (安玄) and Yán Fótiáo (嚴佛調), which confirms the impression that the present formulation in T 225 involves a shift from *araṇa* to *araṇya*. The interlinear commentary found in this part of T 225 then naturally takes this reference to convey that Subhūti was a forest dweller; see T 8.225.479a5: 常善於山澤空淨之行, 故爲佛所稱 and Lai 1983, 95.

135. The Sanskrit manuscript from the Schøyen Collection, edited in Harrison and Watanabe 2006, 119,14 (§9e), reckons him to be *araṇavihāriṇām agryo*, which is also the reading found in T 7.220.981b17: 無諍住最爲第一, T 8.238.768a14: 無諍行最勝說, T 8.239.772c23: 得無諍住中最爲第一, and in D 16 *ka* 124a7+b1: *nyon mongs pa med par gnas pa rnams kyi mchog* (P 739 seems to be lacking text here); other Chinese translations refer to the same quality of absence of conflict as a type of *samādhi*, which is the case for T 8.235.749c10: 得無諍三昧人中最爲第一, T 8.236a.753c18: 得無諍三昧最爲第一, and T 8.237.763a17: 住無諍三昧人中最爲第一. There is thus an overall agreement among these versions to spotlight the theme of absence of conflict.

136. The *Pañcaviṃśatisāhasrikā Prajñāpāramitā*, Kimura 2007, 155,7 and 186,20 (also in Dutt 1934, 123,2 and 145,21), refers to Subhūti twice as foremost in regard to the absence of conflict, *araṇāvihāriṇām agratāyāṃ*. However, as already pointed out by Walleser 1917, 4 and Walser 2018, 235, the *Śatasāhasrikā Prajñāpāramitā*, Ghoṣa 1902, 502,21, rather has the reading *araṇyavihāriṇāṃ . . . agryatāyāṃ*. Chinese versions of the Larger *Prajñāpāramitā* family refer to (the *samādhi* on) the absence of conflict, namely T 5.220.202c15 (= 231a2) and T 7.220.45a15: 住無諍定最爲第一 (with the alternative formulation in T 7.220.52a6: 無諍定聲聞眾中最爲第一) and T 8.223.234a12 and

238b22: 無諍三昧中汝最第一 and 行無諍三昧第一. However, T 8.222.166c20 has much rather a reference to abiding in emptiness 行空第一. This indication in T 222, translated by Dharmarakṣa, thus needs to be added to the count of similar indications in texts extant in Chinese translation: T 26 translated by Gautama Saṅghadeva (on this attribution see Hung and Anālayo 2017 and Radich and Anālayo 2017), T 125 and T 226 (the former could in principle be an instance of rewriting based on the latter, and this is in turn strongly influenced by T 224), and T 224 translated by Lokakṣema. All of these relate Subhūti to the topic of emptiness rather than—or in addition to—relating him to the absence of conflict.

137. In a comment on T 224, Vetter 2001, 73n44 proposes that the "expression *araṇa-vihārin* thus most probably stood in the text that served as the basis for Lokakṣema's translation, but has been represented only with one share of its meaning." Walser 2018, 240, however, finds it "doubtful that the term *araṇavihāra* was in Lokakṣema's manuscript."

138. See Radich and Anālayo 2017, 218.

139. Karashima 2011, 434,7 (= T 8.224.468a17): 如須菩提所說[,] 但說空事. 須菩提亦不見般若波羅蜜者, 亦不見行般若波羅蜜者, 亦不見佛, 亦不見得佛者, 亦不見薩芸若, 亦不見得薩芸若者，亦不見怛薩阿竭，亦不見得怛薩阿竭者，亦不見無所從生, 亦不見無所從生證得之者; see Karashima 2011, 435n382+384 on the addition of 亦不見佛 and on an emendation of an instance of 無有 to read 不見, in keeping with the formulation employed in the remainder of the passage.

140. Wogihara 1932/1935, 28,17: *anyathā 'ham iv' ārya subhūtir aśaktaḥ. na cāraṇāvihāriṇām agratvena viśeṣasadbhāvād bhāṣate ity api śakyate vaktuṃ. mamāpi prajñāvatām agratvaviśeṣasadbhāvād bhāṣaṇaprāpteḥ*. Tsai 2014, 259 aptly qualifies Subhūti's role as involving a "cross-category performance."

141. Karashima 2011, 2,7 (= T 8.224.425c13): 敢佛弟子所說法，所成法，皆持佛威神; Karashima 2010, 491 lists the present instance of 威神 as corresponding to *anubhāva*. In relation to the similar phrasing in T 8.227.537b3: 佛諸弟子, 敢有所說, 皆是佛力, Orsborn 2012, 132 proposes that "what is meant is not the 'Buddha' in terms of Gautama or Śākyamuni, but in terms of realization itself. Teaching through the spiritual power of the 'awakened one' (*buddha*) means that one has oneself become awakened to the nature of *Dharma*." In a comment based on Conze's translation of the Sanskrit counterpart to T 224 and T 227, Osto 2015, 128 suggests the implication of the role taken by Subhūti to be "that Subhūti himself is a *bodhisattva*. How else would he have the necessary insight to understand the profound and paradoxical philosophy of emptiness (*śūnyatā*) as it is found in these texts?" It seems to me that both proposed interpretations underestimate the transformative power accorded by tradition to the notion of *buddhānubhāva*.

An example from the Pāli tradition would be a commentarial gloss on a crucial episode in the narrative of events after the Buddha had just awakened, namely his encounter with the five who had been his former companions during the time of his ascetic practices and had left him in disgust when he abandoned these. The five are on record for having made an agreement that, if he should come to visit them, they were not going to express any respect. Yet, when he actually arrives, they are unable to act according to their earlier agreement and instead receive him with respect; see MN 26 at MN I 171,27 and its parallels MĀ 204 at T 1.26.777c6 and EĀ 24.5 at T 2.125.618c24. This change of behavior is crucially at this junction of the narrative, as the Buddha faces the difficult task of convincing these five that he had reached awakening even though (or rather precisely because) he had given up ascetic practices. According to the Pāli commentary, their change of behavior was the outcome of the Buddha's *anubhāva*; Ps II 191,16: *buddhānubhāvena buddhatejena abhibhūtā attano katikāya ṭhātuṃ nāsakkhiṃsu*. This exemplifies the power associated with such *buddhānubhāva*.

In the present case, the three versions under discussion—Karashima 2011, 2,6 (= T 8.224.425c12), T 8.227.537b2, and Wogihara 1932/1935, 28,3—agree in reporting that Śāriputra's preceding reflection already mentions such *buddhānubhāva* as a possible explanation, with the alternative being that Subhūti will be speaking through his own power. Since this alternative is implicitly dismissed in the reply by affirming *buddhānubhāva*, there seems to be little room left for the idea that Subhūti is speaking by the power of his own realization or that he plays the role of a bodhisattva. Moreover, at later junctions in the Perfection of Wisdom the Buddha explicitly indicates that on one occasion Śakra and on another Śāriputra have also been speaking through the Buddha's power; see Karashima 2011, 209,7 and 214,1 (= T 8.224.444c20 and 445a25): 拘翼,乃作是問.今發汝者,皆佛威神之所致and舍利弗,乃樂作是說,皆佛威神之所致. These instances confirm that the point at stake is not attributing qualities or powers to the speakers themselves, instead of which the overarching concern is to showcase the Buddha's *anubhāva*.

142. This is the 大智度論, a commentary on the *Pañcaviṃśatisāhasrikā Prajñāpāramitā*, with the relevant passage found at T 25.1509.137a22: 佛以眾生信敬阿羅漢諸漏已盡, 命之爲說, 眾得淨信故. 諸菩薩漏未盡, 若以爲說, 諸人不信. 以是故, 與舍利弗, 須菩提, 共說般若波羅蜜 (after 若以爲 adopting the 宋, 元, 明, and 宮 variant 說 instead of 證).
143. T 25.1509.136c26: 須菩提於弟子中, 得無諍三昧最第一. 無諍三昧相, 常觀眾生不令心惱, 多行憐愍. 諸菩薩者, 弘大誓願以度眾生, 憐愍相同, 是故命說; to be precise, this reckons him foremost in the "concentration" (三昧) on the absence of conflict. T 25.1509.137a19: 須菩提常行空三昧, 與般若波羅蜜空相相應, 以是故佛命令說般若波羅蜜.
144. Karashima 2011, 37,3 (= T 8.224.429a5): 須菩提言: 善哉, 舍利弗所解法, 如舍利弗言無異.
145. An example in case can be found in Karashima 2011, 213,2 (= T 8.224.445a18) in the form of the report that, on being invited by the Buddha, Śāriputra illustrates the nature of the Perfection of Wisdom with a series of apt similes.
146. The study is based on findings presented in Nattier 1992. Without intending to join the debate regarding her intriguing suggestion that the *Prajñāpāramitāhṛdaya* may be of Chinese origins, I cannot help but wonder if the term "apocryphal" (used even in the article's title) is appropriate in this context. After all, if her research conclusion is correct, it would merely be a case of recycling already existing material. Moreover, expansions and abridgements are an integral part of the development of *Prajñāpāramitā* literature, and there is no reason why only Indian contributions in this respect deserve to be considered genuine.
147. See in more detail Anālayo 2022a.
148. The need for such an alternative perspective, although without explicitly bringing in the tetralemma, has already been recognized in relation to the *Vajracchedikā Prajñāpāramitā* by Nagatomo 2000, 221–22, in that "the *Sutra* rejects either-or logic in

favour of neither-nor logic," that is, its presentation "is opting for a *third* perspective that cannot be accommodated by either affirmation . . . or negation."

149. AN 2.2.8 at AN I 57,21.

150. Hanayama 1966, 71–74 summarizes research by Hideo Masuda, who distinguishes between two types of negations in *Prajñāpāramitā* texts, the first of which is "absolute" (in the sense of calling for a literal reading) whereas the second is only "relative." In the case of the second, the formulation "'Non-S' in the form of 'Non-S is S' is not a mere negation. These negatives must mean the state of Bodhisattvas in which they completely abandon . . . attachment" (72). The identification of such relative negation confirms the impression that the third option of the tetralemma probably offers a more apt way of reading such passages in *Prajñāpāramitā* texts than relying on the assumption that these involve self-contradiction.

151. Selected examples, chosen somewhat at random to exemplify the currency of this type of opinion in scholarly writings on Mahāyāna in general or *Prajñāpāramitā* in particular, are the following: Conze 1959/2008, 77: "The Hinayana, in rejecting the 'heresy of individuality,' had taught that persons are 'empty of self,' and are in fact conglomerations of impersonal processes, called *dharmas*. The Mahayana now adds that also these impersonal processes are 'empty of self.'" Verboom 1998, 23–24: "the concept of 'empty' in itself was known in the older schools of Buddhism. The constituents were considered to be 'empty' or, more specifically, 'empty of self' (also called *pudgalanairātmyam*). In Early Mahāyāna . . . this concept is no longer limited to the five constituents alone, but relates to all entities (also called *sarvadharmanairātmyam* or *sarvadharmaśūnyatā*)." Skilton 2002, 56: "the insight or knowledge which can be attained by the bodhisattva . . . transcends that of the Śrāvaka path insofar as it deconstructs not only the person, but also the phenomena which make up the person." Salomon 2018, 337: "the central conception of the Mahāyāna sūtras . . . can be summed up in the single concept of 'emptiness' (*śūnyatā*) . . . [t]he principle of emptiness can be understood in historical terms as a radical extension of the traditional Buddhist concept of 'nonself' (*anātman*), applied not only to the illusory sense of individual personality that is a fundamental principle of conservative Buddhism, but to the entire conceptual universe."

152. Sn 937: *samantam* (E$^{e}$: *samantaṃ*) *asāro loko*. Sn 9: *sabbaṃ vitatham idan ti ñatvā* (C$^{e}$: *ñatva*) *loke, so bhikkhu jahāti orapāraṃ*, with similarly worded Indic language parallels in the Gāndhārī *Dharmapada* 87, Brough 1962/2001, 131 (see also Lenz 2003, 67), the Patna *Dharmapada* 412, Cone 1989, 214, and the Sanskrit *Udānavarga* 32.55, Bernhard 1965, 447. Sn 1119: *suññato lokaṃ avekkhassu, mogharāja sadā sato, attānudiṭṭhiṃ ūhacca*. SN 35.85 at SN IV 54,4: *yasmā ca kho, ānanda, suññaṃ attena vā attaniyena vā tasmā suñño loko ti vuccati*, with a similar position taken in the parallel SĀ 232 at T 2.99.56b24. Dhp 279: *sabbe dhammā anattā*, with similarly worded Indic language parallels in the Gāndhārī *Dharmapada* 108, Brough 1962/2001, 134, the Patna *Dharmapada* 374, Cone 1989, 203, and the Sanskrit *Udānavarga* 12.8, Bernhard 1965, 194.

153. Regarding the qualification of lacking an essence or a core, *asāra*, Choong 2006, 60 notes that the triad *rittaka*, *tucchaka*, and *asāraka* in SN 22.95 at SN III 141,2 has a counterpart in the triad *rittaka*, *tucchaka*, and *suññaka* in SN 35.197 at SN IV 174,34, which conveys the impression that the qualification of lacking an essence or a core is closely related to the qualification of being empty; see also the discussion in Huifeng 2016, 223–24.

154. See Anālayo 2023d, 15.

155. It serves as a contemplation leading to the liberation of the mind by emptiness in SN 41.7 at SN IV 296,33 (see also MN 43 at MN I 297,37) and its parallel SĀ 567 at T 2.99.150a3 (see also below n. 194). Alternatively, the same can also lead to the attainment of nothingness in MN 106 at MN II 263,26 and its parallels MĀ 75 at T 1.26.542c18 and Up 4058 at D 4094 *ju* 228b7 or P 5595 *tu* 261a7. The standard approach to the latter is based on the perception that there is nothing (or more literally not anything), a perception that is clearly meant to carry a comprehensive sense.

156. AN 3.134 at AN I 286,18.

157. SN 22.90 at SN III 132,26 and its parallel SĀ 262 at T 2.99.66b14.

158. SN 44.10 at IV 401,5, with parallels in SĀ[2] 195 at T 2.100.444c12 and Up 9031 at D 4094 *nyu* 89a4 or P 5595 *thu* 136b1. The relevant passage in another parallel, SĀ 961, does not have a version of the statement under discussion; see also Anālayo 2023a, 70.

159. T 25.1509.295c5: 三藏中處處說法空; see also below n. 395.

160. Karashima 2011, 326,4 (= T 8.224.456c13): 佛言: 云何? 我常不言: 諸法空? 須菩提言: 如怛薩阿竭所說[:] 法悉空.

161. Walser 2018, 37n17 offers the following assessment: "The earliest reference I have been able to find asserting the Hīnayāna/Mahāyāna distinction as having anything to do with selflessness of persons vs. dharmas is in a commentary on the *Diamond Sutra* ascribed to Vasubandhu. See T. 1511, pp. 788c29–789a2; T. 1513, p. 879c15–16." These two passages associate teachings on the four truths to the lower vehicle or the vehicle of *śrāvaka*s and those on the not-self nature of dharmas to the great vehicle; see T 25.1511.788c29: 不妄說小乘者, 說小乘苦諦等唯是諦故. 不妄說大乘者, 說法無我真如故 and T 25.1513.879c15: 由於聲聞乘說苦等四諦是實不虛, 於其大乘說法無性所顯真如稱實知故.

162. In a discussion of past, present, and future form, T 26.1536.412a22 employs the following formulation: 過去性, 過去類, 過去世攝 . . . 未來性, 未來類, 未來世攝 . . . 現在性, 現在類, 現在世攝; see also Cox 2004, 567 and 589n114–15.

163. In the context of a discussion of the nature of Nirvana, T 26.1543.923c22 comes out with the following statement: 恒住自性, 不捨自性, on which Cox 2004, 585n85 comments that here "the term 自性 is used in an early canonical text with the sense of 'intrinsic nature' (*svabhāva*)." According to an assessment by Akanuma Chizen, summarized in Hanayama 1966, 55, "it is very possible that the Prajñāpāramitā Literature was originally composed just after the establishment of this text," that is, the *Jñānaprasthāna*.

164. In the context of a discussion surveyed by Cox 2004, 559–60, T 27.1545.308a20 reports the following statement: 自性於自性是有, 是實, 是可得 . . . 恒不空 . . . 非不已有, 非不今有, 非不當有.

165. Examples for early Abhidharma works that stand in close interrelationship with *Āgama* literature would be the *Saṅgītiparyāya* and the *Dharmaskandha* of the Sarvāstivāda and the *Vibhaṅga* and the *Puggalapaññatti* of the Theravāda traditions. On proto-Abhidharma in *Āgama* literature see in more detail Anālayo 2014c and Dhammadinnā 2019.

166. A somewhat accidental impact of this notion, evident from the circumstance that the relevant qualification of the objects of the senses as "truly existing" is not applied consistently, can be seen in MĀ 165 at T 1.26.697c20; see also Anālayo 2008d, 7, 2017e, 69, and 2022d, 192. This seems to be about as far as the evidence in *Āgama* literature

reaches, conveying the impression that concerns related to the notion of *svabhāva* emerged too late to be able to make a more substantial impact on this type of text.

167. See below n. 183.

168. Falk and Karashima 2012, 40: *bosisatvo ṇama ṇa vedami ṇa uvalahami, aviṃdamaṇa aṇua + .. [ma] bosisatvo prañaparamidae anuśaśemi?*, Falk and Karashima 2012, 42: *saye hi bosi _ _ _ _ _ _ satvasa prañaparamida uadiśamaṇae ṇa oli + + + + [sa](ṃ) traso avajati*, Falk and Karashima 2012, 46: *[a]yaṃ bosisatvasa aparigra[h · d · ṇa](ma) [sa](ma)[si]*. In a general comment on the notion of emptiness in the *Aṣṭasāhasrikā Prajñāpāramitā*, Nattier 2003a, 180n18 notes the relative rarity of the term *śūnyatā* in the early chapters, in that "[t]he authors of the *Aṣṭa* favor the use of experiential terminology such as 'is not found' (*na saṃvidyate*), 'is not obtained' (*nopalabhyate*), etc." This comment helps appreciate the above extract, which clearly is about emptiness even though the actual term does not occur.

169. As already pointed out by Karashima 2011, 3n17, Lokakṣema's translation only reports that at this point Subhūti deconstructs the notion of a bodhisattva, not yet the notion of the Perfection of Wisdom. This thereby directly targets his audience, as bodhisattvas listening to this teaching are mentioned in the introduction, which identifies two such bodhisattvas by name, namely Maitreya and Mañjuśrī; see Karashima 2011, 2,1 (= T 8.224.425c8): 彌勒菩薩, 文殊師利菩薩等. Harrison 2000, 165 comments that the reference to Mañjuśrī here "has all the appearance of an interpolation." In fact, whereas Mañjuśrī occurs just in this single instance, Maitreya features on several occasions and at times takes an active role in the discussions (Maitreya also takes an active role in what appears to be an addition to the *Pañcaviṃśatisāhasrikā Prajñāpāramitā*; see Conze and Iida 1968). For example, he advises that the teachings just given should not be addressed to those who have only recently embarked on the path to Buddhahood, as that risks that they lose their faith; see Karashima 2011, 134,5 (= T 8.224.438b10): 彌勒菩薩謂須菩提: 不當於新學菩薩, 摩訶薩前說是語. 何以故? 或亡所信. This advice seems particularly pertinent given that Maitreya, as the next Buddha, would presumably be the most advanced bodhisattva in the assembly. Commenting on the Sanskrit version of this advice, Kent 1982, 317 reasons that "difficult doctrines as 'emptiness' and 'the non-existence of all dharmas,' 'should not be taught or expounded upon in front of a *bodhisattva* who is newly set out in the vehicle,'" in that one should "not reveal the complete perfection of wisdom teaching to either potential recruits or new converts, pragmatically choosing instead to reveal them gradually." He sees this as characteristic for "sectarian groups [who] frequently withhold complicated or controversial doctrines from potential converts while the established members attempt to cultivate personal relationships with them." I wonder if it could not be seen simply as a pedagogical skill that is not necessarily confined to sectarian groups. Take the example of students in their first semester at university, where it would similarly be advisable not to confront them immediately with all the problems and challenges of the subject they have chosen, as that could motivate them to withdraw and enroll instead at a different department or even give up university studies altogether.

170. Harrison 1978a, 48 comments on the Sanskrit verb *upalabhate* and related nominal forms like *upalambha*, *upalabdhi*: "Referring primarily to the act of grasping or obtaining, the significance of *upalambha* as a mental function is only imperfectly rendered by 'apprehension' . . . [t]his difficult term, common in Prajñāpāramitā literature, refers to

that mode of cognition which views its objects as existing in themselves; to have such notions about those objects is tantamount to being attached to them."

171. For a discussion of the suggestions offered by Skilton 2002 regarding the significance of *samādhi* in some Mahāyāna *sūtra*s see Anālayo 2025b, 110–14.

172. Nattier 2003a, 62n19 provides a convenient illustration of the relationship between the *Aṣṭasāhasrikā* and the *Pañcaviṃśatisāhasrikā Prajñāpāramitā* by proposing that the latter "consists of the *Aṣṭa* 'sliced' like a loaf of bread and then layered with 'fillings' introduced from other sources. Very little of the text of the *Aṣṭa* has been altered in the process, and only rarely does a crumb of the 'bread' seem to have dropped out. The *Pañca* is thus not simply related to the *Aṣṭa*; it *is* the *Aṣṭa*, with the addition of a number of layers of new material."

173. Zacchetti 2005, 41 comments on T 222 that "from a historical point of view it is very unlikely that it should be called a translation of the *Pañcaviṃśatisāhasrikā Prajñāpāramitā*, if we take this designation as anything more than a loose categorization." It thus seems preferable to avoid a direct attribution of a Sanskrit title that quite probably came into existence much later than the text in question. Bongard-Levin and Hori 1996, 27 propose the usage of "the Larger Prajñāpāramitā" as an umbrella term for the *Pañcaviṃśatisāhasrikā* and the *Aṣṭādaśasāhasrikā*, thereby setting these apart from shorter versions, like the *Aṣṭasāhasrikā*, and the longer *Śatasāhasrikā*. Zacchetti 2005, 41 comments that "not only do I fully endorse the proposal of using the name 'Larger PP [Prajñāpāramitā]' . . . but I would actually propose that we use this appellation systematically for all the texts belonging to this family that are not explicitly identified by titles or colophons as representing a particular version (i.e., essentially for all the earlier texts of this family)."

174. Zacchetti 2005, 187,12 (= T 8.222.150b26): 智慧解空不計吾我, 是爲般若波羅蜜. Boucher 1996, 251 infers "that Dharmarakṣa's Chinese skills significantly improved between the years 267 . . . and 284," and thus prior to his rendering of T 222 completed in 286 (Boucher 1996, 260).

175. Kimura 2007, 110,19: *tadyathā 'pi nāma, subhūte, sattvaḥ sattva iti cocyate, na ca kācit sattvopalabdhiḥ* (also in Dutt 1934, 99,13), with its Tibetan parallel in D 9 *ka* 87b4 or P 731 *nyi* 89a4: *rab 'byor, 'di lta ste dper na: sems can sems can zhes bya bar ming du gdags pa'i ming de ni btags pa tsam ste*. The relevant passage is not without difficulties in T 8.222.162b17: 譬如, 須菩提, 所見人者, 但假託號, 彼亦無名, wherefore in my discussion I rely rather on the Sanskrit version. Other Chinese translations of larger *Prajñāpāramitā* texts do refer to a sentient being: T 7.220.29a28: 如是有情, T 8.221.11b11: 譬如字衆生爲衆, and T 8.223.230c11: 如衆生 (in T 220 and T 223 this is only the second term taken up for discussion, hence the use of 如是 or 如). Elsewhere in T 222, Dharmarakṣa repeatedly uses 衆生, such as in a recurrent reference to 一切衆生. Karashima 1998, 435 comments on the use of 所見 in Dharmarakṣa's translation of the *Saddharmapuṇḍarīka* that in that text it can function as "a particle used to form a phrase with a passive meaning." Occurrences of 所見 in T 222 tend to convey visibility; for a good example see T 8.222.189b8: 眼所見者. In sum, it is not clear to me how to explain the present usage and I will have to leave the solution to those who are better acquainted with Dharmarakṣa's translation idiom.

176. SN 5.10 at SN I 135,19: *nayidha sattupalabbhati* (C^e^ and E^e^: *sattūpalabbhati*)—which thus uses the same verb to designate the not obtaining of a sentient being as the passage from the *Pañcaviṃśatisāhasrikā Prajñāpāramitā* quoted in the previous note—with

parallels in SĀ 1202 at T 2.99.327b8: 無是衆生者, SĀ$^2$ 218 at T 2.100.454c28: 都無有衆生, and Up 9014 at D 4094 *nyu* 82a7 or P 5595 *thu* 128b2: *'di la sems can rnyed ma yin* (Pradhan 1967, 466,2: *na hi sattvotra vidyate*); see also below n. 412.

177. AN 4.34 at AN II 34,12: *yāvatā, bhikkhave, sattā . . . tathāgato tesaṃ aggam akkhāyati*, with parallels in SĀ 902 at T 2.99.225c22: 若有衆生 . . . 於一切如來最第一 and EĀ 21.2 at T 2.125.602a1: 諸有衆生 . . . 如來於中最尊, 最上.
178. SN 35.66 at SN IV 39,22 and its parallel SĀ 230 at T 2.99.56a27 and 56b10.
179. SN 23.2 at SN III 190,3 and its parallel SĀ 122 at T 2.99.40a6.
180. See also Anālayo 2010a, 19n18 and Silk 2013, 198.
181. Karashima 2011, 3,9 (= T 8.224.425c19): 佛使我說菩薩. 菩薩有字, 便著. 菩薩有字無字? Karashima 2011, 3n14 presents an alternative reading of the middle part of this passage in this way: "(If) there is a name for a bodhisattva, then (people) will cling to it. Is there a name for a bodhisattva or not?," followed by noting that "[o]ther versions lack parallels," except for T 8.226.508c7, which reads: 菩薩有字. 爲在何法而字菩薩? 亦不見法, 有法字菩薩.
182. SN 44.1 at SN IV 376,23.
183. Falk and Karashima 2012, 52: *ruo yeva ausa śariputra virahido ruasvabhaveṇa eva vedaṇa saṃña saṃkhara viñaṇo + + + + + [ri]putra virahido viñaṇasvabhaveṇa*. An overcoming of (the notion of) *svabhāva* also features in another early Mahāyāna text extant in Gāndhārī, Bajaur Kharoṣṭhi Fragment 4v11, Schlosser 2022, 130.
184. Williams 1989/2009, 52 explains that the teachings of the *Prajñāpāramitā* texts are made "from the position of a Buddha's perception wherein absolutely nothing has any independent final ultimate existence." The position taken by Orsborn 2012, 370, that in the first two chapters of the *Aṣṭasāhasrikā Prajñāpāramitā* "the doctrine of emptiness was *not* the key point that the authors were trying to convey," seems to rely on relating his structural analysis to explicit occurrences of the term "emptiness." Yet, the present quote from the Gāndhārī manuscript is a good example for the possibility of making a statement that embodies the doctrine of emptiness but does not actually employ the term.
185. Karashima 2011, 24,1 (= T 8.224.427c7): 譬如幻師於曠大處, 化作一大城. 作化人滿其中, 悉斷化人頭.
186. SĀ 265 at T 2.99.69a7, with parallels in T 1.105.501b9 and Up 4084 at D 4094 *ju* 240a4 or P 5595 *tu* 274a8; another two parallel versions, SN 22.95 at SN III 142,10 and T 1.106.502a17, do not provide details about the nature of the magical illusion. The illusionism in Mahāyāna traditions has already been related to relevant passages in *Āgama* literature by Schmithausen 1978, 113–14, who offers the following comments: "Dieser Illusionismus konnte anknüpfen an die im Hīnayāna entwickelte Lehre von der Nichtselbsthaftigkeit und Substanzlosigkeit aller Daseinsfaktoren, insofern diese Lehre . . . gelegentlich überspitzt formuliert und die Wertlosigkeit und Unzuverlässigkeit weltlicher Gegebenheiten sogar mit illusionistisch klingenden Illustrationen wie Zaubertrug und Fata Morgana verdeutlicht worden war"; see also Schmithausen 1973, 180–85. A reference to just consciousness being like an illusion, in line with the indication found in *Āgama* literature, occurs in T 15.624.353c16: 知其識如幻; on this text see below n. 565.
187. Karashima 2011, 25,9 (= T 8.224.427c24): 色如幻無著, 無縛, 無脫, 痛痒, 思想, 生死, 識如幻無著, 無縛, 無脫. 無有邊, 無著, 無縛, 無脫. Regarding 生死 as a referent to the fourth aggregate, Karashima 2010, 421 explains that "[i]n older Chinese translations,

the word 生死 often corresponds to Skt. *saṃskāra*, which indicates that its Middle Indic form *saṃkhāra* was confused with *saṃsāra*," followed by noting that this pattern is not confined to early translations into Chinese but can even occur in Sanskrit texts, such as among manuscripts of the *Saddharmapuṇḍarīka*, Kern and Nanjio 1912, 417,12, in the form of a variation between *sarvasaṃsārabhaya-* and *sarvasaṃskārabhaya-*.

The rendering 生死 used in this way already occurs in translations by Ān Shìgāo (安世高), in relation to which Vetter and Harrison 1998, 213n7 argue that this "is hardly to be explained away by facile recourse to some Prakritic confusion between the two words *saṃskāra* and *saṃsāra*. The former term is in any case notoriously difficult, but it is at least conceivable that here An Shigao had in mind the *saṃskāra*[s] as the forces through which things come into being and pass away, something of which is captured in the English equivalent '(karmic) formations.'" Deleanu 2003, 79n30, in awareness of the aforementioned comment, nevertheless considers it more probable that "the translation of *saṃskāra* as 生死 . . . must have come from a confusion between *saṃskāra* and *saṃsāra*," suggesting as an alternative but less likely explanation that the translator "indulged in a commentarial paranomasia in which *saṃskāra*, as the second member of the twelvefold chain of dependent arising, was equated with or explained as the basic element determining one's *saṃsāra*." Zacchetti 2004, 199n7 draws attention to an "expanded rendition (or paraphrase)" of the second link in dependent arising in the form of 生死精行, found in a text attributed to Ān Shìgāo, T 25.1508.53b7 (see also the phrasing used at 53b9), where the presence of 精行 "seemingly rules out the possibility of a mere confusion *saṃskāra*/*saṃsāra*," thereby corroborating the position taken by Vetter and Harrison 1998, 213n7. According to Greene 2016, 252n17, Ān Shìgāo uses 生死 "to translate *saṃskāra* only in the context of the *skandha*s, never in *pratītyasamutpāda*, where we always find *xing* 行. However conversely, *xing* 行 does occasionally appear in the context of the *skandha*s." Commenting on Ān Shìgāo's usage of 生死 for the fourth aggregate, Vetter 2012, 194–95 reasons: "How to explain this translation? The probably oldest intention of the *twelvefold* dependent origination . . . was: based on 'ignorance' ($^{\text{P}}$*avijjā*/$^{\text{S}}$*avidyā*) emotional factors ($^{\text{P}}$*saṅkhārā*/$^{\text{S}}$*saṃskārāḥ*) like passion and hatred cause birth and death . . . This function of $^{\text{P}}$*saṅkhārā*/$^{\text{S}}$*saṃskārāḥ* might have been the reason why 生死 (in the sense of '*causing* birth and death') was chosen to translate $^{\text{P}}$*saṅkhārā*/$^{\text{S}}$*saṃskārāḥ* in most places where this term indicates the 4th *skandha*."

Given that both explanations advocated above are not only meaningful but also appear to be supported by evidence (the *Saddharmapuṇḍarīka* manuscripts and the phrasing in T 1508, respectively), it seems to me possible to envisage the emergence *and* continuity (at least for some time) of this rendering as resulting from a combination of both (for a somewhat comparable case see below n. 803). Whichever of these two alternatives may have taken the leading role in inspiring the coinage of the rendering 生死, the other alternative could have complemented this by way of providing support for its employment.

The net result is quite a remarkable rendering. The employment of what eventually became the standard rendering, 行, is indeed preferable, as this works also for an arhat or Tathāgata. An arhat or Tathāgata has definitely gone beyond the cycle of rebirths, but the five aggregates are still in existence, although no longer clung to (see Anālayo 2008c, 405–6), including the fourth aggregate. Hence, the rendering 行 would be the appropriate one for the fourth aggregate of an arhat or Tathāgata, conveying a sense of mere functionality. Aside from this limitation in applicability, however, the rendering 生死 has the advantage of suggesting deeper connotations along the lines of the role of *saṃskāras*—as long as ignorance remains active in the background—in fueling the continuity of being subject to *saṃsāra*.

188. Karashima 2011, 25,11 (= T 8.224.427c26): 譬如空無著, 無縛, 無脫.
189. SĀ 265 at T 2.99.69a11: 諸所有識, 若過去, 若未來, 若現在, 若內, 若外, 若麁, 若細, 若好, 若醜, 若遠, 若近 . . . 無所有, 無牢, 無實, 無有堅固; 如病, 如癰, 如刺, 如殺; 無常, 苦, 空, 非我. 所以者何? 以識無堅實故. In addition to the discourse parallels mentioned above in n. 186, a version of the present passage can also be found in Candrakīrti's *Bodhisattvayogācāracatuḥśatakaṭīkā*, Suzuki 1994, 294,19: *evam eva yat kiṃcid vijñānam atītānāgatapratyutpannam ādhyātmikaṃ vā bāhyaṃ vaudārikaṃ vā sūkṣmaṃ vā hīnaṃ vā praṇītaṃ vā yad vā dūre yad vāntike tad bhikṣuḥ paśyen nidhyā yed yoniśaś copaparīkṣeta, tasya tat paśyato nidhyāyato yoniśaś copaparīkṣamāṇasyāsato 'py asya khyāyād riktato 'pi tucchato 'py asārato 'pi rogato 'pi gaṇḍato 'pi śalyato 'py aghato 'py anityato 'pi duḥkhato 'pi śūnyato 'py anātmato 'py asya khyāyāt. tat kasya hetoḥ? kim asmin vijñānaskandhe sāram astīti?* This conveniently exemplifies the importance granted to such type of *Āgama* passages in later traditions.
190. Karashima 2011, 29,5 and 30,5 (= T 8.224.428a24 and 428b2; the key term "self" is based on an emendation of what in the text is 意; see Karashima 2011, 29n235).
191. Dhp 62, with parallels in T 4.210.563b24 and T 4.211.586b4: 我且非我, and in the *Udānavarga* 1.20, Bernhard 1965, 102: *ātmaiva hy ātmano nāsti*.
192. The suggested alternative formulation *attā hi bālassa n' atthi* would result in the same count of eight syllables as found in the actual formulation (and in the other lines) of the verse.
193. See, e.g., SN 35.116 at SN IV 93,6 and its parallels SHT VI 1404V, Bechert and Wille 1989, 120, and SĀ 234 at T 2.99.56c13, according to which the Buddha withdrew to his room right after having delivered a brief statement in front of his disciples, indicating that the end of the world will not be reached by walking. The assembled monastics fail to understand this succinct statement and have to turn to Ānanda for an explanation.
194. SN 41.7 at SN IV 296,33: *suññam idaṃ attena vā attaniyena vā ti, ayaṃ vuccati, bhante, suññatā cetovimutti*, and its parallel SĀ 567 at T 2.99.150a4: 非我, 非我所, 是名空心三昧, see also above n. 155. Although SĀ 567 speaks of the "empty concentration of the mind"—corresponding to "liberation of the mind by emptiness" in SN 41.7—it formulates the actual contemplation in terms of "not self," 非我. This in itself minor variation neatly exemplifies that in *Āgama* literature the denial of the existence of a self and the qualification of being "empty of a self" are often interchangeable. When at times both are mentioned alongside each other, as in the case of the quote given above n. 189, this is probably best read in line with a pervasive tendency in early Buddhist orality to express the basically same meaning with near synonyms.
195. It could be added that it is not clear how far this distinction was indeed prominent at the stage in the development of *Prajñāpāramitā* thought attested in Lokakṣema's translation; see the observation in Vetter 1984, 496n7.
196. In the Sanskrit manuscript from the Schøyen Collection, Harrison and Watanabe 2006, 117,5 (§6), the relevant passage reads as follows: *kolopamaṃ dharmaparyāyaṃm ājānadbhiḥ dharmāḥ eva prahātavyāḥ prāg evādharmāḥ* (a survey of other Sanskrit versions can be found in the same publication). The Chinese and Tibetan versions proceed in this way: T 7.220.980c27: 如來密意而說筏喻法門, 諸有智者法尚應斷, 何

況非法?, T 8.235.749b10: 知我說法如筏喻者, 法尚應捨, 何況非法?, T 8.237.762c14: 解筏喻經, 法尚應捨, 何況非法?, T 8.236a.753b15: 如來常說筏喻法門, 是法應捨, 非捨法故 (adopting the variant 筏 instead of 栰; in this version the final part conveys a different sense), T 8.238.767c2: 如來說筏喻, 法本解法, 如是捨應, 何況非法?,T 8.239.772b20: 如來密意宣說筏喻法門, 諸有智者法尚應捨, 何況非法?, D 16 *ka* 123a3: *chos kyi rnam grangs gzings lta bur shes pa rnams kyis chos rnams kyang spang bar bya na chos ma yin pa rnams lta ci smos zhes gsungs so* (P 739 seems to be lacking text here). The report of the actual delivery of the simile can be found in MN 22 at MN I 135,24: *kullūpamaṃ vo, bhikkhave, dhammaṃ desitaṃ* (E$^e$ lacks *dhammaṃ desitaṃ*) *ājānantehi dhammā pi vo pahātabbā pageva adhammā* and in its parallel MĀ 200 at T 1.26.764c13: 若汝等知我長夜說栰喻法者, 當以捨是法, 況非法耶? Another parallel, EĀ 43.5 at T 2.125.760a26 does not refer back to the earlier delivered simile of the raft and thus only draws out its implications: 善法猶可捨, 何況非法? Yet another parallel, Up 8029 at D 4094 *nyu* 75a6 or P 5595 *thu* 120a7, does refer to the simile but differs in the part that draws out its implications: *dge slong dag, de lta bas na ngas gzings lta bu'i chos kyi rnam grangs bstan pa dag shes nas sngar chos ma yin pa bzhin du chos kyang spang bar bya'o.* A cross-reference to the parable of the raft can be found in MN 38 at MN I 260,35 and its parallel MĀ 201 at T 1.26.767c7. On different interpretations of the parable of the raft see the survey in Choong 2014a. Dutt 1958, 505 comments on the significance of early Buddhist and early Mahāyāna texts sharing this image that, in the Pāli discourses, "the disciples are also taught that the practices prescribed by the Teacher for the purpose of spiritual training should be eschewed like a raft after crossing the stream, for even the least clinging to the spiritual practices would be a hindrance to the attainment of *nirvāṇa*, or complete freedom of mind (*cetaso vimokkha*). Hence it is apparent that Mahāyānism is not altogether a deviation from the original teachings." The above survey of quotations confirms a basic similarity among most of the different articulations of the simile of the raft.

197. Falk and Karashima 2012, 44: *saye rua tistaveti ruaavisaṃkhare caṃrati e + + + + + + + + + + + + + + [saye vi]ñaṇaṃ tistavati [viñana avisaṃkhare carati].*

198. SN 22.79 at SN III 87,8, SĀ 46 at T 2.99.11c7, and Up 1014 at D 4094 *ju* 16b3 or P 5595 *tu* 18a7; see in more detail Anālayo 2023d, 15–17.

199. SN 1.70 at SN I 41,4 (see also Sn 169) and SĀ 1008 at T 2.99.264a12; another parallel, SĀ$^2$ 235 at T 2.100.459b1, conveys a different sense, perhaps the result of an error in transmission or translation.

200. For a more detailed exploration of this topic see Anālayo 2023d.

201. MN 43 at MN I 293,36: *paññā kho, āvuso, abhiññatthā pariññatthā pahānatthā ti.* The parallel MĀ 211 at T 1.26.790c22 defines the purpose of wisdom to be disenchantment, dispassion, and vision according to reality, 智慧者有厭義, 無欲義, 見如真義.

202. See in more detail Anālayo 2024e.

203. See, e.g., Wayman 1957 and Matilal 1980.

204. Schopen 1989, 135n5 reasons that the "repeated emphasis on fear, terror or dread in connection with hearing the Perfection of Wisdom being taught or explained would seem to indicate that the authors of our texts were clearly aware of the fact that what they were presenting was above all else potentially terrifying . . . and that a predictable reaction to it was fear." Williams 1989/2009, 54 points out that the "requirement of completely letting go, 'existential relaxation,' cutting even subtle attachment, is surely an extremely difficult one to fulfil, requiring immense training and application, and

(the sūtras hint) potentially, if taken seriously, very frightening." Westerhoff 2018, 101 comments that the "theory of *dharma*s was the standard Buddhist account of how reality was constituted at the fundamental level, a theory that accounted both for what there is at the rock bottom, and what kind of phenomenology is based on this. If all this is rejected, the audience of the Prajñāpāramitā texts (who we have to imagine as well trained in the theories of the Abhidharma) might well have wondered what, if anything, was left."

205. After recommending that the new bodhisattva receive instructions from a *kalyāṇa-mitra*, the relevant part of the actual instruction in Karashima 2011, 284,12 (= T 8.224.452b5) reads: 是菩薩所布施, 當施與作阿耨多羅三耶三菩. 莫得著色, 痛痒, 思想, 生死, 識. 何以故? 深般若波羅蜜, 薩芸若無所著. 若持戒, 忍辱, 精進, 禪, 智慧[,] 當持是作阿耨多羅三耶三菩. 莫得著色, 痛痒, 思想, 生死, 識. 何以故? 薩芸若無所著. This is followed by commending that the bodhisattva should not delight in the path of an arhat or a Pratyekabuddha.

206. Karashima 2011, 64,1 (= T 8.224.431c10): 善男子, 善女人般若波羅蜜學者, 持者, 誦者, 或當過劇難之中, 終不恐不怖. Stuart 2015a, 274 comments on "a central concern of Buddhist practitioners, the concern with danger and protection," that the "*Aṣṭasāhasrikā* shows a similar concern, but offers the trump of all concerns by asserting the supreme power of the *sūtra* itself," whereas in the *Saddharmasmṛtyupasthānasūtra* that forms the main topic of his study instead "a practitioner successively overpowers evil forces (*mārapakṣa*) and gains the support of wholesome forces (*saddharmapakṣa*)." Without intending to deny that there may indeed be a difference of emphasis in these two texts, it seems to me that indications like the one quoted above can fruitfully be read as comprising the power of the Perfection of Wisdom as a text *together* with the quality of the sixth perfection that the text promotes, thereby also including its actual cultivation undertaken by the practitioner. The perspective I have in mind here can be exemplified with an episode in which Śakra is able to defeat Māra, who is approaching with the intention to create a disturbance. Śakra achieves this by dint of reliance on the Perfection of Wisdom; see Karashima 2011, 84,2 (= T 8.224.434a12): 釋提桓因常作是願: 我會當念般若波羅蜜, 常念, 常持心, 諷誦, 究竟. 釋提桓因心中誦念般若波羅蜜, 且欲究竟, 弊魔便復道, 還去. I would read the measure taken by Śakra as a form of recollection, which combines the power of the object recollected with the power of the subject's practice of recollecting. As already mentioned above in n. 13, it seems to me that a clear distinction between the Perfection of Wisdom as either a text or else a quality is not always straightforward, as occurrences of the term 般若波羅蜜 can be playing on both senses to varying degrees, wherefore I am concerned that opting for the one sense over the other may risk missing out on some of the nuances of the relevant passage.

207. Wogihara 1932/1935, 189,14: *na ca . . . tasya kulaputrasya vā kuladuhitur vā imāṃ prajñāpāramitām udgṛhṇato dhārayato vācayataḥ paryavāpnuvataḥ pravartayamānasyāraṇya-gatasya vā vṛkṣamūlagatasya vā . . . vā tatra tatropasaṃkrāmato vā caṃkramyamāṇasya vā sthitasya vā niṣaṇṇasya vā nipannasya vā bhayaṃ vā bhaviṣyati stambhitatvaṃ vā bhaviṣyati utpatsyate vā*. Although the four postures have not made it into the English translation by Conze 1973/1975, 103, they are covered in the English translation of the *Abhisamayālaṃkārālokā Prajñāpāramitāvyākhyā* by Sparham 2008, 137 and in the unfinished French translation of the *Aṣṭasāhasrikā Prajñāpāramitā* by Burnouf

1852/2022, 80 (the partial German translation by Walleser 1914 does not include the relevant chapter).

208. MN 4 at MN I 21,4 and EĀ 31.1 at T 2.125.666b2.
209. See in more detail Anālayo 2017d, 17f.
210. MN 128 at MN III 157,29 and its parallel MĀ 72 at T 1.26.536c26.
211. See, e.g., Sn 470, Sn 779, Sn 809, and Sn 872.
212. Falk and Karashima 2012, 46: *na hi sa ṇimitado vihatavo.*
213. Falk and Karashima 2012, 56: *saye ruve carati* + + + + + + + + + + .. *[ṇ](i)[miti cara] ti*; see also the discussion in Anālayo 2024b, 31–32.
214. Karashima 2011, 38,6 (= T 8.224.429a11): 爾時, 釋提桓因與四萬天子相隨俱來, 共會, 坐. 四天王與天上二萬天子相隨來, 共會, 坐. 梵迦夷天與萬天子相隨來, 共會, 坐. 梵多會天與五千天子相隨來, 共會, 坐. In *Āgama* literature, celestials tend to keep standing rather than sitting down, presumably reflecting the nature of their celestial bodies as not needing to assume the sitting posture to feel at ease (an exception to this pattern is DN 32 at DN III 194,11 and its Tibetan parallel, Skilling 1994, 462,10). See also below n. 218.
215. On levitation in *Āgama* literature see Anālayo 2016d, 2021c, and 2022d, 237n376.
216. See in more detail Skilling 1992 and 1997, 63–88.
217. This is not to take the position that Abhidharma texts are not amenable to an engagement that is more oriented toward the heart; my point is only that the canonical texts of this genre do not seem to take explicit steps in this direction, unlike *Āgama* literature or early Mahāyāna *sūtras*. According to McDaniel 2008, 93, even the Theravāda commentaries on Abhidharma do not "promote the recitation of Abhidhamma texts at cremation ceremonies or state that individual syllables from the Abhidhamma can be used for ritual protection. Nevertheless, Lao and Thai monastic teachers have used the Abhidhamma in just these ways." Gethin 1998, 204 explains the emic perspective on the power of Abhidharma to be such that "[h]earing it being recited—even without understanding it—can have a far reaching effect. The Abhidhamma catches the very essence of the Dhamma, which means that its sound can operate almost as a charm or spell." In other words, living traditions have certainly been able to assert their needs in relation to Abhidharma texts.
218. The same would then perhaps also be relevant to the translation of the **Pratyutpannasamādhisūtra* attributed to Lokakṣema, 般舟三昧經, which similarly reports various celestials, including Śakra and Brahmā Sahāṃpati, coming to join the assembly; see T 13.418.903a16: 四天王, 釋提桓因, 梵三鉢摩夷亘天, 阿迦貳吒天, 各各與若千億億百千天子俱來到佛所, 前爲佛作禮, 却住一面. A minor detail in this description is that, unlike the case of T 224, here the celestials are not described as sitting down but remain standing to one side. This contrasts to the previous depiction of humans sitting down, T 13.418.903a1–16: 却坐一面, thereby conveying, in line with a standard pattern in *Āgama* literature, that the behavior of humans and celestial visitors differ in this respect (see also above n. 214). Moreover, in the **Pratyutpannasamādhisūtra* the celestials are present from the outset of the actual teachings, rather than coming to join at a later point in the way they do in the Perfection of Wisdom (and thus after the important teachings in the first chapter of this text have already been given).
219. His attainment of stream-entry during a meeting with the Buddha is reported in DN 21 at DN II 288,21, with parallels in Waldschmidt 1932, 111,5 (see also p. 109), DĀ 14 at T 1.1.66a2, MĀ 134 at T 1.26.638c1, T 1.15.250a23, and T 4.203.477c16.

220. SN 11.6 at SN I 224,25, with parallels in SĀ 1222 at T 2.99.333b29 and SĀ$^2$ 49 at T 2.100.390a8.
221. SN 11.5 at SN I 224,12, with parallels in SĀ 1109 at T 2.99.292b7 and SĀ$^2$ 38 at T 2.100.386a12.
222. MN 37 at MN I 253,35, with parallels in SĀ 505 at T 2.99.133c27 and EĀ 19.3 at T 2.125.594a29; for a study of this tale see Anālayo 2011d.
223. Karashima 2011, 77,2 (= T 8.224.433b13): 爾時四萬天人與釋提桓因共來大會.諸天人謂釋提桓因言: 尊者, 當取般若波羅蜜. 當諷誦般若波羅蜜. 佛語釋提桓因: 當學, 拘翼, 般若波羅蜜. 當持經卷. 當諷誦. 何以故? 阿須倫心中作是生念: 欲與忉利天共鬪.阿須倫即起兵上天.是時,拘翼,當誦念般若波羅蜜.阿須倫兵眾即還去.
224. Karashima 2011, 81,4 (= T 8.224.433c25): 釋提桓因從佛所聞般若波羅蜜即受誦. 彼異道人即遙遠遠繞佛一匝, 便從彼間道徑去. As already noted by Drewes 2015, 125 in relation to the corresponding Sanskrit version, the narrative context and the terminology employed here convey that Śakra relies on what he has memorized.
225. Karashima 2011, 84,2 (= T 8.224.434a12): 釋提桓因常作是願: 我會當念般若波羅蜜, 常念, 常持心, 諷誦, 究竟. 釋提桓因心中誦念般若波羅蜜, 且欲究竟, 弊魔便復道, 還去 (see also above n. 206).
226. Ruegg 2004, 18n23 notes that "in one form or another the *topos* of a *mahāyāna* under threat is a familiar one in Mahāyānist literature . . . this *topos* can concern not only menace and attack from outsiders but also internal pressures and decay among its nominal followers."
227. Karashima 2011, 60,2 (= T 8.224.431a27): 梵摩三鉢天及梵天諸天人俱白佛言: 我輩自共護是善男子, 善女人學般若波羅蜜者, 持者, 誦者.
228. In addition, of relevance to the proposed relationship may also be texts in which rebirth in Sukhāvatī appears without standing in a direct relationship to the cult of Amitābha, instead resulting from a range of other religious activities; see the survey and discussion in Schopen 1977/2005.
229. T 11.313.756a21: 不以立婬欲亂意者得生彼佛刹. Regarding the attribution of T 313 to Lokakṣema, Harrison 1993, 166 comments that "[t]he current attribution of the *A-ch'u-fo-kuo-ching* to Lokakṣema must be viewed with some suspicion . . . [i]t is, however, certainly an old text"; see also the discussion in Nattier 2008, 85–86.
230. This condition of the Pure Abodes is not entirely clear in the reference by Halkias 2013, 217n8 to "the *suddhāvāsa* (lit., 'pure abode'), a heaven where 'non-returners' can converse and meet with the Buddha." Just for the record, such meeting and conversation would require that the Buddha pay a visit to such realms (see below n. 344), as the presence of a Buddha is not a characteristic condition of the Pure Abodes.
231. MN 120 at MN III 103,1, which covers rebirth in the five realms of the Pure Abodes; on this presentation see in more detail Anālayo 2019a, 149–50. Strictly speaking, MN 120 does not seem to have a full parallel; see Anālayo 2011b, 678–79.
232. SN 48.57 at SN V 233,11 and Pj II 476,14.
233. SN 6.2 at SN I 139,28 (= AN 4.21 at AN II 20,31), with parallels in SĀ 1188 at T 2.99.322a7, SĀ$^2$ 101 at T 2.100.410a21, and Up 9022 at D 4094 *nyu* 85b4 or Q 5595 *thu* 132a5 (which has only the beginning of the episode, as the quote stops before giving it in full). Here and below, references are to occurrences of Brahmā Sahāṃpati in Pāli discourses and to parallels that refer to a similar action undertaken by a Brahmā, independent of whether these parallels also give his name.

234. SN 47.18 at SN V 167,21 (= SN 47.43 at SN V 185,20), with parallels in SĀ 1189 at T 2.99.322b10, SĀ$^2$ 102 at T 2.100.410b23, and SĀ$^3$ 4 at T 2.101.494b2.
235. SN 6.13 at SN I 154,10, with parallels in SĀ 1191 at T 2.99.322c21 and SĀ$^2$ 104 at T 2.100.411a8.
236. MN 67 MN I 458,16 and one of its two parallels, EĀ 45.2 at T 2.125.771a12; for a comparative study see Anālayo 2011b, 367–70.
237. SN 6.3 at SN I 141,7. In the parallels SĀ 99 at T 2.99.27c6 and SĀ$^2$ 265 at T 2.100.466c17, such an action is rather undertaken by Vaiśravaṇa. This to some extent diminishes the humorous impact of the episode, as the oblations to Brahmā are of course made in the hope of meeting him. In this setting, for Brahmā to appear indeed fits the narrative setting particularly well, with the anticlimax of telling the devotee she should offer the food to a Buddhist monk falling better into place.
238. MN 26 at MN I 168,15. Keown 1992/2001, 42 reasons that the report of "the Buddha's hesitation suggests that although the Buddha was [eventually] moved to teach, teaching is not entailed by the intellectual realisation attained" by him. Webster 2005, 16 comments on the Buddha's hesitation that "he seems to be disinclined towards teaching that which he has discovered," which "might turn Gotama into a Pacceka Buddha." Blomfield 2011, 100 notes that, although "[i]t seems unthinkable that the supreme embodiment of compassion would have considered keeping his wisdom to himself," in MN 26 "Gautama's uncertainty seems real enough, and the Indian tradition of forest hermits, recalled by Buddhist tradition as 'solitary Buddhas,' suggests that remaining in the forest was, indeed, an option for someone in his position. The Discourses record several occasions in Gautama's later life when he showed distaste for the 'bother' that went with his involvement in the world," which "suggest Gautama's abiding love of a peaceful forest life and perhaps a determination to live in his own way, without compromise."
239. Pāli discourses: MN 85 at MN II 93,26 (abbreviated), SN 6.1 at SN I 137,3 (see also SN 21.7 at SN I 234,3, where he repeats his earlier request). *Ekottarikāgama*: EĀ 19.1 at T 2.125.593b1. *Vinayas*: The Dharmaguptaka *Vinaya*, T 22.1428.786c23, the Mahīśāsaka *Vinaya*, T 22.1421.103c22, the *Saṅghabhedavastu* of the Mūlasarvāstivāda *Vinaya*, Gnoli 1977, 129,3, and the Theravāda *Vinaya*, Vin I 5,17; in the case of the last, Sahāṃpati even had to request the Buddha thrice, in contrast to a single request in the Pāli discourses. The *Catuṣpariṣatsūtra*: Waldschmidt 1957, 112,6. The *Lalitavistara*: Lefmann 1902, 394,8 (see also T 3.186.528b4 and T 3.187.603b5). Biographies of the Buddha extant in Chinese: T 3.190.806a12 and T 3.191.952c29.
240. Wogihara 1932/1935, 614,16: *bodhimaṇḍe niṣaṇṇasyālpotsukatāyāṃ cittam avanataṃ na dharmadeśanāyāṃ* (repeated at 615,7), D 12 *ka* 169a6 or P 734 *mi* 182a7: *byang chub kyi snying po la bzhugs pa na, brtson pa chung ba la thugs gzhol bar mdzad de chos bstan pa la gzhol bar ma mdzad do*, T 7.220.823a6: 心作是念: 我所證法微妙, 甚深, 非諸世間卒能信受, T 7.220.898c14: 宴坐思惟不樂說法, 謂作是念: 我法甚深, 非諸世間卒能信受, and T 8.227.562b8: 我欲默然而不說法. The corresponding passage in Lokakṣema's translation, which lacks a counterpart to the above indications, is Karashima 2011, 291,4 (= T 8.224.453a19). A reference to the invitation by Śakra and Brahmā is nevertheless found in another translation by Lokakṣema (see Harrison 1993, 159), T 17.807.751c20: 釋梵從佛求哀, 爲人故使佛說經.
241. For a survey of selected publications on representations in art see Anālayo 2011b, 178n175. For the reports by the Chinese pilgrims see T 51.2085.863b16 (法顯) and T 51.2087.917a27 (玄奘).

242. Jā I 81,9 (for the Tibetan version see Gaffney 2003, 462,9) and Marciniak 2019, 400,13 (also in Senart 1897, 315,6). In both versions, Śakra is part of a larger celestial host that accompanies Brahmā in the attempt to convince the Buddha to teach the Dharma. In the *Jātaka* version, Śakra just comes along, and it is only Brahmā who voices the actual request. In the *Mahāvastu*, however, Śakra is the first to invite the Buddha to teach, which is not successful, whereupon Brahmā reformulates the request. Two separate requests can also be seen in T 3.189.643a1+10, which reports that first Brahmā voiced his invitation, followed by Śakra requesting the Buddha to teach.
243. For a survey of examples see Anālayo 2011a, 18n20+21.
244. Rhi 1994, 220n60 comments that "[i]n Gandhāran representations of the Buddha's life, the scene of the seated Buddha flanked by Brahma and Indra in *añjali* is usually identified as the 'Entreaty to preach' . . . [i]t seems to me that many of such scenes represented a simple scene of worship rather than a fixed iconographical type for the 'Entreaty to preach'."
245. Although the idea conveyed by Figure 2 could indeed be that Brahmā and Śakra are inviting the Buddha to teach, at first sight a problem may appear to be the circumstance that the leaves of the tree under which the seat is placed are not the type to be expected if the idea had been to show the Buddha still seated under the *bodhi* tree (*ficus religiosa*). However, according to relevant *Vinaya* accounts, by the time of this request the Buddha was indeed no longer seated under the *bodhi* tree, as he had in the meantime moved to other places to sit in meditation; see the Dharmaguptaka *Vinaya*, T 22.1428.786b26, the *Mahāvastu* (of the Mahāsāṃghika-Lokottaravādins) Marciniak 2019, 400,1 (also in Senart 1897, 314,13), the Mahīśāsaka *Vinaya*, T 22.1421.103b9, the *Saṅghabhedavastu* of the Mūlasarvāstivāda *Vinaya*, Gnoli 1977, 126,6, and the Theravāda *Vinaya*, Vin I 2,28. This in itself minor detail illustrates the difficulties of being certain whether the depicted scene is indeed portraying the request to teach, as the depiction of a *bodhi* tree, if this had been in line with the textual narratives, would have made the situation fairly clear.
246. MĀ 204 at T 2.26.777a18; see in more detail Anālayo 2011a and 2011b, 178–82.
247. T 1.3.156c14 (this is a partial parallel, in the sense that it parallels the present episode but not some other episodes related to Vipaśyin's birth and youth, found in DN 14 and the Sanskrit version) and Waldschmidt 1956, 148 (10a.1; see also the discussion in his n. 2) or Fukita 2003, 144.
248. Nakamura 2000, 212 concludes that the episode of Brahmā's intervention is "a later interpolation." This may be taking too strong a position. As far as I can see, the possibility of a loss of this episode in those versions where it is no longer found cannot be ruled out, although I would consider this to be the less probable explanation.
249. Mil 232,7; this dilemma occurs in a part of the text that is without a counterpart in the (earlier) Chinese version. Minh Chau 1964, 1 points out that "the three last [of the six] books of the P[āli version] . . . are not available in the C[hinese] version."
250. Mil 233,31: *appossukkatāya cittaṃ nami, no dhammadesanāya; sattānaṃ paṭivedhacintanamānasaṃ yev' etaṃ*.
251. Mil 234,23: *brahme oṇamite tathāgatānaṃ sadevako loko oṇamissati* (in the PTS edition the second term reads *onamite*, which I have adjusted to *oṇamite*, corresponding to the spelling used in the same edition for other occurrences of this verb). For a similar idea see the *Lalitavistara*, Lefmann 1902, 395,16.

252. Ps II 177,12: *jānāti hi bhagavā: mama appossukkatāya citte namamāne mahābrahmā dhammadesanaṃ yācissati.*
253. MN 26 at MN I 168,9: *itiha me, bhikkhave, paṭisañcikkhato appossukkatāya cittaṃ namati, no dhammadesanāya.* Jones 2009, 89 comments that in the early textual sources "there is no hint that the Buddha did not really need to be asked to teach, nor that the Buddha's hesitation was customary for Buddhas. This suggests that the problems later found in the story were not envisaged by its composers."
254. T 4.192.28b19+21: 顧惟本誓願, followed two lines later by 梵天知其念, which then leads on to the request to teach found at T 4.192.28b27.
255. Weller 1928, 249,12: *mchog gnyis.*
256. Johnston 1936/1984, 215n97 comments that "[t]he intention evidently is to remove from the Buddha the reproach of having decided not to preach the Law for the good of the world; the heavenly visitants do not change his resolution . . . but merely strengthen it by their encouragement." In the words of Walters 1999, 276, this episode thereby functions "more as a sort of friendly call than as a charge to preach." As pointed out by Schmithausen 2000a, 120n5, this appears to reflect an attempt to adjust the challenging transmission (of the Buddha's hesitation) to later perspectives, "offenbar ein Versuch, die anstößige Überlieferung der späteren Auffassung anzupassen."
257. Karashima 2011, 41,7 (= T 8.224.429b7): 色不當於中住. 痛痒, 思想, 生死, 識不當於中住. 須陀洹不當於中住, 斯陀含不當於中住, 阿那含不當於中住, 阿羅漢不當於中住, 辟支佛不當於中住, 佛不當於中住. My translation of 色不當於中住, etc., is influenced by its Sanskrit counterpart, Wogihara 1932/1935, 140,4: *na rūpe sthātavyaṃ.*
258. Karashima 2011, 6,4 (= T 8.224.426a6): 欲學阿羅漢法, 當聞般若波羅蜜, 當學, 當持, 當守. Such an indication comes alongside repeated references to teachings or *samādhi*s that are beyond the ken of those pursuing the path to arhat-ship (or to Pratyekabuddhahood).
259. Wogihara 1932/1935, 140,5. In the context of this type of listing, consciousness as one of the six elements stands for the whole of the mind (including the other three mental aggregates). In fact, at times *vijñāna* features in a listing of synonyms together with *citta* and *manas*; see, e.g., SN 12.61 at SN II 94,13 and its parallels in Sanskrit fragments, Chung and Fukita 2020, 113,1, and SĀ 289 at T 2.99.81c7, and for discussions of these three terms, e.g., Johansson 1965, Hamilton 1996, 82–114, Somaratne 2005, and Brahmāli 2009, 49–54.
260. This holds for the Asian editions ($B^e$, $C^e$, and $S^e$) of MN 1 at MN I 6,24, which indicate that *na* ($S^e$ adds *attamanā*) *te bhikkhū bhagavato bhāsitaṃ abhinandun ti.* EĀ 44.6 at T 2.125.766b15: 諸比丘不受其教. Contrary to the indication in Akanuma 1929/1990, 163, closer inspection shows that MĀ 106 and T 56 are more appropriately not reckoned parallels to MN 1; see Anālayo 2008a, 11–12. It follows that EĀ 44.6 is the main parallel relevant to a comparative study of MN 1.
261. Elsewhere the discourses do record a reaction of not delighting in what the Buddha said; see, e.g., MN 87 at MN I 106,22, which reports that the Buddha's visitor got up and left, not delighting in what the Buddha had said. The parallel T 1.91.915a24 proceeds in a similar manner; see also T 4.212.649c21. Another parallel, MĀ 216 at T 1.26.801a11, reports that the visitor left shaking his head, evidently expressing disapproval, given that just before he had contradicted what the Buddha had said. According to EĀ 13.3 at T 2.125.571c12, he rejected the teaching, which had not entered his heart, and left. In all these cases, the episode occurs at the outset of the discourse and leads over to other

events and discussions, rather than being part of the standard conclusion; it moreover involves someone who is not a disciple of the Buddha.

262. Ps I 56,8: *te pañcasatā bhikkhū idaṃ bhagavato vacanaṃ nānumodiṃsu. kasmā? aññāṇakena.*

263. Bodhi 1980/1992, 20 reasons that "[a]lthough this exegetical tradition is certainly plausible, another explanation for the Mūla[pariyāya] Sutta's unique ending is possible as well . . . [i]t may be suggested that the reason for their displeasure was not their inability to understand the Buddha's discourse, but rather the fact that they understood it too well." Ñāṇananda 2015, 286 remarks that the commentators "seem to have interpreted this attitude [of not delighting] as an index to the abstruseness of the discourses . . . we might advance a different interpretation of the attitude of those monks. The declaration that none of the concepts, including that of *Nibbāna*, should be egoistically imagined could have caused displeasure in monks, then as now."

264. T 12.350.193b13: 聞佛說深經皆不解, 不信, 便從衆坐避易亡去; with parallels in T 11.310.637b13, T 12.351.199b27, T 12.352.214c21, T 16.659.282a8, Pāsādika 2015, 83, and Silk 2023, 339 (the last two cases are both §138); see also the comments in Pāsādika 2015, 177n313 and in Silk and Nagao 2022, 688.

265. Karashima 2011, 211,10 (= T 8.224.445a14): 聞是, 恐畏, 即捨還去.

266. MN 1 at MN I 4,19: *nibbānaṃ mā maññi, nibbānasmiṃ mā maññi* (C[e] lacks *nibbānasmiṃ mā maññi*), *nibbānato mā maññi, nibbānaṃ me ti mā maññi, nibbānaṃ mābhinandi. taṃ kissa hetu? pariññeyyaṃ tassā ti vadāmi*. The parallel EĀ 44.6 at T 2.125.766b4 expresses the same matter somewhat differently: 於涅槃, 亦不著於涅槃, 不起涅槃之想. 所以然者, 皆由善分別, 善觀察. Expositions on the need to avoid various modes of conceiving, although without covering the topic of Nirvana and without working through the different types of individuals taken up in MN 1, can be found in SN 35.30 at SN IV 22,5, SN 35.31 at SN IV 23,18, SN 35.90 at SN IV 65,3, and SN 35.91 at SN IV 66,8; the latter two have parallels in SĀ 226 and SĀ 227 at T 2.99.55c4+17, although these do not provide such a detailed breakdown of various modalities of conceiving, here referred to with 計. The same 計 features in a to some extent comparable exposition in a text whose translation is attributed to Lokakṣema; see T 14.458.436a12 and on the translatorship attribution Nattier 2008, 84.

267. Karashima 2011, 47,5 (= T 8.224.430a11): 泥洹亦復如幻.

268. Karashima 2011, 517,4 (= T 8.224.475b8), which repeatedly uses the verb 入. According to Karashima 2010, 387, in its usage by Lokakṣema this verb can convey the sense that one "penetrates (intellectually), comprehends."

269. The listing of the qualities pertinent to awakening does not mention the bases of success (*ṛddhipāda*); see Karashima 2011, 517,16 (= T 8.224.475b25): 亦入於四意止, 亦入於四意斷, 亦入於五根, 亦入於五力, 亦入於七覺意, 亦入於八道. The only parallel to this presentation is T 8.225.506b29, which has the complete list: 四意止, 四意斷, 四神足, 五根, 五力, 七覺意, 八道行 (this has already been noted by Lancaster 1968, 144, who comments that "there is an incomplete reference in T. 224 to thirty-three of the thirty-seven . . . however, T. 225 corrects the text and includes all thirty-seven"). The variation between the two versions in this respect could simply be the result of an error in the original used by Lokakṣema and his team for translation. A to some extent comparable case has been noted by Pagel 1995, 290 for the *Bodhisattvapiṭaka*, where the bases of success are the only item from the listing of *bodhipākṣika*s that does not receive a full treatment.

Without intending to dismiss the possibility of simple transmission error, I would like to note that the bases of success fit the context of qualities pertinent to awakening less well than the other members of this list. The four establishments of mindfulness (*smṛtyupasthāna*), the four right endeavors/abandonments (*samyak pradhāna/prahāṇa*), the five faculties or powers (*indriya* & *bala*), the seven awakening factors (*bodhyaṅga*), and the factors of the noble eightfold path (*āryāṣṭāṅgikamārga*) are quite standard in *Āgama* literature, with a fairly clear meaning and a straightforward relationship to progress to awakening. This does not hold to the same degree for the four bases of success, whose practical implications, in particular regarding the third of the four, remain somewhat obscure and require additional explanation; see Anālayo 2020/2022, 2988.

Another alternative listing can be found in the *Saundarananda* 17.24–26, Johnston 1928, 127,15; as noted by Har Dayal 1932/1970, 82 this "mentions only twenty-eight items." Besides lacking the four bases of success, the *Saundarananda* also refers to the five qualities listed under the alternative headers of being *indriya* or *bala* only once, under the name of the latter. Although this presentation could in principle just be due to poetic license, it does eliminate another less straightforward aspect of the listing, as these two sets refer to basically the same five qualities; see SN 48.43 at SN V 219,11 as well as the **Mahāvibhāṣā*, T 27.1545.726b13 (already noted by Lamotte 1970, 1127).

Now, there is clear evidence of an expansion of the list of thirty-seven qualities pertinent to awakening by way of adding the four absorptions (*dhyāna*) in some reciter traditions; see Anālayo 2022c, 149–57. This leaves open the possibility of envisaging that textual growth could also have happened on earlier occasions, perhaps by way of an expansion of a listing of twenty-eight through a duplication of the five qualities listed as *indriya*s or *bala*s, resulting in the type of list now found in Lokakṣema's translation, followed by adding the four bases of success to become the standard list of thirty-seven qualities pertinent to awakening. However, due to the limitations of the above textual evidence—involving only two instances, both of which allow for alternative explanations—at present this remains only an inconclusive hypothesis.

270. MN 78 at MN II 27,11: *sīlavā hoti no ca sīlamayo, tañ ca cetovimuttiṃ paññāvimuttiṃ yathābhūtaṃ pajānāti, yatth' assa te kusalā sīlā* (C^e and E^e: *kusalasīlā*) *aparisesā nirujjhanti*, with a parallel in MĀ 179 at T 1.26.721a17: 行戒不著戒, 此善戒滅無餘, 敗壞無餘, which thus does not have a counterpart to *tañ ca cetovimuttiṃ paññāvimuttiṃ yathābhūtaṃ pajānāti*.

271. Sn 839: *na diṭṭhiyā na sutiyā na ñāṇena . . . sīlabbatenā pi na suddhim āha, adiṭṭhiyā assutiyā añāṇā* (C^e: *añaṇā*), *asīlatā abbatā no pi tena*, with a parallel in T 4.198.180b11: 亦見聞不爲黠, 戒行具未爲淨, 不見聞亦不癡, 不離行可自淨; see also Anālayo 2022g, 857 and 2023d, 89.

272. Sn 840 reports him making the following and to all appearances approving reference in his reply: *diṭṭhiyā* (S^e adds *ca*) *eke paccenti suddhiṃ*, with a parallel in T 4.198.180b16: 以見可誰有淨.

273. Sn 842: *samo visesī* (C^e: *vihesi*) *uda vā nihīno, yo maññatī* (C^e: *maññati*), *so vivadetha tena*, with a parallel in T 4.198.180b19: 等亦過亦不及, 已著想便分別; Sn 843: *saccan ti so brāhmaṇo kiṃ vadeyya, musā ti vā so vivadetha kena*?, with a parallel in T 4.198.180b21: 有諦人當何言? 已著空誰有諍? In both cases, the second part of the Chinese counterpart proceeds differently. Due to the overall poor quality of the

translation of T 198 (see Anālayo 2023d, 183n231), a translation error appears to be a more probable explanation than assuming a substantially different Indic original.

274. Pj II 548,7.

275. Sn 787: *adhosi so diṭṭhim idh' eva sabban* (E^e^: *sabbā*) *ti* and Sn 913: *sa vippamutto diṭṭhigatehi dhīro.*

276. Deleanu 2000, 88 comments on the emphasis in Mahāyāna texts on the need to transcend all attachments that "[t]he early *arhat* ideal is not so different from this but what gives Mahāyāna its distinctive flavour is pushing the non-attachment, emotional and cognitive, to its utmost logical consequences. Nirvāṇa must be sought without being sought, practice must be done without being practised."

277. This divergence can be confusing, as evident from the assumption by Sander 2000b, 94–96 that Lokakṣema's translation lacks a counterpart to chapters 3 and 4 of the Sanskrit version. This assumption was apparently influenced by the somewhat unclear way of presentation adopted by Conze 1978, 49f and has already been corrected by Falk and Karashima 2013, 97.

278. Wogihara 1932/1935, 182,16.

279. On the development of the idea of merit transfer in *Āgama* literature see Anālayo 2010c.

280. AN 7.58B at AN IV 88,29 (= It 1.3.2 at It 14,21), SHT 412.32V1–2, Sander and Waldschmidt 1980, 64, Tripathi 1995, 167,18, and MĀ 138 at T 1.26.645c17.

281. Khp 8.9 at Khp 7,19.

282. Khp 8.15 at Khp 7,31.

283. Falk and Karashima 2013, 118–20: *vi ye jaṃbudive satva te sarve sadavatiphale p(r)adiṭhavea [ta k](i)[mañas](i) + + + + (p)[ut](r)o vi [ba]hu puña prasavea? aha: bahu bhaṃte bhagava. ado kośiga so ku + + + + + + + .. .. vi ba[hu]daro puño prasaviśati yo prañaparamidae postao parasa likhaṇa.* The terms corresponding in *Āgama* literature to the present reference to a "son of a good family" and "daughter of a good family" (Sanskrit: *kulaputra* and *kuladuhitṛ*; translated by Lokakṣema as 善男子 and 善女人)—the main usage in the *Āgama*s concerns the first of the two, the son of a good family—comprise both laity and monastics, as already noted by Hirakawa 1963, 71–72. However, Hirakawa 1990/1998, 308 suggests that in Mahāyāna texts these two terms instead "refer to lay believers" only, a suggestion that Fronsdal 1998/2014, 145–47 believes to find support in Lokakṣema's translation of the Perfection of Wisdom. It seems to me rather implausible that important indications on the merit potential of the Perfection of Wisdom, such as in the present passage, were explicitly aimed only at lay disciples. Why miss out on the potential of inspiring monastics to engage in the Perfection of Wisdom in the different ways described? A restriction to laity also does not seem to fit some other passages, such as when the memorization and recitation of the Perfection of Wisdom will prevent fear arising in a *kulaputra* or *kuladuhitṛ* who is in forest wilds or else when a *kulaputra* or *kuladuhitṛ* acts as a Dharma teacher on the eighth, fourteenth, or fifteenth day of the lunar calendar; see Karashima 2011, 59,7 + 196,1 (= T 8.224.431a23 + 443c16). Such descriptions seem to have in mind the life of a monastic rather than that of a lay disciple. Considering these together with other passages where the two terms relate more to lay activities, it seems to me that the choice of employing them may well have suggested itself precisely because their previously established usage did not involve a distinction between lay and monastic, making them convenient umbrella terms to refer to any practitioner of the bodhisattva path. On the

use of the terms *kulaputra* and *kuladuhitṛ* not being confined to laity see also Gombrich 1998, 48–50, Harrison 2006, 147n52, and Attwood 2021, 74–75.

284. These four qualities feature in a standard description of the nature of a stream-enterer; see, for example, SN 55.2 at SN V 343,25 and its parallel SĀ 1127 at T 2.99.298c15.

285. The name Kauśika occurs already in *Ṛgveda* I.10.11, Müller 1873/1877, 6,22: *indra kauśika*.

286. At least to some extent a counterpart to the use of hyperbole in this part of the Perfection of Wisdom, which at the same time is also related to the topic of stream-entry, can be seen in the *Abhisamayasaṃyutta*. The first ten discourses in this collection employ striking contrasts to illustrate the amount of *duḥkha* that has been overcome through stream-entry compared to the amount that is still left, with the latter being equivalent to a bit of soil taken up by the Buddha in his fingernail when compared to the whole earth, SN 13.1 at SN II 133,14, to two or three drops of water compared to the great ocean, SN 13.7 at SN II 136,29, or to seven grains compared to the Himalaya, SN 13.9 at SN II 137,26. The parallel SĀ 891 gives a full exposition to only one such example and then presents other alternatives in abbreviation at T 2.99.224b22; see also Choong 2021, 34.

287. Doherty 1983, 121 comments on this imagery (as found in the *Vajracchedikā Prajñāpāramitā*) as follows: "Even though these references to the Ganges river and to its sand-grains have a certain conventional status, in effect they serve to fracture the sense of a natural fidelity between word-image and referent. For example[,] the literal river-image is so multiplied and transposed as to form one mere link in a chain of perspectives which stretches to vanishing point. Whatever claim to a referential validity the image-complex sand-grains/rivers/world systems initially possessed is subsumed in a dizzying multiplication of indices which obliterates any imaginable relationship of the words to an objective reality. This technique of vertiginous hyperbolic expansion is repeated in a variety of spatio-temporal contexts."

288. T 51.2085.859b27: 摩訶衍人則供養般若波羅蜜; the preceding part of this passage mentions worship of Abhidharma and *Vinaya*, the subsequent part refers to Mañjuśrī and Avalokiteśvara et al.; according to Zhao 2023, 4 "the 'Prajñāpāramitā' mentioned in Faxian's passage likely refers to *Prajñāpāramitā* scripture . . . rather than the image of a female bodhisattva." The report by Fǎxiǎn puts into perspective the position taken by Schopen 2000/2005, 5 regarding "evidence for the 'popularity' of the Perfection of Wisdom and the *Aṣṭasāhasrikā* in India. There is such evidence, but it does not come from the third or fourth centuries, but rather from the Pāla Period, and predominantly from the late Pāla Period—that is to say, from the eleventh and twelfth centuries. Then, and only then, do we have any evidence that this literature was even known outside a tiny circle of Buddhist scholastics." Schopen 2000/2005, 12 (and n. 22) approvingly quotes the study by Bareau 1985 of indications provided by Fǎxiǎn's travel account regarding the situation of Mahāyāna in India, showing that he would agree on considering such information to be in principle relevant. It follows that, given Fǎxiǎn's explicit reference to *Prajñāpāramitā* worship, the conclusion proposed by Schopen 2000/2005, 5 is in need of revision. Ruegg 2004, 24n29 also objects that "Schopen avers, p. 4 [= p. 5 of the 2005 reprint], that evidence for the 'popularity' of this work comes 'predominantly from the Late Pala Period, that is, the 11th and 12th centuries', without mentioning that Haribhadra wrote his great comment on it *c.* 800." Yet, Haribhadra could be considered as included in the reference by Schopen 2000/2005,

5 to "a tiny circle of Buddhist scholastics." In contrast, Fǎxiǎn's report does contradict the proposed assessment, as it reflects a common form of worship not confined to "Buddhist scholastics."

Vetter 2003, 68n44 in turn even argues that a cult of *Prajñāpāramitā* literature would already have been in existence in the first century CE, since recurrent references in T 224 to the superiority of worshipping the Perfection of Wisdom compare this to *stūpa* worship but do not refer to the alternative of worshipping Buddha images. Yet, as he notes himself, Lokakṣema's translation does refer to the making of a Buddha image, Karashima 2011, 525,8 (= T 8.224.476b17): 作佛形像; on this passage see also Lancaster 1974a and Rhi 2005, 204–5. Once the text reflects knowledge of the practice of making Buddha images, which obviously serve for the purpose of worship, the absence of explicit references to worshipping Buddha images in discussions of meritorious activities no longer seems to carry that much weight.

289. Anālayo 2010a and 2017a.
290. Karashima 2011, 58,4 (= T 8.224.431a9): 却後無數阿僧祇劫, 汝當作佛, 號字釋迦文. 天上天下於中最尊, 安定世間, 法極明 (the translation is based on the indication in Hirakawa 1997, 374 that 安定 can render *susthita*); see also Karashima 2011, 341,14 (= T 8.224.458b5). On the Dīpaṃkara prediction in general see in more detail Matsumura 2008, 2010, 2011, and 2012.
291. Bv 2.60 at Bv 13,1 and Jā 15,17; for the Tibetan version of the latter see Gaffney 2003, 331,10 (on this Tibetan counterpart see also the discussion in Skilling 1993, 106–8).
292. In Anālayo 2017a, 53–54, I reasoned that this may reflect a custom in ancient Indian art to portray gods and religious teachers with long hair, quite independent of their actual appearance, given that the same procedure holds for Jain saints, even though according to the textual sources of the Jain tradition these plucked out their hair when going forth and therefore could not have had long hair ever after. However, according to Rhi 2023, 2 the mode of depiction evident with Buddha statues "most plausibly stems from the fact that the image of Śākyamuni Buddha was initially created as a representation of the bodhisattva, in other words, Śākyamuni in the stage prior to enlightenment." In relation to evidence from Mathurā and Swāt, Rhi 2023, 4 proposes that "following the so-called aniconic period, the first attempt to represent Śākyamuni in iconic form in both regions started with bodhisattva images, as a preliminary step before creating the Buddha images."
293. MN 26 at MN I 163,30 and its parallel MĀ 204 at T 1.26.776b4 report that Śākyamuni shaved off his hair on going forth. SN 7.9 at SN I 167,33 (= Sn 3.4 at Sn 80,7) and its parallels SĀ 1184 at T 2.99.320b28 and SĀ$^2$ 99 at T 2.100.409a5 indicate that he continued to do so, as they report a brahmin seeing his uncovered head and realizing that Śākyamuni is shaven headed (in Sn 456 the Buddha then confirms that he is indeed shaven headed).
294. MĀ 161 at T 1.26.686c13 and its parallel T 1.76.884a9 refer to a fleshy topknot, 肉髻, as one of the thirty-two marks with which the Buddha was endowed. According to T 76, this topknot shone with light exceeding the light of the sun and the moon. The Pāli parallel, MN 91 at MN II 137,9, reflects an earlier understanding of this physical mark, presumably conveying the idea that his head was well-rounded (see Ps III 386,3), that is, the opposite of having a sort of protuberance.
295. One example can be found in MN 31 at MN I 205,20, MN 128 at MN III 155,15, Senior Kharoṣṭhī fragment 12r11–12, Silverlock 2015, 373, MĀ 72 at T 1.26.536b8, MĀ 185 at

T 1.26.729c22, and EĀ 24.8 at T 2.125.629b6, according to which the guardian of a park inhabited by Buddhist monks tried to stop the Buddha from entering it, failing to realize that the latter was the teacher of these monks. Although in this case it could be that the guardian functions in the narrative as someone who simply had not received sufficient information on the Buddha, such a possibility would not work particularly well for another example in MN 140 at MN III 238,8 and its parallels MĀ 162 at T 1.26.690a27, T 14.511.779c15 and Up 1041 at D 4094 *ju* 35a3 or P 5595 *tu* 38a6, which report that a Buddhist monk stayed overnight in the same room with the Buddha without realizing the latter's identity. Further confirmation can be found in the report in some *Vinaya*s that other monks, on seeing Nanda approach, mistook him for being the Buddha; see the Dharmaguptaka *Vinaya*, T 22.1428.695b15, the Sarvāstivāda *Vinaya*, T 23.1435.130c1, and the Theravāda *Vinaya*, Vin IV 173,10 (the same also occurs in Hoernle 1916, 367, fragment 108b). On this topic see in more detail Guang Xing 2005, 14–15 and Anālayo 2017a, 57–60.

296. See Anālayo 2017a, 61–68.

297. For the recognition that the infant Śākyamuni is endowed with the thirty-two marks and hence has the potential of becoming a Buddha see Sn 690, with counterparts found, e.g., in the *Mahāvastu*, Marciniak 2020, 44,13 (also in Senart 1890, 32,3), and in the *Lalitavistara*, Lefmann 1902, 103,11. A prediction of the infant Vipaśyin in turn occurs in DN 14 at DN II 16,11 and its parallels Waldschmidt 1956, 95 (6a.1) or Fukita 2003, 72, DĀ 1 at T 1.1.4c27, and T 1.2.153c25. A prediction of Maitreya's future Buddhahood, given by the Buddha Śākyamuni, can in turn be found in MĀ 66 at T 1.26.511a14 and T 1.44.830b23; see in more detail Anālayo 2010a, 113–27. Needless to say, Śākyamuni's prediction of Maitreya's Buddhahood implies a clear-cut endorsement of the idea of undertaking the bodhisattva path, which ties in naturally with Śākyamuni's role of recommending such a path in T 224 and other early Mahāyāna *sūtra*s.

298. DN 14 at DN II 16,1 and DĀ 1 at T 1.1.4c20. Another parallel, T 1.2.152b13, does not employ such a specification at all. See in more detail Anālayo 2017a, 87–94.

299. The Sanskrit version, Waldschmidt 1956, 119 (8b.1) or Fukita 2003, 98, gives a description involving the bodhisattva Vipaśyin's father, Bandhumat, and concludes by applying the term *dharmatā* to it. This makes having a father by the name of Bandhumat an invariable feature of all Buddhas, which conflicts with the listing of different names for the fathers of each of the Buddhas in the same text; see Waldschmidt 1956, 79 (3f.1) or Fukita 2003, 46.

300. EĀ 48.3 at T 2.125.788b5: 彌勒有三十二相, 八十種好. An exploration of early stages in the evolution of the idea of Maitreya as the next Buddha can be found in Anālayo 2010a, 95–113 and 2014f; see also Tournier 2017, 165. Karashima 2013c, 178 and 2018a, 181 notes that, previous to my publications in this respect, the lateness of the idea of Maitreya as a future Buddha had already been proposed by him in n. 121 (p. 310) to the second volume of the Japanese translation of the *Dīrghāgama* published in 1997. The present case exemplifies a problem I mentioned in my introduction (see p. 4), in that my ignorance of Japanese prevents me from being up to date regarding research published in that language. Had I been aware of this proposal, I would have happily acknowledged it in my publications on the topic.

301. An example would be T 4.200.249b19; see in more detail Anālayo 2017a, 94–100.

302. An example would be Thī 399 (with Thī-a 241,11); see also Anālayo 2014a and 2017a, 100–101.
303. In using the term "aural/oral intertextuality" I follow Skilling 2014, 511; on the relationship between orality and writing as evident in the Perfection of Wisdom see in more detail Anālayo 2024e.
304. Endo 2013.
305. This has already been noted by Gokuldas De 1951, 26 as a significant contrast between the *Mahāpadānasutta* (DN 14) and the *Buddhavaṃsa*, which he takes to show that at the time of the composition of the former the bodhisattva ideal was not yet known.
306. See above n. 39.
307. The difference can best be exemplified by juxtaposing the earlier and later formulations, with the additional part underlined: DN 30 at DN III 142,16 (repeated in abbreviation and then given in full again at DN III 145,14): *so imaṃ pathaviṃ sāgarapariyantaṃ adaṇḍena asatthena dhammena* ($C^e$ and $S^e$ add *samena*) *abhivijiya ajjhāvasati* and DN 30 at DN III 146,20 (repeated in abbreviation and then given in full again at DN III 177,12): *so imaṃ pathaviṃ sāgarapariyantaṃ akhilam* ($C^e$ and $S^e$: *akhīlam*) *animittam akaṇṭakaṃ iddhaṃ phītaṃ khemaṃ sivaṃ nirabbudaṃ adaṇḍena asatthena dhammena* ($C^e$ and $S^e$ add *samena*) *abhivijiya ajjhāvasati*. Unlike the other three editions, $S^e$ has the underlined part from the outset (= DN III 142,16), which may be a result of a tendency during textual transmission toward standardizing. Rhys Davids and Rhys Davids 1921, 165 translate the underlined part as "void of barrenness, pitfalls or jungle, mighty, prosperous, secure, fortunate, without blemish," and Walshe 1987, 443 as "open, uninfested by brigands, free from jungle, powerful, prosperous, happy and free from perils" (which seems to miss out on *khema*). Rowell 1935, 419n1 comments on the expanded formulation: "I have come across no passage in Pali more like the typical Sanskrit descriptions of the Buddha-kṣetra than this. The Cakkavattī-Sīhanāda-Sutta (*Dīgha* no. XXVI—Vol. iii, p. 75) contains a description of the ideal state of this world under Metteyya . . . but this description is not as close to the familiar Sanskrit Buddha-kṣetra description as" the one found in the present case of DN 30. The additional terms as such are typical of the type of elaboration provided by a commentary. Their appearance in DN 30 can thus safely be taken to reflect the incorporation of commentarial material in the discourse, rather than as reflecting some external influence.
308. MĀ 59 at T 1.1.493b6 only adds 令得安樂 (adopting a CBETA emendation of 藥 to read 樂, in keeping with the formulation found in the remainder of the discourse; elsewhere in the same collection the alternative 令得安隱 occurs, e.g., MĀ 130 at T 1.26.619a8). Moreover, 令得安樂 occurs *after* the description of the wheel-turning king's rule without reliance on weapons.

    I have become aware of the existence of the Tibetan parallel Up 3024 only in the course of the present research, wherefore my earlier study of DN 30 in Anālayo 2017a, 103–35 just takes into account the parallel MĀ 59. Fortunately, however, this does not affect my conclusions, as the case of Up 3024 further supports the inferences I had drawn based on MĀ 59. In relation to the present issue, Up 3024 at D 4094 *ju* 120a6 or P 5595 *tu* 137b8 precedes the reference to the wheel-turning king's rule without reliance on weapons by mentioning the absence of thorns (or obstructions, see below) and of flaws, *tsher ma med cing gnod pa med la*, repeated in D 4094 *ju* 120b3 or P 5595 *tu* 138a5 and D 4094 *ju* 121b7 or P 5595 *tu* 139b4 in the form *'tshe ba med cing gnod pa med pa*. Unlike the case of the additional Pāli terms discussed in the previous note, however, such indications are not confined to the present case of describing the realm of a wheel-turning king, as these recur in Up 2050 at D 4094 *ju* 76b4 or P 5595 *tu* 86b4 (parallel to MN 83 and MĀ 67; see Anālayo 2011b, 466n131) and in Up 4093 at D 4094 *ju* 246a2 or P 5595 *tu* 280b8 (parallel to MĀ 66; see Anālayo 2010a, 115n48). It is possible that, from having originated in the context of Up 3024, in the course of transmission this type of additional specification spread to other descriptions of the realm of a wheel-turning king, in line with the tendency to standardize evident also in the case of S^e^ among the Pāli versions of DN 30.

309. The sequence of listing the marks appears to be influenced by the karmic perspective rather than by the order of listing observed in the first part of DN 30. For a detailed study see Anālayo 2017a, 103–35.

310. Warder 1967, 94 explains that "metrical considerations justify the conclusion that this is a late text standing on the threshold of Classical Sanskrit metrics. It is therefore of great interest to note that in content this *sutta* is an elaborate piece of 'Buddhology' describing in minute detail the thirty-two physical characteristics of the Buddha. In the histories of the religion this iconographic development has often been supposed to be a late development in Early Buddhism, tending to Mahāyāna, and this more or less subjective argument can now be supported by the objective evidence of the metre."

311. For a survey see Anālayo 2022d, 140–51.

312. Another, related testimony to the impact of this notion can be seen in MĀ 161 at T 1.26.687a16+a23+b20, which relates aspects of the Buddha's physical appearance or behavior to his wholesome conduct in the past, 以本善行故; see also Anālayo 2011b, 533. No such indication occurs in the discourse parallels, making it fair to assume that this remark is a later addition, like the case of the karmic exposition in DN 30. Another late indication can be found in a set of verses at the end of EĀ 10.3 at T 2.125.564b16, according to which making offerings leads to accomplishing the awakening of a Buddha and being endowed with the thirty-two marks, 布施成佛道, 三十二相具.

313. DN 30 at DN III 145,17: *imāni kho* (E^e^ adds *te*), *bhikkhave, dvattiṃsa mahāpurisassa* (E^e^ has these two words in the opposite sequence: *mahāpurisassa dvattiṃsa*) *mahāpurisa-lakkhaṇāni bāhirakā pi isayo dhārenti, no ca kho te jānanti: imassa kammassa katattā* (B^e^: *kaṭattā*; S^e^ adds *pe*) *idaṃ* (C^e^and S^e^: *imaṃ*) *lakkhaṇaṃ paṭilabhatī ti* (C^e^: *paṭilabhantī ti*).

314. Wogihara 1930/1936, 378,3: *yathoktaṃ ca lakṣaṇasūtre*. Other examples of expositions relating the marks to former deeds can be found in the *Arthaviniścayasūtra*, Samtani 1971, 55,4 (for a comparison of the relevant portion with DN 30 see Samtani 1962) and in the *Lalitavistara*, Lefmann 1902, 429,3.

315. Although the basic procedure of matching bodily marks with a particular conduct is the same, the actual executions of this procedure differ. A difference in principle is that DN 30 is overall considerably more elaborate, as it also covers the case of a wheel-turning king and follows its prose expositions with verses. Given the contextual setting in the *Bodhisattvabhūmi*, the absence of a reference to a wheel-turning king is obvious, as the concern is to present just the most directly relevant part in the form of the actual correlations. Nevertheless, even these correlations are not necessarily the same, and the sequence of taking these up also differs, showing that the *Lakṣaṇasūtra* on which the *Bodhisattvabhūmi* relies must have differed from the *Lakkhaṇasutta* in the *Dīgha-nikāya*, similar in type to what can emerge when comparing discourses transmitted by different reciter lineages.

316. See also Skilling 2006, 56: "Les *jātaka* jouèrent un rôle essentiel dans le développement de 'la voie du Bodhisattva' (*bodhisattvayāna*) qui, à partir du début de l'ère chrétienne, évolua vers le bouddhisme Mahāyāna, du 'Grand Véhicule.'"
317. See in more detail Anālayo 2010a, 55–71.
318. Basham 1981, 22 proposes that "we may be sure that *Jātakas*, and with them the doctrine of the Bodhisatta, were important elements in popular Buddhism by the time of the carving of the reliefs of Bhārhut *stūpa* railings, which depict about thirty *Jātaka* tales." This seems to propose too early a dating for the bodhisattva ideal; there is a need to distinguish between the popularity of the narratives as such and their interpretation from the viewpoint of the evolving bodhisattva ideal, which is a subsequent step and not necessarily entailed in depictions of the narratives. As pointed out in relation to Bhārhut by Gokuldas De 1951, 18, "the Jātakas of 'Bhārhut' have to be taken in their ordinary sense[,] meaning stories or fables told by the Master in illustration of his Doctrine[,] and not in the special sense in which the Buddhists used them in later times implying birth-stories of the Bodhisatta before he became the Buddha." In the same vein, Cummings 1982, 20 reasons that "there is considerable evidence that most Jātakas at the time of Bhārhut were simply used as parables in illustration of the Doctrine, and did not yet carry any specific significance as stories of the Buddha's previous incarnations." Again, Sarkar 1990, 5 comments on "the sculptures of *Bhārhut* and *Sāñchī* stūpas" that their depictions of "*Jātaka*s were only the illustrations of morals taught by the *Buddha*."
319. The absence of verses has been highlighted by von Hinüber 1998, 182: "Ur-Jātakas sind in eine feste Prosaform gegossen, die von der späteren in der Jātakaṭṭhavaṇṇanā gültigen verschieden ist. Das Fehlen von Versen in den Ur-Jātakas im Suttapiṭaka ist besonders auffällig." He concludes (p. 189): "Der Ursprung der Jātakas, also die Ur-Jātakas, sind Erzählungen ohne Verse, die dem Buddha in seinen Lehrvorträgen in den Mund gelegt wurden. Diesen Erzählungen werden im Vinayapiṭaka Verse beigegeben." Regarding past lives as an animal, Peris 2004, 55–56 reasons that, "though *Jatakam* constituted one of the nine *anga* of Buddhist teaching and certain jatakas were attributed to the Buddha himself in the *Nikayas*, in these he was always a human being," adding in n. 26 that "one exception is the Buddha's identification of himself with the bull Nandivisala in the *Vinaya Pitaka*, (iv. 5–6; cp. The *Nandivisala Jataka* (No. 28)). But this belongs," together with some parts of the *Khuddakanikāya*, to a later textual strata than *Āgama* literature. On this tale see also Anālayo 2010a, 67–68.
320. DĀ 23 at T 1.1.100b$_{11}$: 沙門瞿曇說此事, 不言從他聞, 我默思惟: 沙門瞿曇將無是彼刹利王耶? 或是彼婆羅門大臣耶?
321. DN 5 at DN I 143,$_{15}$ and fragment 408r$_2$, von Criegern 2002, 35; on the formulation in DN 5 see also Klaus 2007, 318–19.
322. Wogihara 1930/1936, 397,$_{11}$: *pūrvenivāsānusmṛtijñānabalena tathāgataḥ pūrvāṃte itivṛttakāṃś ca jātakāṃś ca smṛtvā cittasaṃvegāya cittaprasādāya vineyānāṃ deśayati.*
323. DN 5 at DN I 143,$_{26}$: *ahaṃ* (E$^e$: *ahan*) *tena samayena* (S$^e$ adds *brāhmaṇa*) *purohito brāhmaṇo ahosiṃ tassa yaññassa yājetā ti* and DĀ 23 at T 1.1.100b$_{25}$: 是時, 刹利王爲大祀者, 豈異人乎? 勿造斯觀, 即吾身是也.
324. Fragment 408r4, reconstructed by von Criegern 2002, 49 as follows: *ubhayam apy ahaṃ bhāradvāja samanusmarāmi api rājā kṣatriyo mūrdhābhiṣikta evaṃrūpasya yajñasya yaṣṭā api brāhmaṇaḥ purohitaḥ evaṃrūpasya yajñasya yājayitā.*
325. In the case of another instance of identifying a brahmin chaplain as a former life of the

Buddha, one out of three extant discourse parallels does not report any identification at all; see T 1.8.213c14, in contrast to DN 19 at DN II 251,9 and DĀ 3 at T 1.1.34a9, which present the brahmin chaplain as a former life of the Buddha, an identification also reported in the *Mahāvastu*, Marciniak 2019, 278,12 (also in Senart 1897, 224,5). The absence of such identification in T 8 may be reflecting an earlier stage in textual evolution, when the tale had not yet been turned into a *jātaka*. In fact, another Pāli discourse and its Chinese parallel refer to the same brahmin chaplain without identifying him as a former life of the Buddha; see AN 6.54 at AN III 372,1 (reference here is to his proper name, not to the honorific title mentioned in DN 19 at DN II 232,24) and its parallel MĀ 130 at T 1.26.619c17. The contrast between DN 19 and AN 6.54 in this respect has already been noted by Law 1930a, 172–73 and Gokuldas De 1951, 50. For a comparative survey that covers several other early *jātaka*s see Anālayo 2010a, 59–71.

326. SN 47.6 at SN V 146,18 and SĀ 617 at T 2.99.172c25; see also T 4.212.695a12.

327. Jā 168 at Jā II 58,23: *sakuṇovādasuttaṃ ārabbha kathesi. ekadivasaṃ hi satthā bhikkhū āmantetvā: gocare, bhikkhave, caratha sake pettike visaye ti imaṃ saṃyuttaṃ mahāvagge suttantaṃ kathento*; the identification of the past life is in turn found in Jā 168 at Jā II 60,23: *tadā seno devadatto ahosi, lāpo pana aham evā ti.* The present case has already been noted by Rhys Davids 1903/1997, 195, who comments that "there can be no question as to which is the older document; for the Jātaka quotes as its source, and by name and chapter, the very passage in the Saṃyutta in which the fable originally occurs."

328. See Anālayo 2020d, 113–16.

329. See, e.g., Winternitz 1920/1968, 90, Alsdorf 1977, 25, Norman 1983, 79, Laut 1993, 503, and Anālayo 2010a, 56–58.

330. Boucher 2008, 27 offers the following assessment: "The *Viśvantara* (*Vessantara*) *jātaka* is without a doubt one of the most popular narratives in the Buddhist world. It would be no exaggeration to say that it is rivaled only by the biography of Śākyamuni himself, and in some regions, the story of Viśvantara eclipses even that."

331. See in more detail Anālayo 2016f.

332. Senart 1882, 104,12. The importance of the *jātaka*s for the development of the bodhisattva ideal has already been recognized by Lamotte 1954, 377 and 379, who notes the impact of "les récits de jātaka et les aventures édifiantes où le bodhisattva avait donné le mesure de ses vertus altruistes . . . Vint un moment où, à se nourrir sans cesse de la littérature des jātaka et des avadāna, et à s'exercer à reproduire dans sa vie journalière les gestes altruistes du bodhisattva, le laïc se crut appelé comme son modèle à la suprême et parfaite illumination . . . pour devenir mieux et plus qu'un saint: un buddha pleinement et parfaitement éclairé. Dès lors le Mahāyāna était né." The assumption that this trajectory was confined to lay practitioners is problematic and does not match the actual evidence, be it textual or epigraphic. For a critical reply to a related argument by Lamotte 1954, 379, regarding anti-clericalism supposedly evident in the *Rāṣṭrapālaparipṛcchā*, see Silk 2002, 377–78, and on the topic of the role of laity in general below n. 768.

333. Jā 547 at Jā VI 593,29: *vessantararājā aham evā ti.*

334. As an example of this pattern, von Hinüber 1996/1997, 95–96 mentions the *Chakesadhātuvaṃsa* reporting the erection of six *stūpa*s, each containing a hair of the Buddha, whose "text begins after an introductory verse with the formula *evaṃ me sutaṃ*." Another example is the *Dasabodhisattuppattikathā*, concerned with the arising of ten future Buddhas, where von Hinüber 1996/1997, 99 notes that it adopts the form "of the apocryphal Suttantas beginning *evaṃ me sutaṃ*." On such "apocryphal Suttantas,"

Norman 1994, 279 reports that "[b]y title they are *suttas*; they have the standard canonical opening *evaṃ me sutaṃ ekaṃ samayaṃ* . . . ; the narrative attributes their contents to the Buddha . . . but they are not included in any edition of the Pāli canon. Examples of such literature, however, were apparently known to and accepted as authoritative by Buddhaghosa . . . Manuscripts show that [such] texts are very often transmitted as individual *suttas*, not as [part of] *nikāyas*, and while it would have been difficult to insert a new *sutta* into a *nikāya*, it was easy to add another *sutta* to the collection."

335. For two case studies in the evolution of *Vinaya* narratives see Anālayo 2012a and 2014g.

336. The term is *muṇḍaka samaṇaka*, *muṇḍika śramaṇa*, or *muṇḍaka śramaṇaka* in MN 81 at MN II 46,12, the *Mahāvastu*, Senart 1882, 320,4, and the *Saṅghabhedavastu*, Gnoli 1978, 23,20, with Chinese counterparts in 禿頭沙門 or 髡頭道人 in MĀ 63 at T 1.26.500a21 and T 4.197.172c23. The Pāli commentary explains that the young brahmin's usage of the term *muṇḍaka samaṇaka* expresses contempt, Ps III 280,15: *hīḷento evam āha*. On the term *muṇḍa*/*muṇḍaka* see also Tedesco 1945 and Levman 2011.

337. This has already been noted by Oldenberg 1912a, 189: "Auch ist die Erzählung vielmehr der Verherrlichung des Ghaṭīkāra und seiner frommen Intimität mit dem Buddha jenes Weltalters gewidmet, als der Jotipālas, des Bodhisatta. So ist es meines Erachtens vollkommen in der Ordnung, daß das Jātakakorpus die Geschichte nicht aufgenomen bzw. sie etwa mit einem Vers ausgestattet hat."

338. MN 81 at MN II 51,16 and its parallel MĀ 63 at T 1.26.501b12 indicate that the potter was a stream-enterer, an indication also found in the *Saṅghabhedavastu*, Gnoli 1978, 26,22. MN 81 at MN II 52,2 additionally indicates that he had progressed further and become a nonreturner; see also Anālayo 2011b, 446–47.

339. Karashima 2011, 39,2 (= T 8.224.429a22): 以得須陀洹道, 不可復得菩薩道. 何以故? 閉塞生死道故.

340. Karashima 2011, 43,3 (= T 8.224.429b24): 須陀洹道七死七生, 便度去.

341. MN 81 at MN II 54,18 and its discourse parallel MĀ 63 at T 1.26.503a5, as well as the *Mahāvastu*, Senart 1882, 335,5, the *Saṅghabhedavastu*, Gnoli 1978, 30,14, and T 4.197.173c18. A note of discord in respect to this identification appears at first sight to emerge with the otherwise unrelated EĀ 1.1 at T 1.125.551b20, as this introductory portion to the *Ekottarikāgama* collection identifies the monk Uttara, a disciple of Śākyamuni, with a brahmin named Uttara at the time of the Buddha Kāśyapa, which could in principle be intending the brahmin youth in question. In that case, it would be impossible for that same brahmin to have been a past life of Śākyamuni himself. The identification is doubtful, however, as the name of the young brahmin at the time of Kāśyapa differs in the parallel versions. Whereas MN 81 at MN II 46,4, the *Mahāvastu*, Senart 1882, 319,11, and T 4.197.172c13 speak of Jotipāla/Jyotipāla/火鬘, MĀ 63 at T 1.26.499a28 and the *Saṅghabhedavastu*, Gnoli 1978, 23,1 speak of 優多羅/Uttara. The name Uttara for a young brahmin who will become Śākyamuni Buddha, according to a prediction given in this respect by the Buddha Kāśyapa, occurs also repeatedly in the *Avadānaśataka*, Speyer 1906/1970, 239,7 and 1909/1970, 23,5, 51,8, and 88,1. A commentary on the *Ekottarikāgama*, the 分別功德論, T 25.1507.33a25, has a reference to the episode under discussion: 猶昔火鬘童子誹迦葉佛言: 禿頭沙門何有道? 道難得, 能得道也? 由是後受六年勤苦方乃得道; see also Palumbo 2013, 253. The reference here to 火鬘童子 makes it improbable that EĀ 1.1 would refer to the same person as

優多羅, and my suggestion in this respect in Anālayo 2010a, 75 needs to be revised in the light of this passage in the 分別功德論.

342. See above n. 337.

343. MĀ 63 at T 1.26.503a8: 爾時說法不至究竟, 不究竟白淨, 不究竟梵行, 不究竟梵行訖 . . . 我今說法得至究竟, 究竟白淨, 究竟梵行, 究竟梵行訖. The same type of contrast occurs in MĀ 8 at T 1.26.429c16, MĀ 60 at T 1.26.496a3, MĀ 67 at T 1.26.515a14, MĀ 68 at T 1.26.518b11, MĀ 155 at T 1.26.678a11, and MĀ 160 at T 1.26.684b13, in each case in relation to a former life of Śākyamuni that indeed did not involve teachings leading to the ultimate. In order to make sense of the present passage, one would need to supply "[I]" to the phrase regarding not reaching the ultimate, 不至究竟, etc. Such a supplementation, however, would not work for the other instances of the same formulation, which are clearly meant to convey that the teachings followed by Śākyamuni in these former lives did not reach the ultimate, rather than that he himself did not reach the ultimate. This makes it safe to consider the occurrence of the same phrasing in MĀ 63 to be the result of borrowing an established pericope. The suggested possibility of reading it on its own as conveying the sense "[I] did not reach the ultimate" may in turn explain why this passage was transmitted without undergoing some correction.

344. The descriptions of this visit make it clear that Śākyamuni should be reckoned as already a Buddha by this time, that is, these encounters are not part of his recollection of past lives during the night of his awakening. Besides such clear indications, an additional point is that, unlike celestial travel in general, paying a personal visit to the Pure Abodes may have been considered to require having gained a level of mental purification corresponding to that of its inhabitants—that is, at least nonreturn if not full awakening—in addition to the need to have developed the supernormal ability to visit celestial worlds. Although to the best of my knowledge not expressed explicitly, support for this assumption could be found in the circumstance that some versions report the Buddha stating that he had penetrated the Dharma-element, *dharmadhātu*, enabling him to know various details related to these former Buddhas, which features as a mode of knowledge in addition to being informed by *deva*s. Such a reference occurs in DN 14 at DN II 10,16 and 53,14 (the second instance comes right at the end of the report of the visit to the Pure Abodes and thus reads as if it were meant to refer back to that) and in Waldschmidt 1956, 66 (1b.12) or Fukita 2003, 34; see also DĀ 1 at T 1.1.1c1, which instead speaks of the Dharma nature, 法性.

Another point calling for a comment is that in DN 14 at DN II 2,6 the Buddha introduces his exposition of the six Buddhas as a topic related to former lives, *pubbenivāsa*, repeated at DN II 11,1. DĀ 1 at T 1.1.1c13 and 3c11 even speaks of recollection of past lives, 宿命智, which reads as if it were intending the Buddha's own ability in this respect. In view of the narrative context, however, in particular given the description of the Buddha Śākyamuni's visit to the Pure Abodes in all versions, including DĀ 1, such a reference is best understood to concern the *deva*s of the Pure Abodes recollecting their former lives as disciples of the six Buddhas. The occurrence of somewhat equivocal formulations may be due to the overall trend of relating any story from the past to the Buddha's recollection of his own former lives. Besides being a central force in the generation of *jātaka* tales, this same trend may have also impacted versions of the present discourse during the period of oral transmission, despite the clear indication that the source of Śākyamuni's knowledge about the lives and circumstances of former Buddhas was an encounter with their former disciples now living as *deva*s in the Pure

Abodes, and it was these former disciples—rather than Śākyamuni himself—who recollected various details about the Buddhas whom they had been following.

345. The $E^e$ edition of DN 14 at DN II 53,5 abbreviates without giving the names of the Buddhas between Vipaśyin and Śākyamuni, but these are spelled out in the Asian editions ($B^e$, $C^e$, and $S^e$), including a reference to Kāśyapa*: mayaṃ . . . kassapamhi bhagavatī brahmacariyaṃ caritvā*. The same pattern, with explicit reference to Kāśyapa, holds for the corresponding part in Waldschmidt 1956, 162 (11.7) or Fukita 2003, 160: *vayaṃ kāśyapasya [śrāvakā]*, in DĀ 1 at T 1.1.10b17: [我等皆是]迦葉佛[弟子], and in T 1.3.158b22: [我是]迦葉佛[聲聞弟子].

346. MN 4 at MN I 22,11 and its parallel EĀ 31.1 at T 2.125.666b24; see also the Dharmaguptaka *Vinaya*, T 22.1428.781b7, the *Saṅghabhedavastu*, Gnoli 1977, 117,27, and the *Buddhacarita* 14.2, Johnston 1936/1984, 157. The same report, with the difference of preceding such recollection with the divine eye (rather than having recollection of past lives first, followed by the divine eye), can be found in T 17.757.599c1 (parallel to MN 12 and MN 36), the *Lalitavistara*, Lefmann 1902, 345,3, and the *Mahāvastu*, Marciniak 2020, 170,3 and 353,4 (also in Senart 1890, 132,15 and 284,7).

347. See Anālayo 2010a, 81n83+84 for a survey of sources reporting that Śākyamuni Buddha proclaimed to have had no teacher and that he announced to have realized what was previously not heard. The same phrase *pūrvam ananuśruteṣu dharmeṣu* qualifies realization gained on one's own, as distinct from reliance on *anuśrava*, in MN 100 at MN II 211,16 and its parallel Sanskrit fragment 348r1–2, Zhang 2004, 12; see also SHT IV 165 folio 26Vc, Sander and Waldschmidt 1980, 200. This suggests the point at stake to be that Śākyamuni's awakening was not based on what he had heard from a teacher but rather involved what he reached on his own; see also Nidd I 457,18 and Paṭis I 174,3, which precede *pubbe ananussutesu dhammesu* with *sayambhū anācariyako*. In other words, "previously unheard" means "previously unheard [by Śākyamuni]," that is, not heard by him from some teacher, *ācariya*, who had disclosed the path to awakening to him, instead of which he had to discover this path independently, *sayambhū*, on his own.

In awareness of the first of these two references (the one found in Nidd), Tournier 2017, 125n1 nevertheless sees a contrast between this notion and the comparison of the Buddha's realization to the rediscovery of an ancient city (referenced in Anālayo 2010a, 81n86), commenting: "La réalisation des quatre nobles vérités par le Buddha est présentée comme 'non entendue auparavant' dans plusieurs sources canoniques de toutes les écoles . . . cette formule pourrait s'interpréter comme la marque d'une insistance primaire sur le caractère sans précédent de la réalisation du Buddha. Cependant, dans les mêmes corpus canoniques, le Buddha est présente comme le re-découvreur d'une voie ancienne . . . sans qu'un rapport d'antériorité puisse être établi entre les deux affirmations." In view of the epistemological connotation of the reference to being previously unheard as qualifying realization gained on one's own and thus without a teacher, there would perhaps be no need to see a contrast between this and the simile of rediscovering an ancient city, making it appear less important which of these may be the earlier one. In the context of this simile, the rediscovery is not due to having received information about the path to the city's location from someone else. Similarly, the relevant sources present the Buddha's awakening as something gained without having received information from someone else about the path to liberation.

The city itself, however, would represent the same realization of Nirvana that previous Buddhas had also attained.

The notion that indeed does not sit particularly well with these various sources is rather the idea that Śākyamuni had been a monk disciple of the Buddha Kāśyapa and thus in a recent life had direct contact with liberating teachings; in fact, Ps III 282,18 reports that—in line with what by the time of its composition has become a standard pattern for all bodhisattvas to go forth under a previous Buddha—he had memorized all the teachings given by Kāśyapa and cultivated meditative insight right up to the brink of stream-entry. In view of the standard account that Śākyamuni recollected his past lives in the night of his awakening, he could have easily gained direct access to memories of his time under the Buddha Kāśyapa and the latter's teachings on how to reach awakening, which would no longer fit his claim to have had no teacher and to have not heard about the path to awakening from another.

In sum, when viewed from the perspective of the early Buddhist doctrinal setting, the existence of former Buddhas who on their own realized awakening in the past does not conflict with the notion that others like Śākyamuni or Maitreya can become Buddhas by also realizing the same type of awakening on their own, as long as there is no direct teacher-disciple relationship between any of these in either past or present lifetimes. This perspective changes in other texts, as is already evident in the abovementioned Pāli commentary. With the precedent set by the tale of Śākyamuni as a disciple of Kāśyapa Buddha, this is perhaps unsurprising. The same change of perspective can also be seen reflected in the Perfection of Wisdom in the report that Maitreya is present in its audience, Karashima 2011, 129,9 (= T 8.224.438a14), or in the idea of bodhisattvas who, after having received their prediction, proceed in their future lives from one Buddhafield to another, continuously being in the presence of a Buddha, Karashima 2011, 340,8 (= T 8.224.458a19).

A solution to enable still conceiving of Buddhahood as a realization gained by oneself would then perhaps be for such bodhisattvas to sidestep any recollection of their past lives until after they have successfully realized full awakening. At least in *Āgama* literature recollection of past lives does indeed not seem to be conceived as an essential ingredient of the path to Buddhahood, given that it is not mentioned as having preceded the event of Vipaśyin's awakening reported in DN 14 at DN II 35,22 and its parallels Waldschmidt 1956, 147 (9d.4) or Fukita 2003, 143, DĀ 1 at T 1.1.7c7, and T 1.3.156b21.

This in turn puts into perspective the assertion by Walters 1997, 174 that "*Buddhas* and *arhats* share a virtue that ordinary people do not: they know their previous lives," which he considers to be a "well-established canonical detail." A fairly clear indication to the contrary for the case of arhats can be found in SN 8.7 at SN I 191,22 and its parallels MĀ 121 at T 1.26.610b24, T 1.63.862a4, SĀ 1212 at T 2.99.330b24, and SĀ² 228 at T 2.100.457c11, which list arhats who are just liberated by wisdom, as distinct from those who have gained the three higher knowledges (one of which is recollection of past lives) or who are liberated both ways. This implies that only some arhats were held to have cultivated the ability to recollect their past lives.

348. MĀ 32 at T 1.26.469c24: 世尊迦葉佛時，始願佛道，行梵行；若世尊迦葉佛時，始願佛道，行梵行者，我受持是世尊未曾有法; on this formulation see also Anālayo 2010a, 85n90 and 2017c, 110n33. In the *Madhyamāgama*, the compound 佛道 occurs only in MĀ 32. Most occurrences relate to the present marvel, but one occurrence

instead designates Śākyamuni's actual awakening, T 1.26.471c9: 世尊一時在鬱鞞羅尼連然河邊, 阿闍惒羅尼拘類樹下, 初得佛道. This supports understanding it to refer to Buddhahood itself rather than to the path leading to it. The phrase 始願, which does not recur in the *Madhyamāgama* apart from its usage in the above formulation, could be a rendering of an Indic original corresponding to Sanskrit *ādyapraṇidhāna*; see Hirakawa 1997, 360 and 1268. The term occurs in Abhidh-k IV 110, Pradhan 1967, 266,28: *ādyaṃ praṇidhānaṃ kṛtam*, although with different Chinese counterparts in T 29.1558.95b2: 最初發心 and T 29.1559.249c5: 初發菩提願.

349. MĀ 63 at T 1.26.500b1: 此優多羅童子 . . . 彼於世尊無信敬心, the *Saṅghabhedavastu*, Gnoli 1978, 24,14: *ayaṃ, bhadanta, uttaro māṇavo na buddhe 'bhiprasanno na dharme na saṅghe 'bhiprasannaḥ*, and T 4.197.173a15: 然其不識三尊, 不信三寶, 不見佛, 不聞法, 不供養眾僧.

350. The *Saṅghabhedavastu*, Gnoli 1978, 21,31 and 30,15 (the first provides the occasion for delivering the whole tale; the second has the final conclusion relating his verbal conduct at that time to his six years of ascetic practices at present) and T 4.197.173c22 (repeated in verse at 174a2); see also Ap 387.29–30 at Ap I 301,7 and Bechert 1961, 238–39, or else T 11.310.602a29, T 12.345.162a10, T 12.346.173c15, and for the Tibetan counterparts the translation by Tatz 1994/2001, 62, leading on to discussions that present interesting attempts to interpret the whole episode from the viewpoint of skill in means (for further references see Anālayo 2011b, 444n17 and above n. 341).

351. The testimony provided by the present passage extant only in Chinese translation is one of many instances confirming the appropriateness of the position taken by de Jong 1968, 15 that "no student of Buddhism, even if he [or she] is interested only in Indian Buddhism, can neglect the enormous corpus of Chinese translations." In more general terms, Silk 2022, 758n14 and 764 reasons that "[t]he power of philology is that it, and only it, enables us to approach what people in the past said, and ultimately meant," wherefore, "[i]f our goal . . . is to uncover as much of the textual history of Buddhist literature as possible, I think that full consideration of all preserved evidence is essential, and in this regard the Sanskrit, Chinese and Tibetan sources must be fully utilized." Contrary to a tendency by some scholars to dismiss the importance of Chinese sources—examples would be Schopen 2000/2005, 4, with a critical reply in Harrison 2008/2010, or Shulman 2021, 4n14, with a critical reply in Anālayo 2024c, 71–72—this indeed holds just as much for researching early Mahāyāna as it does for researching early Buddhism.

352. Kv 4.8 at Kv 288,34: *nanu vuttaṃ bhagavatā: kassape ahaṃ, ānanda, bhagavati brahmacariyaṃ acariṃ āyatiṃ sambodhāya. atth' eva suttanto ti? āmantā*. The expression of agreement here is noteworthy, given that such a passage is not found in the relevant Pāli discourse.

353. Gnoli 1977, 20,17: *kāśyapo nāma . . . buddho bhagavān, yasya antike bodhisattvo bhagavān āyatyāṃ bodhāya praṇidhāya brahmacaryaṃ caritvā, tuṣite devanikāye upapannaḥ*.

354. Senart 1882, 329,20: *atha khalv ānanda jyotipālasya bhikṣusya ekarahogatasya pratisaṃlīnasya ayam evarūpaś cetaso parivitarko utpadye: aho punar ahaṃ bhaveyam anāgatam adhvānaṃ tathāgato arhaṃ samyaksambuddho vidyācaraṇasaṃpannaḥ sugato lokavid anuttaraḥ puruṣadamyasārathiḥ śāstā devānāṃ ca manuṣyāṇāṃ ca*.

355. Senart 1882, 332,2: *bhaviṣyasi tvaṃ jyotipāla anāgatam adhvānan tathāgato 'rhan samyaksambuddho vidyācaraṇasampannaḥ sugato lokavid anuttaraḥ puruṣadamya-*

*sārathiḥ śāstā devānāṃ ca manuṣyāṇāṃ ca . . . ihaiva vārāṇasīye ṛṣivadane mṛgadāve dharmacakraṃ pravartayiṣyasi triparivartaṃ dvādaśākāraṃ.*

356. This justification can be seen underlying the Buddha Kāśyapa's statement that all the other assembled monks did become arhats, except for the young brahmin whose future Buddhahood he had predicted; see Senart 1882, 335,1: *sarveṣāṃ imeṣāṃ saptānāṃ bhikṣusahasrāṇāṃ . . . anupādāyāśravebhyaś cittāni vimuktāni sthāpayitvā jyotipālasya bhikṣusya, so pi mahyaṃ vyākṛto ca anuttarāye samyaksaṃbodhaye.*

357. Drewes 2021, 146n4 offers the following assessment: "Anālayo has argued that an older tradition held that Śākyamuni first vowed to attain Buddhahood under the Buddha Kāśyapa (*Genesis*, 84–93), but this is almost certainly incorrect, as Tournier points out (*La formation*, 151–56)." This assessment was probably formulated without awareness of a brief reply to some of the criticism raised by Tournier 2017 in Anālayo 2017c, 110n33+35. Although such a reply in two notes can of course easily be missed, it could already have helped to rectify the impression that my suggestions in this respect are "almost certainly incorrect," a formulation that goes further than what has actually been pointed out by Tournier 2017. As far as I have been able to ascertain, the latter has not identified anything incorrect in my presentation, instead of which he mainly expresses his lack of conviction regarding my conclusions. The question is thus not so much one of being either correct or else incorrect—in fact, my proposal is based on actual textual evidence and is certainly correct in this respect—but rather of evaluating probabilities and the strengths and weaknesses of differing interpretations.

358. On the historical value of the Pāli discourses and by implication of those *Āgama* collections that reflect a comparable level in development, such as the *Madhyamāgama* (T 26), see Anālayo 2012d, in critical reply to Schopen 1985 and Vetter 1994b. Tournier 2017, 154n105 objects to what he apparently perceives as a wholesale rejection of relevant developments in the *Mahāvastu* in Anālayo 2010a, 122n58, set apart from those found in the textual corpus of *Āgama* discourses. In what follows I provide the full text of both relevant notes for the sake of facilitating an accurate assessment.

The note in Tournier 2017, 154n105 reads: "Il n'y a toutefois rien de nettement 'proto-mahāyānique' dans ce type de développement, comme le laisse entendre Anālayo pour rejeter en bloc les évolutions à l'œuvre dans le *Mahāvastu* hors du corps des 'early discourses.' Cf. Anālayo 2010a: 122–123 n. 58." The referenced note 58 in my study in turn reads: "The account of the bodhisattva's meeting with the Buddha Kāśyapa in the *Mahāvastu* does mention such a prediction, Senart 1882, 332,2, which is not found in the parallel versions. On the lateness of the passage containing this prediction see Oldenberg 1912b, 139. This passage seems in line with a general pattern in the *Mahāvastu* to incorporate later elements that reflect embryonic Mahāyāna tendencies, observed by a range of scholars, cf. e.g. Barth 1899, 527, who notes that 'le Mahāvastu a été profondément pénétré d'éléments mahāyānistes'; see also de La Vallée Poussin 1915, 329–30, Winternitz 1920/1968, 192, Law 1930b, 12, Basak 1963, 43, Rahula 1978, 69–79, and Hiraoka 2003, 349–50. Therefore it seems quite probable that an already existing notion of a prediction was adopted in the *Mahāvastu*, whereas to assume that this notion originally arose in the *Mahāvastu* and then influenced the *Madhyama-āgama* Discourse on an Explanation about the Past seems rather improbable" (references in this quote to publications by others have been adjusted to the style of the present book).

As the actual formulation of my note would show, this is not meant to be a rejection "en bloc" but rather an attempt to assess the *probability* of the direction of influence between the two texts, an assessment that does not amount to a wholesale dismissal of the developments at work in the *Mahāvastu*. Moreover, the reference to embryonic Mahāyāna tendencies in that note summarizes what to the best of my knowledge has been the consensus among a range of scholars writing on the *Mahāvastu*, and the authentication strategy of rewriting the tale under discussion by adding a prediction to Buddhahood would seem to be in line with the tendencies identified in this way. At the same time, I agree with Tournier 2017, xvii that the notion "proto-Mahāyāna"—or even of "embryonic Mahāyāna tendencies," the term I had used—needs to be handled with circumspection so as to ensure a full appreciation of the complexity of the dynamics at work.

The reason for setting the *Mahāvastu* apart from the corpus of "early discourses" is simply that it is a *Vinaya* text, as convincingly demonstrated by Tournier 2012. The same applies to the Pāli *Vinaya*, which is also not part of the textual corpus of "early discourses" as such, an assessment obviously not based on considering this text to be in some way "proto-mahāyānic." In fact, Schopen 1995/2004, 94 allocates the finalization of *Vinaya* texts to what he refers to as "the Middle Period of Indian Buddhism." Although this allocation is not without problems (see Anālayo 2023e, 1–2), it is indeed the case that the finalization of *Vinaya* texts appears to have happened later than the finalization of the Pāli discourses and their *Āgama* parallels (except for the *Ekottarikāgama*).

Finally, Tournier 2017, 154 himself considers the *Mahāvastu* version of the tale under discussion to be probably influenced by its textual setting in the same work and thereby by the degree of evolution of the bodhisattva ideal this reflects. This concords with my position, in that it is reasonable to allow for the *Madhyamāgama* to have preserved earlier testimonies to the impact of this tale on the evolution of the bodhisattva ideal, simply because the *Mahāvastu* version appears to be itself influenced by an already existing, developed bodhisattva ideal, rather than contributing to the evolution of this ideal. In the words of Tournier 2017, 154 (see also below n. 366), the notion of an aspiration or vow for Buddhahood (and its prediction) "est davantage l'effet de l'homogénéisation du contenu du *Jyotipālasūtra* avec les récits d'un même cycle narratif que de la trajectoire autonome de ce *sūtra*."

359. See also Radich and Anālayo 2017, 218.

360. Tournier 2017, 152 reasons: "nous ne pouvons suivre l'auteur [= Anālayo 2010a] . . . lorsqu'il suggère que le passage du *Madhyama-Āgama* doit être considéré comme le plus ancien témoin de la formation du concept de *praṇidhāna*." It is indeed not convincing to suggest that the *Madhyamāgama* "must" (doit) be the most ancient testimony. This is precisely why in my discussion in Anālayo 2010a, 88 (quoted by Tournier 2017, 152n93) I speak just of it being "reasonable to assume" that the passage in question "may have preserved a remnant of an incipient stage in the development of the idea." It is not clear to me how what I intended to be a cautiously worded hypothesis could have come to be understood in the way reflected in the above quote.

361. Tournier 2017, 152 reasons that "[r]ien, en effet, dans le contexte narratif de la légende liant Kāśyapa au futur Śākyamuni, ne permet de prouver que la notion même d'aspiration à l'Éveil y ait pris naissance, avant de se diffuser aux récits portant sur le prédécesseurs de Kāśyapa, selon le scénario que propose l'auteur" (= Anālayo 2010a). As in the case of the preceding note, I think it would be helpful to recognize that I am evaluating

probabilities. The idea of proving ("prouver") is not what I have been attempting to do in my study. It is obviously not possible to *prove* that the notion of Śākyamuni's vow to become a Buddha arose from the tale of the young brahmin at the time of Kāśyapa Buddha, and it is also not possible to prove that it did not arise from this tale. What remains are probabilities, and these can be evaluated based on the religio-historical setting, the type of textual evidence at hand, and its narrative context. In the present case, as far as I can see all of these converge on making it probable—but obviously not certain—that this notion may indeed have arisen in the course of retellings of the encounter between the young brahmin and the Buddha Kāśyapa, and that the *Madhyamāgama* reference to an "initial" vow for Buddhahood may be testifying to an interim stage in the evolution of this notion.

362. The present marvel is not limited to a quality or deed of Śākyamuni himself, as it also comprises, at least implicitly, the transformative abilities of the Buddha Kāśyapa. Such a broadening of the scope of what is considered marvelous can also be seen in another marvel, reported in MN 123 at MN III 122,2 (see also above n. 35) but absent from MĀ 32, according to which his mother passed away seven days after Śākyamuni had been born. This marvel also comprises another person in addition to Śākyamuni, in this case his mother; see also Anālayo 2010a, 32–33.

363. According to MĀ 32 at T 1.26.469c27 and the *Saṅghabhedavastu*, Gnoli 1977, 21,1, the life as a young brahmin at the time of the Buddha Kāśyapa was followed by his life in Tuṣita. However, according to the Pāli commentarial tradition, Jā I 47,16, the life that preceded his stay in Tuṣita was as the prince Viśvantara/Vessantara.

364. This impression receives support from the observation by Tournier 2017, 153–54 that the aspiration or vow taken at the time of the Buddha Kāśyapa tends to be minimized or even disappears with texts that operate from the viewpoint of a large number of past Buddhas, together with an allocation of Śākyamuni's embarking on the career of a bodhisattva to a far distant time in the past.

365. An example for a proliferation of encounters with past Buddhas occurs right after the present tale in Senart 1882, 337,18; see also the discussion in Tournier 2017, 175–76. As noted by von Hinüber 2023, 51, the *Mahāvastu* reflects an "endeavour to push the lineage of the Buddha back more and more into an incredibly remote past by inventing ever new names of Buddhas."

366. This assessment concords with the position taken by Tournier 2017, 154: "la seule version canonique du récit de Ghaṭikāra et Jyotipāli qui accorde une place à la notion de *praṇidhāna* est le *Jyotipālasūtra* du *Mahāvastu*. S'il partage, pour l'essentiel, la trame du récit du *Ghaṭikārasutta* pāli et de ses parallèles du *Madhyama-Āgama* et du *Saṅghabhedavastu*, il porte la marque d'une série de révisions qui le distingue de la perspective des trois précédents textes: l'insistance sur le *praṇidhāna* et le *vyākaraṇa*, que l'adjonction du *Jyotipālavyākaraṇa* vient encore asseoir, est l'une de plus significatives. Compte tenu de l'apparition de ces unités micro-textuelles dans les autres récits de la première partie du *Mahāvastu*, cette place faite aux deux actions majeures du progrès spirituel du *bodhisattva* s'explique vraisemblablement par l'influence de ces récits" (see also above the final part of n. 358).

367. Two examples already mentioned by Drewes 2007, 134 are SN 15.3 at SN II 179,25, according to which the tears shed by the members of the audience exceed even the waters of the four great oceans, and SN 56.47 at SN V 455,24, according to which the probability of a human rebirth for those in the lower realms is even less than the

probability of a blind turtle surfacing once every hundred years to put its head through the opening of a yoke floating on the surface of the ocean. The contrast between the four great oceans and the tears features also in the parallels to SN 15.3, SĀ 938 at T 2.99.240c28 and SĀ² 331 at T 2.100.486a22, both of which refer to the river Ganges flowing into these four oceans (the actual comparison in SĀ² 331 then just concerns the water of the Ganges); another parallel, EĀ 51.1 at T 2.125.814a28, from the outset just refers to the water of the river Ganges. Yet another parallel in fragment SHT I 167R4, Waldschmidt, Clawiter, and Holzmann 1965, 95, has preserved a reference to the river Ganges. The simile of the blind turtle in SN 56.47 has parallels in a Gāndhārī manuscript, Allon 2007, and in SĀ 406 at T 2.99.108c7.

368. On instances of the crescendo effect in *Āgama* literature as a counterpart to its usage in the *Aṣṭasāhasrikā Prajñāpāramitā* see Anālayo 2024c. Its employment in the present context can be considered to combine the use of repetition with self-promotion as two aspects identified by Lopez 1995, 41 as characteristic of Mahāyāna *sūtra* literature, in that "the Mahāyāna sūtras have many of the qualities of the Nikāyas—redundancy, stock phrases, reliance on lists . . . The Mahāyāna sūtras differ from the earlier works, however, in their self-consciousness and often exaltation of their own status as texts, as physical objects, with many works being devoted almost entirely to descriptions of benefits to be gained by reciting, copying, and worshipping them."

An example for promotional strategies found in *Āgama* literature would be the Buddha's revelation that in future times monastics will not be keen on the profound teachings given by him that are connected to emptiness (Pāli: *suññatapaṭisaṃyutta*) and will not learn and transmit them, a dire scenario leading to his injunction to the monastics present on this occasion that they should make an effort to learn and transmit such teachings; see SN 20.7 at SN II 267,19 and its parallel SĀ 1258 at T 2.99.345b20. Notably, in this case the whole discourse serves the purpose of textual promotion. This is its overarching concern to such an extent that it does not contain or even reference any actual teaching related to emptiness, and it is left to the Pāli commentary to try to identify what discourses this promotional effort has in mind; see Spk II 229,5.

The commentary then refers to a *Saṅkhittasaṃyutta*, the implication of which is not entirely clear, as such a *saṃyutta* does not appear to be known. Malalasekera 1938/1998, 982 reasons that "[t]he reference is probably to the Saṭṭhipeyyāla," found at SN IV 148,26 to 156,15, but this is just a repetition series related to the three characteristics, without any mention of *suññatā*, so that the proposed identification remains doubtful. A gloss on the same expression *suññatapaṭisaṃyutta* in Spk III 291,9 mentions the *Khajjaniyasutta* (SN 22.79), found in the *Khandhasaṃyutta* at SN III 86,9. At any rate, both references are to a *saṃyutta* or a particular discourse of the *Saṃyuttanikāya*. Given the division among reciters according to the four *nikāya*s (Anālayo 2022d, 120), by the time of the composition of the commentaries the *Saṃyuttanikāya* could be considered as representative of a particular textual community. This would in turn bring the case of the promotional effort articulated in SN 20.7 closer to the wider category of self-promotion of a particular textual community that is characteristic of a range of early Mahāyāna *sūtra*s.

In sum, the present case goes to show that promotional attempts are not confined to early Mahāyāna *sūtra*s, as these can also be found among *Āgama* literature, and that even in relation to the transmission of teachings on emptiness. In fact, both versions of the discourse under discussion quite explicitly warn of the future danger that the discourses related to emptiness will disappear; see SN 20.7 at SN II 267,15 and its parallel SĀ 1258 at T 2.99.345b17. Although they do not employ the hyperbole with which some early Mahāyāna *sūtra*s articulate textual promotion, the fact remains that both versions of the discourse are in their entirety dedicated to such promotional purposes, from beginning to end.

369. Harrison 2022, 659n24 relates this part to a passage in the *Pratyutpannabuddhasaṃmukhāvasthitasamādhisūtra* (3F), Harrison 1978b, 31,24: *gzugs chud mi gzon to, tshor ba dang 'du shes dang 'du byed dang rnam par shes pa chud mi gzon to* (here and elsewhere, I adjust to the Wylie system). In a note to his translation of this passage, Harrison 1990, 37n11 quotes another similar occurrence in the *Ratnacandraparipṛcchāsūtra* (the most directly relevant part reads: *gzugs dang tshor ba dang 'du shes dang 'du byed dang rnam par shes pa med par mi 'gyur ro*) followed by offering the following comment: "That the basic elements of existence 'do not perish' (*chud mi gzon*) or 'do not cease to exist' (*med par mi 'gyur*) is presumably to be understood as a formulation of a non-substantialist rather than eternalist position." In fact, as noted by Salomon 2018, 402n449 in relation to the Gāndhārī manuscript version of the Perfection of Wisdom: "the statement 'Form is impermanent,' which is here attributed to the teachers of the imitation Perfection of Wisdom, does not conflict with the doctrine of genuine Perfection of Wisdom."

370. Falk and Karashima 2013, 116: [*ṇa vaṇa*] *kośiga* [*ruavi*]*ṇaśeṇa* [*ruaaṇicada pa*] + + + + + .. [*daṇa*]*saṃñasaṃ*[*kha*]*ro viñaṇo* [*ṇa ho vaṇa*] *kośiga viñaṇaviṇaśeṇa viñaṇaaṇicada paśi* ++ + + + *evaṃ paśati prañaparamidae pa*[*ḍivaṇa*]*gae carati*. In the case of Lokakṣema's translation, Karashima 2011, 116,3+6 (= T 8.224.437a10+13), it remains uncertain if the Indic original had a version of Sanskrit *prativarṇika*; see also Karashima 2011, 116n692+694.

371. Wogihara 1932/1935, 299,12: *rūpasya kṣaṇād ūrdhvam anavasthānam vināśo rūpānityatā*. The context qualifies form to be *kalpita* or *vikalpita*, and the present part concerns the second type; on *kalpita* and *vikalpita* see in more detail Urban and Griffith 1994. Thompson 2008, 255n22 offers the following assessment: "Some texts speak of a 'counterfeit *prajñāpāramitā*' in which a Bodhisattva teaches impermanence and destruction of *dharmas*," which intends the "Sarvāstivāda analyses of *dharmas* into their arising, [momentary] persisting, decay, and destruction."

372. The relevant exposition in Karashima 2011, 116,1 (= T 8.224.437a8) refers to future sons and daughters of a good family wishing to train in the Perfection of Wisdom for the sake of attaining supreme, complete awakening who are being obstructed by a bad friend teaching the imitation Perfection of Wisdom: 當來善男子, 善女人, 欲得阿耨多羅三耶三菩阿惟三佛, 喜樂學般若波羅蜜, 反得惡知識教掖椷般若波羅蜜. What has been preserved in the Gāndhārī manuscript suggests a similar situation; see Falk and Karashima 2013, 112: *[pra]ñaparamidae paḍivaṃṇiga tatra so kulaputro va kuladhita vi [aṇ]u[tarae saṃ]ma + + + + + duamo ma praṇaśiśati ta paḍivaṃṇiga śrunita*.

373. According to von Rospatt 1995, 28, in the "still-extant Abhidharmapiṭakas . . . as in the Nikāyas/Āgamas, the theory of momentariness is not postulated as a canonical doctrine and is only attested, if at all, as a sectarian stance to be refuted. This implies that the theory developed after the schism of the sects within certain schools and is in that sense a post-canonical development which . . . may date back as far as the first century A.D., possibly even beyond."

374. Karashima 2011, 116,3+6 (= T 8.224.437a10+13): 惡知識; see also T 8.225.486a2+3: 惡友 and T 8.226.518c18+21: 惡師. In contrast, T 8.227.546c2+4 and T 8.228.605a5+11 do not convey any negative evaluation.

375. Wogihara 1932/1935, 298,23: *'bhāvitakāya abhāvitaśīla abhāvitacittā abhāvitaprajñā eḍamūkajātīyā prajñāparihīnās*, D 12 *ka* 63b5 or P 734 *mi* 67a7: *lus ma bsgoms pa tshul khrims ma bsgoms pa sems ma bsgoms pa shes rab ma bsgoms pa shes rab 'chal pa lug ltar lkug pa'i rang bzhin can shes rab yongs su nyams pa dag 'byung ste*, and T 7.220.784c27: 不能善修身戒心慧, 智慧狹劣, 猶如牛羊; a less strongly articulated censure can be found in T 7.220.879b9: 愚癡顛倒.

376. AN 3.47 at AN I 152,5 and its parallel EĀ 22.5 at T 2.125.607c14.

377. Notably, even when the commentary on the *Visuddhimagga* rejects this position, this is still not seen as a dismissal of impermanence but instead correctly identified as an attempt to expound the law of dependent arising. Ñāṇamoli 1991, 829n6 quotes the following assessment: "some misinterpret the meaning of dependent origination thus, 'Without cessation, without arising' (*anuppādaṃ anirodhaṃ*) instead of taking the unequivocal meaning in the way stated," corresponding to Skilling 2018, 62n52: *yathā ca eke anirodhaṃ anuppādan ti ādinā paṭiccasamuppādassa atthaṃ micchā gāhenti, evaṃ gāhe akatvā vuttanayen' eva aviparītaṃ atthaṃ gāhantena.*

378. Karashima 2011, 153,11 (= T 8.224.440a16): 其法者, 爲無所生, 法亦無有滅, 法亦無所從生, 法亦無所從滅; 於法中, 了無有生者, 法亦無所從有而滅. My attempt at translation involves rendering the second and third instances of 從 as "toward," following the indication in Karashima 2010, 94 that in Lokakṣema's usage this character can also convey "towards, to." This alternative meaning fits the case of cessation better than the meaning "from," employed for the first instance of 從 related to arising.

379. In this respect, it is perhaps of interest to note that in one of three early Mahāyāna texts edited by Schlosser 2022, 142, Bajaur Kharoṣṭhi Fragment 11v19, a reference can be found to not coming from anywhere and not going anywhere, which occurs in the context of a description of different insight-related perspectives that also include the aspects of being impermanent, not self, and empty: *aṇicagareṇa aṇatvagareṇa śuñagareṇa . . . akuhicaagamaṇaakuhicagamaṇaagareṇa*. In a comment on this line, Schlosser 2022, 234 notes an occurrence of the notion of not coming from anywhere and not going anywhere in the *Aṣṭādaśasāhasrikā Prajñāpāramitā* from Gilgit, Conze 1974, 65,19, which takes the form *akutaścid āgamanataś ca akvacid gamanataś ca*, applied to the five aggregates. Another relevant reference in Bajaur Kharoṣṭhi Fragment 6r1, Schlosser 2022, 146, seems to relate viewing the aggregates, elements, and sense spheres as permanent and a self to the notion of coming from anywhere and going anywhere: *ime kadhadhaduaïdaṇa ṇice dakṣiśati atva . . . kuhicaagamaṇa(*ku) h(*icagamaṇa) ca bhaveadi* (see also 6r7). These references would concord with the proposed reading of the passage from T 224 quoted in the previous note, and they would also align with the discourse passages surveyed in the notes below.

380. This assertion takes the form of an exchange between the Buddha and *deva*s, who ask him if this is indeed the case, which the Buddha then confirms; see Karashima 2011, 293,11 (= T 8.224.453b4): 諸天子問佛: 何謂隨怛薩阿竭教? 如法無所從生, 爲隨怛薩阿竭教乎? 佛言: 如是, 諸天子. 諸法無所從生[,] 爲隨怛薩阿竭教. The posing of such a query by *deva*s seems to provide a convenient opportunity for the articulation of uncertainty and its resolution, presumably reflecting a type of reaction that

teachers of the Perfection of Wisdom may expect to encounter among their potential audiences.

381. Up 1013 at D 4094 *ju* 14a6 or P 5595 *tu* 15b5: *dge slong, 'du byed sgyu ma lta bu, smig rgyu lta bu . . . ma byung ba las byung zhing byung nas kyang 'jig pa ste. dge slong, de'i phyir 'du byed ni stong pa.* The passage continues by relating emptiness to impermanence. Chung 2008, 84 notes an application to all *dharma*s of this relationship between emptiness and impermanence in the *Yogācārabhūmi*; see Delhey 2009, 184,16: *sarvadharmāñ śūnyān pratyavekṣate nityena yāvad ātmanātmīyeneti.*

382. SĀ 273 at T 2.99.72c13: 不實來實去, which similarly leads on to expounding their empty nature in terms of the absence of permanence and of a self or what belongs to a self. According to a gloss provided in the *Yogācārabhūmi* on the present discourse, identified as such in Yìnshùn 1983, 354 and found at T 30.1579.820c26, conditioned phenomena "come from nowhere and proceed toward nowhere," 來無所從, 往無所至.

383. EĀ 51.8 at T 2.125.819c14: 若眼起時, 則起亦不知來處; 若眼滅時, 則滅亦不知去處 (adopting a 宋, 元, and 明 variant reading that adds 則起 after 時 in the case of arising, in analogy to the case of cessation).

384. Vism 484,6: *na hi tāni pubbe udayā kutoci āgacchanti, na pi uddhaṃ vayā kuhiñci gacchanti.* Notably, Cp-a 299,27 relates this type of insight to those who are established in patience that is in conformity: *tato ca anulomiyaṃ khantiyaṃ ṭhito kevalā ime attattaniyabhāvarahitā dhammamattā yathāsakaṃ paccayehi uppajjanti, vayanti, na kutoci āgacchanti, na kuhiñci gacchanti, na ca katthaci patiṭṭhitā.*

385. SN 12.12 at SN II 13,25, with parallels in SĀ 372 at T 2.99.102a25 and Up 9028 at D 4094 *nyu* 87a6 or P 5595 *thu* 134a5. The basically same problem recurs when Polak 2023 tries to find out who identifies with the aggregates, leading him to posit an agent of clinging that exists apart from the aggregates. This exemplifies how asking a wrongly formulated question results in arriving at wrong conclusions.

386. SN 12.18 at SN II 22,15, with parallels in Chung and Fukita 2020, 175 (abbreviated) and SĀ 303 at T 2.99.86c6.

387. Karashima 2011, 153,9 (= T 8.224.440a15): 過去, 當來, 今現在法無所取, 亦無所捨, 亦無所知, 亦無所得.

388. T 7.220.515c19: 又如虛空, 前, 後, 中際皆不可得 . . . 過去世過去世空, 未來世未來世空, 現在世現在世空; 三世平等, 三世平等空. On the rejection of the three periods of time see also Lancaster 1974/1991, 499.

389. Karashima 2011, 173,9 (= T 8.224.441c25): 色之自然故爲色 . . . 過去色之自然色故 . . . 當來色之自然色故 . . . 今現在 . . . 色之自然色故; Karashima 2011, 173n398 (again 174n400) comments on 自然 that "Lokakṣema seems to have mistaken *a-svabhāvatva* for *svabhāvatva*." A misunderstanding of a negation in an Indic original can indeed easily happen, as can be seen from its apparent recurrence in T 8.226.523b19, T 8.227.551b11, and T 8.228.616a15. Alternatively, the same recurrence may result from being influenced by the precedent set by T 224, given that, as noted by Harrison 2010, 234, there is a "strong tendency in the Chinese translation tradition . . . for newer translations to draw inspiration from, echo, or simply repeat older ones." The Sanskrit version, Wogihara 1932/1935, 405,18, reads: *rūpāsvabhāvatvāt, subhūte, rūpam. . . pūrvāntāsvabhāvaṃ hi, subhūte, rūpam . . . aparāntāsvabhāvaṃ hi, subhūte, rūpam . . . pratyutpannāsvabhāvaṃ hi, subhūte, pratyutpannaṃ rūpam*, with its Tibetan counterpart in D 12 *ka* 104a7 or P 734 *mi* 112a2: *rab 'byor, gzugs ngo bo nyid med pa'i phyir gzugs . . . rab 'byor, gzugs la sngon gyi mtha'i ngo bo nyid med pa'i phyir ro . . . rab*

*'byor, gzugs la phyi ma'i mtha'i ngo bo nyid med pa'i phyir ro . . . rab 'byor, gzugs la da ltar byung ba'i ngo bo nyid med pa'i phyir ro.* A rendering in line with what appears to be the required sense can be seen in T 7.220.801c21: 色以無性爲自性故 . . . 善現, 色前際以無性爲自性故 . . . 色後際以無性爲自性故 . . . 色中際以無性爲自性故; see also T 7.220.885a27: 色以無性爲自性故 . . . 善現, 色前, 後, 中際皆以無性爲自性故. Needless to say, the same applies to the remaining four aggregates.

390. See, e.g., SN 22.62 at SN III 71,15.

391. In the context of arguing that criticism voiced in the *Aṣṭasāhasrikā Prajñāpāramitā* need not be considered as invariably aimed at Sarvāstivāda doctrine, Onishi 1999, 179 (see also 176–77) nevertheless acknowledges that "the Aṣṭa contains references to the Sarvāstivādin notion of the real existence of [phenomena in] the three time-periods and criticizes it." Regarding this notion, Mizuno 1961, 70 explains that the "*Vijñāna-kāya* clearly expresses for the first time the thought of 'the real existence of phenomena in the three states of time,'" whereby this work, reflecting the middle period in the development of the canonical Sarvāstivāda Abhidharma collection, "laid the theoretical foundation of the school" of the Sarvāstivādins. These take the position "that not only the present, but the past and future phenomena also have real existence (as an entity) throughout the three states of time." The relevant discussion in the *Vijñānakāya* begins at T 26.1539.531a27; see also de La Vallée-Poussin 1925/1991, 82–94 and, on the work in general, Willemen, Dessein, and Cox 1998, 66–67, 72–73, and 197–205. On occurrences of this notion in two discourse quotations in the *Abhidharmakośopāyikā-ṭīkā* see Dhammadinnā 2019, 8–14.

392. See in more detail, e.g., Sinha 1983, 85–104, Dhammajoti 2002/2007, 144–80, Dessein 2007a, and Maas 2020, 968–77.

393. See, e.g., MN 63 at MN I 426,10: *sassato loko ti* ($C^e$ and $E^e$: *iti*) *pi, asassato loko ti* ($C^e$ and $E^e$: *iti*) *pi,* with parallels in MĀ 221 at T 1.26.804a26: 世有常, 世無有常 and T 1.94.917b18: 世間有常, 世間無常.

394. See, e.g., Oldenberg 1881/1961, 256–63, Schrader 1904/1905, Beckh 1919, 118–21, Keith 1923/1979, 62–67, Thomas 1927/2003, 201–2, de La Vallée Poussin 1928, Organ 1954, Murti 1955/2008, 36–50, Nagao 1955/1992, 38, Frauwallner 1956/2003, 141–42, Edgerton 1959, 82–83, Tatia 1960, Jayatilleke 1963/1980, 470–76, Smart 1964/1976, 34–35, Warder 1970/1991, 137–41, Robinson 1972, Kalupahana 1975, 177–78, Lamotte 1976, 2003–5, Ruegg 1977, 1–2, Collins 1982, 131–38, King 1983, 263, Pannikar 1989/1990, 61–76, Rigopoulos 1992, 1993, Tilakaratne 1993, 109–21, Oetke 1994, Harvey 1995, 84–87, Holder 1996, 449–50, Vélez de Cea 2004, Manda 2005, Karunadasa 2007, 2013, 129–49, Anālayo 2017f, 13–15, 2018c, 39–44, 2022a 1412–14, and Lin 2022.

395. The idea of such cross-relating could find support in a passage from the *Dà zhìdù lùn* (**Mahāprajñāpāramitopadeśa*), which occurs in the context of a survey of instances of teachings on the emptiness of dharmas found in *Āgama* literature. The passage in question mentions the rejection of another of the positions taken in the standard questionnaire, regarding the identity or difference between the life principle and the body; see T 25.1509.192c29: 若有人言: 身即是神, 若言: 身異於神, 是二雖異, 同爲邪見. 佛言: 身即是神, 如是邪見, 非我弟子; 身異於神, 亦是邪見, 非我弟子. 是經中佛說法空. Although this falls short of explicitly mentioning the case of the world being either eternal or not eternal, given the instance from the standard questionnaire it does mention it seems that, from the perspective of the *Dà zhìdù lùn*, the refusal to affirm

the nature of the world as either eternal or not eternal would probably also qualify as a teaching on the emptiness of dharmas.

396. Karashima 2011, 133,4 (= T 8.224.438b5): 但用無黠故，還墮四顛倒: 無常謂有常 (etc.). The same four perversions recur in Lokakṣema's translation of the **Kāśyapaparivarta* together with the required antidotes—the "medicines" for curing them—which in the case of the perversion of perception under discussion then is indeed the fact of impermanence; see T 12.350.191c25: 四顛倒各自有藥. 何等爲各自有藥? 一者有常以無常爲藥. Notably, at an earlier point the same work dismisses impermanence as one of two extremes, T 12.350.190c17: 有常在一邊, 無常在一邊, 有常無常適在其中. A reading able to accommodate these two statements could be developed by assuming that the rejection of dualistic contrasts need not necessarily be meant to reject impermanence as such. Another text translated by Lokakṣema (see Nattier 2005), T 10.282.453a11, describes how seeing people afflicted by illness motivates a bodhisattva's aspiration in a form that conveniently combines impermanence with emptiness: 十方天下人皆使念無常, 悉入虛空中.

397. Karashima 2011, 330,2 (= T 8.224.457a28): 佛言: 云何? 心前滅, 後復生耶? 須菩提言: 不也. 佛言: 心初生, 可滅不? 須菩提言: 可滅. 佛言: 當所滅者, 寧可使不滅不? 須菩提言: 不也; for translating 當所滅者 I have taken a lead from Karashima 2011, 330n257.

398. Kimura 2009, 6,26: *rūpam anityam iti pratyavekṣate na copalabhate* (also in Dutt 1934, 154,23)—the same of course holds for the other aggregates—with its Tibetan counterpart in D 9 *ka* 162b5 or P 731 *nyi* 162b6: *gzugs mi rtag ces bya bar rtog ste de mi dmigs so.* Some variations occur among the Chinese versions, where T 7.220.54a19: 觀色無常相, 亦不可得 and T 8.223.240a20: 觀色無常相, 是亦不可得 agree with the Sanskrit and Tibetan, but the earliest translation by Dharmarakṣa, T 8.222.175b4, recommends the opposite of *not* contemplating impermanence: 不觀色無常, 色亦不可得. This presumably requires an emendation by deleting the 不 found before the 觀.

399. Karashima 2011,142,4 (= T 8.224.439a8): 其作想者, 譬若雜毒. 何以故? 若設美飯, 以毒著中, 色大甚好而香, 無不喜者. 不知飯中有毒, 愚闇之人食之, 歡喜飽滿. 食欲消時, 久久大不便身. The translation of 想 here and elsewhere is based on the indication by Karashima 2010, 536 that its usage by Lokakṣema can render "sign," corresponding to Sanskrit (and Pāli) *nimitta*. This lack of a clear dividing line between 想 and 相 is in keeping with a recurrent tendency in Chinese translations of Buddhist texts to alternate between these two characters. In fact, 想 and 相 are not only similar in writing (differing just in the addition of the heart radical 心 in the case of the former) and in pronunciation (see Pulleyblank 1991, 337 and 338) but in addition also tend to convey related meanings in their use in Buddhist texts; see also the discussion of relevant usage in Kumārajīva's translation of the *Vajracchedikā Prajñāpāramitā* in Harrison 2010, 240 and Zacchetti 2015a. Notably, Lokakṣema in fact uses 思想 rather than just 想 on its own for the case of the third aggregate of perception. As for the expression 作想, Karashima 2010, 697 indicates that another occurrence of this expression in T 8.224.442c11 corresponds to *nimittato manasikaroti* in the Sanskrit version, Wogihara 1932/1935, 417,26, which makes it fair to assume a similar sense would be relevant to the present context, namely paying attention by means of signs.

400. MN 46 at MN I 316,10 and its parallels MĀ 175 at T 1.26.713a11 and T 1.83.902c15.

401. MN 105 at MN II 260,25. Although Sanskrit fragments have preserved parallels to several other sections of this discourse, these do not seem to cover the present simile;

see Anālayo 2011b, 610n131 (the same holds for the subsequently published fragments in Wille 2015, 88 and Hartmann and Wille 2016).

402. SN 12.66 at SN II 110,1 and its parallel SĀ 291 at T 2.99.82b22 (where the poison has been put into a roadside pond that travelers may wish to drink from).

403. SN 41.7 at SN IV 297,24: *rāgo . . . nimittakaraṇo, doso nimittakaraṇo, moho nimittakaraṇo* and SĀ 567 at T 2.99.150a7: 貪者是有相, 恚, 癡者是有相.

404. I am indebted to Ñāṇananda 2015, 283 for the basic idea of the river simile.

405. What follows is based on extracts from Anālayo 2023d, 3–59, in which I examine in more detail the role of signs and meditative practices related to them, especially the cultivation of signlessness.

406. AN 6.60 at AN III 397,11 and its parallel MĀ 82 at T 1.26.559a21 (adopting the 宋 variant 無相 instead of 無想); see also Anālayo 2023d, 29–30.

407. See above p. 294 for a report of how the Buddha, on the eve of his final Nirvana, crossed the river Ganges by supernatural means and then delivered a poem that plays on the metaphorical sense of using a vehicle for crossing over.

408. Karashima 2011, 180,14 (= T 8.224.442b27): 知色空者, 是曰爲著; 知痛痒, 思想, 生死, 識空者, 是曰爲著; 於過去法, 知過去法, 是曰爲著; 於當來法, 知當來法, 是曰爲著; 於現在法, 知現在法, 是曰爲著. The translation follows the indication in Karashima 2010, 636 that in the present context 知 conveys "perceiving" and related terms like "recognizing," "considering," or "deeming."

409. Karashima 2011, 180,11 (= T 8.224.442b25): 有字者, 便有想. 以故著; on 字 and 便 see Karashima 2010, 41 and 661 (on the translation of 想 see above n. 399). The first part of the quote relates perception to "name" (*nāma*/字). In *Āgama* literature, *nāma* designates a set of mental activities apart from consciousness that comprise, in addition to perception, feeling tone, intention, contact, and attention; see SN 12.2 at SN II 3,34, with a parallel EĀ 49.5 at T 2.125.797b28 (on whose wording see also Anālayo 2020a, 1132), and a more detailed discussion in Anālayo 2018c, 9–14 and 2024a, 82–86. In combination, the mental activities subsumed under the header of *nāma* perform the function of cognizing and recognizing, that is, the function of giving a "name" to something.

410. Karashima 2011, 179,5 (= T 8.224.442b11): 我者清淨.

411. Wogihara 1932/1935, 412,8: *ātmanaḥ paraparikalpitasya paramārthato 'nutpattiviśuddhis*.

412. SN 5.10 at SN I 135,19: *suddhasaṅkhārapuñjo yaṃ*. SĀ 1202 at T 2.99.327b8 reads 唯有空陰聚, which through the employment of "only," 唯, still captures the sense conveyed by the phrase under discussion. The notion of being "empty" serves as the prominent theme in the other two discourse parallels SĀ² 218 at T 2.100.454c28: 假空以聚會 and Up 9014 at D 4094 *nyu* 82a7 or P 5595 *thu* 128b2: *'du byed phung po 'di stong ste*; see also Enomoto 1994, 42 (= Pradhan 1967, 466,2): *śūnyaḥ saṃskārapuñjo 'yaṃ*.

413. T 25.1509.514b22: 如虛空塵水不著, 性清淨故; 般若波羅蜜亦如是, 不生不滅故, 常清淨. 如虛空不可染污, 般若波羅蜜亦如是 . . . 不可染污.

414. MN 51 at MN I 349,2: *brahmabhūtena attanā viharatī ti*.

415. Pérez-Rémon 1980, 118 reasons that occurrences of the expression *brahmabhūtena attanā viharati* "refer to a self that is free from all attachment . . . Such a usage of *attā* gives the term a prominence that could not be expected from people utterly convinced that the basic teaching of early Buddhism was that of absolute *anattā*"; for a survey of scholarly discussions relevant to this expression see Anālayo 2023d, 186n268.

416. Karashima 2011, 167,7 (= T 8.224.441b8): 用是斷法罪故, 死入大泥犁中. 若干百千歲, 若干億千萬歲, 當更若干泥犁中, 具受諸毒痛不可言. 其中壽盡, 轉生他方摩訶泥犁中. 其壽復盡, 展轉復到他方摩訶泥犁中生.

417. Karashima 2011, 168,8 (= T 8.224.441b13): 若諷誦說深般若波羅蜜時, 其心疑於法者, 亦不肯學, 念是言: 非怛薩阿竭所說. 止他人言: 莫得學是! The very opposite type of attitude, being thus the commendable reaction to hearing the Perfection of Wisdom, can be seen described in Karashima 2011, 432,3 (= T 8.224.467c21): 菩薩聞深般若波羅蜜, 信不狐疑, 菩薩作是念: 如佛所說, 諦無異.

418. Karashima 2011, 169,4 (= T 8.224.441b19): 舍利弗, 不當與共坐起, 言語, 飲食. 何以故? 是曹之人誹謗法者, 自在冥中, 復持他人著冥中.

419. MacQueen 1981, 304 comments on another such reference in the *Aṣṭasāhasrikā Prajñāpāramitā* that a rejection of the authenticity of the text "is obviously viewed as very dangerous . . . The efforts . . . to call Mahāyānists back to orthodoxy were seen as a terrible temptation which a member of the new movement (a *bodhisattva*) must reject at all costs."

420. A minor difference is that according to SN 35.135 the Buddha made a point of noting that he had seen this himself, SN IV 126,3: *diṭṭhā mayā, bhikkhave, cha phassāyatanikā nāma nirayā*, whereas the parallel SĀ 210 at T 2.53a13 simply states that there is such a hell, 有六觸入處地獄. The indication in SN 35.135 could be a later addition. Besides not being found in the parallel SĀ 210, it also does not fit the context particularly well. With such a general reference to the nature of hell there is hardly a need for authentication by way of the Buddha emphasizing that he has seen this himself.

421. Spk II 400,8 explains that, although the name *chaphassāyatanika* is applicable to all hells, in the present context the reference is in particular to Avīci, *idam pana avīci mahānirayaṃ sandhāya vuttaṃ*. For the case of heaven, Spk II 400,10 then takes the corresponding description to intend Tāvatiṃsa. Malalasekera 1937/1995, 200 notes that the term *avīci* occurs in the four *Nikāya*s only in DN 26 at DN III 75,11 and AN 3.56 at AN I 159,29, where it functions as an adjective to convey the sense of something being "without an interval" or "uninterrupted," used here to express a density of population. As a noun, the term *avīci* occurs outside of the four *Nikāya*s to designate the hell in which Devadatta was reborn; see It 3.4.10 at It 86,7 (= Vin II 203,11). Although a precise stratification of these texts is not possible, in general material found in the *Vinaya* and the *Itivuttaka* can testify to more developed notions than those reflected in the four *Nikāya*s. If this should hold for the present case as well, then the usage of *avīci* to designate a hell would be slightly later than, and presumably inspired by, the employment of *avīci* to convey the quality of being uninterrupted.

422. MN 50 at MN I 337,7 lists *chaphassāyataniko* as one of several alternative names for the Great Hell, which has a counterpart in 六更 as an alternative name of the great hell mentioned in the parallel MĀ 131 at T 1.26.622a20. The same 六更 occurs in T 1.66.866a18, although here it seems to function more as a qualification of the Great Hell. Another two parallels, T 1.67.868a20 and Up 3021 at D 4094 *ju* 119a4 or P 5595 *tu* 136b4, just refer to the "Great Hell," 大地獄/*dmyal ba chen po*, without bringing in the notion of the six spheres of contact. Overall, this leaves open the possibility that the usage of this notion as a proper name for a hell could be the result of some development.

423. Spk II 400,15: *manussaloko pana vokiṇṇasukhadukkho, idh' eva apāyo pi saggo pi paññāyati.*

424. AN 7.68 at AN IV 128,10 and its parallels MĀ 5 at T 1.26.425a22 and EĀ 33.10 at T 2.125.689a8; in the last case the image is more general and does not specify that the fire or the beautiful woman is being hugged. On this discourse see also below n. 710.
425. EĀ 33.10 at T 2.125.689b15: 比丘當知, 如我今日觀無戒之人所趣向處, 設彼人間者, 形體枯悴, 沸血從面孔出, 便取命終.
426. AN 7.68 at AN IV 131,23 and its parallel MĀ 5 at T 1.26.426a19 refer to a strong person, *balavā puriso*/力士, who forces the mouth open and inserts the hot metal ball; EĀ 33.10 at T 2.125.689b2 has no such specification, so that here the comparison is simply between swallowing the iron ball and swallowing the undeserved food. The ball in AN 7.68 is made of *loha*; for a discussion of the significance of this term see Marino 2019, 33–34.
427. Dhp 308, with Indic language parallels in the Gāndhārī *Dharmapada* 331, Brough 1962/2001, 171, the Patna *Dharmapada* 295, Cone 1989, 180, and the Sanskrit *Udānavarga* 9.2, Bernhard 1965, 169. The notion of a metal ball, apparently also burning, occurs as well in Dhp 371c–d, with Indic language parallels in the Gāndhārī *Dharmapada* 75c–d, Brough 1962/2001, 129, the Patna *Dharmapada* 33c–d, Cone 1989, 112, and the Sanskrit *Udānavarga* 31.31c–d, Bernhard 1965, 418, the last of which explicitly refers to hell. A Chinese version of Dhp 308 comes embedded in a commentary, T 4.212.668b1, which depicts in detail the repercussions of swallowing such a burning iron ball and then points out that such suffering is confined to the present, unlike rebirth in lower realms with their uncountable sufferings, 猶如鐵丸猛火燒赤, 取而吞之, 燒脣, 燒舌, 燒咽, 燒腹下過. 雖有此苦, 自致死亡, 不緣此入地獄, 餓鬼, 畜生受苦無量 (adopting a CBETA emendation of 父 to read 火). Commenting on Dhp 308, Dhp-a III 480,10 refers to the episode leading to the promulgation of the fourth *pārājika* regarding false claims to higher attainments, where the verse indeed occurs at Vin III 90,27. It 2.2.11 at It 43,7 also has this verse, preceded here by a prose passage that predicts rebirth in hell not only for breaches of monastic celibacy but also for unfounded accusations that another monastic has committed such a breach; another occurrence in the same collection is It 3.5.2 at It 90,12. The second of these two unwholesome actions provides the narrative setting for yet another reference to a burning iron ball in SĀ 1075 at T 2.99.280b21 and SĀ$^2$ 14 at T 2.100.378a25 (see also Enomoto 1994, 21), spoken by the Buddha precisely in reference to such an unfounded accusation. In the Pāli tradition, the episode leading up to the Buddha's censure occurs at Vin II 79,36 and Vin III 163,15, which only refer in brief to this censure and presumably for this reason do not employ the verse; for a remarkable study of this episode in different *Vinaya*s, clarifying an aspect of it that has since ancient times been causing perplexity, see Clarke 2008. The relationship to falsehood, evident in this case, is the main theme of another occurrence of this verse in some versions of an instruction given by the Buddha to his son, Rāhula, on the need to be truthful; see Skilling 1996b and Anālayo 2011b, 344n21. A relationship to slander appears to stand in the background to Sn 667, which refers to hot iron balls as the appropriate food. The notion of appropriateness presumably applies to those who engage in slander, as the preceding prose narration reports Kokālika wrongly accusing Sāriputta and Mahāmoggallāna of being under the influence of evil desires; see also Pj II 480,1: *patirūpan ti katakammānurūpaṃ*. Another usage of the same motif of the hot iron ball occurs in a simile in SĀ 1259 at T 2.99.345b25, according to which the predicament of a monastic who goes

begging without sense restraint and ends up burning with sensual desire is comparable to placing an iron ball into fire. The above are just a few selected instances to illustrate different employments of the motif of the burning metal/iron ball; further examples can be found in the notes below.

428. SĀ 241 at T 2.99.58a11: 墮惡趣中, 如沈鐵丸 (repeated for each of the five senses); the parallel SN 35.194 at SN IV 168,20 does not refer to a metal ball or employ any other illustration in relation to the dire prospect of a bad rebirth. For the sixth sense of the mind, the two versions agree in presenting sleep as preferable to thinking detrimental thoughts (which SN 35.194 at SN IV 169,32 relates more specifically to the problem of creating a schism). References to rebirth in bad realms have also been preserved in the Sanskrit fragment parallel, Nagashima 2015, 369–70, Or.15009/537 v4: *anyatamānyatamāṃ durgatiṃ*, Or.15009/539r6: *tisṛṇāṃ durgatīnāṃ anyatamānya*, and Or.15009/539v3: *kariṣyāmi yat tisṛṇāṃ durgat[ī]*.

429. SN 56.43 at SN V 450,31 and SĀ 422 at T 2.99.111b11, in contrast to the Gāndhārī fragment in Marino 2017, 154 (line 13). In the course of a detailed discussion of this reference in the light of its parallels, Marino 2017, 71 notes that a similar description can be found in the *Mahāvastu*, according to which Avīci/Avīcī hell is similar to a burning iron ball; see Marciniak 2022, 316,9 (also in Senart 1882, 15,15).

430. EĀ 21.9 at T 2.125.605b8: 欲者亦無有常.

431. MN 13 at MN I 87,22, MĀ 99 at T 1.26.585c7, T 1.53.847c5, and T 17.737.540a21.

432. SN 19.1 at SN II 255,11 (= Vin III 105,15) and SĀ 509 at T 2.99.135c1; on the role of Mahāmaudgalyāyana in such contexts see also Gifford 2003. The fact that these birds have something to peck at (according to SĀ 509 something to eat, 食) suggests that this sentient being should have at least some meaty parts left, in addition to the bones and tendons that make up the skeleton. A comparable case can be found in the *Mahāvastu*, Senart 1882, 7,4, which reports that the meaty parts eaten by the birds regrow afterward, a narrative detail that helps appreciate how the birds have something to continue pecking at.

433. SĀ 527 at T 2.99.138a15: 有熾熱鐵丸, 從身出入, SĀ 530 at T 2.99.138b20: 食熱鐵丸, and SĀ 533 at T 2.99.138c26: 亦以鐵鉢盛熱, 鐵丸而食之.

434. The relevant passage in the *Mahāvastu*, Senart 1882, 8,2, is still part of a report of what Mahāmaudgalyāyana had been able to witness himself. As noted by Marino 2019, 41, the actual description is closely similar to the torture described in MN 130 (quoted below in my next note), which features victims who are in hell, whereas SĀ 530 (in keeping with the standard pattern of the set of discourses reporting Mahāmaudgalyāyana's visions) concerns something seen while he was on the way into town to beg alms. Zin 2014, 275 points out inconsistencies evident in this part of the *Mahāvastu*, showing that its presentation would have resulted from a combination of material from different sources; see also Tournier 2017, 226, who speaks of an "interpolation de matériaux additionnels." References to the guardians of hell administering a torture that involves burning iron balls can also be found in the *Ekottarikāgama*; see EĀ 42.2 at T 2.125.748c3: 獄卒以熱鐵丸著彼罪人口中, EĀ 50.5 at T 2.125.810c13: 又以熱鐵丸使令吞之, and EĀ 52.8 at T 2.125.828c17: 復令仰臥, 以熱鐵丸使食之. Another type of occurrence involves the Buddha himself swallowing hot iron balls in a former life. One example is found in EĀ 42.3 at T 2.125.751a1: 世尊告曰: 我向作是念, 本未成

道時長處地獄, 呑熱鐵丸, and another example in EĀ 49.7 at T 2.125.801b24: 我自念生死無數 . . . 或在地獄中, 以熱鐵丸噉之; on EĀ 49.7 see also Anālayo 2015d.

435. MN 130 at MN III 186,3 and its main parallels MĀ 64 at T 1.26.505c3 and EĀ 32.4 at T 2.125.676a24. A similar torture is described in DĀ 30.4 at T 1.1.126b15 and in the *Divyāvadāna*, Cowell and Neil 1886, 375,8.

436. MN 130 at MN III 186,30: *taṃ kho panāhaṃ* ($C^e$ and $E^e$: *pana ahaṃ*), *bhikkhave, nāññassa* ($S^e$ adds *kassaci*) *samaṇassa vā brāhmaṇassa vā sutvā vadāmi, api ca* ($S^e$ adds *kho*) *yad eva me* ($B^e$ without *me*) *sāmaṃ* ($E^e$: *sāmañ*) *ñātaṃ sāmaṃ diṭṭhaṃ sāmaṃ viditaṃ, tad evāhaṃ* ($C^e$ and $E^e$: *tam evāhaṃ*) *vadāmī ti*. A similar statement can be found in AN 3.35 at AN I 142,10, which only takes up three divine messengers, whereas MN 130 and its parallels take up five (by way of adding the conditions of being born and being an infant to the divine messengers of old age, disease, and death). A presentation that also takes up only the three divine messengers of old age, disease, and death can be found in DĀ 30.4 at T 1.1.126b19, which does not report the Buddha making a statement comparable to the one in AN 3.35 (or MN 130).

437. Ps IV 231,5: *tattha ekacce therā nirayapālā nāma n' atthi, yantarūpaṃ viya kammam eva kāraṇaṃ kāretī ti vadanti*. In his detailed study of this position, Mori 1997, 460–61 points out that the reference in this commentarial explanation to the position that the guardians of hell are like a puppet, *yantarūpa viya*, seems to correspond to a passage in the 成唯識寶生論, T 31.1591.87b28: 猶如木人能有所作.

438. MĀ 199 at T 1.26.762c20: 彼有善處, 名六更樂. A similar reference is found in the partial Tibetan parallel, Up 2033 at D 4094 *ju* 67b1 or P 5595 *tu* 75a5: *reg pa'i skye mched drug ces bya ba'i mtho ris yod de*. Note that the corresponding part in the Pāli parallel, MN 129 at MN III 177,25 (after the completion of the simile of the wheel-turning king), does not offer any additional specification of heaven.

439. MĀ 199 at T 1.26.761a6: 彼地獄中有獄, 名六更樂. The Pāli parallel, MN 129 at MN III 167,14, instead refers to the Great Hell (*mahāniraya*) made completely of blazing iron; a comparable hell is mentioned in the partial parallel T 1.86.907c26: 泥犁城, which here comes without the qualification of being "great." As noted in Anālayo 2011b, 745, T 86 does not cover the case of the wise person at all. For this reason, it is best considered a partial parallel only.

440. MĀ 199 at T 1.26.759c16: 比丘, 地獄不可盡說, 所謂, 地獄苦.

441. MN 129 at MN III 166,18 and T 1.86.907b22. Some degree of lack of coherence can be identified right at the junction where the exposition of tortures in MĀ 199 starts, as the first torture described at T 1.26.760a22 employs exactly the same text as the second torture at T 1.26.760a28, except for the single difference between a reference to 鐵斧 or else to 鐵釿, with a variant reading in the second case that has precisely 斧 (although, probably erroneously, given as an alternative for 鐵). In other words, there is a fairly clear case of textual doubling right at the juncture where the description of tortures begins, which could have occurred in the course of adding the whole exposition.

The Pāli version shows signs of development also in relation to the topic of a heavenly rebirth, as it provides a detailed account of the seven treasures and four types of success of a wheel-turning king; see MN 129 at MN III 172,14 to 177,5. Besides being absent from MĀ 199, such a detailed coverage seems out of proportion for a simile and can thus with considerable probability be considered the result of a textual expansion.

Compared to MĀ 199, overall MN 129 seems to testify to a more evolved stage in textual development.

442. MĀ 199 at T 1.26.760a23, a pattern that also applies to the Pāli parallel MN 129 at MN III 166,18. This pattern differs from MN 130 and its parallels, where only some of the tortures are administered by the guardians of hell. The difference that emerges in this way could be read in the light of the assessment by Przyluski 1923, 126 that the presentation in MN 129 and its parallels is overall later than the one in MN 130 and its parallels, "le Devadūta est plus archaïque et plus proche de l'antiquité védique, tandis que le Bālapaṇḍita traduit des conceptions plus évoluées."

443. MN 129 at MN III 163,26, MĀ 199 at T 1.26.759b11, and T 1.86.907a19.

444. On the type of hellish punishment that involves some form of burning, Marino 2019, 45–46 offers the following reasoning: "Karma is often said to 'ripen,' to come to fruition, expressed by the Skt. verb √*pac*. In a strange sort of parallel to this, bodies in hell are often tossed in an actual metal pot and 'cooked' or 'boiled,' also expressed by √*pac*, but do not die until the evil karma that conditioned the cooking is exhausted. This suggests that karma associated with certain misdeeds can be effectively 'cooked off' by suffering analogous tortures in hell. When one who takes advantage of almsgivers suffers the maturation of his bad karma by eating hot iron balls, as his karma in a sense 'cooks' him, it is itself 'cooked off.'"

445. DĀ 7 at T 1.1.43b3: 獄鬼無慈, 又非其類, adopting the 宋, 元, and 明 variant 人 instead of 其. Such a remark is not found in the corresponding part of the parallels DN 23 at DN II 322,17, MĀ 71 at T 1.26.526a13, and T 1.45.832a12.

446. Kv XX.3 at Kv 596,13; for a survey of discussions in the *Kathāvatthu* that are related to hell see Braarvig 2009, 260–64.

447. Abhidh-k III 59, Pradhan 1967, 164,12: *kiṃ te narakapālāḥ sattvasaṃkhyātā utāho neti? netyeke*. The passage continues by distinguishing the guardians of hell from the *yamarākṣasas*, which are the attendants of Yama responsible for throwing culprits into hell, having been born into this role as retribution for their cruelty and irascibility in a former life. A problem with this argument is that the description of Yama in MN 130 at MN III 179,13 (= AN 3.35 at AN I 138,12) and in the majority of its partial or complete parallels—DĀ 30.4 at T 1.1.126b21, T 1.42.827a24, T 1.86.909b26, and EĀ 32.4 at T 2.125.674c1—employs the same term "guardians of hell" (*nirayapālā*/獄卒) or else a proper name (旁, explained to be the name of a 泥犁卒) for the attendant(s) who bring the culprit into the presence of Yama *and* for those who later administer various tortures in hell. Another parallel, MĀ 64 at T 1.26.503c25, however, uses a different term for the attendants: 閻王人收. This leaves only one version supporting the idea of distinguishing between the guardians of hell inflicting punishment and Yama's attendant(s). Feer 1892, 205 and Mus 1939, 210 may well be right in proposing that the latter would correspond to the former. Elsewhere in *Āgama* literature the guardians of hell do in fact perform functions in addition to being directly responsible for inflicting tortures. One example is MN 50 at MN I 337,8 and its parallels MĀ 131 at T 1.26.622a20, T 1.66.866a19, and T 1.67.868a20 (the extract quoted in Up 3021 no longer covers this part of the narrative), where the role of the hell guardians is merely to inform the culprit of the passage of time that has elapsed once a particular torture has come to its conclusion. Another example is MN 97 at MN II 186,32 and its parallel MĀ 27 at T 1.26.457a2, where the culprit tries to argue with the guardians of hell, explain-

ing that the misconduct was done on behalf of others (which is, of course, to no avail). The function of the guardians of hell in these two instances—which do not explicitly relate them to an actual inflicting of punishment, although the same may be implicit—resemble to some extent the role of Yama. Such usage supports the impression that Yama's attendants would be the same hell guardians that also have the task of torturing victims.

448. Abhidh-k III 59, Pradhan 1967, 164,19: *katham agninā na dahyante*? A more detailed discussion can be found in the *Viṃśikā*, Silk 2016/2018, 49,3 (also in Lévi 1925, 4,19); see also Mori 1997, 458–59 and Kellner and Taber 2014, 739–40.

449. MĀ 199 at T 1.26.759b28: 猶如晡時,日下高山,影懸向在地.如是彼所有身惡行,口,意惡行,彼於爾時懸向在上.彼作是念:此是我身惡行,口,意惡行,懸向在上.我於本時不作福,多作惡. The parallel MN 129 at MN III 164,24 does not specify that the evildoer is sick. However, an otherwise closely similar description of the evildoer's reflection in AN 4.184 at AN II 174,17 does precede this by indicating that the culprit is gravely sick. It seems fair to assume that such an indication could have been lost in MN 129. A placing at the time of being gravely sick and even close to death also fits the depiction in MN 129 at MN III 165,6 of the culprit's apprehension of being destined to a bad rebirth. The partial parallel T 1.86.907a27 explicitly indicates that the evildoer is sick at this time, 病時, which here even leads to visions of hellish tortures. A similar description of regret being comparable to a shadow can also be found in the *Śrāvakabhūmi* of the *Yogācārabhūmi*, Shukla 1973, 80,15, which also indicates that the person in question is sick, *ābādhiko bhavati*.

450. On the divine messengers see also Anālayo 2007b. Marasinghe 1974, 269 and Siklós 1996, 176 argue that the role of Yama here is not so much one of passing judgement and condemning to hell, instead of which Yama merely reminds the culprit of the divine messengers. In the same vein, Tiefenauer 2018, 99 reasons that "le roi des enfers proclame la loi karmique: 'C'est toi qui a commis ces mauvaises actions (*pāpakamma*) et c'est toi seul qui en subiras les conséquences.' Là-dessus, Yama se tait (*tuṇhī hoti*), n'émettant aucun jugement." However, Tiefenauer 2018, 513 also comments on the presentation in MN 130 that "Yama est à la fois un roi qui dirige l'enfer (*niraya*) et un juge." In fact, in MN 130 at MN III 179,15 (= AN 3.35 at AN I 138,15) the guardians of hell present the culprit to Yama, saying: *imassa devo daṇḍaṃ paṇetū ti*. This points to a role of passing judgment, so that perhaps Yama's remaining silent at the end of the interrogation of the culprit should be understood as expressing a judgment. The corresponding passages in the parallels also convey the impression of Yama having a more active role related to the subsequent punishments; see MĀ 64 at T 1.26.503c28: 唯願天王處當其罪, T 1.42.827a27: 閻羅處此人過罪, and T 1.86.909b29: 願王處是人過罪, where 處 seems to carry the meaning "to judge," as well as EĀ 32.4 at T 2.125.674c4: 當觀此人以何罪治?, which is clearly about imposing a punishment; in fact, here Yama does not remain silent but instead tells the hell guardians to put the culprit into hell, T 2.125.675a29: 速將此人往著獄中. According to MĀ 64 at T 1.26.504c13, once the interrogation is completed, Yama hands the culprit over to the hell guardians, 即付獄卒, which also seems to be more than just remaining silent. In sum, although not always expressed fully, the role of Yama does seem to be that of a judge.

451. Kimura 2009, 93,15: *gaṅgānadīvālukopamān kalpān niraye paceyaṃ* (also in Dutt 1934, 219,6), Ghoṣa 1905, 1461,8: *gaṅgānadīvālukopamān kalpān nirayeṣu vasan tatra chedanabhedanakuṇḍanasnedanapacanāny anubhaveyaṃ*.

452. T 25.1509.177c5: 菩薩見此, 如是思惟: 此苦業因緣, 皆是無明諸煩惱所作. 我當精進懃修六度, 集諸功德, 斷除眾生五道中苦. Perhaps of relevance is also an indication in T 7.220.908c9 that a vision of hell (and other lower realms) can occur in a dream: 若諸菩薩乃至夢中見有地獄.

453. Karashima 2011, 198,1 (= T 8.224.443c29): 三千大千剎土諸天子飛在上, 俱皆觀, 便舉聲, 共嘆曰: 於閻浮利地上, 再見法輪轉. 佛謂須菩提: 無兩法輪爲轉; 亦不想有一法輪轉; 不轉是者, 即般若波羅蜜; where my rendering of 三千大千剎土 takes inspiration from Harrison 1990, 322. Karashima 2011, 199,3 (= T 8.224.444a11): 佛語須菩提: 空者, 無所轉, 亦無轉還, 亦無想, 亦無願, 亦無生死, 亦無所從生, 亦不有轉, 亦不轉還. 作是說者, 是爲說法 (here 無想 corresponds to *animitta* in Wogihara 1932/1935, 443,24; see also above n. 399).

Streng 1982, 93 understands the first of the corresponding indications by the Buddha in the Sanskrit version to point to a shift in conceptions of *bhūtakoṭi*, but the term does not occur explicitly, and it also does not seem to be implicit in the present context; see Wogihara 1932/1935, 442,15: *nedaṃ, subhūte, dvitīyaṃ dharmacakrapravartanaṃ nāpi kasyacid dharmasya pravartanaṃ vā nivartanaṃ vā. evam iyaṃ, subhūte, bodhisattvasya mahāsattvasya prajñāpāramitā*. It seems more straightforward to read the passage as simply a deconstruction of the notion of turning the wheel of Dharma, in keeping with the usual rhetoric of emptiness, and it is this deconstruction that amounts to being an instance of the Perfection of Wisdom.

The notion of a "trichiliomegachiliocosm" is already found among Pāli discourses, in the form of the *tisahassīmahāsahassīlokadhātu* mentioned in AN 3.80 at AN I 228,14. Bodhi 2012, 1662n514 explains that this refers to "*a thousand times* the size of a thousand-to-the-second-power middling world system, in other words, a thousandfold world system cubed."

454. MN 117 at MN III 77,25: *mahācattārīsako dhammapariyāyo pavattito appaṭivattiyo* (C[e]: *appativattiyo*) *samaṇena vā brāhmaṇena vā devena vā mārena vā brahmunā vā kenaci vā lokasmiṃ* (C[e] and S[e]: *lokasmin*). The part that leads up to this statement by providing a contrast between right and wrong path factors occurs also in AN 10.106 at AN V 215,3, which does not have a counterpart to the rebuttal of possible objections or to the above passage reminiscent of terminology used in SN 56.11 (see next note below).

455. SN 56.11 at SN V 423,19: *dhammacakkaṃ pavattitaṃ appaṭivattiyaṃ* (C[e] and E[e]: *appativattiyaṃ*) *samaṇena vā brāhmaṇena vā devena vā mārena vā brahmunā vā kenaci vā lokasmin ti*, with the difference that in this case the statement is made by celestials (as is the case in the Perfection of Wisdom), whereas in MN 117 and its parallels the Buddha himself makes the corresponding statement.

456. MĀ 189 at T 1.26.736c9: 梵輪 and Up 6080 at D 4094 *nyu* 47a6 or P 5595 *thu* 87a4: *tshangs pa'i 'khor lo*.

457. MN 26 at MN I 170,6: *sace hi so imaṃ dhammaṃ suṇeyya khippam eva ājāneyyā ti* and MĀ 204 at T 1.26.777a25: 若聞此者, 速知法次法 (references are to the case of the first of the two teachers, Ārāḍa Kālāma).

458. MN 26 at MN I 171,16, MĀ 204 at T 1.26.777b28, and EĀ 24.5 at T 2.125.618c16.

459. See in more detail Anālayo 2011c.

460. SN 56.11 at SN V 423,13, with discourse parallels in Chung 2006, 94, SĀ 379 at T 2.99.104a9, T 2.109.503c13, T 2.110.504b7, EĀ 24.5 at T 2.125.619b6, and Waldschmidt 1957, 162 (here he becomes an arhat). Discourse quotations of the same occur in the

*Dharmaskandha*, T 26.1537.480a7, the *Abhidharmakośavyākhyā*, Wogihara 1936/1971, 580,13, and the *Abhidharmakośopāyikāṭīkā*, Up 6056 at D 4094 *nyu* 29a6 or P 5595 *thu* 65b1. The same is also reported in several *Vinaya*s, namely the Dharmaguptaka *Vinaya*, T 22.1428.788c7, the *Mahāvastu* (of the Mahāsāṃghika-Lokottaravādins), Marciniak 2019, 426,3 (also in Senart 1897, 333,18), the Mahīśāsaka *Vinaya*, T 22.1421.104c18, the *Saṅghabhedavastu* of the Mūlasarvāstivāda *Vinaya*, Gnoli 1977, 138,6 (where he attains full awakening; notably the *Kṣudrakavastu* of the same Mūlasarvāstivāda *Vinaya*, T 24.1451.292b29 and D 6 *tha* 248b1 or P *de* 235a3, still only refers to his stream-entry, whereas a second report in the same work, T 24.1451.407a15 and D 6 *da* 312b6 or P 1035 *ne* 295b6, instead mentions his full awakening), the Sarvāstivāda *Vinaya*, T 23.1435.448c14, and the Theravāda *Vinaya*, Vin I 11,32. The successful outcome of the Buddha's first sermon features also in several biographies of the Buddha extant in Chinese, such as T 3.189.644c11, T 3.190.812c5, T 3.191.954b1, and T 4.196.148c15. For a comparative study of versions of the Buddha's first sermon see Anālayo 2012b and 2013a.

461. Abhidh-k VI 54c, Pradhan 371,4: *dharmacakram tu dṛṅmārgaḥ*; see also T 29.1558.128b28: 見道似彼故名法輪 and T 29.1559.279c29: 由見道似輪故, 說此法名輪. Paṭis II 162,17 concludes a lengthy discussion of the wheel of Dharma by stating *amatogadhaṃ nibbānaṃ pariyosānaṭṭhena dhammo, taṃ dhammaṃ pavattetī ti dhammacakkaṃ*.

462. Choong 2006, 72: "Die vier Wahrheiten sind deshalb der Inhalt der Aufmerksamkeit vor und nach erfolgter Befreiung. Angesichts der Tatsache, dass Befreiung nur ein Moment der Wendung des Geistes ist, und diese Wendung des Geistes durch die Aufmerksamkeit auf die vier Wahrheiten bewirkt wird, sind diese vier Wahrheiten eben die befreiende Einsicht. Die Tatsache, dass die vier Wahrheiten in ein solch theoretisches Schema gebracht werden, ist nur ein Problem, wenn der Inhalt der Aufmerksamkeit in sprachlicher Form wiedergegeben werden muss. In dem Befreiungszustand können die vier Wahrheiten (zumindest implizit) Inhalt einer *sati* sein, die als ein einziger Erkenntnisakt zu fassen ist." See also Anālayo 2021a.

463. An example would be Sn 840.

464. See, e.g., Dhammadinnā 2021, 104.

465. See, e.g., Frauwallner 1971, 84, Dhammajoti 2002/2007, 586–94, and Dessein 2007b, 28–30.

466. Karashima 2011, 158,2 (= T 8.224.440b24): 具足三合十二法輪爲轉.

467. The formulation for the first two truths proceeds as follows: Kimura 2009, 82,3: *tatra katamad duḥkhajñānaṃ? yad duḥkhasyānutpādajñānam idaṃ duḥkhajñānaṃ. tatra katamat samudayajñānaṃ?* (also in Dutt 1934, 209,1), D 9 *ka* 239b5 or P 731 *nyi* 243a8: *de la sdug bsngal shes pa gang zhe na? sdug bsngal mi* (P has the vowel marker for "i" mistakenly on the previous letter) *skye bar shes pa'o. de la kun 'byung ba shes pa gang zhe na?*, T 7.220.487c25: 云何苦智? 謂若智以無所得而爲方便, 知苦應不生, 是爲苦智. 云何集智?, T 8.221.25b29: 何等爲苦慧? 不生苦是爲苦慧. 何等爲習慧?, T 8.222.194c5: 彼何謂分別? 於苦知苦無所從生亦無所起, 是謂分別苦. 何謂爲曉了所習?, and T 8.223.254c21: 云何名苦智? 知苦不生, 是名苦智. 云何名集智?

468. Pagel 1995, 267 comments on a similar indication in the *Bodhisattvapiṭaka* that "knowledge of suffering is to see that the aggregates are unproduced, that suffering is without origination and destruction," reasoning that "[t]he significance of skill in truth lies not only in the perception of defilement (*duḥkha*/*samudaya*) and purifica-

tion (*nirodha/mārga*), but . . . it also rejects the need for a self to sustain their presence," in the sense of rejecting the assumption that there must be a self that is either defiled or else reaches purification.

469. Tsai 2021, 51 expresses the matter in this way: "The cultivation of *prajnāpāramitā* enables bodhisattvas . . . to guide sentient beings on multiple paths, including *śrāvakayāna*, *pratyekabuddhayāna*, and *bodhisattvayāna*. According to various levels of faculties, motivations, preferences, habits, thoughts, purposes, and environments of sentient beings, different paths should be formulated respectively. Regardless of the path chosen, as long as it is for a good cause, it can serve as a way to alleviate suffering."

470. Karashima 2011, 234,8 (= T 8.224.447a12): 如是, 須菩提, 當來有菩薩棄深般若波羅蜜, 反索枝掖, 爲隨異經術, 便墮聲聞, 辟支佛道地. 譬若男子得象, 觀其腳. 於須菩提意云何? 是男子爲黠不? 須菩提言: 爲不黠. 佛言: 是菩薩有德之人, 爲二輩中有[,] 棄深般若波羅蜜去, 反修學餘經, 得阿羅漢, 辟支佛道. 於須菩提意云何? 是菩薩爲黠不? 須菩提言: 爲不黠. 佛言: 如是當覺知魔爲. The original has an additional reference to 般若波羅蜜 after 反索枝掖, which I have left out, following the suggestion by Karashima 2011, 234n352 that this is "probably superfluous."

471. See, e.g., MN 29 at MN I 192,14 and its parallel EĀ 43.4 at T 2.125.759b11.

472. Wogihara 1932/1935, 504,2: *so 'ndhakāre hastinaṃ labdhvā*, D 12 *ka* 129b7 or P 734 *mi* 139b4: *mun khung nas glang po che zhig rnyed nas*, T 7.220.810c15 (= 891a26): 譬如有人欲觀香象身量大小, 形類勝劣, 得而不觀反尋其跡, T 8.227.556a18: 譬如人得象不觀, 反尋其跡, and T 8.228.625a20: 譬如有人欲觀其象, 雖復得見, 不能真實觀其形相, 是人即自返尋象跡觀取象相.

473. Ud 6.4 at Ud 68,3 and DĀ 30 at T 1.1.128c11; see also T 1.23.289c17, T 3.152.50c24, T 4.198.178b6, T 17.768.704c7, and T 31.1592.98c16.

474. Māra's reflection takes the following forms in Karashima 2011, 483,2 (= T 8.224.472b10): 是人當出我境界, 脫人眾多, and—in the context of another episode—Karashima 2011, 509,3 (= T 8.224.474b25): 得道者, 出我界, 度脫人不可計.

475. DĀ 30 at T 1.1.115a28 and Ps I 34,2. DĀ 30 is a comparatively late discourse concerned with cosmology in a manner that in Pāli texts emerges only with exegetical works; on this discourse see also Anālayo 2014h, 35–44.

476. The same applies to the case of the Perfection of Wisdom, where the deeds of Māra, as already noted by Mäll 2003/2005, 94, cover both "negative states of mind" as well as "certain external obstacles."

477. See in more detail Anālayo 2014d, 117–19.

478. SN 4.16 at SN I 112,16 and SĀ 1102 at T 2.99.290a16.

479. Karashima 2011, 233,3 (= T 8.224.446c27): 菩薩, 摩訶薩書是經時, 左右顧視, 當覺知魔爲. 菩薩, 摩訶薩書是經時, 心邪念不一, 當覺知魔爲. Based on a survey of the different interferences by Māra reported in the Perfection of Wisdom, Giddings 2014, 113 reasons that, even though at first sight the list of Māra's mischievous activities may appear arbitrary, a closer inspection shows "a gradual serialization in which emphasis changes according to the deepening of the disciples' engagement and understanding of the bodhisattva path. These begin with doubts over entering the path and problems with interacting with other pursuants. Next, the doubts develop into anxieties over personal expectations and finally, the occurrence of problems in the relationship between the aspiring bodhisattva and his teacher"; on the depiction of student-teacher problems in the *Aṣṭasāhasrikā* see also Nance 2008, 145.

480. Karashima 2011, 242,17 (= T 8.224.448a22): 稱譽天上快樂: 五所欲悉可自恣. An example in *Āgama* literature of Māra recommending the enjoyment of sense pleasures can be found in SN 5.6 at SN I 132,26, SĀ 1205 at T 2.99.328a27, and SĀ[2] 221 at T 2.100.455c8 (see also Enomoto 1994, 43). His advocacy of rebirth in a celestial realm of the sense sphere occurs in what in all three discourse collections is the next discourse: SN 5.7 at SN I 133,12, SĀ 1206 at T 2.99.328b29, and SĀ[2] 222 at T 2.100.456a6.
481. SN 5.9 at SN I 134,24 (which uses "puppet" to refer to bodily form), SĀ 1203 at T 2.99.327c6, and SĀ[2] 219 at T 2.100.455a21.
482. SN 5.10 at SN I 135,20, SĀ 1202 at T 2.99.327b9, SĀ[2] 218 at T 2.100.454c29, and Up 9014 at D 4094 *nyu* 82a7 or P 5595 *thu* 128b2; see also Enomoto 1994, 42 and for a discussion of the simile Dhammadinnā 2020 and Anālayo 2023e, 453n17.
483. See in more detail Anālayo 2022b, 92–93.
484. SN 5.2 at SN I 129,24, SĀ 1199 at T 2.99.326b6, and SĀ[2] 215 at T 2.100.454a9.
485. Karashima 2011, 308,5 (= T 8.224.454c21): 弊魔來到是菩薩所, 便於邊化作八大泥犁, 其一泥犁中有若干千百千菩薩化作是.
486. Kern and Nanjio 1912, 145,3, T 9.262.20c9 (= T 9.264.155b10), T 9.263.86c3, and D 113 *ja* 55a5 or P 781 *chu* 63a5.
487. This has already been noted by Silk 2014, 181–82; see also Felbur 2015, 276. An example for Citta delivering profound teachings to monks can be found in SN 41.1 at SN IV 282,16 and SĀ 572 at T 2.99.152a2, another example in SN 41.5 at SN IV 292,1 and SĀ 566 at T 2.99.149b14, and yet another example in SN 41.7 at SN IV 296,9 and SĀ 567 at T 2.99.149c20.
488. Study Group on Buddhist Sanskrit Literature 2006, 62,17, T 14.474.527c22, T 14.475.547a15, and T 14.476.572b2.
489. Karashima 2011, 253,3 (= T 8.224.449a19): 其有愛欲心者, 知是爲愛欲心; 其有瞋恚心者, 知是爲瞋恚心; 其有愚癡心者, 知是爲愚癡心. 知愛欲心之本無愛欲心; 知瞋恚心之本無瞋恚心; 知愚癡心之本無愚癡心. 是者, 須菩提, 令我得薩芸若者般若波羅蜜. 何以故? 怛薩阿竭無愛欲心. 用無愛欲心, 悉知其心之本亦無愛欲心. 以是故, 怛薩阿竭心無有愛欲. 何以故? 怛薩阿竭無瞋恚心. 用無瞋恚心, 悉知其心之本亦無瞋恚心. 以是故, 怛薩阿竭心無有瞋恚. 何以故? 怛薩阿竭無愚癡心. 用無愚癡心, 悉知其心之本亦無愚癡心. 以是故, 怛薩阿竭心無有愚癡. 如是, 須菩提, 怛薩阿竭, 阿羅呵, 三耶三佛因般若波羅蜜示現持世間. My translation of 以是故, literally "therefore," as "the reason being" is inspired by the context.
490. On this listing see also Schmithausen 1987, 319–21.
491. Karashima 2011, 256,6 (= T 8.224.449b25): 其心者本淨故, 亦無有想; on the translation of 想 see above n. 399 and on 本淨 Zacchetti 2008, 143n34.
492. The Sanskrit version, Wogihara 1932/1935, 549,17, refers to *alakṣaṇatvād artha-viviktatvāt* (see also Karashima 2011, 256n68), with its Tibetan parallel in D 12 *ka* 146a4 or P 734 *mi* 157a6: *mtshan nyid med cing don gyis dben pa yin pa'i phyir*. The Chinese versions that have a counterpart to the relevant passage agree in only mentioning a single item, which is the absence of signs; see T 7.220.815c21: 無相可得, T 8.225.491c5: 何以故? 無想 (which I suggest could be emended to 無相), T 8.227.558a20: 以無相義故, and T 8.228.630c28: 離諸相.
493. Wogihara 1932/1935, 542,6: *prakṛtiprabhāsvarāṇi, subhūte, tāni cittāni*, D 12 *ka* 142b1 or P 734 *mi* 153a2: *sems de dag rang bzhin gyis 'od gsal ba ste*, and 7.220.815a13: 心本性淨. Another relevant instance with a larger number of parallels is Wogihara 1932/1935, 38,23: *prakṛtiś cittasya prabhāsvarā*, D 12 *ka* 3a3 or P 734 *mi* 3a7: *sems kyi rang bzhin ni*

*'od gsal ba*, T 7.220.763c18: 心性本性淨, T 7.220.866a10: 心本性淨, T 8.225.478c23: 意淨, 光明者, T 8.226.508c16: 心者淨, T 8.227.537b14: 心相本淨, and T 8.228.587b15: 心性淨. As already noted by Zacchetti 2008, 139, Karashima 2011, 4n25, and Huifeng 2017, 205n26, the counterpart to this reference in Lokakṣema's translation does not mention the luminous/pure nature of the mind.

494. MĀ 98 at T 1.26.584a5: 云何觀心如心念處? 比丘者有欲心, 知有欲心如真, 無欲心, 知無欲心如真; 有恚, 無恚; 有癡, 無癡 . . . 如是比丘觀內心如心, 觀外心如心, 立念在心, 有知, 有見, 有明, 有達. 是謂比丘觀心如心. 若有比丘, 比丘尼如是少少觀心如心者, 是謂觀心如心念處, with parallels in MN 10 at MN I 59,29 (= DN 22 at DN II 299,7) and EĀ 12.1 at T 2.125.568c21; for a comparative study see Anālayo 2011b, 87–89 and 2013e, 142–63.
495. See Collett and Anālayo 2014 and Anālayo 2022e.
496. See Anālayo 2020c and 2020e.
497. The gloss on the external modality of contemplating the three mental states under discussion proceeds as follows in Vibh 197,37: *kathañ ca bhikkhu bahiddhā citte cittānupassī viharati? idha bhikkhu sarāgaṃ vāssa cittaṃ sarāgassa cittan ti pajānāti, vītarāgaṃ vāssa cittaṃ vītarāgassa cittan ti pajānāti, sadosaṃ vāssa cittaṃ sadosassa cittan ti pajānāti, vītadosaṃ vāssa cittaṃ vītadosassa cittan ti pajānāti, samohaṃ vāssa cittaṃ samohassa cittan ti pajānāti, vītamohaṃ vāssa cittaṃ vītamohassa cittan ti pajānāti.* The formulation adopted here makes it clear that the contemplation involves mental states that occur in another person. For internal contemplation, the corresponding formulation for the first case of a mental state with lust reads as follows in Vibh 197,16: *kathañ ca bhikkhu ajjhattaṃ citte cittānupassī viharati? idha bhikkhu sarāgaṃ vā cittaṃ sarāgaṃ me cittan ti pajānāti.* This in turn clearly refers to a mental state occurring in the mind of the practitioner. Commenting on the exegesis of *smṛtyupasthāna* in this work, Bronkhorst 1985, 311 reasons that it would have been "composed before the 4 *smṛtyupasthāna*s were given the explanations we now find in the Sūtras."
498. MN 10 at MN I 56,12 (= DN 22 at DN II 291,3) and MĀ 98 at T 1.26.582c12.
499. MN 10 at MN I 61,11 (= DN 22 at DN II 302,14) and MĀ 98 at T 1.26.584a14.
500. Darwin 1872, 365–66 offers the following explanation: "The movements of expression in the face and body . . . serve as the first means of communication between the mother and her infant; she smiles approval, and thus encourages her child on the right path, or frowns disapproval. We readily perceive sympathy in others by their expression . . . The movements of expression . . . reveal the thoughts and intentions of others more truly than do words."
501. Kimura 2009, 77,18: *bodhisattvo mahāsattvaḥ prajñāpāramitāyāṃ carann adhyātmaṃ kāye kāyānupaśyī viharati ātāpī saṃprajānan smṛtimān vinīya loke 'bhidhyādaurmanasye tac cānupalambhayogena* (also in Dutt 1934, 205,12). This can be compared to MN 10 at MN I 56,4 (= DN 22 at DN II 290,11): *bhikkhu kāye kāyānupassī viharati ātāpī sampajāno satimā, vineyya loke abhijjhādomanassaṃ.* A difference in placing is that the Pāli passage occurs at the outset of the exposition of the four establishments of mindfulness, whereas the location of the above passage from the *Pañcaviṃśatisāhasrikā Prajñāpāramitā* is at the conclusion of instructions on the four elements as one of the body contemplations. My choice of these two different locations is motivated by the circumstance that the actual phrasing is particularly close, thereby making it easy to discern the key difference. On comparison, minor differences are that the instructions are addressed to a bodhisattva cultivating the Perfection of Wis-

dom, or else to a monastic, and that the *Prajñāpāramitā* version explicitly refers to internal practice, which in the Pāli instructions feature in a textual portion repeated after each actual exercise, mentioning contemplation done internally, externally, and internally-and-externally. Setting these minor differences aside, however, the main difference would indeed be the reference to *tac cānupalambhayogena*. This reference has a counterpart in the following formulations in the parallels: D 9 *ka* 233a5 or P 731 *nyi* 236b4: *mi dmigs pa'i tshul gyis*, T 7.220.484c24: 以無所得, T 8.222.193a20: 不得, and T 8.223.253b21: 以不可得故; see also Bidyabinod 1927, 8 (plate III figure 2 line 6): *kāye kāyānupaśyī viharati tachchānupalaṃbha*.

502. A more detailed instruction for the case of contemplation of the body can be found in the *Bodhisattvabhūmi*, Wogihara 1930/1936, 259,17: *iha bodhisattvaḥ kāye kāyānudarśī viharaṃ naiva kāyaṃ kāyabhāvato vikalpayati, nāpi sarveṇa sarvam abhāvataḥ, taṃ ca kāyanirabhilāpyasvabhāvadharmatāṃ yathābhūtaṃ prajānāti. iyam asya pāramārthikī kāye kāyānupaśyanā smṛtyupasthānaṃ.*
503. Harrison 1993, 146; on ceremonial dimensions that can influence the choice of the day for presenting to the public the completion of a translation into Chinese see also Hureau 2006. For a detailed discussion of the translatorship attribution of T 418 see Harrison 1990, 221–49. Stated in brief, the prose of the first six chapters would indeed be attributable to Lokakṣema, and the same probably holds for the prose of the remaining chapters, whereas the verses appear to be by someone else.
504. Harrison, Lenz, and Salomon 2018.
505. T 55.2145.47c6 and 48c10.
506. This is the 般舟三昧經, T 13.418.914a5: 自觀意, 觀他人意, 自觀意觀他人意者, 本無意, which clearly speaks of contemplating the mental states of oneself and of another person, as well as both, in what must be a counterpart to the standard indication that such mindfulness practice should be undertaken internally, externally, and internally-and-externally. The Tibetan version, Harrison 1978b, 130,17 (15j), does not employ a comparable specification in its description of contemplation of the mind or of the other establishments of mindfulness. The same holds for the version of this instruction found in T 13.416.888b7.
507. Anālayo 2022c, 59–115.
508. SN 6.5 at SN I 144,17 mentions his attainment of the fire element, which is not reported in the parallels SĀ 1196 at T 1.99.324c20 and SĀ$^2$ 109 at T 2.100.412c22. DN 24 at DN III 27,12 proceeds from the Buddha attaining the fire element to him manifesting a flame of the height of seven palm trees, a depiction not found in the parallels SHT IV 165.5–6, Sander and Waldschmidt 1980, 178, and DĀ 15 at T 1.1.69a25; for a more detailed discussion see Anālayo 2015a, 23–26.
509. DĀ 14 at T 1.1.62c12. In the parallels, a fire-like radiance of the mountain is instead due to the arrival of a host of *devas* to pay the Buddha a visit; see DN 21 at DN II 264,17, Waldschmidt 1932, 67, Nagashima 2015, 380, T 1.15.246b21, MĀ 134 at T 1.26.633a11, T 4.203.476a28, and for a more detailed discussion Anālayo 2015a, 11–20.
510. Allon 2001, 124 line 5, a presentation not supported by parallels in AN 4.36 at AN II 37,26, SĀ 101 at T 2.99.28a23, SĀ$^2$ 267 at T 2.100.467a29, and EĀ 38.3 at T 2.125.717c21; see in more detail Anālayo 2017a, 23–26. On the probable relationship of the Gāndhārī manuscript to a Dharmaguptaka lineage of textual transmission see Salomon 1999, 166–78.
511. DĀ 1 at T 1.1.5a29. Except for a parallel extant in Uighur, Shōgaito 1998, 374 line 2, the

other two parallels do not mention a luminosity of the footprint; see DN 14 at DN II 17,13 and Waldschmidt 1956, 102 (6b.3) or Fukita 2003, 78.

512. SN 51.22 at SN V 283,11.

513. The former occurs in MN 140 at MN III 243,11, not found in the parallels MĀ 162 at T 1.26.691c6, T 14.511.780c2, and Up 1041 at D 4094 *ju* 39b6 or P 5595 *tu* 43a6; see also Stuart 2015b, 272 (§4.1.6). The latter occurs in SN 46.33 at SN V 92,23, AN 3.100.14 at AN I 258,10, and AN 5.23 at AN III 16,19, not supported by the single parallel SĀ 1246 at T 2.99.341c25. For a more detailed discussion see Anālayo 2022c, 79–86.

514. AN 1.6.1–2 at AN I 10,10; see in more detail Anālayo 2022c, 86–104.

515. T 28.1548.697b18.

516. AN 10.62 at AN V 116,15 and its parallels MĀ 52 at T 1.26.487c27 and T 1.36.819c23.

517. Karashima 2011, 273,4 (= T 8.224.451a12): 佛說是經時, 五百比丘僧, 二十比丘尼皆得阿羅漢; 六十優婆塞, 三十優婆夷皆得須陀洹道; 二十菩薩皆逮得無所從生法樂, 皆當於是婆羅劫中受決.

518. In a discussion published earlier, Nattier 2003b, 180 comments on Śākyamuni Buddha: "[W]hat was seen as special about him, in this early period, was not the quality of his enlightenment, nor even of his compassion (for in early Buddhism, as in the Theravāda tradition today, arhats also teach). What was unique about the Buddha was the fact that he was the first person in recent memory who had discovered on his own, without the help of an awakened teacher, the way to escape from rebirth ... The fact that Śākyamuni was described, in the well-known list of 'ten epithets of the Buddha,' as an arhat (among other things) demonstrates the continuity that was perceived between his own achievement and that of his followers."

519. Sasaki 1958, 355 emphasizes that such *kṣānti* refers to a "positive mental disposition or a willing acceptance." Schopen 1989, 139n20 reasons that "to obtain *kṣānti* is the positive expression for the same state which is negatively expressed by such formulae as 'he is not depressed, not cowed, not dejected ... he is not terrified, frightened and does not tremble with fear.' But the opposite of dejection, terror and fear is not patience or endurance, it is rather something more like composure. Note too that in almost every case the absence of fear and dread and the obtainment of *kṣānti* are to take place in regard to the same basic fact, however expressed: the absence of a self. The proper reaction to this fact, and the full realization of its implications, may be expressed either positively by saying 'he obtains composure in regard to it,' or negatively by saying 'he is not terrified, alarmed, frightened, etc.' In the end they are very much the same." Pagel 1995, 185 notes that the role "of *dharmakṣānti* is generally one of support. It represents a mental precondition for the acquisition and retaining of spiritual fruits and prepares the practitioner for the moment when he comes face to face (*abhimukhī*) with reality itself." Nattier 2003a, 244n240 comments on *kṣānti* that "[t]he word is used in early bodhisattva sūtras in two distinct contexts: on the one hand, to describe the optimal reaction of a bodhisattva when he is insulted, injured, or otherwise impinged upon by others (a context in which the emphasis is generally upon the bodhisattva's ability to avoid becoming angry with those who are his tormentors); and on the other, to describe the bodhisattva's reaction to certain cognitive propositions, e.g., the fact that all things are unoriginated (*anutpattikadharmakṣānti*). In both cases the optimal response is much more than 'patience,' but requires the ability to endure torment without responding with anger (in the former case) or fear and disorientation (in the latter)." These helpful

clarifications will hopefully suffice to bring out the nuances to be kept in mind when encountering the standard translation of "patience," which after some deliberation I decided to keep in order to avoid the problems that can manifest with new terminology; see above n. 1.

520. AN 6.101 at AN III 442,20: *nibbānaṃ sukhato samanupassanto anulomikāya khantiyā samannāgato bhavissatī ti ṭhānam etaṃ vijjati; anulomikāya khantiyā samannāgato sammattaniyāmaṃ okkamissatī ti ṭhānam etaṃ vijjati; sammattaniyāmaṃ okkamamāno sotāpattiphalaṃ vā sakadāgāmiphalaṃ vā anāgāmiphalaṃ vā arahattaṃ vā sacchikarissatī ti ṭhānam etaṃ vijjatī ti*. The preceding discourses AN 6.98 to AN 6.100 work through the same mode of presentation but in relation to seeing formations/dharmas as permanent, happiness, and a self, contrasted to seeing them as impermanent, *duḥkha*, and not self; the latter three cases then similarly lead to being endowed with patience in conformity, etc. In addition to these expositions, the notion of patience that is in conformity also occurs in AN 6.88 at AN III 437,13.

In the course of an informative survey of occurrences of similar terminology in Mahāyāna texts, which besides *anutpattikadharmakṣānti* also comprise the distinct notions of *ānulomikadharmakṣānti* and *ānulomikī kṣānti*, Strauch 2010, 38 comments on relevant Pāli literature that "[t]he idea of *ānulomikī kṣānti* seems to have found its way into Pāli Buddhism as well. Although it is occasionally attested in a few *Aṅguttaranikāya* (hereafter AN) texts (*anulomikā khanti*), its *locus classicus* among the Pāli Buddhist texts is certainly the *Paṭisambhidāmagga* (hereafter Paṭis) of the second century CE, where it is found more than fifty times." The reference given in support of the dating is von Hinüber 1996/1997, 60, whose actual position is somewhat less definite, as he only proposes that Paṭis is found in the fifth *Nikāya* "probably because it was composed too late (perhaps 2nd century AD) to be included into the Abhidhammapiṭaka." The phrase "perhaps 2nd century AD" is in turn supported by a reference to Frauwallner 1971, 106, who envisages a development of the canonical Pāli Abhidhamma literature taking place between the second century BCE and the second century CE, and then considers Paṭis to be the latest Abhidhamma work (see also Norman 1983, 87, who gives no specific date for Paṭis and just observes that "[t]he form of the text suggests that it is late . . . the text is later than much of the canon"). Besides the uncertainty of the dating, Paṭis II 236,2 gives a full quote of the four discourses AN 6.98 to AN 6.101, after which it offers explanations (see below n. 522). This makes it quite clear that the set of *Aṅguttara* discourses under discussion constitutes the earlier textual source.

521. On the attainment of stream-entry as already involving a realization of Nirvana see Anālayo 2023d, 63–64.

522. Paṭis II 239,38: *pañcakkhandhe rittato passanto anulomikaṃ khantiṃ paṭilabhati . . . pañcakkhandhe tucchato passanto anulomikaṃ khantiṃ paṭilabhati . . . pañcakkhandhe suññato passanto anulomikaṃ khantiṃ paṭilabhati . . . pañcakkhandhe anattato passanto anulomikaṃ khantiṃ paṭilabhati . . . pañcakkhandhe asārakato passanto anulomikaṃ khantiṃ paṭilabhati*. These are five out of altogether forty insight perspectives with the potential of leading to patience that is in conformity. Maharjan 2022, 106–9 relates advanced stages of patience that is in conformity to the commentarial concept of *anuloma ñāṇa*, which stands for mature insight on the brink of the realization of one of the four levels of awakening. Maharjan 2022, 122 then notes that Ps III 282,16 employs the term *anuloma ñāṇa* also in its description of the path of bodhisattvas, in particular in reference to the level of insight reached at which they stop in order to

avoid the attainment of path and fruit, see above n. 61. This implicitly broadens the relevance of patience that is in conformity beyond progress toward the standard four levels of awakening so as to play a role as well in relation to the path to Buddhahood.

523. SN 22.95 at SN III 141,2, with parallels in SĀ 265 at T 2.99.68c6, T 2.105.501a12, T 2.106.501c20, and Up 4084 at D 4094 *ju* 239a5 or P 5595 *tu* 273a7.

524. An alternative perspective has been proposed by Tournier 2017, 217–18, who suggests rather an influence of the notion of nonreturn. This interesting suggestion is based on a reference in the *Lokānuvartanāsūtra*, Harrison 1982, 216,15 (= Senart 1882, 170,3), to the future Buddha Śākyamuni having been free from passion, *vītarāga*, since the time of his encounter with Dīpaṃkara. Tournier 2017, 218 reasons: "l' épithète *vītarāga* semble bien pouvoir se rapporter à la définition du *bodhisattva* irréversible, à condition de mesurer l'écho existant entre ce type de *bodhisattva* et l'*anāgāmin* . . . une 'condition caractérisée par le non-retour [en ce monde]' (*anāvarttikadharma*). La correspondance terminologique entre la description de l'*anāgāmin* et du *bodhisattva* avancé est particulièrement étroite, ce qui tend à suggérer que le premier d'entre eux, défini en termes d'irréversibilité dès une époque ancienne, a pu constituer une source d'inspiration pour la définition du state où l'aspirant à l'état de *buddha* est assuré de sa réalisation future. L'évocation des *anāgāmin* dans le *Mahāvastu* leur reconnaît l'état de *vigatarāga*; de la même manière, son doublon *vītarāga* est employé ici pour désigner le Bodhisattva. L'absence de passion est également l'attribut des *arhant*, donc des *buddha*, et un autre passage du *Daśabhūmika* affirme que les *bodhisattva* irréversibles (*anivartiya*) doivent, à compter de la huitième *bhūmi*, être considérés comme de parfaits *buddha*. Les *bodhisattva avaivartika* sont donc des *buddha* en puissance de la même manière que les *anāgāmin* sont des *arhant*."

The term *vītarāga* can convey different nuances of meaning, which can perhaps best be exemplified by juxtaposing two instances found in the same textual collection, the *Majjhimanikāya*, both of which occur in relation to the topic of worthiness in respect to receiving gifts. In MN 142 at MN III 255,8 the term *vītarāga* designates the condition of being free from lust in regard to sensual pleasures of a non-Buddhist who features in a hierarchical listing of recipients of gifts below someone who is on the path to stream-entry; in MN 35 at MN I 237,2 the same term *vītarāga* qualifies, together with *vītadosa* and *vītamoha*, the Buddha as a supreme recipient of gifts. Since the term *vītarāga* can evidently carry different connotations, the context of any particular occurrence needs to be considered to ascertain its meaning. From a doctrinal perspective, being free from sensual lust can occur through suppression or through eradication; the former is temporary, unlike the latter. The case of a nonreturner clearly involves freedom from sensual lust through eradication, and it would not be possible to equate the *vītarāga* of the above non-Buddhist recipient with the condition of nonreturn; in fact, the two feature at quite different levels in the hierarchy of recipients of gifts given in MN 142 (and its parallels; see Anālayo 2011b, 815).

In the same vein, the freedom from sensual lust through eradication gained by a nonreturner would not be applicable to the case of the bodhisattva (= the future Buddha Śākyamuni) at the time of his encounter with Dīpaṃkara. In fact, the *Lokānuvartanāsūtra* continues by referring to the Buddha's son, Rāhula, in an evident attempt to negotiate the problem of the incompatibility of the notion of *vītarāga* in its full sense with fathering a son. The same type of challenge also holds for other passages that report Śākyamuni's struggle with sensuality during his quest for awakening; see

Anālayo 2010a, 17n6. It thus seems that the passage from the *Lokānuvartanāsūtra*, which reflects a specific notion of *vītarāga* related to docetic ideas of the nature of a Buddha, is not readily applicable to the general conception of a nonreturner. The attainment of nonreturn is usually defined by way of having eradicated the five lower fetters (one of which is precisely sensual lust, *kāmarāga*), an eradication that does not feature in descriptions of what is characteristic of an irreversible bodhisattva.

With awakening attained, a Buddha is reckoned to have eradicated all ten fetters (including nonsensual lust for what is fine-material and immaterial, *rūparāga* and *arūparāga*). Such eradication marks off not only a Buddha but also an arhat, who similarly differs from a nonreturner in regard to the eradication of the five higher fetters. In contrast, the characteristic quality of a nonreturner, as duly signaled by Tournier 2017, 218 through his addition of "[en ce monde]," concerns not returning to this world in terms of not being reborn in it. An example of the relevant phrasing would be MN 22 at MN I 141,29: *anāvattidhammā tasmā lokā*, with a counterpart in 得不退法, 不還此世 in its parallel MĀ 200 at T 1.26.766b13. The main concern here is freedom from rebirth in other realms except for the Pure Abodes. The same basic meaning can be seen, e.g., in the *Divyāvadāna*, Cowell and Neil 1886, 533,26: *'nāvṛttikadharmiṇyaḥ punar imaṃ lokam*. Notably, the same notion can in turn also be applied to an arhat, who is *anāvattidhamma*/不轉還 . . . 法/*phyir mi ldog pa'i chos can* but in relation to all three realms of existence; see AN 9.26 at AN IV 404,7 and its parallels SĀ 499 at T 2.99.131b8 and Up 7004 at D 4094 *nyu* 53b4 or P 5595 *thu* 94b4. This occurrence confirms that the notion under question is not just about being irreversibly destined to reach full awakening—as is the case for an *avaivartika* bodhisattva—because in the case of an arhat full awakening has already been reached. Instead, the main point is about rebirth: the arhat will not be reborn at all and a nonreturner only once in the Pure Abodes. In contrast, the condition of being an *avaivartika* bodhisattva does not involve having successfully gone beyond the prospect of repeated rebirths.

As far as irreversibility in progress toward awakening is concerned, stream-entry appears to emerge as a preferable candidate for a cross-matching with the path to Buddhahood, given that a stream-entrant is already irreversibly established on the path to awakening. The irreversibility of a stream-entrant finds expression in a standard qualification of being *niyato sambodhiparāyaṇo* found, e.g., in MN 68 at MN I 466,4, with a Chinese counterpart in 定趣正覺 in the parallel MĀ 77 at T 1.26.545c23. If the notion of nonreturn is to be related to the path of a bodhisattva, perhaps the expectation of only one more birth could be made the basis for proposing a relationship to a level more advanced than the *avaivartika* bodhisattva, namely that of the *ekajātipratibaddha* bodhisattva as depicted in Perfection of Wisdom literature.

525. Karashima 2011, 319,6 (= T 8.224.455c22): 亦不疑: 我非阿惟越致地. 亦不言: 我是阿惟越致地. 譬若有人得須陀洹道, 在其地終不疑. A comparable indication can be found in T 11.313.760a7, which likens the nature of a bodhisattva who has become *avaivartika* through rebirth in Akṣobhya's Buddhafield (see T 11.313.760a4) to the nature of a stream-enterer (on the attribution of T 313 to Lokakṣema see above n. 229).

526. SN 25.1 at SN III 225,14+21 (in relation to both the *saddhānusārin* and the *dhammānusārin*): *abhabbo ca* ($C^e$ and $S^e$: *va*) *tāva kālaṃ kātuṃ yāva na sotāpattiphalaṃ sacchikaroti*, a statement repeated in SN 25.2–10. This whole *Saṃyutta* has no known parallel.

527. See, e.g., SN 55.7 at SN V 356,10: *khīnanirayomhi*, with a parallel in SĀ 1044 at T 2.99.273c3: 我地獄盡.

528. Karashima 2011, 309,1 (= T 8.224.454c27), in relation to the 阿惟越致菩薩: 便不復墮泥犁中, 當生天上; see also Karashima 2011, 408,5 (= T 8.224.465a2): 菩薩學如是者, 不入泥犁. Rebirth in lower realms in general then comes up in Karashima 2011, 318,1 (= T 8.224.455c4): 亦不生惡處. 用是比, 用是相, 行具足, 知是阿惟越致菩薩; see also below n. 555.

529. Karashima 2011, 295,10 (= T 8.224.453b29): 當說本無時, 二百比丘僧皆得阿羅漢, 五百比丘尼皆得須陀洹道, 五百諸天人皆逮無所從生法樂, 於中立; 六十新學菩薩皆得阿羅漢道. 佛言: 是六十菩薩過去世時, 各各供養五百佛. 布施求色, 持戒, 忍辱, 精進求色, 禪不知空, 離空. 不得般若波羅蜜, 漚惒拘舍羅.

530. SN 12.20 at SN II 26,5: *yā tatra tathatā avitathatā anaññathatā idappaccayatā, ayaṃ vuccati, bhikkhave, paṭiccasamuppādo*, with parallels in Chung and Fukita 2020, 148,5: *yātra dharmatā dharmastitatā dharmaniyāmatā dharmayathātathā avitathatā ananyathā bhūtaṃ satyatā tavatā yathātathā aviparītatā aviparyastatā idaṃ pratyayatā pratītyasamutpādānulomatā, ayam ucyate pratītyasamutpādaḥ*, SĀ 296 at T 2.99.84b22: 此等諸法, 法住, 法空, 法如, 法爾, 法不離如, 法不異如, 審諦真實, 不顛倒. 如是隨順緣起, 是名緣生法, and Mejor 1991, 69,12 (= Up 3037 at D 4094 *ju* 137a6 or P 5595 *tu* 157b5): *chos rnams kyi gnas pa, chos rnams kyi nges pa, chos rnams kyi ji lta ba nyid, de bzhin nyid, mi 'gyur ba de bzhin nyid, gzhan ma yin pa de bzhin nyid ji lta ba, bden pa, de kho na nyid, ji lta ba bzhin mi 'gyur ba, phyin ci ma log pa, rkyen 'di tsam pa ste, 'di ni rten cing 'brel par 'byung ba go rim las zlog pa ste. 'di ni rten cing 'brel par 'byung ba zhes bya'o*; see also Pāsādika 1989, 59 (§ 195) and the discussion in Guang Xing 2018, 122–26, who also takes into account the related term "such" applied to the four noble truths in, e.g., SN 56.20 at SN V 430,22 and its parallel SĀ 417 at T 2.99.110c4; see also SHT II 51d3+d2R4, Waldschmidt, Clawiter, and Sander-Holzmann 1968, 3.

531. MN 28 at MN I 190,37: *yo paṭiccasamuppādaṃ passati so dhammaṃ passati, yo dhammaṃ passati so paṭiccasamuppādaṃ passatī ti* and MĀ 30 at T 1.26.467a9: 若見緣起便見法, 若見法便見緣起.

532. Karashima 2011, 294,11 (= T 8.224.453b23): 菩薩得是真本無, 如來名. The use of 如來 is rare in T 224, which generally reflects a preference for the transliteration 怛薩阿竭; see Karashima 2006, 356–57 on the underlying language reflected by this transliteration, and for a survey of various Chinese renderings of the term *tathāgata* Anālayo 2017f.

533. For a study of earthquakes in Buddhist literature see Ciurtin 2009 and 2012.

534. Karashima 2011, 295,17 (= T 8.224.453c8).

535. Karashima 2011, 245,4 (= T 8.224.448b25): 魔事一起時, 令深學菩薩爲本際作證, 便墮聲聞中, 得須陀洹道. 如是菩薩, 摩訶薩當覺知魔爲.

536. Karashima 2011, 280,10 (= T 8.224.451c10): 菩薩有信樂, 有定行, 有精進, 欲逮阿耨多羅三耶三菩, 不得深般若波羅蜜, 不學漚惒拘舍羅. 是菩薩便墮阿羅漢, 辟支佛道中. 菩薩有信樂, 有定行, 有精進, 欲逮阿耨多羅三耶三菩, 得深般若波羅蜜, 學漚惒拘舍羅. 是菩薩終不中道懈惰, 過出阿羅漢, 辟支佛道去, 正在阿耨多羅三耶三菩中住.

537. See, e.g., AN 9.20 at AN IV 394,24 and its parallels MĀ 155 at T 1.26.677c8, T 1.73.879c2, and T 1.74.881b12.

538. For a survey see Anālayo 2015f. An instance that does have a parallel is EĀ 38.7 at T 2.125.723a19, which is MN 116 at MN III 68,25; see in more detail Anālayo 2010b.

539. EĀ 35.7 at T 2.125.700b23, EĀ 38.11 at T 2.125.726a16, and EĀ 49.9 at T 2.125.804c12.
540. SN 16.5 at SN II 202,16, SĀ 1141 at T 2.99.301c13, SĀ$^2$ 116 at T 2.110.416b15, and EĀ 41.5 at T 2.125.746a24.
541. EĀ 12.6 at T 2.125.570b16: 三乘之道.
542. EĀ 12.6 at T 2.125.570b6: 我今不從如來教. 所以然者, 若如來不成無上正真道者, 我則成辟支佛; adopting a 宋, 元, and 明 variant that dispenses with 當 before 如來.
543. An alternative explanation proposed by Kloppenborg 1974, 6 is that the motif of the Pratyekabuddha may have served to accommodate pre-Buddhist seers within the Buddhist fold. This seems unconvincing, since non-Buddhist seers would not have been allocated a place above arhats in the hierarchy of recipients of gifts. Moreover, *Āgama* literature occasionally refers to pre-Buddhist seers, showing that there was no felt need to integrate these into the Buddhist fold, and the notion of six former Buddhas already suffices to provide authentication from the past; see in more detail Anālayo 2015f, 20–21 (other parts of the same article also offer a more detailed discussion of the possible function of the motif of Pratyekabuddhas, presented here only in brief).
544. EĀ 23.1 at T 2.125.609b16: 與向須陀洹食者, 獲福不可計. 況復成須陀洹乎, 況向斯陀含, 得斯陀含道; 況向阿那含, 得阿那含道; 況向阿羅漢, 得阿羅漢道; 況向辟支佛, 得辟支佛; 況向如來, 至真, 等正覺, 況成佛及比丘僧.
545. Th 534: *buddhassa mātā pana māyanāmā* (S$^e$: *māyā mahesī*).
546. Bloch 1950, 157,2: *hida buddhe jāte sakyamunī*; see also Falk 2006, 180.
547. Karashima 2011, 462,4 (= T 8.224.470c13): 如是輩菩薩不當字菩薩, 當字爲佛. 何以故? 今得佛不久故.
548. Nakamura 1980/1999, 18 concludes: "The verse claimed to have been proclaimed by the Buddha at his birth was composed very late."
549. MN 123 at MN III 123,21: *aggo 'ham asmi lokassa, seṭṭho 'ham asmi lokassa, jeṭṭho 'ham asmi lokassa, ayam antimā jāti, n' atthi dāni punabbhavo* (B$^e$ and S$^e$ have the *jeṭṭho* and *seṭṭho* statements in the opposite sequence); for a more detailed discussion see Anālayo 2010a, 28–46. A version of this statement can be found in a translation by Lokakṣema, T 17.807.751c12; for a Sanskrit parallel from the *Mahāvastu* see Harrison 1982, 216,19.
550. Examples can be found in the *Lalitavistara*, Lefmann 1902, 84,22 (see also T 3.187.553a23), T 3.184.463c14, T 3.185.473c2, T 3.188.618a19, T 3.189.625a27, and T 3.190.687b10. A reference only to this being his last birth, which nevertheless effectively means that at that time the bodhisattva Śākyamuni was supreme in the world, can be found in such a proclamation in the *Mahāvastu*, Marciniak 2020, 33,11 (also in Senart 1890, 24,8), the *Divyāvadāna*, Cowell and Neil 1886, 389,22, and the *Buddhacarita* 1.15, Johnston 1936/1984, 2.
551. Karashima 2011, 307,1 (= T 8.224.454c13): 是心甚清潔. 清潔過於阿羅漢, 辟支佛道上; the translation follows the indication in Karashima 2010, 39 that in Lokakṣema's usage 道, when occurring in the phrase 辟支佛道, can convey the sense of a "path" rather than of "awakening"; the former appears to be a better fit for the present context, although elsewhere "awakening" seems a better choice. The parallels are as follows: Wogihara 1932/1935, 672,12: *yayā ca, subhūte, cittapariśuddhyā śrāvakapratyekabuddhabhūmim atikrānto bhavati*, D 12 *ka* 180b6 or P 734 *mi* 194a8: *sems rnam par dag pa gang yin pa des nyan thos dang rang sangs rgyas kyis las 'das par 'gyur te*, T 7.220.826b20 (= 901a22): 超聲聞及獨覺地 . . . 應知心常清淨, T 8.225.494c25: 是心淨潔過應儀, 緣一覺上, T 8.226.527a11: 心故清淨, 過聲聞, 辟支佛道地, T 8.227.564b8: 心清淨.

以心清淨故, 能過聲聞, 辟支佛地, and T 8.228.641c9: 得心清淨. 由心清淨故, 即能過於聲聞, 緣覺之地; see also Choong 2014b, 144.

552. Karashima 2011, 340,6 (= T 8.224.458a17): 佛言: 是恒竭優婆夷, 却後當來世名星宿劫, 是中有佛名金華佛. 是優婆夷後當棄女人身, 更受男子形, 却後當生阿閦佛刹. 從阿閦佛刹去, 復到一佛刹. 從一佛刹復生一佛刹 . . . 是優婆夷從一佛刹復到一佛刹, 未嘗不見佛. Regarding 恒竭 (as a correction of 怛竭; in line with the recurrent use of 恒 elsewhere in T 224 to refer to the Ganges), Karashima 2010, 213 explains that this is "an incomplete transliteration of Skt. *Gaṅgadevī* ('the goddess of the Ganges')."

Fronsdal 1998/2014, 214n19 objects to the translation "Goddess of the Ganges," used by Conze 1973/1975, 219, arguing that "since she is given the familiar title *bhaginī* ("sister") it is more likely that Gaṅgadeva [sic] is simply the name of a human woman; Monier-Williams seems to take it as a fairly common name (*A Sanskrit-English Dictionary*, p. 341c)." Following up this reference, it appears that Monier-Williams 1899/1999, 341 just gives the following (under the main header *Gaṅgā*): "-devī, f., N. of a woman," without mentioning *-devā* and also without an explicit indication regarding this name being "fairly common," apart from the fact that the name is listed at all. The Sanskrit version of the *Aṣṭasāhasrikā Prajñāpāramitā* uses Gaṅgadevā (variant Gaṅgādevā), as distinct from its chapter header's usage of Gaṅgadevī.

Regarding the implications of the term "sister," DN 21 at DN II 268,4+6 reports a celestial bard using the term *bhaginī* to refer to the celestial woman with whom he has fallen in love; this shows that the term can in principle be employed to refer to nonhumans. Moreover, the term "sister" does not occur in relation to Gaṅgadevā in Lokakṣema's translation, which qualifies her just as an *upāsikā*, Karashima 2011, 340,6 (= T 8.224.458a17): 優婆夷, for the Sanskrit of which Monier-Williams 1899/1999, 215 gives "a lay female votary of Buddha." Judging from Vin III 27,6, a chief connotation of being an *upāsaka/upāsikā* is the status of not being ordained, as applying the term to oneself serves as a valid way for a monastic to disrobe. A standard definition given in the Pāli commentaries, e.g., at Sv I 234,28, explains that the term *upāsaka* (and by implication *upāsikā*) conveys lay status and having taken refuge, *tattha ko upāsako ti? yo koci saraṇagato gahaṭṭho*.

Gaṅgadevā does not appear to be ordained and her behavior shows that she is a Buddhist disciple, wherefore qualifying her as 優婆夷 is natural and does not seem sufficient to conclude that she must be a human rather than a celestial. As pointed out by Harrison 1987, 88n9, the second part of her name does of course not imply that she must be a celestial, as evident in the example of the philosopher and monk Āryadeva. Hence, a consultation of the description of her behavior would be needed to ascertain her status.

In the narrative setting, she gets up from being seated. In *Āgama* literature such behavior would be in line with what humans usually do, whereas celestials tend to take the standing posture. However, in the version of the Perfection of Wisdom translated by Lokakṣema celestials at times also sit down (see above n. 214), so that getting up from being seated does not mark her as being a human disciple. Having gotten up, she performs an act of worshipping the Buddha with golden flowers, rather than using natural flowers as done by the future Śākyamuni when meeting Dīpaṃkara; see Karashima 2011, 341,13 (= T 8.224.458b4). This gives the impression that these flowers may have been created magically, in which case her act of worship would be more in line with what a celestial is able to do. This is evident in the report in an earlier chapter that Śakra magically created flowers to worship Subhūti; see Karashima 2011, 49,10 (= T 8.224.430a23). Although the idea of holding a golden canopy of flowers features in T 12.362.303b3 as an action undertaken by humans, a version of the present episode in T 7.220.907a4, which employs the same description of an act of worship by scattering golden flowers, 金華散, indicates that the protagonist is a celestial woman, 天女 (nevertheless, the same act in T 8.227.568b11 and T 8.228.648b17 is instead undertaken by a 女人). That Gaṅgadevā receives a prediction of future Buddhahood in turn would be feasible independent of whether she is a human or a celestial disciple, as it concerns a future life. The Perfection of Wisdom, Karashima 2011, 295,11 (= T 8.224.453c1), reports celestials gaining *anutpattikadharmakṣānti*, which makes it fair to assume that celestials could in principle also receive a prediction. In sum, it seems to me difficult to come to a definite decision whether her appearance in the Perfection of Wisdom should indeed be reckoned an instance involving a human rather than a celestial protagonist.

553. Kwan 1985, 55 draws attention to the explanation of the name Akṣobhya as reflecting his dedication, already as a bodhisattva, to remaining completely free of any anger; see T.11.313.752b3: 其菩薩, 摩訶薩用無瞋恚故, 名之爲阿閦, 用無瞋恚故, 住阿閦地. On Akṣobhya in general see also, e.g., Dantinne 1983, Williams 1989/2009, 231–34, Nattier 2000 and 2003b, 185–87, Sato 2004, and Strauch 2010, 45–62.
554. For a Nepalese inscription that uses phrasing similar to the reference to Gaṅgadevā's change of sex in the Sanskrit version (Wogihara 1932/1935, 745,10), see Acharya 2008/2010, 31 and 35.
555. Karashima 2011, 304,7 (= T 8.224.454b25): 阿惟越致 . . . 身不生惡處, 不作女人身.
556. T 27.1545.887a11: 捨非男身, 恒得男身.
557. Wogihara 1930/1936, 94,3: *na ca strī anuttarāṃ samyaksaṃbodhim abhisaṃbudhyate. tat kasya hetoḥ? tathā hi bodhisattvaḥ prathamasyaiva kalpāsaṃkhyeyasyātyayāt strībhāvaṃ vijahāti bodhimaṇḍaniṣadanam upādāya na punar jātu strī bhavati.*
558. Senart 1882, 103,11: *sarvāsu daśabhūmiṣu puruṣā bhavanti.*
559. Jā I 44,20 (= Bv 2.58 at Bv 12,28): *liṅgasampatti*, with its Tibetan counterpart in Gaffney 2003, 329,2: *mtshan mar ldan*; see also Endo 1997/2002, 253–54. Ps IV 122,12 and Mp II 15,7 even proclaim that a woman is unable to have the (fully fledged) aspiration for Buddhahood, *paṇidhānamattam pi itthiyā na sampajjati.*
560. In support of this assessment, Nattier 2003a, 100 refers to research on Indian inscriptions by Schopen 1988/1997, 250, which led him to the conclusion that "the emergence of the Mahāyāna [in inscriptions] in the fourth to fifth centuries coincided with a marked decline in the role of women of all kinds in the practice of Indian Buddhism."
561. Karashima 2011, 511,3 (= T 8.224.474c9).
562. Karashima 2011, 520,2 (= T 8.224.475c26).
563. Note that the circumstance of not receiving a name need not be due to their larger number, as another episode reports the Buddha predicting the future Buddhahood of a large group, simply indicating that they will all have the same name; see Karashima 2011, 437,2 (= T 8.224.468b9): 當於是波羅劫中作佛. 皆同一字 and for other occurrences of this type of procedure Strauch 2010, 49–50. A comparable approach could in principle also have been used in the present case, had it not been for the fact that they are women.
564. Karashima 2011, 531,5 (= T 8.224.477b15): 五百女人即化作男子. In a general com-

ment not related to this specific passage, Romberg 2002, 164 reasons that once "[t]he aim was no longer to become an Arhat, but to become a Buddha . . . [t]his shift made, in fact, the situation for women worse, because a doctrinal foundation was laid for the necessity of changing the sex before being able to become enlightened."

565. T 15.624.361b10: 難以母人自致阿耨多羅三耶三菩提; the present and the two references to T 624 given below in the next note have already been discussed by Harrison 1987, 77–78. The text in question is the 伅真陀羅所問如來三昧經, for which Harrison 1987, 69 gives the Sanskrit title *Drumakinnararājaparipṛcchāsūtra*. Nattier 2008, 85 considers T 624 to be one of the "third-tier texts" among translations attributed to Lokakṣema, in the sense of bearing only a distant relationship to his style. On a potential problem in relation to the two core texts generally considered to be representative of his style see Harrison 2019, 703.

566. T 15.624.362a22: 諸夫人 . . . 壽終已後離於母人, 當得男子, 便生兜術天上. At the same time, this text also reflects a different current, as a listing of different dimensions of skill in means recognizes the possibility that a bodhisattva may manifest in female form to teach women; see T 15.624.358c11: 示現母人身欲多教母人.

The need to leave behind the condition of being a woman comes up again in another text that does appear to be a translation by Lokakṣema, the 阿彌陀三耶三佛薩樓佛檀過度人道經 (T 362); see Harrison 1998b, 556–57 and Nattier 2008, 86–87. Harrison 1998b, 557 and 563 draws attention to Amitābha's aspiration that his Buddhafield be free of women, in that women who wish to be reborn in it become men, as well as to the subsequent confirmation in the description of Sukhāvatī as being indeed without women, since women transform into men on being reborn in it; see T 12.362.301a27: 令我國中無有婦人，女人欲來生我國中者即作男子 and T 12.362.303c8: 無有婦女 . . . 女人往生即化作男子. Here, too, the situation is complex, however, as the position evident in these two quotes changes to some extent with later versions of the same text; see the discussion in Harrison 1998b.

567. Karashima 2011, 273,4 (= T 8.224.451a12): 五百比丘僧, 二十比丘尼皆得阿羅漢; 六十優婆塞, 三十優婆夷皆得須陀洹道.

568. MN 73 at MN I 490,24 and its parallels SĀ 964 at T 2.99.246c14 and SĀ$^2$ 198 at T 2.100.446b13; my reference is in all three cases to the report on female arhats.

569. Karashima 2011, 295,10 (= T 8.224.453b29): 二百比丘僧皆得阿羅漢, 五百比丘尼皆得須陀洹道.

570. T 13.418.919b19: 八百比丘皆得阿羅漢道, 五百比丘尼皆得阿羅漢道. The same ratio recurs in an attainment report in the Sanskrit version of the *_Kāśyapaparivarta_, Pāsādika 2015, 88,8 (§149). In this case, however, the version of the *_Kāśyapaparivarta_ translated by Lokakṣema, T 350, does not have such an indication.

571. See Anālayo 2016c and 2019c, 51–67.

572. Attempts to revive nun orders in the Mūlasarvāstivāda and the Theravāda traditions—followed respectively in the Himalayan regions and in South and Southeast Asia—can meet with remarkably strong resistance, even though close study shows that a revival of the respective nun traditions is legally possible; see Tsedroen and Anālayo 2013, Anālayo 2017g, 2018a, 2018b, Roloff 2020, and Anālayo 2023e, 413–43.

573. MN 115 at MN III 65,24: *aṭṭhānam etaṃ anavakāso yaṃ itthī* (E$^e$: *itthi*) *arahaṃ assa sammāsambuddho*. The same position recurs in AN 1.15 at AN I 28,9, a Pāli discourse with no known parallel.

574. MĀ 181 at T 1.26.723c26 (the reference is to the beginning of the exposition on impossibilities); this significant difference has already been noted by Nagata 2002, 282–83.
575. See in more detail Anālayo 2009a.
576. T 25.1509.237a28: 如是等, 是處, 不是處, 多性經中佛口自說, 諸論議師輩, 依是佛語, 更廣說: 是處, 不是處; see also Lamotte 1970, 1525.
577. On these five see in more detail Silk 2007.
578. For a survey of the listings of impossibilities in the different versions see table 12.5 in Anālayo 2011b, 650–51.
579. The Pāli version is MN 135, which has a large number of parallels, for a survey and discussion of which see Anālayo 2011b, 767–75.
580. This position has not remained uncontested; see, e.g., Paul 1979/1985, Ohnuma 2000, Dimitrov 2004, Anālayo 2015b, and Dhammadinnā 2015, 2015/2016, and 2018.
581. Karashima 2011, 343,9 (= T 8.224.458b18): 須菩提白佛言: 菩薩行般若波羅蜜, 何等爲入空? 何等爲守空三昧? 佛言: 菩薩行般若波羅蜜, 色, 痛痒, 思想, 生死, 識空觀. 當作是觀, 一心作是觀, 不見法. 如是不見法, 於法中不作證. 須菩提言: 佛所說: 不於空中作證. 云何菩薩於三昧中住, 於空中不得證? 佛言: 菩薩悉具足念空, 不得證. 作是觀, 不取證. 作是觀, 觀入處. 甫欲向是時, 不取證. 不入三昧心無所著. 是時不失菩薩法本, 不中道得證. 何以故? 本願悉護薩和薩故, 爲極慈哀故. The phrase 色, 痛痒, 思想, 生死, 識空觀 is remarkable, as the positioning of 觀 seems to follow the syntax of the Indic original rather than the requirements of Chinese syntax; see also Karashima 2011, 343n5 and the preferable formulation in T 8.226.531b9: 觀色空, 觀痛痒, 思想, 生死, 識空.

Another point worth noting is that, even though in general compassion does not play as central a role as it does in later versions of the *Aṣṭasāhasrikā Prajñāpāramitā*, the final part of the above passage testifies to the basic notion of not proceeding directly to the realization of Nirvana, motivated by compassion for all sentient beings and the bodhisattva's original aspiration to take care of them. These are clearly present in the version of the Perfection of Wisdom translated by Lokakṣema. The same can also be seen reflected in other passages in Lokakṣema's translation, such as Karashima 2011, 346,6 (= T. 8.224.458c8): 是菩薩行極大慈, 心念十方薩和薩, 是時持慈心悉施人上, Karashima 2011, 349,1 (= T 8.224.458c28): 故心念一切薩和薩. 持是所念故, 得漚惒拘舍羅, 不中道取證, Karashima 2011, 380,3 (= T 8.224.462a12): 是故爲薩和薩之度, or Karashima 2011, 407,8 (= T 8.224.464c22): 菩薩如是學, 爲極大慈哀; see also the final part of the passage quoted below in n. 583.

Yet another point worth noting concerns the reference in the above passage to 本願, for which Karashima 2010, 32 gives "an original vow." This seems to be more adequate than the rendering as an "earlier resolution" given for the present passage by Choong 2016, 732n15, understood to be comparable to the resolution a meditator forms when entering cessation attainment. Instead, the idea of 本願 in the present context seems to be the orientation toward Buddhahood established at the time of fully embarking on the path of a bodhisattva. This may of course be recalled briefly before entering meditation practice on emptiness, no doubt, but that does not seem to be the most prominent meaning of 本願 in the present context, which conveys the sense of what in Sanskrit would be *pūrvapraṇidhāna* rather than an earlier *adhiṣṭhāna*. A comparison of the effects of this original aspiration with those of the resolution formed before entering cessation attainment in T 13.397.67c8 or T 13.400.509c26 (for the Tibetan see Choong

2016, 734) appears to be meant to illustrate the effect these can have even when one is not able to form conscious thoughts. It is in this sense that the original aspiration of a bodhisattva would operate in a way similar to the resolution related to attaining cessation, not in the sense of the timing when this aspiration or else a resolution will be made, as only the latter necessitates being done just before entering the concentrative attainment; on the problems related to explaining how a prior determination or resolution can have its effect in bringing about eventual emergence even though the practitioner is in the attainment of cessation see Anālayo 2024b, 20–26. In contrast to the case of cessation attainment, as correctly explained by Choong 2016, 752, "the bodhisattva's vows exert force spontaneously and unceasingly on the bodhisattva, so much so that it becomes an underlying attitude."

582. The translation is based on the assumption that 法 in this passage would render *dharmatā* in the present context, which is the reading in the corresponding part of the Sanskrit version, Wogihara 1932/1935, 749,16: *tāṃ dharmatāṃ dharmatayā na samanupaśyet, tāṃ cāsamanupaśyan dharmatāṃ na sākṣātkuryād bhūtakoṭim. evam ukte āyuṣmān subhūtir bhagavantam etad avocat: yad bhagavān evam āha: na bodhisattvena mahāsattvena śūnyatā sākṣātkartavyeti*, etc.

583. Karashima 2011, 348,8 (= T 8.224.458c24): 是菩薩悉爲護薩和薩, 守空三昧向泥洹門, 心念分別. 何等爲分別? 守空三昧, 無相三昧, 無願三昧. 是爲分別. 漚惒拘舍羅使是菩薩不中道取證. 何以故? 漚惒拘舍羅護之故. 故心念一切薩和薩. 持是所念故, 得漚惒拘舍羅, 不中道取證.

Commenting on Lokakṣema's usage of 念, Karashima 2010, 338–40 indicates that this character can have a range of different counterparts in the Sanskrit version, such as *upanidhyāyati*, *pratyavekṣaṇā*, *manasikāra*, *manyate*, *samanvāharati*, and *smṛti*. In the present context, the Sanskrit version in Wogihara 1932/1935, 756,18 proceeds as follows: *yadā bodhisattvo mahāsattva evaṃ cittam abhinirharati: sarvasattvā mamāparityaktāḥ mayaite parimocayitavyā iti. śūnyatāṃ ca samādhivimokṣamukham abhinirharati ānimittaṃ ca samādhivimokṣamukham abhinirharati apraṇihitaṃ ca samādhivimokṣamukham abhinirharati. tadā upāyakauśalyasamanvāgato bodhisattvo mahāsattvo veditavyo*. The relevant counterpart to 心念 would seem to be *cittam abhinirharati*, although the same verb is also used for the three gateways to deliverance, whereas Lokakṣema uses 守 for that purpose, so that perhaps his original used different terms. Moreover, *abhinirharati* is not among the terms listed by Karashima 2010, 338–40 as equivalents to 念 (nor is it included among such equivalents in Hirakawa 1997, 469). In sum, this little exploration hopefully suffices for allowing me the license of translating 念 according to what to my mind seems to fit the context best. In the present case of cultivating deep *samādhi*s, "thought" must have gone into abeyance and would thus not be a suitable rendering of 念. What fits the context well, as far as I can see, would be the presence of *smṛti* in the role of monitoring the meditation practice, by "keeping in mind" and "recollecting" the need to avoid realization midway.

584. AN 3.163 at AN I 299,14 lists *suññato samādhi*, *animitto samādhi*, and *appaṇihito samādhi* as approaches for eradicating a range of defilements, including the three root defilements of *rāga*, *dosa*, and *moha*, thereby implicitly presenting these *samādhi*s as the means for gaining full awakening. Its parallel EĀ 24.10 at T 2.125.630b3 presents the same three *samādhi*s, 空三昧, 無願三昧, and 無相三昧 (emending 想 to read 相), as indispensable for awakening, since one who does not attain these will remain subject

to *saṃsāra* and be unable to awaken, T 2.125.630b$_{10}$: 有不得此三三昧, 久在生死, 不能自覺寤.

585. Karashima 2011, 332,$_{3}$ (= T 8.224.457b$_{12}$): 求想盡者, 設想滅者, 即可滅也. 便得阿羅漢. 是爲菩薩漚惒拘舍羅: 不滅想, 得證, 向無想, 隨是教 (on the translation of 想 see above n. 399).
586. In the context of a survey of skill in means in *Prajñāpāramitā* literature, Pye 1978/2003, 104–5 comments that such skill is "not just a synonym for a compassionate attitude," in that a "bodhisattva *must* use his skilful means to face both ways at once," thereby becoming able "to recognise, unfalteringly, the simple equality of voidness and the existence and needs of living beings." In this way, a bodhisattva "enters the three 'gates of deliverance' while refusing to leave the multitude of beings behind" (107). In the same vein, de Breet 1992, 206 reasons that skill in means "is the (skill in the) balancing act between entering emptiness and not deserting the world with its suffering beings." Nattier 2003a, 155 explains that "*upāya-kauśalya* as used in the *Aṣṭa* thus refers to what might best be described as a 'balancing act.'" In contrast to skill in means as a technique employed by the Buddha to adapt his teachings to the needs and capacities of others, in the Perfection of Wisdom skill in means "is practiced by bodhisattvas . . . and it is a solitary (rather than interpersonal) practice designed to keep the bodhisattva from accidentally . . . slipping into a lower form of enlightenment" (156).
587. For a more detailed study see Anālayo 2021/2023.
588. DN 33 at DN III 220,$_{3}$ and AN 6.79 at AN III 431,$_{26}$.
589. Vibh 325,$_{31}$.
590. The notion of skill in means in the Perfection of Wisdom is of course not confined to the particular modality discussed here. For a survey of various references to skill in means in T 224 see Giddings 2014, 178–81.
591. Th 158; the preceding Th 157 refers to his sensual lust and fondness of adornment.
592. SN 21.8 at SN II 281,$_{15}$, SĀ 1067 at T 2.99.277a$_{25}$, and SĀ$^{2}$ 5 at T 2.100.375a$_{12}$; another parallel, EĀ 18.6 at T 2.125.591a$_{27}$, instead reports just a rebuke by the Buddha, pointing out that his behavior was not different from lay people.
593. AN 8.9 at AN IV 166,$_{19}$, SHT VI 1226.3R–5V, Bechert and Wille 1989, 20–22, SĀ 275 at T 2.99.73a$_{26}$, SĀ$^{2}$ 6 at T 2.100.375a$_{24}$, and Up 2065 at D 4094 *ju* 90a$_{3}$ or P 5595 *tu* 102b$_{2}$.
594. AN 1.14.4 at AN I 25,$_{11}$ and EĀ 4.5 at T 2.125.557c$_{22}$.
595. Jayatilleke 1963/1980, 406 reasons that the basic notion of skill in means corresponds to the ability of "the Buddha in adjusting his sermons to suit the predilections and temperament of his listeners." Gombrich 1996, 17 comments that the "Buddha's 'skill in means' . . . the exercise of skill to which it refers, the ability to adapt one's message to the audience, is of enormous importance in the Pali Canon." In other words, even when the term is not explicitly used, the basic idea of being *skilled* in teaching others the *means* for cultivating what is wholesome and avoiding what is unwholesome can be seen to underlie a range of instructions attributed to the Buddha.
596. See Anālayo 2009b.
597. Ud 7.9 at Ud 79,$_{5}$.
598. Pande 1957, 75 comments that "the author of the prose . . . seems to have grossly misunderstood the . . . verse, which intends 'water' in no more than a merely figurative sense." Such a story is not found in the Chinese parallel, T 4.212.707c$_{20}$.
599. Ud 3.2 at Ud 21,$_{17}$, EĀ 18.7 at T 2.99.591b$_{5}$, and T 4.212.739c$_{1}$.

600. Dhp-a I 115,17 and T 4.212.739b13.
601. See in more detail Anālayo 2016d, 2021c, and 2022d, 237n376.
602. See MN 136 at MN III 209,20 and its parallels MĀ 171 at T 1.26.707a26 and Up 5004 at D 4094 *ju* 264a7 or P 5595 *thu* 7a3.
603. It seems to be more in line with the position taken in the *Hevajra Tantra* II.ii.50, Snellgrove 1959, 50: *rāgena badhyate loko rāgenaiva vimucyate.*
604. Pj II 274,20 and Jā IV 224,9; Pye 1978/2003, 134 comments on a *Jātaka* version of the Nanda narrative (Jā 182) that the "story does not in itself use the technical terminology at all, but it probably comes nearest to the Mahayana sense of skilful means."
605. Karashima 2011, 441,6 (= T 8.224.468c10): 佛語阿難: 持是般若波羅蜜囑累汝 . . . 我每所說餘經, 汝所受, 設令悉散悉亡, 雖有是, 其過少耳. 汝所從佛受般若波羅蜜, 設散設亡, 其過甚大不小. On the reference to 佛經身 in the part I have elided see the discussion in Harrison 1992, 57–58. The second entrustment occurs in Karashima 2011, 533,6 (= T 8.224.477b23).
606. The Dharmaguptaka *Vinaya*, T 22.1428.968b13, the Mahāsāṅghika *Vinaya*, T 22.1425.491b26, the Mahīśāsaka *Vinaya*, T 22.1421.191a16, the Mūlasarvāstivāda *Vinaya*, T 24.1451.407a3, the Sarvāstivāda *Vinaya*, T 23.1435.448b13, and the Theravāda *Vinaya*, Vin II 287,17. In what perhaps is the Haimavata *Vinaya*, T 24.1463.818a14, however, Ānanda's role is just to be present during the communal recitation by the other monks, so he can be asked in case they should forget something. Although this differs from the presentation in the other versions, here, too, Ānanda has the role of being the one who knows the teachings best and therefore can ensure their correct recitation.

    The role tradition accords to Ānanda as the central authority behind the opening phrase "thus have I heard" has been problematized by Skilling 2023 (see also Skilling 2021, 133–37). Regarding this opening phrase, it is worthy of note that a similar reference to "I heard," *sutaṃ me*, occurs in Pāli discourses depicting how someone who has heard a statement being attributed to the Buddha then approaches him to get this verified; see, e.g., MN 71 at MN I 482,4, which here leads to the Buddha clarifying that he has been misrepresented. The passage shows that the reference to having "heard" does not necessarily imply being present at the original delivery of the reported statement. It also exemplifies the need in an oral setting to ascertain whether the Buddha had indeed made a particular statement. Such a need would provide a natural beginning point for a concern with authentication, which need not be considered problematic, *pace* Skilling 2023, 177n18.

    Once the Buddha has passed away, it seems natural for his longtime attendant Ānanda to be invested with the role of providing the authentication earlier available from the Buddha himself, simply because, among disciples still alive at this time, he would have been the one most likely to have been present at a particular teaching event. This would explain why the above-mentioned *Vinaya* accounts of the first *saṅgīti* grant a central role to him in this respect. Needless to say, my point is not to promote accounts of the first *saṅgīti* as historical in all their details but only to understand the function of the role accorded to Ānanda as a discursive strategy for purposes of authentication in an oral setting.

    The Pāli tradition explicitly recognizes the addition of a discourse, still introduced with *evaṃ me sutaṃ*, at the time of the second *saṅgīti*; see Anālayo 2022d, 43 and 218n102. This shows that the traditional viewpoint was not based on interpreting Ānanda's role in relation to the phrase *evaṃ me sutaṃ* in a strictly literal manner. In view of such evidence, there seems to be less of a need of "trying to fit a fluid skein of ideas associated with Ānanda into the rigid regimens of historicity," to borrow the apt wording used by Skilling 2023, 186.

Even Ānanda's absence at a particular teaching event does not appear to have been a problem for tradition, showing once again the absence of a narrowly literal approach. Skilling 2023, 183f identifies a problem in the 大智度論, **Mahāprajñāpāramitopadeśa*, T 25.1509.69b12, which reports Ānanda stating at the first *saṅgīti* that he was not present when the Buddha delivered his first sermon. This supposedly stands in contrast to several accounts of this first sermon that nevertheless begin with the standard phrase "thus I heard." Yet, the next line in the 大智度論, T 25.1509.69b13, reports Ānanda stating that, even though he was not present at that time, he *heard* it in transmission (from others), 展轉聞; see also Lamotte 1944/1981, 102 (the same reference to having "heard," 聞, in transmission recurs in T 53.2122.373b19 and 375c24, mentioned by Skilling 2023, 184). In other words, Ānanda did hear; it is only that he was not an eyewitness to the original delivery of the first sermon.

Regarding this sermon, it is not entirely clear to me why Skilling 2023, 182 considers it to be "hardly a matter-of-fact event that can be reported by a single individual as 'this is what I have heard'," given that the ability to hear is of course not confined to hearing about matter-of-fact events. At any rate, the indication provided in T 1509 concords with what is evident from the presentation in MN 71, in that *sutaṃ* is not confined to hearing at the time of original delivery.

In line with the precedent set by Ānanda himself, the same reference to having "heard" can thus also include other reciters who repeat the text(s) on later occasions, and that does not require that "the 'I' or 'me' does *not* refer to Ānanda but to the *reciter*," as proposed by Skilling 2023, 187. Why not take it to be relevant to both? That is, the phrase "thus have I heard" could well serve to express not only the present reciter's avowal of reproducing with precision a text memorized personally in this form but also the affirmation that this text was passed down by a lineage of reciters harking back to Ānanda. This would be in line with the probable self-identification of the reciters envisaged by Skilling 2021, 136 himself, in that "when they recited the texts they self-identified with Ānanda as he proclaimed the texts at the first recitation." Note that the proposal of such a form of self-identification requires Ānanda in his traditional role and only works if he is considered to have indeed had a central role in the oral transmission of the text in question.

607. SN 22.83 at SN III 105,14 and its parallel in SĀ 261 at T 2.99.66a8; see in more detail Anālayo 2023d, 147–48.

608. AN 11.9 at AN V 322,9: *yathā kathaṃ pana, bhante, siyā bhikkhuno tathārūpo samādhipaṭilābho yathā na cakkhuṃ manasikareyya, na rūpaṃ manasikareyya, na sotaṃ manasikareyya, na saddaṃ manasikareyya, na ghānaṃ manasikareyya, na gandhaṃ manasikareyya, na jivhaṃ manasikareyya, na rasaṃ manasikareyya, na kāyaṃ manasikareyya, na phoṭṭhabbaṃ manasikareyya, na paṭhaviṃ* (B$^e$: *pathaviṃ*) *manasikareyya, na āpaṃ manasikareyya, na tejaṃ manasikareyya, na vāyaṃ manasikareyya, na ākāsānañcāyatanaṃ manasikareyya, na viññāṇañcāyatanaṃ manasikareyya, na ākiñcaññāyatanaṃ manasikareyya, na nevasaññānāsaññāyatanaṃ manasikareyya, na idhalokaṃ manasikareyya, na paralokaṃ manasikareyya, yam p 'idaṃ* (S$^e$: *yam idaṃ*) *diṭṭhaṃ sutaṃ mutaṃ viññātaṃ pattaṃ pariyesitaṃ anuvicaritaṃ manasā, tam pi na manasikareyya; manasi ca pana kareyyā ti? idh' ānanda, bhik-*

*khu evaṃ manasikaroti: etaṃ santaṃ etaṃ paṇītaṃ, yadidaṃ sabbasaṅkhārasamatho sabbūpadhipaṭinissaggo taṇhakkhayo* (Bᵉ: *taṇhākkhayo*) *virāgo nirodho nibbānan ti.* For the sake of ease of reading, I have subdivided my translation into several paragraphs. A more detailed discussion of this and other such passages can be found in Anālayo 2023d, 71–74.

609. MN 122 at MN III 110,16 and its parallels MĀ 191 at T 1.26.738a19 and Skilling 1994, 194,13.

610. MN 121 at MN III 104,6 and its parallels MĀ 190 at T 1.26.737a2 and Skilling 1994, 148,1. Ray 1994, 272 comments on MN 121 and MN 122, considered together with some of the poems in the *Aṭṭhakavagga*, that these "raise the possibility that the teaching of emptiness as found in the early Mahāyāna *sūtras* was hardly, if at all, an innovation."

611. See in more detail Anālayo 2015c, 75–169 and 2024a.

612. Karashima 2011, 443,1 (= T 8.224.468c20): 汝設有慈心於佛者,當受持般若波羅蜜,當恭敬,作禮,供養.設有是行,汝悉爲供養佛,報恩以;汝爲恭敬過去,當來,今現在佛已. 汝慈孝於佛, 恭敬, 思念於佛, 不如恭敬於般若波羅蜜. 愼莫亡失一句; see also below n. 626. A to some extent comparable relationship between upholding the Buddha's teachings and having an attitude of loving kindness toward him, as part of an instruction given by the Buddha to Ānanda, can be found in MN 122 at MN III 117,25 and its parallels MĀ 191 at T 1.26.740b21 and Skilling 1994, 258,12.

613. See below n. 627.

614. After indicating that all the monks present on this occasion were arhats, the text continues, Wogihara 1932/1935, 8,23: *sthāpayitvā yad ut' āyuṣmantam ānandaṃ*. Similar indications can be found in D 12 *ka* 1b5 or P 734 *mi* 2a2: *ma gtogs pa ni 'di lta ste tshe dang ldan pa kun dga' bo*, T 7.220.763b12 and T 7.220.865c9: 除阿難陀, 獨居學地, T 8.226.508b25: 除賢者阿難, T 8.227.537a28: 唯除阿難, and T 8.228.587a13: 唯一尊者住補特伽羅, 所謂阿難. Such an indication is not found in Lokakṣema's translation, Karashima 2011, 1,10 (= T 8.224.425c6), which does not refer to Ānanda at this point nor to the arhat status of other monks present in the assembly. The same holds for T 8.225.478b23 and for the Gāndhārī manuscript; see Falk and Karashima 2012, 28. This difference seems to be simply a reflection of the generally briefer presentation in the earlier versions. In fact, the translation of the **Pratyutpannasamādhisūtra* (般舟三昧經) attributed to Lokakṣema does have such an indication; see T 13.418.902c28: 皆得阿羅漢, 獨阿難未.

615. See in more detail Anālayo 2015e and 2016c, 159–76.

616. T 22.1425.491a22: 如此學人入無學德力自在眾中, 猶如疥癩野干入師子群中 (瘙 has been emended to become 癩).

617. T 24.1451.404a9 and D 6 *da* 304a6 or Q 1035 *ne* 288a1.

618. The Dharmaguptaka *Vinaya*, T 22.1428.967b27, the Haimavata (?) **Vinayamātṛkā*, T 24.1463.818b17, the Mahāsāṃghika *Vinaya*, T 22.1425.492a22, the Mahīśāsaka *Vinaya*, T 22.1421.191b14, the Mūlasarvāstivāda *Vinaya*, T 24.1451.404c23 and D 6 *da* 306b4 or Q 1035 *ne* 290a4, the Sarvāstivāda *Vinaya*, T 23.1435.449c8, and the Theravāda *Vinaya*, Vin II 289,25.

619. See, e.g., Przyluski 1926, 296–98, Migot 1954, 539–40, Frauwallner 1956, 161–63, Bareau 1971, 140, Tilakaratne 2005, and von Hinüber 2008, 25–27.

620. MN 124 at MN III 125,6 and its parallel MĀ 34 at T 1.26.475a21.

621. On this duration see, e.g., Mochizuki 1940.

622. According to MN 124 at MN III 127,7, he had become an arhat within a week, and according to MĀ 34 at T 1.26.475c7 even within three days of being ordained.
623. See in more detail Anālayo 2007a.
624. Cowell and Neil 1886, 396,11.
625. See Anālayo 2010a, 26–27.
626. Karashima 2011, 535,2 (= T 8.224.477c17): 阿難, 汝所當作者, 悉爲已. 汝身亦有慈, 口亦有慈, 心亦有慈. 汝有孝於佛, 不言無有孝 . . . 我語汝[?] 阿難, 是般若波羅蜜從中亡一字, 汝捨, 汝縱不書, 汝都盧以無有慈孝於佛所, 汝以不復見我. 阿難, 汝以不復恭敬於佛. 阿難, 汝以不復隨佛教. On 縱 see Karashima 2010, 671; on the probable implication of the reference to not writing it down, 不書, in this context see Anālayo 2024e, 81–82. The reference to 慈 with the body, etc., in the present context has its Sanskrit counterpart in Wogihara 1932/1935, 990,14 in *maitreṇa kāyakarmaṇā manaāpena*, etc., whereas the same term 慈 in the case of the first entrustment quoted above n. 612, Karashima 2011, 443,1 (= T 8.224.468c20), instead has its counterpart in Wogihara 1932/1935, 871,3 in *hitaiṣitayā premato vā gauravato vā*; see also Karashima 2013b, 284–87 and Jing Guo 2023, 7. In an attempt to bridge these meanings and reflect that the Chinese has the same 慈, I have chosen "kindness," which has the additional advantage of being more easily related to "loving kindness" as the more specific meaning of 慈 when used to designate the first of the four *brahmavihāras*.
627. DN 16 at DN II 144,15: *dīgharattaṃ kho te, ānanda, tathāgato paccupaṭṭhito mettena kāyakammena hitena sukhena advayena appamāṇena, mettena vacīkammena . . . pe . . . mettena manokammena hitena sukhena advayena appamāṇena*; Waldschmidt 1951, 298,5: *(ta)th(āga)ta upasthitas ta (ānanda) maitreṇa kāyakarmaṇā hitena sukhenādvayenāpramāṇena, maitreṇa vākkarmaṇā maitreṇa manaskarmaṇā hitena sukhenādvayenāpramāṇena*; DĀ 2 at T 1.1.25c8: 汝侍我已來, 身行有慈, 無二, 無量, 言行有慈, 意行有慈, 無二, 無量 (adopting the 宋, 元, and 明 variant 已 instead of 以); T 1.5.169b18: 若盡心侍佛二十餘年, 慈仁於佛, 敬身慎口; and T 1.6.184c27: 自汝侍佛已來, 身行常慈, 口行亦慈, 心行亦慈. Yet another version, T 1.7.200b18, does not refer to *maitrī* and instead reports the Buddha referring to Ānanda's bodily, verbal, and mental activities having been pure and free from blemish, 又復見汝身口及意, 皆悉清淨, 無有瑕穢.
628. An example would be DN 34 at DN III 290,16 (E[c] of DN 34 abbreviates; the full formulation is found in DN 33): *uddhaṃ adho tiriyaṃ advayaṃ appamāṇaṃ* and its parallel Schlingloff 1962, 29: *ū(r)dh(va)m (adha)s tiryag advayam apramā(nam)*; both versions apply this string of qualifications to each of the ten totalities. Two Chinese parallels, DĀ 10 and T 13, do not list the ten totalities.
629. Karashima 2011, 184,4 (= T 8.224.442c20): 無有兩法, 用之, 本淨, 故曰爲一. It seems that this instance would need to be added to the assessment regarding the notion of *advaya* by Lancaster 1968, 127, made in the context of a detailed comparative study of T 224 in the light of its parallels, in that "[e]xcept for Chapter I of T. 225, this term seems to be missing from the early text[s]. Since in T. 225, Chapter I belongs to a later tradition, the one occurrence does not belong to the early text." In contrast, "[i]n every case from T. 227 to the translation of T. 228, *advaya* occurs in the Chinese when it is present in the Sanskrit."
630. See, e.g., MN 1 at MN I 3,29 and its parallel EĀ 44.6 at T 2.125.766a24.
631. See, e.g., MN 137 at MN III 220,30 and its parallel MĀ 163 at T 1.26.693b29.

632. MN 121 at MN III 105,6, with parallels in MĀ 190 at T 1.26.737a21 and Skilling 1994, 156,3.
633. The applicability of the qualification of being unified already to the first absorption can be seen in MN 43 at MN I 295,2, MĀ 210 at T 1.26.788c20, and Up 1005 at D 4094 *ju* 8a2 or P 5595 *tu* 8b8 (the last two are strictly speaking parallels to MN 44; the present case is one of several instances of a shifting around of topics between these two similar discourses in different reciter traditions) and again in MN 122 at MN III 111,20, with parallels in MĀ 191 at T 1.26.738b25 and Skilling 1994, 206,3; for occurrences of the same in Pāli discourses with no known parallel see also MN 111 at MN III 25,15 and SN 40.1 at SN IV 263,21.
634. SN 35.205 at SN IV 196,23 and its parallel SĀ 1169 at T 2.99.312c5; see in more detail Anālayo 2022f, 2–5.
635. MN 106 at MN II 265,4, with parallels in MĀ 75 at T 1.26.543a19 and Up 4058 at D 4094 *ju* 229b3 or P 5595 *tu* 262a5.
636. Sn 724 to Sn 765.
637. MN 19 at MN I 114,25 and its parallel MĀ 102 at T 1.26.589a14.
638. See, e.g., SN 35.106 at SN IV 86,18 and its parallel SĀ 218 at T 2.99.54c22.
639. See in more detail Anālayo 2018c, 9–15.
640. See above n. 409.
641. Kimura 2009, 41,25: *mahāsattvo maitrīsahagatena cittena vipulena mahodgatenādvayenāpramāṇenāvaireṇāsapatnenānāvaraṇenāvyāvadhena sarvatrānugatena . . . viharati* (also in Dutt 1934, 181,18).
642. See, e.g., Lamotte 1970, 1250n1, Pagel 1995, 141, Jenkins 1999, 188–214, Maithrimurthi 1999, 250 and 258–62, Schmithausen 2000b, 447, and Martini 2011, 171.
643. The *Śikṣāsamuccaya*, Bendall 1902, 212,12, introduces a basic threefold distinction of *maitrī* (the third being objectless) by quoting the *Akṣayamati(nirdeśa)sutra*, an early version of which, translated by Dharmarakṣa, already has this basic threefold distinction, T 13.403.599a13, although the actual rendering of the third option of objectless *maitrī* is difficult to resolve; the corresponding Sanskrit is *anārambaṇā maitrī anutpattikadharmakṣāntipratilabdhānāṃ bodhisatvānām iti*. The relevant indication in the *Mahāyānasūtrālaṃkāra*, Lévi 1907, 122,1, reads: *anālambanā maitrī . . . anutpattikadharmakṣāntilābhena aṣṭamyāṃ bhūmau*. The *Bodhisattvabhūmi*, Wogihara 1930/1936, 241,17, applies the basic threefold distinction to all four *brahmavihāras*, beginning with *maitrī*. The *Pañjikā* on the *Bodhicaryāvatāra*, Tripathi 1988, 234,29, in turn presents the same threefold distinction in relation to compassion. In view of the reference in DN 16 and some of its parallels to a form of nondual *maitrī* that is particularly directed toward the Buddha, it is perhaps noteworthy that a Mahāyāna version of the Discourse on the Great Nirvana, the 大般涅槃經, employs the same threefold distinction and then indicates that *maitrī* of the type that is without objects is directed toward the Tathāgata; see T 12.374.452c2 (= T 12.375.694c5): 慈有三緣: 一緣眾生, 二緣於法, 三則無緣. . . 無緣者, 緣於如來, 是名無緣 and Lamotte 1970, 1251n1.
644. See, e.g., MN 97 at MN II 195,2 and its parallel MĀ 27 at T 1.26.458b2. The context of this instruction makes it clear that it does not intend absorption attainment but rather is the way cultivation of *maitrī* should be undertaken; see also Anālayo 2022c, 211–13.
645. Vism 297,14 and Abhidh-k VIII 31c, Pradhan 1967, 454,7; see also Dhammajoti 2010 and Anālayo 2022c, 214–30.
646. For a detailed study from a practice-related perspective see Anālayo 2019b.

647. See in more detail Anālayo 2022c, 13–58.
648. For a comparative survey of *dhyāna* descriptions see Meisig 1990.
649. Apart from these standard descriptions, however, in the context of a listing of various skills in relation to absorption attainment, SN 34.5 at SN III 266,14 speaks of being skilled (or not) in respect to the *ārammaṇa*; a reference repeated in the remainder of this *Jhānasaṃyutta*. The commentary, Spk II 353,3, understands the reference to skill in respect to the *ārammaṇa* here to intend skill in respect to the *kasiṇas*. How far this is indeed the meaning relevant to the discourse remains open to question, since in its general usage in Pāli discourses the term *ārammaṇa* has not yet acquired the sense of an "object," which it mainly carries in later texts; see also below n. 653.
650. Vism 118,1 begins its exposition of the actual practice by surveying different potential problems when residing in a particular monastery, before describing how to set up a device with earth that can then be used as the object for concentration.
651. Vism 123,28.
652. Vism 174,19.
653. Nyanatiloka 1952/1988, 250 explains: "*Ārammaṇa* has in the sutta texts only the meaning of 'foundation,' or 'basis,' or 'dependent on' . . . As [a] term for the 6 objects, *rūpārammaṇa, saddā*°, etc., it is first used in the Abh[idhamma] Canon, though the teaching of [the] dependency of the 6 kinds of *viññāṇa* on the 6 sense-objects is an integral part of the suttas." According to Heim and Ram-Prasad 2018, 1113n54, "'[o]bject' for Buddhaghosa is usually '*ārammaṇa*,' which has the implication of phenomenal object, because its root meaning is support or that which is expedient, i.e., support for the experience of it."
654. The basic distinction comes up in a commentary on an injunction by the Buddha to his disciples reported in MN 8 at MN I 46,9, according to which they should meditate, lest they later have regrets. The commentary explains that this injunction refers to these two modalities; Ps I 195,24: *jhāyathā ti ārammaṇūpanijjhānena aṭṭhatiṃsārammaṇāni, lakkhaṇūpanijjhānena ca aniccādito khandhāyatanādīni upanijjhāyatha.* More details on these two modalities can be found in As 167,8. The basic idea would be that meditating on an *ārammaṇa* is the procedure appropriate for *samatha* meditation leading to absorption attainment, whereas meditating instead on a *lakkhaṇa* (e.g., on impermanence, etc.) is relevant for *vipassanā* meditation and the realization of path and fruit.
655. According to Mishra 1988, 3, "[t]he concept of *advaya* is pivotal to [Mahāyāna] Buddhist thoughts . . . Mahāyāna [S]anskrit texts are replete with this word and also, sometimes, with its synonym *advaita*. The exuberant use of this word denotes the great significance of the principle underlying it."
656. An explicit application of a dualistic distinction to alms food, indicated by the use of the term "twofold" (*duvidha*), can be found in AN 10.54 at AN V 100,31, which has a parallel in a similar presentation in MĀ 109 at T 1.26.598c8, although its actual formulation does not have a counterpart to the term "twofold." In both versions, the basic distinction revolves around the either wholesome or else unwholesome repercussions that result from partaking of such food. This is part of an overall distinction made from an ethical point of view. Although this would not be the intention of this passage, nevertheless, by way of extension the same basic distinction could perhaps also be applied to the difference between healthy and poisonous food, which relates to the positive or negative repercussions to be expected from partaking of such food.

657. Karashima 2011, 67,9 (= T 8.224.432a15): 從薩芸若中得佛. Karashima 2011, 88,4 (= T 8.224.434b21): 薩芸若者從般若波羅蜜成. Karashima 2011, 121,2 (= T 8.224.437b13): 皆從般若波羅蜜中學, 得成薩芸若. Karashima 2011, 208,4 (= T 8.224.444c11): 自歸般若波羅蜜者, 爲自歸薩芸若慧已. Karashima 2011, 208,6 (= T 8.224.444c15): 薩芸若慧者, 是般若波羅蜜之所照明. 於般若波羅蜜中住者, 無不解慧. Karashima 2011, 290,11 (= T 8.224.453a6): 佛言: 心向薩芸若, 是爲觀視般若波羅蜜. 須菩提言: 何謂心向薩芸若? 佛言: 心向空[,] 是爲觀薩芸若.

658. Karashima 2011, 407,3 (= T 8.224.464c15): 如是學[,] 爲學薩芸若. 如是學, 爲學般若波羅蜜. 如是學, 爲學怛薩阿竭地, 爲學力, 爲學無所畏, 爲學諸佛法.

659. MN 76 at MN I 519,16: *piṇḍam pi na labhati, kukkuro pi ḍaṃsati* (Ce and Ee: *ḍasati*), *caṇḍena pi hatthinā samāgacchati, caṇḍena pi assena samāgacchati, caṇḍena pi goṇena samāgacchati.*

660. SHT III 942 R3, Waldschmidt, Clawiter, and Sander-Holzmann 1971, 205: *palvalaṃ prapā[ta]ṃ syandanikāṃ gūtho[ḍ]igallaṃ v[ā].*

661. MĀ 188 at T 2.26.734b20: 或行如是道逢惡象, 惡馬, 惡牛, 惡狗... 或墮廁中.

662. SN 4.18 at SN I 114,9, with parallels in SĀ 1095 at T 2.99.288a15 and EĀ 45.4 at T 2.125.772b2.

663. MN 71 at MN I 482,14: *ye . . . evam āhaṃsu: samaṇo gotamo sabbaññū sabbadassāvī, aparisesaṃ ñāṇadassanaṃ paṭijānāti: carato ca me tiṭṭhato ca suttassa ca jāgarassa ca satataṃ samitaṃ ñāṇadassanaṃ paccupaṭṭhitan ti na me te vuttavādino, abbhācikkhanti ca pana maṃ* (Ee and Se: *man*) *te asatā abhūtenā ti.* On the implications of this passage see also Anālayo 2020f, 21–25, and on the topic of the attribution of omniscience to the Buddha in general see Anālayo 2006 and 2014c, 117–27.

664. MN 14 at MN I 92,35, MN 79 at MN II 31,7, MN 101 at MN II 218,1, AN 3.74 at AN I 220,28, and AN 9.38 at AN IV 429,1 (which reports the same claim also made by another teacher, Pūraṇa Kāśyapa). The situation in the respective parallels is as follows: MN 14 has parallels in MĀ 100, T 54, and T 55. The first and last of these three, MĀ 100 at T 1.26.587b18 and T 1.55.850c6, only report Mahāvīra giving instructions to his disciples, without mentioning that he based these on his claim to be omniscient. The corresponding passage in T 1.54.846a17 does not even refer to Mahāvīra. MN 79 has a parallel in MĀ 208, which at T 1.26.784a16 lists Mahāvīra among several teachers claiming omniscience in the following form (784a11): 自說實有薩云然, 一切知, 一切見, 無餘知, 無餘見也. MN 101 and AN 3.74 have parallels in MĀ 19 and SĀ 563 respectively, which at T 1.26.443c5 and T 2.99.147c7 only report Mahāvīra giving instructions to his disciples, without mentioning that he claimed to be omniscient. Parts of AN 9.38 have been preserved in SHT VI 1326.212, Bechert and Wille 1989, 82–83, but these unfortunately do not comprise the relevant passage. In sum, whereas the Pāli discourses repeatedly present Mahāvīra as a claimant to omniscience—which from a historical viewpoint would be correct—only one parallel (MĀ 208) attributes a claim to omniscience to Mahāvīra, and in this instance such a claim does not feature as something specific to him but rather occurs as part of a list of several teachers making the same assertion.

665. In what follows I provide a few examples for such proposals: Warder 1970/1991, 135: "Since other *śramaṇas* had made this claim, or had it made for them, it was perhaps natural that Buddhists should wish to set their teacher at least as high as anyone had suggested it was possible to get." Jaini 1974, 80: "In the face of the extraordinary claims of the Jains for their Tīrthaṅkaras, however, it is inconceivable that the eager followers

of the Buddha could have long refrained from pressing similar claims for their 'enlightened' Master." Werner 1981/2013, 59: "Claims of omniscience had been made in the time of the Buddha for other ascetic teachers, e.g., Mahāvīra (MN 79), and it is understandable that such a claim would eventually be made also for the Buddha." Naughton 1991, 37: "It is very possible that Śākyamuni's disinterested attitude towards the issue of omniscience reflects his real feelings, and that later statements attributed to him where he appears to claim some form of omniscience for himself were interpolations created by disciples who felt uncomfortable comparing their teacher with Mahāvīra, who had claimed a literal kind of omniscience all along."

666. Sv III 896,13 speaks of the *sabbaññubodhisatta*. In the context of a detailed survey of occurrences of the term *bodhisatta* in Pāli texts, Endo 1996, 85 comments that, "[i]f a bodhisatta is 'sabbaññu' (omniscient), then there would be nothing that he should strive for. He is a Buddha himself . . . The usage of the word 'sabbaññubodhisatta' must therefore be understood from a different viewpoint: it . . . has more [an] emotional significance than [an] etymological [one]." The *Mahāvastu* refers to the omniscient being born, Marciniak 2020, 30,9 (also in Senart 1890, 21,16): *sarvajñaḥ jāyate*, a reference that would also not call for a literal reading, as just a little later in the same work the bodhisattva refers to his omniscience as a future event, Marciniak 2020, 31,3 (also in Senart 1890, 22,5): *sarvajño sarvadarśāvī bhaviṣyaṃ*. I am inclined to read in the same light a reference in the Perfection of Wisdom to *mahāsattva*s who know all; see Karashima 2011, 21,9 (= T 8.224.427b18): 摩訶薩者, 悉自了見, 悉了知十方天下人, 十方所有悉曉了知. Note that this passage in fact does not employ Lokakṣema's standard usage of a transliteration of the term omniscience, 薩芸若, which can perhaps be taken to support the impression that this passage may not intend omniscience in a literal sense.

667. AN 4.23 at AN II 23,28: *yaṃ, bhikkhave, sadevakassa lokassa samārakassa sabrahmakassa sassamaṇabrāhmaṇiyā pajāya sadevamanussāya diṭṭhaṃ sutaṃ mutaṃ viññātaṃ pattaṃ pariyesitaṃ anuvicaritaṃ manasā, sabbaṃ* (S$^{e}$: *sammā*) *taṃ tathāgatena abhisambuddhaṃ. tasmā tathāgato ti vuccati*; for the commentary see Mp III 32,18. A comparable statement occurs in the next discourse, AN 4.24 at AN II 25,1, for a detailed study of which see Ñāṇananda 1974/1985.

668. MĀ 137 at T 1.26.645b16: 若有一切盡普正, 有彼一切如來知, 見, 覺, 得.

669. It 1.1.7 at It 3,28 and T 17.765.670a24.

670. See in more detail Anālayo 2014c.

671. This distinct perspective has already been noted by Vetter 2001, 81, who comments on the first chapter of Lokakṣema's translation in particular that "it is also possible that the teaching was offered and used to relativize the final objective of Buddhahood characterized by all-knowingness. Omniscience would then no longer mean the knowledge of all details, but the knowledge that all the details are without essence and real existence. Such a result is easier to reach than an omniscience of individual details." In appreciation of the highlight placed in this way on the basic attitude in the Perfection of Wisdom, it seems to me nevertheless that, if the promoters of the Perfection of Wisdom had downgraded omniscience to nothing but a penetrative insight into phenomena lacking an essence, they would have lost a major component in the attraction and significance of the goal of becoming a Buddha. This holds especially in the early period reflected by the Gāndhārī manuscript and Lokakṣema's translation, a time before compassion became a central motivating factor. In fact, in the Perfection of

Wisdom omniscience is not attributed to just anyone who knows that phenomena are without essence and do not exist as real entities, such as, for example, Subhūti. The shift in perspective may therefore be a more subtle one, in that the *path* to omniscience is not to be found in a closeup on details—trying to discern their distinct characteristics, even their intrinsic nature—but rather in stepping back to realize their thoroughly empty nature.

672. Karashima 2011, 453,4 (= T 8.224.469c2): 若有菩薩，行般若波羅蜜時，思惟十二因緣不可盡. 作是思惟者，出過羅漢，辟支佛道去，正住佛道. My translation of 不可盡 is only tentative; the Sanskrit counterpart in Wogihara 1932/1935, 880,23 appears to be *akṣayatvena* (here applied to each of the links of dependent arising individually), rendered by Conze 1973/1975, 271 as "non-extinction."
673. See in more detail Anālayo 2021b.
674. Jurewicz 2000.
675. See, e.g., Vin I 40,28, the *Catuṣpariṣatsūtra*, Waldschmidt 1962, 378,13, the *Mahāvastu*, Marciniak 2019, 71,2 (also in Senart 1897, 61,3), and a more detail discussion in Anālayo 2023d, 63 and 150–51.
676. The following sources take this investigation only up to consciousness (standing in a reciprocal conditioning relationship with name-and-form): SN 12.65 at SN II 104,30, Chung and Fukita 2020, 96–97, Bongard-Levin, Boucher, Fukita, and Wille 1996, 39, 52, and 78, T 16.713.826c8, T 16.714.828a4 (which does not mention the reciprocal conditioning), and T 16.715.829b16; see also Nagashima 2009, 154, Melzer 2009, 216, and Kudo and Shono 2015, 459. However, SĀ 287 at T 2.99.80c10 and EĀ 38.4 at T 2.125.718b2 take the same investigation further, up to ignorance; see also SN 12.10 at SN II 10,15. For a more detailed discussion of this difference and its potential implications see Pappas and Anālayo 2026; on dependent arising in general see also Anālayo 2018c, 6–17.
677. See above n. 1 for instances where recollection of past lives and the divine eye are shown to lead to mistaken views, which implies that neither of the two is on its own liberating.
678. MN 4 at MN I 22,9 and its parallel EĀ 31.1 at T 2.125.666b22.
679. Gnoli 1977, 118,11. The same work also provides a link between the second and the third knowledge, Gnoli 1977, 118,27, reporting that witnessing the rebirth of sentient beings in accordance with their deeds through the divine eye led to the realization that these sentient beings fare on in the round of rebirth due to the three influxes (*āśrava*) of sensuality, becoming, and ignorance. Hence, the next step for Gautama was to eradicate these influxes in his own mind, which is precisely the function of the third knowledge, *āśravakṣayajñāna*.
680. Such insight into the mechanism of karma is of course not the only potential outcome of recollecting one's own past lives, which can similarly arouse disenchantment with *saṃsāra* due to insight into impermanence (although this would not be directly relevant to the case of Śākyamuni, as he was already sufficiently disenchanted earlier). In principle, these two alternatives are best seen as complementary rather than as conflicting with each other, *pace* Schopen 1983/2005, 210; for a critical examination of the central arguments in Schopen 1983/2005 regarding memories of past lives and karma see Anālayo 2023b.
681. Karashima 2011, 464,6 (= T 8.224.470c20): 疾欲得佛者，索般若波羅蜜，當如薩陀波倫菩薩. For a survey of parallel versions of this tale see Yang 2013, 99–102.

Orsborn 2021a, 9 (based on Orsborn 2012) finds a chiasmic structure (within the tale itself) only evident in later versions and thus not in T 224. For a discussion of Haribhadra's commentary on the Sadāprarudita tale as exemplifying a scheme of four *bhūmis* see Mak 2011.

682. Karashima 2011, 466,8 (= T 8.224.471a24): 汝行時莫念左, 莫念右, 莫念前, 莫念後, 莫念上, 莫念下, 莫念行. 行時, 莫念恐怖, 莫念喜, 莫念食, 莫念飲, 莫念坐, 莫念行道, 莫念中止, 莫念婬, 莫念怒, 莫念癡, 莫念守, 莫念有所得, 莫念內, 莫念外, 莫念色, 莫念痛痒, 思想, 生死, 識, 莫念眼, 莫念耳, 莫念鼻, 莫念口, 莫念身, 莫念心意, 莫念地, 水, 火, 風, 莫念空, 莫念人, 莫念我, 莫念命, 莫念有空, 莫念無空, 莫念行菩薩道, 莫念有經, 莫念無經, 莫念生天上, 莫念生世間, 莫念菩薩善, 莫念菩薩惡, 一切所向念悉斷, 遍無所著. The counterpart to 莫念, which I have rendered somewhat freely as "disengage attentionally," appears to be *na manasikāraṃ utpādayasi* in Wogihara 1932/1935, 927,17, although a later part of the Sanskrit passage then shifts to a different usage; on the complexities surrounding Lokakṣema's usage of 念 see also above n. 583. In the present context, adopting a more literal translation for 莫念 would not work so well for the reference to the three root defilements, as it would risk giving the impression that the task is to ignore manifestations of these, which would not be in keeping with the overall thrust of the training of a bodhisattva described in the Perfection of Wisdom. The same instruction in T 8.225.504a18 also covers the three root defilements, here given in an abbreviated form: 莫念婬, 怒, 癡 (a tendency toward abbreviation in T 225 has already been noted by Lancaster 1969, 250). The corresponding instruction in T 8.227.580b4 enjoins Sadāprarudita to separate himself from the five hindrances, 當離五蓋. Other versions of this instruction extant in Chinese translations of *Prajñāpāramitā* texts do not refer to the root defilements or to the hindrances; see T 6.220.1059b1, T 8.221.141c5, T 8.223.416b1, T 8.228.668b3, as well as a version of this instruction found in the **Mahāprajñāpāramitopadeśa*, T 25.1509.731a14. A version that is not part of *Prajñāpāramitā* literature, however, taking instead the form of a tale in a *Jātaka* collection, T 3.152.43b12, does have a comparable reference to the three root defilements (together with jealousy/envy): 無念 . . . 貪淫, 瞋恚, 愚癡, 嫉妬.

683. Karashima 2011, 479,1 (= T 8.224.472a19): 即得見十方諸佛三昧; and Karashima 2011, 481,4 (= T 8.224.472a26): 薩陀波倫菩薩從三昧覺, 作是念: 諸佛本從何所來, 去至何所? Beyer 1977, 340 comments that in this way "[f]or Sadāprarudita . . . the visionary quest has become a metaphysical one."

684. Karashima 2011, 502,1 (= T 8.224.473c9): 空本無所從來[,] 去亦無所至. 佛亦如是. 無想本無所從來[,] 去亦無所至. 佛亦如 . . . 泥洹本無所從來[,] 去亦無所至. 佛亦如是. On the relationship of the sermon by Dharmodgata (as reported in the Sanskrit version of the *Aṣṭasāhasrikā Prajñāpāramitā*) to the notion of the Buddha's *dharmakāya* see also Makransky 1997, 32–35.

685. T 13.418.905c27: 作是念: 佛從何所來? 我爲到何所? 自念: 佛無所從來, 我亦無所至. 自念: 三處—欲處, 色處, 無想處—是三處意所爲耳. 我所念, 即見. 心作佛. 心自見. 心是佛. 心是怛薩阿竭. I have for the most part followed the translation by Harrison 1998a, 21, except for adjusting to my own terminological preferences and for not attempting to reflect the difference between 意/*manas* and 心/*citta*; on these different terms as referents to the mind see also the discussion above note 259. The relevance of the present passage to the quote from the Perfection of Wisdom in Karashima

2011, 502,1 (= T 8.224.473c9)—see my previous note—has already been noted by Zhao 2020, 264.

686. Harrison 1998a, 3 comments that this passage "contains hints of the early unfolding of the Yogācāra," with a phrasing that "reappears in the *Daśabhūmika-sūtra* in its Sanskrit form: *cittamātram idam yad idaṃ traidhātukam*"; see Vaidya 1967, 32,9. On the significance of this passage for the evolution of *cittamātra* idealism see also Schmithausen 1973, 176. In the context of a survey of the Sadāprarudita tale and the **Pratyutpanna-samādhisūtra*, Zhao 2018, 81–82 points out that "whilst in the Sadāprarudita story, the interpretation for the answer still reflects the classic Prajñāpāramitā or Madhyamaka philosophy, the PSS [= **Pratyutpannasamādhisūtra*] seems to include a forerunner to a more Vijñānavāda-type of thinking." For a comparison of these two texts see also Zhao 2020.

687. Dhp 1: *manopubbaṅgamā dhammā, manoseṭṭhā manomayā*; for the parallels see Anālayo 2023d, 159n28 and for a more detailed discussion Palihawadana 1984, Skilling 2007a, and Agostini 2010.

688. T 8.225.480b18: 意幻爲三界耳; 如三界, 即六根; 如六根, 即五陰 (adopting a 宋, 元, 明, and 宮 variant that adds 如六根 after 根); the suggestion that 意幻 might reflect an Indic original corresponding to *manomaya* assumes that the translator may have failed to distinguish between the plural form *mayā* and *māyā*, a type of error that is not uncommon in Chinese translations, or else that these two had been interchanged in the Indic original, which would have been facilitated by the circumstance that the prior portion of text does refer to *māyā*.

689. Karashima 2011, 515,8 (= T 8.224.475a16): 阿羅漢泥洹空, 無所生. 般若波羅蜜亦空, 無所生如是. 怛薩阿竭般泥洹本等無有異. 般若波羅蜜亦本等無有異如是.

690. MN 72 at MN I 487,29 and its parallels SĀ 962 at T 2.99.246a5, SĀ$^2$ 196 at T 2.100.445b24, and Up 3057 at D 4094 *ju* 158a4 or P 5595 *tu* 182b5; see in more detail Anālayo 2023d, 116–20.

691. Drewes 2021, 169–70 argues that "when Mahāyāna emerged it was not believed to be possible to become a bodhisattva or meaningfully enter the path to Buddhahood in one's present life," as "the initial step of entering the path to Buddhahood was apparently invariably understood to require the presence of a living Buddha, with confidence in one's status being possible only after receiving a Buddha's prediction." Based on this assessment, Drewes 2021, 172 then proposes the following scenario: "When Mahāyāna arose . . . entering the path to Buddhahood was understood to require the fulfillment of specific requirements in a Buddha's presence, and one's status was regarded as tenuous until one received a Buddha's prediction . . . Rather than being the product of a preexisting bodhisattva tradition, it thus seems most likely that Mahāyāna sūtras were responsible for bringing a bodhisattva tradition into existence for the first time . . . Although the precise developments leading up to it remain unclear, at some point a preacher presented a sūtra claiming that those who were able to encounter it and accept its new teachings had already become bodhisattvas in past lives. Since sūtras are infallible, this transformed those who accepted the text's authenticity into an audience of long-established bodhisattvas, ready for the revelation of further texts intended for their use. Responding to this demand, authors used the conceit of presenting the Buddha's special sūtras for bodhisattvas to introduce further teachings, leading to the composition of a vast corpus of the new texts and the emergence of the broad tradition we know as Mahāyāna."

692. Karashima 2011, 465,9 (= T 8.224.471a8): 是時世有佛 . . . 般泥洹以來甚久, 亦不聞經, 亦不見比丘僧.
693. Karashima 2011, 530,12 (= T 8.224.477b9): 諸菩薩悉見十方無央數佛. It is not immediately clear if the five hundred women should be included in the reference to plural "bodhisattvas." Judging from the context, this seems to be the case, as otherwise they would not be able to witness their own prediction. Without witnessing their own prediction, however, it would be difficult to understand what motivated their magical transformation into males. On this reading, then, by this stage of the narrative the five hundred women, who unlike Sadāprarudita have so far never been qualified as bodhisattvas, would in this instance at least be implicitly referred to as bodhisattvas. This could be in recognition of their earlier wholehearted dedication and willingness to sacrifice themselves. The same appears to hold for T 8.225.507c17: 闓士普見諸佛, which also reports their transformation into males (see next note); Hirakawa 1997, 1201 lists 闓士 as a rendering of the term "bodhisattva"; see also Zacchetti 2021, 53n104. In the other versions, which do not report a transformation of the five hundred women into males, the vision of the Buddhas of the ten directions occurs only to Sadāprarudita; see Wogihara 1932/1935, 989,4, T 6.220.1072c26, T 8.227.586b8, and T 8.228.676a25.
694. Karashima 2011, 531,4 (= T 8.224.477b14): 時五百女人却後稍稍皆當作佛如是 . . . 五百女人即化作男子. The parallel version in T 8.225.507c20 reads: 諸女即化爲男. 世世所生不離諸佛, 常以大明教授十方以求作佛. Although T 225 thus reports their transformation into males, it does not describe their future destiny in terms as definite as T 224, only indicating that they are certain to be always reborn in future lives in the presence of Buddhas and will pursue the path to Buddhahood.
695. Note that in the case of Gaṅgadevā, Karashima 2011, 340,6 (= T 8.224.458a17), again a female receives a prediction of her future Buddhahood, and in this case with specific indications regarding the time when this will happen and the name (s)he will have. The prediction is in this case given by the Buddha Śākyamuni, and her original aspiration to become a Buddha took place in the presence of Dīpaṃkara Buddha; see Karashima 2011, 341,10 (= T 8.224.458b1).
696. T 13.418.915c11: 即受持是三昧, 見十方無央數佛, 悉從聞經, 悉受持. 爾時, 諸佛悉語我言: 却後無央數劫, 汝當作佛名釋迦文. The ensuing verse leaves no doubt that this indeed intends the meeting with Dīpaṃkara; see T 13.418.915c19: 憶念我昔定光佛, 於時逮得是三昧, 即見十方無數佛, 聞說尊法深妙義. The same procedure of relying on the Buddhas of the ten directions can be seen in T 13.416.890c17 and in the Tibetan version, Harrison 1978b, 151,9 (17A).
697. After the statement made by the Buddhas, the Tibetan version adds: *zhes lung bstan to*, Harrison 1978b, 151,17, which conveys that the preceding is a formal "prediction." The same holds for the use of 授我記 in T 13.416.890c18, with the difference that here this comes before the actual prediction. The terminology used in these two versions makes it safe to propose that the somewhat informal phrasing 語我言, used in T 13.418.915c13, is best read as also intending an actual prediction.
698. Drewes 2018, 81–82 quotes from a page in the English translation by Lancaster 1968, 224–309 of Lokakṣema's version of the story of Sadāprarudita (another quote from the same work occurs in Drewes 2011, 347n50); both predictions have been rendered by Lancaster 1968, 307–9 (two further English renderings of these predictions in Lokakṣema's translation can be found in Paul 1979/1985, 133–34 and Giddings 2014, 326). On the same page, Drewes 2018, 81 also refers to a page from the English translation of

the **Pratyutpannasamādhisūtra* (T 418) by Harrison 1998a, which offers a rendition of the two passages quoted above in n. 696 (Harrison 1998a, 77). Consultation of these English translations at the time of undertaking the research eventually published in Drewes 2021 could have clarified that the proposed conclusions are in need of revision.

699. Karashima 2011, 465,6 (= T 8.224.471a5): 時忉利天人來下, 在虛空中, 觀見菩薩日日啼哭 . . . 字菩薩爲薩陀波倫. This features as one of several explanations of his name in the **Mahāprajñāpāramitopadeśa*, T 25.1509.732a24: 憂愁啼哭七日七夜, 因是故, 天, 龍, 鬼神號曰常啼; see also the discussion in Yang 2013, 11–12.

700. Yang 2013, 160 notes that the narrative progression here is not entirely clear, when "he only hears the name of the previous buddha in a dream and then leaves for the wilderness. Something in this turning point concerning his motive to leave for the wilderness appears to be missing." She notes that the missing piece can be found in T 3.152.43a21, which is a *Jātaka* version of the Sadāprarudita tale that occurs outside of *Prajñāpāramitā* literature. This text reports detailed instructions to Sadāprarudita on how he should conduct himself by way of abandoning defilements, attachment, and craving, and by stilling thoughts in his mind. Such advice would provide a meaningful background to his decision to withdraw into seclusion.

701. Karashima 2011, 465,13 (= T 8.224.471a14): 自念言: 我惡所致不見佛, 不聞經, 不得菩薩所行法. 是時薩陀波倫菩薩啼哭.

702. Karashima 2011, 468,4 (= T 8.224.471b14): 行, 中道作是念: 去是幾所乃當得般若波羅蜜? 作是念已, 住, 復大啼哭.

703. Karashima 2011, 479,1 (= T 8.224.472a19): 即得見十方諸佛三昧. Harrison 1978a, 47–48 comments that "there can be no doubt that a specific *samādhi* is being referred to in this early version of the *Aṣṭa*. Now, we have no way of knowing whether or not that *samādhi* can be equated with the *pratyutpanna-samādhi*; what is important for our purposes is that, given the production at some time of the *Pratyutpanna-sūtra*, we are liable to regard the experience of the vision of the Buddhas of the ten directions less as a mere dramatic property in the development of the Sadāprarudita story, and more as a specific experience on the path to the Perfection of Wisdom and awakening, an experience which the author of that tale saw as being worthy of elucidation in terms of the doctrine of Śūnyatā, hence its being made the subject of Dharmodgata's sermon." Another relevant point, already mentioned by Harrison 1978a, 47, is that whereas T 224 mentions a single *samādhi*, the Sanskrit version gives a long list of different *samādhi*s; see Wogihara 1932/1935, 940,21 to 942,5. The apparent proliferation evident in this way would be in line with a general suggestion by Lancaster 1976, 200 that listings of various *samādhi*s probably had some meditative experience as their starting point. For a discussion of the position taken by Skilton 2002 regarding the significance of *samādhi* in some Mahāyāna *sūtra*s see Anālayo 2025b, 110–14.

704. Karashima 2011, 481,4 (= T 8.224.472a27): 作是念: 諸佛本從何所來, 去至何所? 作是思惟已, 便復舉聲大哭.

705. Karashima 2011, 471,1 (= T 8.224.471c6): 皆以七寶作城. 其城七重. 其間皆有七寶琦樹. 城上皆有七寶羅縠緹縵以覆城上. 其間皆有七寶交露 . . . 遶城有七重池水 . . . 池中有七寶之船. On the significance of such references to jewels in the Sadāprarudita tale see also Granoff 1998, 349–52.

706. DN 17 at DN II 170,17, Waldschmidt 1951, 306,1 or Matsumura 1988, 3,3, DĀ 2 at T 1.1.21b17, T 1.5.169c21, T 1.6.185b18, T 1.7.201a8, and MĀ 68 at T 1.26.515b26. Detailed discussions of DN 17 from the viewpoint of visualization can be found in Gethin 2006

and Shaw 2021, 168–76. Zhao 2018, 99 and 104 considers the relevant presentation in the Sadāprarudita tale to reflect a transitional position between the type of depiction found in DN 17 and its more mature counterpart in the *Sukhāvatīvyūha*. For an exploration of a possible relationship between such descriptions and altered states of mind see Osto 2018.

707. For a survey of similes in Pāli discourses see Rhys Davids 1907 and 1908 and Hecker 2009.
708. See in more detail Anālayo 2022h.
709. SN 35.200 at SN IV 179,8 and its parallels SĀ 1174 at T 2.99.314c13 and EĀ 43.3 at T 2.125.758c13.
710. AN 7.68 at AN IV 135,3 (which stands alone in reporting that a third group of sixty monks was physically so affected on hearing this teaching that they vomited blood) and its parallels MĀ 5 at T 1.26.427a3 and EĀ 33.10 at T 2.125.689c1. On this discourse see also above n. 424 and 426.
711. MN 10 at MN I 58,9 (= DN 22 at DN II 295,6): *seyyathā pi passeyya sarīraṃ sīvathikāya* (B$^e$: *sivathikāya*) *chaḍḍitaṃ*, MĀ 98 at T 1.26.583b24: 觀彼死屍 and EĀ 12.1 at T 2.125.568b4: 觀死屍.
712. Kimura 2009, 78,12: *yadā śmaśānagataḥ paśyati nānārūpāṇi śmaśāne 'paviddhāni śivapathikāyām ujjhitāni* (also in Dutt 1934, 206,7), D 9 *ka* 235b5 or P 731 *nyi* 239a6: *nam dur khrod na yod pa'i gzugs sna tshogs dur khrod du bor ba . . . mthong na*, T 7.220.485c27: 往至塚間觀所棄屍, T 8.222.193c8: 如今觀身遭諸寒熱, 若其壽終, and T 8.223.254a6: 若見棄死人身 (adopting a 宋, 元, 明, and 宮 variant that dispenses with 是 after 見). A reference to this type of practice can also be found in the translation of the **Pratyutpannasamādhisūtra* attributed to Lokakṣema; see T 13.418.905c10: 比丘觀死人骨著前. In its context, however, this is not an actual instruction to engage in such practice, as it instead features as part of a simile.
713. Matsuda 2021, 70,3: *śayanāsanam āgamya pādau prakṣālya ca smṛtaḥ, mañcake sanniṣīded vā bṛsyāṃ vā pīṭhake 'tha vā* and MĀ 139 at T 1.26.646c25: 還歸至本處, 澡洗於手足, 敷床正基坐.
714. This would be the implication of the recommendation that one should protect the sign (*nimitta*) that has arisen from the vision of a corpse in various stages of decay, which must be referring to the visual image gained from having seen a corpse; see AN 4.14 at AN II 17,2 and its parallels Allon 2001, 128,9, SĀ 879 at T 2.99.221b27, and EĀ$^2$ 11 at T 2.150A.877c7.
715. See Anālayo 2022c, 199–206.
716. Yamabe 1999, 7 notes that the instruction in DN 22 involves "vivid visual images, and one may call this practice 'visualization.'" Moreover, according to Cousins 2003, 4 it seems as if the "cemetery meditation on the stages of decomposition of a corpse is not recorded as a Jain practice and may well have been typically or even uniquely Buddhist at this time." In other words, such a form of visualization appears to be a specific early Buddhist contribution, and as such features as a modality of contemplation of the body that is an integral part of the direct path to liberation.
717. This appears to be well in line with a general observation by Ruegg 1999, 196 that "in the large and indeed very varied body of the expository technical literature of Buddhism—that is, in religious and even in some canonical philosophical works—there is to be found narrative in the narrower as well as the wider senses of the term. In the

same text the two may in fact be juxtaposed, or the expository may be embedded in a narrative, or *vice versa*."

718. MN 93 at MN II 154,$_{29}$ and its parallels MĀ 151 at T 1.26.665b$_{26}$ and T 1.71.878b$_{11}$; see also EĀ 40.9 at T 2.125.742b$_{17}$ (in which case the preceding part is rather a parallel to SN 3.11) and Up 3017 at D 4094 *ju* 110a$_{5}$ or P 5595 *tu* 126a4 (the last is a discourse quotation and has only preserved the tale as such). For relevant Sanskrit fragments, together with an edition and translation of Up 3017, see Dietz 2018.

719. Karashima 2011, 478,$_{2}$ (= T 8.224.472a$_{15}$): 所有者當施與師.

720. This causes another instance of him breaking out into tears; see Karashima 2011, 484,$_{2}$ (= T 8.224.472b$_{12}$): 是時薩陀波倫菩薩賣身不售, 便自宛轉臥地, 啼哭大呼. In this case, although the crying motivates a celestial intervention by Śakra, disguised as a brahmin, this then takes the form of testing Sadāprarudita's willingness to sacrifice his own body for the sake of the Dharma. From the viewpoint of the gradual building up of the narrative, evident in the four previous instances of him weeping, this can be read as standing in continuity with the same basic trajectory of Sadāprarudita becoming less dependent on consolation from others and more able to take matters into his own hands, in the present case to the extent of successfully overcoming the obstruction created by Māra.

    Another point worth mentioning is that, even though Māra has been successful in preventing any potential buyer from seeing or hearing Sadāprarudita, this has affected neither Śakra, which is unsurprising, nor the woman who witnesses his self-sacrifice and then eventually joins him with her following of five hundred women. T 220 and T 227 make up for this minor ambiguity in the progression of the narrative by reporting that, although Māra prevented everyone else, he was unable to do that for this woman: T 6.220.1062c$_{28}$: 唯除城中一長者女宿善根力魔不能蔽 and T 8.227.582b$_{5}$: 唯一長者女魔不能蔽. Perhaps this can then be taken as a first hint of her exceptional character, which becomes quite evident in the remainder of the narrative.

721. Karashima 2011, 485,$_{3}$ (= T 8.224.472b$_{23}$): 婆羅門語薩陀波倫菩薩: 善男子, 今我欲大祠, 欲得人血, 欲得人肉, 欲得人髓, 欲得人心. 卿設能與我者, 我益與卿財. 薩陀波倫菩薩大歡欣報言: 願相與. 薩陀波倫菩薩即取刀, 自刺兩臂. 血大出, 持與之. 復割兩髀裏肉, 持與之. 復自破骨, 持髓與之. 適復欲自刺胸時.

722. Note that in this version a declaration of truth does not feature as the means to restore Sadāprarudita's body to its former condition. Such a belief in the salvific power of a declaration of truth is part of the ancient Indian heritage in general; see Burlingame 1917, Brown 1940, Venkatasubbiah 1940, Coomaraswamy 1944, Brown 1968, Wayman 1968, Brown 1972a and 1972b, Thompson 1998, Hara 2009, and Kong 2012.

723. Karashima 2011, 510,$_{4}$ (= T 8.224.474c$_{5}$): 是時薩陀波倫菩薩及五百女人各自取刀, 處處刺身出血, 持用灑地, 用慈孝於經法故.

724. Karashima 2011, 484,$_{5}$ (= T 8.224.472b$_{15}$), where Śakra's reflection, leading him to transform himself into a brahmin, proceeds as follows: 我當下試之, 知爲至誠索佛, 不但諛諂. 是時釋提桓因來下化作婆羅門.

725. Ohnuma 2007, 64–65 describes the pattern as follows: "Śakra dons some sort of disguise; he never approaches the bodhisattva in his own form . . . [although] the audience always knows that he is Śakra-in-disguise. Using this disguise, Śakra goes to the bodhisattva and requests a part of his body (or makes a generalized plea for help that he knows will result in a gift of the body), and the bodhisattva, with no hesitation,

agrees to give his body away and generally begins the process of doing so. Rather than allowing the bodhisattva to die, however, these stories generally interrupt the gift at some point and make it clear to the audience that the bodhisattva has successfully passed Śakra's 'test' and does not need to lose his life." In sum, "[r]ather than culminating in a tragic loss of life, such stories conclude with a 'happy ending'—with Śakra fully satisfied and the bodhisattva in robust health" (66). Ohnuma 2007, 135 adds that "Śakra tests the bodhisattva for the sake of the reader as much as for his own sake, since the narrative voice of the text . . . already takes the bodhisattva's virtue for granted."

726. The same identification is repeated in Lancaster 1974b, 86. Giddings 2014, 26 objects to this on the grounds that "the purposes are different. Unlike Śibi who gifts his flesh to spare the life of the pigeon from the attacks of the hungry hawk with the expectation of no personal benefits, Sadāprarudita sells his flesh . . . with the full expectation of personal rewards." This consideration may not be granting sufficient room to the notion of developing the perfections that tradition sees at play in any *jātaka*. This can be exemplified by taking as an example the first of the Chinese versions listed in a detailed survey of various versions of this tale by Lamotte 1944/1981, 256n1. T 3.152.1c18 reports that, on being asked for his motivation, King Śibi explains that he has taken the vow to seek Buddhahood, 誓願求佛, and the tale ends by reporting that it is in this way that bodhisattvas practice the perfection of giving, T 3.152.1c24: 菩薩慈惠度無極行布施如是; see also below n. 731. Without going so far as to carry out a comparative study of the various extant versions, this example would already suffice to show that the purposes of the tales of Sadāprarudita and King Śibi converge on the notion of extraordinary acts of self-relinquishment undertaken for the sake of progress toward Buddhahood.

727. See Parlier 1991. For an ancient Greek counterpart to the basic trope of saving a dove, but without the element of self-sacrifice, see Gaál 2017.

728. Lévi 1908, 146–7 refers to three versions in the *Mahābhārata*, III, 130–31, III, 195, and XIII, 32 (in the last case the name of the hero is instead Vṛṣadarbha), as well as to the *Kathāsaritsāgara* I, 7 (summary version), and to a reference in the *Bṛhatkathāmañjarī* I, 3, v. 81; see also Li 2023 on yet another version of the tale in the *Vahnipurāṇa*.

729. T 13.418.919a2: 常當自割其肌供養於善師, 常不愛惜身. A similar instruction can be found in T 13.416.896c12. In the case of the Tibetan version, a relevant reference occurs only in the ensuing verse section; see Harrison 1978b, 202,15 (23X) and 1990, 185n29. Zhao 2018, 83 comments on the above-quoted instruction that "[t]he theme of self-sacrifice is therefore quite vividly stated here and such an extreme form of offering to the *Dharma*-preacher, even when it consists of one's own flesh, is in line with . . . the Sadāprarudita story." On the importance granted to the teacher in Mahāyāna *sūtra* literature see also Skilling 2009b.

730. Kimura 2009, 168,32: *śiro'rthikebhyaḥ śiro dadāti, aṅgārthikebhyo 'ṅgāni dadāti, māṃsaśoṇitamajjārthikebhyo māṃsaśoṇitamajjāno dadāti* (also in Dutt 1934, 264,4).

731. The version of the tale of King Śibi in the **Mahāprajñāpāramitopadeśa*, T 25.1509.88c26, concludes as follows: 如是等種種相, 是檀波羅蜜滿.

732. T 25.1509.92c17: 有知智慧, 有不知智慧.

733. T 25.1509.92c27: 如說般若波羅蜜中: 三事不可得, 亦不著, 是爲具足檀波羅蜜滿.

734. T 25.1509.145a18. Lamotte 1949/1981, 701n2 notes that a version of this narrative can also be found in T 53.2121.69b7.

735. Boucher 2008, 35 comments that "[t]he point here for this Mahāyāna commentator

is that Śāriputra's failing . . . was to regret his gift on account of the recipient's lack of appreciation or worth."

736. De La Vallée Poussin 1903/1913, 380,9: *atha khalu sadāprarudito bodhisattvo mahāsattvas tīkṣṇaṃ śastraṃ gṛhītvā samantādātmānaṃ viddhā samantatastaṃ pṛthivīpradeśaṃ svakena rudhireṇāsiñcadityādi*; see also Changtzu 2012, 88–89 for an exploration of the popularity of the Sadāprarudita tale that covers, among other things, also the present reference and the one quoted below, and Niisaku 2019.
737. Bendall 1902, 38,14: *sadāprarudito bodhisatvo mahāsatvas tīkṣṇaṃ śastraṃ gṛhītvā dakṣiṇaṃ bāhuṃ viddhvā lohitaṃ nisrāvayati sma dakṣiṇaṃ coruṃ viddhvā nirmāṃsaṃ ca kṛtvā asthi bhettuṃ kuḍyamūlam upasaṃkrāmati*, and 41,3: *atha khalu sadāprarudito bodhisatvo mahāsatva iti pratisaṃkhyāya tīkṣṇaṃ śastraṃ gṛhītvā svakāyaṃ samantato viddhvā taṃ pṛthivīpradeśaṃ svarudhireṇa sarvam asiñcat*.
738. Vaidya 1961, 219,4, D 127 *da* 117b6 or P 795 *thu* 125a7, and T 15.639.598a27.
739. Vaidya 1961, 219,8, D 127 *da* 118a1 or P 795 *thu* 125b2, and T 15.639.598b2.
740. Vaidya 1961, 221,29, D 127 *da* 119b7 or P 795 *thu* 127b2, and T 15.639.599a26.
741. Kern and Nanjio 1912, 407,6, D 113 *ja* 151a3 or P 781 *chu* 172b2, T 9.262.53b7 (= T 9.264.188a15), and T 9.263.125b16.
742. Kern and Nanjio 1912, 412,9, D 113 *ja* 153a7 or P 781 *chu* 175a4, and T 9.262.53c26 (= T 9.264.188c3); T 263 does not seem to have a proper parallel to this description, although the next quote below shows that the basic narrative thread would be the same.
743. Kern and Nanjio 1912, 414,3, D 113 *ja* 153b7 or P 781 *chu* 175b5, T 9.262.54a6 (= T 9.264.188c12), and T 9.263.126a19.
744. For a detailed study see Benn 2007.
745. In the course of a detailed account of ordination procedures in the Dharmaguptaka tradition as undertaken in the tradition of Fó Guāng Shān, 佛光山, Taiwan, Orsborn 2021b, 162 reports on the practice of "the burning of precept scars (戒疤). In the past, this involved numerous sets of three cone incense burns on the scalp about 5 cm behind the hairline. However, in FGS [= Fó Guāng Shān] and most Taiwanese ordinations, there has been a gradual move away from multiple sets to a single set of three on the scalp or inside the forearm, or even abandoning the practice altogether. In mainland China, such precept burns have been officially banned, though many monastics still practice them in private, non-officially sanctioned rites."
746. Kovan 2018, 644 reports that "Tibetan Buddhist self-immolations occurring largely from 2009 and inside Tibetan-Chinese territory have been committed by men and women from the middle-aged to, very often, young people in their teens. At least 151 known cases up to mid-2017 have been documented; most, but not all, of these fatal." See also Kovan 2014.
747. Wynne 2022, xi reports: "On Friday April 22, 2022, Wynn Bruce of Boulder, Colorado, committed suicide by setting himself on fire in front of the American Supreme Court in Washington DC. According to a *New York Times* article of April 24, Mr. Bruce was a climate activist and his death was an 'Earth Day' protest against climate change. Apart from environmental activism, however, Wynne Bruce's suicide was apparently also motivated by Buddhism."
748. The episode is found in the *Dasabodhisattuppattikathā*, Saddhatissa 1975, 130,12: *dve vatthāni gahetvā gandhatelena temetvā pādatalato yāva sīsaṃ paḷiveṭhetvā agginā*

*daṇḍadīpakena jhāpetvā sammāsambuddhaṃ pūjemī ti saññāya idaṃ jīvitaṃ pariccajitvā kataṃ padīpapuññaṃ sabbaññutañāṇassa paccayo hotū ti patthanam akāsi.*

749. Saddhatissa 1975, 130,32: *sarīrapadīpapūjābalena dīghaso asītihattho, jīvitadānaphalena navutivassasahassāyuko bhavissati. ekarattiṃ attānaṃ agginā jhāpitapuññaphalassa nissandena buddharaṃsiyā sakalaloke rattindivā niccaṃ dippissanti. candappabhā suriyappabhā appabhāsā bhavissanti.*

750. Cp-a 306,36: *cakkaṅkitehi pādehi bodhimaṇḍūpasaṅkamanāya caraṇadānaṃ, caturoghanittharaṇāya sattānaṃ saddhammahatthadānatthaṃ hatthadānaṃ, saddhindriyādipaṭilābhāya kaṇṇanāsādidānaṃ, samantacakkhupaṭilābhāya cakkhudānaṃ, dassanasavaṇanussaraṇapāricariyādīsu sabbakālaṃ sabbasattānaṃ hitasukhāvaho sabbalokena ca upajīvitabbo me kāyo bhaveyyā ti maṃsalohitādidānaṃ, sabbalokuttamo bhaveyyan ti uttamaṅgadānaṃ deti.*

751. Ud 8.9 at Ud 92,32, Ud 8.10 at Ud 93,18, SĀ 1076 at T 2.99.280c7, and SĀ[2] 15 at T 2.100.378b8. The two Chinese versions precede this feat with a performance of the twin miracle.

A somewhat similar description of self-immolation, as part of a survey of ways in which arhats in Akṣobhya's Buddhafield attain final Nirvana, can be found in T 11.313.757c28: 中有阿羅漢身中自出火，還燒身，而般泥洹；中有阿羅漢般泥洹時，自以功德行如疾風，中有譬如五色雲氣，於空中行便不復知處; see also Boucher 2018, 102 and on the doubtful attribution of this text to Lokakṣema above n. 229. In fact, the Buddha Akṣobhya adopts the same procedure himself; see T 11.313.761a13: 阿閦佛身中自出火，還燒身. This stands in continuity with his giving away parts of his body in previous lives; see T 11.313.754b25: 阿閦如來，無所著，等正覺，行菩薩道時，世世人求手足，及頭，目，肌肉，終不逆人意也. Nattier 2000, 87–88, who already noted these two passages, comments on the latter: "The story of Akṣobhya makes explicit, in other words, the kinds of activities that early Mahāyāna Buddhists believed were required in order to amass the vast amounts of merit needed to procure all the qualities of a Buddha. Using a script supplied at least in part by the *jātaka* tales, these pioneering bodhisattvas had to look forward to thousands of lifetimes of self-sacrifice before Buddhahood could be attained."

Yet another example, attested in a text that has been attributed to Lokakṣema but according to Nattier 2008, 85 is only one of the "third-tier texts" among his translations, in the sense of bearing only a distant relationship to Lokakṣema' style, occurs in the *Ajātaśatrukaukṛtyavinodanāsūtra*. The relevant passage reports how a matricide receives teachings on emptiness, ordains, becomes an arhat, and then, having received the Buddha's permission to enter final Nirvana, levitates up high into the sky and combusts his own body, T 15.626.403c19: 飛在虛空，去地百四十丈，便於是上其身火出還自燒身; see also Harrison and Hartmann 2000, 201–2 and T 15.627.425a23. For a more detailed discussion of this episode see Anālayo (in preparation).

752. SĀ 1076 at T 2.99.280c11: 譬如燒鐵丸，其焰洞熾然，熱勢漸息滅，莫知其所歸. 如是等解脫，度煩惱淤泥，諸流永已斷，莫知其所之. 逮得不動跡，入無餘涅槃, with parallels in Ud 8.10 at Ud 93,23: *ayoghanahatasseva, jalato jātavedaso* (S[e]: *jātavedassa*), *anupubbūpasantassa, yathā na ñāyate gati. evaṃ sammā vimuttānaṃ, kāmabandhoghatārinaṃ, paññāpetuṃ gati natthi, pattānaṃ acalaṃ sukhan* (C[e]: *sukhaṃ*) *ti*, and SĀ[2] 15 at T 2.100.378b12: 譬如熱鐵，椎打星流，散已尋滅，莫知所至. 得正解脫，亦復如是，已出煩惱，諸欲淤泥. 莫能知彼，所趣方所.

753. The alternative verse in Ud 8.9 does concern the passing away of an arhat. From the

viewpoint of comparative study, since a connection to the motif of auto-combustion only receives support from parallels in the case of the verse found in Ud 8.10, it seems that in the case of Ud 8.9 this association could reflect a stage of development subsequent to such a linkage having already become established (through a literal interpretation of the verse found in Ud 8.10). This suggestion can be supported from the viewpoint of content, as the verse in Ud 8.9 does not refer to fire at all, wherefore it is only the verse in Ud 8.10 that could have given rise to a literal interpretation of the type found in the prose. This makes it fair to assume that the tale of auto-combustion had already arisen when the verse in Ud 8.9 came to be associated with the prose narration. The resultant doubling of the same prose narration then would have necessitated introducing the additional specification that in one of the two instances the Buddha reported what had happened earlier, which was applied to the second of the two consecutive discourses.

Reading the verse in Ud 8.9 as a referent to an auto-combustion is in fact not entirely straightforward, as Ud 8.9 at Ud 93,12 refers to the "disintegration" or "breaking up" of the body, *abhedi kāyo* (the remainder of the verse concerns the other four aggregates); a similar reference to the body breaking up recurs in the parallel verse *Udānavarga* 26.16, Bernhard 1965, 322,3: *bhitvā kāyaṃ* (see also the *Prasannapadā*, de La Vallée Poussin 1903/1913, 520,4: *abhedi kāyo*). The same Pāli *abhedi* occurs also in SN 35.189 at SN IV 159,27, where it functions as a synonym to *paribhedi*, both conveying the sense of a breaking up or a splitting apart. Such a sense seems more natural for something solid that is gradually destroyed and reduced to pieces rather than describing a remainderless burning up on a single occasion. The commentary relates *abhedi* to the latter, Ud-a 433,17: *bhijji, anavasesato ḍayhi*, evidently influenced by the already established relationship between verse and prose. Yet, the term as such seems more appropriate for the normal process of a body's gradual decay after death. This can be seen in a recurrent reference in Pāli discourses to the human body being of a nature to fall apart, *aniccucchādanaparimaddanabhedanaviddhaṃsanadhamma*; see, e.g., DN 2 at DN I 76,18, MN 74 at MN I 500,2, SN 35.103 at SN IV 83,28, and AN 9.15 at AN IV 386,23 (giving for each *Nikāya* only one example out of more such occurrences). Just *bhedanadhamma* on its own (followed by *nikkhepanadhamma*) occurs in the same sense of designating the nature of the human body in SN 3.3 at SN I 71,18.

754. The Dharmaguptaka *Vinaya*, T 22.1428.587b25, the Mahāsāṅghika *Vinaya*, T 22.1425.394c8, the Mahīśāsaka *Vinaya*, T 22.1421.15b4, the Mūlasarvāstivāda *Vinaya*, T 23.1442.695c14, the Sarvāstivāda *Vinaya*, T 23.1435.22a14, and the Theravāda *Vinaya*, Vin II 76,24; see also Silk 2008, 160–62 for a survey of the administrative tasks undertaken by this monk.

755. For a more detailed discussion see Anālayo 2012c.

756. Perhaps the results that emerge in this respect from the present research may offer a contribution to an increasing recognition of the potential of the *Āgama* sources even when it comes to research on early Mahāyāna, which at least to some extent still seems to suffer from patterns characterized by Reat 1992, 139–40 in the following terms: "Conze argued [that] the scrupulous historian has no alternative but to regard the texts of the Theravāda and the Mahāyāna as equally reliable—albeit unreliable—versions of the teachings of the historical Buddha and his earliest followers . . . Conze's initially salubrious insistence upon historical rigor has evolved into a North American school of entrenched, uncritical agnosticism regarding the nature of earliest Buddhism . . . In

recent years the emphasis of Buddhist studies in the West has fallen upon what cannot be ascribed to earliest Buddhism—i.e. that virtually nothing can be attributed with any certainty to earliest Buddhism. For many Western scholars, this position has become an indisputable maxim which justifies neglect of . . . the Pāli canon in favor of the more overtly and comfortably 'religious' nature of Mahāyāna practices and scriptures . . . Conze claimed that the Pāli *suttas* appeal to Western rationalism on a preconscious level, and he deplored this appeal as the reason for the scholarly emphasis, in his day, upon Theravāda Buddhism. He failed to note the similarly preconscious and uncritical resentment which these same scriptures inspire in those Westerners who are bent upon defining and discussing religion in terms of belief in a Supreme Being."

757. In the same vein, Bechert 1973, 14 reasons that "in the early stage of the development of Mahāyāna the differences between the doctrines of the two vehicles were not very deep, and . . . the new doctrine had developed from the concepts of the old one without a sharp rupture." According to Jing Yin 2005, 171, "[i]t seems that Mahāyāna philosophy did not suddenly come into being as a result of the composition of particular Mahāyāna *sūtra*s, such as the *Prajñāpāramitā Sūtra*[s], but was the result of a gradual evolution deeply rooted in Nikāya Buddhism."

758. In principle, epigraphy is another important source of information to be taken into account. For the earlier period represented by Lokakṣema's translations, a significant instance would be a reference to Amitābha on an inscribed image pedestal from Govindnagar; see Schopen 1987/2005, Fussman 1999, 541–43, and Acharya 2008/2010, 24–26. This is not directly pertinent to the present study, however, as the Perfection of Wisdom does not refer to Amitābha and instead mentions Akṣobhya.

759. According to Vetter 2001, 71f, the first chapter of Lokakṣema's translation testifies to a lack of relationship between Mahāyāna and the Perfection of Wisdom (he also takes up the **Kāśyapaparivarta*, which I will not pursue here). The main argument in relation to T 224 appears to be that Subhūti as an arhat is someone who has completed his task and could not embark on the path of Mahāyāna. Yet, he teaches the Perfection of Wisdom to bodhisattvas, who apparently are as yet unaware of it. This then supposedly suggests that the Perfection of Wisdom and the Mahāyāna are of different and unrelated origins. Closer inspection shows that this conclusion does not seem to capture the narrative setting adequately. For one, those with whom Subhūti directly interacts in the course of the first chapter are also arhats, namely Śāriputra and occasionally Pūrṇa Maitrāyaṇīputra. They are shown to receive teachings on something that they are as yet unfamiliar with. Moreover, right at its outset the first chapter clarifies that whatever Subhūti teaches stems from the Buddha's might, the latter being of course, according to the traditional perspective, the only one in the whole congregation who has brought the path of a bodhisattva to its successful completion. In fact, the Buddha steps in from time to time to clarify or endorse what Subhūti has said. In other words, the teachings on the Perfection of Wisdom have their source in the Buddha as one who knows from personal experience what it takes for a bodhisattva to reach the final goal of Buddhahood. The circumstance that his main dialogue partners are arhats rather seems to reflect an authentication strategy (on this strategy in general see Silk 2003a, 173–74, quoted above p. 66). The same strategy can be seen, for example, in T 313 (on the attribution of this translation to Lokakṣema see above n. 229). Even though the *sūtra* is in its entirety dedicated to describing Akṣobhya and his Buddhafield, Śākyamuni's main dialogue partners are the arhat Śāriputra and the stream-entrant Ānanda, in

addition to which the arhat Subhūti makes a brief contribution at T 11.313.760b12. This type of presentation does not seem to carry any deeper significance other than facilitating acceptance of this *sūtra* among an audience still accustomed to the traditional setting of the type adopted in *Āgama* literature.

760. Karashima 2011, 27,6 (= T 8.224.428a6): 摩訶衍於天上天下人中正過上,無有與等者; on the meaning conveyed here by 正 see Karashima 2010, 629. A comparable statement for defining the *mahāsattva* takes the following form in Karashima 2011, 21,7 (= T 8.224.427b15): 摩訶薩者天上天下最尊.

761. Karashima 2011, 23,4 (= T 8.224.427c1): 摩訶衍三拔致, which Karashima 2010, 324 explains to reflect "a transliteration of a certain Middle Indic form (e.g. *mahāyāna-*saṃppaṭṭhita*) of Skt. *mahāyāna-saṃprasthita*."

762. Fronsdal 1998/2014, 65 considers it "inappropriate to label the *Daoxing jing* [= T 224] a Mahāyāna text—in part, because it is unlikely the text was so categorized by the community that composed it, and also because the scholarly assumptions relating to the category 'Mahāyāna' have tended to obscure the early bodhisattva movement more than they have helped us understand it." With due acknowledgement granted to the potentially obscuring nature of the notion of a unitary Mahāyāna tradition in some scholarly writings, it seems to me that the proposed assessment fails to do full justice to the evidence provided in Lokakṣema's translation of the Perfection of Wisdom (= *Daoxing jing*) itself, and it excludes from consideration, for no evident reason, the perspective of Buddhist traditions subsequent to the time of composition and their nearly two millennia of engagement with a text perceived as belonging to the category of Mahāyāna *sūtras*. For a critical reply to another case of problematizing the application of the term Mahāyāna *sūtra* in Nattier 2003a, 10, in this instance in relation to the *Ugraparipṛcchā*, see Pagel 2006, 75–76.

763. Wogihara 1932/1935, 509,8: *'vinivartanīyayānaṃ mahāyānam avāpya samāsādya punar eva tad vivarjya vivartya hīnayānaṃ paryeṣitavyaṃ maṃsyante*. The whole passage in which this statement is found has no counterpart in Lokakṣema's translation; see Karashima 2011, 238,7 (= T 8.224.447b14). However, in a different context in Karashima 2011, 9,1 (= T 8.224.426b6) the term 小道 occurs. As noted by Karashima 2010, 541, here 小道 corresponds to *prādeśika jñāna* in the Sanskrit version, Wogihara 1932/1935, 50,17 (with its Tibetan equivalent in D 12 *ka* 5a3 or P 734 *mi* 5b3 in *phyogs gcig pa'i ye shes*). The Chinese counterparts similarly convey the sense of a limited type of wisdom: 有量智 in T 8.227.537c16 and T 8.228.588a15 or 少分智 in T 7.220.764b22 or T 7.220.866c4. This makes it safe to conclude that the single occurrence of 小道 in T 224 does not serve as a rendering of *hīnayāna* (hereby I respectfully venture to disagree with Harrison 1987, 80, who took the present instance in T 224 to be a reference to *hīnayāna*).

764. See also, e.g., Nattier 2007a, 122, and on the problematic nature of this term as such Anālayo 2014e. Regarding the coinage of a *yāna* that is qualified as *hīna*, Skilling 2013b, 76–77 offers the helpful suggestion that "[t]he origins of the notion of the inferiority of the way of the arhat and of the pratyekabuddha may perhaps be sought, in part, in the concept of 'inferior aspiration' (*hīna-adhimutta*, *hīna-adhimuttika*), already found in Pali and early sources." Notably, the *Tarkajvāla*, Eckel 2008, 303,10 (4.1), uses the very term *hīnādhimukta* to refer to those who voice criticism of Mahāyāna teachings as not being spoken by the Buddha. The Pāli counterpart *hīnādhimuttika* features already in several Pāli discourses (the alternative term *hīnādhimutta* seems

to occur mainly in later Pāli texts). Thus, in SN 14.14 at SN II 154,21 (=It 3.3.9 at It 70,3), SN 14.15 at SN II 156,24, and SN 14.16 at SN II 157,10, *hīnādhimuttika* features in contrast to *kalyānādhimuttika*, whereas in AN 6.85 at AN III 435,12 the same term stands in contrast to *paṇītādhimuttika*. From the viewpoint of extant parallels, SĀ 445 (repeated in SĀ 446 and SĀ 447) at T 2.99.115a9 uses 鄙心 to designate a state of mind or mental attitude that is "lowly," "vulgar," or "ignoble," which would correspond well to *hīna*, whereas EĀ 49.3 at T 2.125.795b28 qualifies such persons in strong terms as 惡者 (in contrast to 善者), being "evil" or "bad," *pāpa*. This terminological choice may be influenced by the circumstance that here Devadatta and his followers appear to be exemplifying the case of being *hīnādhimuttika*.

Another, related usage can be found in a standard qualification in Pāli discourses of the act of disrobing as a return to what is *hīna*; see, e.g., SN 16.11 at SN II 217,28: *sikkhaṃ paccakkhāya hīnāyāvattā bhavanti*, with a parallel in the *Mahāvastu*, Marciniak 2019, 56,5 (also in Senart 1897, 47,13): *śikṣāṃ pratyākhyāya daurbalyam āviṣkṛtvā hīnāya 'vartanti kāmehi*; a Gāndhārī version of this type of statement in Marino 2020, 287 reads: *śikṣa pacakhae hiṇae ava[ta]di*. Two Chinese *Āgama* parallels speak of reverting to what is 俗, "common," "rustic," "secular," or "worldly"; see SĀ 1144 at T 2.99.302c19: 捨戒還俗 and SĀ$^{2}$ 119 at T 2.100.417c15: 罷道還俗. Hirakawa 1997, 133 does not list *hīna* among Sanskrit terms possibly rendered by 俗 (unlike the case of 鄙; see Hirakawa 1997, 1174). This makes it doubtful if the Indic originals of SĀ 1144 and SĀ$^{2}$ 119 had a phrasing corresponding to the Pāli version. Nevertheless, the usage of *hīna* in the *Mahāvastu* testifies to a similar evaluation being known in Mahāsāṃghika-Lokottaravāda circles, showing that this qualification is not just an idiosyncrasy of the Pāli tradition. Its significance appears to be that, even though lay practitioners can be highly accomplished and some monastics rather lax, in principle going forth was seen as the appropriate expression for wholehearted dedication to the path to liberation, wherefore disrobing can be qualified as a return to what is *hīna* in comparison.

In sum, the idea of having an aspiration that is *hīna* or else opting for what is *hīna* would fit the perspective of the evolving Mahāyāna sense of identity, in that wholehearted dedication to the path to Buddhahood is in principle superior, wherefore pursuing the awakening of an arhat or Pratyekabuddha can be qualified as *hīna* in comparison.

765. This is the 眾經目錄, T 55.2146.119b3, referring to the 道行般若波羅蜜經, which features under the header of being a 大乘修多羅 (T 55.2146.115a7); for a similar allocation in a seventeenth century catalogue, confirming the continuity of such a sense of identity, see Nanjio 1882/1989, 3.

766. See also Zacchetti 2015b, 185: "In general, *Larger Prajñāpāramitā* texts lay greater emphasis than does the *Aṣṭasāhasrikā* on bodhisattvas' activities for assisting and instructing beings."

767. See above p. 9.

768. The *Pañcaviṃśatisāhasrikā Prajñāpāramitā* offers a relevant indication in this respect by stating that already at the first of altogether ten stages in progress toward Buddhahood a bodhisattva will go forth in each rebirth; see Kimura 2009, 92,10: *sarvajātiṣv avyavakīrṇo 'bhiniṣkrāmati* (also in Dutt 1934, 218,6). Of relevance here may also be a comment by Gombrich 1988/1990, 30 (in the context of an article on the impact of writing on the spread of Mahāyāna teachings), reasoning that the view "that the Mahāyāna is the Buddhism of the laity . . . rests on a misconception of what it was to be a

Buddhist layman in ancient India." A related observation by Williams 1989/2009, 24 takes the following form: "In India generally, religious change was initiated by those who had the time and the influence on their wider religious community, which is to say, Brahmins and renunciates . . . apart from the mythical lay heroes and heroines of the sūtras we have no names of laypeople who contributed to the doctrinal origins of the Mahāyāna. The Mahāyāna sūtras were clearly the products of monks, albeit monks whose vision of the Dharma embraced the possibility of lay practice at the superior level of a Bodhisattva on the path to Buddhahood, and who used lay figures in the sūtras to embody a critique of other monks seen as in some way defective in the light of the message of the sūtra, or [as] having lost the real message and direction of the Dharma." According to Durt 1991, 16, it seems that "the image of laymen Bodhisattvas . . . has been largely metaphorical," although it could be added that the role of lay patronage needs to be kept in mind as well. For a convenient survey of the rise and fall of the theory that the Mahāyāna originated among lay disciples see Drewes 2010a, 55–57.

769. Regarding the uncertain lay status of the protagonist Gaṅgadevā see above n. 552.

770. An example would be an exchange between Śakra and the Buddha in Karashima 2011, 66,9 (= T 224.8.432a5), which reveals worship of a written copy of the Perfection of Wisdom to be more meritorious than worship of a *stūpa* containing relics of the Buddha. Vetter 1994a, 1268–9 suggests that this may have served as "propaganda for a place or places neither famous in connection with Gotama's life nor in connection with a part of his bodily remains, but being in want of pilgrims' support, perhaps for proliferating *prajñāpāramitā*," which according to him then suggests that the proponents of the Perfection of Wisdom "were not, or not sufficiently, backed by traditional centres of pilgrimage." Yet, the actual passage does not give the impression of being about promoting some alternative place of pilgrimage. Instead, the reasoning given for the proposed evaluation of merit is simply that "there is no need for bodily relics," since attaining Buddhahood relies on the Perfection of Wisdom; see Karashima 2011, 67,6 (= T 8.224.432a15): 不用身舍利, 從薩芸若中得佛, 怛薩阿竭爲出般若波羅蜜中. Perhaps the proposed interpretation was influenced by the explicitly stated attempt by Vetter 1994a, 1241 to present an adapted form of the hypothesis by Hirakawa 1963 relating the origin of Mahāyāna to *stūpa* worship, possibly combined with the impact of the supposed cult of the book, for a critical examination of which see Drewes 2007. Harrison 1995, 62 comments on the role of *stūpa* worship that it "is indeed frequently cited as (hitherto) the most meritorious activity conceivable, but the purpose is not to promote it, nor even to forbid it, but to compare it unfavourably with other religious activities or values, e.g., the realisation of *prajñā-pāramitā*, the memorization of *sūtra*s, or the practice of *samādhi*."

771. See Hirakawa 1963, 85–106 for a summary of his arguments in support of this idea. In a critical survey of this position, Sasaki 1997, 94 points out a major problem in the unwarranted assumption that *śrāvakayāna* and *bhikṣu*s are identical, even though there is no reason why some monastics may not have opted for the bodhisattva path; see also Schopen 1991 on the topic of monastic participation in *stūpa* cults and Drewes 2010a, 57 for a summary of critical responses.

A related issue is the attribution of the rise of Mahāyāna to members of the Mahāsāṃghika *nikāya*(s); see Drewes 2010a, 56–58. Harrison 2018, 17 (see also 26n21) explains that "there are many indications that the Mahāsāṃghikas and their various sub-schools have strong links with texts and ideas reflective of the Mahāyāna, enough for one to see how the idea that the Mahāyāna was the exclusive outgrowth of the Mahāsāṃghikas took root, but our view today is much more cautious and nuanced. In short, we assume that the Mahāyāna ran across *nikāya* boundaries right from the start"; see also, e.g., Harrison 1982, Dessein 2009, Skilling 2009a, 203–4, 2013a, Karashima 2015b, 2018a, 2018b, and Tournier 2017, 255–88.

772. As already noted by Harrison 1987, 79–80 in relation to early Mahāyāna texts in general, "there is no evidence to suggest a widespread cult of the great *bodhisattvas*, and no passages recommend devotion to them. They function as symbols rather than as saviours . . . as far as *bodhisattvas* are concerned the *initial* message of the Mahāyāna is clear: people should not worship *bodhisattvas*, they should become *bodhisattvas* themselves."

773. Karashima 2011, 59,7 (= T 8.224.431a23): 善男子, 善女人學般若波羅蜜者, 持者, 誦者, 若於空閑處, 若於僻隈處, 亦不恐, 亦不怖, 亦不畏. Karashima 2010, 293 and 349 gives "a vacant (*or* uninhabited) place, a desert, wilderness" for 空閑處 and "remote, out-of-the-way, isolated" for 僻隈; on 善男子 and 善女人 as not necessarily designating lay practitioners see the discussion above n. 283.

774. Karashima 2011, 370,3 (= T 8.224.461a10): 佛語須菩提: 我不作是說遠離, 教菩薩, 摩訶薩於獨處止, 於樹間止, 於閑處止. Karashima 2010, 613, 134, and 532 gives "detachment, seclusion, solitude" for 遠離, "a solitary place" for 獨處, and "a solitary place, a desert, wilderness" for 閑處.

775. This passage to some degree already puts into perspective the proposal by Ray 1994, 255–60 that a promotion of the ideal of forest renunciation is evident in the verse counterpart to the *Aṣṭasāhasrikā Prajñāpāramitā*, the probably later *Ratnaguṇasaṃcayagāthā* (on the dating see Zacchetti 2015b, 184). According to Ray 1994, 255, "[c]hapter 21 specifically identifies the primary environment of the renunciant bodhisattva: he may 'practise quite detached from villages or cities in a mountain cave, in a remote forest, or in isolated woods' (21.4), dangerous environments where wild beasts roam (21.6)." These two verses supposedly convey that "it is primarily the forest renunciant that the text addresses." However, the quoted verses are not simply commendations of forest renunciation, as they are rather concerned with the problem of pride developed by those who have adopted this lifestyle. In apparent recognition of this, Ray 1994, 255 then adds that "we are told that *even* if one is a devoted *yogin* who practices in the forest, if one develops pride and does not course in *prajñāpāramitā*, one's practice is of little account. By the same token, *even* if one dwells in towns all the time, if one's understanding and aspiration are pure, then one practices rightly (21.4–6)." Yet, the main message appears to be simply that correct practice is what counts, no matter where one may live. In other words, the verses seem to convey a message different from the proposed reading, since they imply that there is no need to go live in forest wilds as long as one has the right understanding and remains without conceit. In a comment on a larger portion of the same part of the text, Karashima 2001, 174 in fact reasons that "[v]erses 3–8 in Chapter XXI in the *Ratnaguṇasaṃcayagāthā* evidently demonstrate that the Sutra is *not* on the side of wilderness monks" (emphasis added).

What appears to be a second argument by Ray 1994, 255 takes the following form: "How is the ideal of the *yogin*-bodhisattva who dwells in the forest characterized? Of the Buddha, it is said approvingly, 'free he wandered without a home' (*Rgs*. 2.3) and this is what the *yogin* should do (20.12)." The Sanskrit term used in verses 2.3 and 20.12

is *aniketacārī*, which when taken in its literal sense would refer to homelessness as the freedom from the impediments of lay life that is gained by going forth, independent of whether the one gone forth then lives in a village or in forest wilds. In a figurative sense, the same term can convey freedom from craving and attachment (see verses 1.6 and 1.10 as well as the gloss on the corresponding Pāli term in Pj II 573,26), which is also not confined to being in forest wilds. The *Mahāvyutpatti*, Sakaki 1926, 45 (no. 577), mentions the *aniketacārī* as the name of a *samādhi*, which is also about a mental quality/practice that does not depend on being in forest wilds. Thus, if the above quote is meant to offer support for an emphasis on dwelling in forest wilds, then the referenced occurrences of *aniketacārī* do not fulfil this purpose.

In the course of surveying various other qualities of a bodhisattva, Ray 1994, 256 and 259 refers to "[t]he bodhisattva, particularly in his primary incarnation as a bodhisattva of the forest," and asserts that "[a]s we have seen, the *Ratnaguṇa* propounds an ideal of forest renunciation." Yet, the remainder of his survey does not provide substantial evidence that confirms this conclusion. This leaves only the above two arguments, where the actual textual evidence does not support the proposed reading. It follows that the proposed assessment of the *Ratnaguṇasaṃcayagāthā* is in need of revision. As already noted by Drewes 2010a, 62, "[a]lthough Ray claims that the *Ratnaguṇasaṃcayagāthā*, the one text he cites that seems likely to be early, advocates forest dwelling, for example, the very passages he cites from this text to support his claim explicitly discourage it"; see also Nattier 2003a, 94n31. Karashima 2001, 174 seems to be right in proposing that "it is evident that the *Ratnaguṇasaṃcayagāthā* as well as the *Aṣṭasāhasrikā Prajñāpāramitā* . . . are not on the side of wilderness monks." Sasaki 2004, 3 points out that "Ray's theory is very similar to Hirakawa's theory on the origin of Mahāyāna Buddhism in that they both assume that people who were neither pure laypeople nor traditional monastic Buddhist *bhikṣus* were the founders of Mahāyāna."

776. A comparable emphasis on internal qualities over external conduct can be seen in SN 35.63 at SN IV 36,1 and its parallel SĀ 309 at T 2.99.88c21. In response to an inquiry about what defines solitary dwelling, in both versions the Buddha clarifies that living in seclusion and forest wilds does not make one a solitary dweller if craving has not been overcome. Conversely, one without craving is indeed a solitary dweller even if not living in seclusion and forest wilds.

777. Another, related consideration is that such teachings are not necessarily found in other texts that we tend to refer to as reflecting "early Mahāyāna." Regarding the *Ugraparipṛcchā*, for example, Nattier 2003a: 179–80 notes that "the *Ugra* lacks anything that could be construed as a 'philosophy of emptiness.'" In clear contrast to *Prajñāpāramitā* texts, "in the *Ugra* such antiessentialist and antireifying arguments are conspicuous by their absence."

778. This ties in with the pertinent reflection offered by Skilling 2005, 107: "But can the study of the evolution of Buddhist thought and practice be framed in such broad, and essentially atemporal, strokes as Śrāvakayāna versus Mahāyāna? Does that not entail *a priori* judgements? At exactly what point does Śrāvakayāna end, and Mahāyāna begin? . . . There is a great deal of common ground, common *imaginaire*, and common ideology."

779. This is in line with one out of two distinct characteristics of Mahāyāna ideologies identified by Skilling 2018, 33–34: "It strikes me that Mahāyāna ideology departs from the early Āgamas on (at least) two major points. First, Mahāyāna advocates the way to

buddhahood, the bodhisatva path . . . Second, Mahāyāna metaphysics assert that all dharmas are unborn and unceasing. Dharmas have no substance or own-being; they are empty, and they cannot be perceived or obtained."

In regard to the second of these two characteristics, at least as far as Early-*Aṣṭa*-Mahāyāna is concerned it seems to me that there can be a way of reading the emptiness rhetoric as standing in continuity with *Āgama* teachings on the need to avoid reification; see in more detail above p. 36. In the context of my present note, this would then leave mainly the first of these two characteristics, in regard to which Skilling 2018, 34 precedes a detailed survey of references in various Mahāyāna texts to the need to ensure the continuity of the lineage of the three jewels with the following observations: "The schools for which information is preserved all seem to have developed theories about the path to Buddhahood and all seem to have accepted the idea that in the present world some could, and even ought to, follow this path. This was a shared concept. The need for future buddhas was clear, if the continuity of Awakened Ones, or of the Awakened Ones, the Dharma, and the Saṃgha, was to be maintained. Some adherents of the Mahāyāna took the idea to the extreme, and prescribed the path to Buddhahood for all and everyone. They went on to insist that the Great Way was the only way to go." In this way, the prescription of the path to Buddhahood as the only viable option emerges as a distinct characteristic of Mahāyāna ideologies when compared with those of other Buddhist traditions. This would indeed mark a difference compared to the bodhisattva ideal in the Theravāda Buddhist traditions, which in turn of course also differs from the early *Āgama*s in respect to the bodhisat(t)va path as such.

Exploring this further, it could be noted that making this path binding on everyone is not needed for ensuring the continuity of the lineage of the three jewels—a concern shared by non-Mahāyāna Buddhist traditions—for which purpose it suffices if at least some pursue the path to future Buddhahood. Moreover, as far as the third jewel of the Saṅgha as an object of recollection is concerned—representing those in progress to or having reached one of the four levels of awakening, distinct from the monastic Saṅgha as an object of refuge (see Anālayo 2008b, 107)—imposing the path to Buddhahood on everyone forestalls the possibility of anyone progressing to these four levels of awakening. This thereby to some extent dismantles the role of the third jewel as a directly accessible object of recollection and source of inspiration. The reason is simply that, once this prescription of the path to Buddhahood as the only viable option has been successfully implemented, there will no longer be any stream-enterers, once-returners, nonreturners, and arhats. In addition, the same move also prevents the possibility of a rectification of misunderstandings of the second jewel, the Dharma, by those who have realized its essence through the attainment of Nirvana. This will have to wait until the distant time in the future when the next Buddha arises and teaches it anew. From this perspective, ensuring the continuity of the lineage of the *three* jewels would seem better served by an approach that allows individuals the free decision either to adopt the path to Buddhahood or else to pursue arhat-ship, in the understanding that aspirants to both goals can offer their distinct, respective contribution to ensuring the continuity of the three jewels.

780. As far as I can see, the same may not hold in a comparable manner for the suggestion by Drewes 2010b, 73 that, "[w]hen applied to people, the term Mahāyāna should be used to refer to any person or group that accepted or accepts the authenticity of Mahāyāna sūtras." I appreciate the attempt to present a simple and pragmatic definition, oriented toward actual living experience and practice. Nevertheless, the problem I see is that

the designation "Mahāyāna *sūtras*" covers quite a heterogenous body of teachings, and not all the members usually included under this designation necessarily self-identify as Mahāyāna. It would not be easy to pinpoint a common denominator that at the same time can be clearly set apart from the type of thought reflected, for example, in the *Buddhāpadāna*, with its plurality of Buddhas in different Buddhafields, and the *Cariyāpiṭaka*, with its specific perspectives on the bodhisattva path, as members of the Pāli canon and thus an integral part of what Theravādins have come to accept as authentic. At least in principle, the *Buddhāpadāna* and the *Cariyāpiṭaka* would also qualify for inclusion in the category of Mahāyāna *sūtra*s, alongside so-called early Mahāyāna *sūtra*s that do not self-identify as Mahāyāna. In short, how to define "Mahāyāna *sūtras*" in such a way that this expression can then indeed be used to delimitate the scope of "Mahāyāna"? One way or another, we need to avoid the circularity of defining Mahāyāna by way of acceptance of Mahāyāna.

This type of problem can be explored further in relation to an assessment by Cutler 1994, 28 of the *Buddhāpadāna* as being an instance of non-Mahāyāna, as "its goal is not 'to recommend to all the *bodhisattva* path aiming at full enlightenment' although this is one of the characteristics of texts belonging to the Mahāyāna." On taking the universalization of the bodhisattva path as a characteristic mark for assigning a text to the Mahāyāna, the *Buddhāpadāna* can indeed be excluded, but then the same also holds for the Perfection of Wisdom and a range of other early "Mahāyāna" *sūtra*s.

781. Notably, a reference to a single *yāna* instead of the standard three does occur in Karashima 2011, 299,6 (= T 8.224.454a19): 佛所說三有德之人: 求阿羅漢, 辟支佛, 佛. 是三不計三. 如須菩提所說, 爲一道耳 (the Sanskrit counterpart, Wogihara 1932/1935, 657,17, suggests that here 道 would render *yāna*). However, this passage has as its speaker Śāriputra, and it appears to be one of several misunderstandings by him featured in various part of the text. In fact, Subhūti replies by deconstructing both the threefold and the single option, rather than affirming the latter: 云何於本無中見三道不, and 云何於本無中可得一道不, with Śāriputra having to reply to both queries in the negative.

782. See, e.g., Silk 2002, 367: "I think it is quite certain, however, that the referent of the term 'Hīnayāna,' when it occurs in Buddhist texts themselves, is never any existent institution or organization, but a rhetorical fiction." In a similar vein, Skilling 2013b, 76 explains that "[t]he Hīnayāna never existed, anywhere or at any time, as an establishment or organization, as a social movement, as a self-conscious historical agent. Nor was Hīnayāna a state or period in the development of Buddhism." A related problem concerns monastic *nikāya* and *yāna* affiliation, which can combine in various ways, in the sense of being distinct axes in a multi-dimensional space of possible identities. Already Przyluski 1926, 362 argued that "il n'y a pas eu seulement un Grand Véhicule issu de l'École Sarvāstivādin; on peut aussi parler, jusqu'à un certain point, d'un mahāyānism *dharmaguptaka*, d'un mahāyānism *mahāsāṃghika*, etc. Cette constatation, outre a son évident intérêt historique, a l'avantage de permettre, sur bien de points, une interprétation nouvelle et plus exacte des documents et des faits." This could in turn be related to references by Xuánzàng (玄奘) to Indian and Sri Lankan practitioners of the Mahāyāna who were at the same time members of the Sthaviranikāya; for Sri Lanka see T 51.2087.934a14: 遵行大乘上座部法 (since Xuánzàng did not visit Sri Lanka himself, this reference needs to be handled with even more circumspection than his descriptions of the situation in India); references relevant to India can be found in T 51.2087.918b14, 929a3, 935c2, and 936c15. The notion of Mahāyāna

Sthaviras is also attested in a Khmer inscription; see Cœdès 1929, 22,3: *vraḥ paṃnvas bhikṣu mahāyāna sthavira* and on the significance of the formulation also Bizot 1988, 111–12 and Skilling 2013b, 149n159.

783. This holds also for evidence relevant to Theravāda. An illustrative example for the apparent impact of the assumption of a basic incompatibility can be seen in Spiro 1970/1982, 62, who in his study of Burmese Buddhism asserts that "the *Bodhisattva* ideal is not found—nor for reasons just suggested, could it be found—in the *Theravāda* tradition," yet on the very same page reports that in Theravāda Burma there has been a long tradition of aspiring to Buddhahood (see the quote above on p. 21). The impact of the paradigmatic contrast between Mahāyāna and Theravāda has apparently prevented noticing that these two statements are incompatible, and that the former assertion would need to be corrected in the light of the actual evidence reported in the second statement.

784. Hartmann 2019, 15 draws attention to a type of problem that appears to hold as well for the present case, namely a "back-projection of terms and perspectives. Whatever is subsumed under the term Mahāyāna in later times will be gratefully classified under the same label when encountered in earlier periods."

785. One example would be a reference in the *Abhidharmakośavyākhyā*, Wogihara 1936/1971, 11,29, to those who consider only *sūtra* to be authoritative; another example would be a reference in the *Atthasālinī* to a rejection of the claim that the Abhidharma is the word of the Buddha, As 28,20: *abhidhammo kena bhāsito ti? na eso buddhabhāsito ti*. The continuity in later times of contestation among members of the Theravāda tradition(s) regarding the authoritativeness of new texts can be seen, for example, in relation to the *Paññāsajātaka* collection; see Anālayo 2023c, 5.

786. See also Greene 2017, 84: "Modern scholars often take the promotion of the bodhisattva path . . . to be a hallmark of Mahāyāna Buddhism. It is also usually supposed that, when first articulated, this was a new and at least somewhat controversial understanding of the goals of Buddhist practice. However[,] if the Mahāyāna endorsement of the bodhisattva path was controversial, its critics left few traces. Though Mahāyāna texts themselves often claim that their teachings were criticized by others, there are in fact no known Indian Buddhist texts that in their own voice mount sustained argument against any feature of Mahāyāna Buddhism. But equally if not more significantly, even when supposed criticisms of it are discussed within Mahāyāna literature so as to refute them, the bodhisattva path itself is never one of the points of contention."

787. This finding would be in line with the observation by Tsai 1997, 17 that the very casting of Mahāyāna in contrast to Hīnayāna "is intricately interwoven with the construction of an essentialist definition of Mahāyāna. An essentialist view assumes that a labeling term, such as Mahāyāna, invariably contains some fundamental features applicable to all the phenomena that bear this very term. However, historical fluctuation, and geographical and documentary diversity create significant challenges to this essentialist approach . . . [which] overlooks both the complexities of individual documents and the disparities among Mahāyāna documents. The biggest challenge to this practice is evidence from the oldest extant Mahāyāna sūtras."

788. Anālayo 2014c.

789. The most directly relevant publication would be Anālayo 2023c, which summarizes my earlier exploration of the term "Buddhism" in Anālayo 2021d, 108–13 and substantially expands my previous discussion of the term "Theravāda" in Anālayo 2013d.

790. The term *buddhadhamma* appears to emerge only in later Pāli literature; on *dhamma-vinaya* see Geiger and Geiger 1920, 56–58.

791. Th 181: *yato ahaṃ pabbajito* (S^e: *pabbajitvā*) *sammāsambuddhasāsane.*

792. T 50.2063.939c12; see also Guang Xing 2013.

793. MN 26 at MN I 164,5 and MN I 165,25 (same again in MN 36, MN 85, and MN 100); all these occurrences of the term are not supported by parallels.

794. See in more detail Anālayo 2013d, 215–17.

795. See MĀ 204 at T 1.26.776b12 and Sanskrit fragment 331v1, Liu 2010, 105–106.

796. See in more detail Anālayo 2023c, 7–14.

797. Identified by Handlin 2016, 180; for a more detailed discussion see Anālayo 2023c, 1–6.

798. My survey is based on the standard rendering 大乘 (occurrences in T 120 are not included in my survey; on the nature of this text see, e.g., Schmithausen 2003, 22); see also Walser 2009, 235–47 for a detailed discussion of occurrences of 大乘 in DĀ 2 together with T 3 and in SĀ 769. In addition to references in Chinese translations, the Tibetan rendering *theg pa chen po* features once in a collection of discourse quotations extant in Tibetan; see Up 3024 at D 4094 *ju* 127a6 or P 5595 *tu* 146a3. This occurrence is of no further relevance to my present concerns, as it does not form part of the actual discourse quotation.

I have not been able to locate occurrences of Lokakṣema's rendering 摩訶衍—or of the possible alternatives 摩訶乘, 無上乘, or 最上乘—among *Āgama* discourses. Another possible candidate would be 大道, which an interlinear commentary in the early *Prajñāpāramitā* translation T 8.225.481a11 uses to explain 大乘. An occurrence of 大道 in the *Prajñāpāramitā* translation by Lokakṣema, Karashima 2011, 538,1 (= T 8.224.478a13) has a parallel only in T 8.225.508a19 and is not found in the other versions (see Karashima 2011, 538n245). In the case of an occurrence of 大道 in the translation of the **Pratyutpannasamādhisūtra* attributed to Lokakṣema, T 13.418.904a20 (other occurrences in verse portions of the same text are not directly relevant, as according Harrison 1990, 248–49 these were not translated by Lokakṣema), the relevant passage in the Tibetan parallel Harrison 1978b, 17,15 (1X) does not employ the term *mahāyāna* (the same holds for T 13.416.874a29). It thus seems that, at least in these two earliest translations by Lokakṣema, 摩訶乘 is probably the standard rendering for the term *mahāyāna* and 大道 may be translating some other Indic term.

A similar situation appears to apply to occurrences of 大道 in *Āgama* literature, instances of which I survey beginning with the *Ekottarikāgama* and then taking up individual translations in their order of occurrence in the Taishō edition. My first example is thus EĀ 38.4 at T 2.125.718b27, which refers to an ancient 大道 in the context of a simile illustrating the Buddha's discovery of dependent arising as the path to awakening. The parallels also refer to an ancient path, differing only in not using the qualification "great"; see SN 12.65 at SN II 105,36: *purāṇaṃ maggaṃ* (S^e: *purāṇamaggaṃ*), Chung and Fukita 2020, 100 (5.29a) and Bongard-Levin, Boucher, Fukita, and Wille 1996, 80,3: *paurāṇaṃ mārgaṃ*, SĀ 287 at T 2.99.80c17: 古仙人道, T 16.713.827b1: 故道, T 16.714.828b23: 舊道, and T 16.715.830a11: 昔人所行之道. The parallels and the context make it safe to conclude that in this instance 道 would be rendering *mārga* rather than *yāna*. Another occurrence of 大道 can be found in the same *Āgama* collection in EĀ 48.4 at T 2.125.791a19. This has 大導 as a 元 and 明 variant reading, which fits the context better, as it matches the corresponding prose in

EĀ 48.4 at T 2.125.791a13. At any rate, the reference is to the name of the attendant of the former Buddha Vipaśyin.

An instance found in an individually translated text occurs in the context of a distinction between four types of practitioners of the path, the foremost among which is the conqueror of the path, i.e., an arhat. The description of this conqueror of the path in T 1.5.167c23 refers to the ability of such a conqueror of the path to cultivate the 大道. The parallels do not have a comparable reference; see DĀ 2 at T 1.1.18b20, T 1.6.183b12, and Waldschmidt 1951, 261 (26.21) for the Tibetan parallel. Although this particular exposition does not feature in DN 16, a Pāli counterpart occurs in Sn 86. Given that the context is about four types of practitioners of the *mārga*, for which T 5 uses 道, it seems fair to assume that the meaning of a *mārga* additionally qualified as "great" may also be relevant to this reference to 大道.

T 1.6.180a29 reports the Buddha referring to his teaching of the 大道 to Nirvana for abandoning *saṃsāra*. Although the parallels do not have such an indication, the context makes it safe to conclude that the reference is to the great path that leads to becoming an arhat. In another reference in the same text, T 1.6.180c27, 大道 occurs in relation to the Buddha's awakening as one of several events that result in an earthquake. The Pāli and Sanskrit parallels, DN 16 at DN II 108,20 and Waldschmidt 1951, 216,19, employ the term *bodhi*, making it probable that the same underlies 道 here. Perhaps such a sense may also be relevant to other occurrences in the same text, although these remain somewhat doubtful. The first of these is part of a set of verses spoken by a monk after the Buddha had recovered from being sick on hearing a recitation of the seven awakening factors. One of these verses in T 1.6.184c16 refers to humans and *deva*s training together and with (mutual?) *maitrī* in the 大道, qualified as true or real. The Sanskrit parallel has preserved a reference to humans and *deva*s, followed in the next line, Waldschmidt 1951, 292,10, by *nirupādāna iva śikhī*. Four occurrences of 大道 in the same work, T 1.6.186b26+28 and 186c1+3, feature in the context of a description of the boundless cultivation of the four *brahmavihāra*s by King Mahāsudarśana, perhaps in the sense that the prior removal of obstructive states to undertaking such cultivation is conducive to 大道. Unlike such instances, where the meaning remains uncertain (at least for me), a reference in T 1.23.292b4 to the 大道 is quite straightforward, as the context show this to intend a rather large road.

Three occurrences of 大道 feature in T 1.33.817b7+15 as well as 817c24. The first two take the form of referring to 佛泥洹大道, which in both instances features as the last in a list of attainments. In the first instance, the preceding three are becoming an arhat, a Pratyekabuddha, or a bodhisattva (as a result of keeping the monastic rules); in the second instance the preceding six are the four levels of awakening (from stream-entry to arhat-ship), Pratyekabuddhahood, and what appears to be a reference to *bodhicitta*. Both instances seem to reflect the influence of already existing Mahāyāna thought; the phrase itself appears to intend the awakening of a Buddha. The third occurrence in T 1.33.817c24 is part of the query of how one can know that in the world 大道 exists, which may also intend some attainment. Attainments listed in parallels are confined to the four levels of awakening (together with those on the path to these four); see AN 8.20 at AN IV 208,3, MĀ 37 at T 1.26.479b1, T 1.34.818c12, and T 35.1.819b28. One of these parallels, T 1.34.818c18, also has a reference to the 大道, which here designates what is cultivated by those coming from the four classes of ancient Indian society once they have become disciples of the Buddha. MĀ 37 at T 1.26.479b23 also combines a reference to the four classes with an indication of their eventual attainment, which here is imperturbable liberation, that is, full awakening.

My last example occurs in T 1.69.872b6+8, whose introductory narration reports that the Buddha had given teachings to a group of householders for the purpose of arousing in the minds of his listeners the 大道意, *bodhicitta*, and reports that these had indeed aroused the 大道心. No such reference is found in the discourse parallels MN 82 at MN II 55,22, Waldschmidt 1980, 363,3, MĀ 132 at T 1.26.623b2, and T 1.68.869a16; for further parallels see Anālayo 2011b, 451. Neither reference in T 69 fits the context, as according to the narrative setting the Buddha had given a teaching to an assembly of householders that a young man from a leading family in town found so deeply inspiring as to make him want to go forth as a monk in order to pursue the path to becoming an arhat. This young man and his wholehearted struggle to get permission to go forth as well as his successful reaching of the final goal and subsequent experiences are the main theme of the discourse. It follows that the teaching reportedly given by the Buddha at the outset could hardly have been about arousing *bodhicitta*, as the young man was much rather inspired to dedicate himself wholeheartedly to the path to arhat-ship.

In sum, as far as I am able to tell, the employment of 道 in the above of references to 大道 in *Āgama* literature appears to reflect an Indic original corresponding to *mārga* or to *bodhi* but not to *yāna*. For this reason, such references are not relevant to my present exploration.

799. DĀ 2 at T 1.1.12c28: 大乘道之輿, 一切渡天人 (with a 宋, 元, and 明 variant reading 導 instead of 道). T 1.6.178b1: 大乘道之典, 一切渡天人. Walser 2009, 246 comments that "the image of a 'great vehicle' appears to be quite natural to the setting" and "does not appear to be forwarding any obviously Mahāyāna agenda. Indeed, this passage may well have been the inspiration for cases such as the *Daśabhūmikasūtra* in which the Mahāyāna is referred to as the *mahāyānapātra* (the Great Boat)"; see Vaidya 1967, 40,6 and T 10.286.521b19: 乘大乘船, and also below n. 802. The expression 大乘道 recurs in the same type of context in T 3.161.387b28.

800. DN 16 at DN I 89,26 and Waldschmidt 1951, 158.

801. The expression is 乘大舶, which can best be appreciated within its context in T 24.1448.23c21: 智人渡大海, 乘舡不作橋. 愚者海爲橋, 江河乘大舶. 世尊已渡河, 婆羅門處岸. "The wise cross the great ocean embarking on a boat and do not construct a bridge. Fools take a bridge for the ocean and *embark on a great boat* for rivers. The Blessed One has already crossed the river; the Brahmin stands on the [other] shore"; see also the German translation in Waldschmidt 1944, 62. The Tibetan parallel, D 1 *kha* 29a2 or P 1030 *ge* 26b7, proceeds differently and therefore does not shed further light on this line; the same holds for a related verse in the *Divyāvadāna*, Cowell and Neil 1886, 56,8 (for further parallels see Nattier 2023, 232–38). One way or another, the verse translated above differs from the one quoted in DN 16 and its Sanskrit parallel, as it is spoken by a lay disciple rather than the Buddha, and the relevant part carries a negative sense by designating the behavior of fools, rather than being applicable to the Buddha.

802. SĀ 769 at T 2.99.200c26+28 lists 婆羅門乘 but at T 2.99.201a1 instead gives 梵乘, each time followed by the 大乘. Another term also used in this context is the celestial vehicle, 天乘. All three are then related to the notion of enabling a martial approach to overcoming defilements, 能調伏煩惱軍者.

803. Regarding this occurrence in SĀ 769, Walser 2009, 240 argues for "the high probabil-

ity that there was a Northern Indic version . . . that refers to the Noble Eightfold Path as the 'mahāyāna.'" In appreciation of the contribution offered in this way, a minor point I would like to clarify concerns his attribution of the translation to Guṇabhadra, which is in line with the information given in T 2.99.1a5. Yet, it would probably be more accurate to attribute the translation of T 99 to Bǎoyún (寶雲) and his Chinese assistants, with Guṇabhadra's role being mainly to read out the Indic text and give his name to the completed translation as a form of authentication. As noted by Glass 2008/2010, 189, since Guṇabhadra had only recently arrived in China, he could hardly have been responsible for the actual work of translation. Nattier 2008, 19 highlights a general tendency where "in many cases a scripture is credited not to the actual translator, but to the foreign participant in the translation process, even if that person's only role . . . was to provide a written text and/or to recite the scripture aloud"; see also Lettere 2020, 271 regarding what appears to have additionally contributed to obfuscating Bǎoyún's role as a translator in general. As far as the possibility of some misunderstanding of the relevant Indic term by Bǎoyún is concerned, there appears to be indeed a *yāna*-related misunderstanding influencing his translation elsewhere in T 99 (mentioned by Walser 2009, 241), namely a mistaking of *ekāyana* as *ekayāna*, resulting in the translation 一乘; see the discussion in Nattier 2007b. At the same time, however, the same misunderstanding—if it is indeed one and not rather a reflection of the Indic original—can also be seen in *Āgama* passages extant in Tibetan translation: *theg pa ni gcig*, found in Up 6029 at D 4094 *nyu* 13a4+13b5 or P 5595 *thu* 46a8+47a1 and in Up 6080 at D 4094 *nyu* 44a2 or P 5595 *thu* 83b1. Since both T 99 and Up appear to be based on Mūlasarvāstivāda originals, it is in principle possible that the same type of original has been correctly translated in these different instances. Since both meanings make sense in the context, it is perhaps not surprising that a confusion could occur, be this in the Indic original or during translation.

804. SN 45.4 at SN V 5,16 and 6,5 refers to the *brahmayāna*; another term also used in this context is the vehicle of Dharma, *dhammayāna*. Like the case of SĀ 769, the listing of alternative terms culminates in a reference to supreme victory in battle. A bilingual Sanskrit and Uighur fragment has not preserved a counterpart to the terms used in either SN 45.4 or SĀ 769 and for this reason is not of direct relevance to the present difference; see von Gabain 1954, 15 (also Waldschmidt 1967, 248).

805. See, e.g., Katz 1984, 189: "Etymologically, the term derives from the Sanskrit root *yā*, 'to go,' giving the sense of going or proceeding, as well as the means of [a] carriage or the vehicle, and is very close in many connotations to *mārga*, the path."

806. Vetter 2001, 64–67 proposes that a sense of "path" underlies Lokakṣema's understanding of the term *mahāyāna* not only in some of his other translations but also in his rendition of the Perfection of Wisdom. Yet, as pointed out by Walser 2009, 224, the underlying idea of a vehicle can be seen in the following passage, Karashima 2011, 28,3 (= T 8.224.428a9): 摩訶衍者亦不見來時, 亦不見去時, 亦不見住處. Walser 2009, 224 offers the following comment: "Here, the repetition of the character 時 adds a temporal dimension to the sentence, ('it is not seen *when* it comes, it is not seen *when* it departs . . .') that would simply not make sense if he understood the *mahāyāna* to be a path. Thus, we can infer that, at least in this translation, Lokakṣema understood *mahāyāna* as a vehicle and not as a path."

807. MN 91 at MN II 139,31 and MĀ 161 at T 1.26.687b25.

808. T 1.76.884b20: 以四等大乘自度尊身又濟眾生. On the translation of T 76 see Nattier 2008, 129–30.

809. T 1.34.818c1: 大乘之味, 志求大願度人民故. On the translator to whom this discourse is attributed see Zürcher 1959/1972, 70.

810. AN 8.20 at AN IV 207,25 (here only given in abbreviation; for the text in full see the preceding AN 8.19 at AN IV 203,7), Ud 5.5 at Ud 56,2, MĀ 37 at T 1.26.479a10, T 1.35.819c4, and EĀ 42.4 at T 2.125.753a28 (this discourse is, strictly speaking, a parallel to AN 8.19); in addition, corresponding presentations can be found in the Dharmaguptaka *Vinaya*, T 22.1428.824c21, the Mahīśāsaka *Vinaya*, T 22.1421.181a27, and the Theravāda *Vinaya*, Vin II 239,32.

811. EĀ 19.8 at T 2.125.595b13: 求於大乘行 (the term 大乘 occurs also thrice in the introduction to the collection, T 2.125.550a12, 550b4, and 550c10, occurrences that are of no relevance to my present purposes).

812. Given that there is evidence for a somewhat free style of translation adopted by Zhú Fóniàn (竺佛念), see above n. 26, it is quite possible for the present occurrence of 大乘 to reflect Zhú Fóniàn's creative approach rather than an Indic original.

813. Walser 2009, 247 concludes his study of the origin of the term *mahāyāna* by proposing that it "appears to be an organic outgrowth of specifically Buddhist appropriations of the Upaniṣadic idea of the *devayāna patha* cross-pollinated with Śrauta metaphors of the sacrifice as chariot and more generally Indic ideas of vehicle *vimāna*s as a reflection of religious practice." Thus, "when we find Mahāyāna texts talking about the *mahāyāna*, they may well be referring to a term that was already in vogue."

814. According to an alternative explanation proposed by Karashima 2001, 171–72 and 2015a, based on studying variants among manuscripts of the *Saddharmapuṇḍarīka* and its Chinese translations, the term *mahāyāna* may result from a Sanskritization of a Prakrit form of *mahājñāna*. In full recognition of the remarkably detailed survey of textual evidence marshalled by Karashima 2015a on this fascinating aspect of the *Saddharmapuṇḍarīka*, I find his conclusions on the wider implications of his findings not necessarily compelling. In the first draft of the present book, I had tried to sidestep this issue, but feedback from one of my reviewers made it clear to me that I should not allow my profound sense of indebtedness, in particular to Karashima 2010 and 2011, to prevent me from clearly articulating where I see things differently. Before getting into that, I need to mention that the supposed choice of (a Prakrit form of) the term *mahājñāna* by early Mahāyānists to designate the goal of their aspirations has already been problematized by Walser 2009, 226n17—a publication not mentioned in Karashima 2015a, suggesting that he may not have been aware of it—whose reasoning I reproduce here for ease of reference:

"1) Since, presumably, the earliest Mahāyānists aspired to become Buddhas, we would expect to find the Buddha lauded as one with Great Knowledge in some authoritative non-Mahāyāna text. Mahāyānists could then tap into the legitimacy of the already established text through the adoption of the term. I have not been able to find the term *mahājñāna* applied to the Buddha in early biographies, though it does appear in later sources.

"2) Barring (1), we should at least expect to find the Buddha's enlightenment experience to be described as a special kind of *jñāna*, preferably a *mahājñāna*, in some other authoritative non-Mahāyāna text (preferably in an *abhidharma* treatise if not in one of the biographies of the Buddha). Again, this appears to be the case only in much later texts.

"3) Finally, in the absence of (1) and (2), at the very least we should expect to find some Mahāyāna text to make a big deal about *jñāna*, preferably about *mahājñāna*. If the term had been so foundational to the early Mahāyāna movement, we should expect to find residual evidence of this fact in existing Mahāyāna texts. Though the term *mahājñāna* does appear in some early Mahāyāna texts[,] its significance is certainly eclipsed by other terms like *prajñāpāramitā*."

In what follows, I examine the proposed hypothesis from the viewpoint of its applicability to the specific case of Lokakṣema's *Prajñāpāramitā* translation, T 224. One issue to be explored is the dating of such early *Prajñāpāramitā* compared to that of the *Saddharmapuṇḍarīka*. Karashima 2015a, 175 takes up the promotion of the "single Buddha-vehicle" in the parable of the burning house, which already occurs in what he reckons to belong to the earliest layer in the development of the *Saddharmapuṇḍarīka* (p. 176). The assumption by Karashima 2015a, 187 that such promotion of Buddhahood as a universal goal is a form of "renaissance" of a position already found in the *Suttanipāta* is unfortunately incorrect; see Anālayo 2016e, 6n8. Instead, the idea that "[e]verybody can obtain Buddha-wisdom equally and should aim at obtaining it" (p. 187) appears to be an innovation testifying to a mature stage in the development of the bodhisattva ideal. Karashima 2015a, 187 reasons that reports of antagonism toward proponents of the *Saddharmapuṇḍarīka* can be read to indicate "that the Lotus Sutra is the oldest text among the so-called Mahāyāna scriptures, which proclaim everybody's possibility of becoming a *buddha*." Yet, this still makes the same text later—and that in relation to a topic closely related to *yāna* terminology—than those "among the so-called Mahāyāna scriptures" in which the path of a bodhisattva still features as an exceptional choice undertaken by a minority; this is the case for T 224.

Another topic to be examined here concerns occurrences of the term *mahāyāna* in T 224. Karashima 2015a, 191 comments on an exchange between Pūrṇa and Subhūti, found toward the final part of the first chapter of the *Aṣṭasāhasrikā Prajñāpāramitā*, that "Pūrṇa's criticism that to relate *mahāyāna* with *prajñāpāramitā* was unreasonable indicates that *mahāyāna* had been originally heterogenous to *Prajñāpāramitā* thought." It is debatable if this is indeed the best way of reading this exchange, given that the Buddha endorses Subhūti's explanation rather than Pūrṇa's criticism; see Karashima 2011, 28,10 (= T 8.224.428a16) and the Sanskrit counterpart in Wogihara 1932/1935, 109,3. The present exchange can perhaps preferably be read in line with an exchange that closely precedes it, where Pūrṇa also features in the role of needing Subhūti to clarify things for him; see Karashima 2011, 25,3 (= T 8.224.427c18) and the Sanskrit counterpart in Wogihara 1932/1935, 91,23. That is, I would take the depiction of "Pūrṇa's criticism that to relate *mahāyāna* with *prajñāpāramitā* was unreasonable" to be intended to portray his lack of understanding.

The above episode is one of several occurrences of the term *mahāyāna* in the first chapter, which is generally considered, at least in part, to reflect a rather early stage in the evolution of this text, even being at times considered the original version of the text before it expanded to its present form; see, e.g., Schmithausen 1977, 37 and Zacchetti 2015b, 177. It is therefore unexpected when Karashima 2015a, 190 argues that, "[a]s an introduction is usually written after the completion of an entire book, Chapter I of the AsP [= *Aṣṭasāhasrikā Prajñāpāramitā*] is thought to have been composed at the very last stage of its compilation" (unfortunately without providing a reference that could help identify to whom the phrase "is thought" refers). The first chapter does not give me the impression of being an introduction compiled after the rest of the text had been composed, and asserting its lateness would require critical engagement with the evidence surveyed and the arguments provided by those scholars who rather consider it to be early. Whatever may be the final word on the earliness of the first chapter, however, references to the term *mahāyāna* in this chapter are already found in Lokakṣema's translation, unlike several other terms and notions that only make their appearance in later members of the *Aṣṭasāhasrikā* textual family; for examples see Lancaster 1968. Thus, the date of the translation of T 224 provides a testimony to such references being already in existence at that time. The significance of this testimony can be related to the case of T 626, mentioned in Karashima 2015a, 186n60, which gives the impression that, unlike later translations, Lokakṣema's translation of this text opts for the reading *mahājñāna* rather than the alternative term *mahāyāna*. This may suggest the absence of a tendency to try to introduce the term *mahāyāna* wherever possible, which in turn would increase confidence in those instances where this term indeed occurs.

Under the header of discussing "[t]he reason for the *yāna* / *jñāna* confusion in the Lotus Sutra," Karashima 2015a, 171 comments on relevant occurrences in the early verse parts of the *Saddharmapuṇḍarīka* that "[w]e may assume, then, in the earliest stage of the transmission of the Lotus Sutra, the Prakrit form **jāna* or *jāṇa* (< OIA. [= Old Indo-Aryan] *jñāna*, *yāna*), which could mean both 'vehicle' and 'wisdom,' had stood in these places and that later, somebody back-formed it to *jñāna* ('wisdom'), while other redactors sanskritized it to *yāna* ('vehicle')." He adds that, "[a]s in Gāndhārī, *yāna* became *yaṇa*, while *jñāna* became *ñaṇa*, the *yāna* / *jñāna* confusion could not have taken place in this Northwestern Indian dialect"; this reasoning would apply to the case of T 224, whose translation was, according to Karashima 2013c, based on a Gāndhārī original. Now, according to Karashima 2015a, 166, the gradual Sanskritization of Buddhist *sūtra*s would have taken place "from the third century onwards." If the proposed Sanskritization resulting in a replacement of *mahājñāna* with the term *mahāyāna* could only have happened from the third century onward, the resultant temporal frame decisively undermines the proposal by Karashima 2015a, 191 that "the notion of *mahāyāna* was adopted from the Lotus Sutra in the *Aṣṭasāhasrikā Prajñāpāramitā*," at least as far as T 224 is concerned. How could the results of a development taking place in India since the third century have had any impact on the formation of a text that was translated in China already in the second century?

In sum, it seems that references in T 224 to the term *mahāyāna*, 摩訶衍, must have come into existence independent of any "confusion" with *mahājñāna*, because this would not have happened in Gāndhārī, and its apparent occurrence as part of a Sanskritization of a Prakrit original—such as in the case of the *Saddharmapuṇḍarīka*—would have emerged at too late a time to be able to impact the formation of T 224 prior to its translation. The conclusion that emerges in this way would align with the apparent dating of the respective texts, given that the earliest strata of the *Saddharmapuṇḍarīka* testifies to a more mature stage of development of the bodhisattva ideal than its early *Prajñāpāramitā* counterpart. At the same time, however, the above does not in any way diminish the remarkable philological contribution to our understanding of the *Saddharmapuṇḍarīka* offered by Karashima 2015a, as it only concerns the applicability of his research conclusions to other texts, in particular to the case of T 224.

815. On references to Mahāyāna in other translations by Lokakṣema (together with T 322 and T 630) see Harrison 1987.
816. Karashima 2011, 27,6 (= T 8.224.428a6); see above n. 760.
817. Karashima 2011, 26,6 (= T 8.224.427c30): 摩訶衍者, 無有正也, 不可得邊幅.
818. Karashima 2011, 28,1 (= T 8.224.428a8): 摩訶衍覆不可復計, 阿僧祇人. 爾故, 呼摩訶衍. Gombrich 1992, 40 comments on the corresponding Sanskrit passage that "here *yāna* is a chariot, not a path," given that the passage conveys "that the vehicle is so big that it has room for an infinite number of creatures"; see Wogihara 1932/1935, 106,25: *ākāśasamatayā atimahattayā tan mahāyānam, yath' ākāśe aprameyāṇām asaṃkhyeyānāṃ sattvānām avakāśaḥ, evam eva bhagavann asmin yāne aprameyāṇām asaṃkhyeyānāṃ sattvānām avakāśaḥ*. A similar articulation of this image continues with the *Pañcaviṃśatisāhasrikā* and *Śatasāhasrikā Prajñāpāramitā*, Kimura 2009, 114,11 (also in Dutt 1934, 231,13) and Ghoṣa 1905, 1530,4.
819. Karashima 2011, 41,7 (= T 8.224.429b6): 菩薩, 摩訶薩摩訶僧那僧涅 摩訶衍三拔致.
820. Karashima 2011, 24,4 (= T 8.224.427c10): 菩薩, 摩訶薩度不可計阿僧祇人, 悉令般泥洹, 無不般泥洹一人也. 菩薩聞是, 不恐, 不畏, 不悉, 不捨去就餘道, 知是則爲摩訶僧那僧涅. My summary of this passage's import is based on the assumption that the double negation in the formulation 無不般泥洹一人也 is due to a misunderstanding of the Indic original and should be emended to a single negation. As indicated by Karashima 2011, 24n187, this is the sense of the relevant passage in the Sanskrit version, Wogihara 1932/1935, 89,20: *na ca sa kaścit sattvo yaḥ parinirvṛto* as well as in the other early Chinese versions T 8.225.480c25: 爲無有人得滅度也 and T 8.226.510c1: 無有人般泥洹者.
821. Karashima 2011, 228,2 (= T 8.224.446b19): 善男子, 善女人聞是波羅蜜者, 以得極尊歡樂摩訶衍功德, 還近阿耨多羅三耶三菩, which is based on an emendation of 勸 to read 歡; see Karashima 2011, 228n307.
822. As the survey provided by Karashima 2010, 352–53 shows, references to 菩薩道 in T 224 can have different Sanskrit counterparts or even none. This reflects the same problem also relevant to my earlier discussion of 大道 above n. 798, in that the usage of 道 can in principle reflect a range of different Indic originals. My discussion in the present context is restricted to those occurrences of 菩薩道 that match *bodhisattvayāna* in the Sanskrit counterpart. Three such occurrences have already been identified by Karashima 2010, 353 in the course of providing selected examples of this type of usage. On the usage of the terms *mahāyāna* and *bodhisattvayāna* in translations attributed to Lokakṣema in general see also Harrison 1987, 72–73.
823. Karashima 2011, 413,11 (= T 8.224.465c9): 行菩薩道者, 乃向佛道乎; here and in the notes below, I reference the corresponding occurrence of the term *bodhisattvayānika* in the Sanskrit version, which in the present case occurs in Wogihara 1932/1935, 829,15.
824. Karashima 2011, 228,8 (= T 8.224.446b26): 我勸助是善男子, 善女人至德學菩薩道; see Wogihara 1932/1935, 492,23.
825. Karashima 2011, 153,9 (= T 8.224.440a14): 菩薩道德之人, 常知: 過去, 當來, 今現在法無所取, 亦無所捨, 亦無所知, 亦無所得 (also quoted above n. 387); see Wogihara 1932/1935, 370,6.
826. Karashima 2011, 237,5 (= T 8.224.447b3): 當來行菩薩道者, 得聞深般若波羅蜜, 不可意, 便棄捨去, 反明聲聞, 辟支佛法, 於中求薩芸若 and Karashima 2011, 238,19 (=

T 8.224.447b24): 甫當來有行菩薩道者，得聞深般若波羅蜜，反持比聲聞法，於聲聞法中，欲得薩芸若，作佛; see Wogihara 1932/1935, 507,11 and 508,12.

827. This impression could be related to a passage in the translation of the **Pratyutpanna-samādhisūtra* attributed to Lokakṣema, which reports the wish that those who cultivate the *bodhisattvayāna* never leave the Mahāyāna; T 13.418.904a19: 行菩薩道未曾離摩訶衍. This case is not entirely straightforward, however, as the Tibetan version, Harrison 1978b, 17,13, just speaks of *byang chub sems dpa'i spyod pa thams cad rgyun mi gcod pa rnams su 'gyur ba*, which thus does not mention Mahāyāna at all and speaks of the aspiration to "become those who never interrupt any of the practices of a bodhisattva" (Harrison 1990, 22), rather than referring to the *bodhisattvayāna*. Nevertheless, T 13.416.874a28 does have such a reference to never leaving the Mahāyāna, 未曾遠離大乘.

828. What emerges in this way can be compared to the summary of the case of the *Ugraparipṛcchā* provided by Nattier 2003a, 195: "For the authors of this sūtra, the Mahāyāna is nothing more, and nothing less, than a synonym of the 'bodhisattva path.' For the *Ugra*, in other words, the Mahāyāna is not a school, a sect, or a movement, but a particular spiritual *vocation*, to be pursued within the existing Buddhist community."

829. This is in itself not a novel realization, as already some forty years ago Rawlinson 1983, 170 reasoned that "[w]e are asking the wrong question if we try and find *an* origin of the Mahayana."

830. See Anālayo 2022d.

831. MN 37 at MN I 251,20: *sabbe dhammā nālaṃ abhinivesāyā ti*, with a parallel in EĀ 19.3 at T 2.125.593c18; for a survey of different translations of this injunction see Skilling 2024, 6–7 and for expositions based on this injunction SN 35.80 at SN IV 50,15 (E[e] lacks *sabbe*) and AN 7.58 at AN IV 88,12. The former provides an exemplification of the degree to which the Pāli tradition does justice to the profundity of this dictum, wherefore a short survey of the key points of this discourse may be an appropriate way of concluding my annotations.

SM 35.80 sets out on the inquiry of whether there is one dharma whose abandoning will result in abandoning ignorance and arousing knowledge. In reply, the Buddha confirms that this exists. The next inquiry then is naturally what that dharma is, which receives the reply that ignorance is the one dharma whose abandoning will lead to the abandoning of ignorance and the arousing of knowledge. The apparent tautology could be on purpose, in the sense of forcing the questioner to shift from ascertaining what exists to trying to find out how to practice. Such a shift indeed happens, as the next question, instead of continuing in the same rut, rather queries how one should know and see to achieve the abandoning of ignorance and the arousal of knowledge. This motivates the Buddha to offer a detailed reply, which sets out on having heard *sabbe dhammā nālaṃ abhinivesāyā ti*. Having heard it, one fully knows any dharma, *sabbaṃ dhammaṃ abhijānāti*; fully knowing any dharma, one penetratively knows any dharma, *sabbaṃ dhammaṃ abhiññāya sabbaṃ dhammaṃ parijānāti*. This appears to call first of all for seeing any dharma as it is, without being influenced by biases and projections, and based on that then seeing through any dharma, in the sense of cultivating insight into its true nature. With this much in place, one sees all signs as otherwise, *sabbaṃ dhammaṃ pariññāya sabbanimittāni aññato passati*. Such seeing as otherwise then applies to each of the senses, from the eye to the mind, as well as to the respective objects, consciousness, contact, and feeling tones arisen in dependence on that contact.

In other words, all dimensions of experience are to be seen as otherwise from what they usually appear to be, and this takes place at the stage of taking up a sign, *nimitta*, as a basic element in perceptual appraisal. The profundity of this instruction resonates in several respects with central concerns articulated in the Perfection of Wisdom.

# References


Abeynayake, Oliver. 1984. *A Textual and Historical Analysis of the Khuddaka Nikāya*. Colombo: Tisara.

Acharya, Diwakar. 2008/2010. "Evidence for Mahāyāna Buddhism and Sukhāvatī Cult in India in the Middle Period: Early Fifth to Late Sixth Century Nepalese Inscriptions." *Journal of the International Association of Buddhist Studies*, 31.1/2: 23–75.

Agostini, Giulio. 2010. "'Preceded by Thought Are the Dhammas': The Ancient Exegesis on Dhp 1–2." In *Buddhist Asia 2. Papers from the Second Conference of Buddhist Studies Held in Naples in June 2004*, edited by Giacomella Orofino and Silvio Vita, 1–34. Kyoto: Italian School of East Asian Studies.

Akanuma Chizen. 1929/1990. *The Comparative Catalogue of Chinese Āgamas & Pāli Nikāyas*. Delhi: Sri Satguru.

Allon, Mark. 2001. *Three Gāndhārī Ekottarikāgama-Type sūtras, British Library Kharoṣṭhī Fragments 12 and 14*. Seattle: University of Washington Press.

———. 2007. "A Gāndhārī Version of the Simile of the Turtle and the Hole in the Yoke." *Journal of the Pali Text Society*, 29: 229–62.

Allon, Mark and Richard Salomon. 2010. "New Evidence for Mahāyāna in Early Gandhāra." *The Eastern Buddhist*, 41.1: 1–22.

Alsdorf, Ludwig. 1977. "Das Bhūridatta-Jātaka. Ein anti-brahmanischer Nāga-Roman." *Wiener Zeitschrift für die Kunde Südasiens*, 21: 25–55.

Anālayo, Bhikkhu. 2005. "The Seven Stages of Purification in Comparative Perspective." *Journal of the Centre for Buddhist Studies*, 3: 126–38.

———. 2006. "The Buddha and Omniscience." *Indian International Journal of Buddhist Studies*, 7: 1–20.

———. 2007a. "The Arahant Ideal in Early Buddhism: The Case of Bakkula." *Indian International Journal of Buddhist Studies*, 8: 1–21 (republished in 2012e).

———. 2007b. "The Divine Messengers." In *Buddhist Studies in Honour of Venerable Kirindigalle Dhammaratana*, edited by Sumana Ratnayaka, 15–26. Colombo: Felicitation Committee for Vihārasthāna Kāryasādhaka Samitiya, Vidumina Pirivena, Maratugoda, Pujapitiya.

———. 2007c. "Who Said It? Authorship Disagreements between Pāli and Chinese Discourses." In *Indica et Tibetica 65: Festschrift für Michael Hahn zum 65. Geburtstag von Freunden und Schülern überreicht*, edited by Konrad Klaus and Jens-Uwe Hartmann, 25–38. Wien: Arbeitskreis für Tibetische und Buddhistische Studien, Universität Wien.

———. 2008a. "Reflections on Comparative Āgama Studies." *Chung-Hwa Buddhist Journal*, 21: 3–21.

———. 2008b. "Theories on the Foundation of the Nuns' Order: A Critical Evaluation." *Journal of the Centre for Buddhist Studies*, 6: 105–42 (republished in 2017h).

———. 2008c. "Upādāna." In *Encyclopaedia of Buddhism*, edited by W. G. Weeraratne, 8.2: 402–8. Sri Lanka: Department of Buddhist Affairs.

———. 2008d. "The Verses on an Auspicious Night, Explained by Mahākaccāna: A Study and Translation of the Chinese Version." *Canadian Journal of Buddhist Studies*, 4: 5–27 (republished in 2012e).

———. 2009a. "The Bahudhātuka-sutta and Its Parallels on Women's Inabilities." *Journal of Buddhist Ethics*, 16: 137–90 (republished in 2012e).

———. 2009b. "The Development of the Pāli Udāna Collection." *Buddhist Studies*, 37: 39–72 (republished in 2015g).

———. 2010a. *The Genesis of the Bodhisattva Ideal*. Hamburg: Hamburg University Press.

———. 2010b. "Paccekabuddhas in the Isigili-sutta and Its Ekottarika-āgama Parallel." *Canadian Journal of Buddhist Studies*, 6: 5–36 (republished in 2016b).

———. 2010c. "Saccaka's Challenge: A Study of the Saṃyukta-āgama

Parallel to the Cūḷasaccaka-sutta in Relation to the Notion of Merit Transfer." *Chung-Hwa Buddhist Journal*, 23: 39–70.

———. 2011a. "Brahmā's Invitation: The Ariyapariyesanā-sutta in the Light of Its Madhyama-āgama Parallel." *Journal of the Oxford Centre for Buddhist Studies*, 1: 12–38 (republished in 2012e).

———. 2011b. *A Comparative Study of the Majjhima-nikāya*. Taipei: Dharma Drum Publishing Corporation.

———. 2011c. "Right View and the Scheme of the Four Truths in Early Buddhism: The Saṃyukta-āgama Parallel to the Sammādiṭṭhi-sutta and the Simile of the Four Skills of a Physician." *Canadian Journal of Buddhist Studies*, 7: 11–44 (republished in 2015g).

———. 2011d. "Śakra and the Destruction of Craving: A Case Study in the Role of Śakra in Early Buddhism." *Indian International Journal of Buddhist Studies*, 12: 157–76 (republished in 2015g).

———. 2012a. "The Case of Sudinna: On the Function of Vinaya Narrative, Based on a Comparative Study of the Background Narration to the First Pārājika Rule." *Journal of Buddhist Ethics*, 19: 396–438 (republished in 2017h).

———. 2012b. "The Chinese Parallels to the Dhammacakkappavattana-sutta (1)." *Journal of the Oxford Centre for Buddhist Studies*, 3: 12–46 (republished in 2015g).

———. 2012c. "Dabba's Self-Cremation in the Saṃyukta-āgama." *Buddhist Studies Review*, 29.2: 153–74 (republished in 2015g).

———. 2012d. "The Historical Value of the Pāli Discourses." *Indo-Iranian Journal*, 55: 223–53 (republished in 2017b).

———. 2012e. *Madhyama-āgama Studies*. Taipei: Dharma Drum Publishing Corporation.

———. 2012f. "Teaching the Abhidharma in the Heaven of the Thirty-Three: The Buddha and His Mother." *Journal of the Oxford Centre for Buddhist Studies*, 2: 9–35 (republished in 2015g).

———. 2013a. "The Chinese Parallels to the Dhammacakkappavattana-sutta (2)." *Journal of the Oxford Centre for Buddhist Studies*, 5: 9–41 (republished in 2016b).

———. 2013b. "Dukkha." In *Encyclopedia of Sciences and Religions*, edited by Anne L. C. Runehov, Lluis Oviedo, and Nina P. Azari, 647–49. Dordrecht: Springer.

———. 2013c. "Mahāyāna in the Ekottarika-āgama." *Singaporean Journal of Buddhist Studies*, 1: 5–43 (republished in 2016b).

———. 2013d. "A Note on the Term Theravāda." *Buddhist Studies Review*, 30.2: 216–35 (republished in 2016b).

———. 2013e. *Perspectives on Satipaṭṭhāna*. Cambridge: Windhorse Publications.

———. 2014a. "Beautiful Eyes Seen with Insight as Bereft of Beauty: Subhā Therī and Her Male Counterpart in the Ekottarika-āgama." *The Journal of the Sati Center for Buddhist Studies*, 2: 39–53 (republished in 2016b).

———. 2014b. "The Brahmajāla and the Early Buddhist Oral Tradition." *Annual Report of the International Research Institute for Advanced Buddhology at Soka University*, 17: 41–59 (republished in 2017b).

———. 2014c. *The Dawn of Abhidharma*. Hamburg: Hamburg University Press.

———. 2014d. "Defying Māra: Bhikkhunīs in the Saṃyukta-āgama." In *Women in Early Indian Buddhism: Comparative Textual Studies*, edited by Alice Collett, 116–39. New York: Oxford University Press (republished in 2015g).

———. 2014e. "The Hīnayāna Fallacy." *Journal of the Oxford Centre for Buddhist Studies*, 6: 9–31 (republished in 2016b).

———. 2014f. "Maitreya and the Wheel-Turning King." *Asian Literature and Translation: A Journal of Religion and Culture*, 2.7: 1–29 (republished in 2017b).

———. 2014g. "The Mass Suicide of Monks in Discourse and Vinaya Literature." *Journal of the Oxford Centre for Buddhist Studies*, 7: 11–55 (republished in 2017h).

———. 2014h. "Three Chinese Dīrgha-āgama Discourses without Parallels." In *Research on the Dīrgha-āgama*, edited by Bhikkhunī Dhammadinnā, 1–55. Taipei: Dharma Drum Publishing Corporation (republished in 2017b).

———. 2014/2015. "Discourse Merger in the Ekottarika-āgama (2): The

Parallels to the Kakacūpama-sutta and the Alagaddūpama-sutta." *Journal of Buddhist Studies*, 12: 63–90 (republished in 2016b).
———. 2015a. "The Buddha's Fire Miracles." *Journal of the Oxford Centre for Buddhist Studies*, 10: 9–42 (republished in 2017b).
———. 2015b. "The Buddha's Past Life as a Princess in the Ekottarika-āgama." *Journal of Buddhist Ethics*, 22: 95–137 (republished in 2016b).
———. 2015c. *Compassion and Emptiness in Early Buddhist Meditation*. Cambridge: Windhorse Publications.
———. 2015d. "Discourse Merger in the Ekottarika-āgama (1): The Parallel to the Bhaddāli-sutta and the Laṭukikopama-sutta, Together with Notes on the Chinese Translation of the Collection." *Singaporean Journal of Buddhist Studies*, 2: 5–35 (republished in 2016b).
———. 2015e. "The First saṅgīti and Theravāda Monasticism." *Sri Lanka International Journal of Buddhist Studies*, 4: 2–17 (republished in 2017h).
———. 2015f. "Pratyekabuddhas in the Ekottarika-āgama." *Journal of the Oxford Centre for Buddhist Studies*, 8: 10–27 (republished in 2016b).
———. 2015g. *Saṃyukta-āgama Studies*. Taipei: Dharma Drum Publishing Corporation.
———. 2016a. "Āgama and aṅga in the Early Buddhist Oral Tradition." *Singaporean Journal of Buddhist Studies*, 3: 9–37.
———. 2016b. *Ekottarika-āgama Studies*. Taipei: Dharma Drum Publishing Corporation.
———. 2016c. *The Foundation History of the Nuns' Order*. Bochum: Projektverlag.
———. 2016d. "Levitation in Early Buddhist Discourse." *Journal of the Oxford Centre for Buddhist Studies*, 10: 11–26 (republished in 2017b).
———. 2016e. "Selected Madhyama-āgama Discourse Passages and Their Pāli Parallels." *Dharma Drum Journal of Buddhist Studies*, 19: 1–61.
———. 2016f. "The Vessantara-Jātaka and Mūlasarvāstivāda Vinaya Narrative." *Journal of the Oxford Centre for Buddhist Studies*, 11: 11–37 (republished in 2017h).
———. 2017a. *Buddhapada and the Bodhisattva Path*. Bochum: Projektverlag.

———. 2017b. *Dīrgha-āgama Studies.* Taipei: Dharma Drum Publishing Corporation.

———. 2017c. "How Compassion Became Painful." *Journal of Buddhist Studies*, 14: 85–113.

———. 2017d. *A Meditator's Life of the Buddha: Based on the Early Discourses.* Cambridge: Windhorse Publications.

———. 2017e. "The 'School Affiliation' of the Madhyama-āgama." In *Research on the Madhyama-āgama*, edited by Bhikkhunī Dhammadinnā, 55–76. Taipei: Dharma Drum Publishing Corporation.

———. 2017f. "Some Renditions of the Term tathāgata in the Chinese *Āgamas*." *Annual Report of the International Research Institute for Advanced Buddhology at Soka University*, 20: 11–21 (republished in 2017b).

———. 2017g. "Theravāda Vinaya and bhikkhunī Ordination." In *Rules of Engagement, Medieval Traditions of Buddhist Monastic Regulations*, edited by Susan Andrews, Jinhua Chen, and Cuilan Liu, 333–67. Bochum: Projekt Verlag.

———. 2017h. *Vinaya Studies.* Taipei: Dharma Drum Publishing Corporation.

———. 2018a. *Bhikkhunī Ordination from Ancient India to Contemporary Sri Lanka.* New Taipei City: Āgama Research Group.

———. 2018b. "Bhikṣuṇī Ordination." In *Oxford Handbook of Buddhist Ethics*, edited by Daniel Cozort and James Mark Shields, 116–34. Oxford: Oxford University Press.

———. 2018c. *Rebirth in Early Buddhism and Current Research.* Somerville, MA: Wisdom Publications.

———. 2019a. "An Ekottarika-āgama Discourse without Parallels: From Perception of Impermanence to the Pure Land." In *Buddhist Path Buddhist Teachings: Studies in Memory of L. S. Cousins*, edited by Naomi Appleton and Peter Harvey, 145–56. Sheffield: Equinox Publishing (republished in 2023e).

———. 2019b. *Mindfulness of Breathing: A Practice Guide and Translations.* Cambridge: Windhorse Publications.

———. 2019c. "Women in Early Buddhism." *Journal of Buddhist Studies*, 16: 33–76 (republished in 2023e).

———. 2020a. "Attention and Mindfulness." *Mindfulness*, 11.5: 1131–38.
———. 2020b. "Early Buddhist Oral Transmission and the Problem of Accurate Source Monitoring." *Mindfulness*, 11.12: 2715–24.
———. 2020c. "External Mindfulness." *Mindfulness*, 11.7: 1632–46.
———. 2020d. *Mindfulness in Early Buddhism: Characteristics and Functions*. Cambridge: Windhorse Publications.
———. 2020e. "Once Again on External Mindfulness." *Mindfulness*, 11.11: 2651–57.
———. 2020f. "The Tevijjavacchagotta-sutta and the Anupada-sutta in Relation to the Emergence of Abhidharma Thought." *Journal of Buddhist Studies*, 17: 21–33 (republished in 2023e).
———. 2020/2022. "The Qualities Pertinent to Awakening: Bringing Mindfulness Home." *Mindfulness*, 13.12: 2979–96.
———. 2021a. "The Buddha's Awakening." *Mindfulness*, 12.9: 2141–48.
———. 2021b. "Dependent Arising and Interdependence." *Mindfulness*, 12.5: 1094–102.
———. 2021c. "The Mind-made Body and Levitation: A Brief Clarification." *Annali di Ca' Foscari, Serie Orientale*, 57: 7–8.
———. 2021d. *Superiority Conceit in Buddhist Traditions: A Historical Perspective*. Somerville, MA: Wisdom Publications.
———. 2021/2023. "Skill in Means and Mindfulness." *Mindfulness*, 14.10: 2323–30 (republished in 2023e).
———. 2022a. "Beyond the Limitations of Binary Thinking: Mindfulness and the Tetralemma." *Mindfulness*, 13.6: 1410–17.
———. 2022b. *Daughters of the Buddha: Teachings by Ancient Indian Women*. Somerville, MA: Wisdom Publications.
———. 2022c. *Developments in Buddhist Meditation Traditions: The Interplay between Theory and Practice*. Barre: Barre Center for Buddhist Studies.
———. 2022d. *Early Buddhist Oral Tradition: Textual Formation and Transmission*. Somerville, MA: Wisdom Publications.
———. 2022e. "Lay Meditation in Early Buddhism." *Mindfulness*, 13.2: 318–25.
———. 2022f. "The Role of Absorption for Entering the Stream." *Journal of Buddhist Studies*, 19: 1–26.

———. 2022g. "Situating Mindfulness, Part 2: Early Buddhist Soteriology." *Mindfulness*, 13.4: 855–62.

———. 2022h. "Visualization in Early Buddhism." *Mindfulness*, 13.9: 2155–61.

———. 2023a. "The Function of Silence in Āgama Literature." *Annual Report of the International Research Institute for Advanced Buddhology at Soka University*, 26: 67–76.

———. 2023b. "Memories of Past Lives in Nikāya/Āgama and Mahāyāna Literature." *Indian International Journal of Buddhist Studies*, 23: 1–22.

———. 2023c. "The Name Theravāda in an Eighteenth-Century Inscription: Reconsidering the Problematization of the Term." In *Śāntamatiḥ: Manuscripts for Life: Essays in Memory of Seishi Karashima*, edited by Noriyuki Kudo, 1–25. Tokyo: International Research Institute for Advanced Buddhology, Soka University.

———. 2023d. *The Signless and the Deathless: On the Realization of Nirvana*. Somerville, MA: Wisdom Publications.

———. 2023e. *Studies in Āgama and Vinaya Literature*. New Delhi: Aditya Prakashan.

———. 2024a. *Abiding in Emptiness: A Guide for Meditative Practice*. New York: Wisdom Publications.

———. 2024b. "Acitta in Early Prajñāpāramitā: Unconsciousness, Cessation Attainment, or Signlessness?" *Indian International Journal of Buddhist Studies*, 24: 1–41.

———. 2024c. "Crescendo Repetitions: From the Madhyama-āgama to the Aṣṭasāhasrikā Prajñāpāramitā." *Annual Report of the International Research Institute for Advanced Buddhology at Soka University*, 27: 49–76.

———. 2024d. *Mindfulness between Early Buddhism and Climate Change*. Barre: Barre Center for Buddhist Studies.

———. 2024e. "Orality and Writing in Early Prajñāpāramitā." *Annual Report of the International Research Institute for Advanced Buddhology at Soka University*, 27: 77–93.

———. 2025a. "Meeting Buddhas Now, Part 1: Meditative Visions of the Buddha and Buddhafields." *Annual Report of the International*

*Research Institute for Advanced Buddhology at Soka University*, 28: 83–108.

———. 2025b. "Meeting Buddhas Now, Part 2: Samādhi, the *Pratyutpannasamādhi-sūtra, and Prajñāpāramitā." *Annual Report of the International Research Institute for Advanced Buddhology at Soka University*, 28: 109–34.

———. In preparation. "The Erosion of Ethics in Emptiness: Infallible Teachers and Inconsequential Matricide."

Appleton, Naomi. 2010. *Jātaka Stories in Theravāda Buddhism: Narrating the Bodhisatta Path*. Surrey: Ashgate.

Assavavirulhakarn, Prapod. 2010. *The Ascendancy of Theravāda Buddhism in Southeast Asia*. Chiang Mai: Silkworm Books.

Attwood, Jayarava. 2021. "Preliminary Notes on the Extended Heart Sutra in Chinese." *Asian Literature and Translation*, 8.1: 63–85.

———. 2022. "The Cessation of Sensory Experience and Prajñāpāramitā Philosophy." *International Journal of Buddhist Thought & Culture*, 32.1: 111–48.

Baba Norihisa. 2005. "On the Order of the Compilation of the Abhidhammapiṭaka and the Khuddakanikāya." *Journal of Indian and Buddhist Studies*, 53.2: 991–94.

Bareau, André. 1955. *Les sectes bouddhiques du Petit Véhicule*. Paris: Publications de l'École Française d'Extrême-Orient.

———. 1971. *Recherches sur la biographie du Buddha dans les Sūtrapiṭaka et le Vinayapiṭaka anciens: II, Les derniers mois, le Parinirvāṇa et les funérailles*. Paris: École Française d'Extrême-Orient.

———. 1985. "Étude du bouddhisme, 1: Aspects du bouddhisme indien décrits par les pèlerins chinois." *Annuaire de Collège de France*, 649–53.

———. 1997. "Le prodige accompli par le Buddha à Saṃkaśya selon l'Ekottara-āgama." In *Lex et Litterae: Studies in Honour of Professor Oscar Botto*, edited by Siegfried Lienhard and Irma Piovano, 17–30. Torino: Edizione dell'Orso.

Barth, A. 1899. [Review of] "Le Mahāvastu, texte sanscrit publié pour la première fois et accompagné d'introductions et d'un commentaire, par É. Senart. 3 vol, in-8°, 1882–1897." *Journal des Savants*, 517–31.

Barua, Dwijendralal. 1946. "'Buddhakhetta' in the Apadāna." In *B. C. Law Volume, Part II*, edited by R. Bhandarkar, K. A. Nilakanta Sastri,

B. M. Barua, B. K. Gosh, and K. Gode, 183–90. Poona: Bhandarkar Oriental Research Institute.

Basak, Radhagovinda. 1963. *A Study of the Mahāvastu-avadāna*. University of Calcutta: Alumni Association.

Basham, A. L. 1981. "The Evolution of the Concept of the Bodhisattva." In *The Bodhisattva Doctrine in Buddhism*, edited by Leslie S. Kawamura, 19–59. Calgary: Canadian Corporation for Studies in Religion.

Bastian, Edward B. 1979. [Review of] "The Prajñāpāramitā Literature, by Edward Conze. Tokyo: The Reiyukai, 1978. 138 pp." *Journal of the International Association of Buddhist Studies*, 2.2: 99–102.

Baums, Stefan. 2022. "The Earliest Colophons in the Buddhist Northwest." In *The Syntax of Colophons: A Comparative Study across Pothi Manuscripts*, edited by Nalini Balbir and Giovanni Ciotti, 15–41. Berlin: De Gruyter.

Bechert, Heinz. 1961. *Bruchstücke buddhistischer Verssammlungen aus zentralasiatischen Sanskrithandschriften: Die Anavataptagāthā und die Sthaviragāthā*. Berlin: Akademie Verlag.

———. 1964. "Zur Frühgeschichte des Mahāyāna-Buddhismus." *Zeitschrift der Deutschen Morgenländischen Gesellschaft*, 113: 530–35.

———. 1973. "Notes on the Formation of Buddhist Sects and the Origins of Mahāyāna." In *German Scholars on India: Contributions to Indian Studies, Volume 1*, edited by Friedrich Max Müller, 6–18. New Delhi: Chowkhamba Sanskrit Office.

———. 1976. "Buddha-Feld und Verdienstübertragung: Mahāyāna-Ideen im Theravāda-Buddhismus Ceylons." *Bulletins de la Classe des Lettres et des Sciences Morales et Politiques*, 62: 27–51.

Bechert, Heinz and Klaus Wille. 1989. *Sanskrithandschriften aus den Turfanfunden, Teil 6*. Stuttgart: Franz Steiner.

Beckh, Hermann. 1919. *Buddhismus (Der Buddha und seine Lehre): I Einleitung, Der Buddha*. Berlin: Göschen.

Bendall, Cecil. 1902. *Çikshāsamuccaya: A Compendium of Buddhistic Teaching Compiled by Çāntideva, Chiefly from Earlier Mahāyāna-sūtras*. St.-Pétersbourg: Commissionnaires de l'Académie Impériale des Sciences.

Benn, James A. 2007. *Burning for the Buddha: Self-Immolation in Chinese Buddhism*. Honolulu: University of Hawai'i Press.

———. 2009. "The Lotus sūtra and Self-Immolation." In *Readings of the Lotus sūtra*, edited by Stephen F. Teiser and Jacqueline I. Stone, 107–31. New York: Columbia University Press.

Bernhard, Franz. 1965. *Udānavarga, Band 1*. Göttingen: Vandenhoeck & Ruprecht.

Beyer, Stephan. 1977. "Notes on the Vision Quest in Early Mahāyāna." In *Prajñāpāramitā and Related Systems: Studies in Honor of Edward Conze*, edited by Lewis Lancaster and Luis O. Gómez, 329–40. Berkeley: University of California Press.

Bidyabinod, B. B. 1927. "Fragment of a Prajnaparamita Manuscript from Central Asia." *Memoirs of the Archaeological Survey of India*, 32: 1–11.

Bingenheimer, Marcus. 2011. *Studies in Āgama Literature: With Special Reference to the Shorter Chinese Saṃyuktāgama*. Taiwan: Shin Weng Feng Print Co.

Bizot, François. 1988. *Les traditions de la pabbajjā en Asie du Sud-Est: Recherches sur le bouddhisme khmer, IV*. Göttingen: Vandenhoeck & Ruprecht.

Bloch, Jules. 1950. *Les inscriptions d'Asoka: Traduites et commentées*. Paris: Société d'Édition Les Belles Lettres.

Blomfield, Vishvapani. 2011. *Gautama Buddha: The Life and Teachings of the Awakened One*. London: Quercus.

Bodhi, Bhikkhu. 1978/1992. *The All-Embracing Net of Views: The Brahmajāla sutta and Its Commentaries, Translated from the Pali*. Kandy: Buddhist Publication Society.

———. 1980/1992. *The Discourse on the Root of Existence: The Mūlapariyāya sutta and Its Commentaries, Translated from the Pali*. Kandy: Buddhist Publication Society.

———. 2012. *The Numerical Discourses of the Buddha: A Translation of the Aṅguttara Nikāya*. Somerville, MA: Wisdom Publications.

Bond, George D. 1988. *The Buddhist Revival in Sri Lanka: Religious Tradition, Reinterpretation and Response*. Columbia: University of South Carolina Press.

Bongard-Levin, Grigorij Maksimovic, Daniel Boucher, Takamichi Fukita, and Klaus Wille. 1996. *The Nagaropamasūtra: An Apotropaic Text from the Saṃyuktāgama; A Transliteration, Reconstruction, and Translation of the Central Asian Sanskrit Manuscripts.* Göttingen: Vandenhoeck & Ruprecht.

Bongard-Levin, Grigorij Maksimovic, and Shin'ichirō Hori. 1996. "A Fragment of the Larger Prajñāpāramitā from Central Asia." *Journal of the International Association of Buddhist Studies*, 19.1: 19–60.

Boucher, Daniel. 1996. *Buddhist Translation Procedures in Third-Century China: A Study of Dharmarakṣa and His Translation Idiom.* PhD thesis, University of Pennsylvania.

———. 2008. *Bodhisattvas of the Forest and the Formation of the Mahāyāna: A Study and Translation of the Rāṣṭrapālaparipṛcchā-sūtra.* Honolulu: University of Hawai'i Press.

———. 2018. "Recruitment and Retention in Early Bodhisattva Sodalities." In *Setting Out on the Great Way: Essays on Early Mahāyāna Buddhism*, edited by Paul Harrison, 95–118. Sheffield: Equinox.

Braarvig, Jens. 2009. "The Buddhist Hell: An Early Instance of the Idea?" *Numen*, 56: 254–81.

Brahmāli, Bhikkhu. 2009. "What the Nikāyas Say and Do Not Say about Nibbāna." *Buddhist Studies Review*, 26.1: 33–66.

Bronkhorst, Johannes. 1985. "Dharma and Abhidharma." *Bulletin of the School of Oriental and African Studies*, 48: 305–20.

———. 2018. "Abhidharma in Early Mahāyāna." In *Setting Out on the Great Way: Essays on Early Mahāyāna Buddhism*, edited by Paul Harrison, 119–40. Sheffield: Equinox.

Brough, John. 1962/2001. *The Gāndhārī Dharmapada: Edited with an Introduction and Commentary.* Delhi: Motilal Banarsidass.

Brown, Norman W. 1940. "The Basis for the Hindu Act of Truth." *Review of Religion*, 5: 36–45.

———. 1968. "The Metaphysics of the Truth Act (*satyakriyā)." In *Mélanges d'Indianisme à la mémoire de Louis Renou*, edited by Louis Renou, 171–77. Paris: Éditions de Boccard.

———. 1972a. "Duty as Truth in Ancient India." *Proceedings of the American Philosophical Society*, 116.3: 252–68.

———. 1972b. "Duty as Truth in the Rig Veda." In *India Major: Congrat-*

*ulatory Volume Presented to J. Gonda*, edited by Jacob Ensink and Peter Gaefkke, 57–67. Leiden: Brill.

Burlingame, Eugene Watson. 1917. "The Act of Truth (saccakiriya): A Hindu Spell and Its Employment as a Psychic Motif in Hindu Fiction." *Journal of the Royal Asiatic Society*, 429–67.

Burnouf, Eugène. 1852/2022. *Aṣṭasāhasrikā Prajñāpāramitā: La Perfection de Sagesse en Huit Mille Stances, traduite du Sanskrit par Eugène Burnouf (1801–1852) éditée par Guillaume Ducœur*. Strasbourg: Université de Strasbourg.

Carter, Martha L. 1990. *The Mystery of the Udayana Buddha*. Napoli: Istituto Universitario Orientale.

Changtzu. 2012. "The Employment and Significance of the Sadāprarudita Jātaka/Avadāna Story in Different Buddhist Traditions." *Buddhist Studies Review* 29.1: 85–104.

Choong Mun-keat. 2021. "A Comparison of the Pāli and Chinese Versions of Jhāna Saṃyutta, Asaṅkhata Saṃyutta, and Abhisamaya Saṃyutta: Early Buddhist Discourses on Concentrative Meditation, the Uncompounded, and Realization." *Journal of the Oxford Centre for Buddhist Studies*, 21: 10–43.

Choong Yoke Meei. 2006. *Zum Problem der Leerheit (śūnyatā) in der Prajñāpāramitā*. Frankfurt: Peter Lang.

———. 2014a. "Divided Opinions among Chinese Commentators on Indian Interpretations of the Parable of the Raft in the Vajracchedikā." In *A Distant Mirror: Articulating Indic Ideas in Sixth and Seventh Century Chinese Buddhism*, edited by Chen-kuo Lin and Michael Radich, 419–69. Hamburg: Hamburg University Press.

———. 2014b. "How Free Is the Bodhisattva in Deliberate Rebirth?" *Dharma Drum Journal of Buddhist Studies*, 14: 129–62.

———. 2016. "The Prajñāpāramitā in Relation to the Three samādhis." *Journal of Indian Philosophy*, 44.4: 727–56.

Chung Jin-il. 2006. "Dharmacakrapravartana-dharmaparyāya of the Sarvāstivāda and Mūlasarvāstivāda Tradition." In *Jaina-Itihāsa-Ratna: Festschrift für Gustav Roth zum 90. Geburtstag*, edited by Ute Hüsken, Petra Kieffer-Pülz, and Anne Peters, 75–101. Marburg: Indica et Tibetica.

———. 2008. *A Survey of the Sanskrit Fragments Corresponding to the Chinese Saṃyuktāgama*. Tokyo: Sankibo.

Chung Jin-il and Fukita Takamichi. 2020. *A New Edition of the First 25 sūtras of the Nidānasaṃyukta*. Tokyo: Sankibo Press.

Ciurtin, Eugen. 2009. "The Buddha's Earthquakes [I]. On Water: Earthquakes and Seaquakes in Buddhist Cosmology and Meditation, with an Appendix on Buddhist Art." *Stvdia Asiatica*, 10.1/2: 59–123.

———. 2012. "'Thus Have I Quaked': The Tempo of the Buddha's Vita and the Earliest Buddhist Fabric of Timelessness [The Buddha's Earthquakes II]." In *Figurations of Time in Asia*, edited by Dietrich Boschung and Corinna Wessels-Mevissen, 21–54. München: Wilhelm Fink Verlag.

Clarke, Shayne. 2008. "The Case of the Nun Mettiyā Reexamined: On the Expulsion of a Pregnant Bhikṣuṇī in the Vinaya of the Mahāsāṅghikas and Other Indian Buddhist Monastic Law Codes." *Indo-Iranian Journal*, 51: 115–35.

Cœdès, G. C. 1929. *Recueil des inscriptions du Siam: Deuxième partie, Inscriptions de Dvāravatī, de Çrīvijaya et de Lăvo*. Bangkok: Bangkok Times Press.

Collett, Alice and Bhikkhu Anālayo. 2014. "Bhikkhave and Bhikkhu as Gender-Inclusive Terminology in Early Buddhist Texts." *Journal of Buddhist Ethics*, 21: 760–97.

Collins, Steven. 1982. *Selfless Persons: Imagery and Thought in Theravāda Buddhism*. Cambridge: Cambridge University Press.

Cone, Margaret. 1989. "Patna Dharmapada." *Journal of the Pali Text Society*, 13: 101–217.

Conze, Edward. 1948/2008. "The Prajñāpāramitā-hṛdaya sūtra." In *Thirty Years of Buddhist Studies: Selected Essays by Edward Conze*, 148–67. New Delhi: Munshiram Manoharlal Publishers.

———. 1952/2008. "The Composition of the Aṣṭasāhasrikā Prajñāpāramitā." In *Thirty Years of Buddhist Studies: Selected Essays by Edward Conze*, 168–84. New Delhi: Munshiram Manoharlal Publishers.

———. 1953. "The Ontology of the Prajnāpāramitā." *Philosophy East and West*, 3.2: 117–29.

———. 1959/2008. "Mahayana Buddhism." In *Thirty Years of Buddhist*

*Studies: Selected Essays by Edward Conze*, 48–86. New Delhi: Munshiram Manoharlal Publishers.

———. 1960/2008. "The Development of Prajñāpāramitā Thought." In *Thirty Years of Buddhist Studies: Selected Essays by Edward Conze*, 121–47. New Delhi: Munshiram Manoharlal Publishers.

———. 1962. *Buddhist Thought in India: Three Phases of Buddhist Philosophy*. London: George Allen & Unwin.

———. 1964. "The Buddha's lakṣaṇas in Prajñāpāramitā." *Journal of the Oriental Institute, Baroda*, 14: 225–29.

———. 1973/1975. *The Perfection of Wisdom in Eight Thousand Lines & Its Verse Summary*. Bolinas, CA: Four Seasons Foundation.

———. 1974. *The Gilgit Manuscript of the Aṣṭādaśasāhasrikāprajñāpāramitā: Chapters 70 to 82, Corresponding to the 6th, 7th and 8th Abhisamayas*. Rome: Istituto Italiano per il Medio ed Estremo Oriente.

———. 1975/1984. *The Large Sutra on Perfect Wisdom with the Divisions of the Abhisamayālaṅkāra*. Berkeley: University of California Press.

———. 1978. *The Prajñāpāramitā Literature: Second Edition Revised and Enlarged*. Tokyo: Reiyukai.

Conze, Edward and Iida Shotaro. 1968. "Maitreya's Question in the Prajñāpāramitā." In *Mélanges d'Indianisme à la Mémoire de Louis Renou*, edited by Louis Renou, 229–42. Paris: Éditions de Boccard.

Coomaraswamy, Ananda K. 1944. "Headless Magicians; And an Act of Truth." *Journal of the American Oriental Society*, 64.4: 215–17.

Cooray, H. S. 1961. "Abhinīhāra." In *Encyclopaedia of Buddhism*, edited by G. P. Malalasekera, 1.1: 94–95. Sri Lanka: Department of Buddhist Affairs.

Cousins, L. S. 2003. "Sākiyabhikkhu/Sakyabhikkhu/Śākyabhikṣu: A Mistaken Link to the Mahāyāna?" *Nagoya Studies in Indian Culture and Buddhism*, 23: 1–27.

Cowell, E. B. and R. A. Neil. 1886. *The Divyāvadāna: A Collection of Early Buddhist Legends, Now First Edited from the Nepalese Sanskrit Mss. in Cambridge and Paris*. Cambridge: University Press.

Cox, Collett. 1995. *Disputed Dharmas: Early Buddhist Theories on Existence; An Annotated Translation of the Section on Factors Dissociated from Thought from Saṅghabhadra's Nyāyānusāra*. Tokyo: International Institute for Buddhist Studies.

———. 2004. "From Category to Ontology: The Changing Role of 'Dharma' in Sarvāstivāda Abhidharma." *Journal of Indian Philosophy*, 32.5/6: 543–97.

Cummings, Mary. 1982. *The Lives of the Buddha in the Art and Literature of Asia*. Ann Arbor: University of Michigan, Center for South and Southeast Asian Studies.

Cutler, Sally Mellick. 1994. "The Pāli Apadāna Collection." *Journal of the Pali Text Society*, 20: 1–42.

Dantinne, Jean. 1983. *La Splendeur de l'Inébranlable (Akṣobhyavyūha)*. Louvain-La-Neuve: Université Catholique de Louvain, Institut Orientaliste.

Darwin, Charles. 1872. *The Expression of the Emotions in Man and Animals*. London: John Murray.

de Breet, Jan A. 1992. "The Concept Upāyakauśalya in the Aṣṭasāhasrikā Prajñāpāramitā." *Wiener Zeitschrift für die Kunde Südasiens*, 36: 203–16.

Deeg, Max. 2006. "Unwirkliche Gegner, Chinesische Polemik gegen den Hīnayāna-Buddhismus." In *Jaina-Itihāsa-Ratna: Festschrift für Gustav Roth zum 90. Geburtstag*, edited by Ute Hüsken, Petra Kieffer-Pülz, and Anne Peters, 103–25. Marburg: Indica et Tibetica.

de Jong, Jan Willem. 1968. *Buddha's Word in China*. Canberra: Australian National University.

de La Vallée Poussin, Louis. 1903/1913. *Mūlamadhyamakakārikās (Mādhyamikasūtras) de Nāgārjuna avec le Prasannapadā Commentaire de Candrakīrti*. Delhi: Motilal Banarsidass.

———. 1915. "Mahāvastu." In *Encyclopædia of Religion and Ethics: Volume VIII, Life and Death–Mulla*, edited by James Hastings, 328–30. Edinburgh: T. & T. Clark.

———. 1925/1991. "La Controverse du Temps e du Pudgala dans le Vijñānakāya." In *Essays on Time in Buddhism*, edited by H. S. Prasad, 79–112. Delhi: Sri Satguru Publications.

———. 1928. "Agnosticism (Buddhist)." In *Encyclopædia of Religion and Ethics: Volume 1, A–Art*, edited by James Hastings, 220–25. New York: Charles Scribner's Sons.

Deleanu, Florin. 1993. "Śrāvakayāna Yoga Practices and Mahāyāna Buddhism." *Waseda Daigaku Daigakuin Bungaku Kenkyūka kiyō bessatsu shigakuhen*, 20: 3–12.

———. 2000. "A Preliminary Study on Meditation and the Beginnings of Mahāyāna Buddhism." *Annual Report of the International Research Institute for Advanced Buddhology at Soka University*, 3: 65–113.

———. 2003. "The Newly Found Text of the An ban shou yi jing Translated by An Shigao." *Journal of the International College for Advanced Buddhist Studies*, 6: 63–100.

Delhey, Martin. 2009. *Samāhitā Bhūmiḥ: Das Kapitel über die meditative Versenkung im Grundteil der Yogācārabhūmi*. Wien: Arbeitskreis für Tibetische und Buddhistische Studien, Universität Wien.

Dessein, Bart. 2007a. "The Existence of Factors in the Three Time Periods: Sarvāstivāda and Madhyamaka Buddhist Interpretations of Difference in Mode, Difference in Characteristic Marks, Difference in State, and Mutual Difference." *Acta Orientalia*, 60.3: 331–50.

———. 2007b. "The First Turning of the Wheel of the Doctrine: Sarvāstivāda and Mahāsāṃghika Controversy." In *The Spread of Buddhism*, edited by Ann Heirman and Stephan Peter Bumbacher, 15–48. Leiden: Brill.

———. 2009. "The Mahāsāṃghikas and the Origin of Mahayana Buddhism: Evidence Provided in the *Abhidharmamahāvibhāṣāśāstra." *The Eastern Buddhist*, 40.1/2: 25–61.

Dhammadinnā, Bhikkhunī. 2015. "Predictions of Women to Buddhahood in Middle-Period Literature." *Journal of Buddhist Ethics*, 22: 481–531.

———. 2015/2016. "Women's Aspirations and Soteriological Agency in Sarvāstivāda and Mūlasarvāstivāda Vinaya Narratives." *Buddhism Law & Society*, 1: 33–67.

———. 2018. "Karma Here and Now in a Mūlasarvāstivāda avadāna: How the Bodhisattva Changed Sex and Was Born as a Female 500 Times." *Annual Report of the International Research Institute for Advanced Buddhology at Soka University*, 21: 63–94.

———. 2019. "Co-textuality of sūtra and Early Abhidharma in the Abhidharmakośopāyikā-ṭīkā's Discourse Quotations." *Journal of Buddhist Studies*, 16: 1–32.

———. 2020. "Bhikṣuṇī Śailā's Rebuttal of Māra's Substantialist View: The Chariot Simile in a sūtra Quotation in the Abhidharmakośopāyikā-ṭīkā." *Indian International Journal of Buddhist Studies*, 21: 1–33.

———. 2021. "Reflections on Truth and Experience in Early Buddhist Epistemology." In *Buddhism in Dialogue with Contemporary Societies*, edited by Carola Roloff, Wolfram Weiße, and Michael Zimmermann, 101–33. Münster: Waxmann.

Dhammajoti, Bhikkhu K. L. 2002/2007. *Sarvāstivāda Abhidharma*. Hong Kong: Centre of Buddhist Studies, University of Hong Kong.

———. 2010. "The apramāṇa Meditation in the Sarvāstivāda with Special Reference to Maitrī-bhāvanā." *Journal of Buddhist Studies*, 8: 165–86.

———. 2011. "From Abhidharma to Mahāyāna: Remarks of the Early Abhidharma Doctrine of the Three yāna-s." *Journal of the Centre for Buddhist Studies*, 9: 153–69.

———. 2023. "Akliṣṭājñāna, vāsanā, jñeyāvaraṇa, and Origins of Mahāyāna." In *To the Heart of Truth, Felicitation Volume for Eli Franco on the Occasion of His Seventieth Birthday*, edited by Hiroko Matsuoka, Shinya Moriyama, and Tyler Neill, 3–58. Wien: Arbeitskreis für Tibetische und Buddhistische Studien.

Dietz, Siglinde. 2018. "Fragments of the Āśvalāyanasūtra." In *Reading Slowly: A Festschrift for Jens E. Braarvig*, edited by Lutz Edzard, Jens W. Borgland, and Ute Hüsken, 125–35. Wiesbaden: Harrassowitz.

Dimitrov, Dragomir. 2004. "Two Female Bodhisattvas in Flesh and Blood." In *Aspects of the Female in Indian Culture*, edited by Ulrieke Roesler and Jayandra Soni, 3–30. Marburg: Indica et Tibetica.

Dohanian, Diran Kavork. 1977. *The Mahāyāna Buddhist Sculpture of Ceylon*. New York: Garland Publishing.

Doherty, Gerald. 1983. "Form Is Emptiness: Reading the Diamond Sutra." *The Eastern Buddhist*, 16.2: 114–23.

Drewes, David. 2007. "Revisiting the Phrase 'sa pṛthivīpradeśaś caityabhūto bhavet' and the Mahāyāna Cult of the Book." *Indo-Iranian Journal*, 50: 101–43.

———. 2010a. "Early Indian Mahāyāna Buddhism I: Recent Scholarship." *Religion Compass*, 4.2: 55–65.

———. 2010b. "Early Indian Mahāyāna Buddhism II: New Perspectives." *Religion Compass*, 4.2: 66–74.

———. 2011. "Dharmabhāṇakas in Early Mahāyāna." *Indo-Iranian Journal*, 54.4: 331–72.

———. 2015. "Oral Texts in Indian Mahāyāna." *Indo-Iranian Journal*, 58.2: 117–41.

———. 2018. "The Forest Hypothesis." In *Setting Out on the Great Way: Essays on Early Mahāyāna Buddhism*, edited by Paul Harrison, 73–93. Sheffield: Equinox.

———. 2021. "The Problem of Becoming a Bodhisattva and the Emergence of Mahāyāna." *History of Religions*, 61.2: 145–72.

Durt, Hubert. 1991. "Bodhisattva and Layman in the Early Mahāyāna." *Japanese Religions*, 16.3: 1–16.

Dutt, Nalinaksha. 1934. *Pañcaviṃśatisāhasrikā Prajñāpāramitā: Edited with Critical Notes and Introduction*. London: Luzac & Co.

———. 1958. "Emergence of Mahāyāna Buddhism." In *The Cultural Heritage of India: Volume I, The Early Phases (Prehistoric, Vedic and Upaniṣadic, Jaina and Buddhist)*, edited by Sarvepalli Radhakrishnan, 503–17. Calcutta: Ramakrishna Mission.

Eckel, Malcolm David. 2008. *Bhāviveka and His Buddhist Opponents*. Cambridge, MA: Harvard University Press.

Edgerton, Franklin. 1959. "Did the Buddha Have a System of Metaphysics?" *Journal of the American Oriental Society*, 79: 81–85.

Endo Toshiichi. 1996. "Bodhisattas in the Pāli Commentaries." *Buddhist Studies*, 25: 65–92.

———. 1997/2002. *Buddha in Theravada Buddhism: A Study of the Concept of Buddha in the Pali Commentaries*. Dehiwela: Buddhist Cultural Centre.

———. 2003. "Views Attributed to Different bhāṇakā (Reciters) in the Pāli Commentaries." *Buddhist Studies*, 31: 1–42.

———. 2005. "The 'Aṭṭhakathā' as Source-Material of the Pāli Commentaries: An Inquiry into the Date of Their Compilation." In *Dhamma-Vinaya: Essays in Honour of Venerable Professor Dhammavihari (Jotiya Dhirasekera)*, edited by Asaṅga Tilakaratne, Endo Toshiichi, G. A. Somaratne, and Sanath Nanayakkara, 33–53. Colombo: Sri Lanka Association for Buddhist Studies.

———. 2013. "'Potthaka' (Book or Manuscript) in the Pāli Commentaries." In *Studies in Pāli Commentarial Literature: Sources, Controversies and Insights*, edited by Endo Toshiichi, 107–19. Hong Kong: Centre of Buddhist Studies, University of Hong Kong.

Enomoto Fumio. 1994. *A Comprehensive Study of the Chinese Saṃyuktāgama: Indic Texts Corresponding to the Chinese Saṃyuktāgama as Found in the Sarvāstivāda-Mūlasarvāstivāda Literature, Part 1: *Saṃgītanipāta*. Kyoto: Kacho Junior College.

Falk, Harry. 2006: *Aśokan Sites and Artefacts: A Source-Book with Bibliography*. Mainz: Philipp von Zabern.

———. 2011. "The 'Split' Collection of Kharoṣṭhī Texts." *Annual Report of the International Research Institute for Advanced Buddhology at Soka University*, 14: 13–23.

Falk, Harry and Karashima Seishi. 2012. "A First-Century Prajñāpāramitā Manuscript from Gandhāra: Parivarta 1 (Texts from the Split Collection 1)." *Annual Report of the International Research Institute for Advanced Buddhology at Soka University*, 15: 19–61.

———. 2013. "A First-Century Prajñāpāramitā Manuscript from Gandhāra: Parivarta 5 (Texts from the Split Collection 2)." *Annual Report of the International Research Institute for Advanced Buddhology at Soka University*, 16: 97–169.

Feer, Léon. 1892. "L'enfer indien." *Journal Asiatique*, 8.20: 185–232.

Felbur, Rafal. 2015. "Vimalakīrtinirdeśa." In *Brill's Encyclopedia of Buddhism: Volume I, Literature and Languages*, edited by Jonathan A. Silk, Oskar von Hinüber, and Vincent Eltschinger, 274–82. Leiden: Brill.

Frauwallner, Erich. 1956. *The Earliest Vinaya and the Beginnings of Buddhist Literature*. Rome: Istituto Italiano per il Medio ed Estremo Oriente.

———. 1956/2003. *Geschichte der indischen Philosophie: I. Band, Die Philosophie des Veda and des Epos, Der Buddha und der Jina, Das Sāṃkhya und das klassische Yoga-System*. Aachen: Shaker Verlag.

———. 1971. "Abhidharma Studien: III. Der Abhisamayavādaḥ; IV. Der Abhidharma der anderen Schulen." *Wiener Zeitschrift für die Kunde Süd- und Ostasiens*, 15: 69–121.

Fronsdal, Gil. 1998/2014. *Dawn of the Bodhisattva Path: The Early Perfection of Wisdom*. Berkeley: Institute for Buddhist Studies.

Fujita Yoshimichi. 2009. "The Bodhisattva Thought of the Sarvāstivādins and Mahāyāna Buddhism." *Acta Asiatica: Bulletin of the Institute of Eastern Culture*, 96.1: 99–121.

Fukita Takamichi. 2003. *The Mahāvadānasūtra: A New Edition Based on Manuscripts Discovered in Northern Turkestan*. Göttingen: Vandenhoeck & Ruprecht.

Fussman, Gérard. 1999. "La place des Sukhāvatī-vyūha dans le Bouddhisme Indien." *Journal Asiatique*, 287.2: 523–86.

Gaál, Balázs. 2017. "King Śibi in the East and the West: Following the Flight of a Suppliant Dove." *International Journal of the Classical Tradition*, 24.1: 1–34.

Gaffney, Sean D. 2003. *The Jatakanidāna: A Critical Study, Tibetan Edition and Annotated Translation*. PhD thesis, School of Oriental and African Studies, University of London.

Garfield, Jay. 1995. *The Fundamental Wisdom of the Middle Way: Nāgārjuna's Mūlamadhyamakakārikā*. New York: Oxford University Press.

Geiger, Magdalene and Wilhelm Geiger. 1920. *Pāli Dhamma, Vornehmlich in der kanonischen Literatur*. München: Verlag der Bayerischen Akademie der Wissenschaften.

Gethin, Rupert. 1998. *The Foundations of Buddhism*. Oxford: Oxford University Press.

———. 2006. "Mythology as Meditation: From the Mahāsudassana sutta to the Sukhāvatīvyūha sūtra." *Journal of the Pali Text Society*, 28: 63–112.

———. 2020. "Schemes of the Buddhist Path in the Nikāyas and Āgamas." In *Mārga, Paths to Liberation in South Asian Buddhist Traditions*, edited by Cristina Pecchia and Vincent Eltschinger, 5–77. Wien: Österreichische Akademie der Wissenschaften.

Ghoṣa, Pratāpacandra. 1902. *Çatasāhasrikā-Prajñā-Pāramitā: A Theological and Philosophical Discourse of Buddha with His Disciples (in a Hundred Thousand Stanzas), Part I Fas. 1*. Calcutta: Asiatic Society.

———. 1905. *Çatasāhasrikā-Prajñā-Pāramitā: A Theological and Philosophical Discourse of Buddha with His Disciples (in a Hundred Thousand Stanzas), Part I Fas. 10*. Calcutta: Asiatic Society.

Giddings, William James. 2014. *A Structuralist Examination of the Origins of the Māra Mytheme and Its Function in the Narrative of the Dàoxíng*

*Bōrě Jīng, the Earliest Complete Recension of the Aṣṭasāhasrikā-prajnā-pāramitā-sūtra*. PhD thesis, King's College, Department of Theology and Religious Studies.

Gifford, Julie. 2003. "The Insight Guide to Hell: Mahāmoggallāna and Theravāda Buddhist Cosmology." In *Constituting Communities: Theravāda Buddhism and the Religious Cultures of South and Southeast Asia*, edited by John Clifford Holt, Jacob N. Kinnard, and Jonathan S. Walters, 71–84. New York: State University of New York Press.

Glass, Andrew. 2008/2010. "Guṇabhadra, Bǎoyún, and the Saṃyuktāgama." *Journal of the International Association of Buddhist Studies*, 31.1/2: 185–203.

Gnoli, Raniero. 1977. *The Gilgit Manuscript of the Saṅghabhedavastu, Being the 17th and Last Section of the Vinaya of the Mūlasarvāstivādin: Part I*. Rome: Istituto Italiano per il Medio ed Estremo Oriente.

———. 1978. *The Gilgit Manuscript of the Saṅghabhedavastu, Being the 17th and Last Section of the Vinaya of the Mūlasarvāstivādin: Part II*. Rome: Istituto Italiano per il Medio ed Estremo Oriente.

Gokuldas De, M. A. 1951. *Significance and Importance of Jātakas: With Special Reference to Bhārhut*. Calcutta: Calcutta University Press.

Gombrich, Richard F. 1988/1990. "How the Mahāyāna Began." *The Buddhist Forum*, 1: 21–30.

———. 1992. "A Momentous Effect of Translation: The 'Vehicles' of Buddhism." In *Apodosis: Essays Presented to Dr. W. W. Cuickshank to Mark His Eightieth Birthday*, 34–46. London: St. Paul's School.

———. 1996. *How Buddhism Began: The Conditioned Genesis of the Early Teachings*. London: Athlone.

———. 1998. "Organized Bodhisattvas." In *Sūryacandrāya: Essays in Honour of Akira Yujama on the Occasion of His 65th Birthday*, edited by Paul Harrison and Gregory Schopen, 43–56. Swisttal-Odendorf: Indica et Tibetica Verlag.

———. 2007. "Popperian Vinaya: Conjecture and Refutation in Practice." In *Pramāṇakīrtiḥ: Papers Dedicated to Ernst Steinkellner on the Occasion of His 70th Birthday*, edited by Birgit Kellner, Helmut Krasser, Horst Lasic, Michael Torsten Much, and Helmut Tauscher,

203–11. Wien: Arbeitskreis für Tibetische und Buddhistische Studien, Universität Wien.

Gómez, Luis O. 1976. "Proto-Mādhyamika in the Pāli Canon[?]" *Philosophy East and West*, 26.2: 137–65.

Granoff, Phyllis. 1998. "Maitreya's Jewelled World: Some Remarks on Gems and Visions in Buddhist Texts." *Journal of Indian Philosophy*, 26.4: 347–71.

Greene, Eric M. 2016. "Pratītyasamutpāda in the Translations of An Shigao and the Writings of His Chinese Followers." In *Text, History and Philosophy: Abhidharma across Buddhist Scholastic Traditions*, edited by Bart Dessein and Weijen Teng, 248–78. Leiden: Brill.

———. 2017. "Doctrinal Dispute in the Earliest Phase of Chinese Buddhism: Anti-Mahāyāna Polemics in the Scripture on the Fifty Contemplations." *Journal of the International Association of Buddhist Studies*, 40: 63–109.

Guang Xing. 2005. *The Concept of the Buddha: Its Evolution from Early Buddhism to the trikāya Theory*. London: Routledge Curzon.

———. 2013. "Maritime Transmission of the Monastic Order of Nuns to China." In *The Emergence and Heritage of Asian Women Intellectuals*, edited by Supakwadee Amatayakul, 111–20. Bangkok: Chulalongkorn University.

———. 2018. "Tathatā: The Creation of the Doctrinal Foundation for Mahāyāna Buddhism." *Journal of Buddhist Philosophy*, 4: 121–38.

Halkias, Georgios T. 2013. *Luminous Bliss: A Religious History of Pure Land Literature in Tibet*. Honolulu: University Press of Hawai'i.

Hamilton, Sue. 1996. *Identity and Experience: The Constitution of the Human Being According to Early Buddhism*. London: Luzac Oriental.

Hanayama Shoyu. 1966. "A Summary of Various Research on the Prajñāpāramitā Literature by Japanese Scholars." *Acta Asiatica: Bulletin of the Institute of Eastern Culture*, 10: 16–93.

Handlin, Lilian. 2016. "A Man for All Seasons: Three Vessantaras in Premodern Myanmar." In *Readings of the Vessantara Jātaka*, edited by Steven Collins, 153–82. New York: Columbia University Press.

Hara Minoru. 2009. "Divine Witness." *Journal of Indian Philosophy*, 37.3: 253–72.

Har Dayal. 1932/1970. *The Bodhisattva Doctrine in Buddhist Sanskrit Literature*. Delhi: Motilal Banarsidass.

Harrison, Paul M. 1978a. "Buddhānusmṛti in the Pratyutpanna-buddha-saṃmukhāvasthita-samādhi-sūtra." *Journal of Indian Philosophy*, 6: 35–57.

———. 1978b. *The Tibetan Text of the Pratyutpanna-buddha-saṃmukhāvasthita-samādhi-sūtra: Critically Edited from the Derge, Narthang, Peking and Lhasa Editions of the Tibetan Kanjur and Accompanied by a Concordance and Comparative Table of Chapters of the Tibetan and Chinese Versions*. Tokyo: Reiyukai.

———. 1982. "Sanskrit Fragments of a Lokottaravādin Tradition." In *Indological and Buddhist Studies: Volume in Honour of Professor J. W. de Jong*, edited by Luis Anna Hercus, F. B. J. Kuiper, T. Rajapatirana, and E. R. Skrzypczak, 211–34. Canberra: Faculty of Asian Studies.

———. 1987. "Who Gets to Ride in the Great Vehicle? Self-Image and Identity among the Followers of the Early Mahāyāna." *Journal of the International Association of Buddhist Studies*, 10.1: 67–89.

———. 1990. *The Samādhi of Direct Encounter with the Buddhas of the Present: An Annotated English Translation of the Tibetan Version of the Pratyutpanna-Buddha-saṃmukhāvasthita-samādhi-sūtra with Several Appendixes Relating to the History of the Text*. Tokyo: International Institute for Buddhist Studies.

———. 1992. "Is the Dharma-kāya the Real 'Phantom Body' of the Buddha?" *The Journal of the International Association of Buddhist Studies*, 15.1: 44–94.

———. 1993. "The Earliest Chinese Translations of Mahāyāna Buddhist sūtras: Some Notes on the Work of Lokakṣema." *Buddhist Studies Review*, 10.2: 135–77.

———. 1995. "Searching for the Origins of the Mahāyāna: What Are We Looking For?" *The Eastern Buddhist*, 28.1: 48–69.

———. 1998a. *The Pratyutpanna Samādhi Sutra Translated by Lokakṣema: Translated from the Chinese (Taishō Volume 13, Number 418)*. Berkeley: Numata Center for Buddhist Translation and Research.

———. 1998b. "Women in the Pure Land: Some Reflections on the Textual Sources." *Journal of Indian Philosophy*, 26: 553–72.

———. 2000. "Mañjuśrī and the Cult of the Celestial Bodhisattvas." *Chung-Hwa Buddhist Journal*, 13.2: 157–93.

———. 2003. "Mediums and Messages: Reflections on the Production of Mahāyāna sūtras." *The Eastern Buddhist*, 35.1/2: 115–51.

———. 2006. "Vajracchedikā Prajñāpāramitā: A New English Translation of the Sanskrit Text Based on Two Sanskrit Manuscripts from Greater Gandhāra." In *Manuscripts in the Schøyen Collection III: Buddhist Manuscripts II*, edited by Jens Braarvig, 133–59. Oslo: Hermes Publishing.

———. 2008/2010. "Experimental Core Samples of Chinese Translations of Two Buddhist sūtras Analysed in the Light of Recent Manuscript Discoveries." *Journal of the International Association of Buddhist Studies*, 31.1/2: 205–49.

———. 2010. "Resetting the Diamond: Reflections on Kumārajīva's Chinese Translation of the *Vajracchedikā* (Diamond sūtra)." *Journal of Historical and Philological Studies of China's Western Regions/*西域歷史語言研究集刊, 3: 233–48.

———. 2018. "Early Mahāyāna: Laying Out the Field." In *Setting Out on the Great Way: Essays on Early Mahāyāna Buddhism*, edited by Paul Harrison, 7–31. Sheffield: Equinox.

———. 2019. "Lokakṣema." In *Brill's Encyclopedia of Buddhism: Volume II, Lives*, edited by Jonathan A. Silk, Richard Bowring, Vincent Eltschinger, and Michael Radich, 700–706. Leiden: Brill.

———. 2022. "Bending Minds and Winning Hearts: On the Rhetorical Uses of Complexity in Mahāyāna sūtras." *Journal of Indian Philosophy*, 50: 649–70.

Harrison, Paul and Jens-Uwe Hartmann. 2000. "Ajātaśatrukaukṛtyavinodanāsūtra." In *Manuscripts in the Schøyen Collection I: Buddhist Manuscripts, Volume I*, edited by Jens Braarvig, 165–216 and 301–2. Oslo: Hermes Publishing.

Harrison, Paul, Timothy Lenz, and Richard Salomon. 2018. "Fragments of a Gāndhārī Manuscript of the Pratyutpannabuddhasaṃmukhāvasthitasamādhisūtra." *Journal of the International Association of Buddhist Studies*, 41: 117–43.

Harrison, Paul and Watanabe Shōgo. 2006. "Vajracchedikā Prajñāpāramitā." In *Manuscripts in the Schøyen Collection III: Buddhist Manuscripts II*, edited by Jens Braarvig, 89–132. Oslo: Hermes Publishing.

Harter, Pierre-Julien. 2022. "Haribhadra: The Voice of Perfect Wisdom." In *The Routledge Handbook of Indian Buddhist Philosophy*, edited by William Edelglass, Pierre-Julien Harter, and Sara McClintock, 497–510. London: Routledge Curzon.

Hartmann, Jens-Uwe. 2019. "The Earliest 'Mahāyāna' sūtra Manuscripts and What They Tell Us." *Hōrin*, 20: 13–22.

Hartmann, Jens-Uwe and Klaus Wille. 2016. "A Folio of a Parallel to the Śalyasūtra or Sunakkhattasutta." In *Manuscripts in the Schøyen Collection III: Buddhist Manuscripts IV*, edited by Jens Braarvig, 151–58. Oslo: Hermes.

Harvey, Peter. 1990. *An Introduction to Buddhism: Teachings, History and Practices*. Delhi: Munshiram Manoharlal.

———. 1995. *The Selfless Mind: Personality, Consciousness and Nirvāṇa in Early Buddhism*. Richmond Surrey: Curzon.

Hecker, Hellmuth. 2009. *Similes of the Buddha: An Introduction*, translated by Bhikkhu Khantipālo and Bhikkhu Piyadhammo. Kandy: Buddhist Publication Society.

Heim, Maria and Chakravarthi Ram-Prasad. 2018. "In a Double Way: Nāmarūpa in Buddhaghosa's Phenomenology." *Philosophy East and West*, 68.4: 1085–115.

Hemasiri, Kadihingala and Sangjingyu. 2022. "The Mahayana Bodhisattva Impact on Sri Lankan Monks with Special Reference to the Bodhicaryāvatāra and Bodhisattva Prārthanā Gāthā." *Sri Lanka International Journal of Buddhist Studies*, 8: 55–63.

Henry, Justin. 2020. "Sri Lanka's Place in the History of South Asian Buddhism." In *Routledge Handbook of South Asian Religions*, edited by Knut A. Jacobson, 124–38. London: Routledge.

Hirakawa Akira. 1963. "The Rise of Mahāyāna Buddhism and Its Relation to the Worship of Stupas." *The Memoirs of the Research Department of the Toyo Bunko*, 22: 57–106.

———. 1990/1998. *A History of Indian Buddhism: From Śākyamuni to Early Mahāyāna*, translated by Paul Groner. Delhi: Motilal Banarsidass.

———. 1997. *Buddhist Chinese-Sanskrit Dictionary*. Tokyo: Reiyukai.

Hiraoka Satoshi. 2003. "The Structure of the Mahāvastu-avadāna." In *Buddhist and Indian Studies in Honour of Professor Sodo Mori*, edited by the Publication Committee for Buddhist and Indian Studies in Honour of Professor Sodo Mori, 349–62. Hamamatsu: Kokusai Bukkyoto Kyokai.

Hoernle, A. F. Rudolf. 1916. *Manuscript Remains of Buddhist Literature Found in Eastern Turkestan*. Oxford: Clarendon Press.

Hofinger, Marcel. 1954. *Le Congres du Lac Anavatapta (Vies de Saints Bouddhiques): Extrait du Vinaya des Mūlasarvāstivādin, Bhaiṣajyavastu, I: Légendes des Anciens (Sthavirāvadāna)*. Louvain: Institut Orientaliste.

Holder, John J. 1996. "The Early Buddhist Theory of Truth: A Contextualist Pragmatic Interpretation." *International Philosophical Quarterly*, 36.4: 443–59.

Holt, John Clifford. 1991. *Buddha in the Crown: Avalokiteśvara in the Buddhist Traditions of Sri Lanka*. Oxford: Oxford University Press.

Huifeng Shi. 2014. "Apocryphal Treatment for Conze's Heart Problems: 'Non-attainment,' 'Apprehension,' and 'Mental Hanging' in the Prajnāpāramitā Hṛdaya." *Journal of the Oxford Centre for Buddhist Studies*, 6: 72–105.

———. 2016. "Is 'Illusion' a Prajñāpāramitā Creation? The Birth and Death of a Buddhist Cognitive Metaphor." *Journal of Buddhist Philosophy*, 1.2: 214–62.

———. 2017. "An Annotated English Translation of Kumārajīva's Xiaŏpĭn Prajñāpāramitā sūtra." *Asian Literature and Translation*, 4.1: 187–236.

Hung Jen-Jou and Bhikkhu Anālayo. 2017. "A Quantitative Textual Analysis of the Translation Idiom of the Madhyama-āgama and the Ekottarika-āgama." In *Research on the Madhyama-āgama*, edited by Bhikkhunī Dhammadinnā, 177–96. Taipei: Dharma Drum Publishing Corporation.

Hureau, Silvie. 2006. "Preaching and Translating on poṣadha Days: Kumārajīva's Role in Adapting an Indian Ceremony to China." *Journal of the International College for Postgraduate Buddhist Studies*, 10: 87–119.

Hurvitz, Leon N. and Arthur E. Link. 1975. *Three Prajñāpāramitā Prefaces of Tao-An: En hommage à M. Paul Demiéville*. Limoges, France: Imprimerie A. Bontemps.

Huyên-Vi, Thích and Bhikkhu Pāsādika. 2002. "Ekottarāgama XXIX." *Buddhist Studies Review*, 19.1: 49–55.

Jaini, Padmanabh S. 1974. "On the sarvajñatva (Omniscience) of Mahāvīra and the Buddha." In *Buddhist Studies in Honour of I. B. Horner*, edited by Lance Cousins, 71–90. Dordrecht: Reidel.

Jayatilleke, K. N. 1963/1980. *Early Buddhist Theory of Knowledge*. Delhi: Motilal Banarsidass.

Jenkins, Stephen Lynn. 1999. *The Circle of Compassion: An Interpretive Study of karuṇā in Indian Buddhist Literature*. PhD thesis, Harvard University.

Jing Guo. 2023. "The Buddhist Concept of 'Filial Piety' in the Context of Early Chinese Buddhist Scripture Translation.' *Religions*, 14.1507: 1–13.

Jing Yin. 2005. "The Bodhisattva Precepts and the Origin of the Mahāyāna School." *Journal of the Centre for Buddhist Studies*, 3: 169–89.

Johansson, Rune E. A. 1965. "Citta, mano, viññāṇa: A Psychosemantic Investigation." *University of Ceylon Review*, 23.1/2: 165–215.

Johnston, Edward Hamilton. 1928. *The Saundarananda of Aśvaghoṣa: Critically Edited with Notes*. London: Oxford University Press.

———. 1936/1984. *Aśvagoṣa's Buddhacarita or Acts of the Buddha in Three Parts: Sanskrit Text of Cantos I–XIV with English Translation of Cantos I–XXVIII, Cantos I to XIV Translated from the Original Sanskrit Supplemented by the Tibetan Version and Cantos XV to XXVIII Translated from the Tibetan and Chinese Versions*. Delhi: Motilal Banarsidass.

Jones, Dhivan Thomas. 2009. "Why Did Brahmā Ask the Buddha to Teach?" *Buddhist Studies Review*, 26.1: 85–102.

Jurewicz, Joanna. 2000. "Playing with Fire: The pratītyasamutpāda from the Perspective of Vedic Thought." *Journal of the Pali Text Society*, 26: 77–103.

Kajiyama Yuichi. 1982a. "On the Meanings of the Words bodhisattva and mahāsattva in Prajñāpāramitā Literature." In *Indological and Buddhist Studies: Volume in Honour of Professor J. W. de Jong on His Sixtieth*

*Birthday*, edited by Luis Anna Hercus, F. B. J. Kuiper, T. Rajapatirana, and E. R. Skrzypczak, 253–70. Canberra: Faculty of Asian Studies.

———. 1982b. "Women in Buddhism." *The Eastern Buddhist*, 25.2: 53–70.

———. 1995. "Prajñāpāramitā and the Rise of Mahāyāna." In *Buddhist Spirituality: Indian, Southeast Asian, Tibetan, and Early Chinese*, edited by Takeuchi Yoshinori, Jan Van Bragt, James W. Heisig, Joseph S. O'Leary, and Paul L. Swanson, 137–54. New York: Crossroad.

Kalupahana, David J. 1975. *Causality: The Central Philosophy of Buddhism*. Honolulu: University Press of Hawai'i.

Karashima Seishi. 1998. *A Glossary of Dharmarakṣa's Translation of the Lotus Sutra*, 正法華經詞典. Tokyo: Soka University.

———. 2001. "Who Composed the Lotus Sutra? Antagonism between Wilderness and Village Monks." *Annual Report of the International Research Institute for Advanced Buddhology at Soka University*, 4: 143–79.

———. 2006. "Underlying Languages of Early Chinese Translations of Buddhist Scriptures." In *Studies in Chinese Language and Culture: Festschrift in Honour of Christoph Harbsmeier on the Occasion of His 60th Birthday*, edited by Christoph Anderl and Halvor Eifring, 355–66. Oslo: Hermes Academic Publishing.

———. 2010. *A Glossary of Lokakṣema's Translation of the Aṣṭasāhasrikā Prajñāpāramitā*, 道行般若經詞典. Tokyo: International Research Institute for Advanced Buddhology, Soka University.

———. 2011. *A Critical Edition of Lokakṣema's Translation of the Aṣṭasāhasrikā Prajñāpāramitā*, 道行般若經校注. Tokyo: International Research Institute for Advanced Buddhology, Soka University.

———. 2013a. "On the 'Missing' Portion in the Aṣṭasāhasrikā Prajñāpāramitā." *Annual Report of the International Research Institute for Advanced Buddhology at Soka University*, 16: 189–92.

———. 2013b. "A Study of the Language of Early Chinese Buddhist Translations: A Comparison between the Translations of Lokakṣema and Zhi Qian." *Annual Report of the International Research Institute for Advanced Buddhology at Soka University*, 16: 273–88.

———. 2013c. "Was the Aṣṭasāhasrikā Prajñāpāramitā Compiled in

Gandhāra in Gāndhārī?" *Annual Report of the International Research Institute for Advanced Buddhology at Soka University*, 16: 171–88.

———. 2015a. "Vehicle (yāna) and Wisdom (jñāna) in the Lotus Sutra: The Origin of the Notion of yāna in Mahāyāna Buddhism." *Annual Report of the International Research Institute for Advanced Buddhology at Soka University*, 18: 163–96.

———. 2015b. "Who Composed the Mahāyāna Scriptures? The Mahāsāṃghikas and Vaitulya Scriptures." *Annual Report of the International Research Institute for Advanced Buddhology at Soka University*, 18: 113–62.

———. 2018a. "Ajita and Maitreya: More Evidence of the Early Mahāyāna Scriptures' Origins from the Mahāsāṃghikas and a Clue as to the School-Affiliation of the Kanaganahalli-stūpa." *Annual Report of the International Research Institute for Advanced Buddhology at Soka University*, 21: 181–96.

———. 2018b. "The Relationship between Mahāsāṃghikas and Mahāyāna Buddhism Indicated in the Colophon of the Chinese Translation of the Vinaya of the Mahāsāṃghikas." *Annual Report of the International Research Institute for Advanced Buddhology at Soka University*, 21: 197–207.

Karunadasa, Y. 2007. "The Unanswered Questions: Why Were They Unanswered? A Re-examination of the Textual Data." *Pacific World, Third Series*, 9: 3–31.

———. 2013. *Early Buddhist Teachings: The Middle Position in Theory and Practice*. Hong Kong: Centre of Buddhist Studies, University of Hong Kong.

Katz, Nathan. 1984. "Prasaṅga and Deconstruction: Tibetan Hermeneutics and the yāna Controversy." *Philosophy East and West*, 34.2: 185–204.

Keith, A. Berriedale. 1923/1979. *Buddhist Philosophy in India and Ceylon*. Delhi: Oriental Books Reprint Corporation.

Kellner, Birgit and John Taber. 2014. "Studies in Yogācāra-Vijñānavāda Idealism I: The Interpretation of Vasubandhu's Viṃśikā." *Asiatische Studien*, 68.3: 709–56.

Kent, Stephen A. 1982. "A Sectarian Interpretation of the Rise of Mahāyāna." *Religion*, 12: 311–32.

Keown, Damien. 1992/2001. *The Nature of Buddhist Ethics*. New York: Palgrave.

Kern, Hendrik and Nanjio Bunyiu. 1912. *Saddharmapuṇḍarīka*. St.-Pétersbourg: Académie Impériale des Sciences.

Kimura Takayasu. 2007. *Pañcaviṃśatisāhasrikā Prajñāpāramitā I-1*. Tokyo: Sankibo Busshorin.

———. 2009. *Pañcaviṃśatisāhasrikā Prajñāpāramitā I-2*. Tokyo: Sankibo Busshorin.

King, Winston L. 1983. "The Existential Nature of Buddhist Ultimates." *Philosophy East and West*, 33.3: 263–71.

Klaus, Konrad. 2007. "Zu der formelhaften Einleitung der buddhistischen sūtras." In *Indica et Tibetica 65: Festschrift für Michael Hahn zum 65. Geburtstag von Freunden und Schülern überreicht*, edited by Konrad Klaus and Jens-Uwe Hartmann, 309–22. Wien: Arbeitskreis für Tibetische und Buddhistische Studien, Universität Wien.

Kloppenborg, Ria. 1974. *The Paccekabuddha, a Buddhist Ascetic: A Study of the Concept of the Paccekabuddha in Pāli Canonical and Commentarial Literature*. Leiden: E. J. Brill.

Kong Choy Fah. 2012. *Saccakiriyā: The Belief in the Power of True Speech in Theravāda Buddhist Tradition*. Singapore: Choy Fah Kong.

Kovan, Martin. 2014. "Thresholds of Transcendence: Buddhist Self-Immolation and Mahāyānist Absolute Altruism Part Two." *Journal of Buddhist Ethics*, 21: 387–430.

———. 2018. "Being and Its Other: Suicide in Buddhist Ethics." In *Oxford Handbook of Buddhist Ethics*, edited by Daniel Cozort and James Mark Shields, 630–49. Oxford: Oxford University Press.

Kuan Tse-fu. 2013. "Mahāyāna Elements and Mahāsāṃghika Traces in the Ekottarika-āgama." In *Research on the Ekottarika-āgama (Taishō 125)*, edited by Bhikkhunī Dhammadinnā, 133–94. Taipei: Dharma Drum Publishing Corporation.

———. 2019. "Moggallāna's Journey to Another Buddha-Field: How a Mahāyāna Narrative Crept into the Ekottarika Āgama (T 125)." *Religions of South Asia*, 13.1: 24–50.

Kudo Noriyuki and Shono Masanori. 2015. "The Sanskrit Fragments Or.15009/601–678 in the Hoernle Collection." In *Buddhist Manuscripts from Central Asia: The British Library Sanskrit Fragments, Volume III.1*, edited by Karashima Seishi, Nagashima Jundo, and Klaus Wille, 419–74. Tokyo: International Research Institute for Advanced Buddhology, Soka University.

Kwan Tai-wo. 1985. *A Study of the Teaching Regarding the Pure Land of Aksobhya Buddha in Early Mahayana*. PhD thesis, University of California.

Lai Whalen W. 1983. "Before the Prajñā Schools: The Earliest Chinese Commentary on the Aṣṭasāhasrikā." *Journal of the International Association of Buddhist Studies*, 6.1: 91–108.

Lamotte, Étienne. 1944/1981. *Le Traité de la Grande Vertu de Sagesse de Nāgārjuna (Mahāprajñāpāramitāśāstra): Tome I, Chapitres I–XV*. Louvain-la-Neuve: Institut Orientaliste.

———. 1949/1981. *Le Traité de la Grande Vertu de Sagesse de Nāgārjuna (Mahāprajñāpāramitāśāstra): Tome II, Chapitres XV–XXX*. Louvain-la-Neuve: Institut Orientaliste.

———. 1954. "Sur la Formation du Mahāyāna." In *Asiatica: Festschrift Friedrich Weller zum 65. Geburtstag gewidment von seinen Freunden, Kollegen und Schülern*, edited by Johannes Schubert and Ulrich Schneider, 377–96. Leipzig: Harrassowitz.

———. 1957. "Khuddakanikāya and Kṣudrakapiṭaka." *East and West*, 7.4: 341–48.

———. 1958. *Histoire du Bouddhisme Indien: Des origines à l'ère Śaka*. Louvain-la-Neuve: Institut Orientaliste.

———. 1970. *Le Traité de la Grande Vertu de Sagesse de Nāgārjuna (Mahāprajñāpāramitāśāstra): Tome III, Chapitres XXXI–XLII*. Louvain-la-Neuve: Institut Orientaliste.

———. 1976. *Le Traité de la Grande Vertu de Sagesse de Nāgārjuna (Mahāprajñāpāramitāśāstra): Tome IV, Chapitres XLII (suite)–XLVIII*. Louvain-la-Neuve: Institut Orientaliste.

———. 1980. *Le Traité de la Grande Vertu de Sagesse de Nāgārjuna (Mahāprajñāpāramitāśāstra): Tome V, Chapitres XLIX–LII, et Chapitre XX (2e série)*. Louvain-la-Neuve: Institut Orientaliste.

Lancaster, Lewis Rosser. 1968. *An Analysis of the Aṣṭasāhasrikā Prajñā-*

*pāramitāsūtra from the Chinese Translations*. PhD thesis, University of Wisconsin.
———. 1969. "The Chinese Translation of the Aṣṭasāhasrikā-prajñāpāramitā-sūtra Attributed to Chih Ch'ien 支謙." *Monumenta Serica, Journal of Oriental Studies*, 28: 246–57.
———. 1974a. "An Early Mahayana Sermon about the Body of the Buddha and the Making of Images." *Artibus Asiae*, 36.4: 287–91.
———. 1974b. "The Story of a Buddhist Hero." *Tsing Hua Journal of Chinese Studies*, 10.2: 83–90.
———. 1974/1991. "Discussion of Time in Mahāyāna Texts." In *Essays on Time in Buddhism*, edited by H. S. Prasad, 499–504. Delhi: Sri Satguru Publications.
———. 1975. "The Oldest Mahāyāna sūtra: Its Significance for the Study of Buddhist Development." *The Eastern Buddhist, New Series*, 8.1: 30–41.
———. 1976. "Samādhi Names in Buddhist Texts." In *Malalasekera Commemoration Volume*, edited by O. H. de Wijesekera, 196–202. Colombo: The Malalasekera Commemoration Volume Editorial Committee.
Laut, Jens Peter. 1993. "Jātaka." In *Enzyklopädie des Märchens: Handwörterbuch zur historischen und vergleichenden Erzählforschung*, edited by Rolf Wilhelm Brednich, 7: 500–507. Berlin: De Gruyter.
Law, Bimala Chun. 1930a. "Chronology of the Pāli Canon." *Annals of the Bhandarkar Oriental Research Institute*, 12.2: 171–201.
———. 1930b. *A Study of the Mahāvastu (Supplement)*. Calcutta: Thacker, Spink & Co.
Lefmann, S. 1902. *Lalita Vistara: Leben und Lehre des Çâkya-Buddha, Textausgabe mit Varianten-, Metren- und Wörterverzeichnis*. Halle: Verlag der Buchhandlung des Waisenhauses.
Lenz, Timothy. 2003. *A New Version of the Gāndhārī Dharmapada and a Collection of Previous-Birth Stories: British Library Kharoṣṭhī Fragments 16 + 25*. Seattle: University of Washington Press.
Lethcoe, Nancy R. 1976. "Some Notes on the Relationship between the Abhisamayālaṅkāra, the Revised Pañcaviṃśatisāhasrikā and the Chinese Translations of the Unrevised Pañcaviṃśatisāhasrikā." *Journal of the American Oriental Society*, 96.4: 499–511.

———. 1977. "The bodhisattva Ideal in the Aṣṭa and Pañca Prajñāpāramitā." In *Prajñāpāramitā and Related Systems: Studies in Honor of Edward Conze*, edited by Lewis Lancaster and Luis O. Gómez, 263–80. Berkeley: University of California Press.

Lettere, Laura. 2020. "The Missing Translator: A Study of the Biographies of the Monk Baoyun 寶雲 (376?–449)." *Rivista degli Studi Orientali, Nuova Serie*, 93.1/2: 259–74.

Lévi, Sylvain. 1907. *Mahāyāna-Sūtrālaṃkāra: Exposé de la doctrine du Grand Véhicule selon le système Yogācāra, édité et traduit. Tome I.–Texte*. Paris: Librairie Honoré Champion.

———. 1908. "Açvaghoṣa: Le Sûtrâlaṃkâra et ses sources." *Journal Asiatique*, 10.12: 57–184.

———. 1925. *Vijñpatimātratāsiddhi: Deux traités de Vasubandhu Viṃśatikā (La Vingtaine), accompagnée d'une explication en prose et Triṃśikā (La Trentaine) avec le commentaire de Sthiramati, original Sancrit publie pour la première fois d'après des manuscrits rapportes du Népal*. Paris: Librairie Ancienne Honoré Champion.

———. 1932. *Mahākarmavibhaṅga (La Grande Classification des Actes) et Karmavibhaṅgopadeśa (Discussion sur le Mahā Karmavibhaṅga): Textes sanscrits rapportés du Népal, édités et traduits avec les textes parallèles en Sanscrit, en Pali, en Tibétains, en Chinois et en Koutchéen*. Paris: Ernest Leroux.

Levman, Bryan. 2011. "The muṇḍa/muṇḍaka Crux: What Does the Word Mean?" *Canadian Journal of Buddhist Studies*, 7: 45–76.

Li Channa. 2019. "Śāriputra." In *Brill's Encyclopedia of Buddhism: Volume II, Lives*, edited by Jonathan A. Silk, Richard Bowring, Vincent Eltschinger, and Michael Radich, 409–19. Leiḍen: Brill.

Li Charles. 2023. "King Śibi in the Vahnipurāṇa: A Critical Edition and Translation of the Śiber Upākhyāna." *Asian Literature and Translation*, 10.1: 1–46.

Lin Qian. 2022. "On the Early Buddhist Attitude toward Metaphysics." *Journal of Indian Philosophy*, 50: 143–62.

Liu Zhen. 2010. *Dhyānāni tapaś ca*, 禅定与苦修. Shanghai: 古籍出版社.

Lopez, Donald S. Jr. 1995. "Authority and Orality in the Mahāyāna." *Numen*, 42.1: 21–47.

Maas, Philipp A. 2020. "Sarvāstivāda Buddhist Theories of Temporality and the Pātañjala Yoga Theory of Transformation (pariṇāma)." *Journal of Indian Philosophy*, 48.5: 963–1003.

MacQueen, Graeme. 1981. "Inspired Speech in Early Mahāyāna Buddhism I." *Religion*, 11: 303–19.

———. 1982. "Inspired Speech in Early Mahāyāna Buddhism II." *Religion*, 12: 49–65.

Maharjan, Sabin. 2022. *The Perfection of kṣānti in Theravāda and Mahāyāna: A Critical Study*. PhD thesis, University of Hong Kong.

Maithrimurthi, Mudagamuwe. 1999. *Wohlwollen, Mitleid, Freude und Gleichmut, Eine ideengeschichtliche Untersuchung der vier apramāṇas in der buddhistischen Ethik und Spiritualität von den Anfängen bis hin zum frühen Yogācāra*. Stuttgart: Franz Steiner.

———. 2004. "Entfaltung des Wohlwollens als eine meditative Übung." *Journal of the International College for Advanced Buddhist Studies*, 7: 165–214.

Mak, Bill M. 2011. "Haribhadra's Commentary (Abhisamayālaṅkārālokā) on the Story of Sadāprarudita (Ch. 30–31 of Aṣṭasāhasrikā Prajnāpāramitā): Sources and Construction of a Mahāyāna Soteriology." In *Ñāṇappabhā: A Felicitation Volume in Honour of Venerable Dr. Pategama Gnanarama Maha Thera*, edited by Rangama Chandavimala and Chandima Wijebandara, 84–97. Singapore: Ti-Sarana Buddhist Association.

Makransky, John. 1997. *Buddhahood Embodied: Sources of Controversy in India and Tibet*. Albany: State University of New York Press.

Malalasekera, G. P. 1937/1995. *Dictionary of Pāli Proper Names: Vol. I, A–Dh*. Delhi: Munshiram Manoharlal.

———. 1938/1998. *Dictionary of Pāli Proper Names: Vol. II, N–H*. Delhi: Munshiram Manoharlal.

Mäll, Linnart. 2003/2005. *Studies in the Aṣṭasāhasrikā Prajñāpāramitā and Other Essays*. New Delhi: Motilal Banarsidass.

Manda Michitoshi. 2005. "The Meaning of Tathāgata in the avyākata Questions." In *Buddhism and Jainism: Essays in Honour of Dr. Hojun Nagasaki on His Seventieth Birthday*, 724–13. Kyoto: Committee for the Felicitation of Dr. Hojun Nagasaki's Seventieth Birthday.

Marasinghe, M. M. J. 1974. *Gods in Early Buddhism: A Study in Their Social and Mythological Milieu as Depicted in the Nikāyas of the Pāli Canon*. Kelaniya: University of Sri Lanka, Vidyalankara Campus Press.

Marciniak, Katarzyna. 2019. *The Mahāvastu: A New Edition, Vol. III*. Tokyo: International Research Institute for Advanced Buddhology at Soka University.

———. 2020. *The Mahāvastu: A New Edition, Vol. II*. Tokyo: International Research Institute for Advanced Buddhology at Soka University.

———. 2022. "The Description of Hells in the Mahāvastu I 9–16 Revisited." In *Guruparamparā: Studies on Buddhism, India, Tibet and More in Honour of Professor Marek Mejor*, edited by Katarzyna Marciniak, Stanisław Jan Kania, Małgorzata Wielińska-Soltwedel, and Agata Bareja-Starzyńska, 295–320. Warsaw: University of Warsaw Press.

Marino, Joseph. 2017. *Metaphor and Pedagogy in Early Buddhist Literature: An Edition and Study of Two sūtras from the Senior Collection of Gāndhārī Manuscripts*. PhD thesis, University of Washington.

———. 2019. "From the Blacksmith's Forge to the Fires of Hell: Eating the Red-Hot Iron Ball in Early Buddhist Literature." *Buddhist Studies Review*, 36.1: 31–51.

———. 2020. "The Gandhari 'Discourse on Pleasure and Pain': Some Thoughts on Similes and Textual Variation in the Connected Discourses." In *Research on the Saṃyukta-āgama*, edited by Bhikkhunī Dhammadinnā, 259–300. Taipei: Dharma Drum Publishing Corporation.

Martini, Giuliana. 2011. "Mahāmaitrī in a Mahāyāna sūtra in Khotanese." *Chung-Hwa Buddhist Journal*, 24: 121–93.

Matilal, Bimal Krishna. 1980. "Ignorance or Misconception? A Note on avidyā in Buddhism." In *Buddhist Studies in Honour of Walpola Rahula*, edited by Somaratna Balasooriya, André Bareau, Richard Gombrich, Siri Gunasingha, Udaya Mallawarachchi, and Edmund Perry, 154–64. London: Fraser.

Matsuda Katsunobu. 2021. "Sanskrit Text and Japanese Translation of the Madhyama-āgama 139 (**Śivapathikā-sūtra*) Based on the Tridaṇḍamāla Manuscript." *Bulletin of the Association of Buddhist Studies, Bukkyo University*, 26: 63–82.

Matsumura Hisashi. 1988. *The Mahāsudarśanāvadāna and the Mahāsudarśanasūtra*. Delhi: Sri Satguru.

Matsumura Junko. 2008. "The Sumedhakathā in Pāli Literature: Summation of Theravāda-Tradition Versions and Proof of Linkage to the Northern Textual Tradition." *Journal of Indian and Buddhist Studies*, 56.3: 1086–94.

———. 2010. "The Sumedhakathā in Pāli Literature and Its Relation to the Northern Buddhist Textual Tradition." *Journal of the International College for Postgraduate Buddhist Studies*, 14: 101–33.

———. 2011. "An Independent sūtra on the Dīpaṃkara Prophecy." *Journal of the International College for Postgraduate Buddhist Studies*, 15: 81–141.

———. 2012. "The Formation and Development of the Dīpaṃkara Prophecy Story." *Journal of Indian and Buddhist Studies*, 60.3: 80–89.

McDaniel, Justin Thomas. 2008. "Philosophical Embryology: Buddhist Texts and the Ritual Construction of a Fetus." In *Imagining the Fetus: The Unborn in Myth, Religion, and Culture*, edited by Vanessa R. Sasson and Jane Marie Law, 91–105. New York: Oxford University Press.

McMahan David L. 2002. *Empty Vision: Metaphor and Visionary Imagery in Mahāyāna Buddhism*. London: Routledge Curzon.

Meisig, Konrad. 1990. "Meditation (dhyāna) in der ältesten Buddhistischen Lehre." In *Ihr Alle Seid aber Brüder*, edited by Ludwig Hagemann, 541–54. Würzburg: Echter.

Mejor, Marek. 1991. *Vasubandhu's Abhidharmakośa and the Commentaries Preserved in the Tanjur*. Stuttgart: Franz Steiner.

Melzer, Gudrun. 2009. "The Sanskrit Fragments Or.15009/151–200 in the Hoernle Collection." In *Buddhist Manuscripts from Central Asia: The British Library Sanskrit Fragments, Volume II.1*, edited by Seishi Karashima and Klaus Wille, 199–226. Tokyo: International Research Institute for Advanced Buddhology, Soka University.

Migot, André. 1954. "Un grand disciple du Buddha, Śāriputra: Son rôle dans l'histoire du Bouddhisme et dans le développement de l'Abhidharma." *Bulletin de l'École Française d'Extrême Orient*, 46: 405–554.

Mingun Sayadaw, Bhaddanta Vicittasārābhivaṃsa Tipiṭakadhara Dhammabhaṇḍāgārika Agga Mahāpaṇḍita Abhidhaja Mahāraṭṭhaguru. 1991. *The Great Chronicle of Buddhas: The State Buddha Sasana Council's Version, Volume One, Part One.* Translated into English by U Ko Lay and U Tin Lwin. Yangon: Ti-Ni Publishing Centre.

Minh Chau, Thich. 1964. *Milindapañha and Nāgasenabhikshusūtra: A Comparative Study Through Pāli and Chinese Sources.* Calcutta: K. L. Mukhopadyay.

Mishra, Kameshwar Nath. 1988. "Advaya (= non-dual) in Buddhist Sanskrit." *The Tibet Journal*, 13.2: 3–11.

Mitra, Rajendralala. 1887/1888. *Aṣṭasāhasrikā Prajñāpāramitā.* Calcutta: Royal Asiatic Society of Bengal.

Mizuno Kōgen. 1961. "Abhidharma Literature." In *Encyclopaedia of Buddhism*, edited by G. P. Malalasekera, 1.1: 64–80. Sri Lanka: Department of Buddhist Affairs.

Mochizuki Shinko. 1940. "The Places of varṣāvasāna during Forty-Five Years of the Buddha's Career after His Enlightenment." In *Studies on Buddhism in Japan, Volume Two*, 29–44. Tokyo: International Buddhist Society.

Monier-Williams, M. 1899/1999. *A Sanskrit-English Dictionary: Etymologically and Philologically Arranged, with Special Reference to Cognate Indo-European Languages.* Delhi: Motilal Banarsidass.

Mori Sodō. 1997. "The Vijñānavādin View as Depicted in the Pāli Commentaries with Special Reference to the Niryapāla-kathā." In *BaudDhavidyāsudhākaraḥ: Studies in Honour of Heinz Bechert on the Occasion of His 65th Birthday*, edited by Petra Kieffer-Pülz and Jens-Uwe Hartmann, 453–64. Swisstal-Odendorf: Indica et Tibetica.

———. 1999. *Mahāyāna Buddhism in Sri Lanka.* Nagoya: ARM Corporation.

Müller, F. Max. 1873/1877. *The Hymns of the Rig-Veda in the Samhita and Pada Texts: Reprinted from the Editio Princeps, Volume One.* London: Trübner and Co.

Murti, T. R. V. 1955/2008. *The Central Philosophy of Buddhism: A Study of the Mādhyamika System.* Oxon: Routledge.

Mus, Paul. 1939. *La lumière sur les six voies: Tableau de la transmigration bouddhique d'après des sources Sanskrites, Pāli, Tibétaines et Chinoises en majeure partie inédites*. Paris: Institut d'Ethnologie.

Nagao G. M. 1955/1992. "The Silence of the Buddha and Its Madhyamic Interpretation." In *Mādhyamika and Yogācāra: A Study of Mahāyāna Philosophies, Collected Papers of G. M. Nagao*, edited by L. S. Kawamura, 35–49. Delhi: Sri Satguru Publications.

Nagashima Jundo. 2009. "The Sanskrit Fragments Or.15009/51–90 in the Hoernle Collection." In *Buddhist Manuscripts from Central Asia: The British Library Sanskrit Fragments, Volume II.1*, edited by Seishi Karashima and Klaus Wille, 128–59. Tokyo: International Research Institute for Advanced Buddhology, Soka University.

———. 2015. "The Sanskrit Fragments Or.15009/501–600 in the Hoernle Collection." In *Buddhist Manuscripts from Central Asia: The British Library Sanskrit Fragments, Volume III.1*, edited by Seishi Karashima, Jundo Nagashima, and Klaus Wille, 347–418. Tokyo: International Research Institute for Advanced Buddhology, Soka University.

Nagata Mizu. 2002. "Transitions in Attitudes toward Women in the Buddhist Canon: The Three Obligations, the Five Obstructions, and the Eight Rules of Reverence." Translated by Paul B. Watt. In *Engendering Faith: Women and Buddhism in Premodern Japan*, edited by Barbara Ruch, 279–95. Ann Arbor: Center for Japanese Studies, University of Michigan.

Nagatomo Shigenori. 2000. "The Logic of the Diamond Sutra: A Is Not A, Therefore It Is A." *Asian Philosophy*, 10.3: 213–44.

Nakamura Hajime. 1980/1999. *Indian Buddhism: A Survey with Bibliographical Notes*. Delhi: Motilal Banarsidass.

———. 2000. *Gotama Buddha: A Biography Based on the Most Reliable Texts, Volume One*. Tokyo: Kosei Publishing Co.

Ñāṇamoli, Bhikkhu. 1991. *The Path of Purification (Visuddhimagga) by Bhadantācariya Buddhaghosa*. Kandy: Buddhist Publication Society.

Ñāṇananda, Bhikkhu K. 1971/1986. *Concept and Reality in Early Buddhist Thought: An Essay on "papañca" and "papañca-saññā-saṅkhā."* Kandy: Buddhist Publication Society.

———. 1974/1985. *The Magic of the Mind in Buddhist Perspective: An Exposition of the Kālakārāma sutta*. Kandy: Buddhist Publication Society.

———. 2015. *Nibbāna: The Mind Stilled, Volumes No. I–VII, Library Edition*. Mādhya Bhāraya: Pothgulgala Dharmagrantha Dharmasravana.

Nanayakkara, S. K. 1972. "Bodhicitta." In *Encyclopaedia of Buddhism*, edited by G. P. Malalasekera, 3.2: 184–89. Sri Lanka: Department of Buddhist Affairs.

Nance, Richard. 2008. "Indian Buddhist Preachers Inside and Outside the sūtras." *Religion Compass*, 2.2: 134–59.

Nanjio Bunyiu. 1882/1989. *A Catalogue of the Chinese Translation of the Buddhist Tripiṭaka: The Sacred Canon of the Buddhists in China and Japan*. Delhi: Classics India Publications.

Nattier, Jan. 1992. "The Heart sūtra: A Chinese Apocryphal Text?" *Journal of the International Association of Buddhist Studies*, 15.2: 153–223.

———. 2000. "The Realm of Akṣobhya: A Missing Piece in the History of Pure Land Buddhism." *Journal of the International Association of Buddhist Studies*, 23.1: 71–102.

———. 2003a. *A Few Good Men: The Bodhisattva Path according to The Inquiry of Ugra (Ugraparipṛcchā)*. Honolulu: University of Hawai'i Press.

———. 2003b. "The Indian Roots of Pure Land Buddhism: Insights from the Oldest Chinese Versions of the Larger Sukhāvatīvyūha." *Pacific World, Third Series*, 5: 179–201.

———. 2005. "The Proto-History of the Buddhāvataṃsaka: The Pusa benye jing 菩薩本業經 and the Dousha jing 兜沙經." *Annual Report of the International Research Institute for Advanced Buddhology at Soka University*, 8: 323–60.

———. 2007a. "Indian Antecedents of Huayan Thought: New Light from Chinese Sources." In *Reflecting Mirrors: Perspectives on Huayan Buddhism*, edited by Imre Hamar, 109–38. Wiesbaden: Harrassowitz Verlag.

———. 2007b. "'One Vehicle' (一乘) in the Chinese Āgamas: New Light on an Old Problem in Pāli." *Annual Report of the International Research Institute for Advanced Buddhology at Soka University*, 10: 181–200.

———. 2008. *A Guide to the Earliest Chinese Buddhist Translations, Texts from the Eastern Han 東漢 and Three Kingdoms 三國 Periods*. Tokyo: Soka University.

———. 2008/2010. "Who Produced the Da mingdu jing 大明度經 (T 225)? A Reassessment of the Evidence." *Journal of the International Association of Buddhist Studies*, 31.1/2: 295–337.

———. 2023. "On Two Previously Unidentified Verses in Zhi Qian's Hybrid Dharmapada." *Annual Report of the International Research Institute for Advanced Buddhology at Soka University*, 26: 215–52.

Naughton, Alex. 1991. "Buddhist Omniscience." *The Eastern Buddhist*, 24.1: 28–51.

Niisaku Yoshiaki. 2019. "Quotations from the Aṣṭāsāhasrikā Prajñāpāramitā in Chapter 18 of the Prasannapadā." *Journal of Indian and Buddhist Studies*, 67.3: 1137–42.

Norman, K. R. 1983. *Pāli Literature: Including the Canonical Literature in Prakrit and Sanskrit of All the Hīnayāna Schools of Buddhism*. Wiesbaden: Otto Harrassowitz.

———. 1994. *Collected Papers, Volume V*. Oxford: Pali Text Society.

Nyanaponika Thera and Hellmuth Hecker. 1997. *Great Disciples of the Buddha: Their Lives, Their Works, Their Legacy*, edited by Bhikkhu Bodhi. Kandy: Buddhist Publication Society.

Nyanatiloka, Bhikkhu. 1952/1988. *Buddhist Dictionary: Manual of Buddhist Terms and Doctrines*. Kandy: Buddhist Publication Society.

Oetke, Claus. 1994. "Die 'unbeantworteten Fragen' und das Schweigen des Buddha." *Wiener Zeitschrift für die Kunde Südasiens*, 38: 85–120.

Ohnuma Reiko. 2000. "The Story of Rūpāvatī: A Female Past Birth of the Buddha." *Journal of the International Association of Buddhist Studies*, 23.1: 103–45.

———. 2007. *Head, Eyes, Flesh, and Bones: Giving Away the Body in Indian Buddhist Literature*. New York: Columbia University Press.

Oldenberg, Hermann. 1881/1961. *Buddha: Sein Leben, Seine Lehre, Seine Gemeinde*. München: Wilhelm Goldmann Verlag.

———. 1912a. "Studien zur Geschichte des buddhistischen Kanon." *Nachrichten von der königlichen Gesellschaft der Wissenschaften zu Göttingen, philologisch-historische Klasse aus dem Jahre 1912*: 155–217.

———. 1912b. "Studien zum Mahāvastu." *Nachrichten von der königlichen Gesellschaft der Wissenschaften zu Göttingen, philologisch-historische Klasse aus dem Jahre 1912*: 123–54.

Onishi Yoshinori. 1999. "Is the Astasāhasrikā Prajnāpāramitā sūtra Really

Arguing against the Sarvāstivādins?" *Buddhist Studies Review*, 16.2: 167–80.

Ooi, Eng Jin. 2022. "Aspiring to Be a Buddha and Life before Liberation: The Colophons of the Siamese Questions of King Milinda." *Manuscript Studies: A Journal of the Schoenberg Institute for Manuscript Studies*, 7.1: 104–29.

Organ, Troy Wilson. 1954. "The Silence of the Buddha." *Philosophy East and West* 4.2: 125–40.

Orsborn, Matthew Bryan. 2012. *Chiasmus in the Early Prajñāpāramitā: Literary Parallelism Connecting Criticism & Hermeneutics in an Early Mahāyāna sūtra*. PhD thesis, University of Hong Kong.

———. 2021a. "Annotated English Translation of the 'Sadāprarudita Avadāna' in Kumārajīva's Xiaǒpǐn Prajñāpāramitā sūtra." *Asian Literature and Translation*, 8.1: 1–46.

———. 2021b. "Śrāvaka Ordination in a Mahāyāna Embrace: Triple Platform Ordination in Chinese Buddhism." *Pacific World, Fourth Series*, 2: 129–71.

Osto, Douglas. 2015. "Orality, Authority, and Conservatism in the Prajñāpāramitā sūtras." In *Dialogues in Early South Asian Religions: Hindu, Buddhist and Jain Traditions*, edited by Brian Black and Dean Laurie Patton, 115–35. Farnham: Ashgate Publishing.

———. 2018. "Altered States and the Origins of the Mahāyāna." In *Setting Out on the Great Way: Essays on Early Mahāyāna Buddhism*, edited by Paul Harrison, 177–205. Sheffield: Equinox.

Pagel, Ulrich. 1995. *The Bodhisattvapiṭaka: Its Doctrines, Practices and Their Position in Mahāyāna Literature*. Tring, UK: Institute of Buddhist Studies.

———. 2006. [Review] "About Ugra and His Friends: A Recent Contribution on Early Mahāyāna Buddhism; A Review Article." *Journal of the Royal Asiatic Society, Third Series*, 16.1: 73–82.

Palihawadana, Mahinda. 1984. "Dhammapada 1 and 2 and Their Commentaries." In *Buddhist Studies in Honor of Hammalava Saddhatissa*, edited by Gatare Dhammapāla, Richard Gombrich, and K. R. Norman, 189–202. Nugegoda: University of Jayewardenepura.

Palumbo, Antonello. 2013. *An Early Chinese Commentary on the Ekottarika-āgama: The Fenbie gongde lun 分別功德論 and the His-*

*tory of the Translation of the Zengyi ahan jing* 增一阿含經. Taipei: Dharma Drum Publishing Corporation.

Pande, Govind Chandra. 1957. *Studies in the Origins of Buddhism*. Allahabad: University of Allahabad, Department of Ancient History, Culture and Archaeology.

Pannikar, Raimundo. 1989/1990. *The Silence of God: The Answer of the Buddha*. New York: Orbis Books.

Pappas, Alexandra and Bhikkhu Anālayo. 2026. *In Love with Wisdom: Ancient Greek and Early Buddhist Philosophies*. New York: Wisdom Publications (forthcoming).

Parlier, Edith. 1991. "La légende du roi des Śibi: Du sacrifice brahmanique au don du corps bouddhique." *Bulletin d'Études Indiennes*, 9: 133–60.

Pāsādika, Bhikkhu. 1989. *Kanonische Zitate im Abhidharmakośabhāṣya des Vasubandhu*. Göttingen: Vandenhoeck & Ruprecht.

———. 2008. "Upāyakauśalya." In *Encyclopaedia of Buddhism*, edited by W. G. Weeraratne, 8.2: 439–42. Sri Lanka: Department of Buddhist Affairs.

———. 2015. *The Kāśyapaparivarta: Edited and Translated*. New Delhi: Aditya Prakashan.

Paul, Diana Y. 1979/1985. *Women in Buddhism: Images of the Feminine in the Mahāyāna Tradition*. Berkeley: University of California Press.

Pérez-Rémon, Joaquín. 1980. *Self and Non-self in Early Buddhism*. The Hague: Mouton Publishers.

Peris, Merlin. 2004. *Greek Story Motifs in the Jatakas*. Colombo: Godage International Publishers.

Polak, Grzegorz. 2023. "Who Identifies with the Aggregates? Philosophical Implications of the Selected khandha Passages in the Nikāyas." *Journal of Indian Philosophy*, 51: 663–85.

Pradhan, Prahlad. 1967. *Abhidharmakośabhāṣya of Vasubandhu*. Patna: Kashi Prasad Jayaswal Research Institute.

Przyluski, Jean. 1923. *La légende de l'empereur Açoka (Açoka-Avadāna) dans les textes indiens et chinois*. Paris: Paul Geuthner.

———. 1926. *Le concile de Rājagṛha: Introduction à l'histoire des canons et des sectes bouddhiques*. Paris: Paul Geuthner.

Pulleyblank, Edwin G. 1991. *Lexicon of Reconstructed Pronunciation in*

*Early Middle Chinese, Late Middle Chinese and Early Mandarin*. Vancouver: UBC Press.

Pye, Michael. 1978/2003. *Skilful Means*. London: Duckworth.

Qing Fa. 2001. *The Development of prajñā in Buddhism from Early Buddhism to the Prajñāpāramitā System: With Special Reference to the Sarvāstivāda Tradition*. PhD thesis, University of Calgary.

Radich, Michael and Bhikkhu Anālayo. 2017. "Were the Ekottarika-āgama and the Madhyama-āgama Translated by the Same Person? An Assessment on the Basis of Translation Style." In *Research on the Madhyama-āgama*, edited by Bhikkhunī Dhammadinnā, 209–37. Taipei: Dharma Drum Publishing Corporation.

Rahula, Telwatte. 1978. *A Critical Study of the Mahāvastu*. Delhi: Motilal Banarsidass.

Ratnayaka, Shanta. 1985. "The bodhisattva Ideal of the Theravāda." *Journal of the International Association of Buddhist Studies*, 8.2: 85–110.

Rawlinson, Andrew. 1977. "The Position of the Aṣṭasāhasrikā Prajñāpāramitā in the Development of Early Mahāyāna." In *Prajñāpāramitā and Related Systems: Studies in Honor of Edward Conze*, edited by Lewis Lancaster and Luis O. Gómez, 3–34. Berkeley: University of California Press.

———. 1983. "The Problem of the Origin of the Mahayana." In *Traditions in Contact and Change: Selected Proceedings of the XIVth Congress of the International Association for the History of Religions*, edited by Peter Slater, 163–70. Calgary: Canadian Corporation for Studies in Religion.

Ray, Reginald A. 1994. *Buddhist Saints in India: A Study in Buddhist Values and Orientations*. New York: Oxford University Press.

Reat, Noble Ross. 1992. "The Śālistamba sūtra and the Origins of Mahāyāna Buddhism." In *Summary Report of the Tenth International Conference of the International Association of Buddhist Studies: UNESCO Headquarters, Paris, France, 18–21 July 1991*, edited by Ananda W. P. Guruge, 137–43. Paris: The Permanent Delegation of Sri Lanka to UNESCO.

Rhi Juhyung. 1994. "From bodhisattva to Buddha: The Beginning of Iconic Representation in Buddhist Art." *Artibus Asiae*, 54.3/4: 207–25.

———. 2005. "Images, Relics, and Jewels: The Assimilation of Images in the Buddhist Relic Cult of Gandhāra—or Vice Versa." *Artibus Asiae*, 65.2: 169–211.

———. 2023. "Why Did the Buddha Not Shave His Head? Buddha Images in the Early Phase of Buddhist Art." *Journal of the International Association of Buddhist Studies*, 46: 1–33.

Rhys Davids, C. A. F. 1907. "Similes in the Nikāyas." *Journal of the Pali Text Society*, 5: 52–151.

———. 1908. "Similes in the Nikāyas." *Journal of the Pali Text Society*, 6: 180–88.

Rhys Davids, T. W. 1903/1997. *Buddhist India*. Delhi: Motilal Banarsidass.

Rhys Davids, T. W. and C. A. F. Rhys Davids. 1910. *Dialogues of the Buddha, Translated from the Pali of the Dîgha Nikâya, Part II.* London: Oxford University Press.

———. 1921. *Dialogues of the Buddha: Translated from the Pali of the Dîgha Nikâya, Part III.* London: Oxford University Press.

Rhys Davids, T. W. and William Stede. 1921/1993. *Pali-English Dictionary*. Delhi: Motilal Banarsidass.

Rigopoulos, Antonio. 1992. "The avyākatāni and the catuṣkoti Form in the Pāli Sutta Piṭaka, 1." *East and West*, 42.2–4: 227–59.

———. 1993. "The avyākatāni and the catuṣkoti Form in the Pāli Sutta Piṭaka, 2." *East and West*, 43.1–4: 115–40.

Robinson, Richard H. 1972. "Some Methodological Approaches to the Unexplained Points." *Philosophy East and West*, 22.3: 309–23.

Roloff, Carola. 2020. *The Buddhist Nuns' Ordination in the Tibetan Canon: Possibilities of the Revival of the Mūlasarvāstivāda Bhikṣuṇī Lineage*. Bochum: Projektverlag.

Romberg, Claudia. 2002. "Women in Engaged Buddhism." *Contemporary Buddhism*, 3.2: 161–70.

Rowell, Teresina. 1935. "The Background and Early Use of the buddhakṣetra Concept: Chapter II. The Field in the Bodhisattva-Career." *The Eastern Buddhist*, 6.4: 379–431.

Rowland, Benjamin, Jr. 1948. "A Note on the Invention of the Buddha Image." *Harvard Journal of Asiatic Studies*, 11.1/2: 181–86.

Ruegg, David Seyfort. 1977. "The Uses of the Four Points of the catuṣkoṭi and the Problem of the Description of Reality in Mahāyāna Buddhism." *Journal of Indian Philosophy*, 5: 1–71.

———. 1999. "Remarks on the Place of Narrative in the Buddhist Literatures of India and Tibet." In *India, Tibet, China: Genesis and Aspects of Traditional Narrative*, edited by Alredo Cadonna, 193–227. Firenze: Leo S. Olschki Editore.

———. 2004. "Aspects of the Investigation of the (Earlier) Indian Mahāyāna." *Journal of the International Association of Buddhist Studies*, 27.1: 3–62.

Saddhatissa, Hammalava. 1975. *The Birth-Stories of the Ten Bodhisattas and the Dasabodhisattuppattikathā: Being a Translation and Edition of the Dasabodhisattuppattikathā*. London: Pali Text Society.

Sakaki Ryōzaburō 1926. 飜譯名義大集 [*Mahāvyutpatti*]. Kyōto: Shingonshū Kyōto Daigaku.

Salomon, Richard. 1999. *Ancient Buddhist Scrolls from Gandhāra: The British Library Kharoṣṭhī Fragments*. London: The British Library.

———. 2008. *Two Gāndhārī Manuscripts of the Songs of Lake Anavatapta (Anavatapta-gāthā): British Library Kharoṣṭhī Fragment 1 and Senior Scroll 14*. Seattle: University of Washington Press.

———. 2018. *The Buddhist Literature of Ancient Gandhāra: An Introduction with Translations*. Somerville, MA: Wisdom Publications.

Samtani, N. H. 1962. "Fresh Light on the Interpretation of the Thirty-Two mahāpuruṣa-lakṣaṇas of the Buddha." *Bhāratī*, 6.1: 1–20.

———. 1971. *The Arthaviniścaya-sūtra & Its Commentary (Nibandhana) (Written by Bhikṣu Vīryaśrīdatta of Śrī-Nālandāvihāra): Critically Edited and Annotated for the First Time, with Introduction and Several Indices*. Patna: K. P. Jayaswal Research Institute.

Sander, Lore. 2000a. "Fragments of an Aṣṭasāhasrikā Manuscript from the Kuṣāṇa Period." In *Manuscripts in the Schøyen Collection I: Buddhist Manuscripts I*, edited by Jens Braarvig, Jens-Uwe Hartmann, Kazunobu Matsuda, and Lore Sander, 1–51. Oslo: Hermes Publishing.

———. 2000b. "Die 'Schøyen Collection' und einige Bemerkungen zu der ältesten Aṣṭasāhasrikā-Handschrift." *Wiener Zeitschrift für die Kunde Südasiens*, 44: 87–100.

———. 2002. "New Fragments of the Aṣṭasāhasrikā Prajñāpāramitā of the Kuṣāṇa Period." In *Manuscripts in the Schøyen Collection III: Buddhist Manuscripts II*, edited by Jens Braarvig, 37–44. Oslo: Hermes Publishing.

Sander, Lore and Ernst Waldschmidt. 1980. *Sanskrithandschriften aus den Turfanfunden, Teil IV*. Wiesbaden: Franz Steiner.

Sarkar, Sadhan Chandra. 1990. *Studies in the Common Jātaka and Avadāna Tales*. Calcutta: Sanskrit College.

Sasaki Genjun H. 1958. "Khanti, kānti, kṣānti." *Journal of Indian and Buddhist Studies*, 7: 354–59.

Sasaki Shizuka. 1997. "A Study on the Origin of Mahāyāna Buddhism." *The Eastern Buddhist*, 30.1: 79–113.

———. 2004. "Araṇya Dwellers in Buddhism." *Buddhist Studies*, 32: 1–13.

Sato Naomi. 2004. "Some Aspects of the Cult of Akṣobhya in Mahāyāna Scriptures." *Journal of Indian and Buddhist Studies*, 52.2: 937–33.

Schlingloff, Dieter. 1962. *Dogmatische Begriffsreihen im älteren Buddhismus. Ia: Daśottarasūtra IX–X*. Berlin: Akademie Verlag.

Schlosser, Andrea. 2022. *Three Early Mahāyāna Treatises from Gandhāra: Bajaur Kharoṣṭhī Fragments 4, 6, and 11*. Seattle: University of Washington Press.

Schmithausen, Lambert. 1973. "Spirituelle Praxis und philosophische Theorie im Buddhismus." *Zeitschrift für Missionswissenschaft und Religionswissenschaft*, 3: 161–86.

———. 1977. "Textgeschichtliche Beobachtungen zum 1. Kapitel der Aṣṭasāhasrikā Prajñāpāramitā." In *Prajñāpāramitā and Related Systems: Studies in Honor of Edward Conze*, edited by Lewis Lancaster and Luis O. Gómez, 35–80. Berkeley: University of California Press.

———. 1978. "Zur Struktur der erlösenden Erfahrung im indischen Buddhismus." In *Transzendenserfahrung, Vollzugshorizont des Heils: Das Problem in indischer und christlicher Tradition*, edited by Gerhard Oberhammer, 97–119. Wien: Institut für Indologie.

———. 1987. "Beiträge zur Schulzugehörigkeit und Textgeschichte kanonischer und postkanonischer buddhistischer Materialien." In *Zur Schulzugehörigkeit von Werken der Hīnayāna-Literatur, Zweiter Teil*, edited by Heinz Bechert, 2: 304–403. Göttingen: Vandenhoeck & Ruprecht.

———. 2000a. "Gleichmut und Mitgefühl: Zu Spiritualität und Heilsziel des älteren Buddhismus." In *Der Buddhismus als Anfrage an Christliche Theologie und Philosophie*, edited by Andreas Bsteh, 119–36. Mödling: Verlag St. Gabriel.

———. 2000b. "Mitleid und Leerheit: Zu Spiritualität und Heilsziel des Mahāyāna." In *Der Buddhismus als Anfrage an Christliche Theologie und Philosophie*, edited by Andreas Bsteh, 437–55. Mödling: Verlag St. Gabriel.

———. 2000c. "A Note on the Origin of ahiṃsā." In *Harānandalaharī: Volume in Honour of Professor Minoru Hara on His Seventieth Birthday*, edited by Ryutaro Tsuchida and Albrecht Wezler, 253–82. Reinbek: Dr. Inge Wezler Verlag für Orientalistische Fachpublikationen.

———. 2003. "Einige besondere Aspekte der 'Bodhisattva-Ethik' in Indien und ihre Hintergründe." *Hōrin: Vergleichende Studien zur japanischen Kultur*, 10: 21–46.

Schopen, Gregory. 1977/2005. "Sukhāvatī as a Generalized Religious Goal in Sanskrit Mahāyāna sūtra Literature." In *Figments and Fragments of Mahāyāna Buddhism in India: More Collected Papers*, edited by Gregory Schopen, 154–89. Honolulu: University of Hawai'i Press.

———. 1983/2005. "The Generalization of an Old Yogic Attainment in Medieval Mahāyāna sūtra Literature." In *Figments and Fragments of Mahāyāna Buddhism in India: More Collected Papers*, edited by Gregory Schopen, 190–220. Honolulu: University of Hawai'i Press.

———. 1985. "Two Problems in the History of Indian Buddhism: The Layman/Monk Distinction and the Doctrines of the Transference of Merit." *Studien zur Indologie und Iranistik*, 10: 9–47.

———. 1987/2005: "The Inscription on the Kuṣān Image of Amitābha and the Character of the Early Mahāyāna in India." In *Figments and Fragments of Mahāyāna Buddhism in India: More Collected Papers*, edited by Gregory Schopen, 247–77. Honolulu: University of Hawai'i Press.

———. 1988/1997. "On Monks, Nuns, and 'Vulgar' Practices: The Introduction of the Image Cult into Indian Buddhism." In *Bones, Stones, and Buddhist Monks: Collected Papers on the Archaeology, Epigraphy, and Texts of Monastic Buddhism in India*, edited by Gregory Schopen, 238–57. Honolulu: University of Hawai'i Press.

———. 1989. "The Manuscript of the Vajracchedikā Found at Gilgit: An Annotated Transcription and Translation." In *Studies in the Literature of the Great Vehicle: Three Mahāyāna Buddhist Texts*, edited by Luis O. Gómez and Jonathan A. Silk, 89–139. Ann Arbor: Center for South and Southeast Asian Studies, The University of Michigan.

———. 1991. "Monks and the Relic Cult in the Mahāparinibbānasutta: An Old Misunderstanding in Regard to Monastic Buddhism." In *From Benares to Beijing: Essays on Buddhism and Chinese Religion in Honor of Jan Yün-hua*, edited by Koichi Shinora and Gregory Schopen, 187–201. Oakville: Mosaic Press.

———. 1995/2004. "Deaths, Funerals, and the Division of Property in a Monastic Code." In *Buddhist Monks and Business Matters: Still More Papers on Monastic Buddhism in India*, edited by Gregory Schopen, 91–121. Honolulu: University of Hawai'i Press.

———. 2000/2005. "The Mahāyāna and the Middle Period in Indian Buddhism: Through a Chinese Looking-Glass." *In Figments and Fragments of Mahāyāna Buddhism in India: More Collected Papers*, edited by Gregory Schopen, 3–24. Honolulu: University of Hawai'i Press.

———. 2005. "On Sending the Monks Back to Their Books: Cult and Conservatism in Early Mahāyāna Buddhism." *In Figments and Fragments of Mahāyāna Buddhism in India: More Collected Papers*, edited by Gregory Schopen, 108–53. Honolulu: University of Hawai'i Press.

Schrader, Otto F. 1904/1905. "On the Problem of Nirvāṇa." *Journal of the Pali Text Society* 157–70.

Senart, Émile. 1882. *Le Mahāvastu: Texte sanscrit publié pour la première fois et accompagné d'introductions et d'un commentaire, tome premier*. Paris: Imprimerie Nationale.

———. 1890. *Le Mahāvastu: Texte sanscrit publié pour la première fois et accompagné d'introductions et d'un commentaire, tome deuxième*. Paris: Imprimerie Nationale.

———. 1897. *Le Mahāvastu: Texte sanscrit publié pour la première fois et accompagné d'introductions et d'un commentaire, tome troisième*. Paris: Imprimerie Nationale.

Shaw, Sarah. 2021. *The Art of Listening: A Guide to the Early Teachings of Buddhism*. Boulder: Shambhala Publications.

Sheravanichkul, Arthid. 2008. "Self-Sacrifice of the bodhisatta in the Paññāsa Jātaka." *Religion Compass*, 2.5: 769–87.

Shimoda Masahiro. 2009. "The State of Research on Mahāyāna Buddhism: The Mahāyāna as Seen in Developments in the Study of Mahāyāna sūtras." *Acta Asiatica: Bulletin of the Institute of Eastern Culture*, 96: 1–23.

Shōgaito Masahiro. 1998. "Three Fragments of Uighur Āgama." In *Bahşi Ögdisi: Festschrift für Klaus Röhrborn*, edited by Jens Peter Laut and Mehmet Ölmez, 363–78. Freiburg/Istanbul: Simurg.

Shukla, Karunesha. 1973. *Śrāvakabhūmi of Ācārya Asaṅga*. Patna: K. P. Jayaswal Research Institute.

Shulman, Eviatar. 2021. "Embodied Transcendence: The Buddha's Body in the Pāli Nikāyas." *Religions*, 12.179: 1–17.

Siklós, Bulcsu. 1996. "The Evolution of the Buddhist Yama." *The Buddhist Forum*, 4: 165–89.

Silk, Jonathan Alan. 1994. *The Origins and Early History of the Mahāratnakūṭa Tradition of Mahāyāna Buddhism with a Study of the Ratnarāśisūtra and Related Materials*. PhD thesis, University of Michigan.

———. 2002. "What, if Anything, Is Mahāyāna Buddhism? Problems of Definitions and Classifications." *Numen*, 49: 355–405.

———. 2003a. "Dressed for Success: The Monk Kāśyapa and Strategies of Legitimation in Earlier Mahāyāna Buddhist Scriptures." *Journal Asiatique*, 291.1/2: 173–219.

———. 2003b. "The Fruits of Paradox: On the Religious Architecture of the Buddha's Life Story." *Journal of the American Academy of Religion*, 71.4: 863–81.

———. 2007. "Good and Evil in Indian Buddhism: The Five Sins of Immediate Retribution." *Journal of Indian Philosophy*, 35: 253–86.

———. 2008. *Managing Monks: Administrators and Administrative Roles in Indian Buddhist Monasticism*. New York: Oxford University Press.

———. 2013. [Review of] "Anālayo, The Genesis of the Bodhisattva Ideal [Hamburg Buddhist Studies 1]." *Indo-Iranian Journal*, 56: 179–99.

———. 2014. "Taking the Vimalakīrtinirdeśa Seriously." *Annual Report of the International Research Institute for Advanced Buddhology at Soka University*, 17: 157–88.

———. 2016/2018. *Materials toward the Study of Vasubandhu's Viṃśikā (I): Sanskrit and Tibetan Critical Editions of the Verses and Autocommentary; An English Translation and Annotations*, Cambridge, MA: Harvard University Press.

———. 2022. "Thinking about the Study of Buddhist Texts: Ideas from Jerusalem, in More Ways than One." *Journal of Indian Philosophy*, 50: 753–69.

———. 2023. "Further Tibetan Sources of the *Kāśyapaparivarta from Dunhang (I)." In *Śāntamatiḥ: Manuscripts for Life, Essays in Memory of Seishi Karashima*, edited by Noriyuki Kudo, 331–45. Tokyo: International Research Institute for Advanced Buddhology, Soka University.

Silk, Jonathan Alan and Nagao Gadjin M. 2022. "History of the *Kāśyaparivarta in Chinese Translations and Its Connection with the Mahāratnakūṭa (Da Baoji jing 大寶積經) Collection." *Journal of the American Oriental Society*, 142.3: 671–97.

Silverlock, Blair Alan. 2015. *An Edition and Study of the Goṣiga-sutra, the Cow-Horn Discourse (Senior Collection Scroll no. 12): An Account of the Harmonious Aṇarudha Monks*. PhD thesis, University of Sydney.

Sinha, Braj Mohan. 1983. *Time and Temporality in Sāṁkhya-yoga and in Abhidharma Buddhism*. New Delhi: Munshiram Manoharlal.

Skilling, Peter. 1992. "The rakṣā Literature of the Śrāvakayāna." *Journal of the Pali Text Society*, 16: 109–82.

———. 1993. "Theravādin Literature in Tibetan Translation." *Journal of the Pali Text Society*, 19: 69–201.

———. 1994. *Mahāsūtras: Great Discourses of the Buddha, Volume I, Texts*. Oxford: Pali Text Society.

———. 1996a. "The sambuddhe Verses and Later Theravādin Buddhology." *Journal of the Pali Text Society*, 22: 151–83.

———. 1996b. "Verses Associated with the Rāhula sūtra." In *Suhṛllekhāḥ: Festgabe für Helmut Eimer*, edited by Michael Hahn, Roland Steiner, and Jens-Uwe Hartmann, 201–26. Swisstal-Odendorf: Indica et Tibetica Verlag.

———. 1997. *Mahāsūtras: Great Discourses of the Buddha, Volume II.* Oxford: Pali Text Society.

———. 2002/2003. "Three Types of bodhisatta in Theravādin Tradition: A Bibliographical Excursion." In *Buddhist and Indian Studies in Honour of Professor Sodo Mori*, edited by the Publication Committee for Buddhist and Indian Studies in Honour of Professor Sodo Mori, 91–102. Hamamatsu: Kokusai Bukkyoto Kyokai.

———. 2005. "Unsettling Boundaries: Verses Shared by Śrāvaka and Māhāyana texts." *Journal of the International College for Advanced Buddhist Studies*, 9: 99–112.

———. 2006. "Le Jātaka: Vies antérieurs et perfection du Bouddha." *Religions et Histoire*, 8: 52–57.

———. 2007a. "'Dhammas Are as Swift as Thought . . .': A Note on Dhammapada 1 and 2 and Their Parallels." *Journal of the Centre for Buddhist Studies*, 5: 23–50.

———. 2007b. "King, Sangha and Brahmans: Ideology, Ritual and Power in Pre-modern Siam." In *Buddhism, Power and Political Order*, edited by Ian Harris, 182–215. London: Routledge.

———. 2009a. "Prakrit Prajñāpāramitās: Northwest, South, and Center: Gleanings from Avalokitavrata and Haribhadra." *Bulletin of the Asia Institute, New Series*, 23: 199–208.

———. 2009b. "Seeing the Preacher as the Teacher: A Note on śāstṛ-saṃjñā." *Annual Report of the International Research Institute for Advanced Buddhology at Soka University*, 12: 73–100.

———. 2013a. "The Samādhirāja-sūtra and Its Mahāsāṃghika Connections." In *Nepalica-Tibetica, Festgabe for Christoph Cüppers, Band 2*, edited by Franz-Karl Erhard and Petra Maurer, 227–36. Andiast: International Institute for Tibetan and Buddhist Studies.

———. 2013b. "Vaidalya, Mahāyāna, and Bodhisatva in India: An Essay towards Historical Understanding." In *The Bodhisattva Ideal: Essays on the Emergence of Mahāyāna*, edited by Bhikkhu Ñāṇatusita, 69–162. Kandy: Buddhist Publication Society.

———. 2014. "Birchbark, bodhisatvas, and bhāṇakas: Writing Materials in Buddhist North India." *Eurasian Studies*, 12.1/2: 499–521.

———. 2018. "How the Unborn Was Born: The Riddle of Mahāyāna Origins." In *Setting Out on the Great Way: Essays on Early Mahāyāna Buddhism*, edited by Paul Harrison, 33–71. Sheffield: Equinox.

———. 2021: *Questioning the Buddha: A Selection of Twenty-Five sutras.* Somerville, MA: Wisdom Publications.

———. 2023: "Evaṃ me sutaṃ: Who Heard What?" *Hualin International Journal of Buddhist Studies*, 6.1: 171–93.

———. 2024. *Buddha's Words for Tough Times: An Anthology.* New York: Wisdom Publications.

———. Forthcoming. "Foreword." In *Buddhist Caves of the Deccan: Issues and Interpretations*, edited by Shrikant Ganvir, 1–12. New Delhi: Kaveri Books.

Skilling, Peter and Santi Pakdeekham. 2013. "Studies in the Epigraphy of Thailand IV: Inscriptions from the Ayutthaya, Thonburi, and Ratanakosin Periods, Part III: Wat Yothanimit Inscription of Chaophraya Phrakhlang (No. 158) Commemorating the Foundation of the Town of Chanthaburi and Wat Yothanimit." *Aséanie*, 32: 185–200.

Skilton, Andrew. 2002. "State or Statement? Samādhi in Some Early Mahāyāna sūtras." *The Eastern Buddhist, New Series*, 34.2: 51–93.

Skorupski, Tadeusz. 2022. "The Provenance and Scope of the Eightfold Path." In *Guruparamparā: Studies on Buddhism, India, Tibet and More in Honour of Professor Marek Mejor*, edited by Katarzyna Marciniak, Stanisław Jan Kania, Małgorzata Wiclińska-Soltwedel, and Agata Bareja-Starzyńska, 355–402. Warsaw: University of Warsaw Press.

Smart, Ninian. 1964/1976. *Doctrine and Argument in Indian Philosophy.* New Jersey: Humanities Press.

Snellgrove, David L. 1959. *The Hevajra Tantra: A Critical Study, Part 2, Sanskrit and Tibetan Texts.* London: Oxford University Press.

Somaratne, G. A. 2005. "Citta, manas and viññāṇa: Aspects of Mind as Presented in Early Buddhist Pali Discourses." In *Dhamma-Vinaya: Essays in Honour of Venerable Professor Dhammavihari (Jotiya Dhirasekera)*, edited by Asaṅga Tilakaratne, Endo Tochiichi, and G. A. Somaratne, 169–202. Colombo: Sri Lanka Association for Buddhist Studies.

Soper, Alexander Coburn. 1959. *Literary Evidence for Early Buddhist Art in China.* Ascona: Artibus Asiae.

Sparham, Gareth. 2006. *Abhisamayālaṃkāra with Vṛtti and Āloka, Vṛtti by Ārya Vimuktisena Ālokā by Haribhadra, Volume One: First Abhisamaya*. Freemont: Jain Publishing Company.

———. 2008. *Abhisamayālaṃkāra with Vṛtti and Āloka, Vṛtti by Ārya Vimuktisena Ālokā by Haribhadra, Volume Two: Second and Third Abhisamaya*. Freemont: Jain Publishing Company.

Speyer, J. S. 1906/1970. *Avadānaçataka: A Century of Edifying Tales Belonging to the Hīnayāna, I*. Osnabrück: Biblio Verlag.

———. 1909/1970. *Avadānaçataka, A Century of Edifying Tales Belonging to the Hīnayāna, Vol. II. Varga 8–10*. Osnabrück: Biblio Verlag.

Spiro, Melford E. 1970/1982. *Buddhism and Society: A Great Tradition and Its Burmese Vicissitudes*. Berkeley: University of California Press.

Stache-Rosen, Valentina. 1968. *Dogmatische Begriffsreihen im älteren Buddhismus II: Das Saṅgītisūtra und sein Kommentar Saṅgītiparyāya*. Berlin: Akademie Verlag.

Strauch, Ingo. 2010. "More Missing Pieces of Early Pure Land Buddhism: New Evidence for Akṣobhya and Abhirati in an Early Mahayana sutra from Gandhāra." *The Eastern Buddhist*, 41.1: 23–66.

———. 2014. "Looking into Water-Pots and over a Buddhist Scribe's Shoulder: On the Deposition and the Use of Manuscripts in Early Buddhism." *Asia*, 68.3: 797–830.

Streng, Frederick J. 1982. "Realization of param bhūtakoṭi (Ultimate Reality-limit) in the Aṣṭasahāsrikā Prajñāpāramitā sūtra." *Philosophy East and West*, 32.1: 91–98.

Stuart, Daniel M. 2015a. *A Less Traveled Path: Saddharmasmṛtyupasthānasūtra Chapter 2, Critically Edited with a Study on Its Structure and Significance for the Development of Buddhist Meditation, Volume I*. Beijing and Vienna: China Tibetology Publishing House and Austrian Academy of Sciences Press.

———. 2015b. *A Less Traveled Path: Saddharmasmṛtyupasthānasūtra Chapter 2, Critically Edited with a Study on Its Structure and Significance for the Development of Buddhist Meditation, Volume II (Appendices)*. Beijing and Vienna: China Tibetology Publishing House and Austrian Academy of Sciences Press.

Study Group on Buddhist Sanskrit Literature. 2006. *Vimalakīrtinirdeśa: A Sanskrit Edition Based on the Manuscript Newly Found at the Potala Palace*. Tokyo: Taisho University Press.

Suzuki Kōshin. 1994. *Sanskrit Fragments and Tibetan Translation of Candrakīrti's Bodhisattvayogācāracatuḥśatakaṭīkā*. Tokyo: Sankibo Press.

Tambiah, S. J. 1976. *World Conqueror and World Renouncer: A Study of Buddhism and Polity in Thailand against a Historical Background*. Cambridge: Cambridge University Press.

Tatia, Nathmal. 1960. "The avyākṛtas or Indeterminables." *Nava-Nālandā-Mahāvihāra Research Publication*, 2: 141–59.

Tatz, Mark. 1994/2001. *The Skill in Means (Upāyakauśalya) sūtra*. Delhi: Motilal Banarsidass.

Tedesco, Paul. 1945. "Sanskrit muṇḍa- 'Shaven.'" *Journal of the American Oriental Society*, 65: 82–98.

Thomas, E. J. 1927/2003. *The Life of Buddha as Legend and History*. Delhi: Munshiram Manoharlal.

Thompson, George. 1998. "On Truth-Acts in Vedic." *Indo-Iranian Journal*, 41.2: 125–53.

Thompson, John M. 2008. *Understanding prajñā: Sengzhao's "Wild Words" and the Search for Wisdom*. New York: Peter Lang.

Tiefenauer, Marc. 2018. *Les enfers Indiens: Histoire multiple d'un lieu commun*. Leiden: Brill.

Tilakaratne, Asaṅga. 1993. *Nirvana and Ineffability: A Study of the Buddhist Theory of Reality and Language*. Sri Lanka: University of Kelaniya, Postgraduate Institute of Pali and Buddhist Studies.

———. 2005. "Personality Differences of Arahants and the Origins of Theravāda: A Study of Two Great Elders of the Theravāda Tradition: Mahā Kassapa and Ānanda." In *Dhamma-Vinaya: Essays in Honour of Venerable Professor Dhammavihari (Jotiya Dhirasekera)*, edited by Asaṅga Tilakaratne, Endo Tochiichi, and G. A. Somaratne, 229–57. Colombo: Sri Lanka Association for Buddhist Studies.

Tournier, Vincent. 2012. "The Mahāvastu and the Vinayapiṭaka of the Mahāsāṃghika-Lokottaravādins." *Annual Report of the International Research Institute for Advanced Buddhology at Soka University*, 15: 87–104.

———. 2017. *La formation du Mahāvastu et la mise en place des conceptions relatives à la carrière du bodhisattva*. Paris: École française d'Extrême-Orient.

———. 2019. "Buddhas of the Past: South Asia." In *Brill's Encyclopedia of*

*Buddhism: Volume II: Lives*, edited by Jonathan A. Silk, Richard Bowring, Vincent Eltschinger, and Michael Radich, 95–108. Leiden: Brill.

Trenckner, V., Dines Andersen, and Helmer Smith. 1924. *A Critical Pāli Dictionary, Vol. 1*. Copenhagen: Royal Danish Academy.

Tripathi, Chandrabhal. 1995. *Ekottarāgama-Fragmente der Gilgit-Handschrift*. Reinbek: Verlag für Orientalistische Fachpublikationen.

Tripathi, Sridhar. 1988. *Bodhicaryāvatāra of Śāntideva with the Commentary Pañjikā of Prajñākaramati*. Darbhanga: Mithila Institute.

Tsai Yao-ming. 1997. *Searching for the Origins of Mahāyāna and Moving toward a Better Understanding of Early Mahāyāna*. PhD thesis, University of California.

———. 2014. "On Justifying the Choice of Mahāyāna among Multiple Paths in Buddhist Teachings: Based on the Prajñāpāramitā-sūtras." In *Scripture:Canon::Text:Context: Essays Honoring Lewis R. Lancaster*, edited by Richard K. Payne, 257–77. Berkeley: Institute of Buddhist Studies and BDK America.

———. 2021. "Critical Reflections on Abiding-Places in the Perfection of Wisdom in Eight Thousand Lines." *International Journal of Buddhist Thought & Culture*, 31.2: 29–57.

Tsedroen, Bhikṣuṇī Jampa and Bhikkhu Anālayo. 2013. "The gurudharma on Bhikṣuṇī Ordination in the Mūlasarvāstivāda Tradition." *Journal of Buddhist Ethics*, 20: 743–74.

Tun, Than. 1956/1978. *History of Buddhism in Burma A.D. 1000–1300*. Mandalay: Burma Research Society.

Unebe Toshiya. 2012. "Not for the Achievement of a sāvaka or paccekabuddha: The Motive behind the bodhisatta's Self-Sacrifice in the Paññāsa-Jātaka." *Buddhist Studies Review*, 29.1: 35–56.

Urban, Hugh B. and Paul J. Griffith. 1994. "What Else Remains in śūnyatā? An Investigation of Terms for Mental Imagery in the Madhyāntavibhāga-Corpus." *Journal of the International Association of Buddhist Studies*, 17.1: 1–25.

Vaidya, P. L. 1960. *Aṣṭasāhasrikā Prajñāpāramitā with Haribhadra's Commentary Called Āloka*. Darbhanga: The Mithila Institute of Post-Graduate Studies and Research in Sanskrit Learning.

———. 1961. *Samādhirājasūtra*. Darbhanga: The Mithila Institute of Post-Graduate Studies and Research in Sanskrit Learning.

———. 1967. *Daśabhūmikasūtram*. Darbhanga: The Mithila Institute of Post-Graduate Studies and Research in Sanskrit Learning.

van Put, Ineke. 2007. "The Names of Buddhist Hells in East Asian Buddhism." *Pacific World, Third Series*, 9: 205–29.

Vélez de Cea, Abraham. 2004. "The Silence of the Buddha and the Questions about the Tathāgata after Death." *Indian International Journal of Buddhist Studies*, 5: 119–41.

Venkatasubbiah, A. 1940. "The Act of Truth in the Ṛgveda." *The Journal of Oriental Research*, 14: 133–65.

Verboom, Arie Willem Cornelis. 1998. *A Text-Comparative Research on "The Perfection of Discriminating Insight in Eight Thousand Lines, Chapter 1."* PhD thesis, Rijksuniversiteit.

Vetter, Tilmann. 1984. "A Comparison between the Mysticism of the Older Prajñāpāramitā Literature and the Mysticism of the Mūlamadhyamaka-kārikās of Nāgārjuna." *Acta Indologica*, 6: 495–512.

———. 1994a. "On the Origin of Mahāyāna Buddhism and the Subsequent Introduction of Prajñāpāramitā." *Asiatische Studien*, 48: 1241–81.

———. 1994b. "Zwei schwierige Stellen im Mahānidānasutta, Zur Qualität der Überlieferung im Pāli-Kanon." *Wiener Zeitschrift für die Kunde Südasiens und Archiv für Indische Philosophie*, 38: 137–60.

———. 2001. "Once Again on the Origin of Mahāyāna Buddhism." *Wiener Zeitschrift für die Kunde Südasiens*, 45: 59–90.

———. 2003. "Arhat und bodhisattva im Daoxing 道行." *Hōrin*, 10: 47–71.

———. 2012. *A Lexicographical Study of An Shigao's and His Circle's Chinese Translation of Buddhist Texts*. Tokyo: International Institute for Buddhist Studies.

Vetter, Tilmann and Paul Harrison. 1998. "An Shigao's Chinese Translation of the *Saptasthānasūtra*." In *Sūryacandrāya: Essays in Honour of Akira Yuyama on the Occasion of His 65th Birthday*, edited by Paul Harrison and Gregory Schopen, 197–216. Swisstal-Odendorf: Indica et Tibetica.

von Criegern, Oliver. 2002. *Das Kūṭatāṇḍyasūtra: Nach dem Dīrghāgama*

*Manuskript herausgegeben und übersetzt*. MA thesis, Ludwig-Maximilians-Universität.

von Gabain, Annemarie. 1954. *Türkische Turfan-Texte VIII*. Berlin: Akademie Verlag.

von Hinüber, Oskar. 1983a. "Die älteste Literatursprache des Buddhismus." *Saeculum*, 34: 1–9.

———. 1983b. "Sieben Goldblätter einer Pañcaviṃśatisāhhasrikā Prajñāpāramitā aus Anurādhapura." *Nachrichten der Akademie der Wissenschaften in Göttingen*, 7: 189–207.

———. 1991. "Das buddhistische Recht und die Phonetik des Pali, Ein Abschnitt aus der Samantapāsādikā über die Vermeidung von Aussprachefehlern in kammavācās." *Studien zur Indologie und Iranistik*, 13/14: 101–27.

———. 1996/1997. *A Handbook of Pāli Literature*. Delhi: Munshiram Manoharlal.

———. 1998. *Entstehung und Aufbau der Jātaka-Sammlung: Studien zur Literatur des Theravāda-Buddhismus I*. Stuttgart: Franz Steiner.

———. 2008. "The Foundation of the Bhikkhunīsaṅgha: A Contribution to the Earliest History of Buddhism." *Annual Report of the International Research Institute for Advanced Buddhology at Soka University*, 11: 3–29.

———. 2009: "Cremated Like a King: The Funeral of the Buddha within the Ancient Indian Cultural Context." *Journal of the International College for Advanced Buddhist Studies*, 13: 33–66.

———. 2023. "Wrestling with the Mahāvastu: Struggling with Structure and Interpretation, A Critical Comment on Recent Researches on a Major Lokottaravāda Vinaya Text." *Indo-Iranian Journal*, 66: 25–95.

von Rospatt, Alexander. 1995. *The Buddhist Doctrine of Momentariness: A Survey of the Origins and Early Phase of This Doctrine up to Vasubandhu*. Stuttgart: Franz Steiner Verlag.

Waldschmidt, Ernst. 1932. *Bruchstücke buddhistischer sūtras aus dem zentralasiatischen Sanskritkanon, herausgegeben und im Zusammenhang mit ihren Parallelversionen bearbeitet*. Leipzig: F. A. Brockhaus.

———. 1944. *Die Überlieferung vom Lebensende des Buddha: Eine vergleichende Analyse des Mahāparinirvāṇasūtra und seiner Textentspre-*

*chungen, erster Teil, Vorgangsgruppe I–IV.* Göttingen: Vandenhoeck & Ruprecht.

———. 1951. *Das Mahāparinirvāṇasūtra: Text in Sanskrit und Tibetisch, Verglichen mit dem Pāli nebst einer Übersetzung der chinesischen Entsprechung im Vinaya der Mūlasarvāstivādins, Auf Grund von Turfan-Handschriften herausgegeben und bearbeitet, Teil II: Textbearbeitung: Vorgang 1–32.* Berlin: Akademie Verlag.

———. 1956. *Das Mahāvadānasūtra: Ein kanonischer Text über die sieben letzten Buddhas, Sanskrit, verglichen mit dem Pāli nebst einer Analyse der in chinesischer Übersetzung überlieferten Parallelversion, auf Grund von Turfan-Handschriften herausgegeben, Teil II: Textbearbeitung.* Berlin: Akademie Verlag.

———. 1957. *Das Catuṣpariṣatsūtra: Eine kanonische Lehrschrift über die Begründung der buddhistischen Gemeinde, Text in Sanskrit und Tibetisch, verglichen mit dem Pāli nebst einer Übersetzung der chinesischen Entsprechung im Vinaya der Mūlasarvāstivādins, auf Grund von Turfan-Handschriften herausgegeben und bearbeitet, Teil I: Der Sanskrit-Text in handschriftlichen Befund.* Berlin: Akademie Verlag.

———. 1962. *Das Catuṣpariṣatsūtra: Eine kanonische Lehrschrift über die Begründung der buddhistischen Gemeinde, Text in Sanskrit und Tibetisch, verglichen mit dem Pāli nebst einer Übersetzung der chinesischen Entsprechung im Vinaya der Mūlasarvāstivādins, auf Grund von Turfan-Handschriften herausgegeben und bearbeitet, Teil III: Textbearbeitung: Vorgang 22–28.* Berlin: Akademie Verlag.

———. 1967. "Zu einigen Bilinguen aus den Turfan-Funden." In *Von Ceylon bis Turfan: Schriften zur Geschichte, Literatur, Religion und Kunst des indischen Kulturraums, Festgabe zum 70. Geburtstag am 15. Juli 1967 von Ernst Waldschmidt,* 238–57. Göttingen: Vandenhoeck & Ruprecht.

———. 1980. "The Rāṣṭrapālasūtra in Sanskrit Remnants from Central Asia." In *Indianisme et Bouddhisme, Mélanges offerts à Mgr. Étienne Lamotte,* edited by André Bareau and Étienne Lamotte, 359–74. Louvain-la-Neuve: Institut Orientaliste.

Waldschmidt, Ernst, Walter Clawiter, and Lore Holzmann. 1965.

*Sanskrithandschriften aus den Turfanfunden, Teil I.* Wiesbaden: Franz Steiner.

Waldschmidt, Ernst, Walter Clawiter, and Lore Sander-Holzmann. 1968. *Sanskrithandschriften aus den Turfanfunden, Teil II.* Wiesbaden: Franz Steiner.

———. 1971. *Sanskrithandschriften aus den Turfanfunden, Teil 3.* Wiesbaden: Franz Steiner.

Walleser, Max. 1914. *Prajñāpāramitā: Die Vollkommenheit der Erkenntnis, nach indischen, tibetischen, und chinesischen Quellen.* Göttingen: Vandenhoeck & Ruprecht.

———. 1917. *Die Streitlosigkeit des Subhūti: Ein Beitrag zur buddhistischen Legendenentwicklung.* Heidelberg: Carl Winter's Universitätsbuchhandlung.

Walser, Joseph. 2009. "The Origin of the Term 'Mahāyāna' (the Great Vehicle) and Its Relationship to the Āgamas." *Journal of the International Association of Buddhist Studies*, 30.1/2: 219–50.

———. 2018. *Genealogies of Mahāyāna Buddhism: Emptiness, Power, and the Question of Origin.* London: Routledge.

Walshe, Maurice. 1987. *Thus Have I Heard: The Long Discourses of the Buddha.* London: Wisdom Publications.

Walters, Jonathan S. 1997. "Stūpa, Story, and Empire: Constructions of the Buddha Biography in Early Post-Aśokan India." In *Sacred Biography in Buddhist Traditions of South and Southeast Asia*, edited by Juliane Schober, 159–92. Honolulu: University of Hawai'i Press.

———. 1999. "Suttas as History: Four Approaches to the Sermon on the Noble Quest (Ariyapariyesana-sutta)." *History of Religions*, 38.3: 247–84.

Wangchuk, Dorji. 2007. *The Resolve to Become a Buddha: A Study of the bodhicitta Concept in Indo-Tibetan Buddhism.* Tokyo: International Institute for Buddhist Studies.

Warder, A. K. 1967. *Pali Metre: A Contribution to the History of Indian Literature.* London: Pali Text Society.

———. 1970/1991. *Indian Buddhism.* Delhi: Motilal Banarsidass.

Watanabe Shōgo. 1994. "A Comparative Study of the Pañcaviṃśatisāhasrikā Prajñāpāramitā." *Journal of the American Oriental Society*, 114.3: 386–96.

Wayman, Alex. 1955. "Notes on the Sanskrit Term jñāna." *Journal of the American Oriental Society*, 75.4: 253–68.

———. 1957. "The Meaning of Unwisdom (avidyā)." *Philosophy East and West*, 7.1/2: 21–25.

———. 1968. "The Hindu-Buddhist Rite of Truth: An Interpretation." In *Studies in Indian Linguistics: Professor M. B. Emenau Ṣaṣṭipūrti Volume*, edited by Bhadriraju Krishnamurti and Murray B. Emeneau, 365–69. Poona: Centre of Advanced Study in Linguistics, Deccan College, and Annamalai University in Studies in Indian Linguistics.

Webster, David. 2005. "The Weary Buddha or Why the Buddha Nearly Couldn't Be Bothered." *Buddhist Studies Review*, 22.1: 15–25.

Weller, Friedrich. 1928. *Das Leben des Buddha von Aśvaghoṣa: Tibetisch und Deutsch*. Leipzig: Verlag von Eduard Pfeiffer.

———. 1934. *Brahmajālasūtra: Tibetischer und mongolischer Text*. Leipzig: Otto Harrassowitz.

Werner, Karel. 1981/2013. "Bodhi and arahattaphala: From Early Buddhism to Early Mahāyāna." In *The Bodhisattva Ideal: Essays on the Emergence of Mahāyāna*, edited by Bhikkhu Ñāṇatusita, 51–67. Kandy: Buddhist Publication Society.

Westerhoff, Jan. 2018. *The Golden Age of Indian Buddhist Philosophy*. Oxford: Oxford University Press.

Wille, Klaus. 2015. "The Sanskrit Fragments Or.15007 in the Hoernle Collection." In *Buddhist Manuscripts from Central Asia: The British Library Sanskrit Fragments, Volume III.1*, edited by Karashima Seishi, Nagashima Jundo, and Klaus Wille, 13–198. Tokyo: International Research Institute for Advanced Buddhology, Soka University.

Willemen, Charles, Bart Dessein, and Collett Cox. 1998. *Sarvāstivāda Buddhist Scholasticism*. Leiden: Brill.

Williams, Paul. 1989/2009. *Mahāyāna Buddhism: The Doctrinal Foundations, Second Edition*. London: Routledge.

Wimalaratana, Bellanwilla. 1994. *Concept of Great Man (mahāpurisa) in Buddhist Literature and Iconography*. Singapore: Buddhist Research Society.

Winternitz, Moriz. 1920/1968. *Geschichte der indischen Literatur, Band 2: Die buddhistische Literatur und die heiligen Texte der Jainas*. Stuttgart: K. F. Koehler.

Witanachchi, C. 1992. "Heaven and Hell." In *Encyclopaedia of Buddhism*, edited by W. G. Weeraratne, 5.3: 421–32. Sri Lanka: Department of Buddhist Affairs.

Wogihara Unrai. 1930/1936. *Bodhisattvabhūmi: A Statement of Whole Course of the Bodhisattva (Being Fifteenth Section of Yogācārabhūmi)*. Tokyo: Sankibo.

———. 1932/1935. *Abhisamayālaṃkār'ālokā Prajñāpāramitāvyākhyā (Commentary on Aṣṭasāhasrikā-prajñāpāramitā) by Haribhadra, Together with the Text Commented On*. Tokyo: The Toyo Bunko.

———. 1936/1971. *Sphuṭārthā Abhidharmakośavyākhyā by Yaśomitra, Part II (IV–VIII Kośasthānam)*. Tokyo: Sankibo Buddhist Book Store.

Wynne, Alexander. 2022. "Editorial: Suicide in Buddhism." *Journal of the Oxford Centre for Buddhist Studies*, 22: xi–xvi.

Yamabe Nobuyoshi. 1999. *The sūtra on the Ocean-Like samādhi of the Visualization of the Buddha: The Interfusion of the Chinese and Indian Cultures in Central Asia as Reflected in a Fifth Century Apocryphal sūtra*. PhD thesis, Yale University.

Yang Hung-Yi. 2013. *A Study of the Story of Sadāprarudita in the Aṣṭasāhasrikā Prajñāpāramitā sūtra*. PhD thesis, University of Sydney.

Yìnshùn 印順. 1983. 雜阿含經論會編 (上). Taipei: 正聞出版社.

Zacchetti, Stefano. 2004. "Teaching Buddhism in Han China: A Study of the Ahan koujie shi'er yinyuan jing T 1508 Attributed to An Shigao." *Annual Report of the International Research Institute for Advanced Buddhology at Soka University*, 7: 197–224.

———. 2005. *In Praise of the Light: A Critical Synoptic Edition with an Annotated Translation of Chapters 1–3 of Dharmarakṣa's Guang zan jing 光讚經, Being the Earliest Chinese Translation of the Larger Prajñāpāramitā*. Tokyo: Soka University.

———. 2008. "Fondamentalmente pura è la mente: La concezione del 'pensiero luminoso' nelle fonti buddhiste cinesi del periodo arcaico". In *Mente e coscienza tra India e Cina*, edited by Emanuela Magno, 131–47. Firenze: Società Editrice Fiorentina.

———. 2015a. "Mind the Hermeneutical Gap: A Terminological Issue in Kumārajīva's Version of the Diamond Sutra." In 漢傳佛教研究的過去現在未來 / *Chinese Buddhism: Past, Present and Future*, 157–94. 宜蘭: 佛光大學佛教研究中心.

———. 2015b. "Prajñāpāramitā sūtras." In *Brill's Encyclopedia of Buddhism: Volume I, Literature and Languages*, edited by Jonathan A. Silk, Oskar von Hinüber, and Vincent Eltschinger, 170–209. Leiden: Brill.

———. 2021. *The Da zhidu lun* 大智度論 *(*Mahāprajnāpāramitopadeśa) and the History of the Larger Prajnāpāramitā: Patterns of Textual Variation in Mahāyāna sūtra Literature*, edited for posthumous publication by Michael Radich and Jonathan Silk. Bochum: Projektverlag.

Zhang Juyan. 2020. "'Buddhas in the Ten Directions': Its Origins in the Early Buddhist Texts and Metamorphosis." *Critical Review for Buddhist Studies*, 27: 9–37.

Zhang Lixiang. 2004. *Das Śaṃkarasūtra: Eine Übersetzung des Sanskrit-Textes im Vergleich mit der Pāli Fassung*. MA thesis, Ludwig-Maximilians-Universität.

Zhao Wen. 2018. *The Conceptions of Seeing the Buddha and Buddha Embodiments in Early Prajñāpāramitā Literature*. PhD thesis, Ludwig-Maximilians-Universität.

———. 2020. "A Narrative in Prajñāpāramitā Literature and the samādhi of Direct Encounter with Present Buddhas (Pratyutpannabuddhasaṃmukhāvasthitasamādhi)." *Journal of the International Association of Buddhist Studies*, 43: 253–74.

———. 2023. "The Story of Sadāprarudita's Search for Dharma and the Worship of the *Prajñāpāramitā sūtra* from India to Sixth-Century China." *Religions*, 14.410: 1–17.

Zhou Chungyang. 2008. *Das Kaivartisūtra der neuentdeckten Dīrghāgama-Handschrift: Eine Edition und Rekonstruktion des Textes*. MA thesis, Georg-August Universität.

Zhutayev, Dar I. 2010. "Sacred Topology of the Buddhist Universe: The buddhakṣetra Concept in the Mahāsāṅghika-Lokottaravādin Tradition." In *Sacred Topology in Early Ireland and India: Religious Paradigm Shift*, edited by Maxim Fomin, Séamus Mac Mathúna, and Victoria Vertogradova, 153–93. Washington: Institute for the Study of Man.

Zin, Monika. 2014. "Imagery of Hell in South, South East and Central Asia." *Rocznik Orientalistyczny*, 67.1: 269–96.

Zürcher, Erik. 1959/1972. *The Buddhist Conquest of China: The Spread and Adaptation of Buddhism in Early Medieval China*. Leiden: E. J. Brill.

———. 1991. "A New Look at the Earliest Chinese Buddhist Texts." In *From Benares to Beijing: Essays on Buddhism and Chinese Religion in Honour of Prof. Jan Yün-Hua*, edited by Koichi Shinohara and Gregory Schopen, 277–304. Oakville: Mosaic Press.

# Image Credits

Fig. 1 © Osmund Bopearachchi
Fig. 2 © Trustees of the British Museum
Fig. 3 © Inagaki Hajime
Fig. 4 © Bhikkhu Ānandajoti
Fig. 5 © Ken and Visakha Kawasaki
Fig. 6 © National Museum of Nepal
Fig. 7 © Marie-Lan Nguyen
Fig. 8 © Staatliche Museen zu Berlin, Museum für Asiatische Kunst, Georg Niedermeiser
Fig. 9 © Clay Gilliland

# Index

# About the Author

Bhikkhu Anālayo is a scholar of early Buddhism and a meditation teacher. He completed his PhD research on the *Satipaṭṭhānasutta* at the University of Peradeniya, Sri Lanka, in 2000 and his habilitation research with a comparative study of the *Majjhimanikāya* in the light of its Chinese, Sanskrit, and Tibetan parallels at the University of Marburg, Germany, in 2007. His over five hundred publications are for the most part based on comparative studies, with a special interest in topics related to meditation and the role of women in Buddhism.

## What to Read Next from Wisdom Publications

**Abiding in Emptiness**
*A Guide for Meditative Practice*
Bhikkhu Anālayo

"Through this book, Ven. Anālayo continues to build bridges between different Buddhist traditions, linking contemplations on emptiness to ancient doctrines and discourses, while highlighting their common heritage. He skillfully opens an avenue for meditative practice on emptiness for all, including contemporary Theravādin practitioners. This practical guide is for all those with a firm grounding in embodied meditation." —Yongey Mingyur Rinpoche

**The Signless and the Deathless**
*On the Realization of Nirvana*
Bhikkhu Anālayo

"To read this extraordinary book is a must not only for specialists but for anybody interested in a deeper understanding of the central issues of Buddhist teaching." —Lambert Schmithausen

**Daughters of the Buddha**
*Teachings by Ancient Indian Women*
Bhikkhu Anālayo

"Bhikkhu Anālayo's book is a brave attempt to introduce the inspiring qualities of spiritual daughters of the Buddha and make their voices heard by skillfully bringing together passages from early Buddhist scriptures. It is an acknowledgment of women's remarkable contribution to the tradition despite some androcentric and misogynist tendencies found in early Buddhist thought." —Professor Hiroko Kawanami, author of *The Culture of Giving in Myanmar*

**Early Buddhist Oral Tradition**
*Textual Formation and Transmission*
Bhikkhu Anālayo

A fascinating investigation into the formation and transmission of the early Buddhist oral tradition. In-depth but still accessible, *Early Buddhist Oral Tradition* is an engrossing and enlightening inquiry into the early Buddhist oral tradition.

**Rebirth in Early Buddhism and Current Research**
Bhikkhu Anālayo

"From his unique perspective as an academic scholar and a monastic, Bhikkhu Anālayo provides a thorough explanation of the early Buddhist doctrine of rebirth and the debates about it in ancient India and early imperial China, as well as a judicious analysis of various phenomena that some people have taken to be evidence for rebirth. This book is essential reading for anyone interested in these fascinating topics." —Evan Thompson, author of *Waking, Dreaming, Being: Self and Consciousness in Neuroscience, Meditation, and Philosophy*

**The Buddhist Literature of Ancient Gandhāra**
*An Introduction with Selected Translations*
Richard Salomon

"There is no doubt that this work will serve as a terrific guidebook especially for those who are interested in Buddhist philology. Therefore, it would not be surprising to find this book added to the curricula of many Buddhist studies programs as well as in the bookshelves of Buddhist scholars around the world." —*International Journal of Buddhist Thought & Culture*

# About Wisdom Publications

Wisdom Publications is the leading publisher of classic and contemporary Buddhist books and practical works on mindfulness. To learn more about us or to explore our other books, please visit our website at wisdom.org or contact us at the address below.

Wisdom Publications
132 Perry Street
New York, NY 10014 USA

We are a 501(c)(3) organization, and donations in support of our mission are tax deductible.

Wisdom Publications is affiliated with the Foundation for the Preservation of the Mahayana Tradition (FPMT).